The first edition of this book was written by Edward de la Billière, Keith Carter and Charlie Loram. The second edition was updated and partly rewritten by Chris Scott with additional research by Lucy Ridout. The third was updated by Jim Manthorpe, the fourth by Stuart Greig and the one you're holding in your hand was updated by Henry Stedman.

Henry Stedman has now completed 11 National Trails and written guides to several of them, including *Hadrian's Wall Path*, *Cleveland Way* and the three books to the *South-West Coast Path*. He is also the author of guides to two other UK long-distance paths, the *Coast to Coast Path* and *Dales Way*. With him on this trek, as usual, was **Daisy**, his (mostly) faithful dog. An experienced long-distance walker, Daisy has completed all the trails above with Henry and her ambition is to walk all 15 National Trails.

Authors

Pennine Way First edition: 2006; this fifth edition: 2019

Publisher Trailblazer Publications
The Old Manse, Tower Rd, Hindhead, Surrey, GU26 6SU, UK
info@trailblazer-guides.com, trailblazer-guides.com

British Library Cataloguing in Publication Data
A catalogue record for this book is available from the British Library

ISBN 978-1-912716-02-9

Editing & layout: Anna Jacomb-Hood **Proofreading**: Clare Weldon
Cartography & illustrations (pp68-71): Nick Hill **Index**: Anna Jacomb-Hood
Photographs (flora): © Bryn Thomas
All other photographs: © Henry Stedman (unless otherwise indicated)

The maps in this guide were prepared from out-of-Crown-copyright Ordnance Survey maps amended and updated by Trailblazer.

Acknowledgements

FROM HENRY: Thanks to everyone who helped with the research of this guide including Sheri and Kieran on Fountains Fell, Iain Grimwood at Clove Lodge (and for the cup of tea), Steve Oxley and Steve Davis. Thanks to Zoë and Henry for allowing me to disappear for a few weeks to work on this project and to Daisy for the company over the entire trek.

At Trailblazer, thanks to: Anna Jacomb-Hood for her usual forensic editing, Nick Hill for maps, Clare Weldon for proofreading and Bryn Thomas, as always, for keeping me busy. I'd also like to Stuart Greig for the previous edition, ex-PWA chairman Chris Sainty and all those readers who wrote in with comments and suggestions, in particular Stuart Blackburne, Kevin Blick, Mick Brewster, Jonathan Brown, Dave Carroll, Iain Chippendale, James Connolly, Mike Cowley, Bill Gallon, Simon Hall, Mats Heder, Nichola Hele, Paul Higinbotham, R Hill, Tony Hutton, Muck Moses, Jolyon Neely, William O'Neill, Mick Scarfe, Simon and Sylvia, John Smithson, Chris Taylor, Rob Till, Paul Valcari, Willemijn W and Vinny Whalley.

A request

The authors and publisher have tried to ensure that this guide is as accurate and up to date as possible. However, things change even on these well-worn routes. If you notice any changes or omissions that should be included in the next edition of this guide, please email us (🖳 info@trailblazer-guides.com) or write to us (address above). Those persons making a significant contribution will be rewarded with a free copy of the next edition.

Warning: hillwalking can be dangerous

Photos – Front cover: Taking a break on Jacob's Ladder, on the way up to Kinder Scout.
This page: Walltown Crags, where the Pennine Way meets and follows Hadrian's Wall.
Previous page: Tackling the knee-knackering descent from Pen-y-ghent.
Overleaf: Drinking in the views from near the top of Shunner Fell.

Updated information will be available on: 🖳 **www.trailblazer-guides.com**

Printed in China; print production by D'Print (☎ +65-6581 3832), Singapore

Pennine Way

138 large-scale maps & guides to 57 towns and villages

PLANNING – PLACES TO STAY – PLACES TO EAT

EDALE TO KIRK YETHOLM

STUART GREIG &
HENRY STEDMAN

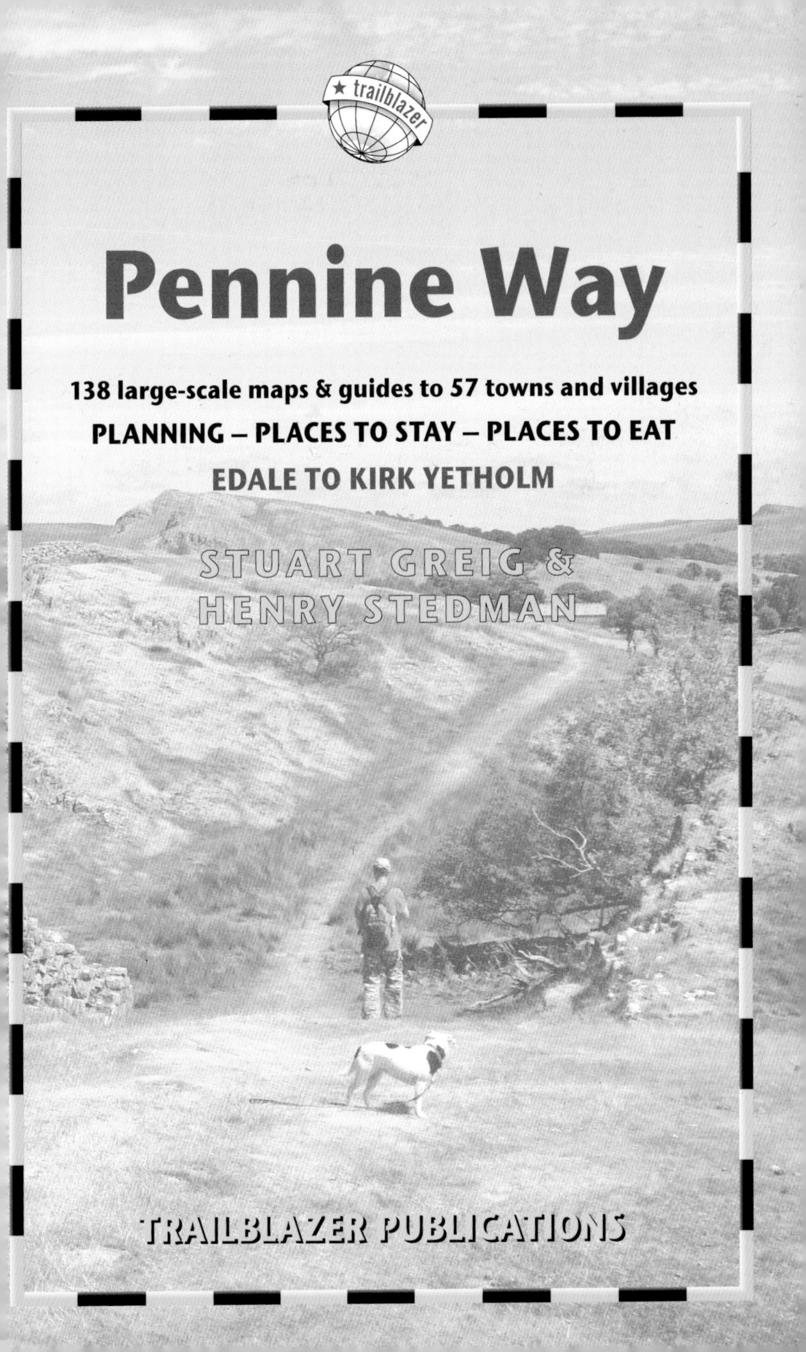

TRAILBLAZER PUBLICATIONS

Contents

INTRODUCTION

About the Pennine Way
History 9 – How difficult is the Pennine Way? 11
How long do you need? 12 – When to go 13

PART 1: PLANNING YOUR WALK

Practical information for the walker
Route finding 17 – GPS 17 – Accommodation 19
Food and drink 24 – Money and other services 27
Walking companies 27 – Information for foreign visitors 28
Walking with dogs 31

Budgeting 32

Itineraries
Village and town facilities 34 – Suggested itineraries 39
The best day and weekend (two-day) walks 39

What to take
Travelling light 44 – How to carry your luggage 44
Footwear 45 – Clothes 45 – Toiletries 46 – First-aid kit 47
General items 47 – Sleeping bag 47 – Camping gear 48
Maps 48 – Sources of further information 50
Recommended reading 51

Getting to and from the Pennine Way
National transport 51 – Getting to Britain 52 – Local transport 53
Public transport map 54 – Public transport services 56

PART 2: THE ENVIRONMENT & NATURE

Conserving the Pennines 60
Government agencies and schemes 60
Campaigning and conservation organisations 62

Flora and fauna
Wild flowers, grasses and other plants 63
Trees, woods and forests 65 – Birds 66 – Mammals 71
Reptiles 73

PART 3: MINIMUM IMPACT WALKING & OUTDOOR SAFETY

Minimum impact walking
Environmental impact 74 – Access and the right to roam 76

Outdoor safety
Avoidance of hazards 78 – Weather forecasts 79 – Blisters 79
Hypothermia, hyperthermia and sunburn 80

PART 4: ROUTE GUIDE & MAPS

Using this guide 81 **Edale** 83

Edale to Crowden 86 (Upper Booth 90, Snake Pass 93, Torside 93, Padfield & Hadfield 98, Crowden 98)

Crowden to Standedge 98 (Standedge 104, Marsden 104, Diggle 104)

Standedge to Calder Valley 106 (Blackstone Edge 110, Mankinholes 110, Todmorden 110, Hebden Bridge 114)

Calder Valley to Ickornshaw 119 (Blackshaw Head 120, Colden 120, Widdop 120, Ponden 124, Stanbury 124, Haworth 125, Ickornshaw 131, Cowling 131)

Ickornshaw to Malham 134 (Lothersdale 136, Earby 136, East Marton 136, Gargrave 140, Airton 142, Kirkby Malham 145, Malham 147)

Malham to Horton-in-Ribblesdale 149 (Horton-in-Ribblesdale 156)

Horton-in-Ribblesdale to Hawes 158 (Hawes 165)

Hawes to Tan Hill 170 (Hardraw 172, Thwaite 175, Muker 176, Keld 177, Tan Hill 180)

Tan Hill to Middleton-in-Teesdale 180 (Bowes Loop alternative route 183, Baldersdale 190, Cotherstone 190, Lunedale 190, Middleton-in-Teesdale 194)

Middleton-in-Teesdale to Dufton 196 (Holwick 198, High Force 198, Forest-in-Teesdale 200, Langdon Beck 202, Dufton 210)

Dufton to Alston 211 (Garrigill 218, Alston 218)

Alston to Greenhead 223 (Knarsdale 226, Kellah 231, Greenhead 231)

Greenhead to Bellingham 234 (Burnhead 238, Once Brewed 238, Stonehaugh 244, Bellingham 244)

Bellingham to Byrness 249 (Byrness 252)

Byrness to Kirk Yetholm 256 (Upper Coquetdale 271, Kirk Yetholm 271, Town Yetholm 272)

APPENDICES & INDEX

Map keys 273 GPS waypoints 274 Taking a dog 282 Index 285

DISTANCE CHART 290

OVERVIEW MAPS & PROFILES 292

Contents

ABOUT THIS BOOK

This guidebook contains all the information you need. The hard work has been done for you so you can plan your trip without having to consult numerous websites and other books and maps. When you're all packed and ready to go, there's comprehensive public transport information to get you to and from the trail and detailed maps (1:20,000) to help you find your way along it.

- Where to stay – from wild camping to B&Bs, hostels and hotels
- Walking companies if you want an organised tour and baggage-carrying services if you just want your luggage carried
- Itineraries for all levels of walkers
- Answers to all your questions: when is the best time to walk, how hard is it, what to pack and the approximate cost of the trip
- Walking times in both directions; GPS waypoints as a back-up to navigation
- Availability and opening times of cafés, pubs, tea-shops, restaurants, and shops/supermarkets along the route
- Rail, bus and taxi information for the towns and villages on or near the Way
- Street maps of the main towns and villages
- Historical, cultural and geographical background information

❑ MINIMUM IMPACT FOR MAXIMUM INSIGHT

Nature's peace will flow into you as the sunshine flows into trees. The winds will blow their freshness into you and storms their energy, while cares will drop off like autumn leaves. **John Muir** (one of the world's first and most influential environmentalists, born in 1838)

Why is walking in wild and solitary places so satisfying? Partly it is the sheer physical pleasure: sometimes pitting one's strength against the elements and the lie of the land. The beauty and wonder of the natural world and the fresh air restore our sense of proportion and the stresses and strains of everyday life slip away. Whatever the character of the countryside, walking in it benefits us mentally and physically, inducing a sense of well-being, an enrichment of life and an enhanced awareness of what lies around us. All this the countryside gives us and the least we can do is to safeguard it by supporting rural economies, local businesses, and low-impact methods of farming and land-management, and by using environmentally sensitive forms of transport – walking being pre-eminent.

In this book there's a section on the wildlife and conservation of the region and a chapter on minimum-impact walking, with ideas on how to tread lightly in this fragile environment; by following its principles we can help to preserve our natural heritage for future generations.

INTRODUCTION

The Pennine Way is the grand-daddy of all the UK National Trails and although its 268-mile (431km) length doesn't qualify it as the longest trail (that honour goes to the mammoth 636-mile long South-West Coast Path), it was the first and is probably the best known of all the National Trails. Surprisingly, it is almost equally loved and loathed by those that walk it and it is certainly a challenge however you decide to tackle it.

As well as physical fitness... above all else a Pennine Wayfarer needs a positive mental attitude.

As well as physical fitness, determination and an ability to smile in the face of a howling wind, above all else a Pennine Wayfarer needs a positive mental attitude. There will be times when you just want to throw in the towel, catch the next train or bus home and never return to the moors again, but you must overcome these moments of weakness if you want to reach Scotland and the Border Hotel.

As you progress, the walking gets easier as you become fitter, the scenery is diverse and engaging and there's always something of interest to see, including an incredible variety of plants and wildlife and some of the best walking to be had in the UK.

The impressive limestone amphitheatre known as Malham Cove (see p147).

The path begins in the Peak District, in the heart of England and cunningly weaves between the old industrial centres of Manchester, Huddersfield, Halifax and Burnley. By sticking as much as possible to the high heather moors between these conurbations it visits Stoodley Pike monument and Top Withins, thought by some to be Wuthering Heights from Emily Brontë's novel.

The path soon leaves the gritstone of the Southern Pennines behind and the rocks become light grey as you enter limestone country through the Airedale Gap and into Malham, the home of the incredible amphitheatre of Malham Cove. A tough day over Fountains Fell and Pen-y-ghent brings you to Horton-in-Ribblesdale, the start and finish of the Yorkshire Three Peaks walk. The Way visits the iconic Yorkshire Dales of Wensleydale and Swaledale and traverses Great Shunner Fell between them. After a quick stop at the highest pub in Great Britain (Tan Hill Inn) you reach the halfway point at Baldersdale. Now your muscles are like steel wires, you hardly feel the weight of your rucksack and you have your sights firmly set on Scotland.

Possibly the best day walk anywhere in the country starts at Middleton-in-Teesdale, taking in three incredible waterfalls and the stunning glacial valley of High Cup, followed the next day, by the highest point on the walk over Cross Fell (2930ft/893m).

Beyond this, you spend a day walking the best section of Hadrian's Wall, before plunging into the forests of Wark and Redesdale, emerging into the town of Bellingham, the last proper outpost of civilisation before the end.

Above: The ruins of Top Withins (see p119), believed to be the inspiration and setting for the Earnshaw's house in Emily Brontë's *Wuthering Heights*. **Below**: View from the trail overlooking Lower Laithe Reservoir, near Haworth.

Technically you've left the Pennines behind now, as you pass through Byrness and over the rolling green mountains of the Cheviot range for the last marathon section into Kirk Yetholm.

You may arrive at the Border Hotel a different person – the walk has certainly had a profound effect on many of the people who have walked it (see the boxes on p12, p30, p31, p33, p36, p37, p38, p42, p43 and p284), but even if not, you've completed one of the planet's great walks. And if you've managed to do it without getting rained on, you really are one in a million!

About the Pennine Way

HISTORY

Anyone walking the Pennine Way today owes a debt of thanks to the journalist Tom Stephenson. When he first proposed 'a long green trail' in 1935 there were no official long-distance footpaths in the UK. He first described 'a Pennine Way from the Peaks to the Cheviots' in an article in the *Daily Herald* in June of that year, in response to a letter from two American ramblers who were looking for suggestions on walks to do in England. America, he said, already had two incredible treks: the 2000-mile (3200km) long Appalachian Trail in the east and the even longer, 2500-mile (4000km) John Muir Trail up the western side of the country. Albeit on a smaller scale, he suggested there was no reason why England couldn't produce a walk to compare with these enterprises.

When Tom Stephenson first proposed 'a long green trail' in 1935 there were no official long-distance footpaths in the UK

It took 30 years of wrangling, negotiation, compromise and even conflict to agree a 256-mile* (412km) route from Edale, along almost the exact route proposed by Stephenson, to Kirk Yetholm in Scotland. The Pennine Way was finally

* now 253 miles (407.5km) or 268 miles (429km) including optional side routes.

❑ Alfred Wainwright and the Pennine Way

Alfred Wainwright is best known for his Coast to Coast Path from St Bees to Robin Hood's Bay although he is also closely associated with the Pennine Way. It is he you must thank for the tradition that still persists: that anyone who completes the Way is rewarded with a half-pint of beer in the Border Hotel in Kirk Yetholm. This was originally paid for by the man himself, although the hotel and brewery foot the bill now. He famously hated the Pennine Way, likening the bliss of finishing with that felt when you stop banging your head on a wall. He suffered from terrible weather and fell victim to the notorious peat bogs on Black Hill (now tamed) and was mightily relieved to be rescued by a companion and a Park Ranger who happened to be passing close by at the time. Thankfully the popularity of the walk has not been unduly affected by his words – perhaps it's the lure of that glass of beer at the end?

The notorious peat bogs on sodden Black Hill, which made the route hard going for early Wayfarers, were tamed with a slab causeway. The area has now been reseeded with grasses. Photo © Stuart Greig.

opened at an official ceremony on Malham Moor on 24th April 1965. Like many 'official' openings, then and now, the path had been in common use for a while before this ceremony took place, with walkers using a pamphlet from the Ramblers' Association (as it was called at the time) to follow the route (see box p33). However, it wasn't until 1969 that the first official Pennine Way guidebook was published, by HMSO, written of course by Tom himself.

The original premise of a natural path, ie 'no concrete or asphalt', meant a much tougher walk for the first Pennine Wayfarers, as much of the path crossed terrain that tended to hold water, not least the dreaded peat bogs! As more and more feet churned the delicate peat into an ever-widening black morass, slabs were laid over the worst of the erosion to protect the environment and, as a result, walkers benefited from certain navigation and dry feet in places where previously neither was guaranteed. The Pennine Way was just the first of many, so if you walk any of the country's long-distance paths (official or otherwise), doff your cap and raise a glass to Tom Stephenson; surely the father of long-distance walking in the UK.

The lovely Green Dragon pub at Hardraw (see p172). How many other pubs can boast their own waterfall?

HOW DIFFICULT IS THE PENNINE WAY?

This book is not intended to mislead, so be prepared for a tough walk, especially if you plan to walk the Way in one go! There are only a few demanding days that you can't break down into smaller chunks (unless you're wild camping), but the real challenge is walking day after day for over two weeks. If you could guarantee good weather for those two or three weeks, that would also reduce the difficulty of the Way, but this is England and on the high moors you really can experience all four seasons in one day.

A paraglider takes advantage of the perfect conditions around Stoodley Pike, high on the hills above Hebden Bridge.

Over recent years the waymarking has improved and slabs across some of the expanses of peat have made navigation easier, but there are still wild and remote sections where navigation skills are required, so the ability to read a map and use a GPS or compass is essential. Half the Pennine Way is on open moorland and a quarter on rough grazing; only a tenth passes through forest, woodland or along riverbanks.

Over the course of the Pennine Way you will climb approximately 40,000ft (12,000m)

Over the course of the Pennine Way you will climb approximately 40,000ft (12,000m), but don't be put off, there are very few steep gradients and even the most serious sufferer of vertigo is unlikely to be troubled. There are about 230 miles (369.5km) on slopes of less than 10°, 20 miles (32km) on slopes of 10-15°, and only 3½ miles (6km) on steep slopes of more than 15°. However, if you can read a map and comfortably walk at least 12 miles (19km) in a day you should manage it; just don't expect every day to be a walk in the park.

'Nothing in life worth having comes easy', or so the saying goes and this applies to the Pennine Way. Many experienced and hill-hardened walkers leave Edale and never finish; but those who do can stand proud and claim to have walked one of the toughest paths in Britain.

Greg's Hut (see p215), the lonely bothy situated by the track known ominously as Corpse Road, is a welcome sight for those descending from Cross Fell, at 893m (2930ft) the highest point on the Pennines.

HOW LONG DO YOU NEED?

However long you take, you're unlikely to complete the Pennine Way faster than Mike Hartley did in 1989. The current record holder completed the route in 2 days, 17 hours and 20 minutes, running without sleep and stopping only twice on the way, one of which was for fish & chips in Alston. Most mortals average 17 days and even that schedule has some long days of well over 20 miles (32km) in it. Trying to fit the Pennine Way into a 14-day holiday is another order of magnitude, with many more challenging days, and would be a step too far for most walkers. A relaxed schedule with a couple of rest days will require 19-21 days.

Most mortals average 17 days and even that schedule has some long days of well over 20 miles (32km)

See pp39-41 for some suggested itineraries covering different walking speeds

Whichever schedule you choose, or have imposed upon you, there are going to be some long days that can only be broken by the flexibility of wild camping (see pp19-20), or by negotiation with B&B owners or taxi drivers for collection from the path and a return the next morning. The final 25½-mile (41km) marathon stage from Byrness to Kirk Yetholm being a prime example of this.

❑ Doing the walk in several stages

I first walked the Pennine Way in 2010 over 17 glorious days in May and it's an experience I will never forget; the accomplishment of a dream I'd had for almost 10 years. It's a long walk! Forgive the statement of the obvious, but few people (including myself) who set out on this endeavour have ever walked such a distance in one go before. It is a supreme test of both physical fitness and mental fortitude and many walkers fail to reach their goal in Kirk Yetholm. Many more just don't have the time to allocate the best part of three weeks to this challenge.

An alternative approach is to walk the Way in stages, breaking the route down into manageable chunks and completing it over one, two or even several years. On my 2010 walk I met a couple who spent one long weekend every year doing a stage of the walk. They were eight years in, with two more to go! For my update I was forced, through circumstances, to break the walk down into several short stages and as I was typically walking alone, I used a car, in conjunction with public transport to shuttle back and forth along the length of the track to complete these linear stages.

Trains alone can be used as far as the Roman Wall, with Bardon Mill station, on the Newcastle–Carlisle line, being two miles from Rapishaw Gap where the Pennine Way leaves the Wall and strikes out north towards Scotland. Beyond this point you will need to rely on a combination of buses and trains to complete your journey.

Between Edale and Bardon Mill there are stations at regular intervals, sometimes right on the Pennine Way, sometimes a two- or three-mile diversion away, but there are enough to provide a degree of flexibility into your stage lengths. I often used a car to drive to one station, park there, catch a train to a station further south and then walk for three or four days back to the car, but this was purely for convenience and I could have managed with just trains alone.

I hope this information, along with the transport maps on p54 and p55, may provide inspiration for anyone who feels that the Pennine Way is out of their reach, for whatever reason. **Stuart Greig** (who updated the previous edition of this guide)

When to go

SEASONS

The **main walking season** in the UK is from Easter (late March/April) to October; in terms of weather and the lack of crowds the best months in which to do the Way are May, June and September.

In terms of weather and the lack of crowds the best months in which to do the Way are May, June and September.

Spring

In the UK, **March** can produce some of the most wintery conditions we experience, especially on the high hills. It may just as easily deliver wonderfully fresh sunny days though; so the best advice we can give is to hope for the best – but prepare for the worst!

The month of **April** is one of the most unpredictable for walkers. The weather can be warm and sunny, though blustery days with showers are more typical; there is a good chance that snow will still be lying on the higher tops. On the plus side, hills are beginning to return to green, there won't be many other walkers about, there will be plenty of wild flowers and the birdsong will be at its best.

By **May** the weather has improved significantly and this is often the driest month of the year, with temperatures at just the right level for walking; not too hot, but warm enough to bask in the sun at lunchtime. The long school summer break is still weeks away so the path will be quiet, wild flowers are out in their full glory and the daylight will outlast your stamina.

Ascending Bleaklow (see p95) in early April. This is one of the most unpredictable months and there may still be some snow on higher ground. Photo © Stuart Greig.

Summer

Of the summer months, **June** probably has the most consistent walking weather and will be much quieter than **late July** and **August** when the UK schools break up for the long summer holiday. Tourist numbers boom and places such as Haworth, Malham and the Yorkshire Dales become bustling hives of colourful waterproofs, traffic blocks the lanes and accommodation becomes scarce. Just because it's summer, don't expect constant sun; there's typically as much rain in August as there is in March, it's just warmer rain.

Autumn

Schools resume in early **September** and quiet returns to many places along the Way. Autumn colours make the rare woodland sections a sheer delight, but even the hills display a pleasant coppery hue as bracken dies back and the heather

❑ FESTIVALS AND ANNUAL EVENTS ALONG THE PENNINE WAY

January to March

• **Montane Spine Race** (🖳 thespinerace.com) Held each January, this is Britain's longest non-stop foot race and competitors must complete all 268 miles of the Pennine Way, in winter, in under 7 days. The 2017 winner, Tom Hollins, finished in an incredible 99 hours 25 mins – yet even this wasn't enough to beat the previous year's record time of 99 hours 17 minutes, set by Eoin Keith.

April to July

• **Yorkshire Three Peaks Challenge** (🖳 threepeakschallenge.uk/yorkshire-three-peaks-challenge, see box p156) Held for 60 years on the last Saturday in April in the area around Horton-in-Ribblesdale.

• **Fellsman Hike** (🖳 fellsman.org.uk) A 60-mile high-level traverse from Ingleton to Threshfield via Dodd Fell (see Map 53, p164) held for over 50 years across two days in April or May. The event challenges the competitors' navigational skills and fitness.

• **Swaledale Arts Festival** (🖳 swaledale-festival.org.uk) Brass bands, jazz and various art and walking events; held over two weeks from late May to early June.

• **Yetholm Festival Week** Second week in June climaxing with a duck race.

• **Edale Country Day** (🖳 edalecountryday.org.uk) Wacky races, wood turning, sheep shearing, morris dancers, brass bands and maypole dancing; held in June.

• **Twice Brewed Roman Wall Show** Sheep and shepherds show on the second Saturday in June.

• **Malham Show** (🖳 malhamdale.com/showindex.htm) Agricultural show and other events, including falconry displays, held in late August.

• **Hawes & District Gala** Held on a Saturday in late June, Hawes Gala has been going for over half a century now and includes fancy dress processions, tug of war contests and fairground rides.

• **Hebden Bridge Arts Festival** (🖳 hebdenbridgeartsfestival.co.uk) Music, comedy, drama, talks and exhibitions held at the end of June and start of July.

For details of other events in **Hebden Bridge** during the year visit 🖳 hebdenbridge.co.uk/events.

August and September

• **Middleton Carnival** (🖳 www.facebook.com/middletoncarnival) is held in Middleton-in-Teesdale in early August.

• **Gargrave Show** (🖳 gargraveshow.org.uk) Over a century old, an agricultural show featuring prize cattle and sheepdog trials; mid August.

• **Dufton Agricultural Show** (🖳 duftonshow.co.uk) Agricultural show and sheepdog trials; last Saturday in August.

• **Bellingham Show & Country Festival** (🖳 bellinghamshow.co.uk) Held on the last Saturday in August; expect country events, wrestling, tug-of-war and lots of live music.

• **Bowes Agricultural Show** (🖳 bowesshow.org.uk) A traditional English agricultural and farming show, held in early to mid September.

• **Three Peaks Cyclocross** (🖳 3peakscyclocross.org.uk) Held on the last Sunday in September and using the path from Pen-y-ghent to Horton; perhaps a day to avoid doing this stage of the Pennine Way.

• **Hardraw Scar Brass Band Festival** (🖳 yhbba.org.uk/hardraw1.html) Running since 1884 in the grounds of the Green Dragon Inn; second Sunday in September.

loses its purple flowers. The path is quieter because there are fewer tourists, but also because the weather becomes more unpredictable; you may well get some wonderfully warm, calm days, but you'll also get more windy and rainy days.

Expect similar conditions in **October** and **November**, with most days being wet and windy and with rare gems in between where the sun shines and the wind relents. Underfoot conditions begin to deteriorate; more rain means the ground becomes soaked and lowland pastures and high Pennine plateaus alike become wet and muddy.

Winter

According to the Christmas cards and Charles Dickens, winter is a month of cold, frosty mornings and snow-draped hills. You will get a scattering of wonderful clear winter days between December and the end of February, but they will be surrounded by windy, rainy days. Even snow, which, once fallen, can add a magical element to the hills, can be disorientating and dangerous if it's falling heavily enough in high places.

As well as the days being much shorter, many B&Bs and guesthouse owners close up to go on their annual holiday and hostels and bunkhouses close for long periods; even some shops close over the winter. As a result, you may struggle to complete the long stages in daylight and that brings its own problems and risks. You

Dropping down off the summit of Pen-y-ghent (see p149).

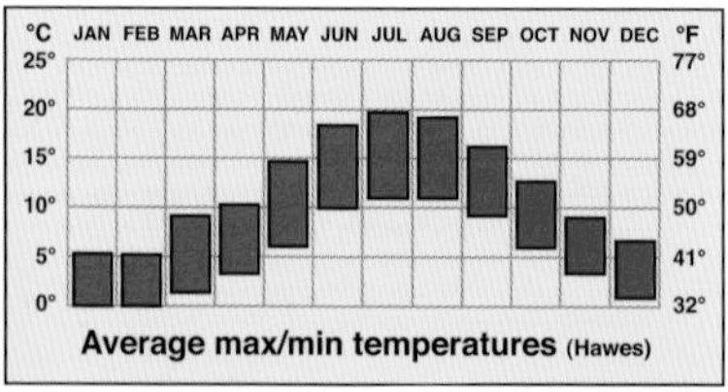
°C JAN FEB MAR APR MAY JUN JUL AUG SEP OCT NOV DEC °F
25° 20° 15° 10° 5° 0°
77° 68° 59° 50° 41° 32°
Average max/min temperatures (Hawes)

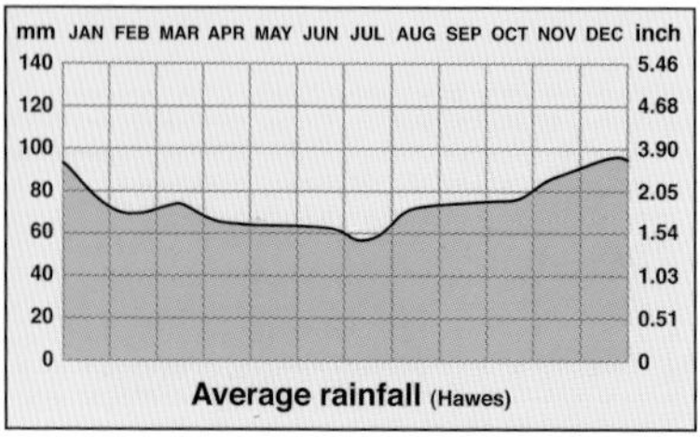
mm JAN FEB MAR APR MAY JUN JUL AUG SEP OCT NOV DEC inch
140 120 100 80 60 40 20 0
5.46 4.68 3.90 2.05 1.54 1.03 0.51 0
Average rainfall (Hawes)

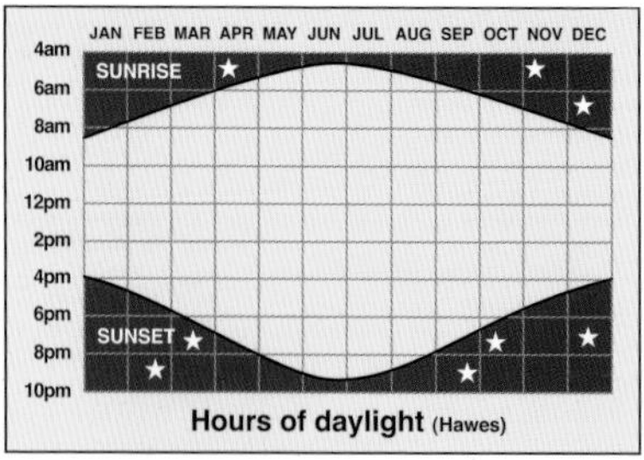
JAN FEB MAR APR MAY JUN JUL AUG SEP OCT NOV DEC
4am 6am 8am 10am 12pm 2pm 4pm 6pm 8pm 10pm
SUNRISE
SUNSET
Hours of daylight (Hawes)

will need to carry more equipment too as you don't want to be caught out climbing Pen-y-ghent in snow and ice without crampons. This will mean your pack is heavier and therefore your speed will drop.

TEMPERATURE, RAINFALL AND DAYLIGHT HOURS

These days the Pennines are certainly less wet than their reputation suggests and if you pick your time of year you can minimise your chances of spending days encased in a waterproof shell. There is no 'right time' of the year to avoid the weather though; if there's anything predictable about the English weather, it's how unpredictable it will be. The charts on these pages can only provide a rough guide.

Between late April and early September the daylight hours will usually exceed the hours you need to or, indeed, wish to walk along the Way. Outside this period though, careful note should be taken of the daylight available to you; leave early and finish early is a good approach to adopt, leaving time in the afternoon as a backup in case of problems or an injury that slows you down.

The hours of daylight chart (see above) gives the sunrise and sunset times for the middle of each month at Hawes, a town about halfway along the Pennine Way which gives a reasonably accurate picture for daylight for the whole trail.

Depending on the weather you can get a further 30-45 minutes of usable twilight after sunset. By this time you should be nearly done anyway, following a clear path to a village bathed in warm lamplight.

● **Opposite Top**: The distinctive chimney of Dale End Textile Mill dominates the view over Lothersdale. **Bottom**: On the top of Fountains Fell (see p149), the views from which are remarkable for their lack of houses, pylons, poles and other signs of civilisation.

● **Overleaf Left**: The glaciated valley known as High Cup (see p198) is one of the most impressive sights on the walk. **Right**: Clearly in need of a drink, Daisy hurries towards Britain's highest pub, the Tan Hill Inn (see p180). **Centre, right**: Built in the 14th century, Thirlwall Castle (see p232) is largely made from stones from nearby Hadrian's Wall. **Bottom**: The imposing rocky escarpment of Whin Sill provides a daunting barrier to those coming from the north – a fact exploited by the Romans, who built their Wall along its top.

PLANNING YOUR WALK 1

Practical information for the walker

ROUTE FINDING

Despite the improvement in waymarks and the many helpful and photogenic wooden signposts, there are still plenty of places where you will stand and think, 'Where's the path gone?' Fortunately, on some open moorlands the presence of slabbed causeways not only makes for easy-going across the mire but also acts as an easy-to-follow trail, even in zero visibility. However, the ability to read a map is the single most-important skill you can acquire before setting out on the Pennine Way. The ability to use a compass or a GPS is the next.

There are sections of the route that are only ever walked by Pennine Wayfarers, so you can't always rely on someone else coming along to help you out. The Pennine Way is very long and the relatively small number of walkers means that, unlike other national trails, you can't simply follow the flow of folk leaving the town or village in the morning. You have to rely on yourself. In many cases there will be a visible path on the ground, made by walkers who have come before you. This may be as subtle as footprints in the early morning dew, a path of flattened grass across a field, or a track as obvious as a wide scar in a peat moor; all of which may help in route finding. The further north you get, the less often these worn paths occur as the number of Pennine Wayfarers diminishes and you become the trailblazer rather than the follower.

GPS

I never carried a compass, preferring to rely on a good sense of direction... I never bothered to understand how a compass works or what it is supposed to do ... To me a compass is a gadget, and I don't get on well with gadgets of any sort. **Alfred Wainwright**

While Wainwright's acolytes may scoff, other walkers will accept GPS technology as an inexpensive, well-established if non-essential, navigational aid. To cut a long story short, within a minute of being turned on and with a clear view of the sky, **GPS receivers** will estab-

---

(Opposite) Top: Lapwing, little owl and curlew, just some of the many birds you may see on the trek. **Middle**: The wonderful High Force (see p200) – just don't get too close to the edge! **Bottom**: A farmhouse by the River Tees on one of the loneliest stretches on the trail: Middleton-in-Teesdale to Dufton.

lish your position as well as elevation in a variety of formats, including the British OS grid system to an accuracy of within a few metres. These days, most **smartphones** have a GPS receiver built in and mapping software available to run on them (see p49).

One thing must be understood, however: **treating GPS as a replacement for maps, map-reading skills and/or a compass is a big mistake**. Although current units are robust, it only takes an electronic malfunction to leave you in the dark. GPS is merely a navigational aid or backup to conventional route finding and, in almost all cases, is best used in conjunction with a paper map. All a GPS should be relied on to do, is stop you exacerbating navigational errors or save you time in correcting them.

Using GPS with this book

In most cases the maps in this book are adequate for route finding, but should you stray from the path you may need to resort to the GPS to bring you back onto both the track and the map. This book includes 309 GPS waypoints that can be pre-loaded into your device before you leave, for just this sort of situation.

Most of the maps in the book contain one or more numbered waypoints, which correlate with the list provided on pp274-81. Here you will find the numbered waypoint, an OS grid reference, the longitude/latitude position in a decimal minute format and a brief description. You'll find more waypoints on bleak moorland sections such as Cross Fell, where a walk can degenerate into a prolonged stumble through thick mist. Typically the end or start of a slabbed section is also marked, as well as cairns and other significant landmarks or turnings. In towns and villages waypoints are less common but in places can still be useful to pin down an unsigned turn down an alleyway, for example.

The GPS waypoints can be used at the point you need them, by manually keying them into your handheld GPS unit, or more easily and with more certain accuracy by downloading the list for free from the Trailblazer website.

The method for uploading the waypoint file into your GPS unit will vary by device and you should check your manufacturer's documentation for instructions on doing this and to ensure your device supports the number of waypoints provided here. The file itself, as well as notes on .gpx files, can be found at: 💻 **trailblazer-guides.com/gps-waypoints**.

© Chris Scott

Some days are clearly better than others.

Many of the top-end GPS devices now include **digital maps**, displayed on a colour screen with your position superimposed on the display. This means you can instantly see your position on an Ordnance Survey map without having to convert map references onto a paper map. These digital maps, depending on their scale and quality, can be expensive and unless you walk regularly it is unlikely it will be easy to justify their expense for the Pennine Way alone. See box on p49 for more information on digital mapping.

Remember that tens of thousands of people walked the Pennine Way before the invention of GPS and before the proliferation of waymarking and other navigational aids such as the slabs that exist today. You don't need to use GPS to walk the Way but if you wish to avoid those inevitable frustrating moments of navigational uncertainty the technology now exists to return you to the path quickly. Think of it as a way of getting you into a hot bath or shower, or in front of the fire in the pub, all the sooner.

ACCOMMODATION

There is no shortage of accommodation along the Pennine Way and the options increase if you're prepared to walk a mile or two off the path, although this is rarely an absolute necessity. Many of the towns and villages on the Way are situated in popular walking areas and have an abundance of walker-friendly establishments, including hotels, B&Bs, hostels, bunkhouses and campsites. This means that you often don't need to book weeks in advance of your walk.

If you plan on walking in the high season (between mid July and early September), however, you are well advised to book at least a few days in advance, especially if your stay coincides with a weekend as accommodation, even in a town with many options, can fill up quickly upon the announcement of a weekend of decent weather (see box p22).

Camping

If you're doing the Pennine Way on a budget you may be considering using campsites for your evening stops. Be aware that facilities at campsites vary wildly between locations and you may just as easily find yourself directed towards a field already occupied by sheep, as pitching on the manicured lawn of a modern, fully equipped 'glamping' site. You may also be letting yourself in for the worst of both worlds – you lack the freedom and exhilaration of sleeping out in the wilds (see below) and the negligible soundproofing of close-packed tents means a rowdy group can ruin your evening.

As long as you avoid packed campsites, the flexibility offered by this approach can pay dividends; there's no need to book accommodation, you can change plans on a whim, or depending on the weather, and you can treat yourself to a more comfortable option whenever it's available.

The only real advantages to campsites over wild camping are the perceived sense of security, the hot shower and toilets and the probable availability of a nearby pub for an evening meal. This last also means that you may be able to dispense with carrying anything other than emergency rations.

Wild camping (See also box p39) Of all the national trails in England, the Pennine Way probably offers the best chance to wild camp along the full length. Huge sections of the route are on high ground beyond the last farm wall or fence and there are plenty of inconspicuous places to pitch a small tent.

Wild camping offers the ultimate outdoor experience in this country, especially in the warm summer months; what could be better than sitting and watching the sun set behind the hills with your warm brew, or a wee dram, in hand? Perhaps, an early start to watch the sun rise? It also allows you to avoid the sometimes unnecessary diversion into town for accommodation, usually downhill with the inevitable uphill slog to return to the path in the morning.

Officially, in England and Wales, you need to seek the permission of the landowner before you can camp anywhere, but this is typically impractical and often impossible. An acceptable compromise, often shared by landowners, can be achieved by following these simple rules:

- Camp late or out of sight of nearby buildings and leave early
- Camp in small groups of no-more than two or three tents
- Never make open fires
- Bury or pack out your toilet waste (see pp75-6)
- Leave no trace of your camp.

If you are spotted by a landowner, as long as you clearly look like a walker in transit they probably won't shoot you but, if they ask you to move on, you must comply. Bedding down late and leaving early should avoid the chances of such a confrontation. Avoid camping beside a gate that is obviously well used and you will reduce your chance of inconveniencing a farmer coming and going from the hills.

In the Pennines there are some **wild camping black spots**: one is Kinder Scout, the first day out of Edale. Because of the high peat-fire risk during very dry and always busy summers it's not unknown for rangers to set out in the evening to harry wild campers. Spare the hassle and save your wild nights until you're over the Snake Pass, if not the A62. Ever busy Hadrian's Wall is also a place you'd want to avoid pitching a tent, particularly as the authorities are concerned that wild campers could disturb/damage/destroy the as-yet unexcavated archaeological remains. As such, we recommend you head for Wark Forest instead.

Camping barns, bunkhouses and hostels [see box p22]

For walkers on a budget this type of accommodation is absolutely perfect; it is available in almost every town and village on the path and you are more likely to be able to just turn up at the door and get a bed, or ring the night before and book one, than if you were using B&B-style accommodation (see opposite).

The quality of the accommodation will vary widely though, so don't expect a room on your own or fluffy pillows and feather duvets; you will typically be sleeping in a dormitory/room with multiple bunk beds. In the height of the season these can be busy places and you need to be prepared for this; a busy bunkhouse kitchen can be a true test of patience and compromise and ear-plugs are an essential part of any hostelling kit list!

For many the appeal of this type of accommodation is the fact that you're bunking with fellow walkers, often following the same trail, and can take the time to sit down, talk and swap 'war stories', rather than just a passing greeting on the trail. Friendships that can span a lifetime are sometimes created in this way.

At the lowest end of the scale is the **camping barn** (£8-15 per person). This may be no more than a roof over your head, a raised wooden sleeping platform, a kitchen area, where you use your own stove, and a toilet with a shower if you're lucky. Assume that you'll need your full camping kit list (apart from the tent) for this type of accommodation.

Bunkhouses provide more facilities and you can expect to pay around £15-22pp per night. For this you will get a bunk bed, cooking facilities, hot showers and maybe even a drying room where you can hang wet gear. You will normally need a sleeping bag although some provide bedding for a small charge. Don't *expect* breakfast or an evening meal, though some bunkhouses do offer these.

There are two main types of **hostel** – privately run businesses and those that are part of the Youth Hostel Association (YHA). They both offer a similar level of service, but prices may vary depending on location and facilities.

If you are planning on using YHA hostels (☎ 0800-019 1700 or ☎ 01629-592700, 💻 yha.org.uk) for the majority of your stops it is worth becoming a member, as non-members pay an additional fee (around £3) per night. You can join online, or at any hostel as you check in. YHA annual membership costs £10/15 for under-26s/over-26s; £5 discount for both if you pay by direct debit. You can either book accommodation online through the YHA website or by phone.

Hostels vary widely in size, age and user demographic. If you don't enjoy sharing an enclosed space with 50 intense children, high on fresh air and freedom from parental guidance, be sure to check in advance at places such as Edale and The Sill on Hadrian's Wall, as these are prime locations for school parties. Members can expect to pay between £15 and £30 per night; you are guaranteed a hot shower and a self-catering kitchen; most hostels provide an evening meal and breakfast for an additional fee. Free wi-fi is available at many hostels.

To find out if any hostels are closing for refurbishment or any other important changes visit the YHA website.

Camping pods and 'glamping'

Acting as a halfway house between camping and staying in a B&B, several sites now have **camping pods** – basic but comfortable 'sleeping sheds', usually simply furnished with a table and sleeping platform, though you'll often have to have your own bedding/sleeping bag. Prices vary widely but the better ones are around the £30pp mark.

Even a walk as remote as the Pennine Way hasn't entirely been immune to the current craze for **glamping** – where the campsite provides you with a luxury tent (often a bell tent or yurt) fitted out with rugs, furniture and a proper bed to sleep in. Indeed, even Edale, right at the start of the trek, now boasts its own (very upmarket) 'glampsite'. It's great fun of course, though not cheap, with prices more akin to an upmarket B&B (or, in Edale's case, an upmarket hotel!) than a campsite.

Bed and Breakfast (B&B)

The title says it all; in this type of accommodation you get a bed for the night and a breakfast in the morning. In most cases you will be staying in someone's home; they may run it as a business with a dozen rooms in a converted farmhouse or you may be sleeping in little Johnny's room now that he's left for university. The quality and facilities of Pennine Way B&Bs range from luxurious to spartan, but they are nearly always clean, tidy and efficient.

The real benefit of B&B accommodation is the fact that you get a room to yourself and you can travel light. A hot shower, or bath, at the end of the day, followed by a good night's sleep and a hearty cooked breakfast are enough to revive most walkers after a gruelling day on the fells. B&Bs in remote locations, where there is no pub nearby, may also offer an evening meal for an additional fee and if booked in advance. Many also offer a packed lunch option.

Any B&B on the Pennine Way will be accustomed to taking in walkers, often dripping wet on their doorstep, wind-blown and mud-spattered. The best ones have drying facilities, some will even do your washing (for a small charge). The psychological boost of putting on clean, dry clothing in the morning should not be underestimated!

❑ Should you book your accommodation in advance?

When walking the Pennine Way it's advisable to have your night's accommodation booked at least by the time you set off in the morning. Although it may compromise your spontaneity, most daily stages are pretty clear cut and booking enables you to enjoy the walk (or suffer its torments) knowing you have a secure bed come nightfall. You need to be particularly careful at weekends, when many people hike the trail and the accommodation can get booked up weeks and sometimes months in advance, particularly during the summer holidays and in those areas where accommodation is, in general, scarce anyway. That said, there's a certain amount of hysteria regarding the booking of accommodation, some insisting you start booking at least six months in advance. Whilst it's true that the earlier you book the more chance you'll have of getting precisely the accommodation you want, booking so far in advance leaves you vulnerable to changing circumstances.

The situation is often not as bad as some suggest, at least not outside the high season (the school holidays from the middle of July to the first week of September). Outside this period, and particularly in April/May or September, as long as you're flexible and willing to take what's offered you should get away with booking just a few nights in advance, or indeed often just the night before. The exceptions to this rule are weekends and places where accommodation is limited, and also if a festival or major event is happening.

If you're planning on staying in **hostels** the same applies though do be careful when travelling out of high season as some YHA hostels have limited opening days/hours between November and March. Once again, it's well worth booking at least one night before, and well before that if it's a weekend or the summer holidays, to make sure the hostel isn't fully booked or shut. Note that **bunkhouses** are often booked by groups on a sole-occupancy basis, particularly in holiday periods, so it is essential to book in advance.

Be aware that generally you will be asked for a **deposit** when you book, which might be non refundable, or a refund may incur an administration charge.

If you have to cancel do try and telephone your hosts; it saves a lot of worry and allows them to provide a bed for someone else.

❑ B&B-style accommodation

• **Rooms** **Single rooms** are likely to be small and their availability is limited. **Twin rooms** have two single beds while a **double** generally has one double bed though sometimes has two single beds that can be separated to make twin beds when required. **Triples** generally have a double and a single, or three single beds, and **quads** often have a double bed with bunk beds/two single beds, or four single beds; thus for a group of three/four people two may have to share a double bed; however, these rooms can also be used as a double or twin.

• **Facilities** An **en suite room** typically attracts a higher rate and often this is just a small shower cubicle with a toilet and basin squeezed into the room. So don't automatically turn your nose up at a **bathroom** across the corridor which could be much more spacious and there's nothing quite as relaxing as a proper bath at the end of a long day. Bathrooms may be shared with other rooms (**shared facilities**) or they may be for the sole use of the guests in a particular room (**private facilities**).

• **Rates** In this guide rates are quoted on a **per person** (pp) per night basis based on two people sharing a room. Rates range from £27.50pp (the pubs in Alston were amongst the cheapest rooms we found) for a bed in a room with a shared bathroom up to £50+pp for a very comfortable room with an en suite, or private, bathroom and all mod cons. Most places listed in this guide are £35-45pp, though a night in some of the hotels en route could be up to £60pp – or even more. Also hotel rates do not always include breakfast so check in advance. Hotels (and some hostels including those owned by the YHA) change their tariffs at a moment's notice in response to the number of visitors, so use the prices in this book as a rough guide. In the low season (Sep-Mar) prices may come down to some extent. Also some places shut over the winter months.

Solo walkers will normally pay a premium for any room other than a single as most places charge a **single occupancy supplement** of between £10 and £30 for multi-bed rooms; there are still some B&Bs that don't charge any extra – but there are also some places that insist that solo walkers pay the full room price. In the height of the season, in some places, you could even be expected to pay the room rate and, unless you pay for two people, there are establishments that won't accept bookings from solo travellers at weekends, as they can usually be sure to fill them with two people. If the rate quoted is for a room (not per person) there may be a discount for single occupancy.

Guesthouses, hotels, pubs and inns

Guesthouses are hotel-like B&Bs. They're generally slightly more expensive but can offer more space, an evening meal and a comfortable lounge for guests.

Pubs and inns often turn their hand to B&B accommodation in country areas and, although these businesses are less personal, you may find the anonymity preferable. They can be good fun if you plan to get hammered at the bar, but not such fun if you're worn out and trying to sleep within earshot of that same rowdy bar. In this case it's best to ask to see the room first or specifically ask for a quiet room. Pubs boasting both rooms and food allow you to avoid an extra walk in the evening through the rain to find an evening meal. Being able to pad down to the bar in just your socks is not to be understated after many days in boots.

Some **hotels** are fantastic places with great character and worth the treat – but more likely they are places you're forced to go to when all the cheaper alternatives are full.

Airbnb

The rise and rise of Airbnb (🖳 airbnb.co.uk) has seen private homes and apartments opened up to overnight travellers on an informal basis. While accommodation is primarily based in cities, the concept is spreading to tourist hotspots in more rural areas, but do check thoroughly what you are getting and the precise location. While the first couple of options listed may be in the area you're after, others may be far too far afield for walkers. At its best, this is a great way to meet local people in a relatively unstructured environment, but do be aware that these places are not registered B&Bs, so standards may vary, yet prices may not necessarily be any lower than the norm.

FOOD AND DRINK

After 20 miles of wind and rain (though it's highly unlikely that every day will be like that!) there really is nothing like sitting down to a good meal and a refreshing drink. The Pennine Way is littered with fine establishments, with grand home-cooked meals and well-tended beer cellars, that fulfil this requirement perfectly. Unfortunately there are also one or two places that seem to thrive despite their obvious mediocrity.

If you wish to sample the best of Britain's beer always choose a pint from a hand-pulled pump; ask the bar staff for a recommendation. Many places will even let you sample a small portion before you order. Yorkshire in particular is renowned for its brewing tradition and a rest day in Hawes will not be wasted in the many pubs.

A busy café, restaurant, pub or hotel is often a sign of a good kitchen, especially if the locals are eating there; your B&B owner will probably be able to make a recommendation, they will have heard the high praise or horror stories from other guests.

The box opposite may offer some inspiration for regional dishes along the Pennine Way.

Breakfast

Most B&Bs, pubs and guesthouses will offer you a **cooked breakfast** to begin your day on the fells. A walker can go a long way on a good 'Full English', certainly all the way to lunch time! Depending on where you are, the items on the plate will vary but normally include: sausages, bacon, fried egg, tomatoes, black pudding and mushrooms. This will usually be served with toast and marmalade, orange juice and tea or coffee. In the northern reaches of the Way and in Scotland the black pudding may be white pudding and potato cakes may make an occasional appearance.

Many places also offer a lighter option – a **continental breakfast**. If you want to get an early start some places may be happy to provide a packed lunch instead of breakfast.

Lunch, cream tea and evening meals

For **lunch** you may like to take a packed lunch from wherever you stayed the night before or buy something in the many bakeries, cafés, and local shops en

❑ Regional dishes

• **Cumberland sausage** Common on pub menus, this is a long, coiled or curved sausage where the meat (pork) inside is chopped rather than minced and pepper, rather than herbs, is added. Served with chips or mashed potato.

• **Yorkshire pudding** This is a hollow, baked batter savoury pudding, typically served with roast beef and gravy on a Sunday, but many pubs serve it all week round and you may sometimes find large versions filled with meat and gravy.

• **Lamb Henry** With all those sheep out on the hills it comes as no surprise that lamb is popular. Lamb Henry is lamb shank/ shoulder cooked slowly, often with mint or rosemary, and served with gravy, chips and some vegetables. It's a cheap but filling meal though is mostly served in the winter months.

© Chris Scott

Lamb Henry with chips

• **Parkin** A Yorkshire ginger cake, said to be the ideal accompaniment to a cup of strong Yorkshire tea.

• **Wensleydale cheese** It's been around a long time but had a surge of popularity thanks to its endorsement by global superstars Wallace and Gromit. You can visit the factory and shop in Hawes (see p165).

• **Bilberry pie** A pastry pie filled with bilberries which are found growing wild across the northern moors in late summer.

• **Curd tarts** Pastry tarts of curd cheese often with currants, best served as an afternoon snack with a cup of tea.

• **Rag pudding** Invented in Oldham, in the 19th century, when this town, was the centre of Lancashire's cotton mill industry, this is a dish of minced meat and onions which is then wrapped in suet pastry and cooked in a cheesecloth.

route. If you need sustenance in the afternoon look out for places serving **cream teas** (a scone served with jam and cream, possibly with a cake or two, and a pot of tea).

Pennine pubs are a great place to unwind in the **evening** and, apart from the few towns with restaurants, are often your only choice for a meal. With Britain's long overdue food revolution continuing apace, pubs have also been forced to become more than drinking dens. Places where your meal flips from freezer to microwave to plate are thankfully in decline. Despite the name, bar meals can be eaten at a regular table and at best have a home-cooked appeal which won't find you staring bleakly at an artfully carved radish entwined around a lone prawn. All menus include some token vegetarian options and, if there is a traditional Pennine Way dish it must be Lamb Henry, found on menus from Edale to Dufton and beyond. How better to recharge your stomach than with a juicy shank of Pennine lamb and a pint of Black Sheep (see box p26). It makes the walk worth walking.

Buying camping supplies

With a bit of planning ahead there are enough shops to allow self-sufficient campers to buy supplies along the way. All the known shops are listed in Part 4. The longest you should need to carry food for is two days. Hours can be irregular in village shops although camp stoves, gas canisters or meths are usually available in general stores. Coleman Fuel is not so widely found.

Drinking water

Very few of us drink enough water during a normal day, never mind when we're working hard climbing hills and walking several miles a day. **A walker should, on average, be drinking between three and four litres per day** in order to maintain optimum hydration and personal well-being.

One of the best ways to carry water is in a hydration pack (such as a Camelback or Platypus), which can be slipped into a purpose-built sleeve in the back of your pack. Access to the water is through a bite-valve at the end of a tube looped over your shoulder and enables you to sip water regularly without stopping to find a water bottle.

On longer days where you aren't likely to encounter a village or a pub, you may want to consider topping up the hydration pack from water sources you find along the path. A lightweight water filter such as the Sawyer Squeeze Filter can be used to clean most water found in UK streams and rivers. The advantage of these sort of devices over a sterilising tablet is speed, simplicity and taste; you can drink straight from the filter or squeeze the water through into your hydration pack – selecting one that closes at the top does help in this regard. A steripen, which uses UV light to kill off any bugs in the water, is a quick and effective alternative though more expensive.

In general terms the higher up a hill you source your water and the faster that water is flowing, the more likely it is to be clean and pure. In many places along the Way the water will be discoloured from the peat it has flowed through to reach the river. This may be off-putting, but doesn't affect the quality of the

❑ Real ales

- **Black Sheep Brewery** (🖳 blacksheepbrewery.com) has been brewing since 1992 and produces a number of cask ales but its most popular is simply called Black Sheep. You'll see it in pubs up and down the Pennine Way.
- **Theakston** (🖳 theakstons.co.uk) brew in the heart of the Yorkshire Dales. Keep a particular eye out for the exceptional, multi-award-winning Old Peculier dark ale, as well as the more easily found Best Bitter.
- **Peak Ales** (🖳 peakales.co.uk) produces a number of award-winning beers from their base on the Chatsworth Estate, including Swift Nick, a traditional English bitter; the amber-coloured Bakewell Best; and Chatsworth Gold, a honey beer. They also brew seasonal (summer and winter) ales. You might find some of these in the pubs in the southern sections of the Way.
- **Timothy Taylor** (🖳 www.timothytaylor.co.uk) is a famous brewery that has been in the business for over 150 years. Their Landlord is a strong pale ale while the award-winning Boltmaker is named after one of their favourite local pubs.

water in any other way, especially if you filter it as well. Use your common sense; avoid standing pools, murky water or water with lots of insects or algae present. If in doubt, filter it.

As refreshing as a pint of beer may be at lunchtime, it is no substitute for water and should be avoided on hot summer days as the alcohol encourages blood flow to the surface of your skin and can result in overheating.

If you are wild camping near running water, please abide by the toilet guidelines provided on pp75-6.

MONEY AND OTHER SERVICES

Cash and a couple of **credit/debit cards** are the best means of paying your way on the walk. Don't expect an **ATM (cash machine)** in every village but remember that many supermarkets/convenience stores now have an ATM, or offer 'cashback' when you buy something – though clearly these are only available during opening hours. It's also worth knowing that **cheques** are accepted in fewer places each year: although some B&Bs will still accept them from a British bank, many hotels and shops/supermarkets no longer do so.

While there may not be banks or ATMs in every village, most **post offices** allow cash withdrawals with a debit card and PIN number. However, as the era of the country post office is in decline, check with the Post Office Helpline (☎ 0345-746 8469) that the post offices en route are still open. Alternatively a quick search on their website (💻 postoffice.co.uk) will elicit a list of banks offering withdrawal facilities through post offices and a list of branches with an ATM.

Wi-fi is available and free almost everywhere, though at times only in public areas and sometimes it is unreliable. Places that didn't have wi-fi at the time of research are noted in the route guide.

Where they exist, special mention is made in Part 4 of other services such as outdoor gear shops, launderettes, pharmacies/chemists, medical centres and tourist information centres. Where we found phone boxes then we noted these on the maps, though these days most have been given over to defibrillators/book exchanges or have simply been vandalised beyond use.

WALKING COMPANIES

If you'd rather someone else made all your holiday arrangements for you the companies on pp30-1 will be able to help. You can either choose just accommodation booking and/or baggage transfer, or a self-guided/guided holiday in which case these will be included.

Baggage transfer and accommodation booking

Baggage transfer means collecting your gear and delivering it to your next accommodation by late afternoon; all you need on the hill is a daypack with essentials. The cost is usually around £10 per bag per day, but varies between companies and you should check firstly that the company covers the whole walk (some do not) and secondly, that there is no minimum number of bags that they require before they will accept a booking. You could also ask your B&Bs

or local taxi firms if they provide an ad-hoc transfer service for specific sections though this will usually be more expensive.

An **accommodation-booking service** means you can arrange the other areas of your holiday, but leave this tricky logistical challenge to someone else.

• **Brigantes Walking Holidays** (☎ 01756-770402, 💻 brigantesenglishwalks.com; Malham) run a family-operated baggage courier service which support trails across the north of England. They charge a minimum of £9 per person per day (single bag limit is 17kg). Contact them for a daily price.

❑ Information for foreign visitors

• **Currency** The British pound (£) comes in notes of £50, £20, £10 and £5, and coins of £2 and £1. The pound is divided into 100 pence (usually referred to as 'p', pronounced 'pee') which come in silver coins of 50p, 20p 10p and 5p, and copper coins of 2p and 1p.

• **Rates of exchange** Up-to-date rates can be found at 💻 xe.com/currencyconverter and at some post offices, or at any bank or travel agent.

• **Business hours** Most **village shops** are open Monday to Friday 9am-5pm and Saturday 9am-12.30pm, though some open as early as 7.30/8am; many also open on Sundays but not usually for the whole day. Occasionally you'll come across a local shop that closes at lunchtime on one day during the week, usually a Wednesday or Thursday; this is a throwback to the days when all towns and villages had an 'early closing day'. **Supermarkets** are open Monday to Saturday 8am-8pm (often longer) and on Sunday from about 9am to 5 or 6pm, though main branches of supermarkets generally open 10am-4pm or 11am-5pm.

Main **post offices** generally open Monday to Friday 9am-5pm and Saturday 9am-12.30pm; **banks** typically open at 9.30/10am Monday to Friday and close at 3.30/4pm, though in some places both post offices and banks may open only two or three days a week and/or in the morning, or limited hours, only. **ATMs** (**cash machines**) located outside a bank, shop, post office or petrol station are open all the time, but any that are inside will be accessible only when that place is open. However, ones that charge, such as Link machines, may not accept foreign-issued cards.

Pub hours are less predictable as each pub may have different opening hours. However, most pubs on the Pennine Way continue to follow the traditional Monday to Saturday 11am to 11pm, Sunday to 10.30pm, but some still close in the afternoon especially during the week and in the winter months.

The last entry time to most **museums and galleries** is usually half an hour, or an hour, before the official closing time.

• **National (Bank) holidays** Most businesses are shut on 1 January, Good Friday (March/April), Easter Monday (March/April), the first and last Monday in May, the last Monday in August, 25 December and 26 December.

• **School holidays** School holiday periods in England are generally as follows: a one-week break mid February, two weeks around Easter, a week in late May, late July to early September, a one-week break late October, and two weeks around Christmas.

• **Documents** If you are a member of a National Trust organisation in your country bring your membership card as you should be entitled to free entry to National Trust properties and sites in the UK.

• **Travel/medical insurance** The European Health Insurance Card (EHIC) entitles EU nationals (on production of the EHIC card) to necessary medical treatment under the UK's National Health Service while on a temporary visit here. However, this is not

• **Pennine Way Bag Transfer** (☎ 01457-857527, 🖳 penninewaybagtransfer.uk; Torside) They cover only the southern portion from Edale to Malham and charge £15 per bag per transfer, with a minimum of two bags required per booking.
• **Sherpa Van Project** (☎ 01748-826917, 🖳 sherpavan.com) Sherpa operates either an **accommodation-booking** and baggage-transfer service, or just a **baggage-transfer service** for the whole walk. The price for the latter depends on which part of the trail you're on though starts at £9.50 per bag per day, with a minimum of two bags per move. Contact them for a quote in full.

a substitute for proper medical cover on your travel insurance for unforeseen bills and for getting you home should that be necessary. Also consider cover for loss or theft of personal belongings, especially if you're camping or staying in hostels, as there may be times when you have to leave your luggage unattended. If you're walking the Pennine Way any time after March 2019 do check, too, what the latest rules are, for Britain will have left the EU that March and you can expect some changes to the legislation.
• **Weights and measures** Britain's illogical mix of metric and imperial measures is undoubtedly a source of confusion for many visitors. For example, in Britain milk can be sold in pints (1 pint = 568ml), as can beer in pubs, though most other liquid including petrol (gasoline) and diesel is sold in litres. The population remains split, too, between those (mainly the older generation) who still use inches (1 inch = 2.5cm), feet (1ft = 0.3m) and yards and those who are happy with millimetres, centimetres and metres; you'll often be told that 'it's only a hundred yards or so' to somewhere, rather than a hundred metres or so. Distances on road and path signs are also given in miles (1 mile = 1.6km) rather than kilometres, and yards (1yd = 0.9m) rather than metres.

Most food is sold in metric weights (g and kg) but the imperial weights of pounds (lb: 1lb = 453g) and ounces (oz: 1oz = 28g) are often displayed too. The weather – a frequent topic of conversation – is also an issue: while most forecasts predict temperatures in centigrade (C), many people continue to think in terms of fahrenheit (F; see temperature chart on p16 for conversions).
• **Time** During the winter the whole of Britain is on Greenwich Meantime (GMT). The clocks move one hour forward on the last Sunday in March, remaining on British Summer Time (BST) until the last Sunday in October.
• **Smoking** Smoking in enclosed public places is banned. The ban relates not only to pubs and restaurants, but also to B&Bs, hostels and hotels. These latter have the right to designate one or more bedrooms where the occupants can smoke, but the ban is in force in all enclosed areas open to the public – even in a private home such as a B&B. Should you be foolhardy enough to light up in a no-smoking area, which includes pretty well any indoor public place, you could be fined £50, but it's the owners of the premises who suffer most if they fail to stop you, with a potential fine of £2500.
• **Telephones** From outside Britain the international country **access code** for Britain is ☎ 44 followed by the area code minus the first 0, and then the number you require. **Mobile phone reception** is variable and can't be relied on; it's said the Vodafone network works best across rural northern England followed by O2 or EE. If you're using a mobile phone that is registered overseas, consider buying a local SIM card to keep costs down.
• **Wi-fi and internet access** See p27.
• **Emergency services** For police, ambulance, fire and mountain rescue dial ☎ 999 (or the EU standard number ☎ 112).

Self-guided walking holidays

These packages usually include accommodation with breakfast and baggage transfer. Some also include personal transfer to and from the walk, and may include secure car parking and even optional lifts between accommodation if you don't feel like walking that day. Each company offers different services, so check the details carefully. The companies can also tailor-make holidays.

- **Absolute Escapes** (☎ 0131-610 1210, 💻 absoluteescapes.com; Edinburgh) Offer the complete path as well as in sections.
- **Alpine Exploratory** (☎ 0131-214 1144, 💻 alpineexploratory.com; Edinburgh) Offer the whole walk over 22-24 nights, or the southern, central or northern part of the route in about a week. In addition they welcome dogs.
- **Brigantes Walking Holidays** (see p28) They offer the full route but are also happy to work on shorter or longer itineraries. Other options include secure car parking in Kirkby Malham and transport to Edale and back from Kirk Yetholm.
- **Contours Holidays** (☎ 01629-821900, 💻 contours.co.uk; Derbyshire) Walks (Apr-Oct) along the whole Way (13-20 days), as well as the southern (6-8 days), central (6-11 nights) and northern (4-6 days) sections and 3-day 'taster' treks.
- **Discovery Travel** (☎ 01983-301133, 💻 discoverytravel.co.uk; Isle of Wight) They have a 19-walking-day/20-night holiday covering the whole route available between April and September but can offer bespoke itineraries to suit.
- **Macs Adventure** (☎ 0141-530886, 💻 macsadventure.com; Glasgow) They offer the complete trek (15-22 days' walking), the northern section (5-7 days), the south (8-9 days) and central (8-10 days) between April and September.
- **Sherpa Expeditions** (☎ 020-8875 5070, 💻 sherpaexpeditions.com; London) Itineraries for the whole path in 19/20 days' walking and also in half sections.
- **The Walking Holiday Company** (☎ 01600-713008, 💻 thewalkingholiday company.co.uk; Monmouth) Offer the complete trail in 21 nights, or any length and any part of the walk according to clients' wishes.
- **Wandering Aengus** (☎ 016974-78443, 💻 watreks.com; Cumbria) Options (6-21 nights) cover the whole route or one-week sections.

❑ Walking the Pennine Way – a personal experience

When I accompanied a friend in fulfilling his lifelong ambition to walk the PW, I thought I was an experienced walker (Dalesway, Camino de Santiago, Machu Pichu etc). Let's just say I finished a lot more experienced than I started, especially crawling to the stone shelter of Little Dun Fell in the mist and pelting needle-rain accompanying Hurricane Ali, with overtrousers billowing around my knees. The conditions, even at the end of one of the driest summers on record and despite the huge bonus of many solid footings over the interminable marshes, were nearly always challenging with rain, wind and penetrating drizzle sometimes obscuring the views or slowing the pace, especially raising the heart rate for the occasional scrambling up rocky paths or over riverside boulders. The views are quite stunning and remind you how beautiful Britain is. The best ones can be accessed in a few weekends but Edale to Kirk Yetholm in 3 weeks, as Wainwright once implied, is only for an elite order of head-bangers!

Steve Davies (2018)

• **Weather Goat Walks** (☎ 0748-387 0210, 💻 kayamy.uwclub.net/wghome.htm; N Yorks) Help with planning and all aspects of walking support from the absolute beginner to the experienced walker; offer free parking.

Guided walking holidays

• **Footpath** (☎ 01985-840049, 💻 footpath-holidays.com) offers the walk for the southern section (based at Hebden Bridge), the central section (based at Hawes) and the northern section (based at Hexham). The holidays (6-7 days) are operated once a year in July-August and are arranged so that it would be possible to walk the whole route.

WALKING WITH DOGS [see pp282-3]

For many, walking without their dog would be as inconceivable as walking without boots, but the Pennine Way is tough, not just for us humans, but for dogs as well. Be sure that your dog is as prepared for the walk as you are. Dog-friendly accommodation is available in many places along the walk, and is specified in the route guide, but your selection will be restricted; all but one of the hostels along the trail do not allow dogs save for registered assistance dogs (take a bow, Greenhead hostel, see p232, the only exception to this rule) and some campsites will also be closed to you if you're walking with your dog.

Although the Pennine Way is a public right of way along its whole length, there are restrictions for dogs in certain places and at certain times of year. Dogs must always be under close control, ideally on a lead, when near livestock and must always be on a lead when walking through areas of ground nesting birds in spring and early summer. There will be signs on stiles and gates to give you adequate warning. Even a well-trained dog will be hard pressed to resist the temptation to chase a fledgling grouse as it flees from cover.

❑ Walking the Pennine Way – a personal experience

I did the whole walk during the hot dry summer of 2013. It took me 20 days, averaging about 15 miles a day. For some of the first four days I was very aware of evidence of the nearby cities such as reservoirs, pylons, masts and drainage channels, which may come as a disappointment if you are looking for a 'wilderness walk'. However I am glad I was patient as this gradually changes when the walk enters the Yorkshire Dales National Park and becomes wilder and more unspoilt through the North Pennines Area of Outstanding Natural Beauty (AONB) until you reach The Cheviots in the Borders which are really remote. It has some spectacular landmarks including High Force, High Cup Nick and Hadrian's Wall. The enormous job of laying flagstones along the boggy areas of the route has helped tame the bogs, so I didn't have any problems. The Pennine Way can be tailored to suit your budget as there is plenty of low-cost accommodation such as hostels and campsites close to the route.

Overall it is a tough but really exhilarating walk which needs preparation and stamina to complete, having a total of 11,350m of ascent. The Pennine Way stretched my boundaries, involving as it does good map-reading skills, some short scrambles and a lot of hill climbing. The route, which has had a lot of restoration work done to it, is the perfect antidote to crowded routes such as Hadrian's Wall, and really deserves a renaissance. **Rucksack Rose (Twitter: @RucksackRose)**

Budgeting

When it comes to budgeting, there is a happy compromise somewhere between the hardened backpacker, who wild camps every night and forages for wild roots, berries and roadkill, and the five-star traveller, who insists on the best accommodation available, baggage transfer as well as fine wines and comestibles in the evening. Your budget depends on the level of comfort you're prepared to lavish upon yourself and, up to a point, how fast you can walk! Even if you're unlikely to come across any Michelin star restaurants along the Pennine Way, there is still a tendency for walkers to under-estimate their budget. Your walking holiday is likely to cost about the same as a fortnight in the sun.

ACCOMMODATION STYLES

Camping

Wild camping and river water is free and if you carried your own dehydrated meals you may conceivably complete the walk without spending any money at all and without contributing anything to the communities through which you pass. Campsites typically charge around £5-7 per person per night. The additional luxuries of an occasional shower, a cooked breakfast and the odd pint and a meal in the evening will probably bring the cost up to £25pp per day.

Bunkhouses, camping barns and hostels

You can't always cook your own food in bunkhouses/camping barns (though all YHA hostels have a kitchen) so costs can rise: £35-40pp per day will allow you to have the occasional meal out and enjoy a few local brews. If staying in a YHA hostel expect to pay around £20pp per night though more in the high season; breakfast costs about £5 as does a packed lunch; for an evening meal expect to pay £9-10. Many hostels are licensed so budget for more if you're a drinker.

B&B-style accommodation

B&B rates per person can range from £27pp to £60pp or more a night but of course you get a good breakfast to set you up for the day. On top of that add £20 to cover both a packed lunch and a pub meal in the evening. B&Bs often quote prices per room rather than per person, so a solo walker can end up paying the full room rate in establishments without single rooms. You'll soon find doing the walk at a relaxed three-week pace could put your budget into four figures.

OTHER EXPENSES

Think carefully about how you're going to get to Edale – fairly straightforward – and back from Kirk Yetholm – more convoluted. If using trains, buy a flexible ticket well in advance to gain a reasonable fare. Note, too, how the fares are cheaper outside of rush hour so for the cheapest price it's often better to travel after 10am. Incidental expenses can add up: soft drinks or beer, cream teas, taxis to take you to a distant pub or back onto the trail in the morning. This does not include finding out that some vital item of your equipment has been left at home or is not performing well. We estimate adding another £100-200 to your total budget for these 'incidentals'.

❑ Walking the Pennine Way over 50 years ago

In August 1963, clad in cotton and wool that was spun, woven and stitched in the smoky industrial towns each side of the Pennine Way, we raced up Grindsbrook. Fuelled by adrenaline, over-confident, we failed to consult the compass and blundered too long amid the mist-shrouded peat hags of Kinder Scout. We didn't make that mistake twice. As far north as Blackstone Edge, and in places beyond, the Way was largely undefined on the ground. Guidebooks were things of the future. Ordnance Survey maps had yet to show the route. A Ramblers' Association leaflet described the line in sufficient detail for us to trace it onto borrowed maps.

We slogged across tussocks, heather, groughs, streams and bogs, occasionally encouraged by the sighting of a boot-print or a wooden stake but referring always to map and compass. Above Hebden Bridge we crossed fields dulled by soot from coal fires, and at the end of the third day our baptism of wet peat and trackless moors was over. We descended into the pastoral greenery of Craven and found our second wind on home ground in the Yorkshire Dales. On our seventh night we soaked in the bath at a B&B in Middleton in Teesdale. Previously we'd stayed in Youth Hostels without showers, making do with strip washes. Men didn't use deodorants then, and our single set of spare clothes was reserved for evenings. Enough said!

The famous crossing of the Pennines via High Cup was, and remains, a highlight of the Way. It was easier than expected, so fit had we become. Arriving in Dufton, we learned our hostel lay two miles away in the village of Knock. Next morning, without map, we negotiated the Cross Fell range in dubious visibility by dint of walking due north until reaching the Old Corpse Road. On a cold September night at Once Brewed hostel we slept snugly on mattresses in rope 'hammocks'. Next day we picked a way through miles of conifers, hoping the infrequent splashes of white paint on tree trunks indicated our route. On the penultimate day we realised our maps of Redesdale were ancient: they showed none of the huge Forestry Commission plantations, but we found our way by compass bearing. The Cheviot ridge gave us our first sight of Scotland as well as a fitting and final test of our stamina.

Our limited knowledge came from Kenneth Oldham's slim volume, *The Pennine Way*. The mass of information now available on websites lay decades ahead. We saw few signposts, and Tom Stephenson's 'long green trail' hadn't been formed, let alone turned into the spreading morass that necessitated the controversial paving. Few pubs served food, but shops were more plentiful than now. We had none of today's technical fabrics, phones, walking poles, GPS, plastic cards or plastic bags. We never dreamed such things might one day exist, and we felt we had the right kit for the job.

I'd never spent more than a week outside my home county, so the Pennine Way was an exceptional adventure. Since then the world has shrunk. The Way may no longer appear exotic, but still it challenges the walker to meet its mental and physical demands. Somewhere between Hadrian's Wall and Bellingham, the northbound Wayfarer will realise success is nigh. For the southbound traveller, an identical moment lightens the rucksack on the level track between Stoodley Pike and Blackstone Edge. Those feelings are worth your walk, and they will carry you with an inner smile all the way to the end. **Peter Stott**

				VILLAGE AND
Place name (Places in brackets are a short walk off the Pennine Way)	**Distance from previous place** miles (km)	**ATM** (in bank, shop or post office)	**Post Office** (# limited PO services)	**Tourist Information/ Visitor Centre (TIC/VC); National Park Centre (NPC) §**
Edale/Nether Booth	Start			**VC**
Upper Booth	1½ (2.5)			
Torside	13½ (21.5)			
(Padfield & Hadfield)				
Crowden	1 (1.5)			
Standedge	11 (17.5)			
(Diggle)				
Blackstone Edge	5½ (9)			
Mankinholes	6 (9.5)			
Calder Valley	3 (5)			
(Hebden Bridge)		✔	✔	**TIC)**
Blackshaw Head	1½ (2.5)			
Colden	½ (1)			
Widdop	2½ (4)			
Ponden & Stanbury	6 (9.5)			
(Haworth)		✔	✔	**TIC)**
Ickornshaw (& Cowling)	5 (8)			
Lothersdale	2½ (4)			
(Earby)		✔	✔)	
East Marton	6 (9.5)			
Gargrave	2½ (4)	✔	✔	
Airton	4 (6.5)			
Kirkby Malham	1½ (2.5)			
Malham	1 (1.5)			**NPC**
Horton-in-Ribblesdale	14½ (23.5)		#	**TIC**
Hawes	13½ (21.5)	✔	✔	**NPC/TIC**
Hardraw	1½ (2.5)			
Thwaite	8 (13)			
(Muker)				
Keld	3 (5)			
Tan Hill	4 (6.5)			
Baldersdale (& Cotherstone)	10 (16)			
Lunedale	3 (5)			
Middleton-in-Teesdale	3½ (5.5)	✔	✔	**TIC**
Holwick	2½ (4)			
High Force	2½ (4)			
(Forest-in-T'dale/Langdon Beck)				
Dufton	14½ (23.5)			

(cont'd on p36) § See also p50

TOWN FACILITIES

Restaurant/ Café/Pub ✓ = one place ✓✓ = two ✓✓✓ = three +	**Food Store**	**Campsite**	**Hostels** YHA/H* **Camping Barn** (CB)/ **Bunkhouse** (B) **Glamping** (G)	**B&B-style accommodation** ✓ = one place ✓✓ = two ✓✓✓ = three +	**Place name** (places in brackets are a short walk off the Pennine Way)
✓✓✓	✓	✓	YHA, CB, B, G	✓✓✓	**Edale/Nether Booth**
		✓	CB		**Upper Booth**
				✓✓	**Torside**
✓				✓✓✓	**(Padfield & Hadfield)**
		✓			**Crowden**
✓		✓		✓	**Standedge**
✓				✓✓✓	**(Diggle)**
✓					**Blackstone Edge**
✓			YHA		**Mankinholes**
					Calder Valley
✓✓✓	✓		H	✓✓✓	**(Hebden Bridge)**
		✓		✓	**Blackshaw Head**
✓	✓	✓			**Colden**
✓					**Widdop**
✓		✓		✓✓	**Ponden & Stanbury**
✓✓✓	✓		YHA	✓✓✓	**(Haworth)**
✓✓✓	✓	✓		✓	**Ickornshaw (& Cowling)**
✓					**Lothersdale**
✓✓✓	✓		H	✓	**(Earby)**
✓✓		✓			**East Marton**
✓✓✓	✓	✓		✓✓	**Gargrave**
✓	✓		CB	✓	**Airton**
✓					**Kirkby Malham**
✓✓✓		✓	YHA, B, G	✓✓✓	**Malham**
✓✓✓	✓	✓	B	✓✓✓	**Horton-in-Ribblesdale**
✓✓✓	✓	✓	YHA	✓✓✓	**Hawes**
✓✓		✓	B	✓✓	**Hardraw**
✓		✓		✓	**Thwaite**
✓✓	✓			✓✓	**(Muker)**
	✓	✓	B, G	✓✓✓	**Keld**
✓		✓	B	✓	**Tan Hill**
✓			B†	✓	**Baldersdale**
		✓			**Lunedale**
✓✓✓	✓	✓		✓✓✓	**Middleton-in-Teesdale**
✓✓		✓	CB	✓	**Holwick**
✓				✓	**High Force**
✓			YHA	✓✓✓	**Forest-in-T'dle/Lgdn Bk)**
✓✓	✓	✓	YHA	✓	**Dufton**

H* = independent hostel B† opening Mar 2019 *(cont'd on p37)*

VILLAGE AND

(cont'd from p34)

Place name (Places in brackets are a short walk off the Pennine Way)	**Distance from previous place** miles (km)	**ATM** (in bank, shop or post office)	**Post Office** (# limited PO services)	**Tourist Information/ Visitor Centre (TIC/VC); National Park Centre (NPC) §**
Garrigill	15½ (25)		✔	
Alston	4 (6.5)	✔	✔	TIC
Knarsdale	7 (11.5)			
Greenhead	9½ (15.5)			
Burnhead	4 (6.5)			
Once Brewed	2½ (4)			NPC/TIC
(Stonehaugh)				
Bellingham	15 (24)	✔	✔	TIC
Byrness	15 (24)			
(Upper Coquetdale)				
Kirk/Town Yetholm	25½ (41)		✔	

❑ Walking the Pennine Way – a personal experience

I remember exactly when I decided I needed to walk the Pennine Way, it was April 2005 and I was driving home from a meeting in Slough; Radio 4 were doing a feature on the 40th birthday of the path. I'd only just started walking, in an effort to lose some weight and the Pennine Way seemed like a worthy goal to aim for. My love of desolate moorland and mist-shrouded hills was still a long way into the future, but it seemed like a challenge, something I could aspire to.

Over the next few years my walking became prolific; I started with small day walks, built up to longer mountain walks in the Lake District and finally, in May 2010, I set out from Edale.

Over the next 17 days I met only the occasional PW walker, if you're walking the Pennine Way alone, you need to be happy with your own company. I loved the quiet, the solitude on the hills and the emptying of the mind that resulted in having no other responsibility than getting up each morning and putting one foot in front of the other. No other path has offered me that sense of calm and inner peace. It was a joy and a pleasure, as well as a physical and mental challenge at times; it is, after all a long path!

My arrival in Kirk Yetholm, dripping in sweat on a blistering hot day, after walking about 26 miles from Byrness in 10 hours, was welcomed by no-one. A witty local at the bar in the Border Hotel asked me if it was raining outside and the barmaid made no remark when I asked for the Pennine Way book to sign. The path is a personal challenge, don't do it for anyone but yourself.

Stuart Greig (Twitter: @LoneWalkerUK)

TOWN FACILITIES

(cont'd from p35)

Restaurant/ Café/Pub ✔ = one place ✔✔= two ✔✔✔= three +	**Food Store**	**Campsite**	**Hostels** YHA/H* **Camping Barn** (CB)/ **Bunkhouse** (B) **Glamping** (G)	**B&B-style accommodation** ✔ = one place ✔✔= two ✔✔✔= three +	**Place name** (places in brackets are a short walk off the Pennine Way)
✔	✔	✔		✔✔✔	**Garrigill**
✔✔✔	✔	✔	YHA	✔✔✔	**Alston**
✔		✔		✔	**Knarsdale**
✔✔		✔	H, CB, B	✔✔✔	**Greenhead**
✔				✔	**Burnhead**
✔		✔	YHA, B	✔✔✔	**Once Brewed**
		✔			**(Stonehaugh)**
✔✔✔	✔	✔	B, G	✔✔	**Bellingham**
✔	✔	✔	G	✔	**Byrness**
		✔	B		**(Upper Coquetdale)**
✔✔	✔	✔	H	✔✔✔	**Kirk/Town Yetholm**

H* = independent hostel

❑ Walking the Pennine Way – a personal experience

It started for me as a trip with a friend who later dropped out leaving me with the daunting prospect of doing the Pennine Way as my first trail, and alone!

I expected a few problems along the way and ended up packing way too much equipment into my rucksack to cover as much as possible. Even though I had made a couple of trial weekend treks, the weight was a complete killer.

The first half was difficult and engulfed by setbacks. On day one my train was late into Manchester, resulting in me missing the connection to Edale! A cancellation later found me taking another route and walking directly to Crowden for my first night's sleep. I actually went back after to complete the first day's walking.

By the time I got to Thornton-in-Craven my ill-fitting boots meant I had to come away to buy new boots and restart a few days later. The second part was much more enjoyable, my rucksack repacked with less in it, the new boots, and better weather, at least until High Cup Nick, where the weather was so terrible I only knew I was there because the ground vanished! Dufton Hostel was wonderful and I made some lifelong friends there in the pub that night, who completed the walk with me and we still walk together every year. For all of us who walked the rest of the Way, the icing on the cake was spending our last night at Davidson's Linn, a beautiful spot, enhanced only slightly by curry and malt whisky.

I plan to do it again one day, in one go, with no break in the middle. I think there are two secrets to enjoying the Pennine Way; travel as light as possible and take enough time to enjoy the scenery. The walk really is possible for anyone and provided memories that will stay with me forever; from fording swollen streams at Black Hill to the biggest plate of food I have ever seen in Bellingham.

Mark Smith (Twitter: @markj_smith)

Itineraries

All walkers are individuals. Some like to cover large distances as quickly as possible, others like to stroll along and stop frequently – indeed this natural variation in pace is what causes most friction in groups. You may want to walk the Pennine Way all in one go, tackle it over a series of weekends, or use the trail for linear day walks; the choice is yours. This book has been divided into stages, and many will use it that way, but these are not rigid. Instead, the book has been designed to make it easy for you to plan your own optimal itinerary.

The **planning map** (see inside back cover) and **table of village/town facilities** (see pp34-7) summarise the essential information. Alternatively, have a look at the **suggested itineraries** (opposite, p40 & p41) and choose your preferred type of accommodation and pace. There are also suggestions for those who want to experience the best of the trail over a day or a weekend (see opposite). The **public transport maps and service table** (pp54-9) will also be useful.

Having made a rough plan, turn to Part 4, where you will find summaries of the route, full descriptions of the accommodation options, suggestions for where to eat and information about other services in each village and town; as well as the detailed trail maps.

Which direction?

Most people walk the Pennine Way **south to north**. There are practical reasons for this; the prevailing south-westerly wind and rain are behind you, as is the

❏ Walking the Pennine Way – a personal experience

I used to love walking around Edale as a teenager and made my first attempt at the Pennine Way when I was 16. Woefully ill-prepared we aborted after 3 days when my companion got sick. Now 62, newly retired, and a lot wiser, I made it on my second attempt, end-to-end in 19 days.

A lot has changed in the meantime. Underfoot has improved a lot, and signage is much better, no more wandering between walls of peat trying to hold a compass bearing while your boots disappear at each step. There is even an app which tells you where you are! This is all good and helps you appreciate what has not changed and why I love the Pennine Way. The wildness and rough beauty of the moors, the bucolic, green dales, the welcoming villages and pubs and the no-nonsense locals that you meet along the way.

The other thing that remains is the wind. It is rare that you know the exact wind speed when you are out on the hills but my friend and I happened to be blown off our feet on Great Dun Fell at the exact time that the weather station there was officially recording gusts up to 175km/hr. With the wisdom of age, and because we could not physically stand, we slid and crawled down off the ridge, skirted round the summit of Cross Fell and eventually made it to Garrigill. The Pennine Way certainly retains its teeth. So I still haven't completely cracked Cross Fell, but I will be back.

Steve Oxley (2018)

sun. Head north–south if you want a better face tan! The maps in Part 4 give timings for both directions and, as route-finding instructions are on the maps rather than in blocks of text, it ought to be straightforward using this guide back to front.

THE BEST DAY AND WEEKEND (TWO-DAY) WALKS

Not everyone is able to devote the best part of three weeks to walking the Pennine Way in one continuous journey. That doesn't mean, however, that you can't sample the delights of the path and this section may help your decision-making process by describing some of the one- and two-day walk options that

WILD CAMPING* AND CAMPSITES (▲)

	Relaxed pace		Medium pace		Fast pace	
Night	Place	Approx distance miles (km)	Place	Approx distance miles (km)	Place	Approx distance miles(km)
0	Edale		Edale		Edale	
1	Crowden ▲	16 (25.5)	Crowden ▲	16 (25.5)	Black Hill	20½ (33)
2	Standedge ▲	11 (17.5)	Blackstone Edge	16½ (26.5)	Blackshaw Hd	22½ (36)
3	Withens Moor	11 (17.5)	Walshaw	15½ (25)	Pinhaw Beacon	18½ (30)
4	Withins Height	12 (19.5)	Pinhaw Beacon	13½ (21.5)	Fountains Fell	20½ (33)
5	East Marton ▲	15½ (25)	Fountains Fell	20½ (33)	Hawes ▲	20½ (33)
6	Fountains Fell	16½ (26.5)	Dodd Fell	16 (25.5)	Sleightholme	18½ (30)
7	Old Ing Moor	11 (17.5)	Keld ▲	17 (27.5)	Middleton	14½ (23.5)
8	Gt Shunner Fell	15½ (25)	(Rest day)	0 (0)	Rail wagon	6 (9.5)
9	Tan Hill ▲	10½ (17)	Deepdale Beck	12 (19.5)	Greg's Hut	23 (37)
10	Deepdale Beck	8 (13)	Rail wagon	14½ (23.5)	Glendue Burn	18½ (30)
11	Middleton ▲	8½ (13.5)	High Cup	10 (16)	Wark Forest	20½ (33)
12	Rest day	0 (0)	Greg's Hut	13 (21)	Byrness Hill	25 (40)
13	High Cup	16 (25.5)	Alston ▲	10 (16)	Kirk Yetholm#	24½ (39.5)
14	Greg's Hut	13 (21)	Glendue Burn	8½ (13.5)		
15	Alston ▲	10 (16)	Wark Forest	20½ (33)		
16	Glendue Burn	8½ (13.5)	Deer Play	14½ (23.5)		
17	Wark Forest	20½ (33)	Coquet Head	13½ (21.5)		
18	Deer Play	14½ (23.5)	Kirk Yetholm#	21½ (34.5)		
19	Byrness Hill	10½ (17)				
20	Windy Gyle	12 (19.5)				
21	Kirk Yetholm#	12½ (20)				

* Wild camping obviously allows overnighting where you please. Where possible the approximate locations of wild camps have been proposed on the fells, ie where discreet and unobtrusive stays are most easily made. Most places have also been chosen for their scenic appeal, the vicinity of Glendue Burn being a notable but unavoidable exception. On other days the ideal distance – be it 'relaxed' or 'fast' – puts you so near a town it's simpler to stay on a campsite or even at a B&B. The flexibility of wild camping enables greater daily distances to be covered so the three proposed itineraries above may not take as many days.

▲ Campsite # The campsite is in Town Yetholm, not Kirk Yetholm.

are available. This is by no means a definitive list, it simply selects some of the highlights of the Way.

The day walks are mostly circular so you can return to the start point without relying on public transport, or you could simply backtrack from the point at which the walks leave the Way. Some of these walks use paths not covered in the maps in this book, so you will need the appropriate Ordnance Survey maps to complete them. The correct map is identified in the text for each walk.

However, in order to maximise your time on the Pennine Way and to try and simulate the experience those end-to-enders will get, the two-/three-day walks described here are linear and will typically require the use of public transport (or two vehicles) to get back home, or back to your car at the start. With the inclusion of a couple of long stages, it is possible to complete the whole route using this method, even if the dwindling supply of frequent bus services north of the Wall conspires against you.

STAYING IN HOSTELS, BUNKHOUSES & CAMPING BARNS

	Relaxed pace		Medium pace		Fast pace	
Night	Place	Approx distance miles (km)	Place	Approx distance miles (km)	Place	Approx distance miles(km)
0	Edale		Edale		Edale	
1	Torside*	16 (25.5)	Torside*	16 (25.5)	Torside*	16 (25.5)
2	Standedge*	11 (17.5)	Standedge*	11 (17.5)	Mankinholes	22½ (36)
3	Mankinholes	11½ (18.5)	Mankinholes	11½ (18.5)	Ick & Cowling*	18½ (30)
4	Haworth§	11½ (18.5)	Ick & Cowling*	18½ (30)	Malham	17½ (28)
5	Earby•	14 (22.5)	Malham	17½ (28)	Horton-in-Rib	14½ (23.5)
6	Malham	10½ (17)	Horton-in-Rib	14½ (23.5)	Keld	26 (42)
7	Horton-in-Rib	14½ (23.5)	Hawes	13½ (21.5)	Middleton-in-T*	20½(33)
8	Hawes	13½ (21.5)	(Rest day)	0 (0)	Dufton	19½ (31.5)
9	(Rest day)	0 (0)	Keld	12½ (20)	Alston	19½ (31.5)
10	Keld	12½ (20)	Baldersdale†	14 (22.5)	Greenhead	16½ (26.5)
11	Baldersdale†	14 (22.5)	Langdon Beck	14 (22.5)	Bellingham	21½ (34.5)
12	Middleton-in-T*	6½ (10.5)	Dufton	12 (19.5)	Byrness	15 (24)
13	Langdon Beck	7½ (12)	Alston	19½ (31.5)	Kirk Yetholm	25½ (41)
14	Dufton	12 (19.5)	Greenhead	16½ (26.5)		
15	Garrigill*	15½ (25)	Once Brewed	6½ (10.5)		
16	Knarsdale*	11 (17.5)*	Bellingham	15 (24)		
17	Greenhead	9½ (15.5)	Byrness	15 (24)		
18	Once Brewed	6½ (10.5)	Kirk Yetholm	25½ (41)		
19	Bellingham	15 (24)				
20	Byrness	15 (24)				
21	Upper Coquetdale	13 (21)*#				
22	Kirk Yetholm	12½ (20)				

** No hostel/bunkhouse/barn; stay in B&B*

† If bunkhouse at Baldersdale hasn't reopened the nearest B&B is at Cotherstone

§ 3½ miles (6km) to/from town each way • 1½ miles (2km) to/from town each way

 # Add 2 miles (3km) to collection point at Trows or 3½ miles (5.5km) to Barrowburn

One-day circular walks

- **Edale to Kinder Downfall** (see p86) **returning by the old route over Kinder Scout and Grindsbrook Clough** At around **10 miles (16km)** this route will let you experience the start of the Pennine Way as it is today and as it was originally. The crossing of the Kinder plateau should be done with care, good navigation skills and ideally in fine weather. (Explorer OL1)
- **Rochdale Canal to Top Withins** (see p119) **returning via Dean Gate and Hebden Dale** Follow the Pennine Way from the Rochdale Canal at Charlestown across Heptonstall Moor to Top Withins, where you will need to dodge the Brontë tourists before returning along Dean Gate and any one of a dozen footpaths through Hebden Dale back to the canal, a round trip of around **11 miles (17.7km)** in all. (Explorer OL21)
- **Airton to Malham Tarn** (see p136) **returning along the same path** Sometimes an 'out and back' path is rewarding, allowing you to see the land-

STAYING IN B&B-STYLE ACCOMMODATION

	Relaxed pace		Medium pace		Fast pace	
Night	**Place**	**Approx distance** miles (km)	**Place**	**Approx distance** miles (km)	**Place**	**Approx distance** miles(km)
0	Edale		Edale		Edale	
1	Torside	15 (24)	Torside	15 (24)	Torside	15 (24)
2	Standedge	12 (19.5)	Standedge	12 (19.5)	Mankinholes	23½ (38)*
3	Hebden Bridge*	14½ (23.5)	Hebden Bridge*	14½ (23.5)	Ponden & Stanbury	13½ (21.5)
4	Ponden & Stanbury	10½ (17)	Ickornshaw & Cowling	15½ (25)	Malham	22½ (36)
5	Thornton-in-C*	12 (19.5)	Malham	17½ (28)	Horton-in-Rib	14½ (23.5)
6	Malham	10½ (17)	Horton-in-Rib	14½ (23.5)	Keld	26 (42)
7	Horton-in-Rib	14½ (23.5)	Hawes	13½ (21.5)	Middleton-in-T	20½ (33)
8	Hawes	13½ (21.5)	(Rest day)		Dufton	19½ (31.5)
9	(Rest day)		Keld	12½ (20)	Alston	19½ (31.5)
10	Keld	12½ (20)	Cotherstone*	14 (22.5)	Greenhead	16½ (26.5)
11	Cotherstone*	14 (22.5)	Forest in T'dale Langdon Beck	14 (22.5)	Bellingham	21½ (34.5)
12	Forest in T'dale Langdon Beck	14 (22.5)	Dufton	12 (19.5)	Byrness	15 (24)
13	Dufton	12 (19.5)	Alston	19½ (31.5)	Kirk Yetholm	25½ (41)
14	Garrigill	15½ (25)	Greenhead	16½ (26.5)		
15	Knarsdale	11 (17.5)	Once Brewed	6½ (10.5)		
16	Greenhead	9½ (15.5)	Bellingham	15 (24)		
17	Once Brewed	6½ (10.5)	Byrness	15 (24)		
18	Bellingham	15 (24)	Kirk Yetholm	25½ (41)		
19	Byrness	15 (24)				
20	Upper Coquetdale	13 (21)*#				
21	Kirk Yetholm	12½ (20)				

** Additional distance to B&B accommodation from Pennine Way*

 # No B&B but self-catering/bunkhouse accommodation possible

scape from different perspectives. This is one such walk; starting at Airton and taking in Malham Cove and Malham Tarn as well as the wonderful Watlowes valley. Around **12 miles (19.3km)**. (Explorer OL2)

• **Horton-in-Ribblesdale to Cam End** (see p158) **returning via the Ribble Way** Climb out of Horton on the Pennine Way along a lovely lane as far as the logging road at Cam End, where you turn left and drop down to pick up the Ribble Way back into Horton. There are some splendid views of the Yorkshire Three Peaks along this **13-mile (21km)** route. (Explorer OL2)

• **Thwaite to Tan Hill** (see p170) **returning via West Stones Dale road** This walk takes you round the foot of Kisdon Hill, a rustic track with great views into the head of Swaledale, before striking out across East Stonesdale Moor to the enigmatic Tan Hill Inn. Return by the same path, or the quiet West Stonesdale road for a walk of around **14 miles (22.5km)**. (Explorer OL30)

• **Middleton-in-Teesdale to High Force** (see p196) **returning via Holwick Scars** The best waterfall walk in the country – unless you decide to walk on to Cauldron Snout (an extra 11 miles/18km) – along the Pennine Way to High Force and using the high-level route up Holwick Scars and over Crossthwaite Common to return to Middleton, around **13 miles (21km)** in all. (Explorer OL31 & OL19)

• **Dufton to High Cup** (see p211) **returning via Harbour Flatt** Follow the Pennine Way in reverse from Dufton, up to the incredible glacial bowl of High Cup then take the lofty path along its eastern lip, down Middle Tongue and around the nose of Middletongue Crag, passing the farm of Harbour Flatt and back along the lane to Dufton, for an exhilarating **10-mile (16km)** walk. (Explorer OL19)

• **Greenhead to Once Brewed** (see p234) Another 'out and back' day walk, but justified on the basis that the path is accompanied by the Roman Wall and what you miss on the way out you may spot on the way back. You walk a total of about **14 miles (22.5km)** beside some of the finest sections of the Wall; ramparts, milecastles and turrets are all visited. (Explorer OL43)

❑ Walking the Pennine Way – a personal experience

There were a few raised eyebrows when I announced that I was going to walk the Pennine Way on my own. Non-walking friends worried about my safety. Walking friends wondered if I would finish. Happily, they were all wrong. I encountered nothing but kindness and respect and I finished in 18 days wishing it would go on forever. Never once did I think about quitting and to anyone considering it I'd say walk your own walk. Your mind is by far your greatest asset or your greatest liability. The first and last hour of every day are the hardest – no matter how long or short the day is.

Highlight: sharing the last day with my husband and getting my certificate at the Border Hotel. Lowlight: sharing a YHA room with a girl who snored louder than an express train.

Top tip: ignore anyone who says that you can't get lost – trust me, you can. If you think you need to stop and consult the map – you do!

I loved every single soggy exhausting moment of it and I'd do it again in a heartbeat except that I worry that it won't be as good second time and I'd rather keep those wonderful memories. **Janet Donnelly (Twitter: @celebrantjanet)**

Two- and three-day linear walks

• **Edale to Standedge** (see p86) This **30-mile (50km)** walk takes in the Kinder Scout, Bleaklow and Black Hill massifs and offers a chance to experience some of the best 'Dark Peak' walking there is. Where there's gritstone there's also peat, but thankfully the worst of the mire is now slabbed, so although you may not keep your boots dry, you are unlikely to be swallowed whole! The railway stations at Edale and Marsden will facilitate your travel and a Torside B&B will break the journey into two days.

• **Gargrave to Horton-in-Ribblesdale** (see p134) This **22-mile (35km)** section may be within the reach of some as a day walk, using the stations at Gargrave and Horton, both on the Leeds–Carlisle line to facilitate transfer. However, it is best experienced as a weekend walk, with a break in Malham before tackling the tough stretch over Fountains Fell and Pen-y-ghent down into Horton.

• **Horton-in-Ribblesdale to Bowes** (see p158) This is best undertaken as a three-day walk, totalling, as it does, **around 42 miles (68km)**. The route includes the waterfall in Hardraw, an ascent of Great Shunner Fell, the experience of a lifetime at Tan Hill Inn and the crossing of the desolate Sleightholme Moor. The railway station in Horton is a great starting point but a second car, or a bus or taxi to Kirkby Stephen station, will be needed for the return leg.

• **Dufton to Greenhead** (see p211) The high point of the Pennine Way on Cross Fell is also the highlight of this section, unless you decide to extend it slightly to take in the Roman Wall, which could be done by using Bardon Mill station (Newcastle–Carlisle Line) instead of Haltwhistle; both require a diversion of a couple of miles from the Wall. Indeed the start point of Dufton is three miles (5km) from Appleby station, but a taxi can whisk you over this short distance easily enough. Expect to cover **about 40 miles (64km)** on this walk.

• **Bellingham to Kirk Yetholm** (see p249) Both ends of this **40-mile (64km)** section of the Way require some logistical jiggery-pokery, as neither has a railway station within easy reach. The 25-mile (40km) stretch over the Cheviot range can be broken down using the accommodation options described on p259 & p261, or make use of one of the mountain shelters that exist, both have sleeping space for three or four people in comfort. Better still, yomp the whole ridge in one go and feel what it must be like to have walked all the way from Edale.

❑ Walking the Pennine Way – a personal experience

The first time I walked the Pennine Way, south to north, was magic. I enjoyed it so much I decided to do it again, north to south. The countryside is a given – fantastic – but the weather can be totally unpredictable, which adds to the experience; however, the outstanding memory, each time, was of the people I met and how friendly they were.

Each time I camped most of the way. There was one time I asked a farmer for permission to pitch on his land and ended up helping him with a new born calf. Unforgettable! I didn't plan ahead and relied on picking up supplies locally, or, more often than not, eating in pubs. Camping outside Tan Hill Inn was wonderful, waking up with the ducks in the morning. The Pennine Way is one of walking's great 'must do's' and it will more than repay the effort. **Gordon Green (Twitter: @aktovate1)**

What to take

The tales of Pennine Wayfarers, broken and beaten by their huge loads are easy enough to find on the internet. Taking too much is an easy mistake to make when you don't know what to expect and many over-compensate by packing everything they think may be needed. This isn't a problem if you plan on using a baggage-transfer service, but will be if you intend carrying it all yourself.

The ability to pack light comes with experience and requires a degree of discipline. Every ounce you remove from your load will enable you to walk that little bit further, make the day that little bit easier and reduce the strain on feet that need to carry you over 250 miles. Be careful in your selection of equipment and ruthless in your decision to take something at all.

If you've done any hill-walking you will probably have most of the equipment you need, but if you are starting fresh look out for online deals and special offers in the outdoor supermarkets; shopping around can save you a small fortune. However, be aware of cheap, low-quality products; 'buy cheap, buy twice' is often very true and you need equipment to last the full length of the trail.

TRAVELLING LIGHT

Baggage-transfer services (see pp27-9) enable you to walk every day with nothing more than a daypack, water, lunch, waterproofs and the other bare essentials. This lightweight approach and the fact that you can have clean clothes every day appeals to many walkers. Consider, though, the feeling of setting out from Edale with everything you need to walk over 250 miles to Kirk Yetholm and the sense of satisfaction that may engender upon arrival.

HOW TO CARRY YOUR LUGGAGE

Today's **rucksacks** are hi-tech affairs that make load-carrying as tolerable as can be expected. Don't get hung up on anti-sweat features; unless you use a wheelbarrow your back will always sweat. It's better to ensure a good fit, especially in the back-length if you are above average height. In addition to hip belts, an unelasticated cross-chest strap will keep the pack snug; it can make a real difference. If you're camping you'll need a much larger pack, probably no less than 60-litres' capacity. Staying in hostels, 40 litres should be ample, and for those eating out and staying in B&B-style accommodation a 30- to 40-litre pack should suffice; anything less than this and you will almost certainly be using a baggage transfer service. It is worth noting that baggage carriers will impose a weight limit on your bag of around 17-20kg.

Although many rucksacks claim to be waterproof, this isn't always the case so it is worth using a strong plastic **bin liner**. It's also handy to **compartmentalise** the contents into coloured or distinguishable bags so you know what is where. Take **plastic bags** for wet things, rubbish etc; they're always useful. Finally, pack the most frequently used things so they are readily accessible.

FOOTWEAR

Boots

If you have to get one item of equipment right, it's your boots. Although modern boots don't need 'breaking in' the way boots used to, you would still be a brave (or possibly foolish) person to turn up at Edale with a pair of boots you'd never tried before. **Always test equipment** before a long walk and this is all the more true for boots; a weekend walk with the pack weight you intend to use on the Pennine Way should be enough to tell you what you need to know.

Boot selection is best done with the advice of a professional, so an online purchase or an outdoor supermarket may not be the best place, unless you are repeat buying boots. **Fit and comfort are paramount** – there's nothing worse than descending a long stony track, such as the Corpse Road off Cross Fell, and finding your boots don't protect your feet from the surface beneath. You have about half a million steps to do along the Way, so choose wisely. Most reputable outdoor stores will let you try boots at home, around the house, for a few days and allow you to return them if you find they don't fit. Expect to pay £100 or more for a good pair. All boots can be transformed with **shock-absorbing after-market insoles**. Some are thermally moulded to your foot in the shop but the less-expensive examples are also well worth the investment.

If you get bad **blisters** refer to p79 for blister-avoidance strategies.

Although not essential, it's a treat to have **alternative footwear** when not on the trail to give your feet a break or let boots dry. Sport sandals or flip-flops are all suitable as long as they're light.

Socks

A **two-layer** approach to socks helps to prevent blisters; the idea being that the inner sock stays with your foot and the outer sock moves with your boot, which reduces friction on the skin and thereby blisters. A thin liner sock works best for this, with a thicker, cushioning sock used for the outer layer. Foot care is one of those places where you don't want to cut corners, so consider Merino wool for the liner socks, they are light, tough and seem, miraculously, to fail to hold smells!

CLOTHES

Tops

Multiple layers of clothing provide the most effective and flexible approach to upper body protection. Three layers typically provides enough flexibility for an English spring or summer walk.

A quick-drying synthetic **base layer**, or better still a Merino wool layer that stays fresh for weeks, may be enough on its own for warm days, or for when you're working hard up the face of Pen-y-ghent. A warm **mid layer**, typically a fleece or wind shirt will add some protection when you reach the summit and begin to cool down, or for those days when the sun just refuses to shine. Finally, a waterproof **outer layer**, or 'shell' is your final defence against strong winds, rain and really cold days. A good-quality jacket will have vents that you can open to allow some air to flow around your upper body, while still repelling the worst of the rain. It would also be useful to help prevent hypothermia. The layers can be mixed and matched depending on how bad the weather is. Summer rain showers are often warm enough to leave the fleece in your pack and quickly throw the outer shell over your base layer.

Avoid cotton; as well as being slow to dry, when it's wet cotton saps away body heat and will cause chafing if worn next to the skin. Take a change of base layers (including underwear); if you hand wash underwear in the evening, it may not be dry by the time you leave in the morning.

A **spare set of 'evening' clothes** will guarantee you always have something clean and dry to change into at the end of the day, which makes life more comfortable for your companions as well as yourself. Having a spare set of clothes also provides an emergency layer in case you or someone you're with goes down with hypothermia (see p80).

Leg wear

Your legs will probably feel the cold less than any other part of your body so, unless you're walking at the extreme ends of the season, a lightweight, quick-drying pair of **synthetic trousers** will almost certainly suffice. Denim jeans are cotton and the same advice applies to these as it did earlier – jeans tend to chafe once wet and they stay wet for much longer than synthetic materials.

Waterproof overtrousers can be awkward and time-consuming to put on and can generate as much internal moisture through sweat as they repel in a light shower; consider a pair of quick-drying trousers instead.

On a warm day you may also want to consider **shorts** – some trousers allow you to zip off the bottom half of the legs and turn previously long trousers into shorts. Check that you can do this without having to take your boots off though, or convert them first thing, before you set out.

Gaiters are not as essential as they once were. The slabs have tamed the worst of the bogs, but you may be surprised how well they serve to protect your boots and lower legs when walking through long wet vegetation.

Headwear and other clothing

A peaked cap or a full-brimmed **hat** such as a Tilley will help with UV protection on sunny days, but even in the summer you should always pack a woolly hat and **gloves** to combat wind chill on an exposed summit.

TOILETRIES

Besides **toothpaste** and a brush, **liquid soap** can also be used for shaving and washing clothes, although a ziplock bag of detergent is better if you're laundering regularly. Carry **toilet paper** and a lightweight **trowel** to bury the results out on the fells (see pp75-6). Less obvious items include **ear plugs** (for hostel dormitories and campsites), **sun screen**, **moisturiser** and, particularly if camping, **insect repellent** (though we never encountered any, some people claim to have been bitten half to death by midges, particularly when camping by water) and a **water filter bottle or purification system**.

FIRST-AID KIT

Apart from aching limbs your most likely ailments will be blisters so a first-aid kit can be tiny. **Paracetamol** helps numb pain, but as long as you are not asthmatic **Ibuprofen** is more effective against pain with inflammation although rest, of course, is the cure. **'Moleskin'**, **'Compeed'**, or **'Second Skin'** all treat blisters. An **elastic knee support** is a good precaution for a weak knee.

A few sachets of **Dioralyte** or **Rehydrat** powders will quickly remedy mineral loss through sweating. Also consider taking a small selection of different-sized **sterile dressings** for wounds.

GENERAL ITEMS

Essential

Carry a **compass** and know how to use it with a map; also take a **whistle** (see p78) and a **mobile phone** for emergencies, but don't rely on getting a signal in remote places; a **hydration pack** (at least two litres); a **headtorch** with spare **batteries**; **emergency snacks** which your body can quickly convert into energy; a **penknife**, **watch**, **plastic bags**, **safety pins** and **scissors**.

Useful

If you're not carrying a proper bivi bag or tent a compact **foil space blanket** is a good idea in the cooler seasons. A compact **camera** is a great way to capture and record memorable moments – though most people will have this facility on their smartphone. A **notebook** or journal and a **paperback** for the evenings can now be combined in a mobile device such as a Kindle or small electronic tablet (but remember to wrap it safely against water). A **flask** for tea, coffee or hot soup will pay its own way if you're walking in the cooler parts of the year. Also consider **sunglasses**, a small pair of **binoculars** and a **music player** (and batteries).

Walking poles are a personal choice and not something you should take unless you usually walk with them; the Pennine Way is not a place to test new equipment of any sort. However, significant benefits can be gained from using one, or a pair of poles.

SLEEPING BAG

If you're camping or planning to stay in camping barns you'll need a sleeping bag. Some bunkhouses offer bedding but you'll keep your costs down if you don't have to hire it. Most hostels provide bedding and insist you use it.

A **two-season bag** will do for indoor use, but if you can afford it or anticipate outdoor use, go warmer; it's better to be too warm than too cold. Sleeping bags come in two main types: **synthetic and down** (goose is better than duck). Synthetic bags are usually cheaper but weigh more than a down bag rated for a similar temperature range (around £100 compared to £200 or more). A synthetic bag deals with damp much better than a down bag, retaining some thermal properties, but down water-repellent treatments are becoming more common and this difference is now less significant.

CAMPING GEAR

If you have no desire to camp on the hills (wild camping) you may well get away with a cheap festival **tent** for campsites; you can pick these up for under £25. You will need something a little more technical for the hills though, something able to stand up to buffeting from the wind and properly waterproof. Expect to pay around £100 for a good one-man tent and anything up to £300 for a lightweight, two-man example. Aim to select a tent weighing no more than 2kg and remember that you need to be very good friends with anyone you intend to share a two-man tent with!

The technology associated with inflatable **sleeping mats** has developed rapidly over the last few years and you will sleep much better with one beneath your sleeping bag. They are lightweight, incredibly comfortable and pack away small. Self-inflating mattresses are usually more robust, slightly cheaper but also a little less comfortable than the modern 'air-bed' mattresses produced by brands such as Thermarest and Exped.

Give serious consideration to **cooking gear**. The variety of stoves and fuels is bewildering, each with their own merits and pitfalls. Consider using pubs and cafés as an alternative to carrying any cooking gear at all. There is nothing quite like a hot drink before you turn in for the night though. A good-quality water hydration pack can also be turned into a hot water bottle.

MAPS

The hand-drawn maps in this book cover the trail at a scale of just under 1:20,000 but are in a strip, the scale equivalent to two miles wide. In some places, particularly on high moors where navigation points are scant, a proper **topographical map** and a compass could be of great use. But, as mentioned on p17, when the mist comes down and all landmarks disappear, a **GPS** used with a map comes into its own.

❑ Talking the talk

Although we all speak English after a fashion, the finely honed ear will perceive at least five distinct accents along the Pennine Way, each with its own dialect, with greetings being most evident to the walker. These will be most noticeable in deeply rural areas, particularly among agricultural workers who may sound unintelligible to an unacclimatised foreigner.

From the High Peak of northern Derbyshire ('*ahyallrait*?') you'll flit between the cultural frontier of erstwhile county rivals, Yorkshire and Lancashire, who both share a curt 'ow do?' Then, as you leave the Dales another invisible boundary is crossed and the accent takes on the distinctive 'Geordie' tones of County Durham and Northumberland ('allreet?') before your final linguistic watershed over The Cheviots into Scotland where a barely discernible nod means you've a new friend for life.

❑ Digital mapping

Taking OS-quality maps with you on the hills has never been so easy. Most modern smartphones have a GPS chip so you will be able to see your position overlaid onto the digital map on your phone. Almost every device with built-in GPS functionality now has some mapping software available for it. If you don't have a smartphone or would prefer a dedicated handheld GPS device, Garmin has an extensive range (£100 to £600), all compatible with the GPS waypoints that can be downloaded for this walk from the Trailblazer website (🖳 trailblazer-guides.com/gps-waypoints).

There are several software packages and apps on the market today (see below) that provide Ordnance Survey and other maps for a PC or smartphone. Maps are supplied electronically by direct download over the internet. The maps are then loaded into an application, also available by download, from where you can view them, print them and create routes on them.

Digital maps are normally purchased for an area such as a National Park, but user-defined areas are also available allowing you to create a custom map for the length of the Pennine Way. When compared to the multitude of OS Explorer maps that are needed to cover the walk, digital maps can be very competitively priced. Once you own the electronic version of the map you can print any section of the map you like, as many times as you like.

The real value of digital maps, though, is the ability to draw a route directly onto the map from your computer or smartphone. The map, or the appropriate sections of it, can then be printed with the route marked on it. Additionally, the route can be viewed directly on your smartphone or uploaded to a GPS device.

Smartphones and GPS devices should complement, not replace, the traditional method of navigation (a map and compass) as any electronic device can break or, if nothing else, run out of battery. Remember that the battery life of your phone will be significantly reduced, compared to normal usage, when you are using the built-in GPS and running the screen for long periods.

- **Anquet** (🖳 www.anquet.com) has the Pennine Way Northern Section (from £19.81) and Southern Section (from £17.83) using OS 1:25,000 mapping.
- **Ordnance Survey** (🖳 www.ordnancesurvey.co.uk) will let you download and then use their UK maps (1:25,000 scale) on a mobile or tablet without a data connection for a subscription of £3.99 for one month or £19.99 for a year (on their current offer).
- **Harvey** (🖳 www.harveymaps.co.uk) sell their Pennine Way North (1:40,000 scale) and Pennine Way South (1:40,000 scale) as a download for £20.49 for each map.
- **Memory Map** (🖳 www.memory-map.co.uk) currently sell OS 1:25,000 mapping covering the whole of the UK for £100.

Stuart Greig

In Britain the **Ordnance Survey** (🖳 ordnancesurvey.co.uk) maps are peerless. Their orange 1:25,000-scale 'Explorer' series features pin-sharp cartography and detail that makes navigation a doddle. From south to north nine sheets cover the Pennine Way: **OL1** The Peak District – Dark Peak area; **OL21** South Pennines; **OL2** Yorkshire Dales – Southern & Western areas; **OL30** Yorkshire Dales – Northern & Central Areas; **OL31** North Pennines – Teesdale & Weardale; **OL19** Howgill Fells & Upper Eden Valley; **OL43** Hadrian's Wall; **OL42** Kielder Water and Forest; **OL16** The Cheviot Hills. Packing such a stack of maps, especially the bulky laminated weatherproof versions, is a chore. Walkers either post them ahead or mark the Way and trim off the flab with a pair of scissors.

OS Explorers are the ultimate Pennine maps but there is a series of handy maps which give the big picture during planning and work fine on the trail as a back up to this book's maps: Harvey Maps (🖳 harveymaps.co.uk) produce a set of three waterproof maps covering Pennine Way South: Edale to Horton, Pennine Way Central: Horton to Greenhead; and Pennine Way North: Greenhead to Kirk Yetholm (all 2013) in a series of north-oriented strip panels at a scale of 1:40,000. The panels cover a broader area each side of the path and, crucially, they include the OS grid to work with GPS. Alternatively consider the two AZ Adventure Series maps (🖳 az.co.uk) for the Way: South (Edale to Bowes) and North (Bowes to Kirk Yetholm). They are lightweight, cheap (£8.95), use OS's mapping on the same 1:25,000 scale as their Explorer series and have an index.

❑ SOURCES OF FURTHER INFORMATION

Trail information

- **Pennine Way National Trail** (🖳 nationaltrail.co.uk/pennine-way) The website provides an interactive map with accommodation guide, events and information as well as FAQs and even GPS waypoints.
- **Pennine Way Association** (PWA; 🖳 penninewayassociation.co.uk) A charity that campaigned to protect the national trail; though the PWA closed in 2016, as we go to press their website still has lots of useful info and links.

Tourist information centres, Visitor centres and National Park centres

Most **tourist information centres (TICs)** are open daily from Easter to September/ October, and thereafter more limited days/hours. Unless you have a specific query, they're usually of little use to an organised walker once underway. There are TICS at Haworth (see p128) and Alston (p218); at Horton-in-Ribblesdale (p156) and Middleton-in-Teesdale (p194) the TIC is unofficial/run by volunteers so services are more limited. There are **visitor centres** with some tourist information at Edale (p83), Hebden Bridge (p114), Once Brewed (p238) and Bellingham (p244).

The Pennine Way goes through the Peak District, Yorkshire Dales and Northumberland national parks; see box p60 for contact details; both Malham (p147) and Hawes (p166) are **national park centres** and have some tourist information.

Organisations for walkers

- **Backpackers Club** (🖳 backpackersclub.co.uk) For people interested in lightweight camping. Members receive a quarterly magazine, access to a comprehensive information service (including a library) and a farm-pitch directory. Membership costs £15 per year, family £20, under 18s and over 65s £8.50.
- **The Long Distance Walkers' Association** (🖳 ldwa.org.uk) An association of people with the common interest of long-distance walking. Membership includes a journal, *Strider*, three times per year giving details of challenge events and local group walks as well as articles on the subject. Individual membership costs £13 a year whilst family membership for two adults and all children under 18 is £19.50 a year.
- **Ramblers** (formerly Ramblers Association; 🖳 ramblers.org.uk) Looks after the interests of walkers throughout Britain. They publish a large amount of useful information including their quarterly *Walk* magazine. Annual membership costs £35.85/47.85 individual/joint (concessionary rates also available).

RECOMMENDED READING

- *Pennine Walkies*, Mark Wallington (Arrow, 1997) describes in wry humour, the highs and lows of walking the Way with a crazy dog.
- *Pennine Way Companion*, Alfred Wainwright (ed Chris Jesty; Frances Lincoln, 2012) Updated edition of Wainwright's guide to the Pennine Way, in the same style as his Lakeland Pictorial Guides.
- *End to End – An Adventure on the Pennine Way*, Dean Carter (Kindle, 2013) A wonderfully honest account of a personal journey along the Way; not a guide-book, but it will certainly help to prepare you for what's to come.
- *Walking Home: Travels with a troubadour on the Pennine Way*, Simon Armitage (Faber & Faber 2012) Another personal account, this time from someone walking from Scotland back home, describing the highs and lows of walking the Pennine Way.
- *The Pennine Way*, Roly Smith, photographs John Morrison (Frances Lincoln, 2011) A beautifully illustrated celebration of the Pennine Way, including its history and geography, deserving of space on any walker's coffee-table.
- *Wainwright on the Pennine Way* Alfred Wainwright, Derry Brabbs (2014) New edition of a 1985 book in which legendary fell walker Alfred Wainwright teams up with photographer Derry Brabbs to provide a large-format, coffee-table style overview of the path.
- *RSPB Pocket Guide to British Birds*, Simon Harrap (RSPB, 2012).

Getting to and from the Pennine Way

Travelling to the start of the Pennine Way by public transport makes sense in so many ways. There's no need to trouble anyone for a lift or worry about your vehicle while walking, there are no logistical headaches about how to return to your car when you've finished the walk, it's a big step towards minimising your ecological footprint and, if you book in advance, you can take advantage of some really cheap fares. Quite apart from that, you'll simply feel your holiday has begun the moment you step out of your front door, rather than when you've slammed the car door behind you.

NATIONAL TRANSPORT

By rail

Frequent and direct rail connections to Edale from both Manchester and Sheffield make these two cities the most obvious gateways to the start of the Pennine Way. The 30- or 45-minute train journey makes them very convenient as well. At the northern terminus of the walk you need to aim for Berwick-upon-Tweed, which is reached via two bus journeys from Kirk Yetholm, via Kelso, and will take at least 2¼ hours.

❑ Getting to Britain

• **By air** There are plenty of cheap flights from around the world to London's airports: Heathrow, Gatwick, Luton, London City and Stansted. However, Manchester (🖳 manchesterairport.co.uk) and Edinburgh (🖳 edinburghairport.com) airports are the closest to the start and finish points of the Pennine Way and both have plenty of international flights. There are also airports at Newcastle (🖳 newcastleairport.com) and Leeds (🖳 leedsbradfordairport.co.uk). Visit the airport websites to see which airlines fly there and from where.

• **From Europe by train** Eurostar (🖳 eurostar.com) operates a high-speed passenger service via the Channel Tunnel between a number of cities in Europe (particularly Paris, Brussels and Amsterdam) and London (St Pancras International). See below for details of how to get to and from the start/end of the walk by train from London; all the railway stations in London have connections to the London underground. For more information about rail services from Europe contact your national rail company or Railteam (🖳 railteam.eu).

• **From Europe by coach** Eurolines (🖳 eurolines.eu) have a huge network of long-distance coach services connecting over 500 cities in 25 European countries to London. Flix Bus (🖳 global.flixbus.com) also operates low-cost coach services to London. Check carefully, however: often, once such expenses as food for the journey are taken into consideration, it does not work out that much cheaper than taking a flight, particularly when compared to the fares on some of the budget airlines.

• **From Europe by car** P&O Ferries (🖳 poferries.com) and DFDS Seaways (🖳 dfdsseaways.com) are just two of the many ferry operators that operate services between Britain and continental Europe; the main routes are between all the major North Sea and Channel ports. Direct Ferries (🖳 directferries.co.uk) lists all the main operators/routes and sells discounted tickets.

Eurotunnel (🖳 eurotunnel.com) operates 'Le Shuttle', a shuttle train service for vehicles via the Channel Tunnel between Calais and Folkestone taking one hour between the motorway in France and the motorway in Britain.

East Midlands Trains (🖳 eastmidlandstrains.co.uk) have direct services from St Pancras mainline station to Sheffield; change there to Northern Rail services to Edale (see box p59). Alternatively, Virgin Trains (🖳 virgintrains.co.uk) operate from Euston station to Manchester (from where you can also change to a Northern train to Edale). Cross Country Trains (🖳 crosscountrytrains.co.uk) also provide services to both Sheffield and Manchester.

At the end of the walk, or if you are walking north to south, you will need LNER's (London North Eastern Railway; 🖳 lner.co.uk) King's Cross to Edinburgh service as it calls at Berwick-upon-Tweed.

There are stations on the Pennine Way at Edale, Hebden Bridge, Gargrave and Horton-in-Ribblesdale. Other useful stations with good bus services linking them to various parts of the Way include Huddersfield, Marsden, Skipton, Darlington, Appleby, Bardon Mill, Haltwhistle and Hexham. Services are provided by LNER (see above), Northern and Trans-Pennine Express (see box p59).

National Rail (☎ 03457-484950, 24hrs, 🖳 nationalrail.co.uk) has timetable and fare information for rail travel in the whole of Britain. You can buy tickets through the relevant rail operator, in person at a railway station, or online at 🖳 thetrainline.com or 🖳 qjump.co.uk. It's worth planning ahead, at least two weeks, as it's the only way to save a considerable amount of money. It helps to be as flexible as possible and don't forget that most discounted tickets carry some restrictions; check what they are before you buy your ticket. Travel on a Friday may be more expensive than on other days of the week.

Megatrain (🖳 uk.megabus.com/products/megatrain) offers low-cost inter-city train services; destinations include Manchester, Leeds and Berwick-upon-Tweed.

By coach (long-distance bus)

National Express (see box below) is the principal coach operator in Britain. There are services from most towns in England and Wales to a number of towns and cities on or near the route. **Megabus** (🖳 uk.megabus.com) operates low-cost services from all over Britain to Manchester, Sheffield, and Newcastle. Fares start from just £1 plus a 50p booking fee.

Travel by coach is usually cheaper than by train but takes longer. Advance bookings carry discounts so be sure to book at least a week ahead. If you don't mind an uncomfortable night there are overnight services on some routes.

By car

Both Edale and Kirk Yetholm are easily reached using the motorway and A-road network from the rest of Britain. Unless you're just out for a day walk however, you'd be better leaving the car at home as there is nowhere safe to leave a vehicle unattended for a long period.

LOCAL TRANSPORT

Getting to and from most parts of the Pennine Way is relatively simple due to the public transport network including trains, coaches and local bus services.

The public transport map on pp54-5 gives an overview of routes which are of particular use to walkers and the table on pp56-9 lists the operators (and their contact details), the route details and the approximate frequency of services in both directions. Note that services may be less frequent in the winter months or stop completely. It is also essential to check services before travelling as details may change. If the operator details prove unsatisfactory contact traveline (☎ 0871-200 2233, daily 8am-8pm, 🖳 traveline.info), which has timetable information for the whole of the UK; details about services in Scotland are also available on 🖳 travelinescotland.com. Local timetables can also be picked up from tourist information centres along the Way.

❑ **National Express** (🖳 nationalexpress.com)
350 Stansted to Manchester via Mansfield, Sheffield & **Crowden**, daily 1/day
plus Mansfield to Liverpool via Sheffield & **Crowden**, daily 1/day
561 London to Skipton via Keighley, daily 2/day
564 London to Halifax via Sheffield & Huddersfield, daily 3/day
591 London to Edinburgh via Newcastle & Berwick-upon-Tweed, 1/day

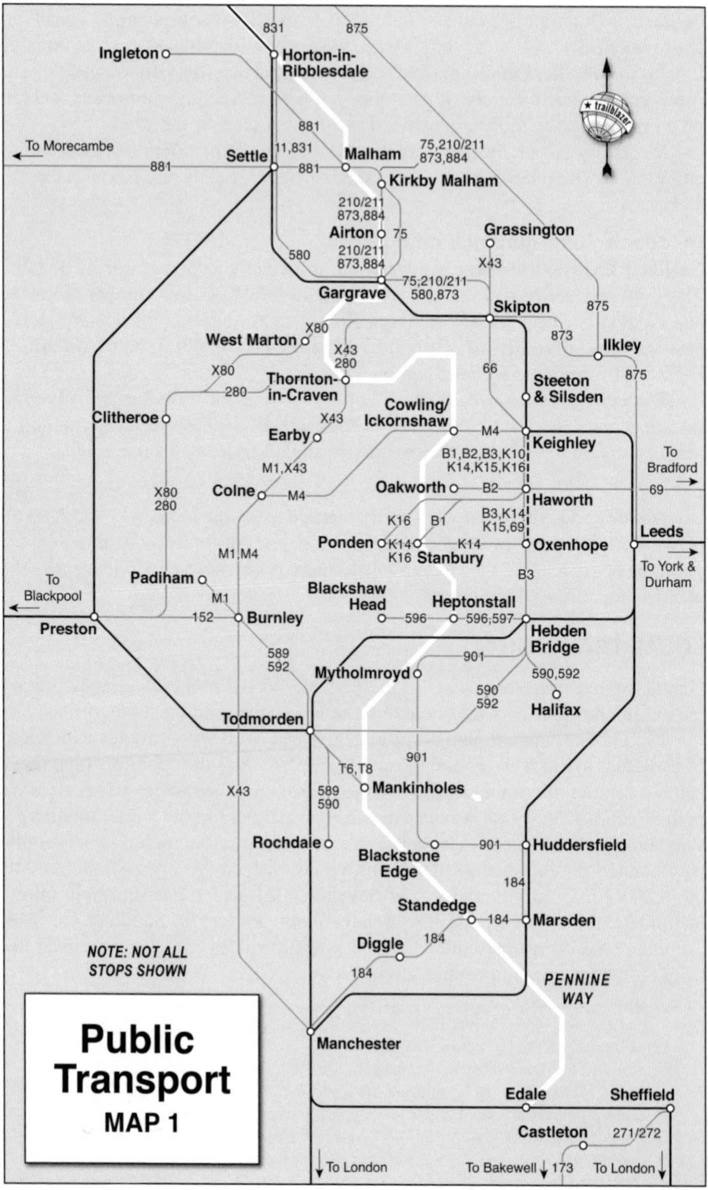
Public Transport
MAP 1
NOTE: NOT ALL STOPS SHOWN
PENNINE WAY
Ingleton
Horton-in-Ribblesdale
831
875
881
To Morecambe
Settle
11,831
Malham
75,210/211
873,884
Kirkby Malham
210/211
873,884
Airton
75
Grassington
580
X43
Gargrave
75,210/211
580,873
Skipton
875
873
Ilkley
West Marton
X80
X43
280
66
Steeton & Silsden
Thornton-in-Craven
Cowling/ Ickornshaw
M4
Keighley
Clitheroe
Earby
B1,B2,B3,K10
K14,K15,K16
To Bradford
M1,X43
Oakworth
B2
69
Colne
Haworth
X80
280
K16
B1
B3,K14
K15,69
Leeds
Ponden
K14
Stanbury
Oxenhope
M1,M4
To York & Durham
B3
To Blackpool
Padiham
Blackshaw Head
Heptonstall
M1
596
596,597
Preston
152
Burnley
Hebden Bridge
901
589
592
Mytholmroyd
590,592
590
592
Halifax
Todmorden
T6,T8
Mankinholes
X43
589
590
Rochdale
Blackstone Edge
Huddersfield
184
Standedge
Marsden
Diggle
Manchester
Edale
Sheffield
Castleton
271/272
To London
To Bakewell
173

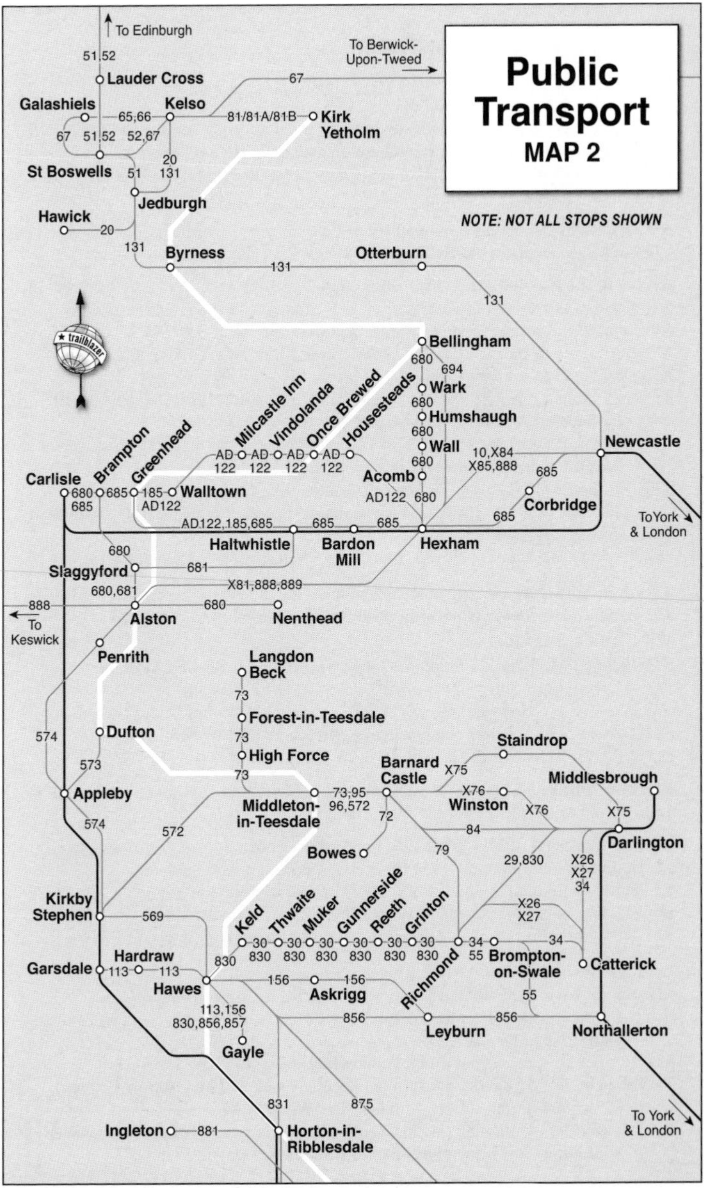
Public Transport
MAP 2
NOTE: NOT ALL STOPS SHOWN
To Edinburgh
To Berwick-Upon-Tweed
Lauder Cross
Galashiels
Kelso
Kirk Yetholm
St Boswells
Jedburgh
Hawick
Byrness
Otterburn
Bellingham
Wark
Humshaugh
Wall
Acomb
Milcastle Inn
Vindolanda
Once Brewed
Housesteads
Carlisle
Brampton
Greenhead
Walltown
Newcastle
Corbridge
Hexham
Haltwhistle
Bardon Mill
To York & London
Slaggyford
Alston
Nenthead
To Keswick
Penrith
Langdon Beck
Forest-in-Teesdale
High Force
Dufton
Appleby
Staindrop
Barnard Castle
Middlesbrough
Middleton-in-Teesdale
Winston
Darlington
Bowes
Kirkby Stephen
Keld
Thwaite
Muker
Gunnerside
Reeth
Grinton
Richmond
Brompton-on-Swale
Catterick
Garsdale
Hardraw
Hawes
Askrigg
Leyburn
Northallerton
Gayle
Ingleton
Horton-in-Ribblesdale
To York & London
trailblazer

❑ PUBLIC TRANSPORT SERVICES

Bus services

Notes: • Not all stops are listed

• Many bus services in rural areas operate on a hail-and-ride basis ie the driver will stop to set passengers down or pick them up as long as it's safe to do so.

• The services listed were operating at the time of research but it is essential to check as often they change.

ADAPT (☎ 01434-600599, 🖳 adapt-ne.org.uk) (SEE MAP 1)

694 Kielder to Hexham via **Bellingham**, Tue & Fri 1/day

Arriva in the North-East (🖳 arrivabus.co.uk/North-East) (SEE MAP 2)

X26 Colburn to Darlington via Catterick & Richmond, Mon-Sat 2/hr, Sun 1/hr
X27 Scotton to Darlington via Catterick & Richmond, Mon-Sat 1/hr
X75 Darlington to Barnard Castle via Staindrop, Mon-Sat 1/hr, Sun 5/day
X76 Darlington to Barnard Castle via Winston, Mon-Sat 1/hr
85 Newcastle to Carlisle via Corbridge, Hexham, Bardon Mill, Haltwhistle, **Greenhead** & Brampton, Mon-Sat 1/hr,
Sun & Bank Hols Newcastle to Hexham 1/hr and Hexham to Carlisle 5/day (services operated in conjunction with Stagecoach 685)
830 Darlington to Gayle via Richmond, Grinton, Reeth, Gunnerside, **Muker**, **Thwaite**, **Keld** & **Hawes**, May to mid Oct Sun & Bank Hols 1/day (Northern Powergrid Country Bus)
857 Gayle to Masham via **Hawes**, Sun 1/day (Wensleydale Wanderer DalesBus)

Arriva in Yorkshire (🖳 arrivabus.co.uk/North-East) (SEE MAPS 1 & 2)

831 Settle to **Hawes** via **Horton-in-Ribblesdale**, Apr-mid Oct Sun 1/day (Ribblehead Ranger)
873 Ilkley to **Malham** via Skipton, **Gargrave**, **Airton** & **Kirkby Malham**, Apr-mid Oct Sun & Bank Hols 2/day plus 1/day to Skipton
875 Wakefield to **Hawes** via Leeds & Ilkley, Apr-mid Oct Sun 1/day (Dalesman)
884 Dewsbury to **Malham** via **Gargrave**, **Airton** & **Kirkby Malham**, Apr-mid Oct Sun & Bank Hols 1/day (Craven Link; Dales Bus)

Blackburn Bus Company (☎ 01254-670583, 🖳 lancashirebus.co.uk) (SEE MAP 1)

152 Preston to Burnley, Mon-Sat 2/hr, Sun 1/hr

Borders Buses (☎ 01289-308719, 🖳 bordersbuses.co.uk) (SEE MAP 2)

51 Jedburgh to Edinburgh via St Boswells, Mon-Sat 6/day, Sun 3/day
52 Kelso to Edinburgh via St Boswells & Lauder Cross, Mon-Sat 6/day, Sun 2/day
67 Galashiels to Berwick via St Boswells & Kelso, Mon-Sat 8/day, Sun 3-5/day
81 **Kirk Yetholm** to Kelso Mon-Fri 2/day term-time only (see also Peter Hogg)

Burnley Bus (☎ 0345-604 0110, 🖳 lancashirebus.co.uk) (SEE MAP 1)

M1 Barnoldswick to Padiham via Burnley, **Earby** & Colne, Mon-Sat 2/hr, Barnoldswick to Burnley via **Earby** & Colne, Sun 1/hr plus Colne to Padiham via Burnley Sun 1/hr
M4 Burnley to Keighley via Colne & **Cowling**, Mon-Sat 2/hr, Sun 6/day
X43 Manchester to Skipton via Burnley, Barnoldswick & **Thornton-in-Craven**, Mon-Sat 2/hr plus 2/hr to Burnley (The Witch Way)
Manchester to Grassington via Burnley, Barnoldswick, **Thornton-in-Craven** & Skipton, Sun 7/day plus 4/day to Burnley & 1/day to Skipton

Cumbria Classic Coaches (🖳 cumbriaclassiccoaches.co.uk) (SEE MAP 2)
569 Ravenstonedale to **Hawes** via Kirkby Stephen, Apr-end Oct Tue 1/day
572 Ravenstonedale to Barnard Castle via Kirkby Stephen, Wed 1/day (in summer the service also calls at **Middleton-in-Teesdale**)
574 Penrith to Kirkby Stephen via Appleby & Long Marton, Tue 1/day

First (🖳 firstgroup.com/ukbus) (SEE MAP 1)
184 Huddersfield to Manchester via **Marsden**, Brun Clough **(Standedge)** & Diggle, Mon-Sat 1/hr, Sun 6/day (First Greater Manchester)
271/272 Sheffield to Castleton, daily approx 1/hr (First South Yorkshire; see also Hulleys of Baslow)
589 Burnley to Rochdale via **Todmorden**, Mon-Sat 1/hr (First Halifax, Calder Valley & Huddersfield; FHCVH)
590 Rochdale to Todmorden, Mon-Fri & Sun 1/hr, Rochdale to Halifax via Todmorden & Hebden Bridge, Sat 1/hr (FHCVH)
592 Halifax to Burnley via Hebden Bridge & Todmorden, daily 1/hr plus Mon-Sat 2/hr to Todmorden and Easter to Sep Halifax to Hebden Bridge 1/hr (FHCVH)

Go North East (☎ 0191-420 5050, 🖳 www.simplygo.com) (SEE MAP 2)
10 Newcastle to Hexham, Mon-Sat 2/hr, Sun 1/hr
X81 **Alston** to Hexham, Mon-Sat 1/day
X84 Newcastle to Hexham, Mon-Sat 1/hr
X85 Newcastle to Newbrough via Hexham, Mon-Sat 1/hr
185 Haltwhistle to Birdoswald via **Greenhead** & Walltown, Mon-Sat 3/day
680 Hexham to **Bellingham** via Acomb, Wall, Humshaugh & Wark, Mon-Sat 7-8/day
681 **Alston** to Haltwhistle via **Slaggyford**, Mon-Sat 2/day
AD122 (**Hadrian's Wall Country Bus**; 🖳 assets.goaheadbus.com, or 🖳 hadrianswallcountry.co.uk/travel/bus)
Hexham to Haltwhistle circular route via Chesters Fort, Housesteads, **Once Brewed** (The Sill Visitor Centre), Vindolanda, **Milecastle Inn**, Walltown & **Greenhead**, end Mar to end Sep daily 9/day, but note that not all services stop at all stops

Hodgsons Buses (☎ 01833-630730, 🖳 hodgsonsbuses.com) (SEE MAP 2)
73 **Langdon Beck** to Barnard Castle via **High Force**, Newbiggin, **Middleton-in-Teesdale**, **Forest-in-Teesdale**, Wed only 2/day plus 1/day to **Middleton-in-Teesdale**
79 Richmond to Barnard Castle, Mon-Sat 4/day

Hulleys of Baslow (☎ 01246-582246, 🖳 hulleys-of-baslow.co.uk) (SEE MAP 1)
173 Bakewell to Castleton, Mon-Sat 4/day
271/272 Sheffield to Castleton, Mon-Sat 3/day (see also First)

Keighley Bus Company (🖳 keighleybus.co.uk) (SEE MAP 1)
B1 Keighley to **Stanbury** via **Haworth**, Mon-Sat 1/hr
B2 Keighley to Oakworth via **Haworth**, daily 1/hr
B3 Keighley to **Hebden Bridge** via **Haworth** & Oxenhope, daily 1/hr
K10 Leeming to Keighley via **Haworth**, Mon-Fri 2/day
K14 Keighley circular route to Oxenhope, **Haworth**, **Stanbury** & **Ponden**, Sun 6/day
K15 Keighley circular route to Oxenhope, Leeming & **Haworth**, Mon-Sat 2-3/day

(cont'd on p58)

PLANNING YOUR WALK

❑ PUBLIC TRANSPORT SERVICES

Bus services *(cont'd from p57)*

K16 Keighley circular route to **Stanbury** via **Ponden** & **Haworth**, Mon-Sat 5-6 day
66 Keighley to Skipton, Mon-Sat 2/hr, Sun 1/hr
69 Oxenhope to Bradford via **Haworth**, Mon-Fri 1/day

Kirkby Lonsdale Coach Hire (🖳 kirkbylonsdalecoachhire.co.uk) (SEE MAPS 1 & 2)
75 Skipton to **Malham** via **Gargrave** & **Kirkby Malham**, Sat only 2/day
580 Skipton to Settle via **Gargrave**, Mon-Sat 1/hr
881 Morecambe to Ingleton via Settle & **Malham**, Sun 1/day plus Ingleton to Malham Sun 2/day

Little White Bus (aka Upper Wensleydale Community Partnership; ☎ 01969-667400, 🖳 littlewhitebus.co.uk) (SEE MAP 2)
30 (Swaledale Shuttle) **Keld** circular route to **Thwaite**, **Muker**, Gunnerside, Reeth, Grinton, Reeth & Richmond, early Apr-early Nov Mon-Sat 2-3/day
113 (Garsdale Station Shuttle) Gayle to Garsdale via **Hawes** & **Hardraw**, Mon-Sat 4/day, Sun & bank hols 2-3/day. Additional journeys can be provided on a pre booked basis; the office (see above) is open Mon-Fri 9am-5.30pm, Sat 9am-12.30pm, or out of hours call the driver on ☎ driver 07816-986448.
156 (Wensleydale Voyager) Gayle to Leyburn via **Hawes**, Askrigg & Aysgarth, Mon-Sat 6-9/day
856 (Acorn Wensleydale Flyer) Northallerton to Gayle via **Hawes** & Leyburn, Sun 3/day (see also Procters Coaches)

NYCC (North Yorkshire County Council; 🖳 northyorks.gov.uk/bus-timetables) (SEE MAPS 1 & 2)
11 Settle to **Horton-in-Ribblesdale**, Mon-Sat 3/day plus Tosside to Settle
210/211 Skipton to **Malham** via **Gargrave**, **Airton** & **Kirkby Malham**, Mon-Fri 2/day

Peter Hogg of Jedburgh (☎ 01835-863755, 🖳 roadhoggs.net) (SEE MAP 2)
20 Kelso to Hawick via Jedburgh, Mon-Sat 3-5/day, Sun 4/day
81/81A/81B Kelso to **Kirk Yetholm** circular route via **Town Yetholm**, Mon-Sat 7/day (See also Borders Buses)
131 Newcastle to Jedburgh via Otterburn & **Byrness**, Mon-Sat 1/day plus Kelso to Newcastle Mon-Fri 1/day

Preston Bus (☎ 01772-253671, 🖳 www.prestonbus.co.uk) (SEE MAP 1)
X80 Preston to Skipton via Clitheroe & West Marton, Mon-Sat 1/day, Clitheroe to Skipton via West Marton, Sun 2/day
280 Preston to Skipton via Clitheroe & **Thornton-in-Craven**, Mon-Sat 8/day, Clitheroe to Preston, Sun 3/day

Procters Coaches (☎ 01677-425203, 🖳 procterscoaches.com) (SEE MAP 2)
29 Darlington to Richmond, Mon-Sat 6/day
34 Darlington to Richmond via Catterick & Brompton-on-Swale, Mon-Sat 4/day
55 Northallerton to Richmond via Brompton-on-Swale, Mon-Sat 3/day
856 Northallerton to **Hawes** via Leyburn, Sun & Bank Hols 3/day (see also Little White Bus)

Robinson's (☎ 01768-351424) (SEE MAP 2)
573 Appleby circular route including **Dufton**, Fri 2/day

Scarlet Band Bus & Coach (☎ 01740-654247, 🖳 scarletbandbuses.co.uk) (SEE MAP 2)

72 **Bowes** to Barnard Castle, Mon-Fri 2/day
84 Darlington to Barnard Castle, Mon-Sat 3/day
95 **Middleton-in-Teesdale** to Barnard Castle via **Cotherstone,** Mon-Sat 4/day
96 **Middleton-in-Teesdale** to Barnard Castle via **Cotherstone**, Mon-Sat 5/day

Stagecoach (🖳 stagecoachbus.com) (SEE MAP 2)
685 Newcastle to Carlisle via Corbridge, Hexham, Haltwhistle, **Greenhead** & Brampton, Mon-Sat 1/hr,
Sun & Bank Hols Newcastle to Hexham 1/hr and Hexham to Carlisle 5/day (operated in conjunction with Arriva North East 85)

Telfords Coaches (🖳 telfordscoaches.com) (SEE MAP 2)
680 **Alston** to Carlisle via **Slaggyford** & Brampton, Tue & Thur in term time 1/day plus **Alston** to Brampton via **Slaggyford** 1/day

TLC Travel (☎ 01274-727811, 🖳 www.tlctravelltd.co.uk) (SEE MAP 1)
596 **Hebden Bridge** to Blackshaw Head via Heptonstall, daily 1/hr
597 **Hebden Bridge** to Heptonstall circular route, Mon-Sat 1/hr
901 Huddersfield to **Hebden Bridge** via Blackstone Edge & Mytholmroyd, 1/hr
T6 **Mankinholes** to Todmorden circular, daily 7-10/day
T8 **Mankinholes** to Todmorden circular, daily 6-7/day

Wright Brothers' Coaches (☎ 01434-381200, 🖳 wrightscoaches.co.uk) (SEE MAP 2)
680 **Alston** to Nenthead, Mon, Wed & Fri 1-2/day
888 Newcastle to Keswick via Hexham & **Alston**, July to end Sep daily 1/day
889 **Alston** to Hexham, Mon-Fri 1/day

Rail services

Note: not all stops are listed (SEE MAPS 1 & 2)

Northern Rail (☎ 0800 200 6060, 🖳 northernrailway.co.uk)
- Manchester Piccadilly to Sheffield via **Edale**, daily 1/hr
- Manchester Victoria (V) to Huddersfield via **Marsden**, daily 1/hr
- Manchester Piccadilly to Hadfield, daily 2/hr
- Leeds to Manchester (V) via **Hebden Bridge** & Todmorden, Mon-Sat 2/hr, Sun 1/hr
- Leeds to Preston via **Hebden Bridge** & Todmorden, daily 1/hr
- Leeds to Blackpool North via **Hebden Bridge** & Todmorden, daily 1/hr
- Leeds to Carlisle via Keighley, **Gargrave**, Skipton, Settle, **Horton-in-Ribblesdale**, Garsdale, Kirkby Stephen & Appleby, Mon-Sat 8/day, Sun 5-6/day (note: not all services stop at Gargrave)
- Newcastle to Carlisle via Hexham & Haltwhistle, daily 1/hr; some services also call at Bardon Mill which is two miles off the Pennine Way and is a stop on Arriva's & Stagecoach's shared 85/685 bus service.

Trans Pennine Express (🖳 tpexpress.co.uk)
- Manchester to Newcastle via Leeds, York & Durham, Mon-Sat 1/hr, Sun 8/day
- Manchester to Middlesbrough via Leeds, York, Northallerton, Darlington, daily 1/hr

See p126 for information about **Keighley & Worth Valley Railway** and p166 for details about **DalesRail**'s seasonal Sunday Blackpool to Carlisle service

2

THE ENVIRONMENT & NATURE

Conserving the Pennines

GOVERNMENT AGENCIES AND SCHEMES

Government responsibility for the countryside is handled in England by **Natural England** (🖳 gov.uk/government/organisations/natural-england). Natural England is responsible for 'enhancing biodiversity and landscape and wildlife in rural, urban, coastal and marine areas; promoting access, recreation and public well-being, and contributing to the way natural resources are managed, so they can be enjoyed now and by future generations'. Amongst other things it designates the level of protection for areas of land, as outlined below, and manages England's national trails (see box opposite).

The highest level of landscape protection is the designation of land as a **national park** which recognises the national importance of an area in terms of landscape, biodiversity and as a recreational resource. The Pennine Way passes through three National Parks: the Peak District (🖳 peakdistrict.gov.uk), the Yorkshire Dales (🖳 yorkshiredales.org.uk) and Northumberland (🖳 northumberlandnationalpark.org.uk). Although they wield a considerable amount of power and can easily quash planning applications from the local council, their management is always a balance between conservation, the needs of visitors, and protecting the livelihoods of those who live within the park.

Land which falls outside the remit of a National Park but which is nonetheless deemed special enough for protection may be designated an **Area of Outstanding Natural Beauty** (**AONB**; 🖳 landscapesforlife.org.uk), the second level of protection after National Park status. The North Pennines is one such AONB (🖳 northpennines.org.uk). Designated in 1988, it is valued for its upland habitats and wildlife, containing a third of England's upland heathland and a third of its blanket bog. These fragile habitats make the North Pennines one of England's most important regions for upland wildlife – it is home to the majority of England's black grouse along with around 22,000 breeding pairs of waders.

Of course, it wouldn't get AONB status unless it was a beautiful area; the moors, hills and wooded valleys certainly make it so. And it is the underlying geology that gives the region its character which

❑ National Trails

The Pennine Way was the first of the National Trails in England and Wales; the officially designated long-distance paths, now supported and funded by Natural England and Natural Resources Wales. There are now 15 National Trails in England and Wales, totalling approximately 2500 miles (4000km) of path, each one looked after by a National Trail Officer who co-ordinates the management, maintenance and marketing of the trail, with the assistance of volunteers and other agencies.

A similar system of trails exists in Scotland, where they are called **Long Distance Routes**.

led to the area being designated a UNESCO European Geopark (🖳 europeangeoparks.org) in 2003, the first in Britain. A year later it became a founding member of the Global Geoparks Network (🖳 globalgeopark.org).

National Nature Reserves (NNRs) are places where wildlife comes first. They were established to protect the most important areas of wildlife habitat and geological formations in Britain, and as places for scientific research. This does not mean they are 'no-go areas' for people. It means that visitors must be careful not to damage the wildlife of these fragile places. Kinder Scout (see box p86) is a NNR.

Local Nature Reserves (LNRs) are for both people and wildlife. They are living green spaces in towns, cities, villages and countryside which are important to people, and support a rich and vibrant variety of wildlife. They are places which have wildlife or geology of special local interest. These can be created by local authorities or councils.

Sites of Special Scientific Interest (SSSIs) purport to afford extra protection to unique areas against anything that threatens the habitat or environment. They range in size from a small site where orchids grow, or birds nest, to vast swathes of upland, moorland and wetland.

The country through which the Pennine Way passes has its share of SSSIs but they are not given a high profile for the very reason that this would draw unwanted attention. They are managed in partnership with the owners and occupiers of the land but it seems this management is not always effective.

Special Areas of Conservation (SACs) are areas which have been given special protection under the European Union's Habitats Directive. They provide increased protection to a variety of wild animals, plants and habitats and are a vital part of global efforts to conserve the world's biodiversity.

❑ Other statutory bodies

- **Historic England** (🖳 historicengland.org.uk) was created in April 2015 as a result of dividing the work done by English Heritage (see box p62). It is the government department responsible for looking after and promoting England's historic environment and is in charge of the listing system, giving grants and dealing with planning matters.
- **Forestry Commission** (🖳 forestry.gov.uk) Government department for establishing and managing woods and forests for a wide variety of uses; see box p65.

CAMPAIGNING AND CONSERVATION ORGANISATIONS

The idea of conservation started back in the mid 1800s with the founding of the Royal Society for the Protection of Birds (see box below). The rise of its membership figures accurately reflects public awareness and interest in environmental issues as a whole: it took until the 1960s to reach 10,000, but rocketed to 200,000 in the 1970s and had mushroomed to over one million by the year 2000. There are now many campaigning and conservation groups – see box below for the details of some. Independent of government but reliant on public support, they can concentrate their resources either on acquiring land which can then be managed purely for conservation purposes, or on influencing political decision-makers by lobbying and campaigning.

The huge increase in public interest and support during the last 20 years indicates that people are more conscious of environmental issues and believe that it cannot be left to our political representatives to take care of them for us without our voice. We are becoming the most powerful lobbying group of all; an informed electorate.

❑ Campaigning/conservation organisations and charities

• **National Trust** (NT; 🖳 nationaltrust.org.uk) A charity with over 4 million members which aims to protect, through ownership, threatened coastline, countryside, historic houses, castles and gardens, and archaeological remains for everybody to enjoy.

NT land/properties on the Pennine Way include Kinder Scout (see box p86), Housesteads Fort (see box p234; though it is managed by English Heritage, see below), Malham Tarn and Moor (see p149) in Yorkshire Dales National Park, Marsden Moor and Hardcastle Crags near Hebden Bridge.

• **Royal Society for the Protection of Birds** (RSPB; 🖳 rspb.org.uk) The largest voluntary conservation body in Europe now has 200 nature reserves in the UK. The closest reserves to the Pennine Way are Geltsdale, off the A689 west of Knarsdale (off Map 99, p229), and Dove Stone, west of Wessenden Head (off Map 12, p101).

• **The Wildlife Trusts** (🖳 wildlifetrusts.org) The umbrella organisation for the 47 wildlife trusts in the UK; the trust is concerned with all aspects of nature conservation and manages around 2300 nature reserves. Wildlife trusts along the Pennine Way include Broadhead Clough (near Hebden Bridge), Globe Flower Wood (near Malham), Brae Pasture (near Horton), Hannah's Meadow (right on the Pennine Way), Greenlee Lough (just north of Hadrian's Wall) and Yetholm Loch (near Kirk Yetholm).

• **English Heritage** (🖳 english-heritage.org.uk) English Heritage looks after, champions and advises the government on historic buildings and places in England. However, in April 2015 it was divided into a new charitable trust that retains the name English Heritage and a non-departmental public body, Historic England (see p61). English Heritage cares for over 400 historic buildings, monuments and sites and manages parts of Hadrian's Wall (see National Trust above) and also Bowes Castle.

• **Woodland Trust** (🖳 www.woodlandtrust.org.uk) The trust aims to conserve, restore and re-establish native woodlands throughout the UK.

• **Butterfly Conservation** (🖳 butterfly-conservation.org) was formed in 1968 by some naturalists who were alarmed at the decline in the number of butterflies, and moths, and who aimed to reverse the situation. They now have 31 branches throughout the British Isles and operate 33 nature reserves and also sites where butterflies are likely to be found.

Flora and fauna

WILD FLOWERS, GRASSES AND OTHER PLANTS

Many grasses, wild flowers, heather, mosses and liverworts (lichen-type plants with liver-shaped leaves) owe their continued existence to man's land management; global warming notwithstanding, if left to its own devices much of the land would return to the natural state of temperate regions: the woodland of 10,000 years ago. Rare breeds of livestock are often excellent grazers for rough grassland because they are hardier so do not have to be fed extra food that will then over fertilise the ground. They also seem to be more selective in what they eat (and taste better too).

Intensive agriculture took its toll on the wild flower population in the same way that it did on the birds and mammals. The flowers are making a comeback but it is illegal to pick many types of flowers now and the picking of most others is discouraged; it is always illegal without the landowners' permission, no matter what the type. Cut flowers only die, after all. It is much better to leave them to reseed and spread and hopefully magnify your or someone else's enjoyment another year. Spring and early summer is the best time to see wild flowers.

Bogs and wet areas

Look out for **cotton grass** (not actually a grass but a type of sedge), **deer-grass, cloudberry** (a dwarf blackberry with a light orange berry when ripe that can be used as a substitute for any fruit used in puddings and jams) and the **insect-eating sundew**. Drier areas of peat may be home to **crowberry** (a source of vitamin C) and **bilberry** (see below).

Peat itself is the ages-old remains of vegetation, including **sphagnum mosses** (see box p87). This type of moss is now rare, but may be found in 'flushes' where water seeps out between gritstone and shale. Also look out for **bog asphodel, marsh thistle** and **marsh pennywort**.

Woodlands

Not much grows in coniferous plantations because the dense canopy prevents light getting in. But in oak woodlands the floor is often covered with interesting plants such as **bilberries**, whose small, round black fruit is ripe for picking from July to September and is much tastier than the more widely commercially sold

> **❑ Why are flowers the colour they are?**
> The vast majority of British wild flowers range in colour from yellow to magenta and do not have red in them; the poppy is the most notable exception. This is because most flowers are insect pollinated as opposed to being pollinated by birds. Birds see reds best, insects see yellow to magenta best.

American variety. It's recommended in jams, jellies, stews and cheesecake. Bilberry pie is known in Yorkshire as 'mucky-mouth pie', for reasons you can work out, and is eaten at funerals. **Moorland cowberry** (also used in jams), **wavy hair grass** and **woodrush** are other species you may see. Other shrubs to look out for include **guelder rose** and **bird cherry**.

Higher areas

Much of the high land is peaty and many types of grass turn brown in winter. Those present include **matgrass, heath rush, bent, fescues** and **wavy hair grass**. Flowers include **tormentil** and **harebell**.

Heather is the main plant of higher areas and is carefully farmed for grouse. It is burnt in strips over the winter to ensure new growth as a food supply for the birds. It has many uses, including as a tea and flavouring beer, and makes a very comfortable mattress on a warm, sunny afternoon. When it flowers around August time, the moors can turn purple. **Bracken**, **gorse** and **tufted hair grass** are all signs that the land is not being intensively managed.

Lower areas

These places are where you'll see the most flowers, whose fresh and bright colours give the area an inspiring glow, particularly if you have just descended from the browns and greens of the higher, peaty areas.

On valley sides used for grazing you may see **self heal, cowslips** (used to make wine and vinegar), **bloody cranesbill** and **mountain pansy**. **Hawthorn** seeds dropped by birds sprout up energetically and determinedly but are cropped back by sheep and fires. This is a good thing; these shrubs can grow to 8 metres (26ft) and would try to take over the hillsides to the detriment of the rich grasslands. They do, however, have a variety of uses: the young leaves are known as 'bread and cheese' because they used to be such a staple part of a diet; the flowers make a delicious drink and when combined with the fruit make a cure for insomnia. **Rushes** indicate poor drainage.

❑ Orchids

These highly prized plants, the occasional object of professional thefts, are often mistakenly thought to grow only in tropical places. They come from one of the largest families in the world and their range is in fact widespread, right up to the Arctic Circle in some places. In Britain over 40 types grow wild and you'd be unlucky not to see any on the Pennine Way, especially in quarries and on hillsides. The **lady's slipper**, first discovered in Ingleborough in 1640, the **narrow-lipped helleborine**, which grows in Northumberland, and the **frog orchid** are just some you may come across. The **early purple orchid** (see photo opposite) is made into a drink called Saloop, which was popular before coffee became the staple.

Although they have a tendency to grow on other plants, orchids are not parasites, as many believe; they simply use them for support. They are distinctive as having one petal longer than the other two and many growers say they're no more difficult to grow at home than many other houseplants. With their flowers being generally spectacular and the wonderful strong scent they're well worth the effort.

Common Vetch
Vicia sativa

Meadow Cranesbill
Geranium pratense

Heartsease (Wild Pansy)
Viola tricolor

Lousewort
Pedicularis sylvatica

Germander Speedwell
Veronica chamaedrys

Common Dog Violet
Viola riviniana

Self-heal
Prunella vulgaris

Heather (Ling)
Calluna vulgaris

Harebell
Campanula rotundifolia

Early Purple Orchid
Orchis mascula

Bell Heather
Erica cinerea

Common Butterwort
Pinguicula vulgaris

Gorse
Ulex europaeus

Meadow Buttercup
Ranunculis acris

Marsh Marigold (Kingcup)
Caltha palustris

Bird's-foot trefoil
Lotus corniculatus

Water Avens
Geum rivale

Tormentil
Potentilla erecta

Primrose
Primula vulgaris

St John's Wort
Hypericum perforatum

Yellow Rattle
Rhinanthus minor

Common Ragwort
Senecio jacobaea

Hemp-nettle
Galeopsis speciosa

Cowslip
Primula veris

Honeysuckle
Lonicera periclymemum

Dog Rose
Rosa canina

Forget-me-not
Myosotis arvensis

Scarlet Pimpernel
Anagallis arvensis

Common Fumitory
Fumaria officinalis

Wood Sorrel
Oxalis acetosella

Ramsons (Wild Garlic)
Allium ursinum

Common Hawthorn
Crataegus monogyna

Ox-eye Daisy
Leucanthemum vulgare

Silverweed
Potentilla anserina

Yarrow
Achillea millefolium

Hogweed
Heracleum sphondylium

C4 Common flora

Cotton Grass
Eriophorum angustifolium

Spear Thistle
Cirsium vulgare

Common Knapweed
Centaurea nigra

Rowan (tree)
Sorbus aucuparia

Herb-Robert
Geranium robertianum

Red Campion
Silene dioica

Bluebell
Hyacinthoides non-scripta

Rosebay Willowherb
Epilobium angustifolium

Foxglove
Digitalis purpurea

The **adder** (see p73) is the only common snake in the north of England, and the only venomous one of the three species in Britain.

Also look out for **bird's eye primrose, white clover** and the grasses such as **crested dog's tail** and **bent.**

TREES, WOODS AND FORESTS

Woods are part of Britain's natural heritage as reflected in the folklore, Little Red Riding Hood and Robin Hood for example, and also in its history with the hunting grounds of Henry VIII and his subsequent felling of the New Forest to construct the fleets that led to Britannia 'ruling the waves'. To the west of Edale, at the start of the walk, is the small town of Chapel-en-le-Frith. Translated, its name means 'chapel in the forest' because it used to be a small clearing in an enormous forest that stretched to Edale and beyond.

Ten thousand years ago as Europe emerged from the Ice Age but before man started to exert his influence on the landscape, 90% of the country was wooded. In 1086 when William the Conqueror ordered a survey it had declined to 15% and it then shrank to 4% by the 1870s. When the Forestry Commission (see box below) was established woodland cover in Britain was 5% but by 1949 it had grown to 6.5%. A survey in 2011 found that there were 2,982,000 hectares of woodland across England, Scotland and Wales, representing 13% of Britain's land area. What these figures disguise is that a huge proportion of the tree cover today, as opposed to 900 years ago or even 100 years ago, is made up of plantations of conifers. Although the Forestry Commission was largely responsible for encouraging the vast numbers of acres of coniferous woodland, it is now a driving force behind diversification of tree species in woodlands. Responding to the criticism of 'blanket conifers' the Forestry Commission began a complete restructuring of Kielder Forest in the late 1970s. Some areas were felled early, others late to break up the even-aged plantations, streamsides were cleared, in scale with the vast landscape which frequently meant over 200 metres wide, broadleaves were planted.

Oak and broadleaf woodlands

Oak trees are one of the most common species in England. There are two native species: the **common** and the **sessile**. Sessile woodlands are generally remnants of the woodland of William the Conqueror's time and before. Broadleaf woods that is deciduous (annual leaf-shedders), hardwood, including **beech,**

> **❑ The Forestry Commission**
> The Forestry Commission (🖳 forestry.gov.uk) was established in September 1919 with the goal of restoring Britain's timber reserves after WW1. It states its mission is to be 'responsible for protecting, expanding and promoting the sustainable management of woodlands.' It is comprised of three divisions: Forestry Commission England; Forestry Commission Scotland; and Forest Research. However, responsibility for the trees in Scotland will be devolved to Scotland in April 2019. (Responsibility for the trees in Wales was devolved to Natural Resources Wales in 2013). Forestry Commission England works with two agencies: Forestry England (originally Forest Enterprise England) and Forest Research.

❑ Fungi, micro-organisms and invertebrates

In the soil beneath your feet and under the yellow leaves of autumn are millions, possibly billions, of organisms beavering away at recycling anything that has had its day and fallen to decay. One gram of woodland soil contains an estimated 4000-5000 species of bacteria. Almost all of them are unknown to science and the vitally important role they play in maintaining the natural balance of our ecosystems is only just beginning to be appreciated. Many scientists now believe these organisms actually run the earth. Research into them is at an early stage but as one American academic put it, 'As we walk across leaf litter we are like Godzilla walking over New York City.'

sycamore, birch, poplar and **sweet chestnut**, have grown by over 30% since 1980. However, they still only account for about 1% of the Yorkshire Dales National Park. In areas of poorer soil you will also see 'pioneer' species such as **rowan, silver birch, downy birch** and the much rarer **aspen**. In a natural environment these improve the soil for longer-lasting species such as oak.

Coniferous woodland

The extent of the demise of Britain's native woodlands was not fully comprehended until after WW2 when politicians realised Britain had had an inadequate strategic reserve of timber in two world wars. The immediate response was to plant fast-growing low-management trees such as the North American **Sitka spruce** across the agriculturally unviable land of the British uplands. The mass-planting continued apace into the 1970s and '80s with big grants and tax breaks available to landowners and wealthy investors.

You can see the result of this 'blanket planting' in the northern Pennines; acres of same-age trees with such a dense canopy that nothing grows beneath. However, one positive is that these forests are virtually the only habitat where almost no insecticide is used. Many probably think moorland is the same but sheep are dipped in some of the most noxious chemicals in use today and then put out on the moors onto which the insecticide gradually washes off.

There are now efforts under way to replant felled coniferous timber with a wider range of species and the number of conifer plantations has fallen by 7% in the past 20 years. These new woodlands are not only planted for timber, but also promote recreation, tourism and are good for wildlife. Kielder Forest now produces 400,000 tonnes of timber a year, the majority going into construction timber, with smaller wood from the tops of the trees going to the Egger chipboard plant in nearby Hexham.

BIRDS

You will see plenty of birds on your walk and the best way of identifying them is through their song. Each species sings a different tune, and not just for your pleasure. It is their way of letting others know that their territory is still occupied and not up for grabs, as well as a mating signal. The dawn chorus is such a cacophony because most avian fatalities take place at night, so when they

> **❑ Field guide apps**
> There are also several field guide **apps** for smartphones and tablets, including those that can aid in identifying birds by their song as well as by their appearance. One to consider is: 💻 merlin.allaboutbirds.org.

wake and are still alive they have to let opportunist home-hunters know it. They also have a call, or alarm, which is different again from the song.

Some birds, such as the swallow, perform incredible annual migrations, navigating thousands of miles to exactly the same nest they occupied the previous summer. Research suggests that some birds ingest their own organs to keep themselves fuelled for the flight. Swifts are believed to fly non-stop for up to two years, only coming down at the end of that period to lay eggs. They can also survive cold periods by entering a state of torpor.

Streams, rivers and lakes

Both the **great-crested grebe** and the **little grebe** live on natural lakes and reservoirs. In spring you can see the great-crested grebe's 'penguin dance', where they raise themselves from the water breast to breast by furiously paddling their feet, and then swing their heads from side to side. They also have their full plumage, including an elaborate collar that could well have served as inspiration for the Elizabethans. They nearly became extinct in Britain in the 19th century, but have now recovered despite plenty of enemies including pike, rooks, mink and even the wake from boats, which can flood their nests. The little grebe is small and dumpy but very well designed for hunting sticklebacks under water.

Yellow wagtails are summer visitors that are as likely to be seen on lakesides as in water meadows, pasture and even moors. How do you recognise them? They have a yellow underneath, unlike the **grey wagtail** which has a black chin and then a yellow belly. If the bird is by a fast-flowing stream it will almost certainly be a grey wagtail.

Reservoir water tends to be relatively acidic so supports little wildlife except wildfowl including **goosanders**, especially in winter, and the similar-looking **red-breasted mergansers**. They are both members of the sawbill family which use serrated bill edges to seize and hold small fish. The trout in the reservoirs will have been introduced for anglers.

In streams and rivers you may see **common sandpipers**. Most of them head for Africa in the winter, but about 50 are thought to brave it out in ever-milder Britain. You might see them stalking insects, their head held fixed and horizontal before a sudden snap marks the hunt to an end.

Dippers are the only songbirds that can 'fly' underwater or walk along streambeds. You may see them 'curtseying' on rocks in the middle of swift-flowing streams before they dive under the surface. They fly extremely quickly, because their small wings are designed for maximum efficiency in the water and are far too small to keep the huge bodies airborne without enormous amounts of flapping and momentum.

Woodland

GREEN WOODPECKER
L: 330MM/13"

Although rare in the Pennines, broad-leaved woodland harbours a variety of birdlife. You may see, or more likely hear, a **green woodpecker**, the largest woodpecker in Britain. They are very shy and often hide behind branches. They trap insects by probing holes and cavities with their tongue, which has a sticky tip like a flycatcher.

The further north you go the more likely you are to see **pied flycatchers**, summer visitors from Africa. The male can have multiple mates and is known to keep territories well over a mile apart, perhaps to keep a quiet life.

Nuthatches are sparrow sized with blue backs, orange breasts and a black eye-stripe, and have the almost unique ability to clamber up and down trunks and branches. Here all year, in summer they eat insects and in the autumn crack open acorns and hazelnuts with hard whacks of their bill.

Treecreepers cling to trees in the same way as nuthatches and woodpeckers. They have a thin, downward-curved bill that is ideal for picking insects out of holes and crevices. They are brown above and silvery-white underneath, which should help you distinguish them from the similar sized and behaviourally similar **lesser-spotted woodpecker**, which is black and white and not seen on the more northern sections of the Way. The male woodpecker also has a red crown.

Coniferous woodland is not home to much wildlife, because the tree canopy is too dense. You may, however, see nesting **sparrowhawks**, Britain's second most common bird of prey. They suffered a big decline in the 1950s due to the use of pesticides in farming. In all the British raptor (bird of prey) species the female is larger than the male, but the male sparrowhawk is one of the smallest raptors in Britain. It feeds entirely on fellow birds and has long legs and a long central toe for catching and holding them. It has a square-ended tail and reasonably short wings for chasing birds into trees.

BLACK GROUSE
L: 580MM/23"

You may also see **short-eared owls** in young plantations because of the preponderance of short-tailed vole, their principal prey. They also hunt over open moors, heaths and rough grasslands. This owl is probably the one that is most often seen in daylight. It has two ear-tufts on the top of its head which are, you've guessed it, shorter than the **long-eared owl**'s. You may also see a **black grouse** (see box p160), also known as **black game**.

Conifer plantations provide temporary havens for them while they try to regain some of their numbers. The males, black cocks, perform in mock fights known as a lek in front of the females, grey hens. This happens year-round and if you see one fluffing up the white of its tail and cooing like a dove don't necessarily expect to see a female present; they are quite happy to perform for anyone.

Coniferous woods are also home to the greeny-yellow **goldcrest**, Britain's smallest bird. It weighs less than 10 grams but along with the **coal tit** is possibly the dominant species in coniferous woods. Because it is one of the few species that can exploit conifers it is growing in number.

Moor, bog and grazing

Many birds have developed to live in the wettest, windiest, most barren places in England; the places along which the best of the Pennine Way passes. On heather moors you will almost certainly see **red grouse** (see also box, p160), for whom the heather is intensively managed to ensure a good supply of young shoots for food. They are reddy brown, slightly smaller than a pheasant and likely to get up at your feet and fly off making a lot of noise.

Moorland is also home to Britain's smallest falcon, the **merlin**. The male is slate-grey, the female a reddish brown. They eat small birds, catching them with low dashing flights. Their main threat comes from the expense of maintaining moorland for grouse shooting; as costs grow, fewer and fewer farmers are doing this and with the disappearance of the moor we will see the disappearance of the merlin. Another moorland raptor is the **short-eared owl** (see opposite).

Bogs are breeding grounds for many species of waders, including the **curlew**, the emblem of Northumberland National Park, if not the Pennine Way. Long-legged, brown and buff coloured, they probe for worms and fish with their long, downward-curving bill. The curlew's forlorn bleat will follow you across many a moor.

Snipe live in wet areas. They are smaller than a grouse, but they share very similar plumages. They have particularly long bills for feeding in water and rely on being camouflaged rather than escaping predators by flight, and hence often get up right at your feet. Once airborne their trajectory is fast and zigzags.

In summer **golden plover** live in upland peaty terrain, are seen in pairs and will be visible to walkers (as well as audible because of their plaintive call); in winter they are seen in flocks and in lowland grassland. They are a little larger than a snipe, have golden-spotted upper parts and can be recognised by their feeding action of running, pausing to look and listen for

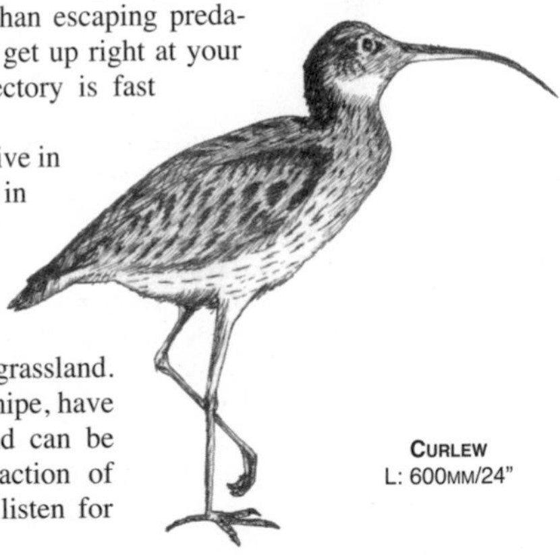

Curlew
L: 600mm/24"

food (seeds and insects) and bobbing down to eat it.

SKYLARK
L: 185MM/7.25"

Dunlins also live in peaty terrain and are half the size of a golden plover but not dissimilar in colouring to the inexperienced eye. They are a very common wader.

You may also see but are more likely to hear the continuous and rapid song of the **skylark**. They tend to move from moorland to lower agricultural land in the winter. Just bigger than a house sparrow, they have brown upper parts and a chin with dark flakes and a white belly.

Patches of gorse and juniper scrub are often chosen as a nesting site for **linnets**, which flock together during the winter but operate in small colonies at other times. They are small birds that will also be seen on open farmland, as will the slightly larger yellowhammer, recognisable by its yellow head and chest. It too nests in gorse and juniper bushes.

The **lapwing** is relatively common, quite large and can be recognised by its wispy black plume on the back of its head and, in summer, the aerial acrobatics of the male. They fly high to dive steeply down, twisting and turning as if out of control before pulling out at the last minute.

LAPWING/PEEWIT
L: 320MM/12.5"

The **meadow pipit** is a small, and a classic, LBJ (little brown job). They make plenty of noise and on a still day climb to about 15 metres (50ft) and then open their wings to parachute gently down. They can sometimes be recognised by their white outer tail feathers as they fly away from you. The **wheatear** is a small grey bird with white tail feathers and its call is a hard 'tack'. It is seen in western and northern Britain in summer but winters in central Africa.

The **peregrine falcon** (see opposite) had a hard time in the 20th century, being shot during WW2 to protect carrier pigeons and then finding it hard to rear their young after eating insects that had fed on pesticide-soaked plants. Their comeback is therefore a sign that things are picking up again in the British countryside.

Buildings and cliffs

Swallows, **house martins** and **swifts** nest in barns and other buildings. They are hard to tell apart, but as a simple guide: swallows are the largest, are blue-black above and have a white belly and a long-forked tail; swifts are the next down in size, are essentially all black with a shallow forked tail that is usually closed and probably fly the fastest; house martins are the smallest, have a relatively short tail and a completely white underneath and, most usefully for identification purposes, a white rump (on top, near the tail). As a walker, you may be able to relate to why a non-breeding swift will fly 100 miles to avoid rain. If insects are bugging you, thank nature for swifts. A single one will eat 10,000 of the pesky buzzers a day, so think how many more bites you would suffer if it were not for them.

Peregrine falcons, **kestrels** and **jackdaws** (similar to a crow but with a whitish back of the head) nest on cliffs. At Malham Cove the RSPB have set up a peregrine-viewing site (see box p147) allowing visitors to see the resident pair on the limestone cliffs. The kestrel, Britain's most common and most familiar bird of prey, also nests in man-made structures and is sometimes seen in city centres. It can be distinguished from the sparrowhawk, the second most common raptor, by its pointed wings and hovering when hunting. The male has a blue-grey head and a rich chestnut-coloured back, while the female is a duller chestnut both above and on her head. Jackdaws are very common in villages and towns; if you see a crow-like bird sitting on a chimney top, reckon on it being a jackdaw.

BARN OWL
L: 355MM/14"

Owls may also nest in cliffs and barns. You are most likely to see a little owl, which is a non-native resident that will often occupy the same perch day after day. Local knowledge can be useful for finding one of these.

Barn owls have been affected by intensive agriculture and are on the decline but are also one of the most widely distributed birds in the world.

MAMMALS

Roe deer are the smallest of Britain's native deer, and are hard to see. They normally inhabit woodland areas but you may see one in grassland or, if you're very lucky, swimming in a lake. The males (bucks) claim a territory in spring and will chase a female (doe) round and round a tree before she gives in to his pursuit. This leaves circles of rings round the base of the tree, which are known as 'roe rings'.

Badgers like to live in deciduous woodland. Their black-and-white striped heads make them highly recognisable, but you're most likely to see them at night. They are true omnivores eating almost anything including berries, slugs and dead rabbits. The female (sow) gathers dry grasses and bracken in February for her nest. She then tucks them between her chin and forequarters and shuffles backwards, dragging them into her home (sett). The young are born blind in February and March and stay underground until spring.

Foxes are common wherever there are animals or birds to be preyed on, or dustbins to scavenge from, which is just about everywhere. Britain is estimated to have 40 times the fox population of northern France. They are believed to have been here since before the last Ice Age when the sabre-toothed tiger would have prevented them from enjoying their current supremacy in the food chain.

Although now banned, fox hunting is an emotive countryside issue. A lot of conservationists believe that the fox itself is the best control of its numbers. If an environment is unsuitable they tend not to try and inhabit it and, like some marsupials, a pregnant vixen will reabsorb her embryos if conditions are unfavourable for raising cubs. Foxes do a useful job eating carrion, which sometimes includes dead lambs and rabbits. If they could learn to lay off the capercaillie and other protected birds they'd even get the RSPB on their side.

The **otter** is a sensitive indicator of the state of our rivers. They nearly died out in the last century due to a number of attacks on them, their habitat and their environment, but law has protected them since 1981. Due to the work of conservationists they're now making a comeback, but even small amounts of pollution can set back the efforts to give them a strong foothold in the wild. They are reclusive so you'll be incredibly lucky if you see one. They not only eat fish, but water voles and small aquatic birds. Their most successful hunting tactic is to launch a surprise attack from below as an otter's eyes are set on the top of its head and they have unique muscles that compensate for the visual distortion caused by water.

Mink were introduced from North America and only exist in the wild because they escaped or were set free from mink farms. They are one of the most serious pests in the countryside; as they are an alien species, nature has yet to work out how to balance their presence. They spend a lot of time in rivers feeding on aquatic birds and fish and can be distinguished from otters by their considerably smaller size and white chin patch.

The **stoat** is a small but fierce predator. They are native and fairly widespread and can be recognised by their elongated and elegant form, reddy-brown coats and white bellies. They are very adaptable, moving in wherever they can find a den, including old rabbit burrows, and may live for up to 10 years. Minks, stoats, polecats, otters, badgers, weasels (the world's smallest carnivores) and pine martens are all from the same family.

The **red squirrel** is native, unlike the grey squirrel, but it is now rare to see one. They are smaller than their reviled grey cousins and feature a vibrant red coat and fabulously bushy tail (although their coat turns a little browner in winter). Note, too, the tufts that grow at the tips of their ears. Despite their rarity, people often see them on the Pennine Way, either near the YHA hostels in Dufton and Alston, or near Hadrian's Wall. The alien **grey squirrel** has played a big part in the demise of the red squirrel, partly because it is able to eat the red squirrel's food before it ripens. Efforts to reintroduce the red squirrel have not had a great deal of success, partly because they're reluctant to move from tree to tree along the ground and therefore need a dense tree canopy.

The **common shrew** is a tiny animal that lives in woodland and hedgerows. It needs to eat every four hours, and in a 24-hour period will eat insects weighing twice its body weight, using its long sensitive nose to sniff them out. It spends a lot of time underground eating earthworms. The mother and babies are sometimes seen traversing open ground in a train-like procession, with each shrew holding the tail of the one in front. It is the second most common British mammal.

The **mole** is armed with powerful forearms that it uses to burrow a network of underground tunnels that act as traps for unsuspecting earthworms. They patrol these every four hours, either eating all the visitors on the spot or gathering them up to save for later after immobilising them through decapitation.

In woodland or anywhere near buildings you may see the smallest of Britain's resident species of **bat**, the **pipistrelle**. Bats have been here consistently since the Ice Age and are now a protected species. Even though the pipistrelle weighs a tiny 3-8 grams (about the same as a single clove of garlic, or two sheets of kitchen roll), in one night it may eat as many as 3500 insects. Bats and dormice are the only British mammals truly to hibernate throughout the whole winter from October to April. They will wake, however, if the temperature increases to unseasonal levels.

REPTILES

The **adder**, or viper, is Britain's only venomous snake but is harmless if left alone. It can be recognised by a black zig-zag down its back and is found in woodland and moorland. Adders hibernate in winter and when possible laze around in the morning and evening sun in spring and summer, eating everything from slugs to small birds. The males fight for females by rearing up and twisting themselves round each other as if trying to climb a tree; victory is often down to length. While this strenuous activity is going on the females are still asleep. They wake to find the victorious male rubbing his body against her and sticking his tongue out. It may sound all too familiar to many.

Although the **slow worm** looks like a snake it is, in fact, a legless lizard, sharing its notched tongue (rather than a snake's forked tongue), moveable eyelids (snakes have no eyelids) and fixed jaw (snakes have a free jaw for swallowing large prey); they eat slugs and insects and inhabit thick vegetation and rotting wood. The **common lizard** inhabits grass, in woods, moorland or grassland; they feed on insects and spiders.

BUTTERFLIES AND MOTHS

Butterfies you may see include the **red admiral**, **peacock** and the **painted lady** which can, on first flutter, be mistaken for a **small tortoiseshell** but look up close and you'll spot several differences to the markings including, most noticeably, the absence of a blue border at the bottom edge of its wings which is present on the tortoiseshell; the painted lady's story is significantly more interesting too as it will have migrated thousands of miles from North Africa to feed on the wildflowers here in late summer. Another eye-catching butterfly is the **green hairstreak**, though to fully appreciate its metallic green wings you need to see it at rest with its wings folded up; in flight it actually looks a fairly dull brown colour.

In mid summer you may see the **emperor moth**, a spectacular moor-dwelling moth that feeds on the heather. Both the brown hindwings and grey forewings have striking 'eye' markings on them, fooling the predators by making them think they are up against a much larger creature.

3 MINIMUM IMPACT & OUTDOOR SAFETY

Minimum impact walking

Britain has little wilderness, at least by the dictionary definition of land that is 'uncultivated and uninhabited'. But parts of the Pennine Way include the closest we have and it's a fragile environment. Trapped between massive conurbations, the Peak District and South Pennines in particular are among the most crowded recreational areas in England and inevitably this has brought its problems. As more and more people enjoy the freedom of the hills so the land comes under increasing pressure and the potential for conflict with other land-users is heightened. Everyone has a right to this natural heritage but with it comes a responsibility to care for it too.

ENVIRONMENTAL IMPACT

A walking holiday in itself is an environmentally friendly approach to tourism. The following are some ideas on how you can go a few steps further in helping to minimise your impact on the environment while walking the Pennine Way. Some of the latter practices become particularly relevant if you are wild camping.

Use public transport

As more and more cars are added to Britain's road network, traffic congestion is becoming a much more common occurrence, particularly on the motorway network, but increasingly also in rural areas as people head to the countryside. The roads in the Peak District and Yorkshire Dales can become very busy, especially in the summer and on Bank Holiday weekends. Despite popular myth, public transport is regular and frequent in many places, although some rural outposts only see a bus once a week. If public transport services aren't used they will decline even faster than they have in recent years.

Never leave litter

'Pack it in, pack it out'. Leaving litter is antisocial so carry a degradable plastic bag for all your rubbish, organic or otherwise and even other people's too, and pop it in a bin in the next village. Or better still, reduce the amount of litter you take with you by getting rid of packaging in advance.

Don't leave litter even if it is biodegradable. Apple cores and especially banana skins and orange peel are unsightly, encourage flies, ants and wasps and so ruin a picnic spot for others. A piece of orange peel left on the ground takes six months to decompose; silver foil 18 months; a plastic bag 10 years; clothes 15 years; and a can 85 years. In high-use areas such as the Pennine Way take all your litter with you.

Buy local

Look and ask for local produce to buy and eat. Not only does this cut down on the amount of pollution and congestion that the transportation of food creates, so-called 'food miles', it also ensures that you are supporting local farmers and producers.

Erosion

Stay on the main trail The effect of your footsteps may seem minuscule but when they are multiplied by thousands of walkers each year they become rather more significant. Although it can be a bit much to ask when the actual pathway is waterlogged, avoid taking shortcuts, widening the trail or creating more than one path; your footprints will be followed by many others. When slabs have been laid, please use them, even if the surrounding landscape is dry. The stones protect the delicate peat from erosion and allow the regrowth of grasses which stabilise the peat bog.

Consider walking out of season The maximum disturbance caused by walkers coincides with the time of year when nature wants to do most of its growth and recovery. In high-use areas, like that along much of the Pennine Way, the trail often never recovers. Walking at less busy times eases this pressure while also generating year-round income for the local economy. Not only that, but it may make the walk more enjoyable as there are fewer people on the path and (where it's open) there's less competition for accommodation.

Respect all flora and fauna

Care for all wildlife you come across and tempting as it may be to pick wild flowers leave them so the next people who pass can enjoy them too. Don't break branches off or damage trees in any way. If you come across wildlife keep your distance and don't watch for too long. Your presence can cause considerable stress particularly if the adults are with their young or in winter when the weather is harsh and food scarce. Young animals are rarely abandoned. If you come across deer calves or young birds keep away so that their mother can return.

Outdoor toiletry

As more and more people discover the joys of the outdoors, answering the call of nature is becoming an increasing issue. In some national parks in North America visitors are provided with waste alleviation gelling (WAG) bags and are required to pack out their excrement. Ideally this should be the case in the UK; similar bags are available online and in some outdoors stores. Human excrement is not only offensive to our senses but, more importantly, can infect water sources.

Where to go Wherever possible **use a toilet**. Public toilets are marked in this guide and you'll also find facilities in pubs and cafés.

If you do have to go outdoors choose a site **at least 30 metres away from running water**. Carry a small trowel and **dig a hole** about 15cm (6") deep to bury your excrement. It will decompose quicker when in contact with the top soil or leaf mould. Do not squash it under rocks as this slows down the composting process. However, do not attempt to dig any holes on land that is of historical or archaeological interest, such as around Hadrian's Wall.

Toilet paper and tampons Toilet paper decomposes slowly and is easily dug up by animals. It can then blow into water sources or onto the trail. The best method for dealing with it is to **pack it out**, along with tampons and sanitary towels; don't be tempted to burn the paper as this could lead to fire spreading, especially in a dry moorland environment.

ACCESS AND THE RIGHT TO ROAM

Right to roam

Following a concerted effort by groups such as the Ramblers (see box p50) and the British Mountaineering Council, the principle of access to open countryside and registered common land was finally allowed under the Countryside and Rights of Way Act 2000, affectionately known as CroW. In England, the act came into effect in full in 2005, creating a new right of access to the English countryside for recreation on foot.

End of
Access Land

© Chris Scott

This confusing sign does not mean 'no access for walkers' but advises that you're leaving a Right to Roam area and thereafter must stick to footpaths.

There are restrictions, of course: some land (such as gardens, parks and cultivated land) is excluded, and high-impact activities such as driving a vehicle, cycling, and horse-riding may not be permitted. The act also: gives greater protection to SSSIs (see p61) and AONBs (see p60); lists habitats and species important to biological diversity in England; and covers the conduct of those walking with dogs (see pp31 and pp282-3).

❑ **Lambing and grouse shooting**

Lambing takes place between mid March and mid May; during this period dogs should not be taken along the path. Even a dog secured on a lead can disturb a pregnant ewe. If you see a lamb or ewe that appears to be in distress contact the nearest farmer.

Grouse shooting is an important part of the rural economy and management of the countryside. Britain is home to 20% of the world's moorland, and is under a duty to look after it. The season runs from 12 August to 10 December but shooting is unlikely to affect your walk.

❑ The Countryside Code

The Countryside Code, originally described in the 1950s as the Country Code, was revised and relaunched in 2004, in part because of the changes brought about by the CRoW Act (see opposite); it was updated again in 2012, 2014 and also 2016. The Code seems like common sense but sadly some people still appear to have no understanding of how to treat the countryside they walk in.

An adapted version of the 2016 Code, launched under the logo 'Respect. Protect. Enjoy.', is given below:

Respect other people

• **Consider the local community and other people enjoying the outdoors** Be sensitive to the needs and wishes of those who live and work there. If, for example, farm animals are being moved or gathered keep out of the way and follow the farmer's directions. Being courteous and friendly to those you meet will ensure a healthy future for all based on partnership and co-operation.

• **Leave gates and property as you find them and follow paths unless wider access is available** A farmer normally closes gates to keep farm animals in, but may sometimes leave them open so the animals can reach food and water. Leave gates as you find them or follow instructions on signs. When in a group, make sure the last person knows how to leave the gate. Follow paths unless wider access is available, such as on open country or registered common land (known as 'open access land'). Leave machinery and farm animals alone – if you think an animal is in distress try to alert the farmer instead. Use gates, stiles or gaps in field boundaries if you can – climbing over walls, hedges and fences can damage them and increase the risk of farm animals escaping. If you have to climb over a gate because you can't open it always do so at the hinged end. Also be careful not to disturb ruins and historic sites.

Stick to the official path across arable/pasture land. Minimise erosion by not cutting corners or widening the path.

Protect the natural environment

• **Leave no trace of your visit and take your litter home** Take special care not to damage, destroy or remove features such as rocks, plants and trees. Take your litter with you (see pp74-5); litter and leftover food doesn't just spoil the beauty of the countryside, it can be dangerous to wildlife and farm animals.

Fires can be as devastating to wildlife and habitats as they are to people and property – so be careful with naked flames and cigarettes at any time of the year.

• **Keep dogs under effective control** This means that you should keep your dog on a lead or in sight at all times, be aware of what it's doing and be confident it will return to you promptly on command.

Across farmland dogs should always be kept on a short lead. During lambing time they should not be taken with you at all. Always clean up after your dog and get rid of the mess responsibly – 'bag it and bin it'. (See also p31 and pp282-3).

Enjoy the outdoors

• **Plan ahead and be prepared** You're responsible for your own safety: be prepared for natural hazards, changes in weather and other events. Wild animals, farm animals and horses can behave unpredictably if you get too close, especially if they're with their young – so give them plenty of space.

• **Follow advice and local signs** In some areas there may be temporary diversions in place. Take notice of these and other local trail advice.

Outdoor safety

AVOIDANCE OF HAZARDS

In walking, as in life, most hazards can be avoided through the application of common sense and with some forethought and planning. The Pennine Way is not an expedition into the unknown, you will probably meet people every day, but some sections are remote and you need to be prepared for problems and adverse conditions.

Always **ensure you have adequate clothing** (see pp45-6) for the season; in the UK that means you will always have a waterproof jacket with you, it is also a good idea to keep a spare set of dry clothes. Carry **enough food and water** to see you through the day and consider some high-calorie, long-lasting emergency rations in case you have an extended day; Kendal Mint Cake is often carried for this purpose. Maps, a compass, whistle and torch are essentials, a GPS is great, and a first-aid kit and mobile phone will be useful in an emergency.

See below for details about what to do in the event of an emergency.

Safety on the Pennine Way

Your safety is your responsibility! Organisations are there to help you if an emergency arises, but you should make every effort to ensure you stay safe in the first place. Here are some tips that may help:

- Make sure that somebody knows your plans for every day you are on the trail. This could be a friend or relative whom you have promised to call every night, or the establishment you plan to stay in at the end of each day's walk. That way, if you fail to turn up or call, they can raise the alarm.
- If visibility is suddenly reduced and you become uncertain of the correct trail, wait. You'll find that mist often clears, at least for long enough to allow you to get your bearings. If you are still uncertain – and the weather does not look like improving – return the way you came to the nearest point of civilisation and try again another time when conditions have improved.
- Fill your water container at every opportunity; carry some high-energy snacks.
- Always carry a torch, compass, map, whistle and wet-weather gear with you.
- Be extra vigilant if walking with children, dogs or the unfit.

Dealing with an accident

- Use basic first aid to treat the injury to the best of your ability.
- Try to work out exactly where you are. If possible leave someone with the casualty while others go to get help. If there are only two people, you have a dilemma. If you decide to get help leave all spare clothing and food with the casualty.
- In an **emergency**, six short blasts on a whistle, and six flashes of a torch after dark, repeated regularly, will identify you as in trouble. A last resort is to dial

☎ 999, ask for the Police and Mountain Rescue: they will need to know your exact location, the nature of the injuries, the number of casualties, and your phone number.

WEATHER FORECASTS

The UK has notoriously unpredictable weather and the Pennine range, like any mountainous area, generates its own weather patterns as well. A check of the weather forecast before you leave in the morning could help you avoid a dangerous situation later in the day. Hostels, TICs and some good B&Bs will have that morning's summary pinned up by the door. If you have wi-fi or a mobile signal, most smartphones have free access to internet weather services; ideally a mountain weather service such as MWIS (see below) as the weather on the high tops can be much more extreme than in the valleys and lowlands.

If the forecast is really bad, consider either an alternative low-level route if there is one, or a rest day if plans allow, or a taxi to your next accommodation if they don't. Some baggage-transfer services allow you to ride with the bags, but check with them first if this is part of their service. Even on what should be a fine day, ensure you have waterproofs in your pack, just in case.

Access to forecasts

The **UK Met Office** (💻 www.metoffice.gov.uk) has a comprehensive range of services, including weather apps for iPhone, Android, Windows Phone and Kindle, a service for mountain areas and national parks, a Mobile Weather service that can be accessed from any web-enabled mobile and direct access to a forecaster (this last is a premium service costing around £21 for 1-24 calls, full details on the website).

The **Mountain Weather Information Service** (MWIS; 💻 www.mwis.org.uk) has a very detailed service for the high hills of the Peak District and the Yorkshire Dales, which is also available to all web-enabled mobile phones.

BLISTERS

The Pennine Way is no place for experimenting with new equipment and this applies particularly for new boots. Even though most new boots do not require 'breaking in' any more they do need to be tested for comfort before you set out. Blisters are often caused by wet feet, so waterproof boots may help; try to avoid getting them wet inside, perhaps by using gaiters, although these aren't to everyone's taste. Airing your feet at rest stops is a great policy and always address hotspots as soon as they develop.

Zinc oxide will help reduce a hotspot, but if you leave it too long and it develops into a blister you will need a 'moleskin' patch or a blister plaster such as Compeed. Avoid popping blisters if at all possible as this can lead to infection. If the skin breaks, clean it with an antiseptic wipe or cream and cover it with a non-adhesive dressing, taped into place.

HYPOTHERMIA, HYPERTHERMIA & SUNBURN

Also known as **exposure**, hypothermia occurs when the body can't generate enough heat to maintain its normal temperature, usually as a result of being wet, cold, unprotected from the wind, tired and hungry. It's usually more of a problem in upland areas on the moors or, of course, outside summer. Hypothermia is easily avoided by wearing suitable clothing, carrying and eating enough food and drink, being aware of the weather conditions and keeping an eye on the condition of your companions. Feeling cold and tired is par for the course on the Pennine Way, but along with shivering, these are the early symptoms of hypothermia; so find (or fashion) shelter as soon as possible and get into whatever dry clothes you have.

If symptoms worsen just adding layers will not help, you will need to add warmth, either in the form of a hot drink, food or fire or through the sharing of body warmth with a companion; this is best achieved through skin-to-skin contact in a sleeping bag or bivi bag. If symptoms aren't addressed behaviour may become erratic, speech slurred and co-ordination poor, leading eventually to unconsciousness, followed by coma and even death. Do not delay in seeking medical assistance, including mountain rescue.

Although uncommon, it is possible to suffer from **heat exhaustion**, even in the north of England. Brought on by a long, strenuous walk in hot temperatures, the symptoms are a result of the loss of body fluids and salts and a sufferer may feel faint, nauseous and sweat heavily. Additional symptoms include: skin that feels hot to the touch, a rapid heart rate, feeling confused and urinating less often.

A person with heat exhaustion should be moved quickly to somewhere cool and given fluids, preferably water, to drink. Follow this, if possible, with a weak salt solution of one teaspoon of salt per litre of water and assist the casualty to drink it. If spotted and addressed quickly, they should start to feel better within half an hour. Certain groups of people – including diabetics using insulin, people with kidney, heart or circulation problems and the young and elderly – are more at risk of getting heatstroke (see below) and should seek medical attention as soon as possible.

Heatstroke (hyperthermia) is a much more serious problem altogether. It occurs when the body's temperature becomes dangerously high due to excessive heat exposure. The body is no longer able to cool itself and starts to overheat. Early symptoms will include a high body temperature and an absence of sweating, followed by erratic behaviour, slurred speech and poor co-ordination, leading eventually to convulsions, coma and possibly death.

Rehydration is not enough; shade the victim and sponge them down, wrap them in wet towels or soak their lower layers, fan them, and get help immediately; this is an emergency situation, dial ☎ 999.

Sunburn can happen, even in northern England and even on overcast days. The only surefire way to avoid it is to cover exposed skin, especially your head, or smother yourself in at least factor 30+ sunscreen throughout the day. A broad brimmed hat will reduce sunburn to your head much better than a baseball cap, which just shades your eyes.

ROUTE GUIDE & MAPS 4

Using this guide

The trail guide has been divided into 15 stages (walking from south to north, the direction taken by 80% of walkers on the Pennine Way), though these are not to be taken as rigid daily itineraries since people walk at different speeds and have different interests.

The **route overviews** introduce the trail for each of these stages. They're followed by **navigation notes** that will help you identify and overcome potential route-finding trouble-spots. To enable you to plan your itinerary, practical information is presented on the trail maps; this includes walking times for both directions, all places to stay and eat, as well as useful shops and other services. Further details are given in the text under the entry for each place. For an overview of all this information see the town and village facilities table, pp34-7.

TRAIL MAPS

Scale and walking times

The trail maps are to a **scale** of just under 1:20,000 (1cm = 200m; $3^{1}/_{8}$ inches = one mile).

Walking times are given along the side of each map; the arrow shows the direction to which the time refers. The black triangles indicate the points between which the times have been taken. See box below about walking times.

These time-bars are a rough guide and are not there to judge your walking ability; actual walking times will be different for each individual. There are so many variables that affect walking speed from the weather conditions to how many beers you drank the previous evening as well as how much you are carrying. After the first hour or two of walking you'll be able to see how your speed relates to the timings on the maps.

> ❑ **Important note – walking times**
>
> Unless otherwise specified, **all times in this book refer only to the time spent walking**. You will need to add 20-30% to allow for rests, photography, checking the map, drinking water etc, not to mention time simply to stop and stare.
>
> When planning the day's hike count on 5-7 hours' actual walking.

Up or down?

The trail is shown as a dashed line. An arrow across the trail indicates the slope; two arrows show that it is steep. The arrows always point up hill. If, for example, you are walking from A (at 80m) to B (at 200m) and the trail between the two is short and steep, it would be shown thus: A – – – >>- – – B. Reversed arrow heads indicate a downward gradient.

Other map features

The numbered GPS waypoints refer to the list on pp274-81. Features are marked on the map when they are pertinent to navigation. In order to avoid cluttering the maps and making them unusable not all features have been marked each time they occur.

ACCOMMODATION

Apart from in large towns where some selection has been necessary, all accommodation on or close to the trail is marked on (or indicated off) the maps with details in the accompanying text.

Details of each place are given in the accompanying text. The number of **rooms** of each type is given at the beginning of each entry, ie: **S** = Single, **D** = Double room, **T** = Twin room with two beds, **Tr** = Triple room and **Qd** = Quad. Note that many of the triple/quad rooms have a double bed and one/two single beds (or bunk beds) thus for a group of three or four, two people would have to share the double bed but it also means the room can be used as a double or twin.

Rates quoted for B&B-style accommodation are **per person (pp)** based on two people sharing a room for a one-night stay; rates are usually discounted for longer stays. Where a single room **(sgl)** is available the rate for that is quoted if different from the rate per person. The rate for single occupancy **(sgl occ)** of a double/twin room may be higher. The per person rate for three/four sharing a triple/quad is generally lower. At some places the only option is a **room rate**; this will be the same whether one or two people (or more if permissible) use the room. The rates quoted were accurate at the time of research but may well change. See box on p23 for more information on rates.

The text also mentions whether the rooms are **en suite**, or if they have **private**, or **shared, facilities** (in either case this may be a bathroom or shower room just outside the room). For those who prefer a relaxed soak at the end of the day ◆ signifies that a **bath** is available in, or for, at least one room.

Also noted is whether the premises allow **dogs to stay** (🐕 – see also pp282-3), subject to prior arrangement, and any associated charges; and if **packed lunches** (Ⓛ) are available (usually these must be requested in advance ie by or on the night before). **Wi-fi** is available almost everywhere so the text only notes where, at the time of research, it was not available.

Several B&B proprietors based a mile or two off the trail will, subject to prior arrangement, be happy to collect walkers from the nearest point on the trail and take them back the next morning; a small charge may be payable though.

The route guide

EDALE [Map 1, p85]

Surrounded by hills and providing access to hundreds of miles of footpaths, it's no surprise that Edale is a mecca for walkers from all over the UK. This ancient and beautiful village comprises a scattering of stone cottages, an impressive village church and an old pub; at weekends it is home to hundreds of visitors. Some of these will be embarking on the Pennine Way and this walk and the village have become synonymous. Upon arrival, visitors are drawn towards the focal point of the village, the Old Nag's Head (see p86), and for Pennine Wayfarers this is an absolute must, as it's the official start point for the walk.

See p14 for details about Edale Country Day in June.

Transport

All great adventures should start with a train journey and the Pennine Way is no different, so the best way to arrive in Edale is by **train**. (Indeed, given that there are no bus services to Edale, train is pretty much the only way to to arrive, at least if you're relying on public transport.) There are frequent connections – services are operated by Northern Rail (see box on p59) – from both Sheffield (30 mins away) and Manchester (45 mins away) and you are unlikely to step onto Edale platform alone.

Undoubtedly a very scenic way to approach Edale is by **car**, using the minor road from the south, over Mam Tor, to see the Vale of Edale spread out below and the village nestled amongst the heather moors around it. If you plan on parking your car here for a few days, give Andrew Critchlow of Shaw Wood Farm a call (☎ 07792-446753); he has a field behind the farmhouse, just five minutes from the station. He usually charges around £2-3 per day, with all money going to charity. The village's official car park (see Map 1) charges £5.20 a day, or £6.20 overnight.

For a **taxi** try SOS Taxis Grindleford (☎ 07541-101076).

Services

Pop into **The Moorland Centre** (Peak District National Park Centre; ☎ 01433-670207, 🖳 visitpeakdistrict.com; Feb half-term & Mar Mon-Fri 10am-3.30pm, Sat & Sun 9.30am-4.30pm, Apr-Sep daily 9.30am-5pm, Oct Mon-Fri 10am-3.30pm, Sat, Sun & bank hols 9.30am-4.30pm, Nov & Feb Sat & Sun 9.30am-4.30pm, Dec & Jan closed except for Boxing Day to New Year's Day 9.30am-3.30pm). **Edale Visitor Centre** here has maps, guidebooks, snacks, souvenirs, and a limited selection of outdoor clothing. Note that the centre closes for approximately half an hour most days for staff to have a lunch break. See also box p87.

At the top end of the village there's **Cooper's Rural Merchants** (☎ 01433-670220; Apr-Oct Mon-Thur 9am-4pm, Fri & Sat 8.30am-9pm, Sun 8.30am-5pm, Nov-Mar Fri-Sun 9am-4pm; note that between Sep and Mar days/hours can be variable – see their Facebook page for details) which caters for walkers' needs. They sell groceries, such as bread, eggs & ham, as well as camping equipment and also specialist gins, whiskies and locally brewed beer; they accept card payment but don't offer cashback. There are limited **post office** services here on Wednesday morning. This is the last shop you will see, unless you divert from the route, until Hebden Bridge (which itself is off the trail).

There is basically no mobile phone coverage but you may get a weak signal on the road just above the railway station. However, there are two public **phones** in the village.

Where to stay

The first day out from Edale requires a full day's walking and is one of the toughest first days of any long-distance walk in the UK. Unless you can arrive early it makes sense, therefore, to stay the night in the village, or very close by. The popularity of Edale makes it important to secure your accommodation prior to arrival, especially if, like most walkers, you plan to begin the Pennine Way at the weekend.

Note that some B&Bs may not be keen to take solo travellers at weekends unless they pay the full room rate.

In Edale There are two **campsites** in the centre of the village both of which are open most of the year (just closing at times in winter). ***Fieldhead*** (☎ 01433-670386, 🖳 fieldhead-campsite.co.uk; no WI-FI; 🐕) by the Moorland Centre, charges from £7pp. There are toilets, showers (20p) and basic drying facilities. Booking is recommended at weekends in the summer months.

Cooper's Camp and Caravan Site (☎ 01433-670372; space for 120 tents; no WI-FI; 🐕 but on a lead at all times), at **New Fold Farm** up the hill by the post office, charges £7.50/14 for one person/two in a tent (cash only). Shower (20p) and toilet facilities are available. Booking is essential for Bank Holiday weekends and is subject to a minimum of three nights; at other times it is first come first served.

Edale Camping Barn (☎ 01433-670273; Mar-Nov) is 10 minutes' walk to the east of the village at **Cotefield Farm**. It's a simple **camping barn** (sleeping eight) with outside (chemical) toilet, water tap and cooking area but there's no electricity or hot water. It costs from £8.50pp (bring everything as if you were camping except for a tent) but the barn is available only for group bookings at weekends (Fri & Sat) nights.

There is a second bunk barn advertised in Edale, ***Ollerbrook Farm Bunkhouse*** (☎ 01433-670235, 🖳 ollerbrookfarm.co.uk), but it's unlikely you'll be able to stay here unless you're part of a group of at least six people; manage to do so and you'll find there are actually two bunkhouses housing a total of 34 beds (£15-20pp).

Walkers requiring **B&B** have a limited choice. ***Ollerbrook Barn*** (☎ 01433-670200, 🖳 ollerbrookbarn.co.uk; 3D all en suite, 1Tr private bathroom; ▼; Ⓛ; 🐕) is a beautiful ivy-clad converted barn in a quiet spot away from the village. B&B costs £35-45pp (sgl occ £40-45). If arranged in advance they are happy to pick people up from Edale station free of charge.

Between the church and the pub is ***Stonecroft*** (☎ 01433-670262, 🖳 stonecroftguesthouse.co.uk; 2D en suite, 1S with private facilities; Ⓛ) which costs £52.50-60pp (sgl from £62, sgl occ full room rate). Note there is a minimum two-night stay at weekends.

Another cosy spot is ***Western House*** (☎ 01433-670014, western.house@btinternet.com; 1D en suite; ▼; 🐕), just above the Old Nag's Head pub, which charges from £42.50pp (sgl occ £65).

❏ Peak & Northern Footpath Society (PNFS)

The PNFS (🖳 peakandnorthern.org.uk) has been providing informative, durable and, many people would say, beautiful signposts for walkers for over a hundred years. In addition, the charitable organisation has installed a number of toposcopes and erected several bridges to help walkers across rivers and streams. Their distinctive square, green, metal-plate signs can be found at various points along the Pennine Way. There are seven PNFS signs on the Pennine Way path – see how many you can spot!

As well as installing signposts and bridges, the PNFS is a staunch defender of the rights of walkers across the north of England. The oldest-surviving regional footpath society in the UK, it was founded in the days when there were no rights to roam and landowners fiercely defended their moorland estates, often with teams of bailiffs employing physical force. The society's roots are deeply entwined with the struggle of walkers and ramblers to gain access to the fells and hills and we all owe them a debt of thanks for their activities and campaigning – as well as for their wonderful signposts.

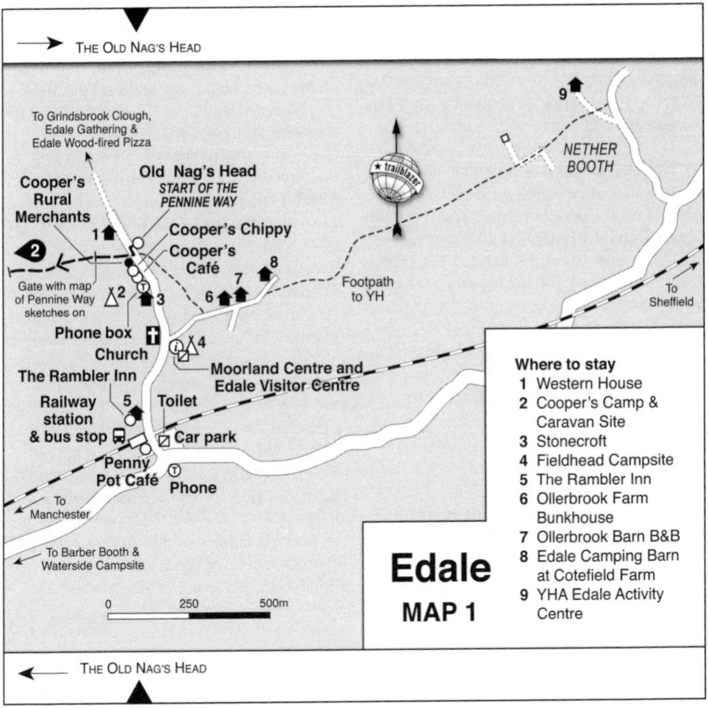

THE OLD NAG'S HEAD
To Grindsbrook Clough, Edale Gathering & Edale Wood-fired Pizza
Cooper's Rural Merchants
Old Nag's Head
START OF THE PENNINE WAY
Cooper's Chippy
Cooper's Café
Gate with map of Pennine Way sketches on
Phone box
Church
The Rambler Inn
Railway station & bus stop
Toilet
Car park
Penny Pot Café
Phone
Moorland Centre and Edale Visitor Centre
Footpath to YH
NETHER BOOTH
To Sheffield
To Manchester
To Barber Booth & Waterside Campsite
0
250
500m
Edale
MAP 1
Where to stay
1 Western House
2 Cooper's Camp & Caravan Site
3 Stonecroft
4 Fieldhead Campsite
5 The Rambler Inn
6 Ollerbrook Farm Bunkhouse
7 Ollerbrook Barn B&B
8 Edale Camping Barn at Cotefield Farm
9 YHA Edale Activity Centre
THE OLD NAG'S HEAD

Originally built as the Railway Hotel, ***The Rambler Inn*** (☎ 01433-670268, 💻 dorbiere.co.uk/the-rambler-inn; 3D/2T/2Tr/2Qd, all en suite; ☕; Ⓛ; 🐕 bar only) charges from £45pp (sgl occ £85).

At the top of Edale's accommodation tree is the new ***Edale Gathering*** (off Map 1; ☎ 01433-670612, 💻 edalegathering.com; ☕; 🐕; lodge apartments open all year, tents Apr-Dec). **Glamping** doesn't get any more fabulous than this, with four tented safari lodges sleeping six (1D/2T) all kitted out with wood-burning stoves, roll-top baths with showers and fully equipped open-plan kitchen/dining areas. They have also restored an old 19th-century shooting lodge for larger parties, with apartments for 4/6 people. It's all rather luxurious and lovely but note that the accommodation has to be booked for a minimum of two/four nights and prices can be eye-watering – with the tented lodges around £645 for (the minimum) four nights, and the shooting lodge often over £370/500 per night (minimum two nights). The site lies about a quarter of a mile above the start of the trail at the very top of the village.

In Nether Booth Most nights ***YHA Edale*** (also known as YHA Edale Activity Centre; bookings ☎ 0345-371 9514, 💻 yha.org.uk/hostel/yha-edale-activity-centre; 1 x 6-, 3 x 3-, 3 x 4-bed rooms en suite, 2 x 1, 3 x 2-, 3 x 3- 2 x 4-, 5 x 6-, 6 x 8-, 2 x 12-bed rooms; Ⓛ; open all year) may seem more of a 157-bed 'hyperactivity centre' over-run with school kids than the old ramblers' hostel it once was. So beware before making the 1½-mile walk east of Edale village, especially in the summer holidays as the hostel is usually fully booked with groups but at any time of the year it is best to book in advance. Dorm beds cost from £13pp, private rooms from £29. Meals are available and there is a bar as well as laundry and drying facilities. You can reach the hostel via a network of footpaths from the village or along the road.

In Barber Booth This small hamlet is about half a mile south-west of Edale (off Map 1) or just under one mile south-east of Upper Booth (off Map 2) and if you're really stuck for accommodation ***Waterside Campsite*** (☎ 01433-670215; 40 pitches; no WI-FI; 🐕 on lead; Easter to Sep) offers **camping** from £5.50pp (£3 per vehicle). Showers, toilets and hot/cold water are available. Booking is essential for bank holiday weekends and a minimum stay of three nights is required.

Where to eat and drink

Being the traditional start of the Pennine Way, a meal at ***The Old Nag's Head*** (☎ 01433-670291, 🖳 dorbiere.co.uk/the-old-nags-head; food served Mon-Fri noon-9pm, Sat noon-9pm, Sun noon-8pm, also Sat & Sun 8.30-11.45am; 🐕) at the top of the village is a must. Try the 'Hiker's Special', a cumberland sausage with a beef & vegetable pasty, chips, veg and gravy (£10.95).

The alternative is the less iconic ***The Rambler Inn*** (see Where to stay; Mon-Sat noon-9pm, Sun to 8pm) down the road or, in the daytime, try ***Penny Pot Café*** (Mon-Fri 10am-4.30pm, Sat & Sun 8.30am-4.30pm) near the station, or ***Cooper's Café*** (☎ 01433-670401; Mar-Oct Thur-Fri & Mon 9am-4pm, Sat & Sun 8am-5pm, Nov-Feb Fri-Sun 9am-4pm. Note that they expect to be closed on Tue and Wed in the summer months; 🐕) near the start of the trail.

In the same building but with a separate entrance is ***Cooper's Chippy*** (Mar-Sep Fri 4-8pm, Sat 5-9pm, extra days added in the school summer hols, winter Fri only), a fish & chip shop.

Completing the list of dining options, there's a pizza company, ***Edale Wood Fired Pizza*** (☎ 01433-670202, or ☎ 07583 547711, 🖳 edalewoodfiredpizza.com) that appears most weekends from 4pm just past Edale Gathering (see Where to stay).

EDALE TO CROWDEN — MAPS 1-9

Route overview

16 miles (25.5km) – 2600ft (793m) of ascent – 5¾-7¼ hours*

As can be seen from the above, the Pennine Way throws you straight in at the deep end. If the weather is poor, it may also test your navigation and equipment as you skirt around the notorious Kinder Scout (see box below) and ascend the remote summit of Bleaklow. The days of wading knee deep through peat bog

❑ Kinder Scout – a bit of history

Kinder Scout, a hugely popular recreational area, with Manchester and Sheffield just a curlew's whistle away, became synonymous with the so-called 'right to roam' when in 1932 it was the scene of a mass 'trespass' in which thousands of people demonstrated their belief that wild land should be accessible to all by marching across the plateau. It took a while but the event eventually led to the National Parks and Access to the Countryside Act of 1949. Today rights of access to the countryside have improved further with the Countryside & Rights of Way Act 2000 (see p76).

In October 2009 Kinder Scout plateau became a National Nature Reserve (NNR; see p61). In all, 800 hectares of blanket bog and sub-alpine dwarf shrub heath were afforded the protection that NNR status should bring. The National Trust, who own the land, have plans to restore much of the damaged habitat; repairing eroded patches and aiding the recovery of sphagnum moss – see box opposite.

* Your walking day will be longer than this! See **important note on walking times** on p81.

are long gone however, thanks to the use of stone slabs, reclaimed from demolished cotton mills and laid over the worst of the bogs to prevent erosion and provide, almost incidentally, a dry path and perfect navigation aid for walkers.

Having left Edale you pass through sheep pastures, the hamlet of **Upper Booth** (Map 2) and along a lane, all the time the hills encroaching closer and closer. The path soon arrives at the picturesque bridge at the foot of **Jacob's Ladder** (Map 3) and the first stiff climb of the walk up to the towering **Edale Rocks**. Here you begin the classic edge walk around **Kinder Scout** passing impressive gritstone outcrops to reach **Kinder Downfall** (Map 4). If you're lucky you may see water cascading down over the edge and if you're even luckier you may see it being blown upwards by the wind as it whistles up the valley and onto the plateau.

Kinder Scout route

For many years the official route of the Pennine Way took walkers up Grindsbrook Clough and across the summit of Kinder Scout to Kinder Downfall. The majority of this route is beautiful and rugged, with the ascent beside Grinds Brook being one of the classic walking routes in the Peak District. Unfortunately the next section across the plateau of Kinder Scout proved the undoing of too many walkers – lost or enmired in the deep peat troughs (called *groughs*) on the wild and pathless plateau. The result was a change in route along a lower path with much simpler navigation and a chance to arrive at Kinder Downfall in mostly clean boots.

Unless you are an experienced walker with excellent navigation skills and a love of peat haggs, this side route is not recommended. Even in the height of summer this route can be extremely muddy and the lack of landmarks can

❑ Moors for the Future

Based at The Moorland Centre in Edale, the Moors for the Future Partnership was established with a Heritage Lottery Fund grant in 2003. It was given a remit to: restore and conserve our important moorland resources; raise awareness of the value of this environment; and to develop expertise on how to protect and manage the moors in a sustainable way in the Peak District and South Pennines.

Peat bogs, such as those on the summit of Bleaklow and Kinder Scout, play an important environmental role as carbon dioxide (CO_2) banks, storing large amounts of the greenhouse gas. As these delicate landscapes are eroded, through pollution, overgrazing, summer wildfires and the weather, the CO_2 is slowly leaked back into the atmosphere. It is estimated that the UK's peat bogs store the equivalent of ten times the country's total CO_2 emissions. Erosion of the southern Pennine hills is causing the release of something like the CO_2 emission of a large town every year.

The work carried out by Moors for the Future Partnership on Kinder and Bleaklow includes projects such as spreading geotextiles to stabilise the bare peat, building footpaths and applying lime, seed and fertiliser and re-introducing **sphagnum** (see p63), a key peat-building moss. The best example of their work for the Pennine Wayfarer is the transformation of Black Hill (Map 12), from a peaty wasteland just a few years ago, to a more healthy revegetated moorland – better for wildlife, water quality and retaining carbon in the soil. More information on the work carried out can be found on their website (🖳 moorsforthefuture.org.uk).

make navigation by compass very tricky. If anyone still feels the urge to take this route an OS map and the OS grid references in the text below provide the best way of following it.

At the head of Grindsbrook Clough head west along the slabs that begin at SK 10528 87225, for about three-quarters of a mile (1.2km), until you reach a junction of streams at SK 09511 87271, where you head north. The path soon disappears and you need to make your way as best you can across the peat bogs (mostly north-north-west) to a thin path that begins beside a stream at SK 09160 88242. Follow this path to a cairn at SK 08901 88368 where you head north and then west, following the stream to Kinder Downfall and a return to the official route.

Note: nowhere on this route is suitable for wild camping.

Keeping to the edge, you'll soon arrive at the steep, stepped descent to a cross-roads of paths. Be sure to keep straight ahead, turning right here (too soon) will leave you with a long road walk to recover the path. Cross William Clough (a *clough* is a stream) and a short distance ahead you reach **Mill Hill**; turn right across the bare peat expanse of featherbed moss, now thankfully slabbed, to meet the A57 at **Snake Pass** (Map 6). Snake Pass Inn (see p93) is a mere 5-mile (8km) round trip along the road, but to save time (and if you have brought sandwiches) a better idea for lunch may be to find a sheltered spot beside the path.

Devil's Dike awaits and a long, steady ascent of Bleaklow. The path follows a sunken course between walls of peat, meandering all the way, crossing small streams and the occasional open expanse of cotton-grass if the season is right. In good weather this is a joy to walk, the section up and beside **Hern Clough** (Map 7) being the highlight. In bad weather and poor visibility in particular this can be a nervous test of navigation. The path is mostly obvious though and

❑ Peat

The Way has not become synonymous with miles of spirit-sapping bogs for nothing. Paving slabs have alleviated much of the misery, but why is it so darn soggy?

Peat and the underlying geology are to blame. The British Isles (and indeed much of the landmass of planet earth) was once covered in trees. Everywhere except the highest mountains and sandy beaches was wooded. Sabre-toothed tigers prowled in the forests alongside elephants and rhinos. Today these ancient woodlands and rampaging carnivores are no longer around. The reason for the disappearance of this habitat is not a natural phenomenon but the activities of early man.

When early Britons felled primeval forests for building and farming, ground-water was no longer absorbed and evaporated by the trees. Add the impermeability of the underlying gritstone and the saturated vegetation rotted where it lay, forming the peat, which you squelch through today. So, next time your boots fill with black peaty soup, don't curse nature, curse your axe-wielding forebears instead.

© Chris Scott

Wet feet? Blame the cavemen!

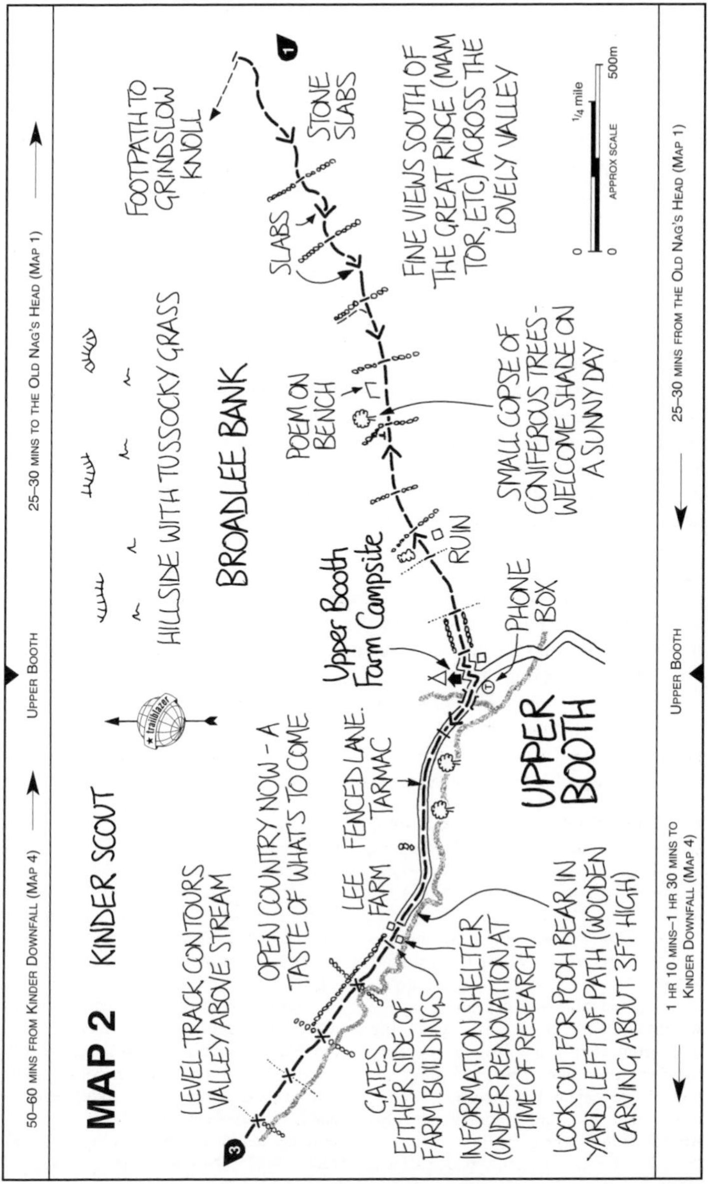
MAP 2
KINDER SCOUT
50–60 MINS FROM KINDER DOWNFALL (MAP 4)
25–30 MINS TO THE OLD NAG'S HEAD (MAP 1)
UPPER BOOTH
1 HR 10 MINS–1 HR 30 MINS TO KINDER DOWNFALL (MAP 4)
25–30 MINS FROM THE OLD NAG'S HEAD (MAP 1)
trailblazer
LEVEL TRACK CONTOURS VALLEY ABOVE STREAM
OPEN COUNTRY NOW – A TASTE OF WHAT'S TO COME
LEE FARM
FENCED LANE. TARMAC
GATES EITHER SIDE OF FARM BUILDINGS
INFORMATION SHELTER (UNDER RENOVATION AT TIME OF RESEARCH)
LOOK OUT FOR POOH BEAR IN YARD, LEFT OF PATH (WOODEN CARVING ABOUT 3FT HIGH)
UPPER BOOTH
Upper Booth Farm Campsite
PHONE BOX
RUIN
HILLSIDE WITH TUSSOCKY GRASS
BROADLEE BANK
POEM ON BENCH
SMALL COPSE OF CONIFEROUS TREES – WELCOME SHADE ON A SUNNY DAY
SLABS
STONE SLABS
FOOTPATH TO GRINDSLOW KNOLL
FINE VIEWS SOUTH OF THE GREAT RIDGE (MAM TOR, ETC) ACROSS THE LOVELY VALLEY
0 1/4 mile
0 500m
APPROX SCALE

ROUTE GUIDE AND MAPS

knee-high stone blocks are interspersed along the length carrying the acorn symbol of the National Trail.

Bleaklow Head is soon reached, an impressive cairn with a stake marking the nominal summit – a huge expanse of peat, rocks and grassy hummocks can't really be called a summit. The exit from Bleaklow isn't obvious, but a stone block guide post points the way and it's mostly downhill now to Torside, still four miles (6.5km) and two hours away. On the way you'll follow **Clough Edge**, a lofty path with great views down to your destination. The steep descent brings you to the B6105 road (Map 9) where, since the YHA hostel at Crowden closed, you have probably arranged to be picked up by someone from your accommodation for the night – unless you're booked to stay at the nearest B&B (see p93), or prefer to walk the two miles plus along the Longdendale Trail or road to the other B&B options in the area (see also p98). Sixteen miles down, 240 to go!

Navigation notes

The path is obvious and clear as far as Kinder Low (Map 3), at which point it becomes somewhat faint and intermittent across the sandy rock-strewn area beside the trig point, but keep an eye out for the cairns beside the path, or better still use a GPS if you lose the faint track. If you find the Kinder Low trig point on your left at any point you've gone wrong. But if, having passed the trig point, you then make for the escarpment to the north of it and keep to the edge you'll be on the right track.

The trickiest part of the day is the summit of Bleaklow Head (Map 7), but providing you seek out the two knee-high, stone block guide markers that are located beside the huge summit cairn, you should end up going in the right direction. GPS waypoints are provided and the summit cairn is an excellent reference for a compass bearing. The final troublespot is encountered at the end of the descent down Wildboar Grain (Map 8). Before you turn right (north-west) down Torside Clough, you need to scramble up the steep slope on the other side of the junction of rivers. There is a path, but it's not obvious until you look for it. At the top of the scramble there's an acorn post to prove you're still on the path.

UPPER BOOTH [Map 2, p89]

Located 1¼ miles (2km) into the Pennine Way, Upper Booth can make a nice warm up the night before you start your walk proper.

The main reason you would come is to stay at ***Upper Booth Farm Campsite*** (☎ 01433-670250, 🖳 upperboothcamping.co.uk; Ⓛ; 🐕; Mar-Nov depending on the weather/ground conditions). **Camping** costs from £6pp and a space in the very basic **camping barn** (🐕), with room for up to 12 people but with no water, heating or electricity, is from £10pp. The site also has toilet and shower facilities. Note that there is no WI-FI or mobile phone signal; also dogs must be under under strict control at all times and cleaned up after and waste disposed of in the bins provided. Booking is essential for both for weekends in the summer and bank holidays (and you need to book a minimum of three-nights over bank holiday weekends). Packed lunches and 'take to your tent' basic meals are available if arranged in advance. Fresh free-range eggs and milk can be bought at this award-winning farm where conservation and business can be seen working hand in hand; an excellent example of how hill farming can be a sustainable and integral part of the local economy and community.

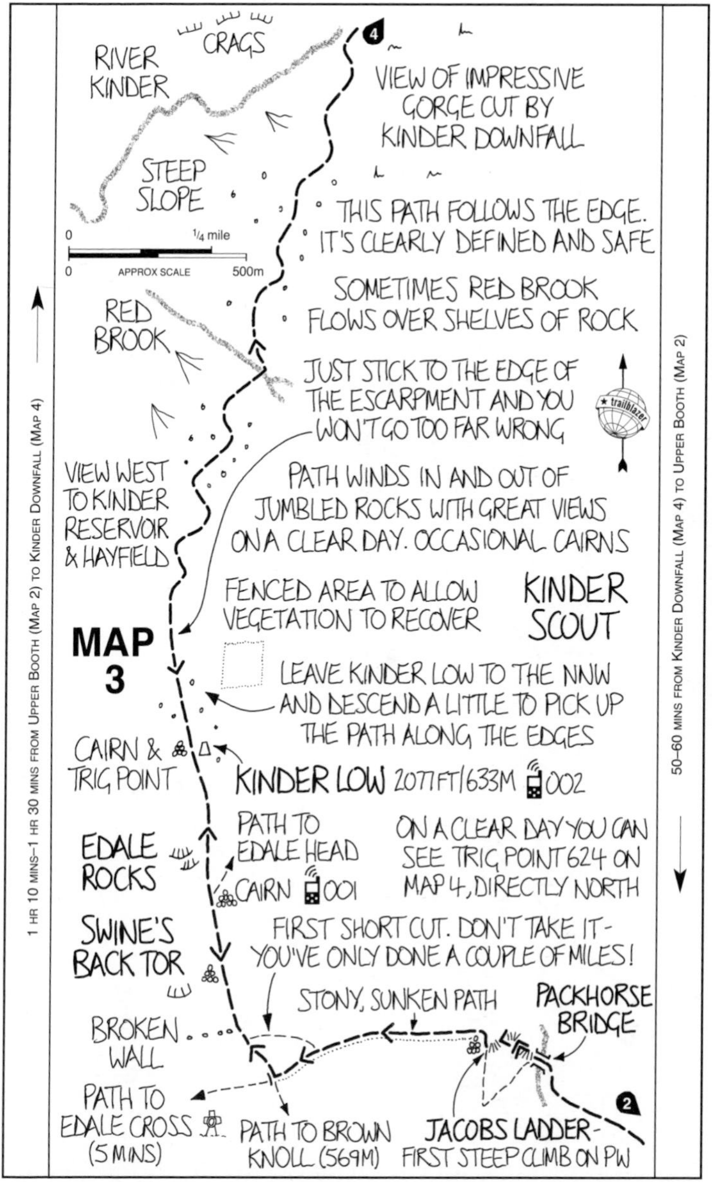
1 HR 10 MINS–1 HR 30 MINS FROM UPPER BOOTH (MAP 2) TO KINDER DOWNFALL (MAP 4)
50–60 MINS FROM KINDER DOWNFALL (MAP 4) TO UPPER BOOTH (MAP 2)
MAP 3
4
CRAGS
RIVER KINDER
VIEW OF IMPRESSIVE GORGE CUT BY KINDER DOWNFALL
STEEP SLOPE
THIS PATH FOLLOWS THE EDGE. IT'S CLEARLY DEFINED AND SAFE
0 1/4 mile
0 APPROX SCALE 500m
SOMETIMES RED BROOK FLOWS OVER SHELVES OF ROCK
RED BROOK
JUST STICK TO THE EDGE OF THE ESCARPMENT AND YOU WON'T GO TOO FAR WRONG
★ trailblazer
VIEW WEST TO KINDER RESERVOIR & HAYFIELD
PATH WINDS IN AND OUT OF JUMBLED ROCKS WITH GREAT VIEWS ON A CLEAR DAY. OCCASIONAL CAIRNS
FENCED AREA TO ALLOW VEGETATION TO RECOVER
KINDER SCOUT
LEAVE KINDER LOW TO THE NNW AND DESCEND A LITTLE TO PICK UP THE PATH ALONG THE EDGES
CAIRN & TRIG POINT
KINDER LOW 2071FT/633M 002
PATH TO EDALE HEAD
CAIRN 001
ON A CLEAR DAY YOU CAN SEE TRIG POINT 624 ON MAP 4, DIRECTLY NORTH
EDALE ROCKS
SWINE'S BACK TOR
FIRST SHORT CUT. DON'T TAKE IT - YOU'VE ONLY DONE A COUPLE OF MILES!
STONY, SUNKEN PATH
PACKHORSE BRIDGE
BROKEN WALL
PATH TO EDALE CROSS (5 MINS)
PATH TO BROWN KNOLL (569M)
JACOBS LADDER - FIRST STEEP CLIMB ON PW
2

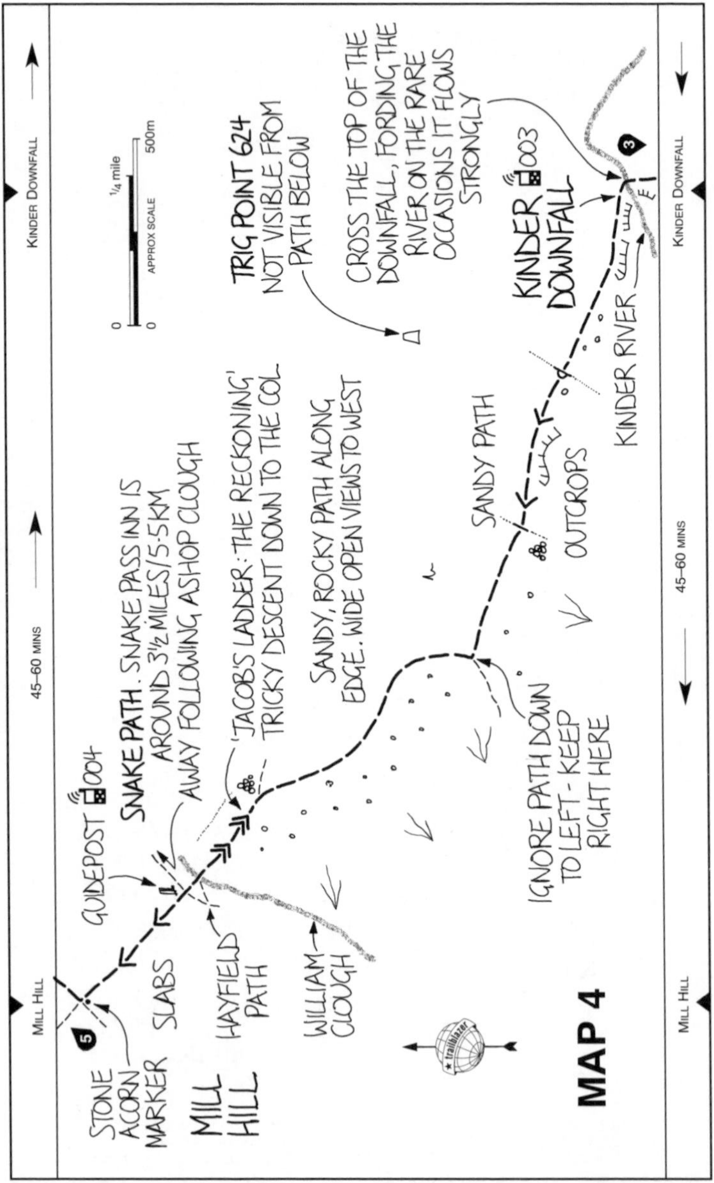

MAP 4
KINDER DOWNFALL
MILL HILL
45–60 MINS
APPROX SCALE
0
0
¼ mile
500m
TRIG POINT 624 NOT VISIBLE FROM PATH BELOW
CROSS THE TOP OF THE DOWNFALL, FORDING THE RIVER ON THE RARE OCCASIONS IT FLOWS STRONGLY
KINDER DOWNFALL
003
KINDER RIVER
SANDY PATH
OUTCROPS
'JACOB'S LADDER': THE RECKONING' TRICKY DESCENT DOWN TO THE COL
SANDY, ROCKY PATH ALONG EDGE. WIDE OPEN VIEWS TO WEST
SNAKE PATH. SNAKE PASS INN IS AROUND 3½ MILES/5.5KM AWAY FOLLOWING ASHOP CLOUGH
GUIDEPOST
004
IGNORE PATH DOWN TO LEFT - KEEP RIGHT HERE
STONE ACORN MARKER
SLABS
HAYFIELD PATH
WILLIAM CLOUGH
MILL HILL
trailblazer

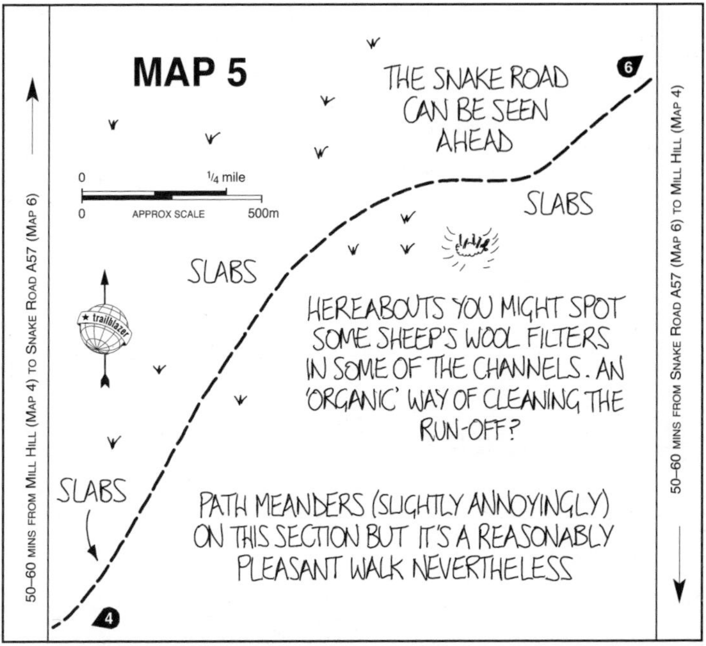
MAP 5
THE SNAKE ROAD CAN BE SEEN AHEAD
0 1/4 mile
0 APPROX SCALE 500m
SLABS
SLABS
trailblazer
HEREABOUTS YOU MIGHT SPOT SOME SHEEP'S WOOL FILTERS IN SOME OF THE CHANNELS. AN 'ORGANIC' WAY OF CLEANING THE RUN-OFF?
SLABS
PATH MEANDERS (SLIGHTLY ANNOYINGLY) ON THIS SECTION BUT IT'S A REASONABLY PLEASANT WALK NEVERTHELESS
50–60 MINS FROM MILL HILL (MAP 4) TO SNAKE ROAD A57 (MAP 6)
50–60 MINS FROM SNAKE ROAD A57 (MAP 6) TO MILL HILL (MAP 4)
6
4

SNAKE PASS [Map 6, p94]

From Snake Pass, ***Snake Pass Inn*** (off Map 6; ☎ 01433-651480, 🖳 contact@thesnakepassinn.com; 4D/2Tr, all en suite; ☕; WI-FI but variable; Ⓛ; 🐕 bar and apartments only) charges £42.50-49.50pp (sgl occ £85-90) for **B&B**. They also have four **apartments** (two sleeping up two people from £140, one for four and one for five people); at the time of research they provide basic accommodation but the new owners of the pub plan to upgrade them.

The inn, 2½ miles east down the A57, is full of history and character with a good choice of beer and meals in the bar. **Food** is served (summer Mon-Thur noon-8.30pm, Fri & Sat to 9pm, Sun & bank hols noon-7pm, winter hours may vary) and the bar is generally open from 11am. Of course a detour here means you probably wouldn't make the Torside Valley that night. You can also reach it by taking Snake Path (see Map 4).

TORSIDE [Map 9, p97]

As you descend the Pennine Way from Clough Edge you reach Torside and the B6105 road.

The Old House B&B (☎ 01457-857527, 🖳 oldhouse.torside.co.uk; 2D/1T/1Tr, all en suite; ☕; no WI-FI; Ⓛ), only 500m west up the road, is friendly and a walkers' favourite. Facilities include a drying cupboard. They also have an **annex** which can be let on a **B&B** basis (3Qd – two rooms with double bed and bunk beds, the other just with bunk beds; shared facilities; Ⓛ; 🐕) though it has a microwave, toaster and kettle so walkers can make their own breakfast. B&B costs from £32.50/40pp (sgl occ from £37.50/80) for shared/en suite facilities per night but they also offer a 2-night Pennine Way package (from £52.50/£60pp, sgl occ room rate) with, for example, transport to Edale on the first morning and they will then take your luggage to Standedge, Marsden or Diggle after the second night, though variations are possible. Look at their website for the latest prices. They don't provide evening meals but offer a lift to the Peels Arms (see p98) and will collect up to 9pm (from £3pp; a taxi back after 9pm costs about £10). ***Windy Harbour*** (off Map 9; ☎ 01457-853107, 🖳 windyharbour.co.uk; 5D/1T, all en suite; Ⓛ; 🐕) is two miles along the B6105 en route to Padfield, but if you call or book ahead they'll come and pick you up where the B6105 crosses the trail. For **B&B** they charge from £40pp (sgl occ £50). **Food** is offered (Mon-Sat noon-8.30pm, Sun noon-4pm), or take a 10-min walk to the Peels Arms, see p98).

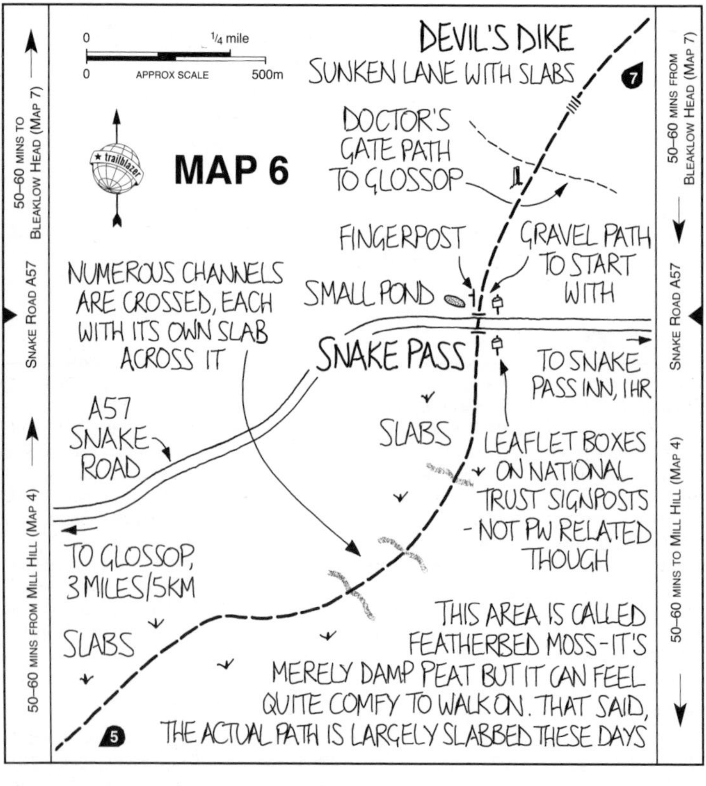
50–60 MINS TO BLEAKLOW HEAD (MAP 7)
SNAKE ROAD A57
50–60 MINS FROM MILL HILL (MAP 4)
0
1/4 mile
0
APPROX SCALE
500m
trailblazer
MAP 6
DEVIL'S DIKE
SUNKEN LANE WITH SLABS
7
DOCTOR'S GATE PATH TO GLOSSOP
FINGERPOST
GRAVEL PATH TO START WITH
NUMEROUS CHANNELS ARE CROSSED, EACH WITH ITS OWN SLAB ACROSS IT
SMALL POND
SNAKE PASS
TO SNAKE PASS INN, 1HR
A57 SNAKE ROAD
SLABS
LEAFLET BOXES ON NATIONAL TRUST SIGNPOSTS - NOT PW RELATED THOUGH
TO GLOSSOP, 3 MILES/5KM
SLABS
THIS AREA IS CALLED FEATHERBED MOSS - IT'S MERELY DAMP PEAT BUT IT CAN FEEL QUITE COMFY TO WALK ON. THAT SAID, THE ACTUAL PATH IS LARGELY SLABBED THESE DAYS
5
50–60 MINS FROM BLEAKLOW HEAD (MAP 7)
SNAKE ROAD A57
50–60 MINS TO MILL HILL (MAP 4)

❑ Important note – walking times

All times in this book refer only to the time spent walking. You will need to add 20-30% to allow for rests, photography, checking the map, drinking water etc.

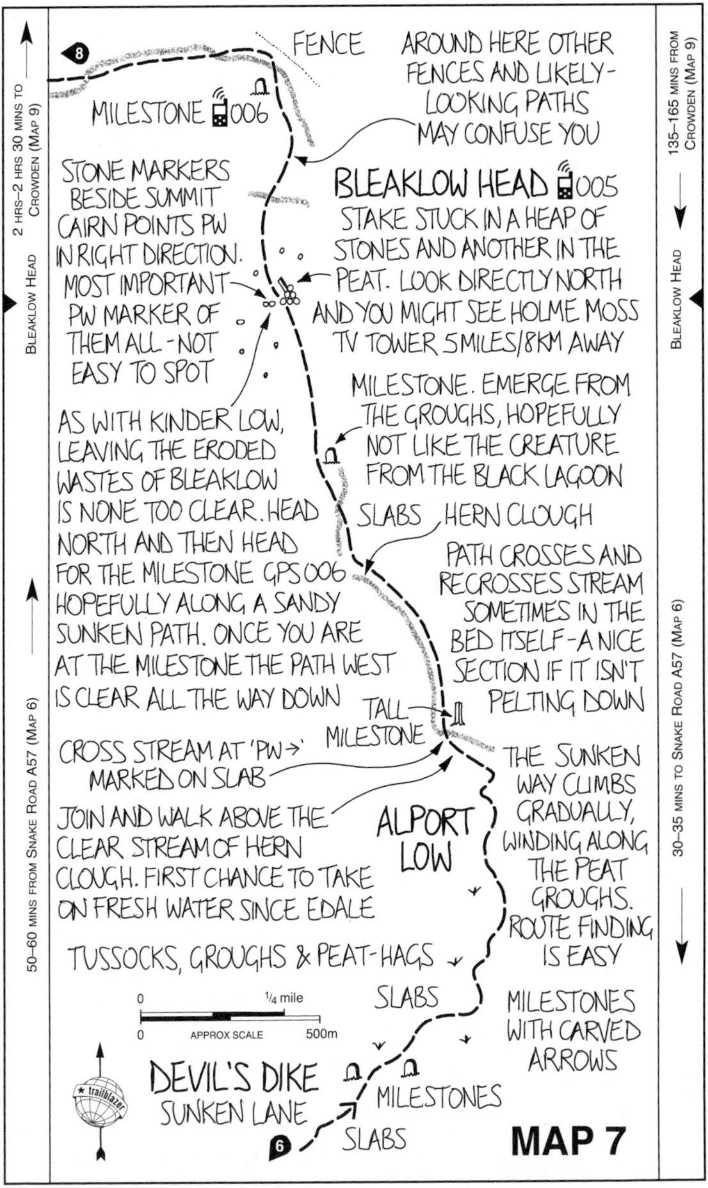
2 HRS–2 HRS 30 MINS TO CROWDEN (MAP 9)
BLEAKLOW HEAD
50–60 MINS FROM SNAKE ROAD A57 (MAP 6)
135–165 MINS FROM CROWDEN (MAP 9)
BLEAKLOW HEAD
30–35 MINS TO SNAKE ROAD A57 (MAP 6)
8
FENCE
AROUND HERE OTHER FENCES AND LIKELY-LOOKING PATHS MAY CONFUSE YOU
MILESTONE 006
STONE MARKERS BESIDE SUMMIT CAIRN POINTS PW IN RIGHT DIRECTION.
MOST IMPORTANT PW MARKER OF THEM ALL - NOT EASY TO SPOT
BLEAKLOW HEAD 005
STAKE STUCK IN A HEAP OF STONES AND ANOTHER IN THE PEAT. LOOK DIRECTLY NORTH AND YOU MIGHT SEE HOLME MOSS TV TOWER 5MILES/8KM AWAY
MILESTONE. EMERGE FROM THE GROUGHS, HOPEFULLY NOT LIKE THE CREATURE FROM THE BLACK LAGOON
AS WITH KINDER LOW, LEAVING THE ERODED WASTES OF BLEAKLOW IS NONE TOO CLEAR. HEAD NORTH AND THEN HEAD FOR THE MILESTONE GPS 006 HOPEFULLY ALONG A SANDY SUNKEN PATH. ONCE YOU ARE AT THE MILESTONE THE PATH WEST IS CLEAR ALL THE WAY DOWN
SLABS
HERN CLOUGH
PATH CROSSES AND RECROSSES STREAM SOMETIMES IN THE BED ITSELF - A NICE SECTION IF IT ISN'T PELTING DOWN
TALL MILESTONE
CROSS STREAM AT 'PW→' MARKED ON SLAB
THE SUNKEN WAY CLIMBS GRADUALLY, WINDING ALONG THE PEAT GROUGHS. ROUTE FINDING IS EASY
JOIN AND WALK ABOVE THE CLEAR STREAM OF HERN CLOUGH. FIRST CHANCE TO TAKE ON FRESH WATER SINCE EDALE
ALPORT LOW
TUSSOCKS, GROUGHS & PEAT-HAGS
SLABS
0
1/4 mile
0
APPROX SCALE
500m
MILESTONES WITH CARVED ARROWS
trailblazer
DEVIL'S DIKE SUNKEN LANE
MILESTONES
6
SLABS
MAP 7

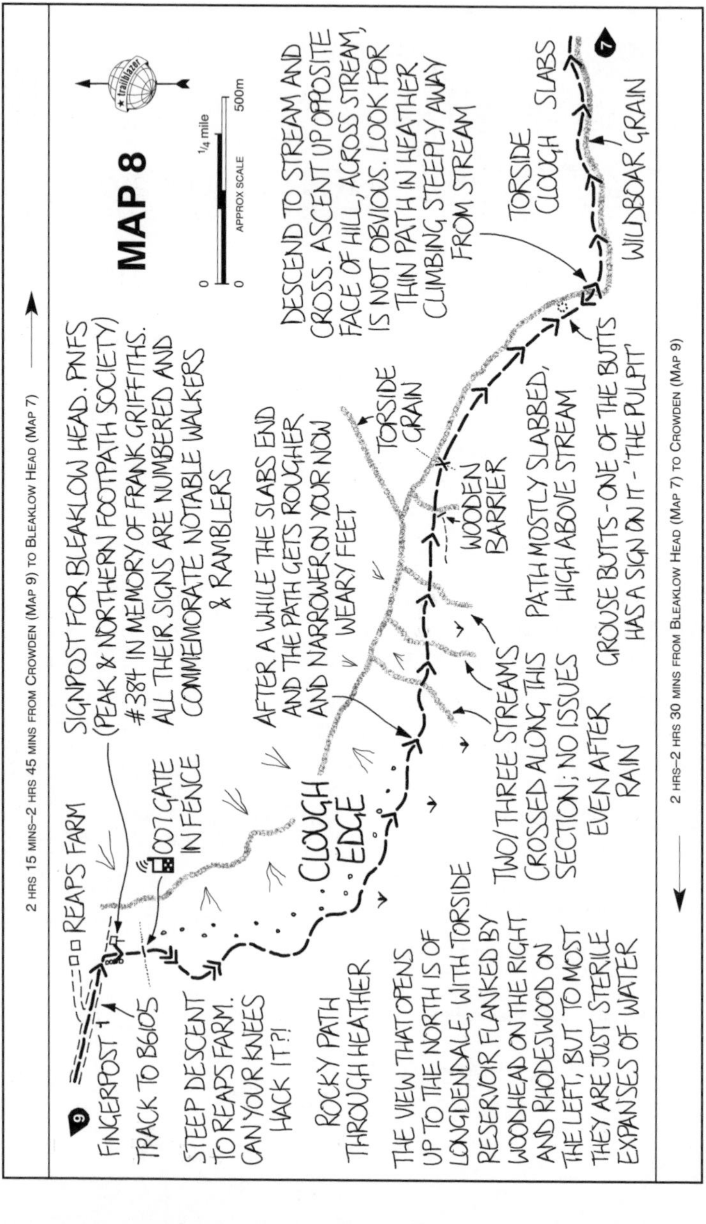

2 HRS 15 MINS–2 HRS 45 MINS FROM CROWDEN (MAP 9) TO BLEAKLOW HEAD (MAP 7)
MAP 8
1/4 mile
500m
APPROX SCALE
0
0
9
FINGERPOST
TRACK TO B6105
REAPS FARM
STEEP DESCENT TO REAPS FARM. CAN YOUR KNEES HACK IT?!
007 GATE IN FENCE
SIGNPOST FOR BLEAKLOW HEAD. PNFS (PEAK & NORTHERN FOOTPATH SOCIETY) #384 IN MEMORY OF FRANK GRIFFITHS. ALL THEIR SIGNS ARE NUMBERED AND COMMEMORATE NOTABLE WALKERS & RAMBLERS
ROCKY PATH THROUGH HEATHER
CLOUGH EDGE
THE VIEW THAT OPENS UP TO THE NORTH IS OF LONGDENDALE, WITH TORSIDE RESERVOIR FLANKED BY WOODHEAD ON THE RIGHT AND RHODESWOOD ON THE LEFT, BUT TO MOST THEY ARE JUST STERILE EXPANSES OF WATER
AFTER A WHILE THE SLABS END AND THE PATH GETS ROUGHER AND NARROWER ON YOUR NOW WEARY FEET
TWO/THREE STREAMS CROSSED ALONG THIS SECTION; NO ISSUES EVEN AFTER RAIN
TORSIDE GRAIN
WOODEN BARRIER
PATH MOSTLY SLABBED, HIGH ABOVE STREAM
GROUSE BUTTS - ONE OF THE BUTTS HAS A SIGN ON IT - 'THE PULPIT'
DESCEND TO STREAM AND CROSS. ASCENT UP OPPOSITE FACE OF HILL, ACROSS STREAM, IS NOT OBVIOUS. LOOK FOR THIN PATH IN HEATHER CLIMBING STEEPLY AWAY FROM STREAM
TORSIDE CLOUGH
SLABS
WILDBOAR GRAIN
7
2 HRS–2 HRS 30 MINS FROM BLEAKLOW HEAD (MAP 7) TO CROWDEN (MAP 9)

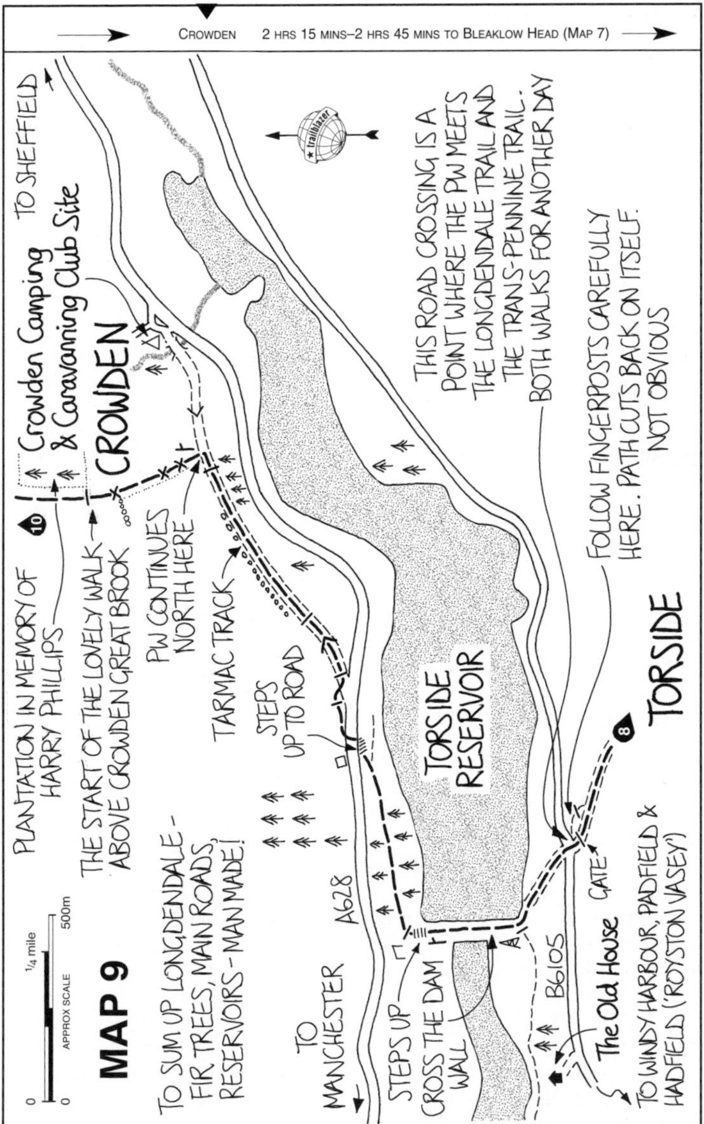

MAP 9
APPROX SCALE
0 1/4 mile
0 500m
Crowden 2 hrs 15 mins–2 hrs 45 mins to Bleaklow Head (Map 7)
Crowden 2 hrs–2 hrs 30 mins from Bleaklow Head (Map 7)
TO SHEFFIELD
Crowden Camping & Caravanning Club Site
CROWDEN
PLANTATION IN MEMORY OF HARRY PHILLIPS
10
THE START OF THE LOVELY WALK ABOVE CROWDEN GREAT BROOK
PW CONTINUES NORTH HERE
TARMAC TRACK
STEPS UP TO ROAD
TO SUM UP LONGDENDALE - FIR TREES, MAIN ROADS, RESERVOIRS - MAN MADE!
A628
TO MANCHESTER
STEPS UP
CROSS THE DAM WALL
TORSIDE RESERVOIR
B6105
The Old House
GATE
TO WINDY HARBOUR, PADFIELD & HADFIELD ('ROYSTON VASEY')
8
TORSIDE
FOLLOW FINGERPOSTS CAREFULLY HERE. PATH CUTS BACK ON ITSELF. NOT OBVIOUS
THIS ROAD CROSSING IS A POINT WHERE THE PW MEETS THE LONGDENDALE TRAIL AND THE TRANS-PENNINE TRAIL. BOTH WALKS FOR ANOTHER DAY

PADFIELD & HADFIELD

[off Map 9, p97]

Padfield is about 2½ miles to the west, adjacent to Hadfield, better known to many as the fictional 'Royston Vasey' from the 1990s TV series *League of Gentlemen*; not a distinction most 'local people' would cherish in reality. Hadfield also has a **railway station** with a frequent service to Manchester Piccadilly operated by Northern Rail (see box p59).

Peels Arms (☎ 01457-852719, 🖳 peelsarms.co.uk; 🐕 back bar only), Temple St, is the best place for a meal (**food** served Mon-Fri noon-2.30pm & 5-9pm, Sat noon-9pm, Sun noon-8pm) and a drink but note that the pub closes in the afternoon during the week. There are good homemade pies and Wainwright beer. Just over the road is ***White House Farm*** (☎ 01457-854695, 🖳 thepennineway.co.uk/whitehousefarm; 2T en suite/1D private bathroom; ▼; Ⓛ; 🐕) with B&B from £30pp (sgl occ £40).

A little closer to Hadfield railway station, about 3 miles/5km from Torside and easily accessible from the Longdendale Trail you may have used to reach Hadfield from Crowden, is ***Hikers & Bikers*** (☎ 07973-376124; 3T, all en suite; ▼; WI-FI), at 105 Station Rd. A bed costs from £26.50pp (sgl occ from £32); breakfast is available at ***Leah's at 105*** (☎ 07903-257196; Mon-Fri 7am-2pm, Sat & Sun 9am-1pm; 🐕) downstairs.

CROWDEN [Map 9, p97]

For some years Crowden was synonymous with the YHA hostel but this is no longer the case if you're walking the Pennine Way as it has closed; the site is now an Outdoor Education Centre.

The only option is **camping** at ***Crowden Camping and Caravanning Club Site*** (☎ 01457-866057, 🖳 campingandcaravanningclub.co.uk; 45 pitches; 🐕; late Mar/early Apr to early Nov), on Woodhead Rd, with good facilities including a shop, laundry facilities and a drying room. They charge from £6.20pp for non members; booking is advised. Note that there is a two-night minimum stay during the summer high season.

The only public transport service is the National Express **coach** (No 350), see box p53.

CROWDEN TO STANDEDGE — MAPS 9-15

Route overview

11 miles (17.5km) – 2300ft (701m) of ascent – 5-6¼ hours

Another classic Peak District walk awaits, with a mixture of remote moorland and reservoir access roads, wide views and plenty of hills. There is a similar amount of height gain as yesterday, so this stage is no pushover.

The day starts with a series of short climbs taking you away from Torside and up to the gritstone outcrops of **Laddow Rocks** (Map 10). Almost half the day's total ascent is in these first three miles or so, but the height gain pays dividends, weather permitting, with outstanding views all around. Keep one eye on the path though, for it is one of the only exposed stretches on the Pennine Way, with a sharp drop off down to your right. This high-level path soon drops to meet **Crowden Great Brook** (Maps 10-11), where wild campers will find an excellent wide flat pitch, before a long, gentle climb (on slabs now), up to the recently transformed **Black Hill** (Map 12). No longer a barren, black wasteland of peat bog, it is now green and lush thanks to much replanting and sheep control (see box p87).

(cont'd on p103)

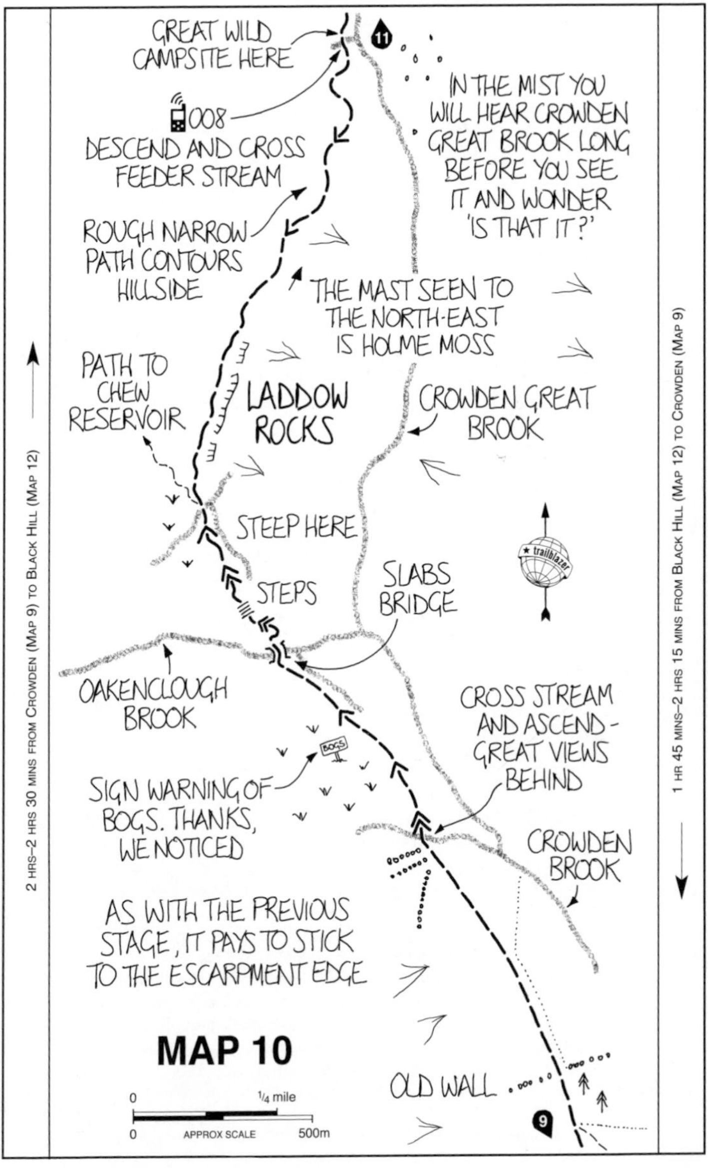
GREAT WILD CAMPSITE HERE
008
DESCEND AND CROSS FEEDER STREAM
IN THE MIST YOU WILL HEAR CROWDEN GREAT BROOK LONG BEFORE YOU SEE IT AND WONDER 'IS THAT IT?'
ROUGH NARROW PATH CONTOURS HILLSIDE
THE MAST SEEN TO THE NORTH-EAST IS HOLME MOSS
PATH TO CHEW RESERVOIR
LADDOW ROCKS
CROWDEN GREAT BROOK
STEEP HERE
STEPS
SLABS BRIDGE
trailblazer
OAKENCLOUGH BROOK
CROSS STREAM AND ASCEND - GREAT VIEWS BEHIND
BOGS
SIGN WARNING OF BOGS. THANKS, WE NOTICED
CROWDEN BROOK
AS WITH THE PREVIOUS STAGE, IT PAYS TO STICK TO THE ESCARPMENT EDGE
MAP 10
OLD WALL
0
1/4 mile
0
APPROX SCALE
500m
2 HRS–2 HRS 30 MINS FROM CROWDEN (MAP 9) TO BLACK HILL (MAP 12)
1 HR 45 MINS–2 HRS 15 MINS FROM BLACK HILL (MAP 12) TO CROWDEN (MAP 9)

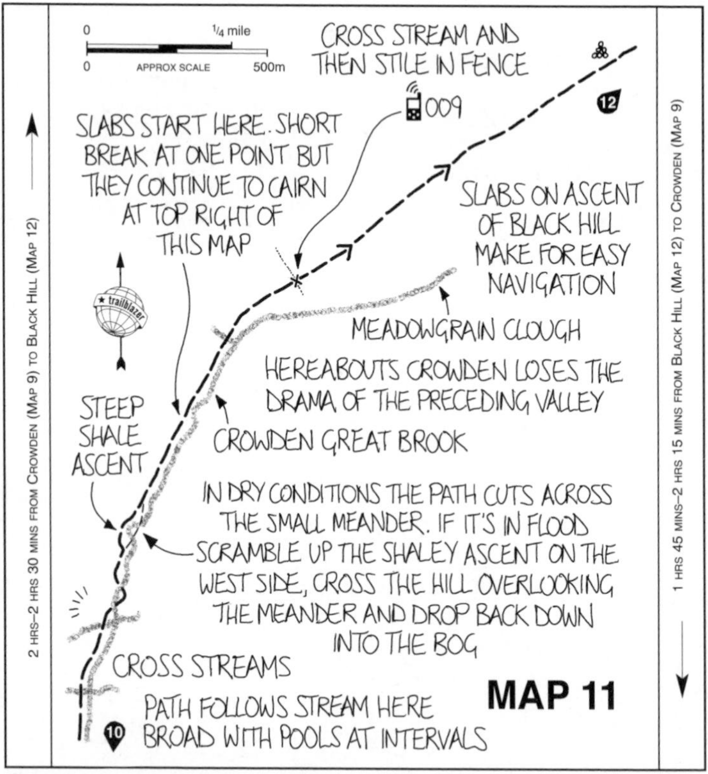

0 ¼ mile
0 APPROX SCALE 500m
CROSS STREAM AND THEN STILE IN FENCE
009
12
SLABS START HERE. SHORT BREAK AT ONE POINT BUT THEY CONTINUE TO CAIRN AT TOP RIGHT OF THIS MAP
SLABS ON ASCENT OF BLACK HILL MAKE FOR EASY NAVIGATION
trailblazer
MEADOWGRAIN CLOUGH
HEREABOUTS CROWDEN LOSES THE DRAMA OF THE PRECEDING VALLEY
STEEP SHALE ASCENT
CROWDEN GREAT BROOK
IN DRY CONDITIONS THE PATH CUTS ACROSS THE SMALL MEANDER. IF IT'S IN FLOOD SCRAMBLE UP THE SHALEY ASCENT ON THE WEST SIDE, CROSS THE HILL OVERLOOKING THE MEANDER AND DROP BACK DOWN INTO THE BOG
CROSS STREAMS
MAP 11
PATH FOLLOWS STREAM HERE BROAD WITH POOLS AT INTERVALS
10
2 HRS–2 HRS 30 MINS FROM CROWDEN (MAP 9) TO BLACK HILL (MAP 12)
1 HRS 45 MINS–2 HRS 15 MINS FROM BLACK HILL (MAP 12) TO CROWDEN (MAP 9)

❑ Emley Moor Transmitter Mast **[off Map 12]**

At 1084ft (330m), Emley Moor Mast is the tallest free-standing structure in the UK and can be seen clearly for much of the second day along the Pennine Way, assuming the mist isn't down! As you stand on the summit of Black Hill the beautifully tapered concrete structure is over 10 miles distant; because of its 'significant architectural or historic interest' it was granted Grade II Listed status in 2003. The mast transmits radio and TV signals to millions of people across the north of England.

On the bitterly cold and windy evening of 19th March 1969 a build-up of ice and snow on top of the tower that stood there at the time, caused the guide wires to fail and the cylindrical steel structure buckled and collapsed, partially destroying the nearby Emley Moor Methodist Chapel and missing the local school bus by just a few minutes. Miraculously no-one was seriously injured. A temporary mast was quickly raised and the tower seen today was built over the next couple of years, this time out of concrete instead of steel.

In 2018 it was announced that over the next five years a new tower will be built beside the current one.

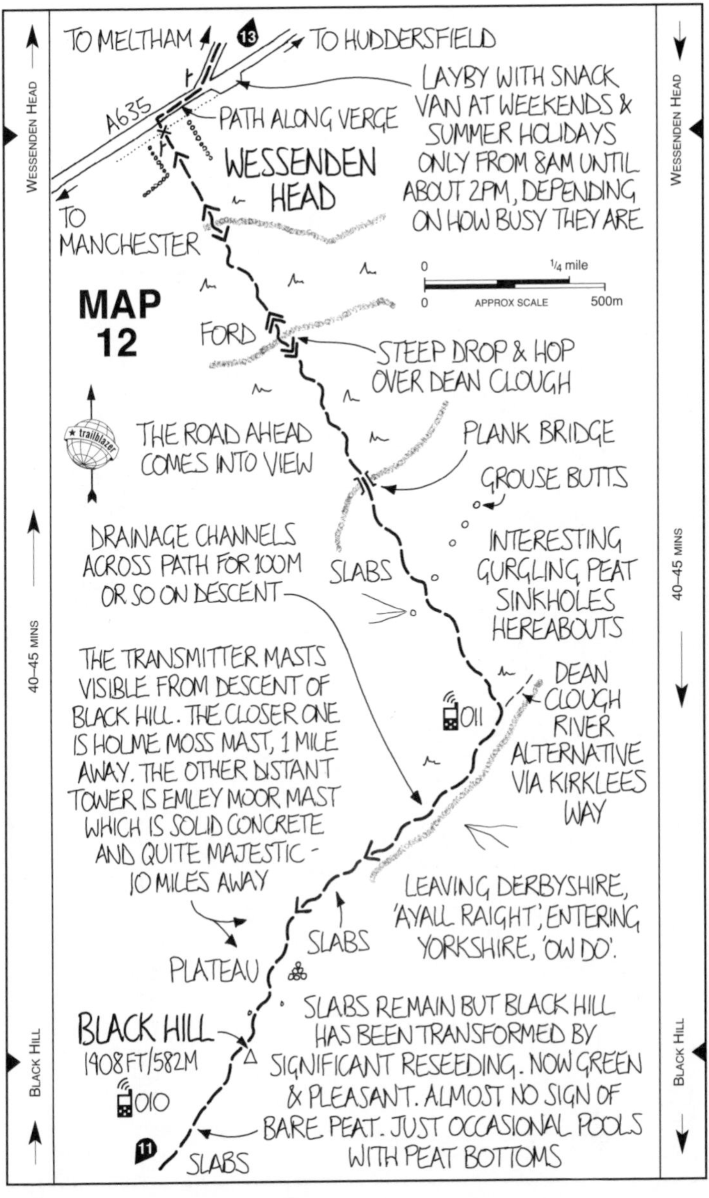
TO MELTHAM
13
TO HUDDERSFIELD
A635
LAYBY WITH SNACK VAN AT WEEKENDS & SUMMER HOLIDAYS ONLY FROM 8AM UNTIL ABOUT 2PM, DEPENDING ON HOW BUSY THEY ARE
PATH ALONG VERGE
WESSENDEN HEAD
TO MANCHESTER
0 1/4 mile
0 APPROX SCALE 500m
MAP 12
FORD
STEEP DROP & HOP OVER DEAN CLOUGH
trailblazer
THE ROAD AHEAD COMES INTO VIEW
PLANK BRIDGE
GROUSE BUTTS
DRAINAGE CHANNELS ACROSS PATH FOR 100M OR SO ON DESCENT
SLABS
INTERESTING GURGLING PEAT SINKHOLES HEREABOUTS
THE TRANSMITTER MASTS VISIBLE FROM DESCENT OF BLACK HILL. THE CLOSER ONE IS HOLME MOSS MAST, 1 MILE AWAY. THE OTHER DISTANT TOWER IS EMLEY MOOR MAST WHICH IS SOLID CONCRETE AND QUITE MAJESTIC - 10 MILES AWAY
011
DEAN CLOUGH RIVER
ALTERNATIVE VIA KIRKLEES WAY
LEAVING DERBYSHIRE, 'AYALL RAIGHT'; ENTERING YORKSHIRE, 'OW DO'.
SLABS
PLATEAU
BLACK HILL 1908FT/582M
SLABS REMAIN BUT BLACK HILL HAS BEEN TRANSFORMED BY SIGNIFICANT RESEEDING. NOW GREEN & PLEASANT. ALMOST NO SIGN OF BARE PEAT. JUST OCCASIONAL POOLS WITH PEAT BOTTOMS
010
11
SLABS
WESSENDEN HEAD
40–45 MINS
BLACK HILL
WESSENDEN HEAD
40–45 MINS
BLACK HILL

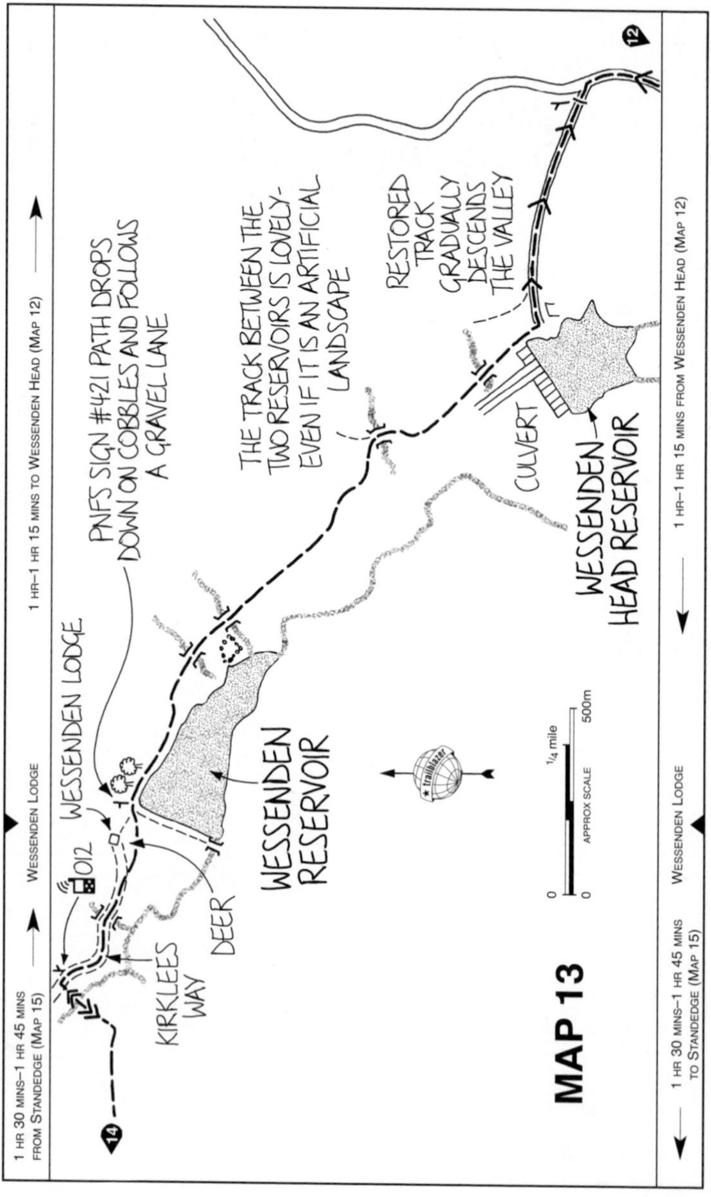

1 HR 30 MINS–1 HR 45 MINS FROM STANDEDGE (MAP 15)
WESSENDEN LODGE
1 HR–1 HR 15 MINS TO WESSENDEN HEAD (MAP 12)
WESSENDEN LODGE
0121
PNFS SIGN #421 PATH DROPS DOWN ON COBBLES AND FOLLOWS A GRAVEL LANE
THE TRACK BETWEEN THE TWO RESERVOIRS IS LOVELY- EVEN IF IT IS AN ARTIFICIAL LANDSCAPE
RESTORED TRACK GRADUALLY DESCENDS THE VALLEY
KIRKLEES WAY
DEER
WESSENDEN RESERVOIR
CULVERT
WESSENDEN HEAD RESERVOIR
MAP 13
0
1/4 mile
0
500m
APPROX SCALE
trailblazer
1 HR 30 MINS–1 HR 45 MINS TO STANDEDGE (MAP 15)
WESSENDEN LODGE
1 HR–1 HR 15 MINS FROM WESSENDEN HEAD (MAP 12)

(cont'd from p98) Dropping down from Black Hill you may see the majestic spire of Emley Moor Mast on the far horizon (see box on p100) and the much-closer Holme Moss Mast across the moor, before meeting the A635; if you've arrived on a weekend morning there may even be a van doing a roaring trade in bacon butties and tea. Sit with your back to the road and admire the hills behind, because ahead the Way follows a series of access roads, linking together a string of reservoirs.

Although not completely devoid of scenic value this man-made landscape feels harsh in comparison to the natural, remote beauty of Kinder and Bleaklow. Once you pass beyond **Wessenden Head**, and the **Wessenden reservoirs** (Map 13) you at least return to moorland. A lovely track takes you between **Swellands and Black Moss reservoirs** (Map 14) and down to **Redbrook Reservoir** (Map 15) and the goal for the day, the **Standedge Cutting** at Brun Clough Reservoir car park on the A62. Unless you have arranged for a lift you are likely to have to continue walking till you reach your accommodation for the night. The walking is fairly unstrenuous, though the midges can be relentless near the reservoirs.

Navigation notes

Thanks to the good path out of Crowden and the judicious use of slabs across the worst sections of bogs, this stage has surprisingly few navigational challenges. The only possible area of confusion may arise if you are forced, by particularly heavy rain, to navigate around the flooded meander of Crowden Great Brook (Map 11). In which case the river should be easy to see and follow until you reach the slabs at GPS 009.

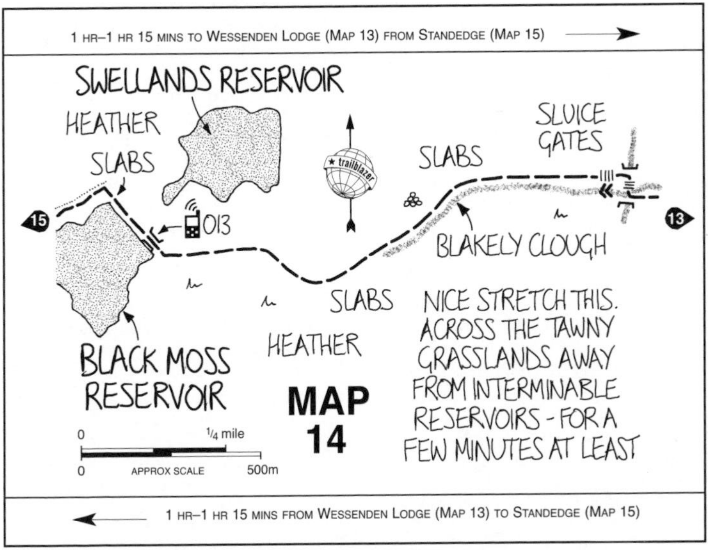
1 HR–1 HR 15 MINS TO WESSENDEN LODGE (MAP 13) FROM STANDEDGE (MAP 15)
SWELLANDS RESERVOIR
HEATHER
SLABS
SLUICE GATES
SLABS
trailblazer
013
15
13
BLAKELY CLOUGH
SLABS
NICE STRETCH THIS. ACROSS THE TAWNY GRASSLANDS AWAY FROM INTERMINABLE RESERVOIRS - FOR A FEW MINUTES AT LEAST
HEATHER
BLACK MOSS RESERVOIR
MAP 14
0
1/4 mile
0
APPROX SCALE
500m
1 HR–1 HR 15 MINS FROM WESSENDEN LODGE (MAP 13) TO STANDEDGE (MAP 15)

STANDEDGE [Map 15]

Arriving on the busy A62 at Standedge, the prospect of a bed does not look too promising. The area here is called Standedge but **Standedge Cutting** refers to where the Rochdale Canal, and road and railway tunnels have been carved through the Pennines.

The Carriage House (☎ 01484-844419, 🖳 thecarriage-house.co.uk; no WI-FI; Ⓛ; 🐕 bar and campers only), on the road towards Marsden, offers **camping** for £5pp with bath/shower (50p) and toilet facilities. If booked in advance and they have B&B guests they can provide breakfast for campers; they will also do basic food shopping. **B&B** (2S/3D/2Tr, all en suite; ▼) costs from £40pp (sgl/sgl occ from £50). The pub specialises in Turkish **food** but they also have a full pub menu (food served Mon, Wed & Thur 5.30-8.30pm, Fri noon-9pm, Sat noon-9.30pm, Sun noon-8pm). The pub is often closed on Tuesdays throughout the year but campers can still camp.

First's No 184 **bus** service passes through Standedge (and Marsden; see below) regularly; see pp54-9.

MARSDEN [off Map 15]

If you prefer to go to Marsden where there are more services, short of waiting for First's No 184 bus service (see pp54-9), the quickest way (two miles) is to take the Standedge Trail eastwards from the southern end of Redbrook Reservoir (Map 15).

Marsden has a Co-op **supermarket** (daily 7am-11pm) with an **ATM**, some B&B accommodation, a chip shop, some cafés and a restaurant. Pennine Wayfarers suffering from sore feet already may find relief at **Mountain Feet** (☎ 01484-842144, 🖳 mountainfeet.com; Tue, Wed & Fri 10am-5.30pm, Thur to 8pm); they specialise in foot function and expert footwear fitting and they can also sometimes fix boots bought elsewhere. All the services are within five minutes of the **railway station** (Marsden is on Northern Rail's Manchester–Huddersfield line) and, of course, First's **bus** service No 184; see pp54-9.

At the end of Manchester Rd, the main street leading away from the station, but close to the town's facilities, is ***The New Inn*** (☎ 01484-841917, 🖳 newinnmarsden.co.uk; 4D/2Qd, all en suite; ▼; Ⓛ; 🐕); **B&B** costs £37.50-44.50pp (sgl occ £45-69). **Food** is served Mon-Fri noon-2.30pm & 5-9pm, Sat, Sun & Bank Hols 8.30am-8pm. The menu may include a minted lamb mince pie with chips, mushy peas & gravy (£9.95), and their fixed-price lunch menu (£6.95/9.95 for 1/2 courses) is great value.

Olive Branch Inn (☎ 01484-844487, 🖳 olivebranch.uk.com), on the main Manchester Rd, has a mouthwatering menu (**food** served Tue-Thur 6.30-9pm, Fri 6.30-9.30pm, Sat 1-9.30pm, Sun 1-8pm) of seafood, game and poultry; a fixed price menu (two courses with wine £18) is available up to 8pm (Mon-Sat only). **B&B** (3D, all en suite; ▼; WI-FI) costs from £45pp (sgl occ £70); they also do a dinner, bed & breakfast deal (from £85pp) and there are some good last-minute deals too – see the website for details.

DIGGLE [Map 15]

On the outskirts of Diggle about 1½ miles south-west of the Pennine Way (all steeply downhill) is ***New Barn*** (☎ 01457-873937, 🖳 andrhodes1@btinternet.com; 1S/1T/1Tr shared facilities/1D en suite; ▼; Ⓛ; 🐕 but in stables only), Harrop Green Lane, which

ROUTE GUIDE AND MAPS

❑ Where to stay: the details

▼ means at least one room has a bath; Ⓛ signifies that a packed lunch is available if requested in advance; 🐕 signifies that dogs are welcome in at least one room but always by prior arrangement. A charge may also be payable (see also pp282-3).

WI-FI is available at most places but see p82.

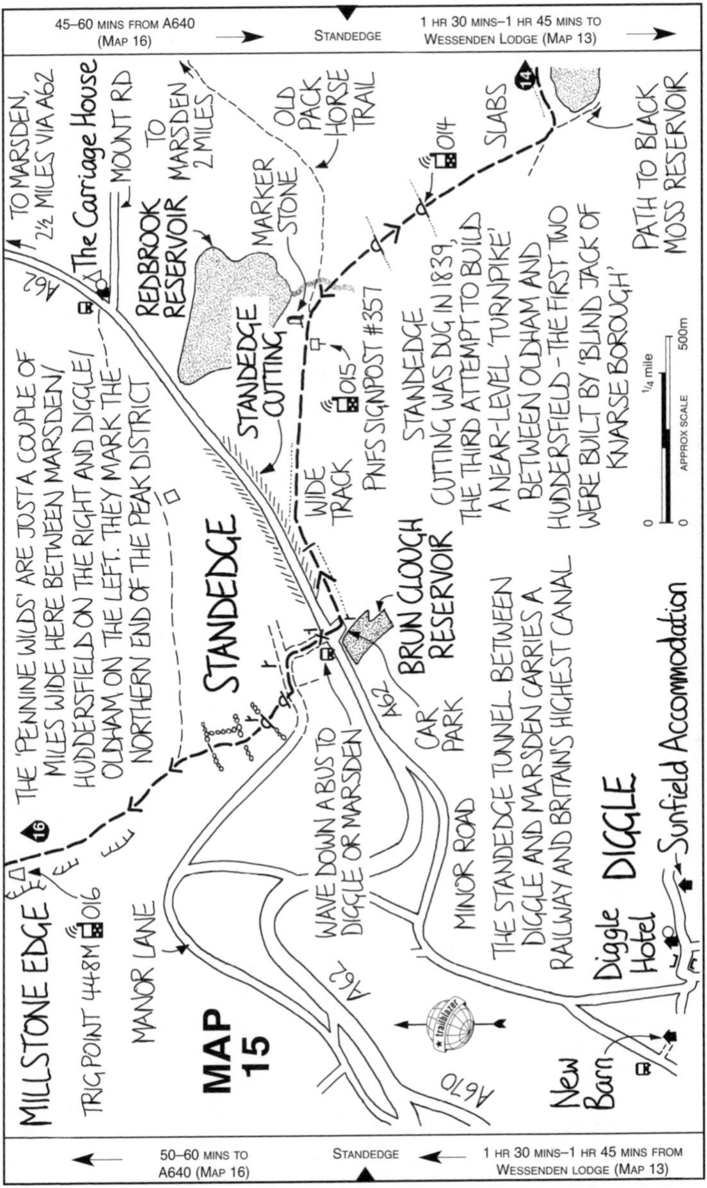
45–60 MINS FROM A640 (MAP 16)
STANDEDGE
1 HR 30 MINS–1 HR 45 MINS TO WESSENDEN LODGE (MAP 13)
MAP 15
MILLSTONE EDGE
TRIG POINT 448M 016
16
MANOR LANE
A62
A670
THE 'PENNINE WILDS' ARE JUST A COUPLE OF MILES WIDE HERE BETWEEN MARSDEN/ HUDDERSFIELD ON THE RIGHT AND DIGGLE/ OLDHAM ON THE LEFT. THEY MARK THE NORTHERN END OF THE PEAK DISTRICT
STANDEDGE
WAVE DOWN A BUS TO DIGGLE OR MARSDEN
MINOR ROAD
CAR PARK
BRUN CLOUGH RESERVOIR
THE STANDEDGE TUNNEL BETWEEN DIGGLE AND MARSDEN CARRIES A RAILWAY AND BRITAIN'S HIGHEST CANAL
DIGGLE
Diggle Hotel
Sunfield Accommodation
New Barn
STANDEDGE CUTTING
WIDE TRACK
015
PNFS SIGNPOST #357
STANDEDGE CUTTING WAS DUG IN 1839, THE THIRD ATTEMPT TO BUILD A NEAR-LEVEL 'TURNPIKE' BETWEEN OLDHAM AND HUDDERSFIELD - THE FIRST TWO WERE BUILT BY 'BLIND JACK OF KNARSE BOROUGH'
0 1/4 mile
0 APPROX SCALE 500m
TO MARSDEN, 2½ MILES VIA A62
The Carriage House
MOUNT RD
REDBROOK RESERVOIR
TO MARSDEN 2 MILES
MARKER STONE
OLD PACK HORSE TRAIL
014
SLABS
14
PATH TO BLACK MOSS RESERVOIR
50–60 MINS TO A640 (MAP 16)
STANDEDGE
1 HR 30 MINS–1 HR 45 MINS FROM WESSENDEN LODGE (MAP 13)

[**Diggle** *cont'd*] charges from £35pp (sgl/sgl occ £35/38) for **B&B**. They have drying facilities. You can take First's No 184 **bus** (see pp54-9) from the stop opposite back up to the Way next morning.

Down in Diggle why not treat yourself at ***Diggle Hotel*** (☎ 01457-872741, 🖳 www.gigglehotel.co.uk; 2T/1D/1Qd, all en suite; Ⓛ), a family-run free house (Mon bar only from 5pm; **food** served Tue-Thur noon-8pm, Fri & Sat to 9pm, Sun to 7pm) with several real ales. Look out on the menu for rag pudding (a local speciality of mince and onions wrapped in suet pastry) with chips, mushy peas & gravy (£10.95). Rooms are also available here from £40pp (sgl occ £45-50), with breakfast an extra £8.95.

Sunfield Accommodation (☎ 01457-874030, 🖳 sunfieldaccom.co.uk; 5D/1T, all en suite; Ⓛ), to the east of Diggle Hotel, charges from £32.50pp (sgl occ £40). They can offer a lift back to the trail the next morning if required and packed lunches must be requested at the time of booking.

STANDEDGE TO CALDER VALLEY — MAPS 15-22

Route overview

14½ miles (23.5km) – 1400ft (426m) of ascent – 5¾-7½ hours

This section is punctuated by road crossings and trig points – four of the former and three of the latter – with a huge monolith of a monument at Stoodley Pike to round off the day. The path almost completely loses the sense of remoteness you'll have been experiencing so far and the conurbations of Lancashire and Yorkshire squeeze the Pennine Way into a narrow corridor, almost smothering it in the process. The walk planners have done all they can to avoid urban walking, however, so this day still retains some scenic highpoints.

Millstone Edge (Map 15) is the first of several gritstone edges you'll need to traverse. The Pennine Way is joined for a while by the Oldham Way (Map 16) before they part company and you reach the **A640 road** between Huddersfield and Oldham/Manchester.

The high, airy path across **White Hill** (Map 17) with its trig point is soon interrupted by the A672, where there may be a ***tea (snack) van***, and then almost immediately beyond that, the soaring arch of the bridge across the **M62 Trans-Pennine Motorway**. The 65ft (20m) high bridge is perhaps the most impressive motorway crossing of any footpath in the country. Thank the foresight of Ernest Marples, the Transport Minister at the time and a keen walker, for its existence.

The crossing of the peaty expanse of **Redmires** (Map 18) has been tamed by the slabs and the climb up to the gritstone splendour of **Blackstone Edge** and its trig point is now much easier. The modern concrete guide marker stands in stark contrast to the ancient **Aiggin Stone** just beyond, which has been guiding travellers for over 600 years and the road you join for a few short yards is thought to be even older, possibly even as old as the Romans. Arriving at ***The White House*** (see p110) marks the end of the moorland scenery. It's rare that a pub pops up so opportunely so make the most of this former packhorse inn. **Wild campers** will find a good pitch in the disused quarry just before the pub and another, about a mile beyond it, in another quarry on Light Hazzles Edge.

The pretence of remoteness that you may have shrouded yourself in all day is gone, as you walk along a wide gravel track beside three reservoirs. As you round the corner at the end of the last of these, Stoodley Pike comes into view, still some two miles (3km) distant along a fine path over the charming **Coldwell**

Hill (Map 20). Before reaching the monument you'll pass **Withen's Gate**, which is the point at which anyone destined for **Mankinholes** (see p110) should turn left, or continue on to **Stoodley Pike** (Map 21, see box p114), an impressive stone monolith. The path now drops steadily and steeply in places, from the

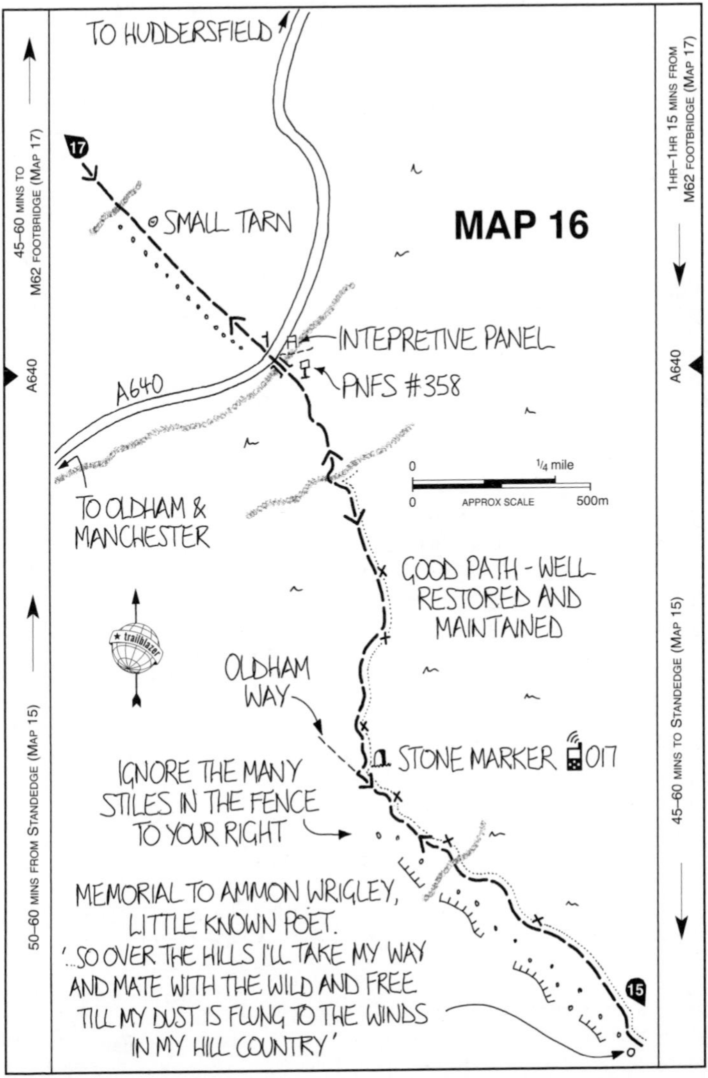
TO HUDDERSFIELD
45–60 MINS TO M62 FOOTBRIDGE (MAP 17)
1HR–1HR 15 MINS FROM M62 FOOTBRIDGE (MAP 17)
17
SMALL TARN
MAP 16
INTEPRETIVE PANEL
A640
A640
A640
PNFS #358
0
¼ mile
0
APPROX SCALE
500m
TO OLDHAM & MANCHESTER
GOOD PATH - WELL RESTORED AND MAINTAINED
OLDHAM WAY
STONE MARKER 017
IGNORE THE MANY STILES IN THE FENCE TO YOUR RIGHT
50–60 MINS FROM STANDEDGE (MAP 15)
45–60 MINS TO STANDEDGE (MAP 15)
MEMORIAL TO AMMON WRIGLEY, LITTLE KNOWN POET.
'...SO OVER THE HILLS I'LL TAKE MY WAY
AND MATE WITH THE WILD AND FREE
TILL MY DUST IS FLUNG TO THE WINDS
IN MY HILL COUNTRY'
15

open moor, through fields to meet a wide farm track. This in turn winds downhill though **Callis Wood** into the **Calder Valley** and towards **Rochdale Canal**.

If your accommodation lies in Hebden Bridge you have another couple of miles as the path turns right along the canal into the town. You can break this canal walk at ***The Stubbing Wharf*** (see p118) before arriving in the slightly eccentric and wonderfully lively town of **Hebden Bridge** (Map 22a).

Navigation notes

There is little chance of going astray; even in winter-white-out conditions the path is obvious and mostly well signed. Blackstone Edge may be the only exception, but provided you stay high, the cairns and stakes should see you through to Aiggin Stone.

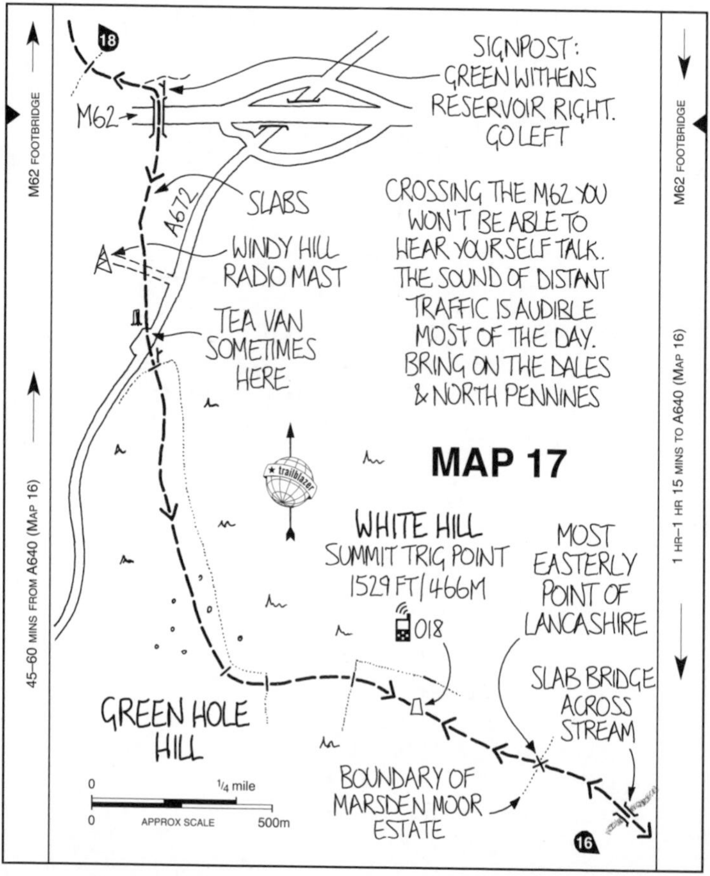

M62 FOOTBRIDGE
45–60 MINS FROM A640 (MAP 16)
M62 FOOTBRIDGE
1 HR–1 HR 15 MINS TO A640 (MAP 16)
18
SIGNPOST: GREEN WITHENS RESERVOIR RIGHT. GO LEFT
M62
A672
SLABS
WINDY HILL RADIO MAST
TEA VAN SOMETIMES HERE
CROSSING THE M62 YOU WON'T BE ABLE TO HEAR YOURSELF TALK. THE SOUND OF DISTANT TRAFFIC IS AUDIBLE MOST OF THE DAY. BRING ON THE DALES & NORTH PENNINES
trailblazer
MAP 17
WHITE HILL
SUMMIT TRIG POINT 1529 FT/466M
018
MOST EASTERLY POINT OF LANCASHIRE
SLAB BRIDGE ACROSS STREAM
GREEN HOLE HILL
BOUNDARY OF MARSDEN MOOR ESTATE
0 1/4 mile
0 APPROX SCALE 500m
16

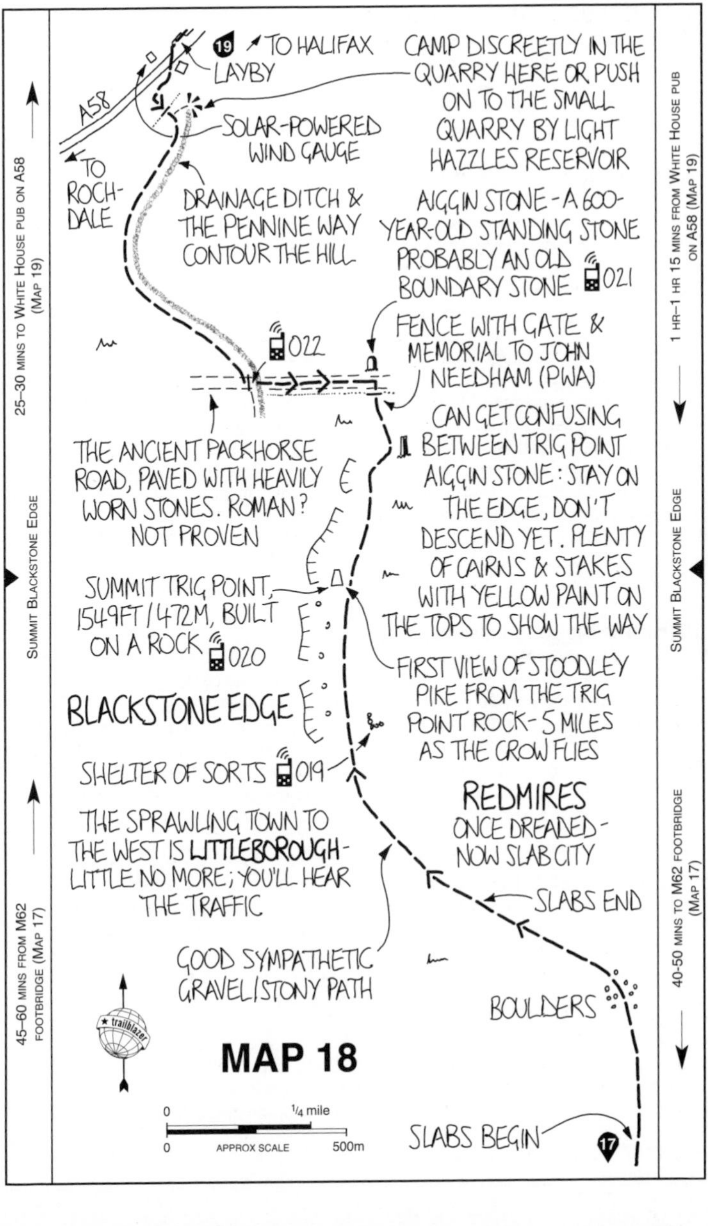
25–30 MINS TO WHITE HOUSE PUB ON A58 (MAP 19)
SUMMIT BLACKSTONE EDGE
45–60 MINS FROM M62 FOOTBRIDGE (MAP 17)
1 HR–1 HR 15 MINS FROM WHITE HOUSE PUB ON A58 (MAP 19)
SUMMIT BLACKSTONE EDGE
40-50 MINS TO M62 FOOTBRIDGE (MAP 17)
19
TO HALIFAX
A58
LAYBY
TO ROCHDALE
CAMP DISCREETLY IN THE QUARRY HERE OR PUSH ON TO THE SMALL QUARRY BY LIGHT HAZZLES RESERVOIR
SOLAR-POWERED WIND GAUGE
DRAINAGE DITCH & THE PENNINE WAY CONTOUR THE HILL
AIGGIN STONE - A 600-YEAR-OLD STANDING STONE PROBABLY AN OLD BOUNDARY STONE 021
022
FENCE WITH GATE & MEMORIAL TO JOHN NEEDHAM (PWA)
THE ANCIENT PACKHORSE ROAD, PAVED WITH HEAVILY WORN STONES. ROMAN? NOT PROVEN
CAN GET CONFUSING BETWEEN TRIG POINT AIGGIN STONE: STAY ON THE EDGE, DON'T DESCEND YET. PLENTY OF CAIRNS & STAKES WITH YELLOW PAINT ON THE TOPS TO SHOW THE WAY
SUMMIT TRIG POINT, 1549FT/472M, BUILT ON A ROCK 020
BLACKSTONE EDGE
FIRST VIEW OF STOODLEY PIKE FROM THE TRIG POINT ROCK - 5 MILES AS THE CROW FLIES
SHELTER OF SORTS 019
REDMIRES
ONCE DREADED - NOW SLAB CITY
THE SPRAWLING TOWN TO THE WEST IS LITTLEBOROUGH - LITTLE NO MORE; YOU'LL HEAR THE TRAFFIC
SLABS END
GOOD SYMPATHETIC GRAVEL/STONY PATH
BOULDERS
trailblazer
MAP 18
0
1/4 mile
0
APPROX SCALE
500m
SLABS BEGIN
17

BLACKSTONE EDGE [Map 19]

The White House (☎ 01706-378456, 🖳 thewhitehousepub.co.uk; **food** served Mon-Sat noon-2pm & 6.30-9.30pm, Sun & bank hols noon-9pm; no 🐕) is a perfectly serviceable place for a pint or a meal – however, note that it closes between 2.30pm and 6.30pm on Monday to Saturday.

TLC Travel's No 901 **bus** service (see pp54-9) calls by the pub en route between Huddersfield and Hebden Bridge.

MANKINHOLES [Map 20, p112]

Unless you're content to curl up in a curlew's nest, the only accommodation between Standedge and the Calder Valley is in Mankinholes. It means a diversion off the route and unless you retrace your steps to Withen's Gate to rejoin the trail proper, you'll have missed out part of the Pennine Way and the resultant guilt could torment you for eternity.

Most walkers continue down to the Calder Valley but unless you haul on up the other side, the bright lights of Hebden Bridge also require a diversion of a mile or two. The traditional ***YHA Mankinholes*** (☎ 0345-371 9751, 🖳 yha.org.uk/hostel/mankinholes; 1 x 6-bed room en suite, 2 x 2-, 4 x 4-, 1 x 6-bed rooms share facilities; no WI-FI; Mar-early Nov) is an old manor house charging from £15pp for a dorm bed and from £25 for a private room. Check in is from 5pm. It has a drying room and a basic food shop but does not provide meals so you'll have to cook your own or go to ***The Top Brink Inn*** (☎ 01706-812696, 🖳 topbrink.com; 🐕; **food** served Apr-Sep daily noon-9.30pm, rest of year Mon-Fri noon-2.30pm & 5-9.30pm, Sat, Sun & Bank Holidays noon-9.30pm) in **Lumbutts**. The menu includes mixed grill (£17.95), cumberland sausage & mash (£8.50) and a range of vegetarian dishes. Note that the pub closes in the afternoon during the week in the winter months.

TLC Travel's T6/T8 **bus** operates between here and Todmorden; see pp54-9.

TODMORDEN [off Map 20, p112]

If you are short of cash or need some retail therapy, Todmorden (or simply 'Tod' to locals; 🖳 visittodmorden.co.uk) provides **shops**, **supermarkets**, **pubs**, **restaurants** and **ATMs**. TLC Travel's T6/T8 **bus** and First's No 589, 590 & 592 call here. It is also a stop on various **railway** services operated by Northern (see p59).

For **B&B**, try ***Two Hoots Cottage Guest House*** (☎ 07792-447356, 🖳 twohootsguesthouse.co.uk; 1D or T private bathroom; ☕; Ⓛ) on Lee Bottom Rd, about a mile away from Stoodley Pike. The smart room costs from £40pp (sgl occ £45). If requested in advance evening meals are available for around £15 for two courses.

❑ The Hebden Bridge Loop

If you're visiting Hebden Bridge for any reason (and we strongly advise that you do), you can take a short-cut from the Pennine Way shortly after Lower Rough Head Farm. This is actually part of the Hebden Bridge Loop, a walk that was established by the Hebden Bridge Walkers Action to coincide with the 50th anniversary of the Pennine Way. The loop is 6km (3¾ miles) long and adds an extra 2km to the direct route. To return to the national trail purists will want to retrace their steps back to the point where they left it; but those who are more relaxed about such things may instead prefer to follow the Loop north to Hebden Bridge and return to the trail at Hebble Hole, taking in the rather lovely village of **Heptonstall,** where there are some pubs that serve food, on the way. The places where the Loop meets the Pennine Way are marked on maps 21 and 23. You can read more about the Loop (including a route guide and map) by visiting 🖳 hebdenbridgeloop.org.uk.

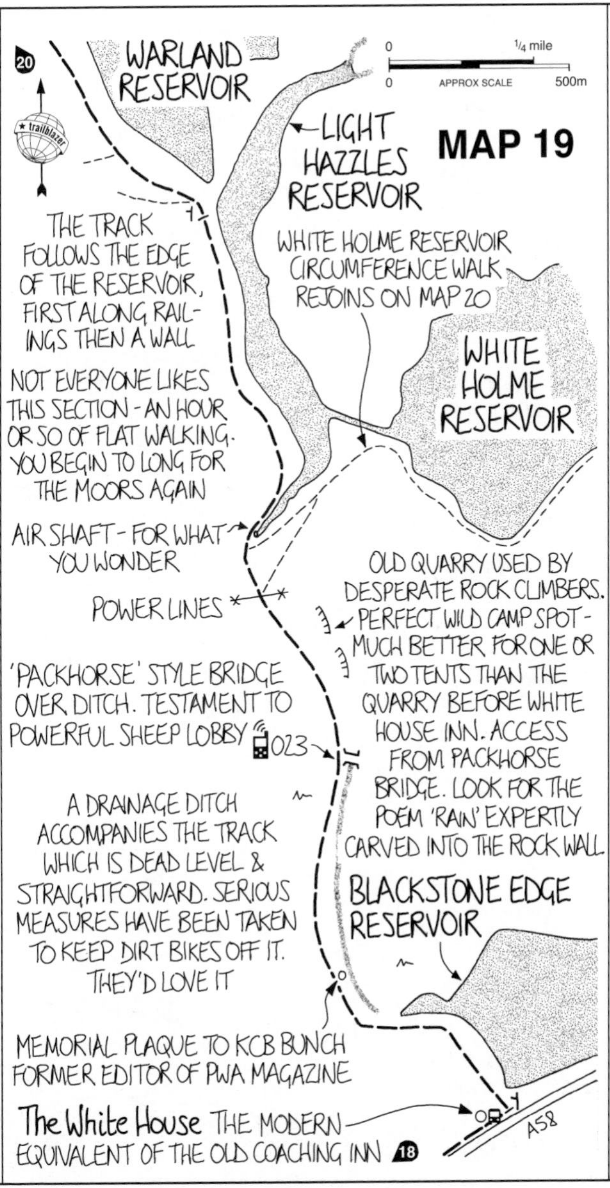

20
WARLAND RESERVOIR
0
¼ mile
0
APPROX SCALE
500m
LIGHT HAZZLES RESERVOIR
MAP 19
THE TRACK FOLLOWS THE EDGE OF THE RESERVOIR, FIRST ALONG RAILINGS THEN A WALL
WHITE HOLME RESERVOIR CIRCUMFERENCE WALK REJOINS ON MAP 20
WHITE HOLME RESERVOIR
NOT EVERYONE LIKES THIS SECTION - AN HOUR OR SO OF FLAT WALKING. YOU BEGIN TO LONG FOR THE MOORS AGAIN
AIR SHAFT - FOR WHAT YOU WONDER
POWER LINES
OLD QUARRY USED BY DESPERATE ROCK CLIMBERS. PERFECT WILD CAMP SPOT - MUCH BETTER FOR ONE OR TWO TENTS THAN THE QUARRY BEFORE WHITE HOUSE INN. ACCESS FROM PACKHORSE BRIDGE. LOOK FOR THE POEM 'RAIN' EXPERTLY CARVED INTO THE ROCK WALL
'PACKHORSE' STYLE BRIDGE OVER DITCH. TESTAMENT TO POWERFUL SHEEP LOBBY
023
A DRAINAGE DITCH ACCOMPANIES THE TRACK WHICH IS DEAD LEVEL & STRAIGHTFORWARD. SERIOUS MEASURES HAVE BEEN TAKEN TO KEEP DIRT BIKES OFF IT. THEY'D LOVE IT
BLACKSTONE EDGE RESERVOIR
MEMORIAL PLAQUE TO KCB BUNCH FORMER EDITOR OF PWA MAGAZINE
The White House THE MODERN EQUIVALENT OF THE OLD COACHING INN
18
A58

1 HR 30 MINS–2 HRS TO STOODLEY PIKE (MAP 21)

THE WHITE HOUSE PUB ON THE A58

1 HR 20 MINS–1 HR 45 MINS FROM STOODLEY PIKE (MAP 21)

THE WHITE HOUSE PUB ON THE A58

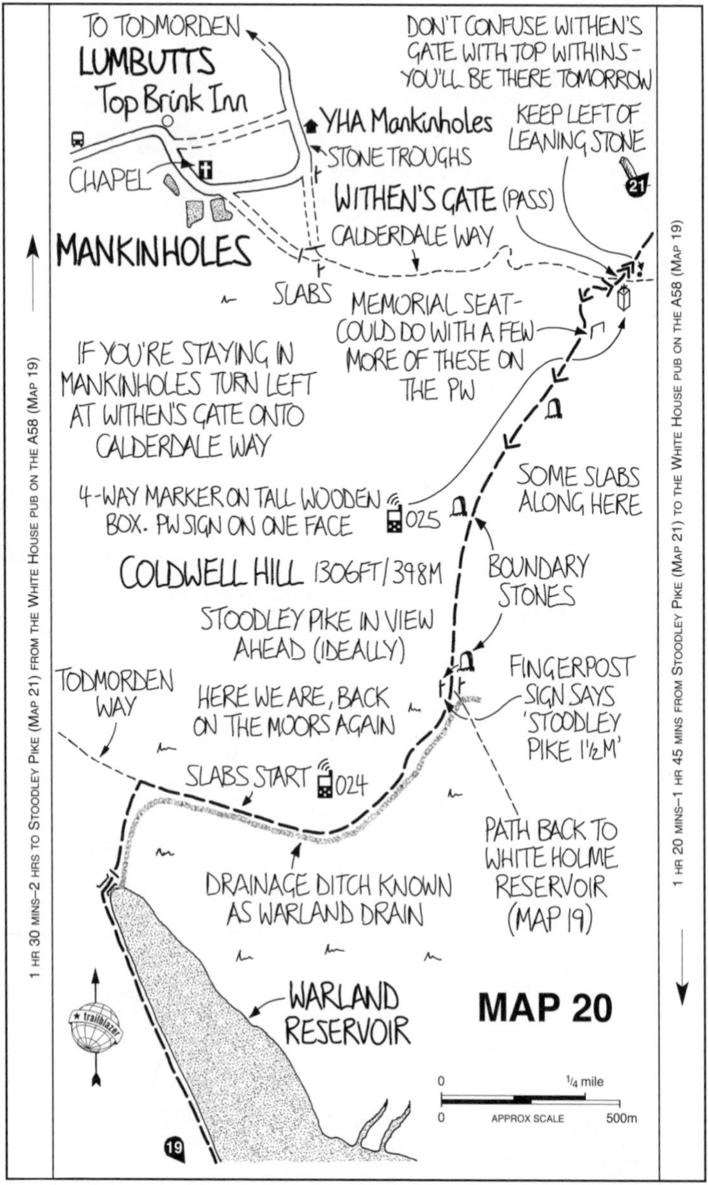

1 hr 30 mins–2 hrs to Stoodley Pike (Map 21) from the White House pub on the A58 (Map 19)
1 hr 20 mins–1 hr 45 mins from Stoodley Pike (Map 21) to the White House pub on the A58 (Map 19)
TO TODMORDEN
LUMBUTTS
Top Brink Inn
DON'T CONFUSE WITHEN'S GATE WITH TOP WITHINS - YOU'LL BE THERE TOMORROW
YHA Mankinholes
KEEP LEFT OF LEANING STONE
STONE TROUGHS
CHAPEL
WITHEN'S GATE (PASS)
CALDERDALE WAY
MANKINHOLES
SLABS
MEMORIAL SEAT- COULD DO WITH A FEW MORE OF THESE ON THE PW
IF YOU'RE STAYING IN MANKINHOLES TURN LEFT AT WITHEN'S GATE ONTO CALDERDALE WAY
SOME SLABS ALONG HERE
4-WAY MARKER ON TALL WOODEN BOX. PW SIGN ON ONE FACE
025
COLDWELL HILL 1306FT/398M
BOUNDARY STONES
STOODLEY PIKE IN VIEW AHEAD (IDEALLY)
TODMORDEN WAY
FINGERPOST SIGN SAYS 'STOODLEY PIKE 1½M'
HERE WE ARE, BACK ON THE MOORS AGAIN
SLABS START
024
PATH BACK TO WHITE HOLME RESERVOIR (MAP 19)
DRAINAGE DITCH KNOWN AS WARLAND DRAIN
WARLAND RESERVOIR
MAP 20
trailblazer
0
¼ mile
0
APPROX SCALE
500m
21
19

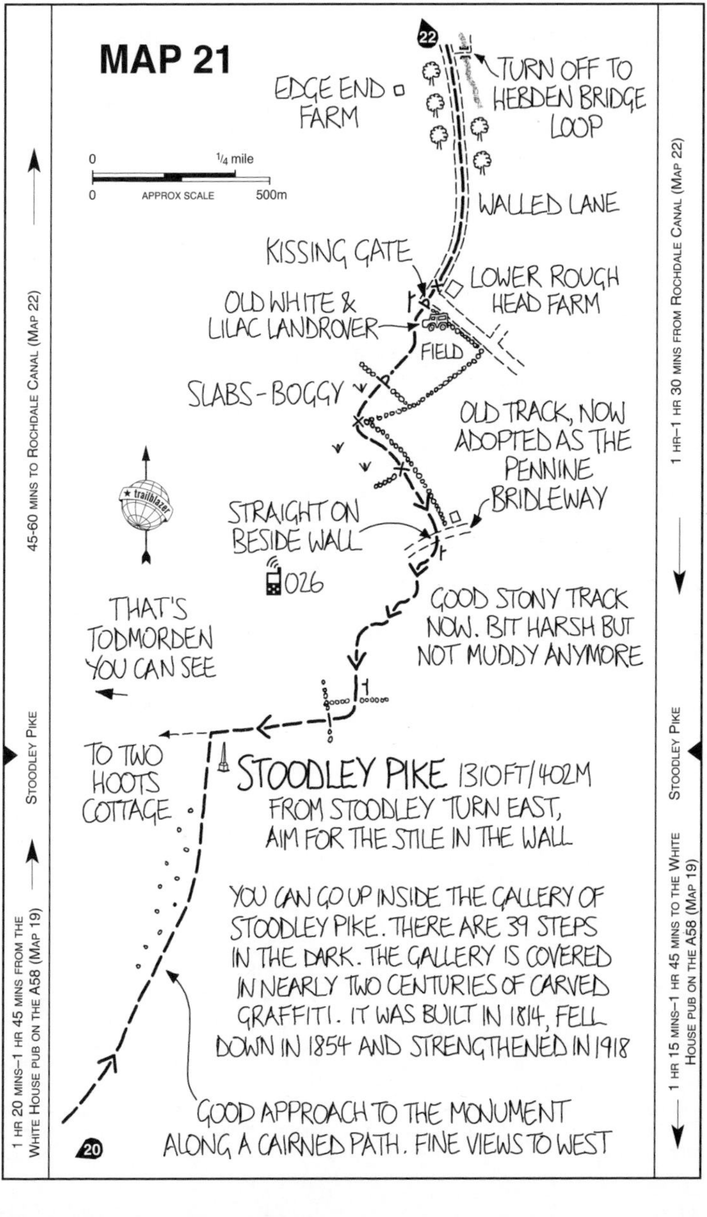
MAP 21
0 1/4 mile
0 APPROX SCALE 500m
EDGE END FARM
TURN OFF TO HEBDEN BRIDGE LOOP
WALLED LANE
KISSING GATE
LOWER ROUGH HEAD FARM
OLD WHITE & LILAC LANDROVER
FIELD
SLABS - BOGGY
OLD TRACK, NOW ADOPTED AS THE PENNINE BRIDLEWAY
STRAIGHT ON BESIDE WALL
026
GOOD STONY TRACK NOW. BIT HARSH BUT NOT MUDDY ANYMORE
THAT'S TODMORDEN YOU CAN SEE
TO TWO HOOTS COTTAGE
STOODLEY PIKE 1310FT/402M
FROM STOODLEY TURN EAST, AIM FOR THE STILE IN THE WALL
YOU CAN GO UP INSIDE THE GALLERY OF STOODLEY PIKE. THERE ARE 39 STEPS IN THE DARK. THE GALLERY IS COVERED IN NEARLY TWO CENTURIES OF CARVED GRAFFITI. IT WAS BUILT IN 1814, FELL DOWN IN 1854 AND STRENGTHENED IN 1918
GOOD APPROACH TO THE MONUMENT ALONG A CAIRNED PATH. FINE VIEWS TO WEST
22
20
45-60 MINS TO ROCHDALE CANAL (MAP 22)
STOODLEY PIKE
1 HR 20 MINS–1 HR 45 MINS FROM THE WHITE HOUSE PUB ON THE A58 (MAP 19)
1 HR–1 HR 30 MINS FROM ROCHDALE CANAL (MAP 22)
STOODLEY PIKE
1 HR 15 MINS–1 HR 45 MINS TO THE WHITE HOUSE PUB ON THE A58 (MAP 19)

❑ Stoodley Pike [Map 21, p113]

This needle-shaped monument above the Calder Valley (Calderdale) was erected on a site where there had been an ancient burial cairn, assumed to be that of a chieftain. It seems plausible, the height being a commanding one and the ideal spot to erect a memorial. It was also an ideal site for a beacon since the chain that warned of the approach of the Spanish Armada included Halifax's Beacon Hill and Pendle Hill above Clitheroe, Stoodley being the link between the two.

Be that as it may, in 1814 it was decided to celebrate the defeat of Napoleon by erecting a monument by public subscription. Local bigwigs were quick to put their name down; then as now a chance to appear influential was not to be missed. Unfortunately Napoleon escaped from Elba, raised his armies and overthrew the restored monarchy, cutting short the erection of the monument. After Wellington finally put paid to Napoleon at Waterloo, work began again and it was completed before the end of 1815. Disaster struck in 1854 when the tower collapsed as the country was going to war again, this time in the Crimea, an evil omen indeed. Rebuilt, it has survived to this day although it is said it wobbled a bit on the eve of the Falklands War (1982).

For walkers along the Pennine Way the 120ft (37-metre) high spire is a landmark that beckons from afar. Inside the graffiti-decked gallery you can climb the 39 steps in the dark. Roughly at the 40-mile (60km) mark from Edale, Stoodley Pike marks a change in the countryside. The peat moors are largely behind you and ahead lie more pastoral scenes as the gritstone gives way to limestone.

HEBDEN BRIDGE [Map 22a, p117]

It was along the Calder Valley that the Industrial Revolution was born and Hebden Bridge, a half-hour stroll east of the Pennine Way along the Rochdale Canal towpath, is well worth the short detour.

Since the mills closed the town has attracted a large 'alternative' population (in 2013 *The Times* named it the coolest place in Britain to live); as a result there are plenty of lively pubs, restaurants, interesting shops and a vibrant arts scene. **Picture House cinema** (🖳 hebdenbridgepicturehouse.co.uk) shows afternoon matinées and the main programme is at 7.30pm daily. There are regular performances at the **Little Theatre** (🖳 hblt.co.uk).

See p14 for details about the Arts Festival in June/July, and other festivals.

If you need to save energy, visit **HB Alternative Technology Centre** (🖳 alternativetechnology.org.uk; Mon-Fri 10am-5pm, Sat noon-5pm, Sun noon-4pm; free but donations welcome) by the canal. The exhibitions change but feature aspects of energy use both in the home and outside.

Transport

[See also pp54-9] There are frequent **trains** (operated by Northern Rail) from Leeds, Bradford, Manchester and Preston.

Hebden Bridge is also a stop on several **bus** services including: First's Nos 590 & 592; TLC Travel's Nos 596, 597 & 901; and Keighley Bus's B3.

Services

Hebden Bridge Visitor Centre (☎ 01422-843831, 🖳 hebdenbridge.co.uk; daily 10am-5pm) is at Butler's Wharf on New Rd in the middle of the town. They have information about accommodation but are no longer able to book it.

Lloyds Bank has an **ATM** as does the Co-op **supermarket** (Mon-Sat 6am-10pm, Sun 11am-5pm) on the main road. There are two smaller supermarkets, Nisa (daily 7am-11pm) and One Stop (daily 6am-11pm) almost next to each other in the centre of town. There's also a **post office** (Mon-Fri 9am-5.30pm, Sat 9am-12.30pm) on Holme St. Mountain Wild (Mon-Sat

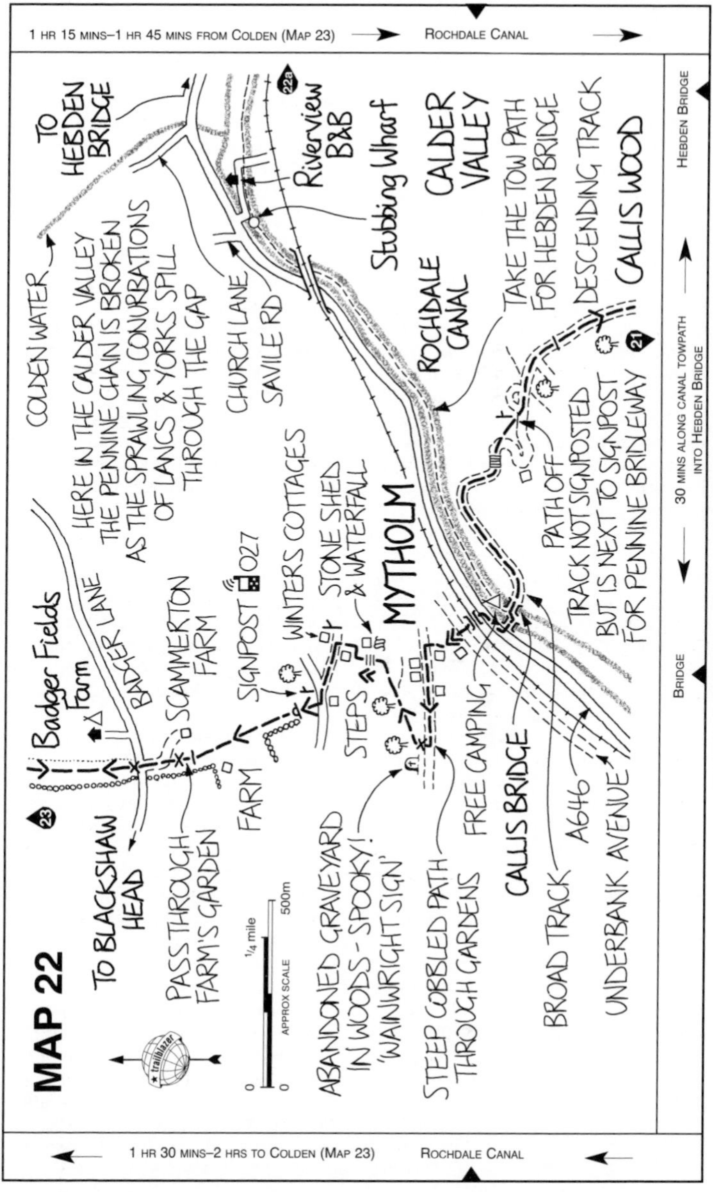
MAP 22
1 HR 15 MINS–1 HR 45 MINS FROM COLDEN (MAP 23)
ROCHDALE CANAL
1 HR 30 MINS–2 HRS TO COLDEN (MAP 23)
ROCHDALE CANAL
HEBDEN BRIDGE
BRIDGE
30 MINS ALONG CANAL TOWPATH INTO HEBDEN BRIDGE
APPROX SCALE
0
1/4 mile
0
500m
23
22a
21
TO BLACKSHAW HEAD
PASS THROUGH FARM'S GARDEN
FARM
ABANDONED GRAVEYARD IN WOODS - SPOOKY! 'WAINWRIGHT SIGN'
STEEP COBBLED PATH THROUGH GARDENS
FREE CAMPING
CALLIS BRIDGE
BROAD TRACK
A646
UNDERBANK AVENUE
Badger Fields Farm
BADGER LANE
SCAMMERTON FARM
SIGNPOST 027
WINTERS COTTAGES
STEPS
STONE SHED & WATERFALL
MYTHOLM
COLDEN WATER
HERE IN THE CALDER VALLEY THE PENNINE CHAIN IS BROKEN AS THE SPRAWLING CONURBATIONS OF LANCS & YORKS SPILL THROUGH THE GAP
CHURCH LANE
SAVILE RD
TO HEBDEN BRIDGE
Riverview B&B
Stubbing Wharf
CALDER VALLEY
ROCHDALE CANAL
TAKE THE TOW PATH FOR HEBDEN BRIDGE
DESCENDING TRACK
CALLIS WOOD
PATH OFF
TRACK NOT SIGNPOSTED BUT IS NEXT TO SIGNPOST FOR PENNINE BRIDLEWAY
trailblazer

ROUTE GUIDE AND MAPS

9am-5pm, Sun 11am-4.30pm) on Crown St sells **walking gear** and there's a **chemist**, Boots (Mon-Sat 9am-5.30pm, Sun 11am-4pm), nearby.

Where to stay

There are no campsites in town, though it is possible to '**wild camp**' (Map 22) alongside the canal; speak with the boat-owners there (they're a friendly and amenable bunch) who pay a peppercorn rent to use the riverbank.

If you'd rather use a **hostel**, there's a reasonable one on the far side of town. ***Hebden Bridge Hostel*** (aka ***Mama Weirdigan's***; ☎ 01422-843183, 🖳 hebdenbridgehostel.co.uk; 1D/1Tr/6Qd, 1x6-bunk-bed room, all en suite; Easter to early Nov) on the eastern side of town. A bed in the bunk room (note that bedding is not provided in this) costs from £16pp; dorm beds (single sex and mixed available) cost from £20pp and the double room costs from £27.50pp (sgl occ £35 Mon-Wed only, room rate rest of week). Rates include a light (organic) breakfast. Note that the hostel is vegetarian so fresh meat/fish cannot be brought onto the premises.

Angeldale Guest House (☎ 01422-847321, 🖳 angeldale.co.uk; 1D or T/1D both en suite, 1D or T private facilities; ▼; Ⓛ; early Feb-Dec), at the top of Hangingroyd Lane, is also fairly central with **B&B** from £35/40pp for private facilities/en suite (sgl occ from £54 but room rate at the weekend). There is a minimum two-night stay over bank holiday weekends.

The White Lion Hotel (☎ 01422-842197, 🖳 whitelionhotel.net; 2D or T/8D, all en suite; ▼; Ⓛ; 🐕), Bridge Gate, charges £57.50-85pp (sgl occ full room rate) for B&B.

Croft Mill (☎ 01422-846836, 🖳 croftmill.com; 13 self-contained apartments sleeping 2-4 people; ▼; WI-FI), just off Albert St, comes highly recommended: 'Quiet, top of the range, with helpful, interested owners'. An apartment costs from £54.50pp (sgl occ rate on request). This rate includes a generous continental 'breakfast pack', and the full cooking facilities (with a couple of supermarkets close by) mean that you could save money on dinner by cooking your own; also it would be easy to make your own packed lunch for the next day.

Almost as far from the Pennine Way as you can get in Hebden Bridge, situated at the far eastern end of the town is ***Laurel End House B&B*** (☎ 01422-846980, 🖳 www.laurelend.com; 1D/1T share bathroom, 1Qd en suite; ▼; Ⓛ; 🐕); it is nonetheless still within close proximity to the town's facilities. Bed and continental breakfast costs from £32.50pp (sgl occ £55). There is a supplement of £3pp for a cooked breakfast.

Thorncliffe B&B (☎ 01422-842163, 07949 729433, 🖳 thorncliffe.uk.net; 1D en suite/1D private bathroom; ▼) is on Alexandra Rd, off Birchcliffe Rd; it is a steep walk (about 5 mins) up from Market St. Expect a nice spacious room and good continental breakfasts as well as a selection of cereal bars and fruit in the room on arrival. They charge from £37.50pp (sgl occ £55).

Riverview B&B (Map 22; ☎ 01422-844943, ☎ 07715-582378, 🖳 riverviewbnb.co.uk; 1D/1T, private facilities; ▼; Ⓛ; 🐕) is on Stubbing Drive; it is less than a mile from the Pennine Way, along the towpath on the route into Hebden Bridge. B&B here costs from £42.50pp (sgl occ £55).

Where to eat and drink

If sandwiches and Full English Breakfasts (FEBs) are getting a bit repetitive, make the most of the variety and choice in Hebden. For example, where else on the Pennine Way can you tuck into some delicious Himalayan fare such as that provided by the ***Tibetan Kitchen*** (☎ 01422-292306, 🖳 tibetankitchen.co.uk; Wed-Sun and bank hol Mons noon-7pm) on Market St? The *shasha chicken* (a lightly battered chicken stir fry; £8) is particularly good.

Market St also contains some particularly good cafés, our favourite being ***Mooch*** (☎ 01422-846954, 🖳 moochcafebar.wordpress.com; 🐕; food Mon-Fri 9am-7pm, Sat 10am-7pm, Sun 10am-6pm) which serves drinks in the evenings. Dog-friendly and pleasant to humans too, they serve food that is both ethically sourced and eclectic, with

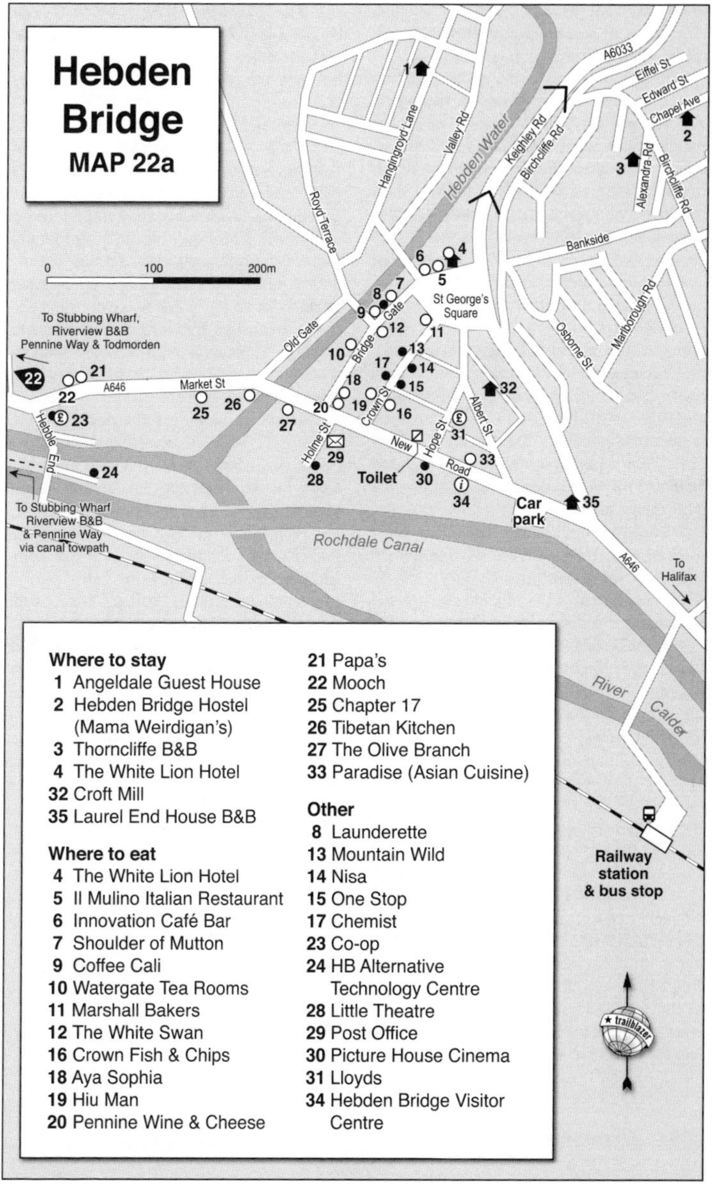
Hebden Bridge
MAP 22a
0
100
200m
To Stubbing Wharf, Riverview B&B Pennine Way & Todmorden
To Stubbing Wharf Riverview B&B & Pennine Way via canal towpath
To Halifax
A6033
A646
Eiffel St
Edward St
Chapel Ave
Alexandra Rd
Birchcliffe Rd
Keighley Rd
Valley Rd
Hangingroyd Lane
Royd Terrace
Hebden Water
Bankside
Marlborough Rd
Osborne St
St George's Square
Old Gate
Bridge Gate
Crown St
Market St
Hebble End
Holme St
New Road
Hope St
Albert St
Toilet
Car park
Rochdale Canal
River Calder
Railway station & bus stop
trailblazer
Where to stay
1 Angeldale Guest House
2 Hebden Bridge Hostel (Mama Weirdigan's)
3 Thorncliffe B&B
4 The White Lion Hotel
32 Croft Mill
35 Laurel End House B&B
Where to eat
4 The White Lion Hotel
5 Il Mulino Italian Restaurant
6 Innovation Café Bar
7 Shoulder of Mutton
9 Coffee Cali
10 Watergate Tea Rooms
11 Marshall Bakers
12 The White Swan
16 Crown Fish & Chips
18 Aya Sophia
19 Hiu Man
20 Pennine Wine & Cheese
21 Papa's
22 Mooch
25 Chapter 17
26 Tibetan Kitchen
27 The Olive Branch
33 Paradise (Asian Cuisine)
Other
8 Launderette
13 Mountain Wild
14 Nisa
15 One Stop
17 Chemist
23 Co-op
24 HB Alternative Technology Centre
28 Little Theatre
29 Post Office
30 Picture House Cinema
31 Lloyds
34 Hebden Bridge Visitor Centre

breakfasts ranging from the full English (£6.50) to a vegan soya yogurt pot with maple syrup, dates & goji berries (£4).

In the heart of town in the pedestrianised section is the licensed ***Watergate Tea Rooms*** (☎ 01422-842978, 🖳 watergatetearooms.com; daily 10am-4.30pm) which does great lunches such as Welsh rarebit (£4.20) as well as a giant Yorkshire pudding with sausages & gravy (£5.80). Both a 'full English' breakfast and a veggie version (both generally available till noon) cost £7.50; a smaller version (£4.70) is also available. A little further on is ***Coffee Cali*** (Mon-Fri 8.30am-5pm, Sat & Sun 9am-5pm), with reasonable coffee that makes a nice accompaniment to their grilled ciabattas (£3.95). Still further on, ***Innovation Café Bar*** (☎ 01422-844094, 🖳 innovationhebdenbridge.co.uk; Mon-Sat 9.45am-5pm, Sun 11am-5pm; WI-FI), in **Hebden Bridge Mill**, does a decent range of hot and cold sandwiches (£3.75-5).

For evening dining, next door is ***Il Mulino*** (☎ 01422-845986, 🖳 ilmulino.co.uk; Mon-Sat 6-10pm) which does a superb range of Italian food, including a wide choice of pasta dishes (from £8.45) and pizzas (from £7.55). From Italy we move east along the Mediterranean coast to ***Aya Sophia*** (☎ 01422-845337, 🖳 ayasophia.co.uk; food daily noon-10pm) with Greek and Turkish specialities from £9.95 including a lovely vegetable moussaka (£11.95).

At ***The Olive Branch*** (☎ 01422-842299, 🖳 theolivebranchrestaurants.com; food daily noon-10pm) you can get a pizza from £9.50, or a *pide* (Turkish equivalent) from £11.95. Down the road at No 17 there's ***Chapter 17*** (☎ 01422-648240, 🖳 chapter17.co.uk; Wed & Sun 11am-8pm, Thur & Fri 11am-9pm, Sat 10am-10pm), a bar and restaurant serving fairly classic English fare with set menu prices in the evening of £11.50/16.50/20.50 for 1/2/3 courses, and a nice line in burgers (£10.95) and sandwiches (£4.25-6.25) during the day.

The Stubbing Wharf (Map 22; ☎ 01422-844107, 🖳 stubbing.co.uk; food served daily noon-9pm; 🐕), situated between the river and the canal, provides pub food.

On Bridge Gate, off the square, ***Shoulder of Mutton*** (Mon-Sat noon-8.30pm, Sun noon-8pm) serves tapas-style platters (4 items for £10.95), though it can get truly hectic on a hot weekend afternoon in summer. ***The White Swan*** is more traditonal and slightly cheaper, serving mainly classic pub grub as well as a pork pie platter at lunch for £5.95. While at the northern end of the town, ***The White Lion*** (see Where to stay) does imaginative fare (Mon-Sat noon-8.45pm, Sun to 7.45pm) from around £12, though their burgers are £10.50.

If you're looking for a pasty or pork pie to take away, ***Marshall Bakers*** (Mon-Sat 9.30am-5pm, Sun 10.30am-5pm) sits right in the heart of the action on St George's Sq, or for something more refined try ***Pennine Wine & Cheese*** (☎ 01422-843121, 🖳 penninewineandcheese.com; Mon-Sat 9.30am-5pm, Sun 11am-5pm) at the southern end of Bridge Gate, with made-to-order sandwiches to go.

If you prefer fast food, ***Crown Fish & Chips*** (Mon-Wed 11.30am-1.15pm & 4-6.15pm, Thur & Fri to 7.15pm, Sat 11.30am-6.15pm, Sun noon-5.45pm) provides the traditional English menu and you can eat in or take away as you please. The western end of the town is served by ***Papa's*** (☎ 01422-844374, 🖳 papashx.com; Sun-Thur 5pm-midnight, Fri & Sat to 1am) which has a selection of pizzas, kebabs and burgers. Indian food is available at the eastern end of the town at ***Paradise*** (☎ 01422-845823, 🖳 paradiseasiancuisine.com; Sun-Thur 5pm-midnight, Fri & Sat to 1am). There's also a Chinese, ***Hiu Man*** (Tue-Thur & Sun 5-10.30pm, Fri & Sat to 11pm) on Crown St.

CALDER VALLEY TO ICKORNSHAW MAPS 22-31

Route overview

15½ miles (25km) – 3100ft (945m) of ascent – 5½-7½ hours

It hasn't exactly been easy to this point, but hopefully by day four the aches and pains are beginning to subside and you've found your walking legs, because you're going to need them for today. Only a couple of other days along the Pennine Way have a higher height gain than this section.

This stretch starts with one of the hardest ascents of the whole walk, a lung-bursting 1000ft (304m) climb in the first two miles (3.2km) as the Way ascends through **Mytholm** (Map 22) passing ***Badger Fields Farm*** (see p120). The effort is compensated for by the varied scenery of lanes, steps, passages and fields; you eventually reach **Colden** (Map 23, see p121) and then Mount Pleasant Farm, one of the last houses before the open expanse of **Heptonstall Moor** (Map 24), where you will find the first wild camping opportunity since leaving Hebden Bridge or, if you prefer a campsite, the path to ***Hebden Camping*** (see p120).

The moor is crossed on a good path which then drops down to the lush, green beauty spot at **Graining Water** (Map 25). Make the most of it, because the next few miles are either along reservoir access roads or on the harsh gravel paths beside them. You'll pass two of the three **Walshaw Dean reservoirs** (Maps 25 & 26) before, thankfully, turning your backs on them and climbing the moorland path up **Withins Height** (Map 27) to the old farmhouse of Top Withins that many associate with Emily Brontë's *Wuthering Heights*. In the summer this place is bristling with tourists.

From here many choose to divert from the Pennine Way to visit **Haworth** (3½ miles, 5.5km, 1½hrs), for the full immersive Brontë experience. An overnight stay here will break up this long section and allow an afternoon of sightseeing and indulgence in this wonderful village. You can follow the scenic **Brontë Way** (Maps 27 & 28), from Top Withins, past the waterfalls, down to your accommodation. If you ignore this literary diversion and proceed along the Pennine Way, the path drops down across moorland to **Ponden** and a rather contrived path around the reservoir of the same name. Another long ascent lies beyond, only 800ft (244m) this time though, and you are rewarded with the crossing of the heather-clad **Ickornshaw Moor** (Map 30), past the wooden huts (called cowlings) and down, across fields into the tiny village of **Ickornshaw** (Map 31). However, many people make the short diversion into Cowling with its slightly wider choice of accommodation.

Navigation notes

Trying to find the Pennine Way path among the myriad of other green footpaths leaving Hebden Bridge is a bit like trying to find a needle in a haystack! The route through the maze is well signed though and you'll be walking slowly up the steep slope so will have little trouble spotting them.

The crossing of Heptonstall Moor (Map 24) is aided by slabs and a well-trodden path and provided you don't miss the sharp right turn at GPS 030 that takes you down to Gorple Cottages, this potentially tricky section should be a breeze. Similarly, the path from Walshaw Dean Middle Reservoir across the moor may look desolate on the map, but the slabs are here too and the signposts which prevent the day-trippers from straying from the path serve just as well.

Leaving Ickornshaw Moor is more likely to cause confusion than the crossing of it, so keep an eye out for the left turn at GPS 045, down through the fields to the waterfall at Lumb Head (Map 31). There is a path around Lower Summerhouse Farm, but it is well signed and exits into the field beyond at almost the same point.

BLACKSHAW HEAD [Map 22, p115]

Where the trail crosses Badger Lane there is ***Badger Fields Farm*** (☎ 01422-845161, 🖳 badgerfields.com; 2T/1D shared facilities, ☛; Ⓛ; 🐕 campers only; Mar to early Nov) where Mrs Whitaker offers **B&B** from £41pp (sgl occ £52), with drying facilities. **Camping** costs £6pp; use of a shower is £2 (towel rental £1), and breakfast (£10 in house, £8 for a breakfast sandwich and hot drink) is available for campers if booked by the night before.

COLDEN [Map 23]

Within a mile of leaving the valley, you will see signs pointing the way to **Aladdin's Cave**, promising untold excesses such as sweets, cakes, groceries and drinks. This is ***Highgate Farm*** (☎ 01422-842897) run by the redoubtable May Stocks who has a natural instinct for what wayfarers want and has provided for them accordingly. Besides the **shop** (daily 7am-9pm), May allows basic **camping** (🐕 on lead) for free for walkers staying one night; there are toilet facilities and a cold water tap. A fine selection of pies and cakes can be bought here, saving you the toil of carrying them up the hill from Hebden Bridge.

The New Delight Inn (☎ 01422-844628, 🖳 newdelightinn.co.uk; 🐕; bar Mon-Thur 5-11pm, Fri 3-11pm, Sat & Sun noon-11pm; **food** served Thur & Fri 5-8pm, Sat noon-8pm, Sun to 6pm), at **Jack Bridge**, provides a haven for thirsty or just plain miserable Pennine Way walkers with a friendly atmosphere and a well-tended cellar.

The Inn also now runs the campsite next door: ***Hebden Camping*** (☎ New Delight Inn, 🖳 hebdenbridge-camping.co.uk; 🐕; closed Nov) charges £5 for a tent and walker plus £3.50 per additional walker. Shower and toilet facilities are available.

WIDDOP [Map 25, p123]

The next pub north from Colden is the ***Packhorse Inn*** (☎ 01422-842803, 🖳 thepackhorseinn.pub; WI-FI; 🐕; **food** Easter to end Sep Tue 6.30-9pm, Wed-Sat noon-2pm & 6.30-9pm, Sun noon-7pm, Oct to Easter Wed-Thur 6.30-9pm, Fri & Sat noon-2pm & 6.30-9pm, Sun noon-7pm), a few hundred metres off route. If you spent the night in Hebden, lunchtime could be about now but note that they're closed Mondays year-round and only open at 5.30pm on Tuesday (Easter to end Sep); between October and Easter they are closed on Monday and Tuesday and only open from 5.30pm on Wednesday & Thursday.

❑ Important note – walking times

All times in this book refer only to the time spent walking. You will need to add 20-30% to allow for rests, photography, checking the map, drinking water etc.

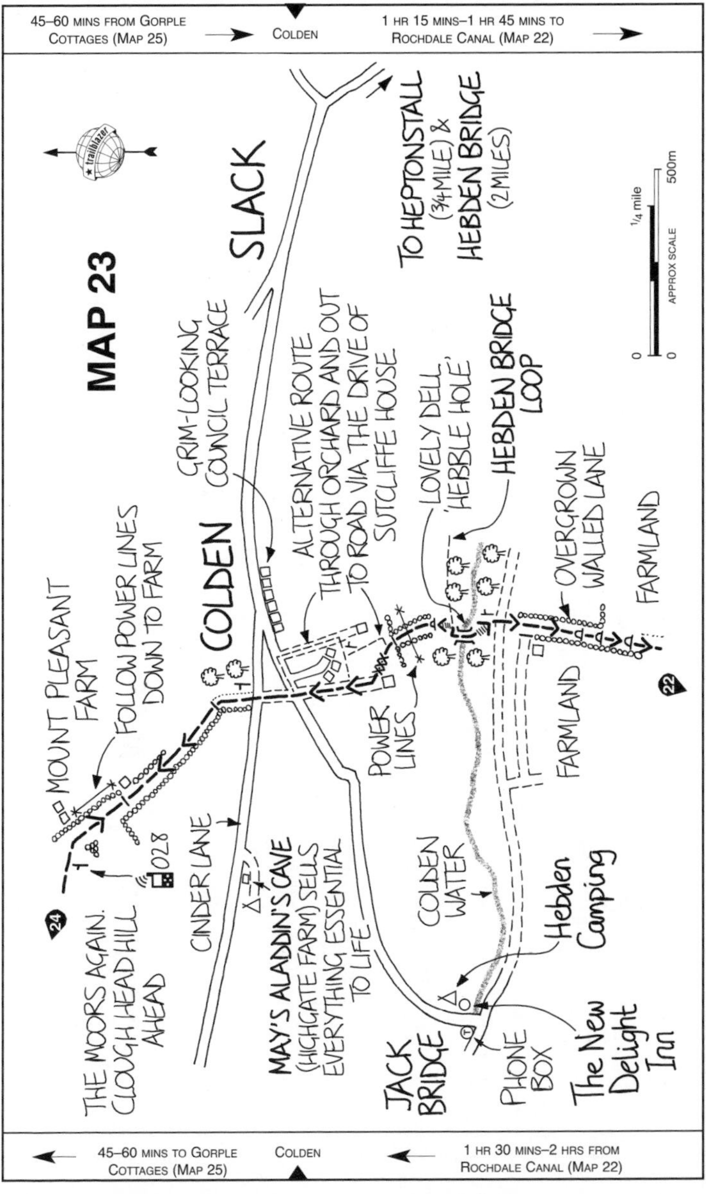
45–60 mins from Gorple Cottages (Map 25)
Colden
1 hr 15 mins–1 hr 45 mins to Rochdale Canal (Map 22)
MAP 23
trailblazer
SLACK
TO HEPTONSTALL (3/4 MILE) & HEBDEN BRIDGE (2 MILES)
1/4 mile
0
500m
APPROX SCALE
GRIM-LOOKING COUNCIL TERRACE
ALTERNATIVE ROUTE THROUGH ORCHARD AND OUT TO ROAD VIA THE DRIVE OF SUTCLIFFE HOUSE
LOVELY DELL 'HEBBLE HOLE'
HEBDEN BRIDGE LOOP
OVERGROWN WALLED LANE
FARMLAND
COLDEN
MOUNT PLEASANT FARM
FOLLOW POWER LINES DOWN TO FARM
POWER LINES
FARMLAND
22
0.28
CINDER LANE
COLDEN WATER
Hebden Camping
24
THE MOORS AGAIN. CLOUGH HEAD HILL AHEAD
MAY'S ALADDIN'S CAVE (HIGHGATE FARM) SELLS EVERYTHING ESSENTIAL TO LIFE
JACK BRIDGE
PHONE BOX
The New Delight Inn
45–60 mins to Gorple Cottages (Map 25)
Colden
1 hr 30 mins–2 hrs from Rochdale Canal (Map 22)

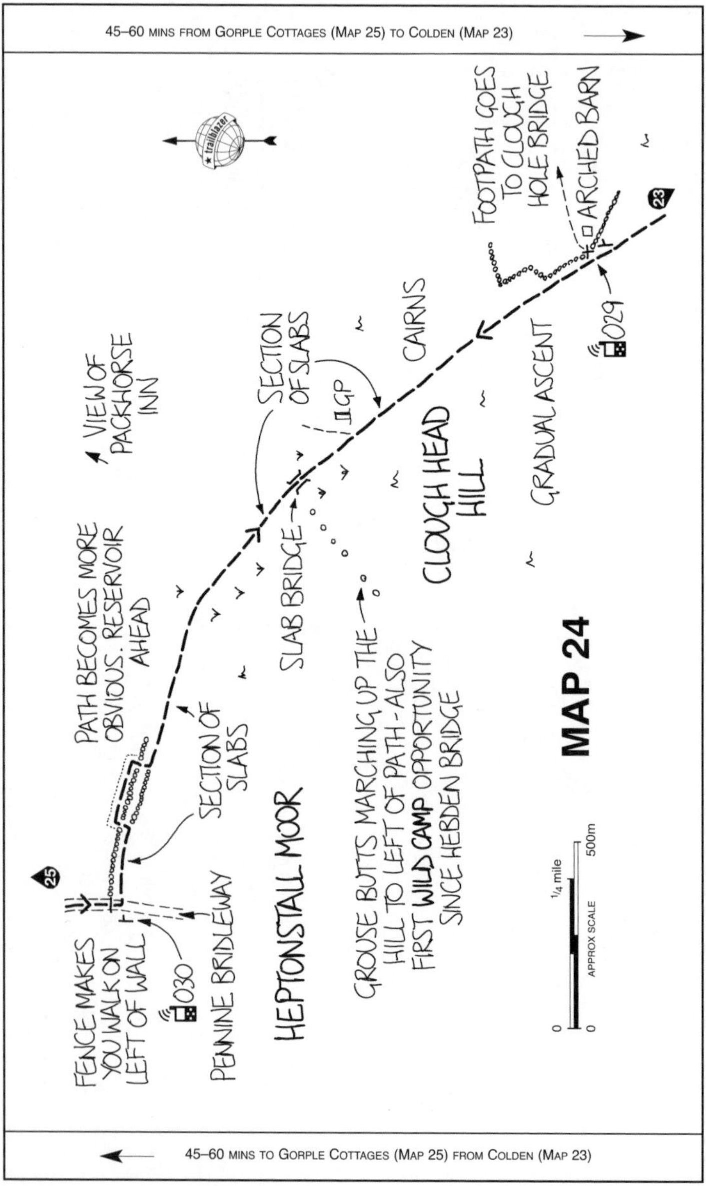
45–60 MINS FROM GORPLE COTTAGES (MAP 25) TO COLDEN (MAP 23)
45–60 MINS TO GORPLE COTTAGES (MAP 25) FROM COLDEN (MAP 23)
MAP 24
FENCE MAKES YOU WALK ON LEFT OF WALL
030
PENNINE BRIDLEWAY
HEPTONSTALL MOOR
SECTION OF SLABS
PATH BECOMES MORE OBVIOUS. RESERVOIR AHEAD
VIEW OF PACKHORSE INN
SLAB BRIDGE
SECTION OF SLABS
GP
GROUSE BUTTS MARCHING UP THE HILL TO LEFT OF PATH - ALSO FIRST WILD CAMP OPPORTUNITY SINCE HEBDEN BRIDGE
CLOUGH HEAD HILL
CAIRNS
GRADUAL ASCENT
029
FOOTPATH GOES TO CLOUGH HOLE BRIDGE
ARCHED BARN
25
23
APPROX SCALE
1/4 mile
500m
0
0

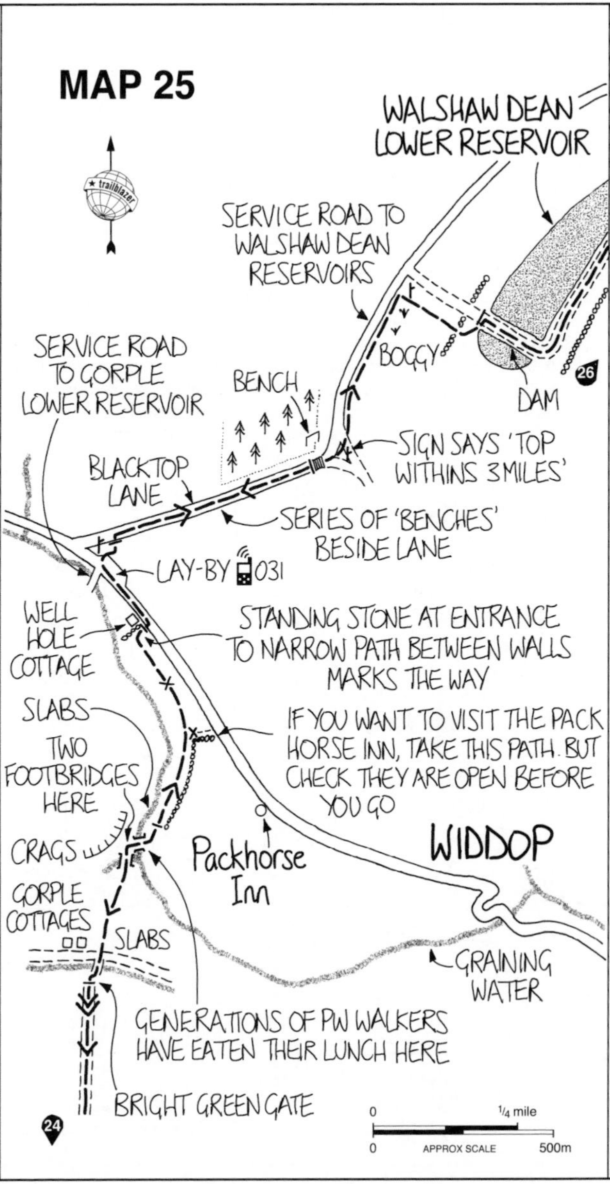

MAP 25
trailblazer
WALSHAW DEAN
LOWER RESERVOIR
SERVICE ROAD TO
WALSHAW DEAN
RESERVOIRS
BOGGY
DAM
26
SERVICE ROAD
TO GORPLE
LOWER RESERVOIR
BENCH
BLACKTOP
LANE
SIGN SAYS 'TOP
WITHINS 3 MILES'
SERIES OF 'BENCHES'
BESIDE LANE
LAY-BY 031
WELL
HOLE
COTTAGE
STANDING STONE AT ENTRANCE
TO NARROW PATH BETWEEN WALLS
MARKS THE WAY
SLABS
TWO
FOOTBRIDGES
HERE
IF YOU WANT TO VISIT THE PACK
HORSE INN, TAKE THIS PATH. BUT
CHECK THEY ARE OPEN BEFORE
YOU GO
CRAGS
Packhorse
Inn
WIDDOP
GORPLE
COTTAGES
SLABS
GRAINING
WATER
GENERATIONS OF PW WALKERS
HAVE EATEN THEIR LUNCH HERE
BRIGHT GREEN GATE
24
0 1/4 mile
0 APPROX SCALE 500m

1 HR 30 MINS TO 2 HRS TO TOP WITHINS (MAP 27)

45–60 MINS FROM TOP WITHINS (MAP 27)

GORPLE COTTAGES

GORPLE COTTAGES

PONDEN [Map 28, p127]

Ponden is now much smaller than it was when weaving was dominant in the area.

On the west side of the reservoir ***Ponden Guest House*** (☎ 01535-644154, 💻 pondenhouse.co.uk; 2T shared bathroom/ 1D en suite, 1Tr en suite; ☕; WI-FI; Ⓛ; 🐕) is a tastefully converted old barn right on the trail. **B&B** costs £37.50-42.50pp (sgl occ from £45) or you can **camp** round the back for £5pp (toilet/shower available). Breakfast for campers (£5.50) and packed lunches are available if booked in advance; alternatively you can walk the mile to the Old Silent Inn (see below), the nearest pub.

Keighley Bus Company's K14/K16 **bus** services (see pp54-9) call in at the eastern end of Ponden Lane on the way to Stanbury.

STANBURY [Map 28, p127]

If Ponden Guest House is full and you have no intention of staying in Haworth, a walk down Ponden Lane takes you to the ***Old Silent Inn*** (☎ 01535-647437, 💻 oldsilentinnhaworth.co.uk; 6D/1T/1Tr, all en suite; Ⓛ; 🐕), an upmarket hostelry which gained its name after Bonnie Prince Charlie hid out here in 1688 with a nod and a wink from the locals. To do likewise will cost from £47.50pp (sgl occ full room rate) for **B&B**.

The menu (**food** served summer Mon-Fri noon-2.30pm & 5-8.30pm, Sat noon-8.30pm, Sun noon-7.45pm) here includes steak & Old Peculier pie (£14.95), and

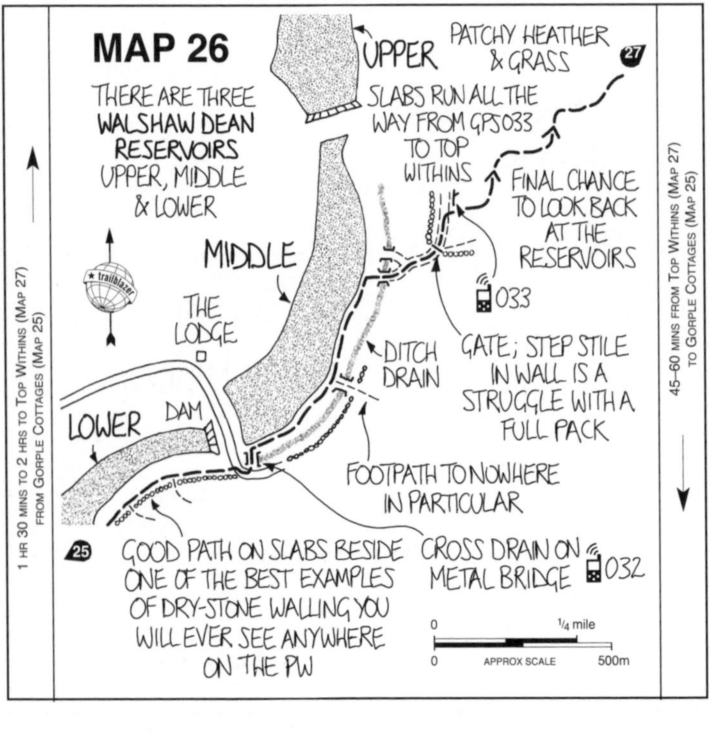
MAP 26
THERE ARE THREE WALSHAW DEAN RESERVOIRS UPPER, MIDDLE & LOWER
UPPER
MIDDLE
LOWER
DAM
THE LODGE
trailblazer
PATCHY HEATHER & GRASS
27
SLABS RUN ALL THE WAY FROM GPS033 TO TOP WITHINS
FINAL CHANCE TO LOOK BACK AT THE RESERVOIRS
033
DITCH DRAIN
GATE; STEP STILE IN WALL IS A STRUGGLE WITH A FULL PACK
FOOTPATH TO NOWHERE IN PARTICULAR
25
GOOD PATH ON SLABS BESIDE ONE OF THE BEST EXAMPLES OF DRY-STONE WALLING YOU WILL EVER SEE ANYWHERE ON THE PW
CROSS DRAIN ON METAL BRIDGE
032
0
1/4 mile
0
APPROX SCALE
500m
1 HR 30 MINS TO 2 HRS TO TOP WITHINS (MAP 27) FROM GORPLE COTTAGES (MAP 25)
45–60 MINS FROM TOP WITHINS (MAP 27) TO GORPLE COTTAGES (MAP 25)

lamb shoulder (£15.75). Note that in the winter months they may close all day on Monday and re open from 5pm on Tuesday.

If this doesn't suit, Keighley Bus's B1 and K14/K16 **bus** services (see pp54-9) stop here en route to Keighley via Haworth.

HAWORTH **[Map 28a, p129]**

The Pennine Way does not go through Haworth, but there are good reasons for taking the detour off the path, via **Brontë Way**, to seek whatever solace may be required: refreshment, accommodation (which is in short supply on the Way itself), literary inspiration; all are there in abundance but the extra 3½ miles (6km) down also involves 3½ miles back up!

This gritstone town's appeal is firmly based on its association with the Brontë sisters. Year-round the streets throng with visitors, most of whom have probably never read the works of Emily, Charlotte or Anne. However, such is the romantic appeal of the family, whose home can still be visited, that crowds continue to be drawn here from all over the world.

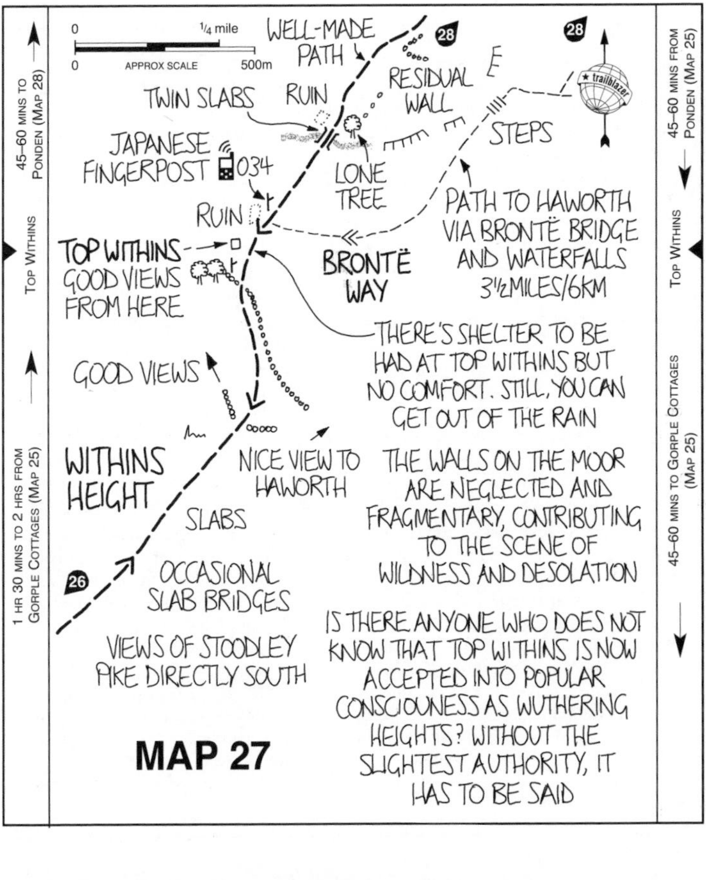

45–60 MINS TO PONDEN (MAP 28)
TOP WITHINS
1 HR 30 MINS TO 2 HRS FROM GORPLE COTTAGES (MAP 25)
0 ¼ mile
0 APPROX SCALE 500m
WELL-MADE PATH
28
28
RESIDUAL WALL
TWIN SLABS
RUIN
STEPS
trailblazer
JAPANESE FINGERPOST
034
LONE TREE
RUIN
PATH TO HAWORTH VIA BRONTË BRIDGE AND WATERFALLS 3½MILES/6KM
TOP WITHINS GOOD VIEWS FROM HERE
BRONTË WAY
THERE'S SHELTER TO BE HAD AT TOP WITHINS BUT NO COMFORT. STILL, YOU CAN GET OUT OF THE RAIN
GOOD VIEWS
WITHINS HEIGHT
NICE VIEW TO HAWORTH
THE WALLS ON THE MOOR ARE NEGLECTED AND FRAGMENTARY, CONTRIBUTING TO THE SCENE OF WILDNESS AND DESOLATION
SLABS
26
OCCASIONAL SLAB BRIDGES
VIEWS OF STOODLEY PIKE DIRECTLY SOUTH
IS THERE ANYONE WHO DOES NOT KNOW THAT TOP WITHINS IS NOW ACCEPTED INTO POPULAR CONSCIOUSNESS AS WUTHERING HEIGHTS? WITHOUT THE SLIGHTEST AUTHORITY, IT HAS TO BE SAID
MAP 27
45–60 MINS FROM PONDEN (MAP 25)
TOP WITHINS
45–60 MINS TO GORPLE COTTAGES (MAP 25)

Haworth is a major destination on the UK tour circuit for Japanese visitors; you'll have spotted PW signs in Japanese near Top Withins.

Brontë Parsonage Museum (☎ 01535-642323, 🖳 bronte.org.uk; daily Apr-Oct 10am-5.30pm, Nov-Dec & Feb-Mar 10am-5pm; £8.50) is at the top of the town. It tells the fascinating story of the family (see box below) and their tragic life including the only son, Branwell, who gave his life up to riotous living. With such talented sisters, who could blame him?

The **railway station** here is a stop on the **Keighley & Worth Valley Railway Line** (☎ 01535-645214, 🖳 kwvr.co.uk; July & Aug daily 4-9/day, Sep-June weekends, school & bank holidays only 4-9/day; return ticket £12, day rover £18), a preserved line which runs steam trips between Keighley (where it links up with the main Leeds–Settle–Carlisle line) and Oxenhope. Oakworth, one of the other stops on the line, is where part of *The Railway Children* was filmed.

Transport

[See also pp54-9] Frequent **bus** services here include Keighley Bus Company's B1, B2, B3, K10, K14, K15, K16 and No 69.

❏ The Brontës of Haworth

Haworth cannot be separated from the Brontës. Their home, the Parsonage, still stands and is open to the public, attracting tens of thousands of visitors every year from across the world. A shop sells the complete works in book form, on disc and on tape plus lavender-scented pot-pourris.

The churchyard above which the Parsonage stands can be a haunting place on a wet evening, calling to mind Mrs Gaskell's account of life in Haworth. Standing at the top of the village, the graveyard's eternal incumbents poisoned the springs which fed the pumps from which the villagers drew their water. Small wonder that typhoid and fever often afflicted the community. Mrs Gaskell's description sums up the oppressive nature of Haworth in Victorian times, an echo of which can be heard even today:

The rain ceased, and the day was just suited to the scenery – wild and chill – with great masses of cloud, glooming over the moors, and here and there a ray of sunshine ... darting down into some deep glen, lighting up the tall chimney, or glistening on the windows and wet roof of the mill which lies couching at the bottom. The country got wilder and wilder as we approached Haworth; for the last four miles we were ascending a huge moor at the very top of which lies the dreary, black-looking village. The clergyman's house was at the top of the churchyard. So through that we went – a dreary, dreary place, literally paved with rain-blackened tombstones, and all on the slope.

Mrs Gaskell *The Life of Charlotte Brontë*, 1857

The three Brontë sisters, Emily (*Wuthering Heights*, 1847), Charlotte (*Jane Eyre*, 1847) and Anne (*The Tenant of Wildfell Hall*, 1848), were brought up by their father and an aunt – after the death, in 1821 from cancer, of their mother – in the Parsonage where Reverend Brontë had taken a living in 1820. The only boy in the family, Branwell, had every hope and expectation lavished on him, taking precedence over his more talented sisters as the son, but squandered his life in drink and drugs, dying in 1848. The lonely, unassuming sisters wrote under male pseudonyms but still their talents went largely unrecognised during their lifetimes and they all died comparatively young from the unhealthy conditions that plagued their village. Today their reputation as novelists endures, and *Wuthering Heights* in particular – set so obviously in the Haworth locality – continues to entrance readers with its vivid portrait of thwarted passion and unfulfilled lives shaped by the bleak, unforgiving landscape of the Yorkshire moors.

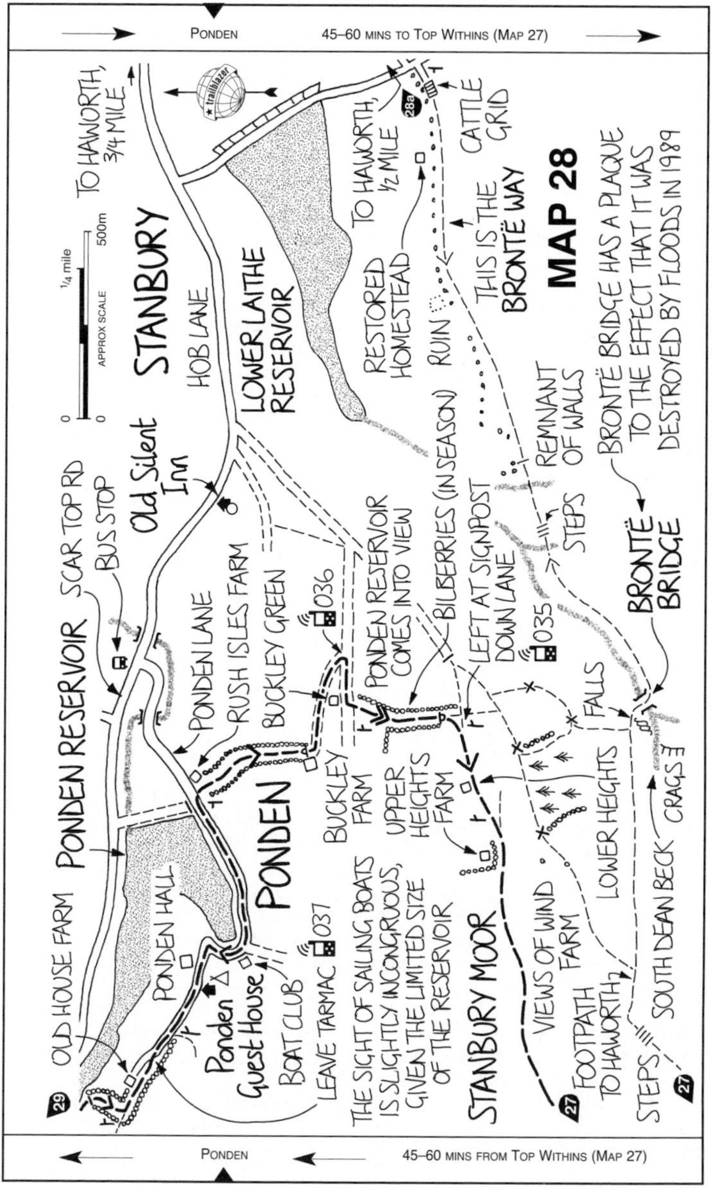
PONDEN
45–60 MINS TO TOP WITHINS (MAP 27)
TO HAWORTH, 3/4 MILE
trailblazer
STANBURY
HOB LANE
LOWER LAITHE RESERVOIR
TO HAWORTH, 1/2 MILE
28a
CATTLE GRID
RESTORED HOMESTEAD
RUIN
THIS IS THE BRONTË WAY
MAP 28
BRONTË BRIDGE HAS A PLAQUE TO THE EFFECT THAT IT WAS DESTROYED BY FLOODS IN 1989
REMNANT OF WALLS
BILBERRIES (IN SEASON)
STEPS
BRONTË BRIDGE
LEFT AT SIGNPOST DOWN LANE
035
FALLS
PONDEN RESERVOIR COMES INTO VIEW
036
BUCKLEY GREEN
RUSH ISLES FARM
PONDEN LANE
SCAR TOP RD BUS STOP
Old Silent Inn
PONDEN RESERVOIR
0 1/4 mile
APPROX SCALE
0 500m
OLD HOUSE FARM
PONDEN HALL
PONDEN
BUCKLEY FARM
UPPER HEIGHTS FARM
LOWER HEIGHTS
Ponden Guest House
BOAT CLUB
LEAVE TARMAC
037
THE SIGHT OF SAILING BOATS IS SLIGHTLY INCONGRUOUS, GIVEN THE LIMITED SIZE OF THE RESERVOIR
STANBURY MOOR
VIEWS OF WIND FARM
FOOTPATH TO HAWORTH
STEPS
SOUTH DEAN BECK
CRAGS
29
27
27
PONDEN
45–60 MINS FROM TOP WITHINS (MAP 27)

For a **taxi** call Brontë Taxis (☎ 01535-644442, 💻 brontetaxis.co.uk).

Services

Haworth has services aplenty including a **post office** (Mon-Fri 9am-1pm & 1.30-5.30pm, Sat 9am-12.30pm, a Spar **supermarket** (daily 7.30am-10.30pm) near the station, **pharmacy** (Mon-Fri 9am-6.30pm, Sat 10am-12.30pm), an army-surplus-cum-**outdoor shop** (Snowdens of Haworth; Mon & Wed-Fri 9am-5pm, Tue & Sat to 4pm), souvenir shops and newsagents.

The **visitor information centre** (TIC; ☎ 01535-642329, 💻 visitbradford.com/discover/Haworth.aspx; daily Apr-Sep 10am-5pm, Oct-Mar 10am-4pm; note that they open at 10.30am on Wednesdays) is at the top of the cobbled Main St in a commanding position that's hard to miss.

There are no banks in Haworth, but there are **ATMs** in the Spar supermarket and the post office at the top of town.

Where to stay

YHA Haworth (☎ 0345-371 9520, 💻 yha.org.uk/hostel/haworth; Ⓛ; Feb-Sep) is on Longlands Drive on the eastern side of town, 1½ miles up a long hill, passing most of the other services on the way. This grand Victorian mansion has 89 beds (1 x 6-bed en suite, 2 x 1-, 1 x 2-, 1 x 3-, 4 x 4-, 5 x 6-, 1 x 7-, 3 x 8-bed rooms shared facilities) but the popularity of the town means that it gets very busy at peak times. A dorm bed costs from £13pp, private rooms from £25. The hostel is licensed and meals are available; there is also a laundry room and drying facilities.

Weavers Guesthouse (☎ 01535-643209, 💻 weaversguesthouse.co.uk; 1S/2T/3D, all en suite; ▼; Ⓛ), at 15 West Lane, charges £39.50-49.50pp (sgl from £55, sgl occ £64-84).

Halfway down the hill on Main St is ***The Fleece Inn*** (☎ 01535-642172, 💻 fleeceinnhaworth.co.uk; 2S/1T/5D/2D or T, all en suite; ▼; Ⓛ; 🐕); it is one of the best pubs in town and has rooms for £42.50-50pp (sgl £50-55, sgl occ from £65) – the rates include 10% off any meals taken at the bar and even a voucher for a complimentary 'tasting tray' of Timothy Taylor ales. At the bottom of Main St ***The Old Registry*** (☎ 01535-646503, 💻 theoldregistryhaworth.co.uk; 8D, all en suite; ▼; WI-FI), 2-4 Main St, is furnished with an eye for detail and an emphasis on luxury and pampering; some rooms come with a whirlpool bath. B&B costs £40-57.50pp Sun-Thur (sgl occ from £65); a two-night minimum stay applies most weekends (Fri & Sat) and the rate then is £42.50-67.50pp (sgl occ rates on request).

Ye Sleeping House (☎ 01535-645992, 💻 yesleepinghouse.co.uk; 1S/1Tr share bathroom, 1Qd en suite; ▼; Ⓛ; 🐕 if it has its own bedding), at 8 Main St, is the perfect place to do what the name says. B&B here costs £32.50-41pp (sgl from £35, sgl occ rates on request).

Not far away, on Sun St, is ***Haworth Old Hall Inn*** (☎ 01535-642709, 💻 hawortholdhall.co.uk; 1D or T/1D, both en suite; Ⓛ; 🐕 bar only) which charges £40-50pp (sgl occ full room rate) for B&B.

Rosebud Cottage (☎ 01535-640321, 💻 rosebudcottage.co.uk; 1S/3D/1T, all en suite; ▼; Ⓛ), 1 Belle Isle Rd, is a well-run establishment charging £37.50-42.50pp (sgl £40-45, sgl occ from £65).

Brontë Hotel (☎ 01535-644112, 💻 bronte-hotel.co.uk; 2S/1T/3D/3Tr, all en suite, 1S/2T shared facilities; ▼; Ⓛ), Lees Lane, is a larger establishment not far from the YHA hostel and might be just the ticket for a group of walkers wanting accommodation under the same roof. It's geared for over-nighters and has good clean rooms with ample scope for eating and drinking downstairs (see Where to eat). You can expect to pay from £45pp (sgl £40-50, sgl occ from £50) for B&B.

Ashmount Country House (☎ 01535-645726, 💻 ashmounthaworth.co.uk; 11D/1T, all en suite; ▼; Ⓛ), on Mytholmes Lane, charges £39.50-137.50pp (sgl occ full room rate); several rooms have a hot tub.

❑ Where to stay: the details
See p82 for details of the symbols used in the text

ROUTE GUIDE AND MAPS

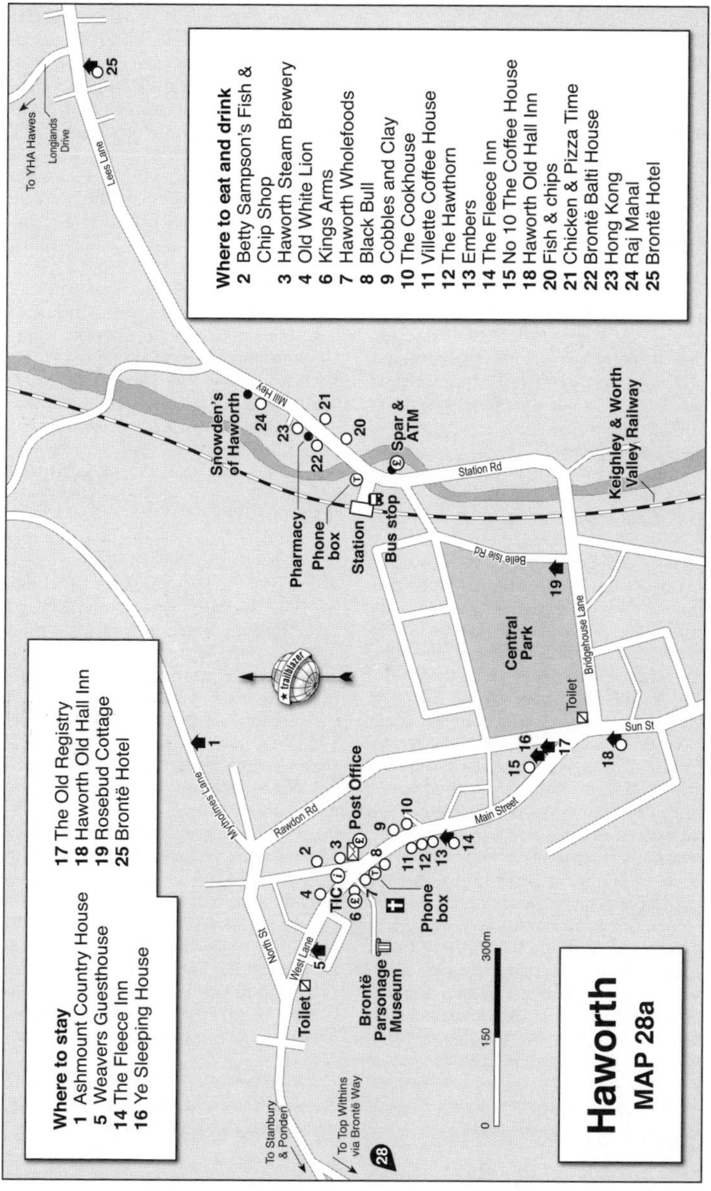
Haworth
MAP 28a
Where to stay
1 Ashmount Country House
5 Weavers Guesthouse
14 The Fleece Inn
16 Ye Sleeping House
17 The Old Registry
18 Haworth Old Hall Inn
19 Rosebud Cottage
25 Brontë Hotel
Where to eat and drink
2 Betty Sampson's Fish & Chip Shop
3 Haworth Steam Brewery
4 Old White Lion
6 Kings Arms
7 Haworth Wholefoods
8 Black Bull
9 Cobbles and Clay
10 The Cookhouse
11 Villette Coffee House
12 The Hawthorn
13 Embers
14 The Fleece Inn
15 No 10 The Coffee House
18 Haworth Old Hall Inn
20 Fish & chips
21 Chicken & Pizza Time
22 Brontë Balti House
23 Hong Kong
24 Raj Mahal
25 Brontë Hotel
To YHA Hawes
Longlands Drive
Lees Lane
Mill Hey
Snowden's of Haworth
Pharmacy
Phone box
Station
Bus stop
Spar & ATM
Station Rd
Keighley & Worth Valley Railway
Belle Isle Rd
Central Park
Bridgehouse Lane
Toilet
Sun St
Main Street
Rawdon Rd
Mytholmes Lane
Post Office
TIC
North St
West Lane
Toilet
Brontë Parsonage Museum
Phone box
To Stanbury & Ponden
To Top Withins via Brontë Way
28
0
150
300m

Haworth *(cont'd)*
Where to eat and drink

Haworth Old Hall Inn (see Where to stay; food served daily noon-9pm) stands apart from the other pubs here and is particularly recommended for its real ales. A range of bar meals in generous portions is available.

Another place to consider is ***Brontë Hotel*** (see Where to stay; food served Mon-Sat noon-2pm & 5-8.30pm, Sun noon-8.30pm); it is open to non residents though it's quite far away if not staying there.

The cobbled Main St has a plethora of eating places. ***The Fleece Inn*** (see Where to stay; food served Mon-Sat 10am-9pm, Sun to 8pm) has a real fire (in winter) and real ales (Timothy Taylor) too. It's a good place to try some local food and main courses are around £10; they have a pie night on Wednesday.

For lunches and afternoon teas you can't do better than ***Villette Coffee House*** (☎ 01535-644967; daily in summer 8.30am-5/6pm – until the last customer leaves – and in winter daily but their opening hours depend on demand; 🐕) where there are such delights as Yorkshire curd tarts, large flat Yorkshire parkins (£1.95) and delicious sticky ginger buns (70p); their Brontë breakfast is a feast for £6.30.

No 10 The Coffee House (🖳 10thecoffeehouse.co.uk; Wed-Sun & Bank Holiday Mondays 12.30-6pm, Sat & Sun from 11.30am) serves a variety of teas and freshly ground coffees, as well as home-made cakes (from £4.50) and scones (from £2.50) baked daily on the premises, in a relaxing environment. A substantial afternoon tea (from £18.50pp) is available but must be reserved in advance.

Haworth Steam Brewery (☎ 01535-646059, 🖳 haworthsteambrewery.co.uk; bar Sun-Wed 11am-6pm, Thur-Sat 11am-11pm; food daily 11am-3.30pm, Thur-Sat 6-8.30pm; no WI-FI; 🐕 during the day only) is a micro-brewery and restaurant at the top of the cobbled Main St. There is an extensive food menu (mains cost from £8 for the liver & onions) and also a range of beers including seasonal ones.

Betty Sampson's (☎ 01535-642336; Tue-Thur 11.30am-3pm, Fri 11.30am-3pm & 4.30-7pm, Sat & Sun 11.30am-5pm; small 🐕) is a traditional chippy with plenty of special offers including two haddock & chips with two cans of drink and a side for £13 for takeaway. Nearby is ***Haworth Wholefoods*** (☎ 01535-649217, 🖳 haworthwholefoods.co.uk; Mon-Sat 9am-5pm, Sun 10am-5pm), home of the delicious Pennine Way pasty (£2.75), a wonderfully filling vegetarian concoction.

Cobbles and Clay (🖳 cobblesandclay.co.uk; daily 8.45am-5pm) is more than just a café; you can paint a plate whilst enjoying four drop pancakes (from £4), or a sandwich. Below it is ***The Cookhouse*** (☎ 01535-640336, 🖳 thecookhousehaworth.co.uk; daily 9.30am-4.30pm; 🐕) which is one of the few cafés where dogs are welcome and boasts a large menu with excellent coffee and a decent afternoon tea (£12.95).

Shuffle further down the hill and you'll come across a couple of more formal dining options. ***The Hawthorn*** (☎ 01535-644477, 🖳 thehawthornhaworth.co.uk; food Mon-Wed 10am-3pm, tea & cakes till 5pm, Thur-Sat the same plus 6-9pm, Sun 10am-7pm; 🐕 downstairs only) is a 'gastropub' in a lovely old Georgian building with a roaring log fire, wood panelled walls and a frequently changing menu with mains starting at £15 for the herb & spelt risotto.

Nearby, ***Embers*** (☎ 01535-642809, 🖳 embersofhaworth.co.uk; food Wed-Sat 6-9pm, Sun noon-4pm & 6-8.30pm) is a more modern affair with an eclectic menu, with mains from £12.55 for pie of the week up to £22.95 for the beef Wellington.

In the eastern, non-touristy, part of town is a collection of takeaways and restaurants. ***Raj Mahal*** (☎ 01535-643890; Wed-Thur & Sun 5.30-10pm, Fri & Sat to 11pm), 51 Mill Hey, is a notable Indian restaurant, or try the nearby ***Brontë Balti House***.

There are also **takeaways**: ***Hong Kong***, a Chinese; ***Chicken & Pizza Time***; and another ***fish & chip*** shop.

ICKORNSHAW [Map 31, p133]
The Pennine Way crosses the busy A6068 between Colne and Keighley at Ickornshaw. To blend in say 'Ick-corn-sher', with the emphasis on the 'corn' and no one need ever know your dark secret.

Ickornshaw is an off-shoot of Cowling which is a quarter of a mile off route to the east.

Squirrel Wood Campsite (☎ 07973-353027, 💻 squirrelwoodcampsite.co.uk)

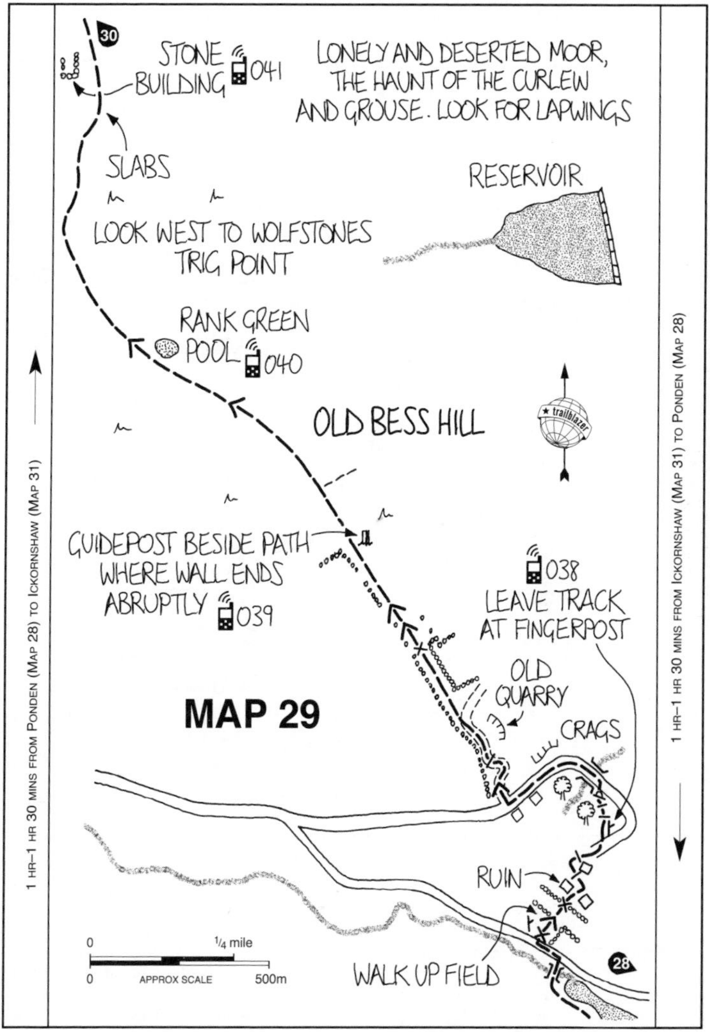
STONE BUILDING 041
LONELY AND DESERTED MOOR, THE HAUNT OF THE CURLEW AND GROUSE. LOOK FOR LAPWINGS
SLABS
RESERVOIR
LOOK WEST TO WOLFSTONES TRIG POINT
RANK GREEN POOL 040
OLD BESS HILL
GUIDEPOST BESIDE PATH WHERE WALL ENDS ABRUPTLY 039
038
LEAVE TRACK AT FINGERPOST
OLD QUARRY
CRAGS
MAP 29
RUIN
WALK UP FIELD
0 1/4 mile
0 APPROX SCALE 500m
1 HR–1 HR 30 MINS FROM PONDEN (MAP 28) TO ICKORNSHAW (MAP 31)
1 HR–1 HR 30 MINS FROM ICKORNSHAW (MAP 31) TO PONDEN (MAP 28)

lies just 100m from the path, has toilet and hot shower facilities and charges **campers** from £10pp (Mar-end Sep; 🐕 but note that dogs aren't allowed on bank holiday weekends). The site also has a **bunkhouse** sleeping 8 (from £15pp), **shepherds hut** (1D; £48), two **camping pods** (sleeping up to two people; £25), and a '**hedgehog lodge**' (£42; up to three people but bedding isn't provided). Most usefully of all, there is a communal hut where you can charge your phones and use the kettle to make a cup of tea. All in all, it's a great campsite.

The site is well signposted from the trail which is just as well as apparently there has been some confusion between this site and nearby ***Winterhouse Barn*** (☎ 01535-632234, 🖳 winterhouse1947@aol.com; 1S/1D, both en suite; ▼; Ⓛ; 🐕), that lies between it and the trail. This is the nearest **B&B** (and one that is recommended for its 'excellent location close to PW and very helpful owners') and they do also allow **camping** for £7pp in a field round the back with a toilet and shower block (bacon sandwich from £3). B&B here costs from £35pp (sgl/sgl occ £39). They don't do evening meals but there are now several options in Cowling (see below).

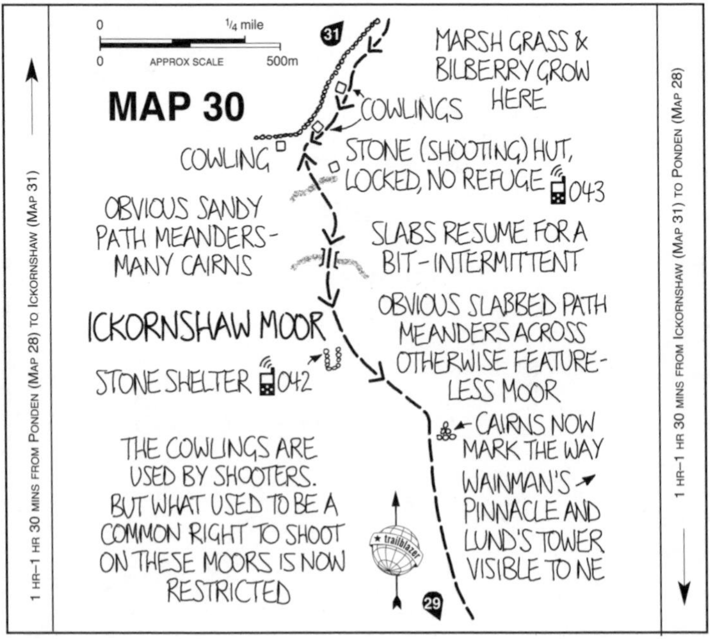
1 HR–1 HR 30 MINS FROM PONDEN (MAP 28) TO ICKORNSHAW (MAP 31)
0
¼ mile
0
APPROX SCALE
500m
MAP 30
31
MARSH GRASS & BILBERRY GROW HERE
COWLINGS
COWLING
STONE (SHOOTING) HUT, LOCKED, NO REFUGE 043
OBVIOUS SANDY PATH MEANDERS - MANY CAIRNS
SLABS RESUME FOR A BIT - INTERMITTENT
ICKORNSHAW MOOR
OBVIOUS SLABBED PATH MEANDERS ACROSS OTHERWISE FEATURE-LESS MOOR
STONE SHELTER 042
CAIRNS NOW MARK THE WAY
THE COWLINGS ARE USED BY SHOOTERS. BUT WHAT USED TO BE A COMMON RIGHT TO SHOOT ON THESE MOORS IS NOW RESTRICTED
WAINMAN'S PINNACLE AND LUND'S TOWER VISIBLE TO NE
trailblazer
29
1 HR–1 HR 30 MINS FROM ICKORNSHAW (MAP 31) TO PONDEN (MAP 28)

COWLING [Map 31]

Cowling has been reinvigorated by the refurbishment and re-opening of the local pub, ***Bay Horse Inn*** (☎ 01535-531992, 🖳 bayhorsecowling.co.uk; bar Sun-Thur noon-midnight, Fri & Sat noon-1am; food served Wed-Fri 5-9pm, Sat noon-9pm & Sun noon-8pm). The menu includes standard pub fare (from £8.25) and 'gourmet pies' (£10.95).

There is a friendly **chip shop** (***Cowling Chippy***; 🖳 cowlingchippy.blogspot.co.uk; Tue-Sat 11.30am-2pm, Tue-Thur 4.30-7pm,

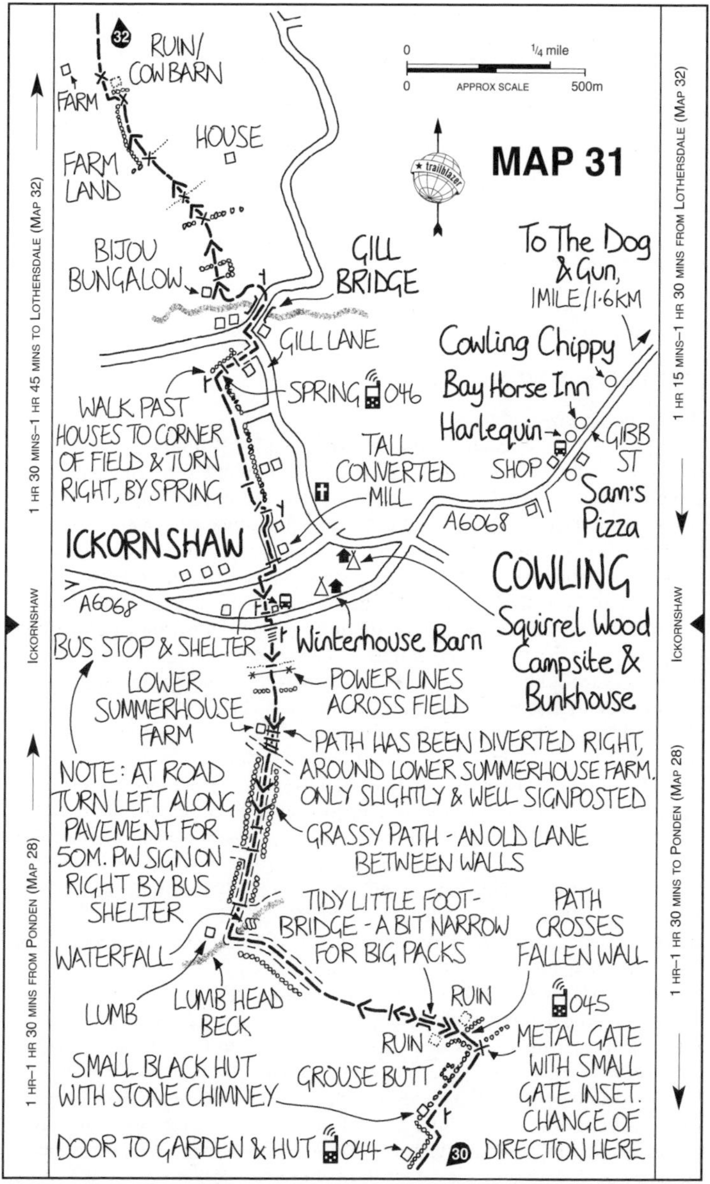
MAP 31
0 1/4 mile
0 APPROX SCALE 500m
trailblazer
1 HR 30 MINS–1 HR 45 MINS TO LOTHERSDALE (MAP 32)
1 HR 15 MINS–1 HR 30 MINS FROM LOTHERSDALE (MAP 32)
ICKORNSHAW
1 HR–1 HR 30 MINS FROM PONDEN (MAP 28)
1 HR–1 HR 30 MINS TO PONDEN (MAP 28)
32
RUIN/ COW BARN
FARM
HOUSE
FARM LAND
BIJOU BUNGALOW
GILL BRIDGE
To The Dog & Gun, 1MILE/1·6KM
GILL LANE
Cowling Chippy
Bay Horse Inn
SPRING 046
WALK PAST HOUSES TO CORNER OF FIELD & TURN RIGHT, BY SPRING
Harlequin
GIBB ST
SHOP
TALL CONVERTED MILL
Sam's Pizza
A6068
ICKORNSHAW
COWLING
A6068
BUS STOP & SHELTER
Winterhouse Barn
Squirrel Wood Campsite & Bunkhouse
LOWER SUMMERHOUSE FARM
POWER LINES ACROSS FIELD
PATH HAS BEEN DIVERTED RIGHT, AROUND LOWER SUMMERHOUSE FARM. ONLY SLIGHTLY & WELL SIGNPOSTED
NOTE: AT ROAD TURN LEFT ALONG PAVEMENT FOR 50M. PW SIGN ON RIGHT BY BUS SHELTER
GRASSY PATH - AN OLD LANE BETWEEN WALLS
TIDY LITTLE FOOT-BRIDGE - A BIT NARROW FOR BIG PACKS
PATH CROSSES FALLEN WALL
WATERFALL
LUMB
LUMB HEAD BECK
RUIN
045
RUIN
METAL GATE WITH SMALL GATE INSET. CHANGE OF DIRECTION HERE
SMALL BLACK HUT WITH STONE CHIMNEY
GROUSE BUTT
DOOR TO GARDEN & HUT 044
30

Fri to 7.30pm) which has some indoor seating as well as the usual takeaway service.

Further up the street, ***Sam's Pizza*** (☎ 01535-448466, 🖳 samspizzas.weebly.com; Thur & Sun 4.30-9.30pm, Fri & Sat to 10pm), selling kebabs and burgers as well as 12-14" pizzas. Between the two is ***Harlequin*** (☎ 01535-633223, 🖳 harlequin-bistro.co.uk; Wed-Fri noon-2pm & 5.30-9pm, Sat 5.30-9pm, Sun noon-7pm), the smartest place in town with mains starting at £10.95 for the mushroom risotto.

The village is also lucky enough to have a useful **shop** (Village Local; Mon-Sat 8.30am-8pm, Sun 9am-3pm).

If you're in the village on a Monday you may not be able to get a meal here, so the next nearest place to eat is ***Dog & Gun*** (☎ 01535-633855, 🖳 dog-and-gun-inn.co.uk; **food** served daily noon-9pm; no WI-FI; 🐕 bar area only) another mile down the road. The menu is extensive, very good value, and includes meat & potato pie (£8.75) as well as fish dishes, sizzlers, hot & cold baguettes and baked potatoes.

The only **bus** service is Burnley Bus's M4; see pp54-9 for details.

ICKORNSHAW TO MALHAM — MAPS 31-41

Route overview

17 miles (27.5km) – 2500ft (762m) of ascent – 6¾-9¾ hours

Nearly all the day's ascent is achieved in the first four miles (6.4km) and the latter half of the day sees a distinct change in scenery; from the dark gritstone and black peat of the Peak District to the light grey limestone and green grass of the Yorkshire Dales. You can lighten the load a little by forgoing a packed lunch as there are opportunities along the way to stop and take on refreshments.

Leaving Ickornshaw via **Gill Bridge** the path makes a short, sharp climb up **Cowling Hill**, then there's another up and over and down into **Lothersdale** (Map 32), with its incongruous chimney. It's probably too early for the Hare & Hounds (see p136) to be open, so it's out of the village and up into the fields for the climb up to **Elslack Moor** (Map 33) and the highpoint of the day at the trig point at **Pinhaw Beacon**. Take a moment to admire the views; on a clear day you may be able to identify Pen-y-ghent. The rest of the day is mostly low level, through fields and pastures as you transition from one geography to the next.

The Way then drops down to **Thornton-in-Craven** (Map 34); a village with few amenities for the walker other than a shady seat beneath the trees just before you reach the road, bus services (Preston Bus No 280 & Burnley Bus X43; see pp54-9) and ***Harrison's Café*** (☎ 01282-841148; summer daily 10am-4pm, winter hours variable) at Thornton Hall Country Park. The menu includes an all-day breakfast, soup of the day, cakes and sandwiches. It's about 800m from where the Way crosses the A56 in Thornton.

However, most press on, over **Langber Hill** (Map 35) to the **Leeds–Liverpool canal**, with its famous double bridge carrying the very busy A59 past **East Marton**. As you leave the canal keep an eye out for ***Abbots Harbour*** (see p136), a lovely café and almost perfectly situated for lunch.

The path then goes through lush green fields, over **Scaleber Hill** (Map 36) – this will cause no problems to the hardened walker you now are – and down into the wonderful oasis of **Gargrave** (Map 37). For Pennine Wayfarers, this is the gateway to the Dales and offers all the refreshment options a walker could

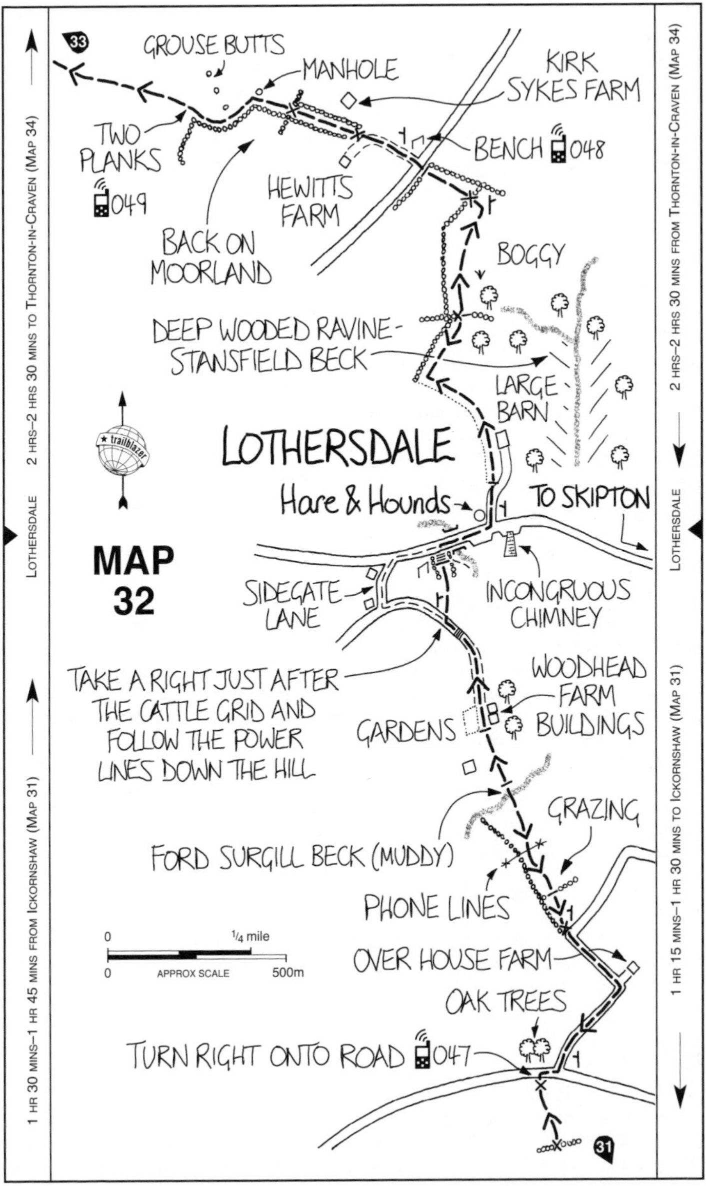
MAP 32
33
GROUSE BUTTS
MANHOLE
KIRK SYKES FARM
TWO PLANKS
049
BENCH 048
HEWITTS FARM
BACK ON MOORLAND
BOGGY
DEEP WOODED RAVINE-STANSFIELD BECK
LARGE BARN
LOTHERSDALE
Hare & Hounds
TO SKIPTON
SIDEGATE LANE
INCONGRUOUS CHIMNEY
TAKE A RIGHT JUST AFTER THE CATTLE GRID AND FOLLOW THE POWER LINES DOWN THE HILL
WOODHEAD FARM BUILDINGS
GARDENS
GRAZING
FORD SURGILL BECK (MUDDY)
PHONE LINES
OVER HOUSE FARM
OAK TREES
TURN RIGHT ONTO ROAD 047
31
0 1/4 mile
0 APPROX SCALE 500m
trailblazer
2 HRS–2 HRS 30 MINS TO THORNTON-IN-CRAVEN (MAP 34)
LOTHERSDALE
1 HR 30 MINS–1 HR 45 MINS FROM ICKORNSHAW (MAP 31)
2 HRS–2 HRS 30 MINS FROM THORNTON-IN-CRAVEN (MAP 34)
LOTHERSDALE
1 HR 15 MINS–1 HR 30 MINS TO ICKORNSHAW (MAP 31)

need. Stopping is mandatory, even if it's just for a bag of sweets from ***Dalesman Café*** (see p142).

Beyond Gargrave the Way climbs steadily through the fields of **Eshton Moor** (Map 38) and then down to meet the River Aire which you cross again, the first time having been in Gargrave, and then walk beside for the remainder of this section, through **Airton** (Map 39), where a diversion to Town End Farm Shop's ***Tea Room*** (see p145) is possible, past **Hanlith Hall** and finally into **Malham**, a tourist hot-spot at the edge of limestone country. Have a good night's rest in this friendly village, for tomorrow hills await.

Navigation notes

The number of fields, stiles and gates on today's route will inevitably lead to confusion and although the path on the ground is often not obvious, especially on the way into Gargrave, the signage is mostly excellent. Keeping one eye (and a finger) on the map and the other on the lookout for Pennine Way markers should be enough to see you through. If all else fails drag the GPS from your pack and lock onto the next waypoint.

LOTHERSDALE [Map 32, p135]

At the time of research the ***Hare & Hounds*** (☎ 01535-631200, 🖳 hareandhounds lothersdale.co.uk; 🐕) had just been taken over by new people; they weren't serving food but expect to soon (daily noon-9pm). The menu will include home-made traditional pub food.

EARBY [Map 34, p138]

Earby is quite a large community but it doesn't have much accommodation.

However, the former YHA hostel is due to re-open early in 2019 as ***Earby Friends of Nature House*** (☎ 01282-842349, 🖳 thefriendsofnature.org.uk/houses/earby; 1 x 2-, 2 x 6-, 1 x 7-bed rooms; shared facilities; Mar/Easter to early Nov). There will be a kitchen (the house will be self-catering only), dining room, lounge and drying room. At the time of research it was not certain what the rates would be.

On the northern side of Earby ***Grange Fell B&B*** (☎ 01282-844991, 🖳 grangefell .com; 2D, shared facilities; Ⓛ) welcome walkers and they charge from £35pp, even if it's single occupancy. They have a drying room, provide fresh eggs from their hens and also make their own jams and preserves.

In Earby itself ***Aspendos*** has pizzas and kebabs to take away, ***Morgan's Café*** (Mon-Fri 9am-2pm, Sat & Sun 9am-1.30pm), an Indian, ***Madras*** (☎ 01282-843943; Sun-Thur 5-10.30pm, Fri & Sat to 11pm), a ***Chinese takeaway*** and two ***fish & chip*** shops (both closed Sunday), a **bakery**, a **general store** cum **post office** (Mon-Sat 9am-10pm, Sun 10am-9pm), a **chemist** (Mon-Fri 8.30am-6.30pm, Sat 9am-2pm) and a Co-op **supermarket** (daily 6am-10pm) with **ATM**.

Burnley Bus's M1 **bus** calls here (see pp54-9).

EAST MARTON [Map 35, p139]

East Marton is a hidden treasure known only to canal users and walkers looking for a mooring or way station alongside the PW.

Abbots Harbour (☎ 01282-843207; 🐕; Apr-end Sep Mon-Wed & Fri 10am-4pm, Sat 10am-5pm, Sun 9am-5pm, closed Thur all year, Oct-end Mar also closed Fri and most of Feb) deserves an accolade for its atmosphere and **food**; it is a cracking good place to eat. *(cont'd on p140)*

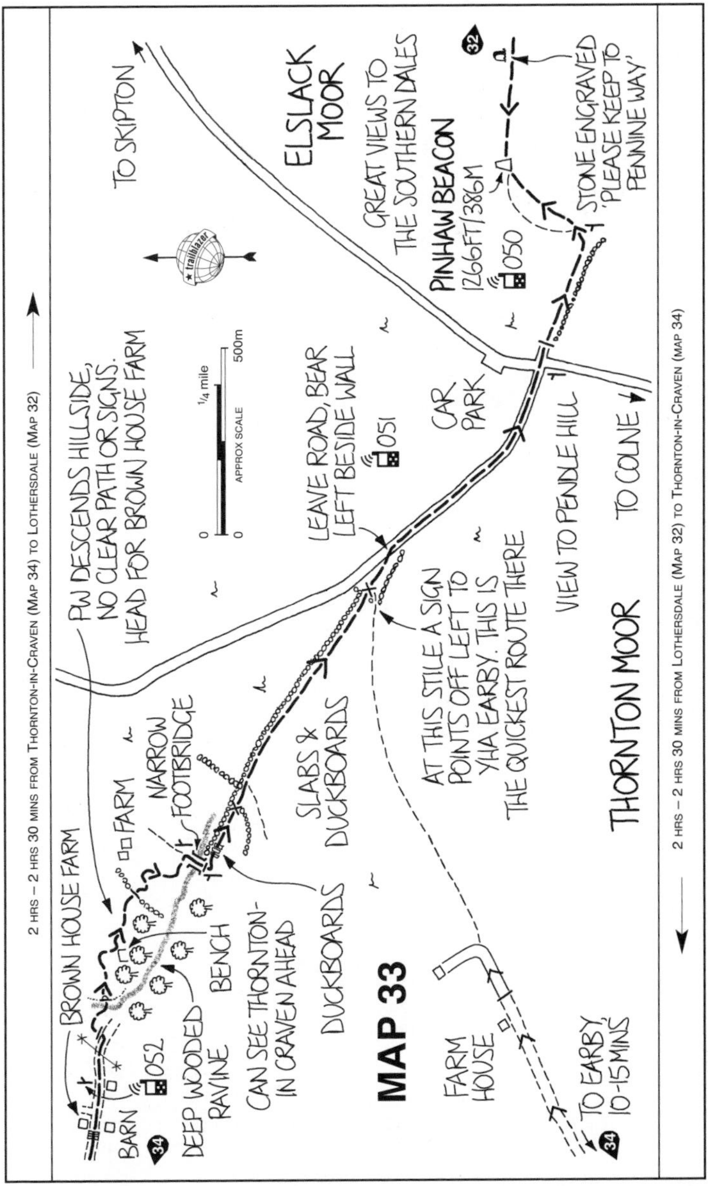
2 HRS – 2 HRS 30 MINS FROM THORNTON-IN-CRAVEN (MAP 34) TO LOTHERSDALE (MAP 32)
2 HRS – 2 HRS 30 MINS FROM LOTHERSDALE (MAP 32) TO THORNTON-IN-CRAVEN (MAP 34)
MAP 33
TO SKIPTON
ELSLACK MOOR
GREAT VIEWS TO THE SOUTHERN DALES
32
PINHAW BEACON 1266FT/386M
050
STONE ENGRAVED 'PLEASE KEEP TO PENNINE WAY'
PW DESCENDS HILLSIDE, NO CLEAR PATH OR SIGNS. HEAD FOR BROWN HOUSE FARM
APPROX SCALE
0
1/4 mile
0
500m
LEAVE ROAD, BEAR LEFT BESIDE WALL
051
CAR PARK
TO COLNE
VIEW TO PENDLE HILL
AT THIS STILE A SIGN POINTS OFF LEFT TO YHA EARBY. THIS IS THE QUICKEST ROUTE THERE
THORNTON MOOR
SLABS & DUCKBOARDS
NARROW FOOTBRIDGE
FARM
BROWN HOUSE FARM
BENCH
DUCKBOARDS
CAN SEE THORNTON-IN CRAVEN AHEAD
DEEP WOODED RAVINE
052
BARN
34
FARM HOUSE
TO EARBY, 10-15 MINS
34

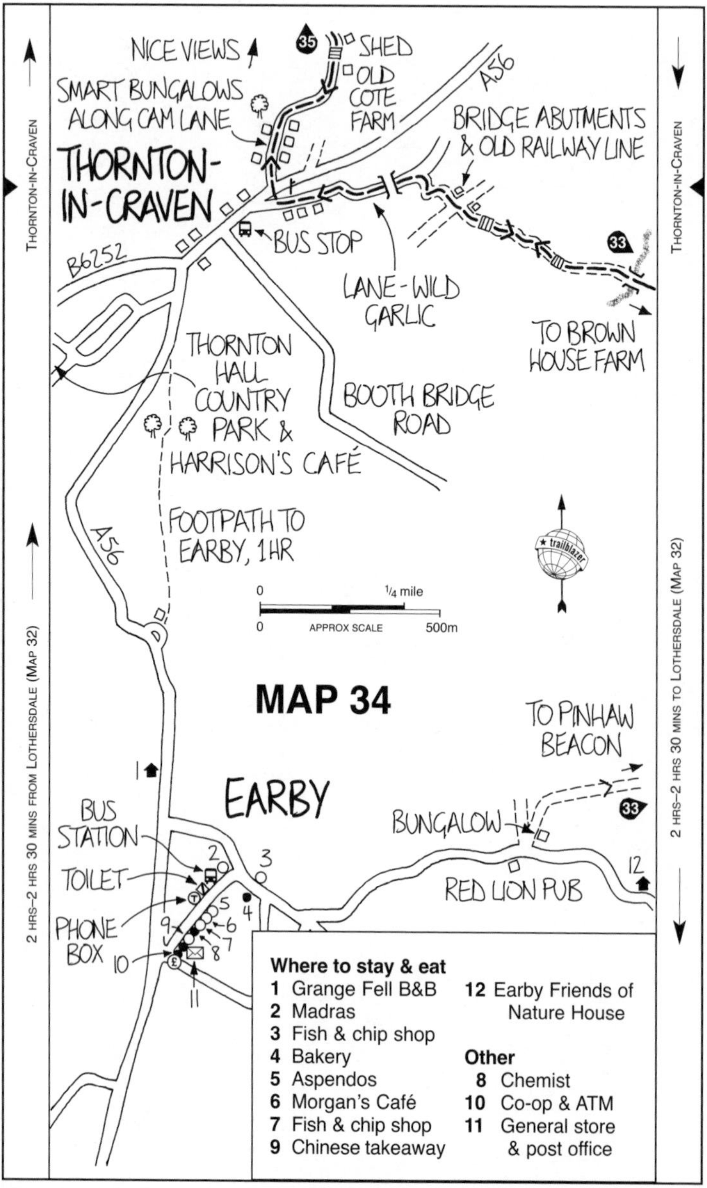

THORNTON-IN-CRAVEN
THORNTON-IN-CRAVEN
2 HRS–2 HRS 30 MINS FROM LOTHERSDALE (MAP 32)
2 HRS–2 HRS 30 MINS TO LOTHERSDALE (MAP 32)
NICE VIEWS
35
SHED
OLD COTE FARM
A56
SMART BUNGALOWS ALONG CAM LANE
THORNTON-IN-CRAVEN
BRIDGE ABUTMENTS & OLD RAILWAY LINE
BUS STOP
33
B6252
LANE - WILD GARLIC
TO BROWN HOUSE FARM
THORNTON HALL COUNTRY PARK & HARRISON'S CAFÉ
BOOTH BRIDGE ROAD
FOOTPATH TO EARBY, 1HR
A56
0
¼ mile
0
APPROX SCALE
500m
trailblazer
MAP 34
TO PINHAW BEACON
EARBY
BUS STATION
TOILET
PHONE BOX
BUNGALOW
33
RED LION PUB
Where to stay & eat
1 Grange Fell B&B
2 Madras
3 Fish & chip shop
4 Bakery
5 Aspendos
6 Morgan's Café
7 Fish & chip shop
9 Chinese takeaway
12 Earby Friends of Nature House
Other
8 Chemist
10 Co-op & ATM
11 General store & post office

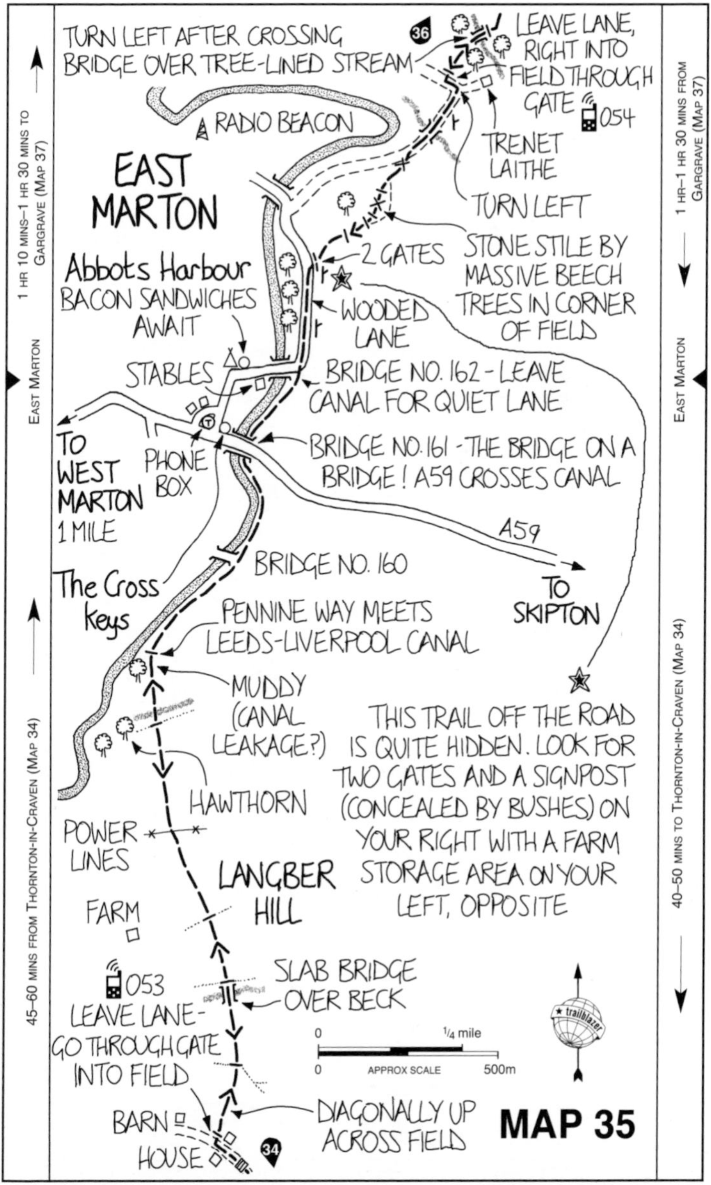
TURN LEFT AFTER CROSSING BRIDGE OVER TREE-LINED STREAM
36
LEAVE LANE, RIGHT INTO FIELD THROUGH GATE
054
RADIO BEACON
TRENET LAITHE
EAST MARTON
TURN LEFT
STONE STILE BY MASSIVE BEECH TREES IN CORNER OF FIELD
2 GATES
Abbots Harbour
BACON SANDWICHES AWAIT
WOODED LANE
STABLES
BRIDGE NO. 162 - LEAVE CANAL FOR QUIET LANE
TO WEST MARTON 1 MILE
PHONE BOX
BRIDGE NO. 161 - THE BRIDGE ON A BRIDGE! A59 CROSSES CANAL
A59
TO SKIPTON
BRIDGE NO. 160
The Cross Keys
PENNINE WAY MEETS LEEDS-LIVERPOOL CANAL
MUDDY (CANAL LEAKAGE?)
THIS TRAIL OFF THE ROAD IS QUITE HIDDEN. LOOK FOR TWO GATES AND A SIGNPOST (CONCEALED BY BUSHES) ON YOUR RIGHT WITH A FARM STORAGE AREA ON YOUR LEFT, OPPOSITE
HAWTHORN
POWER LINES
LANGBER HILL
FARM
SLAB BRIDGE OVER BECK
053
LEAVE LANE - GO THROUGH GATE INTO FIELD
0
1/4 mile
0
APPROX SCALE
500m
trailblazer
BARN
HOUSE
DIAGONALLY UP ACROSS FIELD
34
MAP 35
1 HR 10 MINS–1 HR 30 MINS TO GARGRAVE (MAP 37)
EAST MARTON
45–60 MINS FROM THORNTON-IN-CRAVEN (MAP 34)
1 HR–1 HR 30 MINS FROM GARGRAVE (MAP 37)
EAST MARTON
40–50 MINS TO THORNTON-IN-CRAVEN (MAP 34)

(cont'd from p136) A bacon sandwich costs £3.10, all-day breakfast inc tea or coffee £7.25. You can also **camp** here; £5pp will see you securely ensconced, with toilet and shower facilities at your disposal.

The Cross Keys (☎ 01282-844326, 🖳 thecrosskeys.uk.com; bar open daily from 11.30am in summer; **food** served summer Tue-Fri noon-2.30pm & 5.30-8.30pm, Sat noon-2.30pm & 5.30-9pm, Sun noon-6pm; 🐕 bar area) is the nearest pub, up the lane facing the main road. The menu includes standard pub food starting at £10 for the cheese & onion pie; sandwiches (Tue-Sat noon-2.30pm) cost from £6.50. Note that the pub is closed on Monday and Tuesday in the winter months.

Should you need to get out of town fast ring SD Cars (☎ 01282-814310) for a **taxi**. Preston Bus' No X80 **bus** (see pp54-9) stops in **West Marton**, a mile away, en route between Preston and Skipton.

GARGRAVE [Map 37a, p142]

This small attractive town has most things you will want. Say 'hello' to the River Aire which you'll be following later in the day.

See p14 for details of the agricultural show here in August.

Services

All the shops here are on the main road and close together. There is a **pharmacy**, a well-stocked Co-op **supermarket** (daily 7am-10pm) with an **ATM** and a **post office** (Mon, Wed-Fri 9am-12.30pm & 2-5.15pm, Tue & Sat mornings only).

Transport

Gargrave is a stop on Northern Rail's Leeds to Carlisle **railway** line (see p59).

Bus services calling here include: Kirkby Lonsdale Coaches' Nos 580 & 75; NYCC's No 210 & 211; and Arriva's (seasonal) No 873 & 884. For more details of the service see pp54-9.

Where to stay

Since the accommodation options here are limited plan ahead or take a bus (see above) to Skipton (see 🖳 welcometoskipton.com

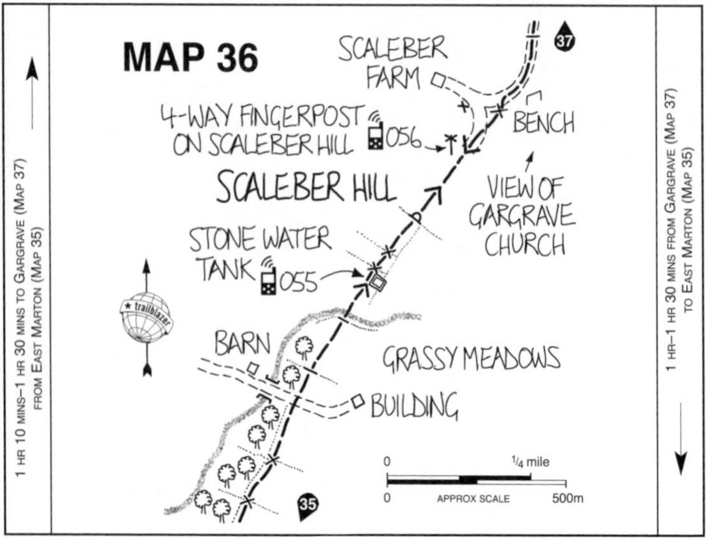
MAP 36
1 HR 10 MINS–1 HR 30 MINS TO GARGRAVE (MAP 37)
FROM EAST MARTON (MAP 35)
1 HR–1 HR 30 MINS FROM GARGRAVE (MAP 37)
TO EAST MARTON (MAP 35)
37
SCALEBER FARM
4-WAY FINGERPOST ON SCALEBER HILL
056
BENCH
SCALEBER HILL
VIEW OF GARGRAVE CHURCH
STONE WATER TANK
055
trailblazer
BARN
GRASSY MEADOWS
BUILDING
0
1/4 mile
0
APPROX SCALE
500m
35

for details of the many accommodation possibilities there as well as other information).

Coming off the Pennine Way, just before the bridge, you'll pass ***Masons Arms*** (☎ 01756-749304, 🖳 masonsarmsgargrave.co.uk; 3D/2T/1Qd, all en suite; ☕; Ⓛ; 🐕), on the corner close to the church. It has rooms from £37.50pp (sgl occ from £55, but full room rate on a Fri or Sat night); breakfast costs £5 extra for the continental version, £8.50 for the full English.

The Old Swan Inn (☎ 01756-749232, 🖳 old-swan-inn.co.uk; 1D/1T/1Tr, all en suite; ☕; clean 🐕) charges from £40pp (sgl occ £50) for B&B.

Head east out of town on the A65 and you'll get to ***Eshton Road Caravan Site*** (☎ 01756-749229; 🐕) with **camping** for £8pp; toilet and shower facilities are available but the shower block closes in the winter months. It is advisable to book ahead if wanting to stay here at a weekend in the summer months.

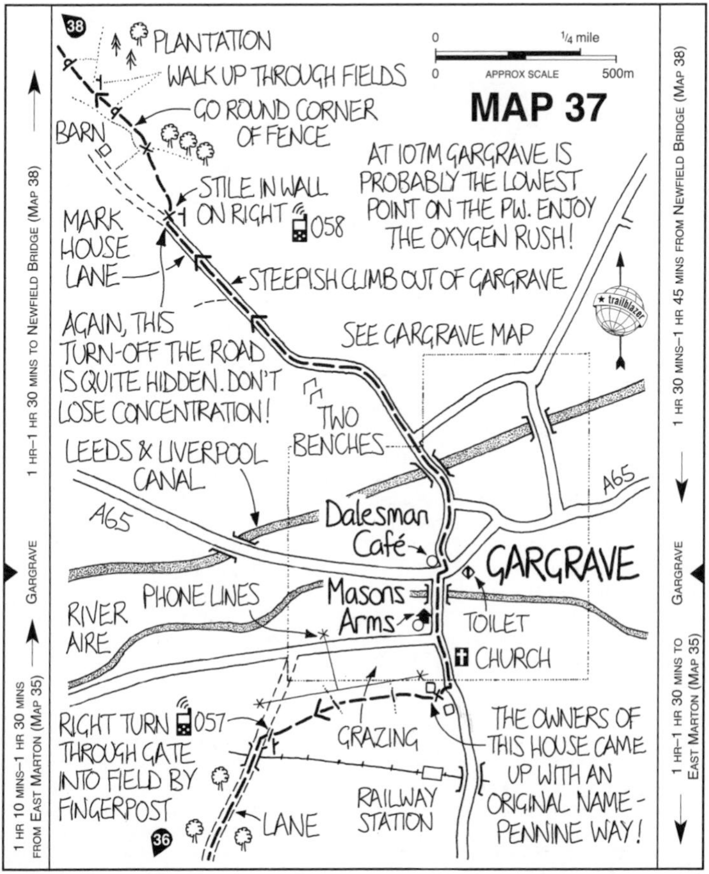
MAP 37
0 ¼ mile
0 APPROX SCALE 500m
38
PLANTATION
WALK UP THROUGH FIELDS
GO ROUND CORNER OF FENCE
BARN
STILE IN WALL ON RIGHT
058
AT 107M GARGRAVE IS PROBABLY THE LOWEST POINT ON THE PW. ENJOY THE OXYGEN RUSH!
MARK HOUSE LANE
STEEPISH CLIMB OUT OF GARGRAVE
AGAIN, THIS TURN-OFF THE ROAD IS QUITE HIDDEN. DON'T LOSE CONCENTRATION!
SEE GARGRAVE MAP
TWO BENCHES
LEEDS & LIVERPOOL CANAL
A65
A65
Dalesman Café
GARGRAVE
RIVER AIRE
PHONE LINES
Masons Arms
TOILET
CHURCH
RIGHT TURN 057 THROUGH GATE INTO FIELD BY FINGERPOST
GRAZING
THE OWNERS OF THIS HOUSE CAME UP WITH AN ORIGINAL NAME - PENNINE WAY!
RAILWAY STATION
LANE
36
trailblazer
1 HR–1 HR 30 MINS TO NEWFIELD BRIDGE (MAP 38)
GARGRAVE
1 HR 10 MINS–1 HR 30 MINS FROM EAST MARTON (MAP 35)
1 HR 30 MINS–1 HR 45 MINS FROM NEWFIELD BRIDGE (MAP 38)
GARGRAVE
1 HR–1 HR 30 MINS TO EAST MARTON (MAP 35)

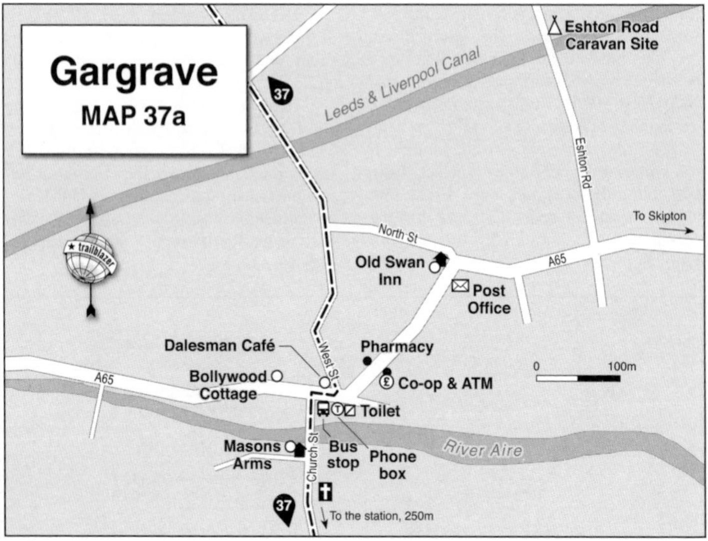
Gargrave
MAP 37a
Eshton Road
Caravan Site
Leeds & Liverpool Canal
37
Eshton Rd
To Skipton
North St
A65
Old Swan
Inn
Post
Office
trailblazer
Dalesman Café
Pharmacy
West St
0
100m
Bollywood
Cottage
Co-op & ATM
A65
Toilet
Masons
Arms
Church St
Bus
stop
Phone
box
River Aire
37
To the station, 250m

Where to eat and drink

As you cross the bridge over the River Aire you will face ***Dalesman Café*** (☎ 01756-749250; Tue & Thur-Sat 9am-4.30pm, Wed & Sun and some Bank Hol Mons 10am-4.30pm; 🐕), a well-primed place for some tucker. It offers a great range of good-value food: a 'Dalesman Lunch' with ham, Wensleydale cheese & chutney is £6.90; home-made cakes are £2; soup (always vegetarian) is £3.95 as well as indulgences such as quality ice-cream, mint cake, and around 200 varieties of old-fashioned sweets sold out of jars in the old-fashioned way. They always have something gluten-free on the menu.

Nearby is a very good Indian restaurant, ***Bollywood Cottage*** (☎ 01756-749252, 💻 bollywoodcottage.co.uk; Tue-Thur 5-11pm, Fri & Sat 5pm-midnight, Sun 5-10.30pm). To eat in there are biryani dishes from £8.95, tandooris from £7.25.

Masons Arms (see Where to stay; food served daily noon-8.30pm) has interesting pub food costing around £8.95-12.50, though specials cost up to £18.95.

The Old Swan Inn (see Where to stay; bar daily noon to 11pm; food served daily noon-2.30pm & 6-9pm) has a variety of traditionally themed rooms such as a flagstone floor 'Snug' with an open fire in winter, and a 'Parlour' with a darts board. The menu largely consists of the usual pub favourites such as bacon-wrapped Yorkshire chicken breast, burgers and gammon steak; mains start at £9.95.

AIRTON [Map 39, p144]

Right by the left bank of the river, Airton is home to little more than two places to stay: ***Airton Barn*** (☎ 01729-830263, 💻 airtonbarn.org.uk; one bunk room with six bunk beds; shared facilities; WI-FI) located at the Meeting House, has a camping barn which is open to anyone. A bunk bed costs from £17pp but if they are full they have fold out mattresses and airbeds, making a total capacity of 18 people. There are shower facilities and access to two kitchens. Sheet and pillow/pillow case and duvet are provided; sheet, duvet cover and pillow slips (£5 per stay) can be rented. Evening meals

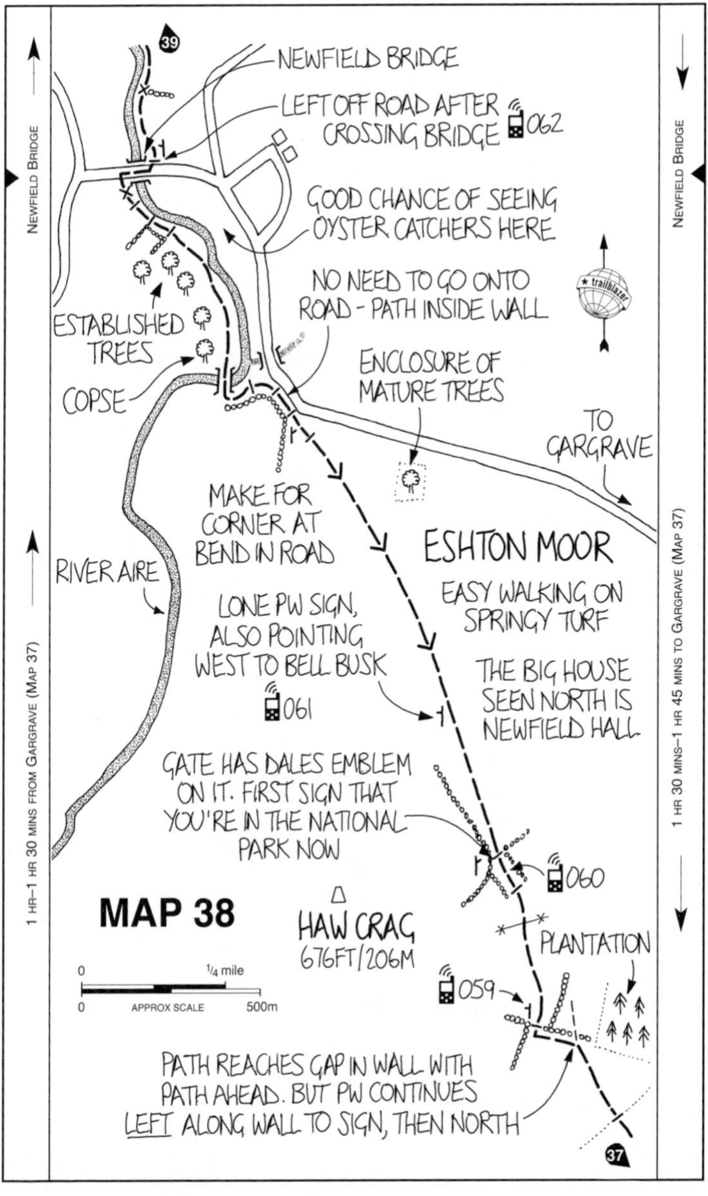
NEWFIELD BRIDGE
LEFT OFF ROAD AFTER CROSSING BRIDGE
062
GOOD CHANCE OF SEEING OYSTER CATCHERS HERE
NO NEED TO GO ONTO ROAD - PATH INSIDE WALL
ESTABLISHED TREES
COPSE
ENCLOSURE OF MATURE TREES
TO GARGRAVE
MAKE FOR CORNER AT BEND IN ROAD
ESHTON MOOR
RIVER AIRE
EASY WALKING ON SPRINGY TURF
LONE PW SIGN, ALSO POINTING WEST TO BELL BUSK
061
THE BIG HOUSE SEEN NORTH IS NEWFIELD HALL
GATE HAS DALES EMBLEM ON IT. FIRST SIGN THAT YOU'RE IN THE NATIONAL PARK NOW
060
MAP 38
HAW CRAG
676FT/206M
PLANTATION
059
0
1/4 mile
0
APPROX SCALE
500m
PATH REACHES GAP IN WALL WITH PATH AHEAD. BUT PW CONTINUES LEFT ALONG WALL TO SIGN, THEN NORTH
39
37
NEWFIELD BRIDGE
1 HR–1 HR 30 MINS FROM GARGRAVE (MAP 37)
NEWFIELD BRIDGE
1 HR 30 MINS–1 HR 45 MINS TO GARGRAVE (MAP 37)

ROUTE GUIDE AND MAPS

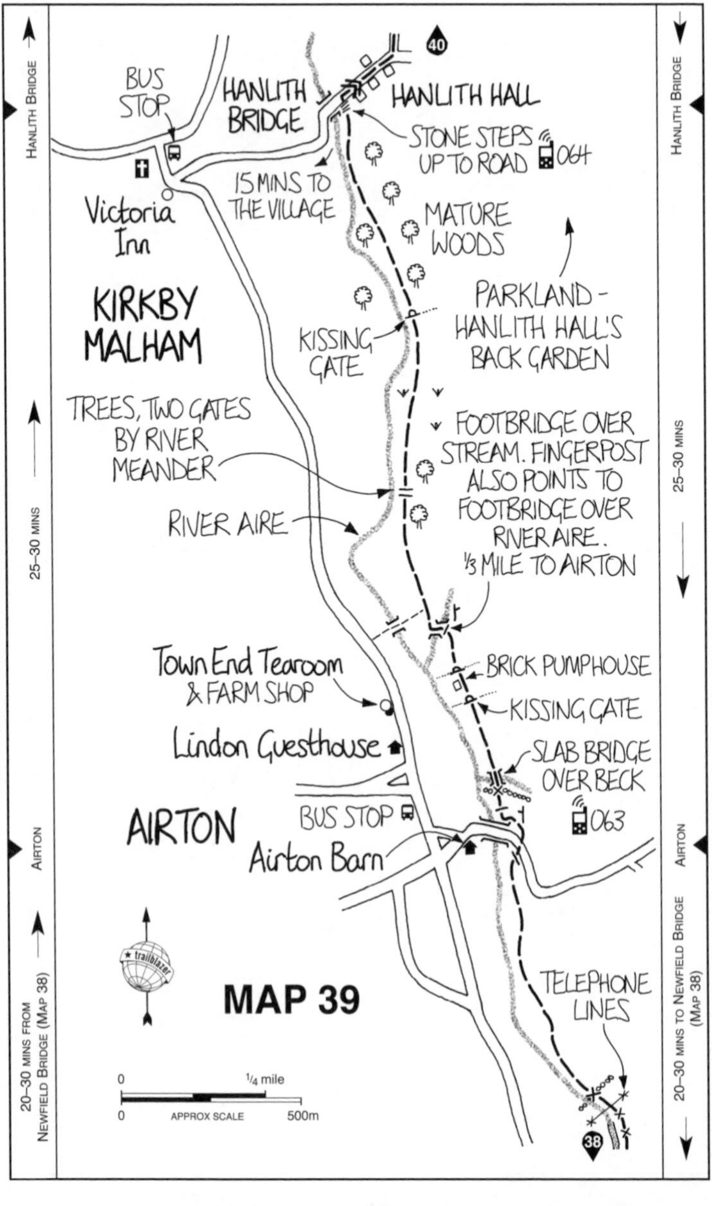

HANLITH BRIDGE
HANLITH BRIDGE
BUS STOP
HANLITH BRIDGE
HANLITH HALL
STONE STEPS UP TO ROAD
064
15 MINS TO THE VILLAGE
Victoria Inn
MATURE WOODS
KIRKBY MALHAM
PARKLAND - HANLITH HALL'S BACK GARDEN
KISSING GATE
TREES, TWO GATES BY RIVER MEANDER
FOOTBRIDGE OVER STREAM. FINGERPOST ALSO POINTS TO FOOTBRIDGE OVER RIVER AIRE. 1/3 MILE TO AIRTON
RIVER AIRE
25–30 MINS
25–30 MINS
Town End Tearoom & FARM SHOP
BRICK PUMPHOUSE
KISSING GATE
Lindon Guesthouse
SLAB BRIDGE OVER BECK
AIRTON
BUS STOP
063
Airton Barn
AIRTON
AIRTON
trailblazer
MAP 39
TELEPHONE LINES
20–30 MINS FROM NEWFIELD BRIDGE (MAP 38)
20–30 MINS TO NEWFIELD BRIDGE (MAP 38)
0
1/4 mile
0
APPROX SCALE
500m
40
38

are not available here but they do have some basic supplies (tins etc) and if you expect to arrive after 5pm the staff there are happy to collect any food order from Town End Farm Shop (see column opposite).

The other place, towards the other end of the scale, is ***Lindon Guesthouse*** (☎ 01729-830418, 🖳 lindonguesthouse.co.uk; 1T/4D, all en suite; Ⓛ; 🐕 but bedding not provided), which is a little way out of the village along the Malham road. The house is better appointed than the average Pennine Way walker may expect. B&B costs from £37.50pp (sgl occ £60); evening meals (£15.95) are available subject to prior arrangement.

Town End Farm Shop (☎ 01729-830902, 🖳 townendfarmshop.co.uk; Tue-Sat 9.30am-5pm, Sun & Bank Hol Mons 10am-5pm) is a farm shop and ***tea room*** (hot food served till 3pm, tea room closes at 4pm; 🐕) which is located a little further along the road, towards Kirkby Malham. There is a handy footpath and footbridge over the Aire, just to the north of the farm if you wish to shortcut back onto the Pennine Way.

NYCC's Nos 210 & 211 **bus services** call here en route between Skipton and Malham, as does Kirkby Lonsdale Coaches' No 75 (Sat only). Arriva's (seasonal) Nos 873 & 884 also call here. See pp54-9 for details.

KIRKBY MALHAM [Map 39]

Standing back from the river, this village is another gem, carefully preserved by its inhabitants and unspoilt by anything as common as a shop. The church has a set of stocks into which anyone putting up a satellite dish would probably be clapped and pelted with rotting fruit.

Victoria Inn (☎ 01729-830499; bar Tue-Thur 3-11pm, Fri & Sat noon-11pm, Sun & bank hols noon-10.30pm) serves standard pub fare (**food** Tue-Sun & bank hol Mon noon-7pm); main dishes are around £7.90-11.90. However, at the time of research its future was uncertain so do check before going.

NYCC's No 210/211 **bus** service calls here as do Kirkby Lonsdale Coaches' No 75 and Arriva's No 873 & 884 services; see pp54-9 for details.

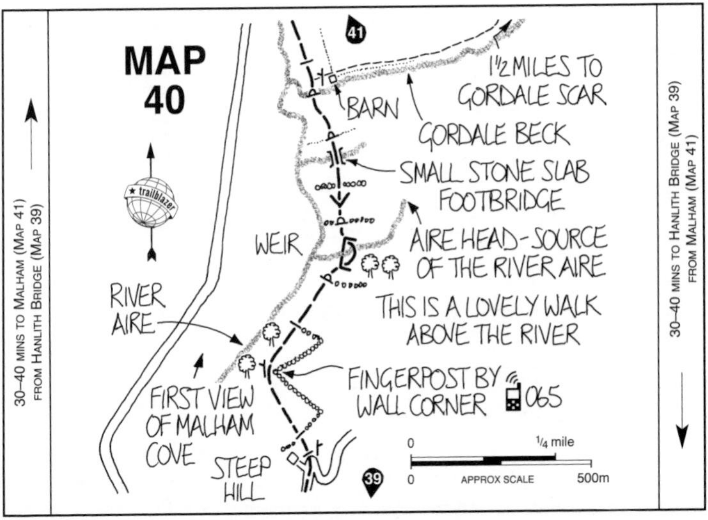
MAP 40
30–40 MINS TO MALHAM (MAP 41) FROM HANLITH BRIDGE (MAP 39)
30–40 MINS TO HANLITH BRIDGE (MAP 39) FROM MALHAM (MAP 41)
41
1½ MILES TO GORDALE SCAR
BARN
GORDALE BECK
SMALL STONE SLAB FOOTBRIDGE
AIRE HEAD-SOURCE OF THE RIVER AIRE
WEIR
THIS IS A LOVELY WALK ABOVE THE RIVER
RIVER AIRE
FINGERPOST BY WALL CORNER 065
FIRST VIEW OF MALHAM COVE
STEEP HILL
39
0
¼ mile
0
APPROX SCALE
500m

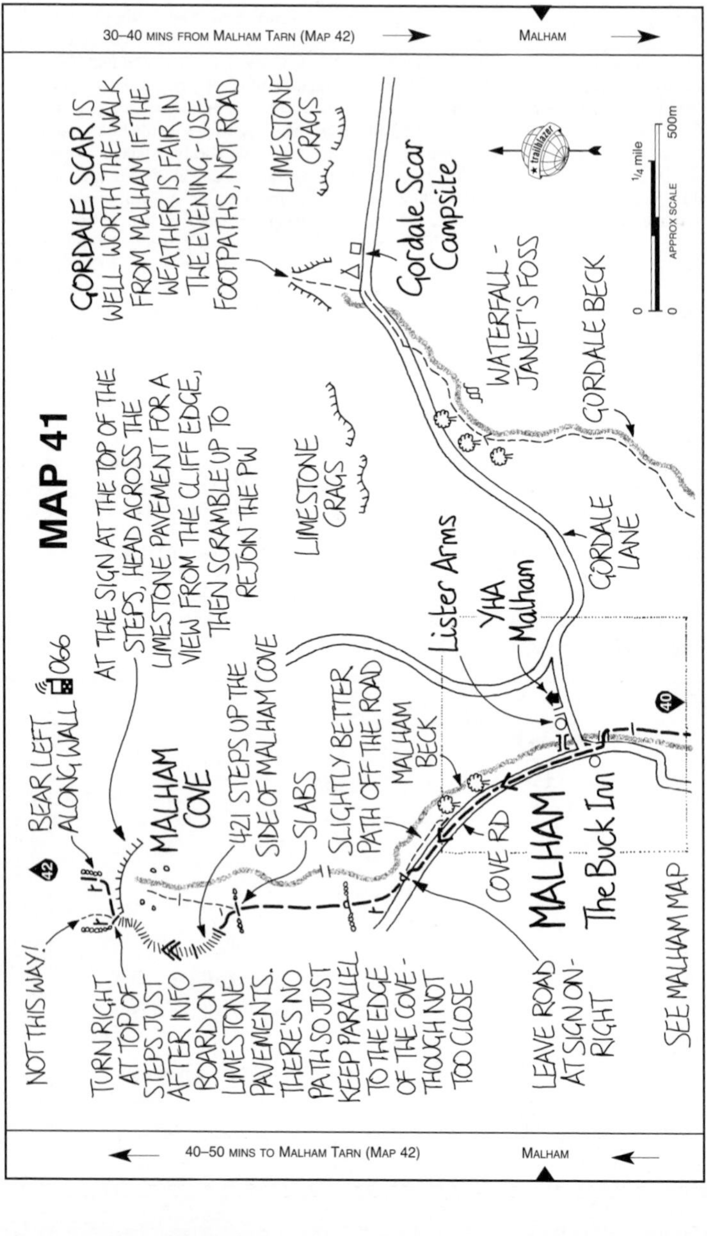
MAP 41
30–40 MINS FROM MALHAM TARN (MAP 42)
MALHAM
40–50 MINS TO MALHAM TARN (MAP 42)
MALHAM
GORDALE SCAR IS WELL WORTH THE WALK FROM MALHAM IF THE WEATHER IS FAIR. IN THE EVENING - USE FOOTPATHS, NOT ROAD
LIMESTONE CRAGS
Gordale Scar Campsite
WATERFALL - JANET'S FOSS
GORDALE BECK
AT THE SIGN AT THE TOP OF THE STEPS, HEAD ACROSS THE LIMESTONE PAVEMENT FOR A VIEW FROM THE CLIFF EDGE, THEN SCRAMBLE UP TO REJOIN THE PW
LIMESTONE CRAGS
Lister Arms
YHA Malham
GORDALE LANE
BEAR LEFT ALONG WALL
066
42
MALHAM COVE
421 STEPS UP THE SIDE OF MALHAM COVE
SLABS
SLIGHTLY BETTER PATH OFF THE ROAD
MALHAM BECK
40
MALHAM
The Buck Inn
COVE RD
NOT THIS WAY!
TURN RIGHT AT TOP OF STEPS JUST AFTER INFO BOARD ON LIMESTONE PAVEMENTS. THERE'S NO PATH SO JUST KEEP PARALLEL TO THE EDGE OF THE COVE - THOUGH NOT TOO CLOSE
LEAVE ROAD AT SIGN ON RIGHT
SEE MALHAM MAP
trailblazer
0
1/4 mile
0
500m
APPROX SCALE

MALHAM **[Map 41a]**

Probably the busiest village between Haworth and the Roman wall, Malham is world-renowned for its incredible limestone amphitheatre and more recently its peregrine falcons (see box below). A wise walker will aim to arrive in Malham during the week, or certainly outside the school holiday period, as accommodation is often booked up well in advance. This was once a mining village known for calamine, the ore which produces zinc.

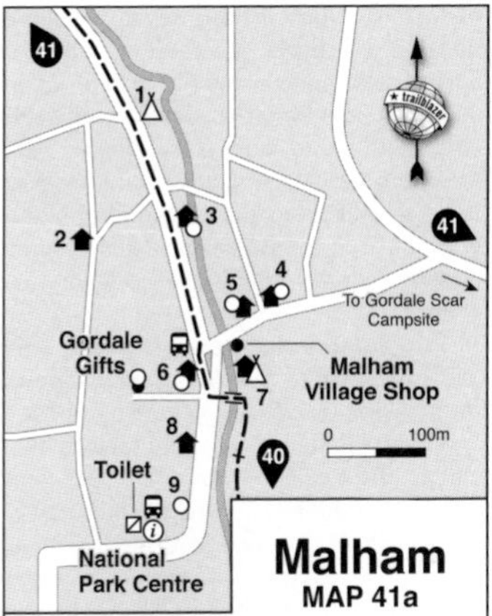
41
1
2
3
4
5
Gordale Gifts
6
7
8
9
To Gordale Scar Campsite
Malham Village Shop
0
100m
40
Toilet
National Park Centre
41
Malham
MAP 41a

Where to stay and eat
1 Riverside Campsite at Town Head Farm
2 Hill Top Farm Bunkhouse
3 Beck Hall B&B
4 YHA Malham
5 Lister Arms
6 The Buck Inn
7 Miresfield Farm (B&B & camping)
8 River House Hotel
9 Old Barn Café

Services

Malham National Park Centre (NPC; ☎ 01729-833200, 🖳 yorkshiredales.org.uk; Easter-Oct daily 10am-5pm, Nov-Dec & Feb-Mar Sat & Sun 10am-4pm) is just to the south of the village and is worth a visit for its interactive displays about the geology and history of the area, as well as general information about the region and Yorkshire Dales National Park. The town's **website** (🖳 malhamdale.com) is also useful for information about the area in general, including yet more accommodation (what follows on p148 is a selection).

A small **general store** (Malham Shop; ☎ 01729-830319) is located right on the bridge in the heart of the village, but its rather unconventional opening times, 'weekends and most afternoons' make it hard to rely on for walkers. If it's open it's worth popping in just to see what can be achieved in such a small space – Dr Who's TARDIS has nothing on this place. The stock is very limited, however, though it's the last chance to buy anything until Hawes. **Gordale Gifts & Outdoor Wear** (☎ 01729-830285; daily 10am-5pm, hours variable in Dec-Jan) is the place to get socks and bootlaces; you can also have a cup of tea here.

See p14 and the box below for details of events held here in the summer.

Transport

[See pp54-9] NYCC's 210/211 **bus** call here as do Kirkby Lonsdale Coaches' No 75 & 881 as well as Arriva's No 873 & 884.

For a 24-hour **taxi** service call Skipton & Craven Taxis (☎ 01756-701122).

Where to stay

Even though there is a good supply of accommodation here visitor numbers are

❑ Peregrine falcon viewing

Every year the RSPB run a peregrine-viewing site at **Malham Cove** (Map 41) where a resident pair of these raptors nest on the limestone cliffs. The site is right in the bowl of the cove and RSPB wardens are on hand with telescopes during the nesting season; this is generally March/April-July (Thur-Mon 10.30am-4.30pm) but the staff at the National Park Centre (see Services) will know the days/hours nearer the time.

high so it's worth making advance reservations. If it's B&B you're after, note that during peak times some places will accept bookings only for a **two-day stay at weekends** and, as in some other places, solo travellers need expect no favours on pricing. As far as room quantities and ambience goes, most of the B&Bs in Malham can be classified in the 'small hotel' category. It's a busy place.

To **camp** in an awesome setting walk one mile east to ***Gordale Scar Campsite*** (Map 41; ☎ 01729-830333; 🐕; Apr/May-Sep/Oct), Gordale House Farm, where they charge from £3pp plus £2-3 per tent. There's a toilet and shower block.

North of the village there's spacious camping at ***Riverside Campsite*** at **Town Head Farm** (☎ 01729-830287, 🖳 malhamdale.com/camping.htm; no WI-FI; 🐕 on a lead; Easter to Oct); they charge from £7pp; shower (£1) and toilet facilities available. If the weather is good it is possible to camp outside their official season so contact them to check. Camping (£5pp) is also possible at ***Miresfield Farm*** (see column opposite; 🐕); toilets are available.

There's **bunkhouse** accommodation at ***Hill Top Farm*** (☎ 01729-830320, 🖳 malhamdale.com/bunkbarn.htm; 2 x 2-, 1 x 3-, 1 x 4-, 1 x 6, 1 x 15-bed room; 🐕); there are also showers, a drying room and a fully equipped kitchen and it costs from £20pp. However, it is important to note that the bunkhouse is only available for sole occupancy (ie group bookings) in school holidays and at weekends and they don't take bookings from individuals until near the requested date.

Near the centre of the village is the very popular ***YHA Malham*** (☎ 0345-371 9529, 🖳 yha.org.uk/hostel/malham; WI-FI in communal areas; Ⓛ). The 81-bed (1 x 3-, 2 x 2-, 1 x 6-bed rooms en suite, 8 x 4-, 4 x 6-, 1 x 8-bed rooms shared facilities) purpose-built hostel now boasts two **camping pods** too (each sleeps up to two adults; from £24 per pod) as well as a licensed ***café/restaurant*** which is also open to non residents, though as always there is a self-catering kitchen. There is also a drying room and laundry facilities as well as a **shop** selling basic food supplies. A dorm bed costs from £13pp, private rooms from £29.

Miresfield Farm (☎ 01729-830414, 🖳 sharpyref@hotmail.co.uk; 5D/5T, all en suite; Ⓛ; 🐕) charges from £32pp (sgl occ £45). ***Beck Hall*** (☎ 01729-830729, 🖳 beckhallmalham.com; 16D/5D or T, all en suite; 🍲; 🐕) is in a nice setting across a footbridge by the river. They have a wide range of rooms and charge from £40pp (sgl occ full room rate); there is a minimum two night-stay requirement at weekends. Packed lunches are not provided but you can order a sandwich from their menu the night before.

If you're looking for more comfort try ***The Buck Inn*** (☎ 01729-830317, 🖳 thebuckmalham.co.uk; 9D/1T, all en suite; 🍲; Ⓛ; 🐕); B&B costs £37.50-57.50pp (sgl occ £69-110). Over the road ***Lister Arms*** (☎ 01729-830444, 🖳 listerarms.co.uk; 2D or T/16D/5Qd, all en suite; 🍲; Ⓛ; 🐕) charges from £52.50pp (sgl occ £95) for B&B.

B&B at ***River House Hotel*** (☎ 01729-830315, 🖳 riverhousemalham.co.uk; 2D or T/6D, all en suite; 🍲; Ⓛ; 🐕) costs £35-60pp (sgl occ £60-99). The hotel has a drying room and laundry service.

Where to eat & drink

Lister Arms (see Where to stay; food served in the restaurant and bar daily noon-9pm) has a great menu: main courses cost £11-18.50, though steaks are £21-28.

Pub grub is also served at ***The Buck Inn*** (see Where to stay; food daily noon-8.30pm) – try the Malham and Masham pie (beef, onions & mushrooms) for £12.75 – and at ***Beck Hall*** (see Where to stay; daily 8-10am for breakfast then noon-8.45pm) with mains starting at £12.95 for the vegetarian option of aubergine curry.

There's also ***Old Barn Café*** (☎ 01729-830486, 🖳 oldbarnmalham.co.uk/cafe.html; early Feb-late Oct daily 9.30am-5pm, to 5.30pm on Sat & Sun in the summer, Nov-mid Feb Sat & Sun 9.30am to dusk; 🐕) near the National Park Centre. An all-day breakfast costs £6.70, jacket potatoes are £5-6; they also serve home-made cakes as well as afternoon teas.

You can also get tea and cake (to 4pm) at ***Gordale Gifts*** (see Services).

MALHAM TO HORTON-IN-RIBBLESDALE MAPS 41-48

Route overview

14½ miles (23.5km) – 2900ft (884m) of ascent – 6-8 hours

> Note that there aren't many options for getting food or snacks on this stage so stock up before you go.

This probably won't feel like the shortest day on the Pennine Way so far; it includes two tough climbs and some of the most exciting scenery to date, including one of the highlights of the whole walk at **Malham Cove** (Map 41). Malham's famous limestone amphitheatre, the site of an ancient waterfall to rival Niagara and home now to peregrine falcons and birdwatchers, is encountered almost immediately on leaving the village. The ascent of the steps beside the Cove doesn't count as one of the two tough climbs, but it will have you breathing more heavily, as will the climb out of **Watlowes** (Map 42), the impressive limestone valley beyond.

The Way passes **Malham Tarn**, an unusual lake in porous limestone country and a haven for waterfowl and more birdwatchers, before reaching **Tennant Gill Farm** (Map 43), and the foot of **Fountains Fell** (Map 44; see box below). A mostly obvious path leads up this 900ft (274m) of ascent with incredible views all around – note the complete lack of reservoirs, pylons and chimneys! As you reach the wall at the top of the climb, you'll get the first sight of Pen-y-ghent, meaning 'hill of the winds', one of the 'Yorkshire Three Peaks' and your next target. Descending from Fountains Fell you follow a quiet country lane which provides a perfect panorama of the stepped profile of **Pen-y-ghent** (Map 46), which you will shortly be ascending. At its base the 600ft (183m) climb appears ferocious and quite daunting, but is actually much easier than it looks and the summit, with its trig point and shelter, is sublime.

The path down to **Horton-in-Ribblesdale** (Maps 46-48), on the other hand, can be quite jarring, hardened as it is to support the hundreds of thousands of 'Three Peakers' (see box p156) who use it every year. You may find you survived the ascent, only to be done in by the descent! *(cont'd on p156)*

❑ Coal mining on Fountains Fell **[Map 44, p152]**

Named after its original owners, the Cistercian monks of Fountains Abbey near Ripon, Fountains Fell possessed substantial coal deposits beneath its cap of millstone grit. It probably still does, but not in sufficient quantity to make extraction economically viable. The most active period of coal extraction was the early 1800s when a road was constructed to the summit plateau where shafts were sunk. The remnants of this road now constitute the generally agreeable gradient of the Pennine Way.

The output of coal was estimated at around 1000 tons a year which required some 10,000 packhorse loads to carry it away.

Very little now remains of the coal industry on Fountains Fell and the shafts have mostly been filled in. The ruins of the colliery building are in evidence but give no real idea of what was once a flourishing industry. Spare a thought for the miners who had to work in this inhospitable place, spending the week in makeshift accommodation (known as 'shops') within yards of their labours and getting up in the small hours to trudge to work in all weathers.

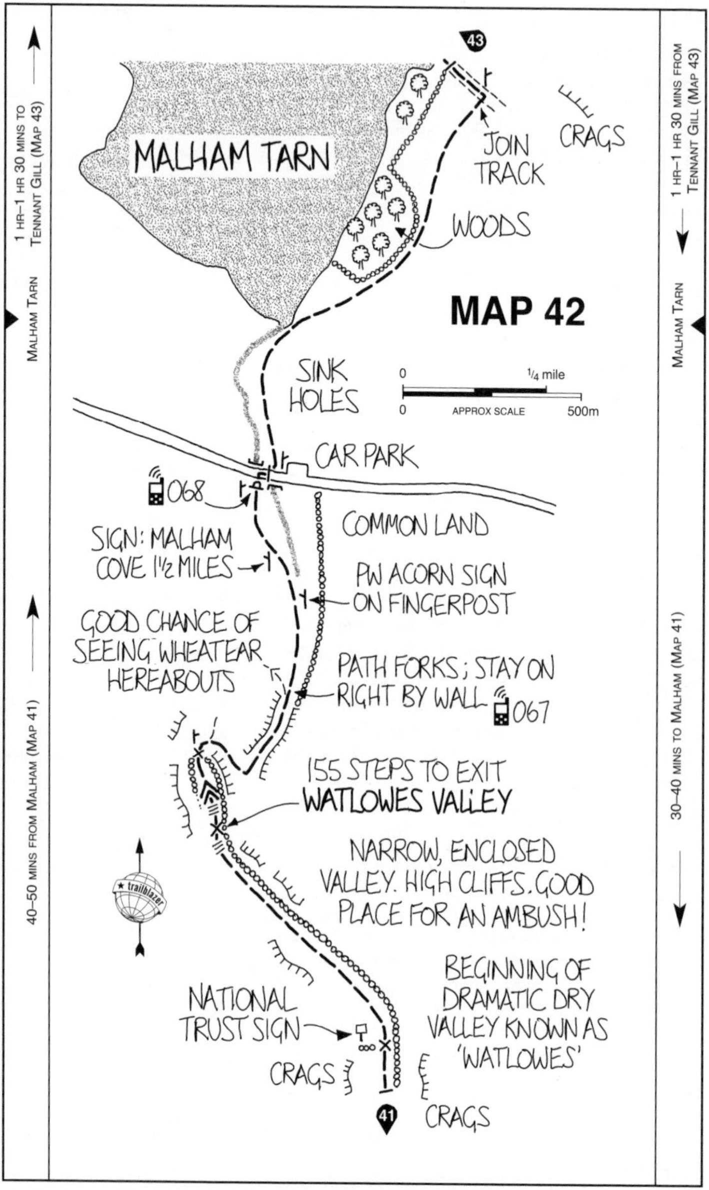
MAP 42
1 HR–1 HR 30 MINS TO TENNANT GILL (MAP 43)
MALHAM TARN
40–50 MINS FROM MALHAM (MAP 41)
1 HR–1 HR 30 MINS FROM TENNANT GILL (MAP 43)
MALHAM TARN
30–40 MINS TO MALHAM (MAP 41)
43
CRAGS
JOIN TRACK
WOODS
SINK HOLES
0 1/4 mile
0 APPROX SCALE 500m
CAR PARK
068
COMMON LAND
SIGN: MALHAM COVE 1½ MILES
PW ACORN SIGN ON FINGERPOST
GOOD CHANCE OF SEEING WHEATEAR HEREABOUTS
PATH FORKS; STAY ON RIGHT BY WALL
067
155 STEPS TO EXIT
WATLOWES VALLEY
NARROW, ENCLOSED VALLEY. HIGH CLIFFS. GOOD PLACE FOR AN AMBUSH!
trailblazer
BEGINNING OF DRAMATIC DRY VALLEY KNOWN AS 'WATLOWES'
NATIONAL TRUST SIGN
CRAGS
CRAGS
41

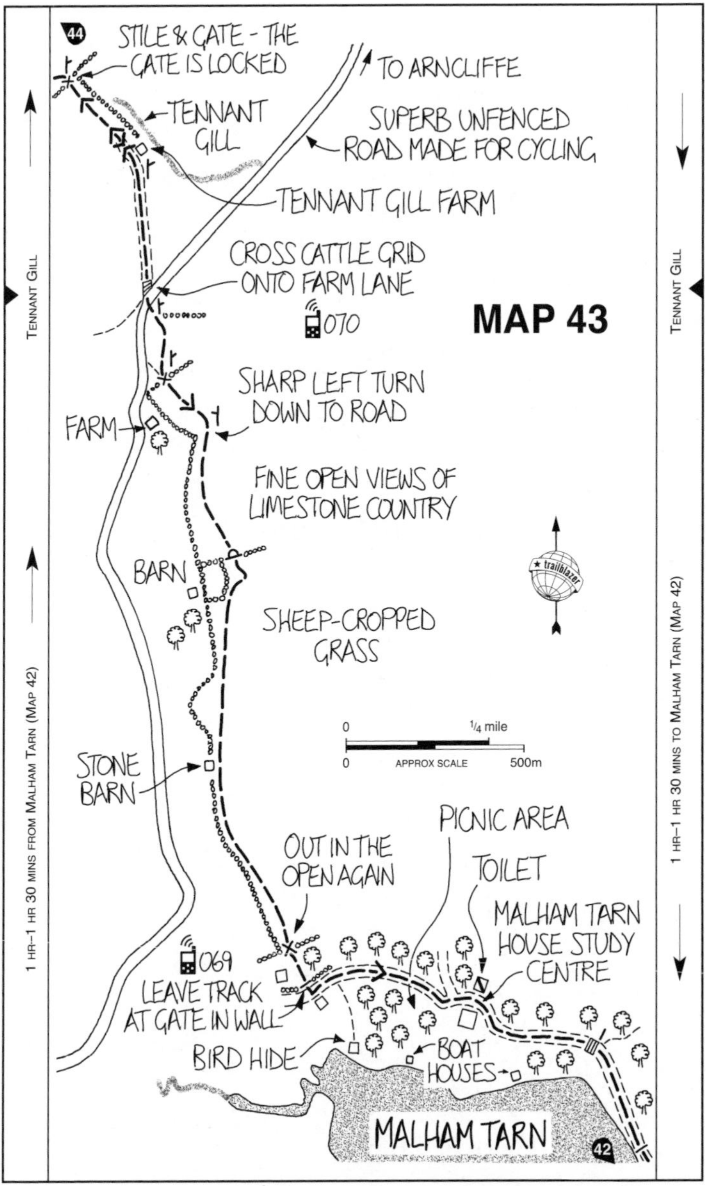
44
STILE & GATE - THE GATE IS LOCKED
TO ARNCLIFFE
TENNANT GILL
SUPERB UNFENCED ROAD MADE FOR CYCLING
TENNANT GILL FARM
CROSS CATTLE GRID ONTO FARM LANE
070
MAP 43
SHARP LEFT TURN DOWN TO ROAD
FARM
FINE OPEN VIEWS OF LIMESTONE COUNTRY
BARN
trailblazer
SHEEP-CROPPED GRASS
0
1/4 mile
0
APPROX SCALE
500m
STONE BARN
PICNIC AREA
OUT IN THE OPEN AGAIN
TOILET
MALHAM TARN HOUSE STUDY CENTRE
069
LEAVE TRACK AT GATE IN WALL
BIRD HIDE
BOAT HOUSES
MALHAM TARN
42
TENNANT GILL
1 HR–1 HR 30 MINS FROM MALHAM TARN (MAP 42)
TENNANT GILL
1 HR–1 HR 30 MINS TO MALHAM TARN (MAP 42)

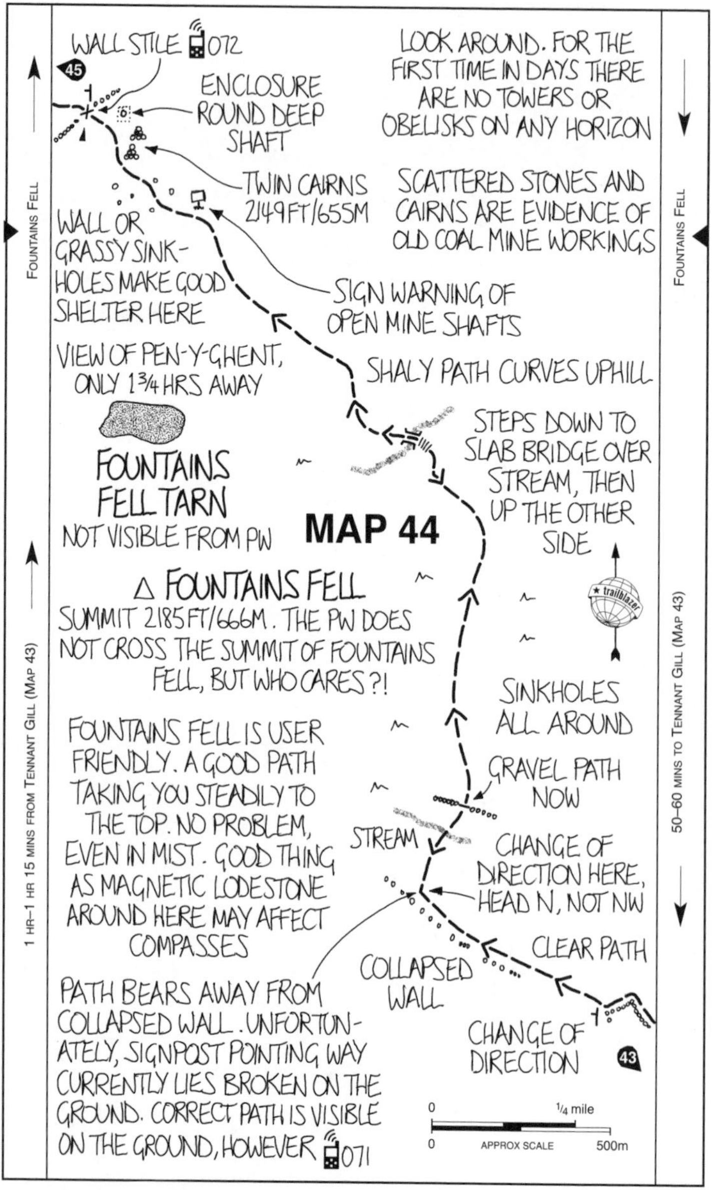

WALL STILE 072
45
ENCLOSURE ROUND DEEP SHAFT
LOOK AROUND. FOR THE FIRST TIME IN DAYS THERE ARE NO TOWERS OR OBELISKS ON ANY HORIZON
TWIN CAIRNS 2149FT/655M
SCATTERED STONES AND CAIRNS ARE EVIDENCE OF OLD COAL MINE WORKINGS
WALL OR GRASSY SINK-HOLES MAKE GOOD SHELTER HERE
SIGN WARNING OF OPEN MINE SHAFTS
VIEW OF PEN-Y-GHENT, ONLY 1¾ HRS AWAY
SHALY PATH CURVES UPHILL
STEPS DOWN TO SLAB BRIDGE OVER STREAM, THEN UP THE OTHER SIDE
FOUNTAINS FELL TARN
NOT VISIBLE FROM PW
MAP 44
△ FOUNTAINS FELL
SUMMIT 2185FT/666M. THE PW DOES NOT CROSS THE SUMMIT OF FOUNTAINS FELL, BUT WHO CARES?!
trailblazer
SINKHOLES ALL AROUND
FOUNTAINS FELL IS USER FRIENDLY. A GOOD PATH TAKING YOU STEADILY TO THE TOP. NO PROBLEM, EVEN IN MIST. GOOD THING AS MAGNETIC LODESTONE AROUND HERE MAY AFFECT COMPASSES
GRAVEL PATH NOW
STREAM
CHANGE OF DIRECTION HERE, HEAD N, NOT NW
CLEAR PATH
COLLAPSED WALL
PATH BEARS AWAY FROM COLLAPSED WALL. UNFORTUNATELY, SIGNPOST POINTING WAY CURRENTLY LIES BROKEN ON THE GROUND. CORRECT PATH IS VISIBLE ON THE GROUND, HOWEVER 071
CHANGE OF DIRECTION
43
0 ¼ mile
0 APPROX SCALE 500m
FOUNTAINS FELL
1 HR–1 HR 15 MINS FROM TENNANT GILL (MAP 43)
FOUNTAINS FELL
50–60 MINS TO TENNANT GILL (MAP 43)

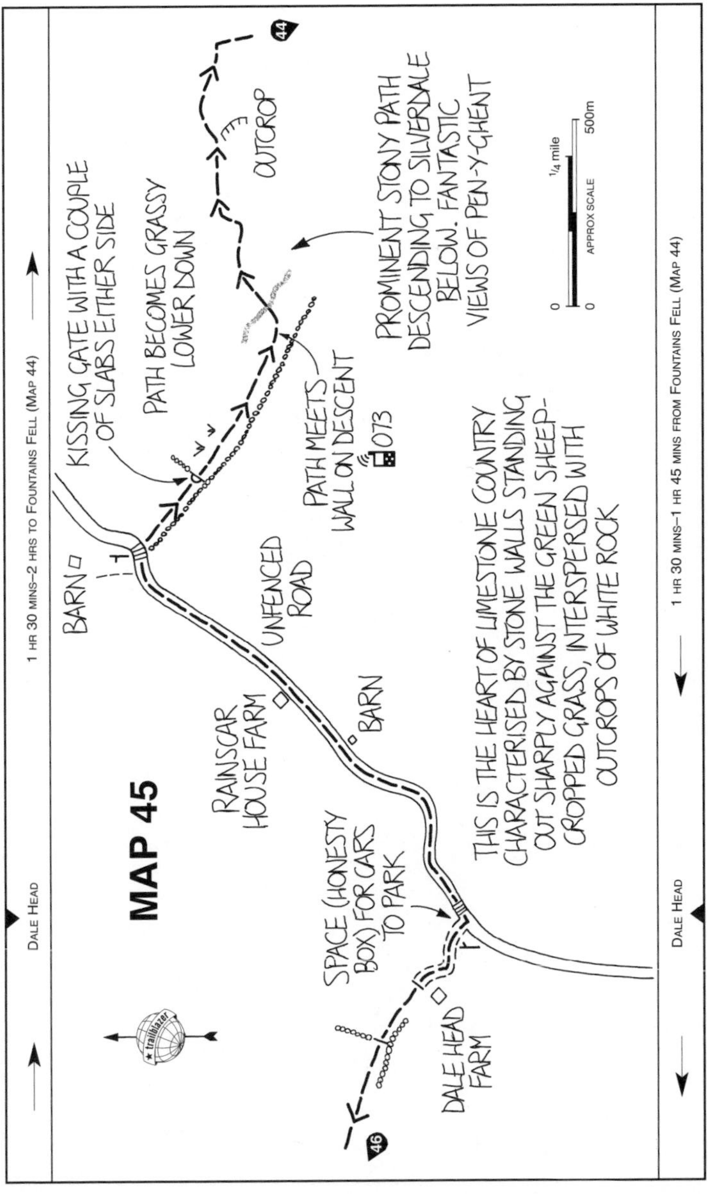
MAP 45
1 HR 30 MINS–2 HRS TO FOUNTAINS FELL (MAP 44)
DALE HEAD
44
KISSING GATE WITH A COUPLE OF SLABS EITHER SIDE
PATH BECOMES GRASSY LOWER DOWN
OUTCROP
PROMINENT STONY PATH DESCENDING TO SILVERDALE BELOW. FANTASTIC VIEWS OF PEN-Y-GHENT
BARN
UNFENCED ROAD
PATH MEETS WALL ON DESCENT
073
RAINSCAR HOUSE FARM
BARN
THIS IS THE HEART OF LIMESTONE COUNTRY CHARACTERISED BY STONE WALLS STANDING OUT SHARPLY AGAINST THE GREEN SHEEP-CROPPED GRASS, INTERSPERSED WITH OUTCROPS OF WHITE ROCK
SPACE (HONESTY BOX) FOR CARS TO PARK
DALE HEAD FARM
46
APPROX SCALE
0
1/4 mile
0
500m
1 HR 30 MINS–1 HR 45 MINS FROM FOUNTAINS FELL (MAP 44)
DALE HEAD

2 HRS–2 HRS 30 MINS FROM DALE HEAD (MAP 45) TO HORTON-IN-RIBBLESDALE (MAP 48)

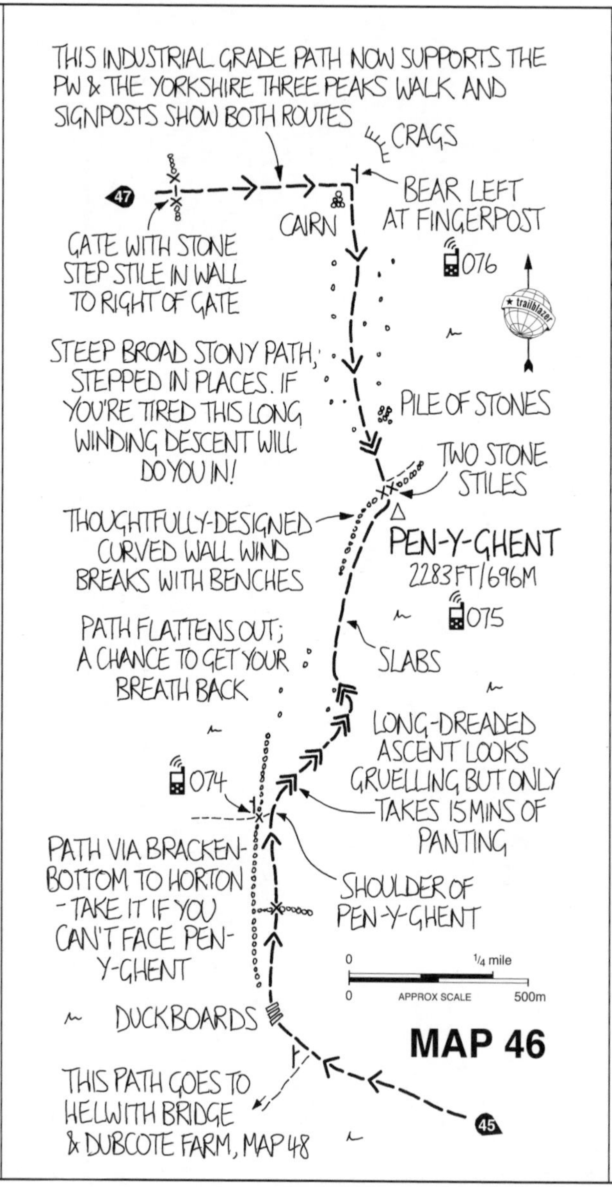
THIS INDUSTRIAL GRADE PATH NOW SUPPORTS THE PW & THE YORKSHIRE THREE PEAKS WALK AND SIGNPOSTS SHOW BOTH ROUTES
CRAGS
47
BEAR LEFT AT FINGERPOST
CAIRN
GATE WITH STONE STEP STILE IN WALL TO RIGHT OF GATE
076
trailblazer
STEEP BROAD STONY PATH; STEPPED IN PLACES. IF YOU'RE TIRED THIS LONG WINDING DESCENT WILL DO YOU IN!
PILE OF STONES
TWO STONE STILES
THOUGHTFULLY-DESIGNED CURVED WALL WIND BREAKS WITH BENCHES
PEN-Y-GHENT
2283FT/696M
075
PATH FLATTENS OUT; A CHANCE TO GET YOUR BREATH BACK
SLABS
LONG-DREADED ASCENT LOOKS GRUELLING BUT ONLY TAKES 15 MINS OF PANTING
074
PATH VIA BRACKENBOTTOM TO HORTON - TAKE IT IF YOU CAN'T FACE PEN-Y-GHENT
SHOULDER OF PEN-Y-GHENT
0
1/4 mile
0
APPROX SCALE
500m
DUCKBOARDS
MAP 46
THIS PATH GOES TO HELWITH BRIDGE & DUBCOTE FARM, MAP 48
45

2 HRS–2 HRS 30 MINS FROM HORTON-IN-RIBBLESDALE (MAP 48) TO DALE HEAD (MAP 45)

2 HRS–2 HRS 30 MINS FROM DALE HEAD (MAP 45) TO HORTON-IN-RIBBLESDALE (MAP 48) →

1 HR 45 MINS–2 HRS 15 MINS FROM LING GILL BRIDGE (MAP 50) TO HORTON-IN-RIBBLESDALE (MAP 48) →

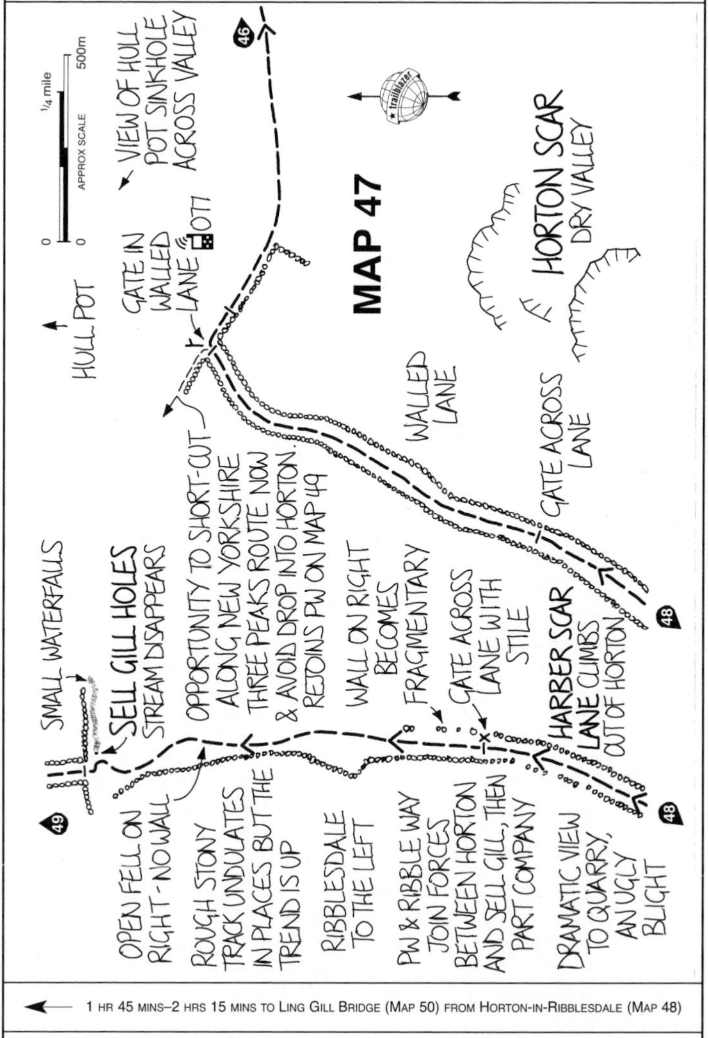

0
1/4 mile
APPROX SCALE
0
500m
VIEW OF HULL POT SINKHOLE ACROSS VALLEY
46
HULL POT
GATE IN WALLED LANE
trailblazer
MAP 47
HORTON SCAR
DRY VALLEY
WALLED LANE
GATE ACROSS LANE
48
SMALL WATERFALLS
SELL GILL HOLES
STREAM DISAPPEARS
OPPORTUNITY TO SHORT-CUT ALONG NEW YORKSHIRE THREE PEAKS ROUTE NOW & AVOID DROP INTO HORTON. REJOINS PW ON MAP 49
WALL ON RIGHT BECOMES FRAGMENTARY
GATE ACROSS LANE WITH STILE
HARBER SCAR LANE CLIMBS OUT OF HORTON
49
OPEN FELL ON RIGHT - NO WALL
ROUGH STONY TRACK UNDULATES IN PLACES BUT THE TREND IS UP
RIBBLESDALE TO THE LEFT
PW & RIBBLE WAY JOIN FORCES BETWEEN HORTON AND SELL GILL, THEN PART COMPANY
DRAMATIC VIEW TO QUARRY, AN UGLY BLIGHT
48

← 1 HR 45 MINS–2 HRS 15 MINS TO LING GILL BRIDGE (MAP 50) FROM HORTON-IN-RIBBLESDALE (MAP 48)

← 2 HRS–2 HRS 30 MINS TO DALE HEAD (MAP 45) FROM HORTON-IN-RIBBLESDALE (MAP 48)

Navigation notes

The improved signage over Fountains Fell has removed the only lingering potential point of difficulty on this section of the Way. The path round Fountains Fell is clear, even in the thickest mist, and the signs point out any changes in direction. Pen-y-ghent is so busy the path has to be industrial to cope with the footfall and as such is almost impossible to lose.

HORTON-IN-RIBBLESDALE

[Map 48]

There are no services along the route until you get to Horton, a famous landmark on the Pennine Way, as much for the presence of Pen-y-ghent Café (see below) as for the charm of the village itself.

Services

Although it was temporarily closed when we went to press, we hope the invaluable **Pen-y-ghent Café** (see also Where to eat; ☎ 01729-860333; mid Feb to mid Nov Mon & Wed-Fri 9am-5.30pm, Sat 8am-5.30pm, Sun 8.30am-5.30pm, closed Tue; weekends only Jan to mid Feb but depending on the weather) will now have reopened. It doubles as the **tourist information centre** (and can provide weather forecasts and advice on accommodation) and also sells **camping gear**, snacks, maps & books. The Bayes family who run it are very helpful, friendly, immensely knowledgeable about the area and generally provide a superb service for walkers. As well as operating a check-in/check-out service for day-walkers in the area, since the Pennine Way was opened they've kept a Pennine Way book for Wayfarers to sign as they pass. There are so many volumes there's now quite a library but it's a wonderful record of everyone who's passed along the Way. Be sure to sign it.

Limited **post office** services (Mon 3.30-6pm, Thur 9-11.30am) are provided in the Crown Hotel (see Where to stay).

Transport

[See also pp54-9] Horton is a stop on Northern Rail's Leeds–Carlisle line so **trains** are frequent, making it an ideal place to begin or end a walk along the Way. Dales Rail's seasonal Sunday service also calls here.

The only **bus** services to call here are NYCC's No 11 to and from Settle and Arriva's seasonal Sunday-only 831 service.

For a **taxi** call Settle Taxis (☎ 01729-822219).

Where to stay

In the centre of the village **camping** at ***Holme Farm*** (☎ 01729-860281; 🐕) costs £2 per tent plus £3pp; there are shower (£1) and toilet facilities. Booking is recommended; it is open all year.

At the southern end of the village, through the car park behind the Golden Lion, is ***3 Peaks Bunkroom*** (☎ 0787 084 9419, ☎ 01729-860380, 💻 3peaksbunkroom.co.uk; WI-FI), a converted barn with 40 beds in two rooms (20 beds per room); they charge £15-17.50pp. They do not provide bedding so if you stay here you will

❏ Fell running

Whilst puffing steadily up the Cam High Road (see Maps 51 & 52), you may be ignominiously overtaken by a wiry person in brief shorts, the scantiest of vests and strange-looking lightly studded shoes. He or she is a fell runner, a participant in a sport that is taken very seriously hereabouts. The routes involve the muddiest tracks and the steepest hills, the sort of terrain that most people would dismiss as un-runnable. It goes to extremes too, and the **Yorkshire Three Peaks Challenge** is one of them. On this event people have to run 26 miles (42km) from Pen-y-ghent Café up three peaks – Pen-y-ghent, Whernside and Ingleborough – which you can see around you, and back in less than 12 hours; the fastest time is less than three hours. See also p14.

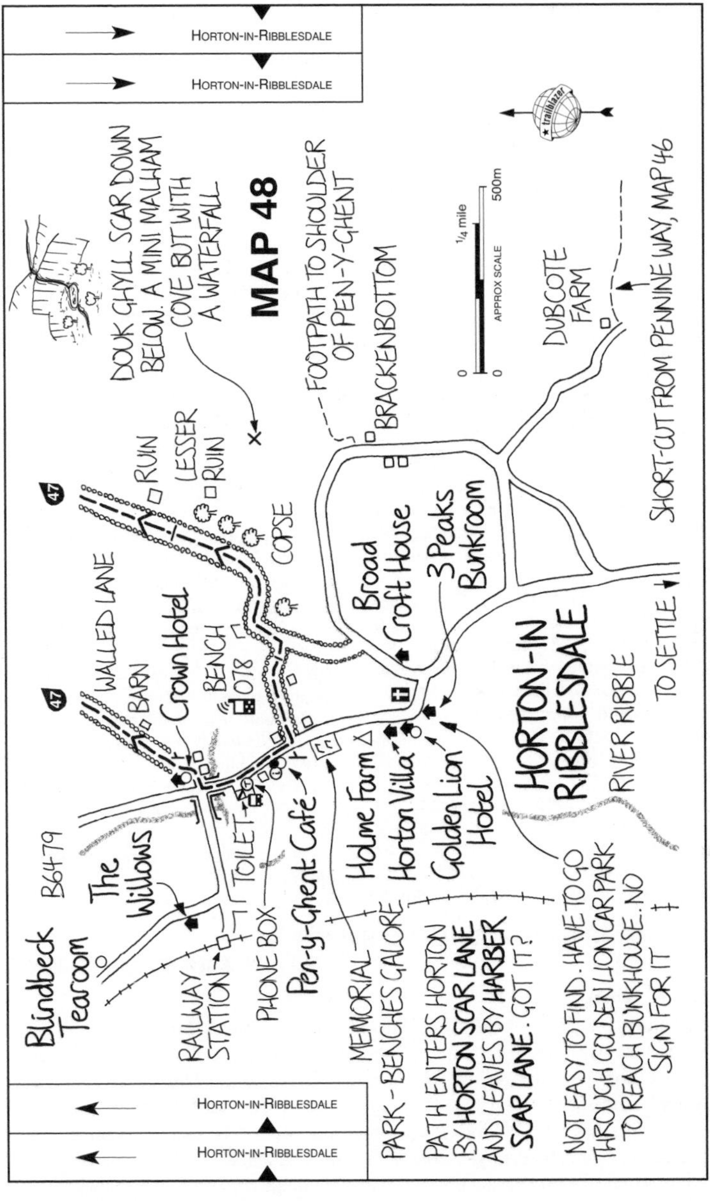
HORTON-IN-RIBBLESDALE
HORTON-IN-RIBBLESDALE
MAP 48
DOUK GHYLL SCAR DOWN BELOW. A MINI MALHAM COVE BUT WITH A WATERFALL
FOOTPATH TO SHOULDER OF PEN-Y-GHENT
BRACKENBOTTOM
0
1/4 mile
APPROX SCALE
0
500m
trailblazer
DUBCOTE FARM
SHORT-CUT FROM PENNINE WAY, MAP 46
47
47
RUIN
LESSER RUIN
COPSE
WALLED LANE
BARN
Crown Hotel
BENCH
078
Broad Croft House
3 Peaks Bunkroom
HORTON-IN RIBBLESDALE
TO SETTLE
RIVER RIBBLE
Blindbeck Tearoom
B6479
The Willows
TOILET
RAILWAY STATION
PHONE BOX
Pen-y-Ghent Café
MEMORIAL
Holme Farm Δ
Horton Villa
Golden Lion Hotel
PARK - BENCHES GALORE
PATH ENTERS HORTON BY HORTON SCAR LANE AND LEAVES BY HARBER SCAR LANE. GOT IT?
NOT EASY TO FIND. HAVE TO GO THROUGH GOLDEN LION CAR PARK TO REACH BUNKHOUSE. NO SIGN FOR IT
HORTON-IN-RIBBLESDALE
HORTON-IN-RIBBLESDALE

need a sleeping bag, pillow & towel. However, note that they do not accept bookings for fewer than five people but if a group is booked and individuals don't mind sharing they will accept single bookings; if not they are likely to send you to The Golden Lion (see below).

Crown Hotel (☎ 01729-860209, 🖳 crown-hotel.co.uk; 1S/1Tr/1D or T shared facilities, 3D/2Tr/2Qd all en suite; ♥; no WI-FI; Ⓛ) is particularly convenient as it's right on the Way. They charge approx £46-47.50pp (sgl £55-65, sgl occ £60-95) but contact them as the rates sometimes vary especially in the low season. They generally require advance bookings of at least two nights at the weekend.

The ***Golden Lion Hotel*** (☎ 01729-860206, 🖳 goldenlionhotel.co.uk; 1D/1D or T/2T/1Tr, all en suite; WI-FI downstairs only; Ⓛ) charges from £37.50pp (sgl occ from £55 but room rate at weekends) for B&B. They also have 15 beds in a **bunk room** (£12pp) with shower and toilet facilities. Breakfast may be available if there are B&B guests staying.

Horton Villa (☎ 07960 126681, 🖳 hortoninribblesdalebedandbreakfast.co.uk; 2D both en suite, 1T/1Tr shared facilities; ♥; Ⓛ) is right next to the Golden Lion and has been recommended. Breakfasts are standard fare with a daily special such as scrambled egg and smoked salmon. They charge £37.50-42.50pp (sgl occ rates on request) and recommend booking in advance. However, between April and October they only accept advance bookings of at least two nights at the weekend (Fri & Sat).

The Willows (☎ 01729-860200, 🖳 thewillowshorton.co.uk; 1D/2T, all with private facilities; ♥; WI-F; Ⓛ) charges from £45pp (sgl occ £70, though it's room rate at weekends); minimum advance booking of two nights at weekends between March and October. Breakfast is available from 6am.

Broad Croft House (☎ 01729-860419, 🖳 broadcrofthouse.co.uk; 1D/1D or T/1T, all en suite; Ⓛ) charges from £42.50pp (sgl occ from £65). Generally they don't accept bookings for one night only at weekends in the main season but contact them to check.

Where to eat and drink

Hopefully now open again, as old as the Pennine Way itself, the legendary ***Pen-y-ghent Café*** (see Services) is the obvious port of call being a 'One Stop Shop' for the walker as well as serving home-made cakes (about £2), sandwiches, filling staples such as beans on toast, vegetable soup with a roll, and chilli con carne. They also now have a number of vegan & gluten-free products.

Other options are the ***Crown Hotel*** (see Where to stay; pub grub served daily noon-2pm & 6-9pm; times vary in the winter; mains from £10.50), which has a nice garden round the back, and ***Golden Lion Hotel*** (see Where to stay; 🐕; bar food served Mon-Thur 3-9pm, Fri & Sat noon-9.30pm, Sun noon-9.30pm).

Just outside the northern end of the village is ***Blindbeck Tea Room*** (☎ 01729-860396, 🖳 blindbeck.co.uk; Mon-Tue & Thur-Fri 10am-6pm, Sat & Sun usually 9am-6pm; they may close earlier in the winter months; WI-FI) which serves home-made cakes and scones as well as hot and cold snacks.

HORTON-IN-RIBBLESDALE TO HAWES

MAP 48, MAP 47, MAPS 49-55

Route overview

13½ miles (21.5km) – 1700ft (518m) of ascent – 6¼-6¾ hours

For anyone who spent the night in Horton the day begins with the almost traditional climb out of the village; those who opted to do the Three Peaks short cut will avoid this. The path ascends along the narrow **Harber Scar Lane** (Maps 47 & 48) with the views behind (if you ignore the scar of the quarry) being an easy excuse for a breather as you soak them in. A decent space between your Full English and this immediate climb out of the village may pay dividends here.

The day ahead consists of wall-enclosed stony tracks, old packhorse trails, used for centuries as thoroughfares over the wild limestone moors and a final descent across moorland and fields into Hawes. It has to be said that the ever-present walls on this section tend to mute the exhilaration of being out on the moors, but do make for easy navigation. With limestone comes pot holes and there are many examples within easy reach of the Pennine Way. At the one at **Sell Gill Holes** (Map 47) the water from Sell Gill Beck disappears down into a gaping hole in the ground.

❑ Packhorse bridges

What is a packhorse bridge? The simple answer is that it is a bridge that was built so that packhorses and their loads could cross an obstruction, usually a river or fast-flowing stream. Packhorse bridges had certain characteristics which separated them from other bridges; they are defined as being no more than six feet wide, built prior to 1800 and have known packhorse associations.

The use of packhorses to carry goods goes back to the transport of salt which was a very important product from early times. The main routes were from Cheshire but smaller salt pans existed down much of the east and south coast and some of these routes can still be followed on old Salters roads. Wool also became very important and in 1305 over 45,000 sacks of wool were carried and exported. The peak period for packhorses was between 1650 and 1800 when all manner of goods were carried, including fish to London as well as corn, coal, charcoal and, in the Pennines, lead and iron ores as well as wool and wool products.

Goods were carried in panniers which were slung on wooden pack frames on the side of the horse. To ensure that there was adequate clearance the parapets on packhorse bridges were very low or entirely absent. When the trade ceased, parapets were often added to the bridge for the safety of pedestrians. Over the years many routes have either disappeared or been upgraded to roads and in the latter case this usually meant that the bridge disappeared.

Old routes can often be traced by the names of the pubs en route such as the Packhorse Inn, beside the Pennine Way beyond Hebden Bridge. In Yorkshire, the term 'Woolpack' indicates a packhorse route. The horses which carried the packs were known in Northern England either as Galloways or Jaegers which was a breed of packhorse from Germany. As well as pubs there are other words which indicate packhorse routes. A 'badger' was a pedlar who was licensed to carry corn from an important market to smaller markets and several badger stones exist. Stoops were guide posts and jagger, which is a corruption of jaegar is a name found on some routes.

The packhorse bridges on or near the Pennine Way include the following: **Edale** (at Ordnance Survey grid reference SK123 860 near the Old Nags Head, on Monks Road route); **Barber Booth** (SK088 861 at the foot of Jacob's Ladder on Monks Road route); **Standedge** (SE012 101, Thieves Bridge, close to where the Way crosses Thieves Clough); **Alcomden at Holme Ends** (SD956 321, 150 metres off the Way on the ascent to Walshaw Dean Lower Reservoir); **Beaumont Clough** (SD980 261, just off the Way at Edge End Farm descending from Stoodley Pike, on the path to Hebden Bridge); **Lower Strines** (SD959 285, near to Lower Strines Farm on Colden Water, visible from the Way); and **Ling Gill** (SD803 789, between Horton and Hawes).

Other packhorse bridges slightly further off the Way can be found at: **Hayfield** (SK050 870); **Marsden** (SE046 117 and SE029 121); **Hebden Bridge** (SD993 273 and SD992 278); **Haworth** (SE020 376 and SE015 375); and **Ravenseat** (NY862 034 after Keld, which is an alternative route to Tan Hill). **William Gallon**

ROUTE GUIDE AND MAPS

The Way now crosses **Jackdaw Hill** (Map 49; 1312ft/400m) on an old trading route. The landscape is known as 'karst'; a geographical term derived from an area of Slovenia and characterised by limestone scars, clints, ravines and dried river beds. The reserve at **Ling Gill** (Map 50), with its deep ravine, protects important native tree species. Just beyond is the **packhorse bridge** (see box on p159), at **Ling Gill Bridge**, with its fading inscription, and the route continues out onto the open expanse of Cam Fell. Here the path meets the harsh logging road at **Cam End**, which provides immense views to all three of the Yorkshire Three Peaks as well as Ribblehead Viaduct and also carries the Pennine Way to **Cam High Road** (Maps 51 & 52), the route of an old Roman road.

Kidhow Gate (Map 53) has long been used by farmers to gather their sheep before driving them to market and it also marks the point at which the path leaves the tarmac to join **West Cam Road** (Map 53), another old drove route above the lush valley of Snaizeholme, hugging the lip of **Dodd Fell** on your right with the valley dropping away to the left. Hills surround you, the sky is huge, the path unravels easily and the moorland walking is straightforward down **Rottenstone Hill** (Map 54) and into Hawes, which is visible long before you reach it, beckoning on down to its numerous pubs, cafés and shops. Make the most of the facilities in **Hawes** (Map 55) as they aren't replicated for another 35 miles (56km), until you reach Middleton-in-Teesdale.

Navigation notes

The only chance of going wrong on this section is the descent of Rottenstone Hill, where the path isn't always obvious on the ground and you may be dodging boggy sections if it's been raining recently. Even in bad visibility it would be hard to go too far wrong though. If in doubt aim for the half-size wooden gate at GPS 087 on Map 54.

❑ Black (and red) grouse

Pennine Way walkers are unlikely to get as far as Bowes without seeing, or at least hearing, red grouse. Their distinctive nagging croak, which has been likened to the warning 'go-back, go-back, go-back', is a familiar sound on wild heather moors, as familiar as the lonely bubbling call of the curlew or the insistent pipe of the golden plover.

While the red grouse is the primary target of many a landowner's gun, the black grouse is a different matter altogether. Shot almost to extinction across most of Northern England, it is now only plentiful in the Scottish hills where the vast space and better cover have enabled it to survive in some numbers. In the Pennines only a few remain and these are carefully protected by gamekeepers and conservationists alike. Most keepers now appreciate the bird for its own sake and, like their changing attitudes to birds of prey, are simply glad it has survived.

In Baldersdale (see p190) black grouse have been seen near the former YHA hostel where their curious courtship ritual was described to me by the warden. The hen birds line up on the branch of a tree like spectators grabbing the best seats in the stands to watch the cock birds perform their 'lek', a display acted out on a piece of prepared ground on which they parade, each trying to outdo the others in their strutting and posturing. Their lyre-shaped tail feathers are fanned out in a magnificent demonstration to win the hens' affections.

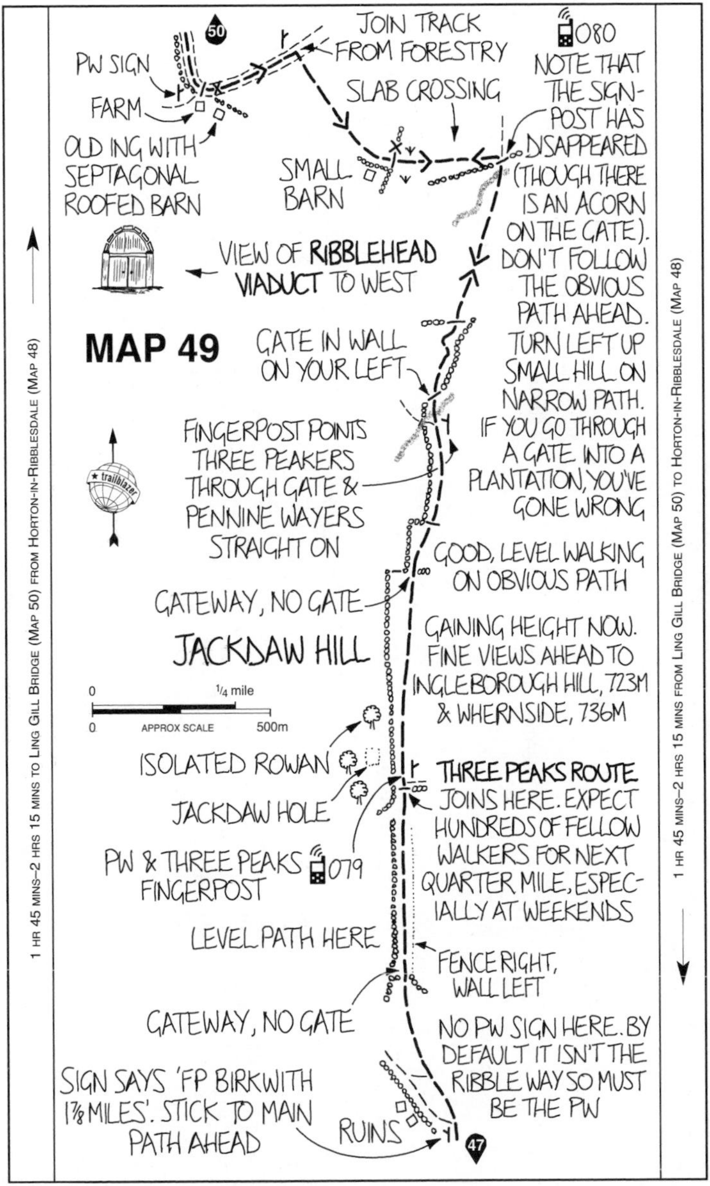
MAP 49
JOIN TRACK FROM FORESTRY
080
NOTE THAT THE SIGN-POST HAS DISAPPEARED (THOUGH THERE IS AN ACORN ON THE GATE). DON'T FOLLOW THE OBVIOUS PATH AHEAD. TURN LEFT UP SMALL HILL ON NARROW PATH. IF YOU GO THROUGH A GATE INTO A PLANTATION, YOU'VE GONE WRONG
PW SIGN
FARM
OLD ING WITH SEPTAGONAL ROOFED BARN
SLAB CROSSING
SMALL BARN
VIEW OF RIBBLEHEAD VIADUCT TO WEST
GATE IN WALL ON YOUR LEFT
FINGERPOST POINTS THREE PEAKERS THROUGH GATE & PENNINE WAYERS STRAIGHT ON
GOOD, LEVEL WALKING ON OBVIOUS PATH
GATEWAY, NO GATE
JACKDAW HILL
GAINING HEIGHT NOW. FINE VIEWS AHEAD TO INGLEBOROUGH HILL, 723M & WHERNSIDE, 736M
0
1/4 mile
0
APPROX SCALE
500m
ISOLATED ROWAN
JACKDAW HOLE
THREE PEAKS ROUTE JOINS HERE. EXPECT HUNDREDS OF FELLOW WALKERS FOR NEXT QUARTER MILE, ESPECIALLY AT WEEKENDS
PW & THREE PEAKS FINGERPOST
079
LEVEL PATH HERE
FENCE RIGHT, WALL LEFT
GATEWAY, NO GATE
NO PW SIGN HERE. BY DEFAULT IT ISN'T THE RIBBLE WAY SO MUST BE THE PW
SIGN SAYS 'FP BIRKWITH 1⅞ MILES'. STICK TO MAIN PATH AHEAD
RUINS
50
47
trailblazer
1 HR 45 MINS–2 HRS 15 MINS TO LING GILL BRIDGE (MAP 50) FROM HORTON-IN-RIBBLESDALE (MAP 48)
1 HR 45 MINS–2 HRS 15 MINS FROM LING GILL BRIDGE (MAP 50) TO HORTON-IN-RIBBLESDALE (MAP 48)

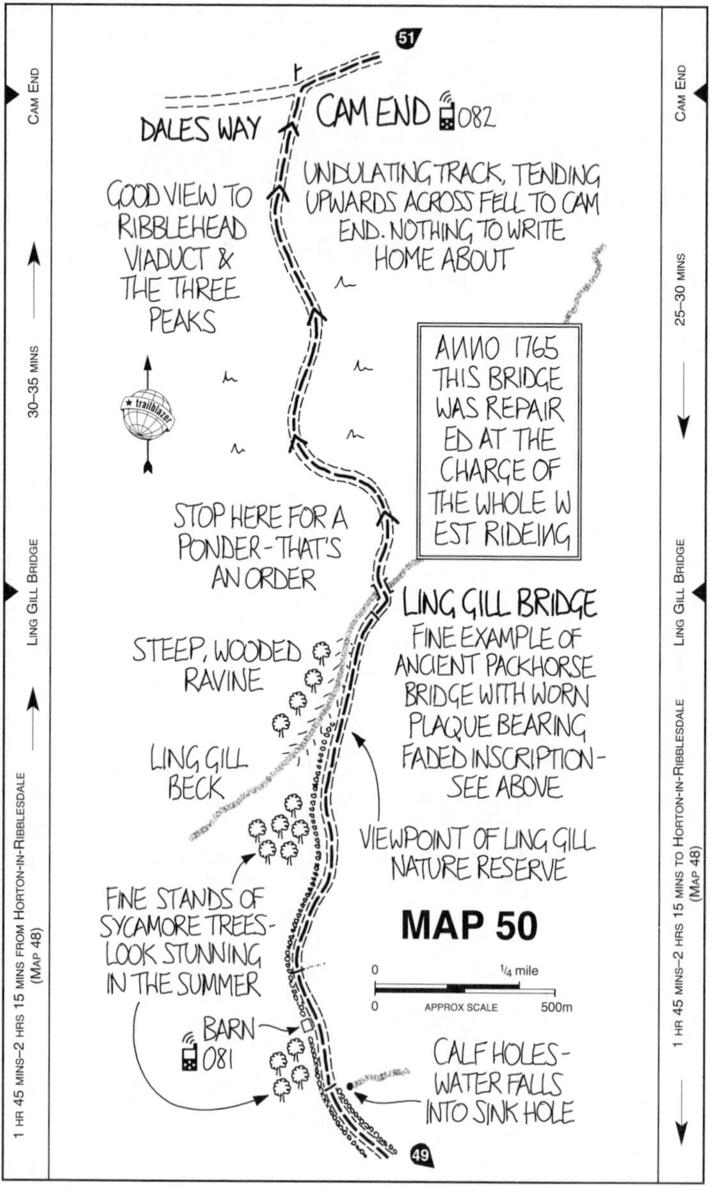

CAM END
30–35 MINS
LING GILL BRIDGE
1 HR 45 MINS–2 HRS 15 MINS FROM HORTON-IN-RIBBLESDALE (MAP 48)
CAM END
25–30 MINS
LING GILL BRIDGE
1 HR 45 MINS–2 HRS 15 MINS TO HORTON-IN-RIBBLESDALE (MAP 48)
51
DALES WAY
CAM END 082
GOOD VIEW TO RIBBLEHEAD VIADUCT & THE THREE PEAKS
UNDULATING TRACK, TENDING UPWARDS ACROSS FELL TO CAM END. NOTHING TO WRITE HOME ABOUT
trailblazer
ANNO 1765 THIS BRIDGE WAS REPAIR ED AT THE CHARGE OF THE WHOLE W EST RIDEING
STOP HERE FOR A PONDER - THAT'S AN ORDER
LING GILL BRIDGE
FINE EXAMPLE OF ANCIENT PACKHORSE BRIDGE WITH WORN PLAQUE BEARING FADED INSCRIPTION - SEE ABOVE
STEEP, WOODED RAVINE
LING GILL BECK
VIEWPOINT OF LING GILL NATURE RESERVE
FINE STANDS OF SYCAMORE TREES - LOOK STUNNING IN THE SUMMER
MAP 50
0
1/4 mile
0
APPROX SCALE
500m
BARN
081
CALF HOLES - WATER FALLS INTO SINK HOLE
49

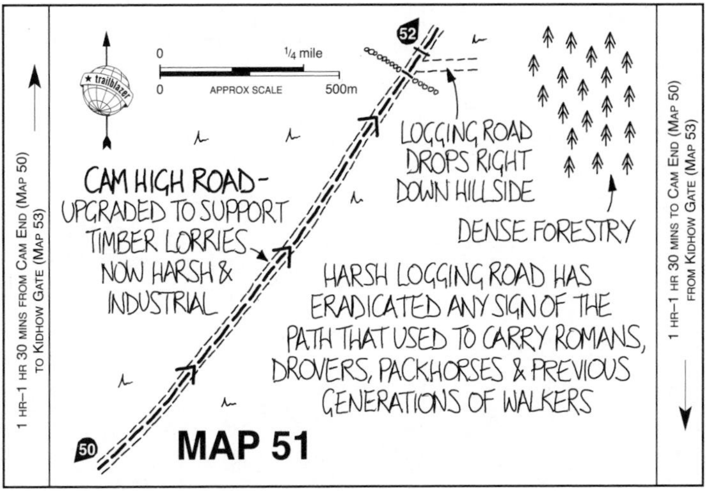
1 HR–1 HR 30 MINS FROM CAM END (MAP 50) TO KIDHOW GATE (MAP 53)
1 HR–1 HR 30 MINS TO CAM END (MAP 50) FROM KIDHOW GATE (MAP 53)
0 1/4 mile
0 APPROX SCALE 500m
52
LOGGING ROAD DROPS RIGHT DOWN HILLSIDE
CAM HIGH ROAD - UPGRADED TO SUPPORT TIMBER LORRIES NOW HARSH & INDUSTRIAL
DENSE FORESTRY
HARSH LOGGING ROAD HAS ERADICATED ANY SIGN OF THE PATH THAT USED TO CARRY ROMANS, DROVERS, PACKHORSES & PREVIOUS GENERATIONS OF WALKERS
50
MAP 51

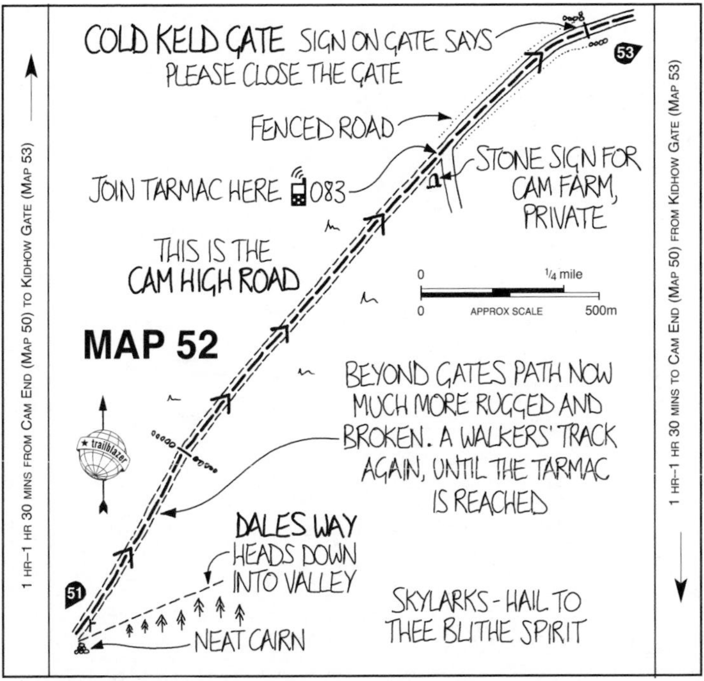
1 HR–1 HR 30 MINS FROM CAM END (MAP 50) TO KIDHOW GATE (MAP 53)
1 HR–1 HR 30 MINS TO CAM END (MAP 50) FROM KIDHOW GATE (MAP 53)
COLD KELD GATE SIGN ON GATE SAYS PLEASE CLOSE THE GATE
53
FENCED ROAD
JOIN TARMAC HERE 083
STONE SIGN FOR CAM FARM, PRIVATE
THIS IS THE CAM HIGH ROAD
0 1/4 mile
0 APPROX SCALE 500m
MAP 52
BEYOND GATES PATH NOW MUCH MORE RUGGED AND BROKEN. A WALKERS' TRACK AGAIN, UNTIL THE TARMAC IS REACHED
DALES WAY HEADS DOWN INTO VALLEY
51
NEAT CAIRN
SKYLARKS - HAIL TO THEE BLITHE SPIRIT

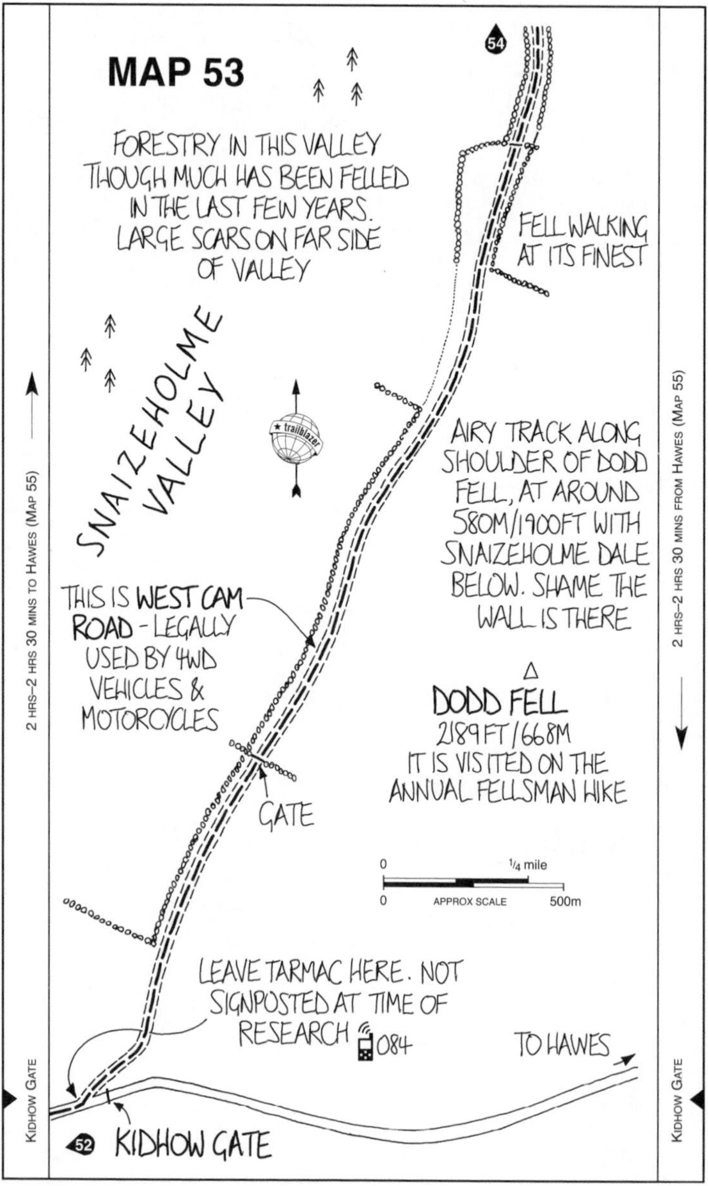
MAP 53
FORESTRY IN THIS VALLEY THOUGH MUCH HAS BEEN FELLED IN THE LAST FEW YEARS. LARGE SCARS ON FAR SIDE OF VALLEY
SNAIZEHOLME VALLEY
FELL WALKING AT ITS FINEST
AIRY TRACK ALONG SHOULDER OF DODD FELL, AT AROUND 580M/1900FT WITH SNAIZEHOLME DALE BELOW. SHAME THE WALL IS THERE
THIS IS WEST CAM ROAD - LEGALLY USED BY 4WD VEHICLES & MOTORCYCLES
DODD FELL
2189FT/668M
IT IS VISITED ON THE ANNUAL FELLSMAN HIKE
GATE
0
1/4 mile
0
APPROX SCALE
500m
LEAVE TARMAC HERE. NOT SIGNPOSTED AT TIME OF RESEARCH 084
TO HAWES
KIDHOW GATE
54
52
2 HRS–2 HRS 30 MINS TO HAWES (MAP 55)
2 HRS–2 HRS 30 MINS FROM HAWES (MAP 55)
KIDHOW GATE
KIDHOW GATE

HAWES **[Map 55a, p169]**

At 850ft (259m) above sea level, Hawes is the highest town in England that still holds a regular market on Tuesdays. It's a down-to-earth Yorkshire town with a vibrant centre full of pubs and cafés. If you're in need of a break this could be the place to relax for a day or so. There's plenty to see: a good local museum, a traditional ropemaker – and this is the home of the world-famous Wensleydale cheese.

At the award-winning **Wensleydale Creamery** (☎ 01969-667664, 🖳 wensleydale.co.uk; Easter to Oct daily 9am-4pm, winter daily but hours vary so contact them) the 900-year-old art of local cheese-making was nearly lost, only to be saved by

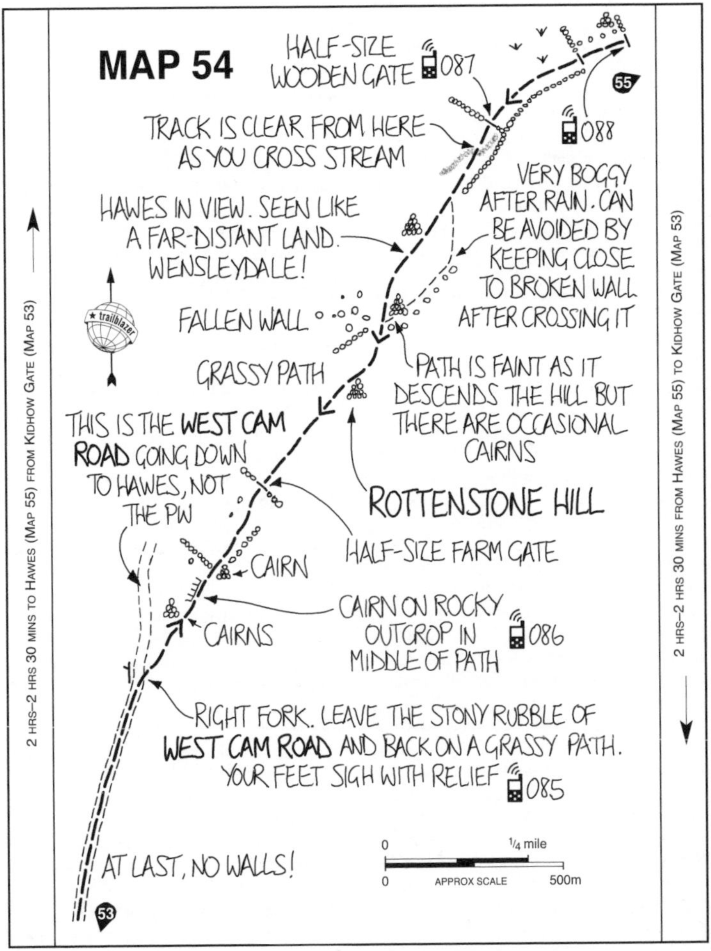
MAP 54
2 HRS–2 HRS 30 MINS TO HAWES (MAP 55) FROM KIDHOW GATE (MAP 53)
2 HRS–2 HRS 30 MINS FROM HAWES (MAP 55) TO KIDHOW GATE (MAP 53)
HALF-SIZE WOODEN GATE 087
55
088
TRACK IS CLEAR FROM HERE AS YOU CROSS STREAM
VERY BOGGY AFTER RAIN. CAN BE AVOIDED BY KEEPING CLOSE TO BROKEN WALL AFTER CROSSING IT
HAWES IN VIEW. SEEN LIKE A FAR-DISTANT LAND. WENSLEYDALE!
trailblazer
FALLEN WALL
GRASSY PATH
PATH IS FAINT AS IT DESCENDS THE HILL BUT THERE ARE OCCASIONAL CAIRNS
THIS IS THE WEST CAM ROAD GOING DOWN TO HAWES, NOT THE PW
ROTTENSTONE HILL
HALF-SIZE FARM GATE
CAIRN
CAIRN ON ROCKY OUTCROP IN MIDDLE OF PATH
CAIRNS
086
RIGHT FORK. LEAVE THE STONY RUBBLE OF WEST CAM ROAD AND BACK ON A GRASSY PATH. YOUR FEET SIGH WITH RELIEF
085
0
¼ mile
0
APPROX SCALE
500m
AT LAST, NO WALLS!
53

the international popularity of Wensleydale-cheese-munching characters Wallace & Gromit. Blending Wensleydale with cranberries soon became a best-seller, and now there's an array of Wensleydale cheeses with blends including apricot, pineapple, mango & ginger, and garlic & chives for the delectation of gourmet *fromageurs*. Phone in advance if you want to go on the Cheese Experience Tour (£3.95) as cheese is not made every day. See also Where to eat.

Dales Countryside Museum (☎ 01969-666210, 🖳 www.dalescountrysidemuseum.org.uk; daily Feb-Oct 10am-5pm, Nov-Dec 10am-4.30pm, last entry to the museum one hour before closing; adults £4.80, children under 16 free) is informative; see also Services. Nearby **The Ropemaker** (W R Outhwaite & Son; 🖳 www.ropemakers.co.uk; Mon-Fri 9am-5.30pm) is not something you'll find in every town.

See p14 for details of events held here.

Transport

The nearest **railway station** is 13 miles away at Garsdale, on Northern Rail's Carlisle–Leeds services see box p59 for details) and Dales Rail's (🖳 communityrail lancashire.co.uk/lines/dalesrail/seasonal) seasonal Blackpool–Carlisle service.

The best way to get there is by **taxi** (try Country Taxis ☎ 01969-667096, 🖳 www.countrytaxis.com), unless you are here at the right time to get Little White Bus's No 113 (Garsdale Station Shuttle) **bus**, which operates at scheduled times though is also a demand-responsive service so you can book it; see box pp54-9 for details. This company actually provides a vital transport link between Hawes and the outside world, with their No 156 (Wensleydale Voyager: Gayle to Leyburn) being the town's most frequent service; for while Hawes is on a number of other **bus** routes, they seem to run on Sunday & Bank Hols only, including Arriva's (seasonal) 830, 831, 857 & 875 and Proctor's Coaches No 856. The exception is Cumbria Classic Coaches (seasonal) 569 service which leaves on a Tuesday.

Services

Both Hawes National Park Centre and the **tourist information centre** (same phone and opening hours, 🖳 yorkshiredales.org.uk) are in Dales Countryside Museum (see column opposite).

A useful website for information on the town is 🖳 wensleydale.org.

There's a Spar **supermarket** (Mon-Sat 7.30am-6pm, Sun 9am-5pm) while Elijah Allen & Sons (Mon-Sat 7.45am-5.30pm) is a wonderful old **grocery store** that shows how it used to be done and has been run by the same family since 1870. On Tuesdays there's a street **market**.

For **outdoor gear** there's Three Peaks (Mon-Sat 10am-4.30pm, Sun 11am-2pm), which has a selection of boots if yours have had it, or try Stewart R Cunningham (Mon-Sat 9am-5.30pm, Sun 9.30am-4.30pm).

The **post office** (Mon-Fri 9am-5.30pm, Sat to 12.30pm) and library with **internet access** (£2.50 for 30 mins on a computer; free WI-FI) share both opening times and premises at The Neukin on Market Place, a small cul-de-sac just off the main street. There's also a **launderette** (Mon-Tue & Thur-Sat 9.30am-4pm), a **chemist** (Mon-Sat 9am-5.30pm), and both the HSBC and Barclays branches have **ATMs** and there's one by the public toilets too.

Where to stay

There are two places where you can **camp**: ***Bainbridge Ings Caravan and Camping Site*** (☎ 01969-667354, 🖳 bainbridge-ings-countrypark.co.uk; 🐕), three-quarters of a mile east of Market Place, where you can pitch your tent (£8pp for walkers) in beautiful countryside. There are toilet, shower (20p) and laundry (coin-operated machines) facilities. Booking is recommended in the school summer holidays.

The second option is ***YHA Hawes*** (bookings ☎ 0345-371 9120, 🖳 yha.org.uk/hostel/hawes; Ⓛ; Mar/Apr-Oct); the comparatively bland exterior of this place belies the fact that it has all the trimmings inside, including 52 **beds** (2 x 2- en suite, 4 x 2-, 3 x 3-, 1 x 4-, 2 x 6-, 1 x 7-, 1 x 8-bed rooms) from £13pp (private rooms from £29); some rooms have bunk beds and some single

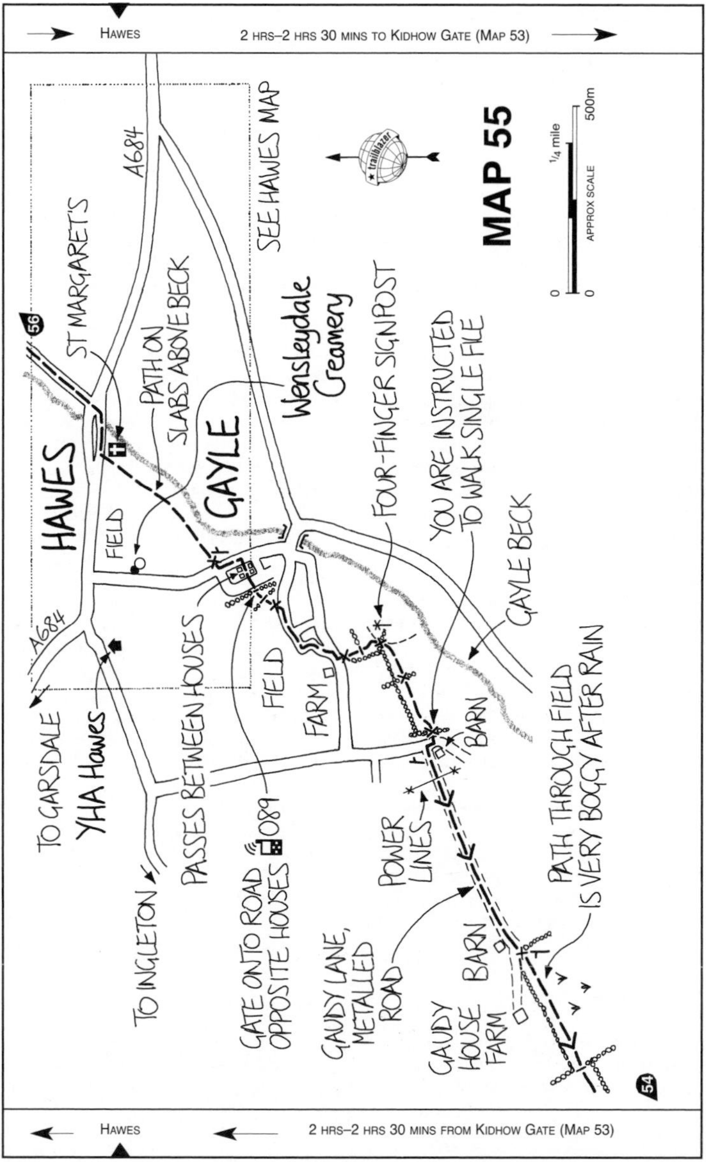
HAWES
2 HRS–2 HRS 30 MINS TO KIDHOW GATE (MAP 53)
HAWES
2 HRS–2 HRS 30 MINS FROM KIDHOW GATE (MAP 53)
MAP 55
APPROX SCALE
1/4 mile
500m
0
0
trailblazer
SEE HAWES MAP
A684
A684
ST MARGARET'S
HAWES
GAYLE
FIELD
PATH ON SLABS ABOVE BECK
Wensleydale Creamery
FOUR-FINGER SIGNPOST
YOU ARE INSTRUCTED TO WALK SINGLE FILE
GAYLE BECK
FIELD
FARM
BARN
PATH THROUGH FIELD IS VERY BOGGY AFTER RAIN
TO GARSDALE
YHA Hawes
TO INGLETON
PASSES BETWEEN HOUSES
089
GATE ONTO ROAD OPPOSITE HOUSES
POWER LINES
GAUDY LANE, METALLED ROAD
GAUDY HOUSE FARM
BARN
56
54

beds. It opens at 5pm. Meals are available and the hostel has a licence. There is also a self-catering kitchen and a drying room.

There's a clutch of **B&Bs** to the east of town which include ***Wensleydale House*** (☎ 01969-666020, 🖳 wensleydalehouse.co.uk; 2D or T/1D, all en suite; ▼; Ⓛ), who do B&B from £42.50pp (sgl occ £60) and across the road ***Crosby House*** (☎ 01969-667322, 🖳 crosbyhousehawes.co.uk; 2D/1D or T, all en suite; ▼; Ⓛ) is equally comfortable and charges from £42.50pp (sgl occ £75). They also have a single room which is joined to a double so can be used for a group of three; if the double is not booked they are happy to let the single as a single room (from £60) but only at the last minute.

Of the pubs offering accommodation, the finest is the 16th-century ***White Hart*** (☎ 01969-667214, 🖳 whitehartcountryinn.co.uk; 3D/2T, all en suite; ▼; Ⓛ; 🐕), on Main St, where all rooms are fitted with plasma TVs with DVD player; B&B costs from £50pp (sgl occ £60).

Laburnum House (☎ 01969-667970, 🖳 laburnumhouse.org.uk; 1T/1D/1Tr, all en suite; ▼; Ⓛ; 🐕; Feb-Dec), The Holme, has rooms costing from £35pp (sgl occ £45) and is just off Market Place.

Also just off Market Place, is ***Herriot's*** (☎ 01969-667536, 🖳 herriotsinhawes.co.uk; 1S/2T/2D/1Tr, all en suite; ▼; Ⓛ; 🐕) which charges from £41pp (sgl/sgl occ £50/75); they have an art gallery and a café (see Where to eat).

Fair View House (☎ 01969-667348, 🖳 fairview-hawes.co.uk; 2S share shower room, 1D/1D or T/1Tr, all en suite; Ⓛ; Mar-mid Nov) is another imposing Victorian property where B&B costs from £42.50pp (sgl £45, sgl occ rates on request).

Probably the best **hotel** is ***Cockett's*** (☎ 01969-667312, 🖳 cocketts.co.uk; 1S/7D/2D or T/1Tr, all en suite; ▼; Ⓛ), which charges from £42.50pp (sgl/sgl occ from £48/55). Two of the rooms have four-poster beds.

B&B at ***The Board Inn*** (☎ 01969-667223, 🖳 theboardinn.co.uk; 1S private facilities, 2D/2D or T, all en suite; ▼; Ⓛ; 🐕) costs £45-50pp (sgl from £45, sgl occ in a double £90) while at ***The Bull's Head Guesthouse*** (☎ 01969-667437; 1D private bathroom, 3D/1Tr, all en suite; ▼; Ⓛ; 🐕) the rate for B&B is from £40pp (sgl occ £60). Note that the sign outside may still say The Bull's Head Hotel but this is not a hotel.

Where to eat and drink

Calvert's Restaurant at Wensleydale Creamery (see p165) is open every day (food served 11.30am-3.30pm) and there is also the ***1897 Coffee Shop*** on the same site (food daily 9am-4.30pm); note that both places shut an hour earlier in winter.

On Market Place, at the western end of the high street, is ***Penny Garth Café*** (☎ 01969-667066, 🖳 pennygarthcafe.co.uk; summer Mon-Fri 10am-4pm, Sat & Sun 9am-9pm, winter days and hours are variable), a legendary lunch stop for bikers but equally welcoming to Pennine Way walkers. They have picnic tables on the street out front where you can tuck into sausage, egg & chips (£4.95) and large English breakfasts (£6.50) amongst other delights. They also serve pizza (Sat & Sun 5-9pm).

Back in town, ***Bay Tree Café & Bistro*** offers quiches and hot or cold baguettes with tasty fillings while a fine dinner in town is waiting for you at ***Cockett's*** (see Where to stay; Wed-Mon 6.30-8.30pm) where a rack of lamb will cost £16.95. Well worth the slog from Horton, if not Edale itself!

❑ Where to stay: the details

▼ means at least one room has a bath; Ⓛ signifies that a packed lunch is available if requested in advance; 🐕 signifies that dogs are welcome in at least one room but always by prior arrangement. A charge may also be payable (see also p82).

WI-FI is now available at most hostels, pubs and cafés as well as places offering B&B-style accommodation (but not always at campsites) so it is no longer specified.

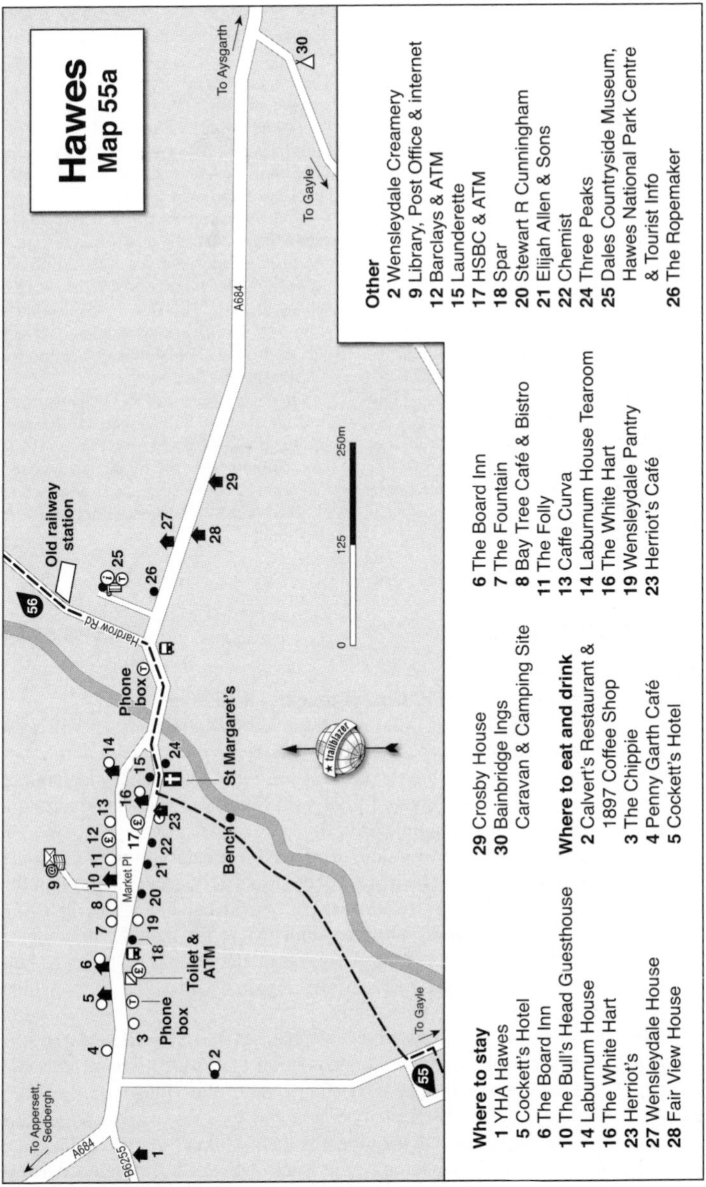
Hawes
Map 55a
To Aysgarth
To Gayle
A684
30
Old railway station
56
Hardrow Rd
25
26
27
28
29
0
125
250m
Phone box
14
15
16
13
12
11
10
9
8
7
6
5
4
3
2
1
17
18
19
20
21
22
23
24
Market Pl
St Margaret's
Bench
Toilet & ATM
Phone box
To Gayle
55
To Appersett, Sedbergh
A684
B6255
trailblazer
Where to stay
1 YHA Hawes
5 Cockett's Hotel
6 The Board Inn
10 The Bull's Head Guesthouse
14 Laburnum House
16 The White Hart
23 Herriot's
27 Wensleydale House
28 Fair View House
29 Crosby House
30 Bainbridge Ings Caravan & Camping Site
Where to eat and drink
2 Calvert's Restaurant & 1897 Coffee Shop
3 The Chippie
4 Penny Garth Café
5 Cockett's Hotel
6 The Board Inn
7 The Fountain
8 Bay Tree Café & Bistro
11 The Folly
13 Caffe Curva
14 Laburnum House Tearoom
16 The White Hart
19 Wensleydale Pantry
23 Herriot's Café
Other
2 Wensleydale Creamery
9 Library, Post Office & internet
12 Barclays & ATM
15 Launderette
17 HSBC & ATM
18 Spar
20 Stewart R Cunningham
21 Elijah Allen & Sons
22 Chemist
24 Three Peaks
25 Dales Countryside Museum, Hawes National Park Centre & Tourist Info
26 The Ropemaker

None of the above allows dogs on their premises but if you're walking with man's best friend a couple of cafés will open their doors to you: ***The Folly*** (☎ 01969-666852; daily 10am-4pm, days/hours variable in winter; 🐕) is a busy little place but one that always greets you and your pooch with a smile. Their sandwiches are great (from £3.95 – though you need a big mouth to manage one!) and their cakes delicious too. It's only a little place, and it shares its premises with a second-hand clothes store, but we really like it here. Note that they accept cash only. Canines are also welcome at ***Herriot's*** (see Where to stay; Thur-Tue 11am-3pm), which serves light lunches, cream teas and cakes. They also make a lot of what they serve including some excellent homemade soups and bread (£4.75).

The White Hart (see Where to stay; bar open all day; food served daily noon-3.30pm & 5-8.30pm) is a welcoming locals' pub and it provides a square meal from around £12.95.

You can also get bar meals at ***The Fountain*** (💻 fountainhawes.co.uk; daily noon-2.30pm & 6-8pm) and ***The Board Inn*** (see Where to stay; food daily noon-2.30pm & 6-8pm, Sun noon-2.30pm only). The latter does a mean plate of Cumberland sausage and Yorkshire pud (£11.75).

Wensleydale Pantry (☎ 01969-667202; Apr-Oct Sun-Fri 8.30am-8pm, Sat to 8.30pm, Nov-Mar daily 8.30am-4.30pm) has meals for around £10-12.

On the corner is ***Caffe Curva*** (daily 9am-4.30pm); it has a small outside terrace and does wonderful filled rolls for £5.95. Close by, ***Laburnum House Tearoom*** (see Where to stay; Feb-Dec Fri-Wed 10am-4pm; 🐕) serves home-made food – including a lovely Wensleydale cream tea (£4.50pp) – in a nice setting.

If you've been craving a change from steak & ale pie and Cumberland sausage, you're now in luck, for close to the YHA is ***The Chippie*** (💻 thechippiehawes.co.uk; Tue-Sat 11.30am-2pm & 5-9pm, Sun 11.30am-6pm), a traditional English fish & chip shop.

HAWES TO TAN HILL — MAPS 55-64

Route overview

16 miles (25.5km) – 3300ft (1005m) of ascent – 8-10 hours

The limestone of the southern Dales is behind you now and the path will soon return, for a short while at least, to the peat landscapes encountered at the start of the walk. First though you have a pleasant stroll through Wensleydale, out of Hawes, across hay meadows chock full of wild flowers in early summer but a delight to walk through at any time of year.

If you've been tormented by rain since leaving Edale you may get some compensation from a visit to **Hardraw Force** (waterfall); access is through the Green Dragon Inn in **Hardraw** (Map 56). This side excursion is only delaying the inevitable ascent of **Great Shunner Fell** (Map 59) though; standing at 2349ft (716m) this is Yorkshire's third highest mountain, but no ropes or helmets are required, just strong calf muscles to carry you along the 4½-mile (7.4km) track from the pub to the summit.

The long, gentle descent towards Swaledale and into **Thwaite** (Map 61) is rewarded with a ***café*** in Kearton Country Hotel (see p175), where you can recharge your batteries before the next climb, out of the village, up the steep slopes of **Kisdon Hill**. In early September you may look down and see the marquees of the annual show held in the little village of Muker (see p176). The path around Kisdon is splendid, leading to the head of Swaledale along a narrow, rocky track with incredible views into Swinner Gill and onto East Stonesdale Moor.

All too soon the path forks and anyone staying in **Keld** (Map 62) needs to head straight on, while folk bound for Tan Hill turn right, over the footbridge. Keld has many more beds than Tan Hill, but most of them will have been booked months in advance by walkers doing Wainwright's Coast to Coast walk (another Trailblazer title that your bookshelf should not be without!).

Walkers aiming for Tan Hill still have work to do; four more miles (6.4km) and 800ft (244m) of ascent, first along a narrow lane between walls, reminiscent of the departure from Horton, and then along a wide, peat-cushioned path around the edge of **Stonesdale Moor** (Map 63) with ***Tan Hill Inn*** (Map 64, see p181) soon appearing in the distance; a welcome sight.

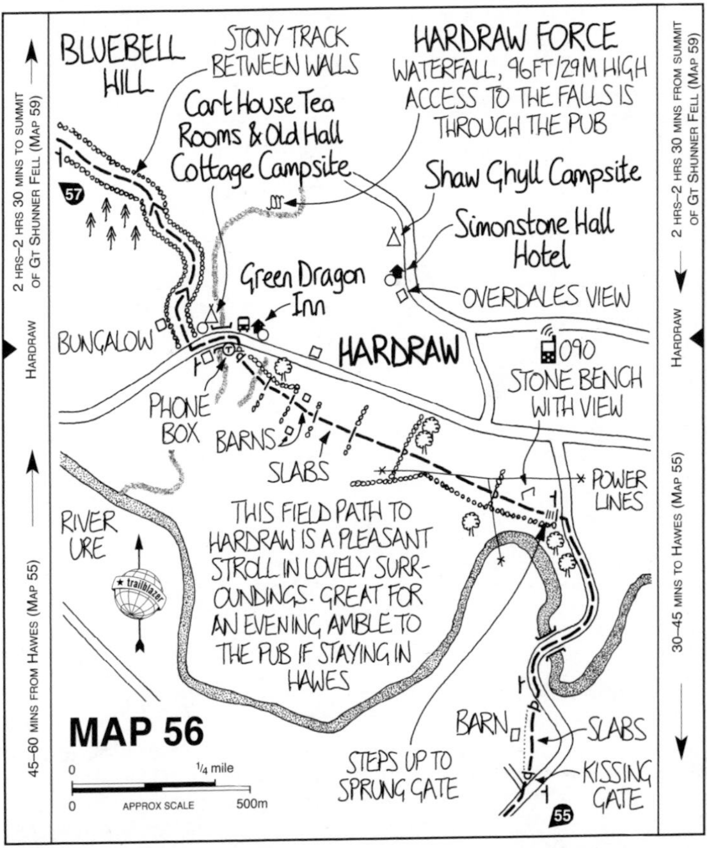
2 HRS–2 HRS 30 MINS TO SUMMIT OF GT SHUNNER FELL (MAP 59)
HARDRAW
45–60 MINS FROM HAWES (MAP 55)
BLUEBELL HILL
STONY TRACK BETWEEN WALLS
HARDRAW FORCE
WATERFALL, 96FT/29M HIGH
ACCESS TO THE FALLS IS THROUGH THE PUB
Cart House Tea Rooms & Old Hall Cottage Campsite
Shaw Ghyll Campsite
Simonstone Hall Hotel
Green Dragon Inn
OVERDALES VIEW
BUNGALOW
HARDRAW
090
STONE BENCH WITH VIEW
PHONE BOX
BARNS
SLABS
POWER LINES
RIVER URE
trailblazer
THIS FIELD PATH TO HARDRAW IS A PLEASANT STROLL IN LOVELY SURROUNDINGS. GREAT FOR AN EVENING AMBLE TO THE PUB IF STAYING IN HAWES
MAP 56
0
1/4 mile
0
APPROX SCALE
500m
STEPS UP TO SPRUNG GATE
BARN
SLABS
KISSING GATE
57
55
2 HRS–2 HRS 30 MINS FROM SUMMIT OF GT SHUNNER FELL (MAP 59)
HARDRAW
30–45 MINS TO HAWES (MAP 55)

Navigation notes

A close eye on the map between Hawes and Hardraw will avoid you getting lost in the fields and once you've found the lane out of Hardraw, the navigation over Great Shunner Fell and down into Thwaite is child's play, thanks mainly to the slabs. Things can get a little confusing between Thwaite and Keld though you shouldn't get lost for too long and you should be on an easy street all the way to the open fell beyond East Stonesdale Farm, the other side of Keld.

From here the path can be sketchy in places, especially on the open moorland sections and if night has beaten you, or the mist is down, this does need careful concentration. If you do lose the path, you always have the road, which is downhill to your left and that will take you all the way to Tan Hill Inn.

HARDRAW [Map 56, p171]

Hardraw's ***Green Dragon Inn*** (☎ 01969-667392, 🖳 thegreendragoninnhardraw.com; 1D/6D or T/1Tr, all en suite, ☕; Ⓛ; 🐕 only in the bar and in the rooms in the separate building) is known for its fine ales. **B&B** costs from £47.50pp (sgl occ rates on request). Two of the rooms are in the pub, the others are in a separate building and

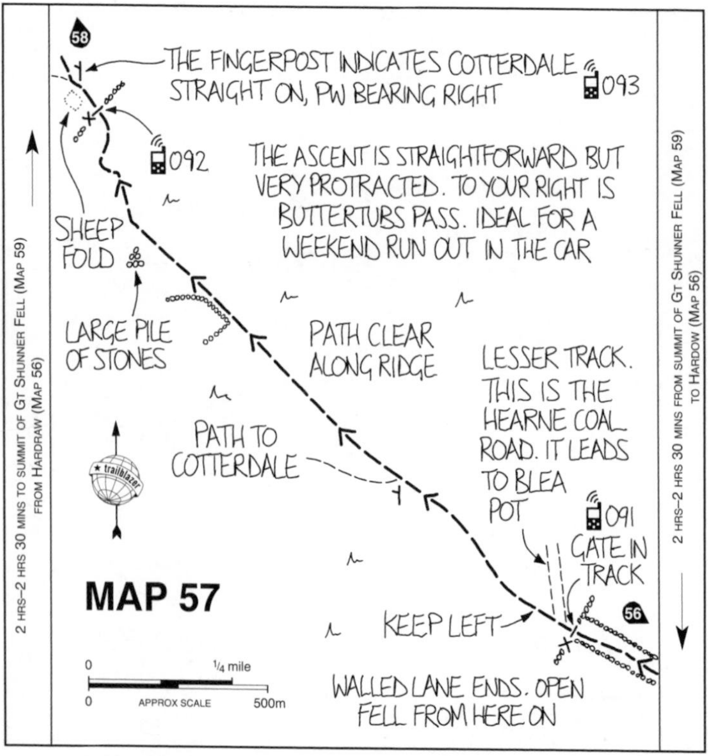
58
THE FINGERPOST INDICATES COTTERDALE STRAIGHT ON, PW BEARING RIGHT
093
092
THE ASCENT IS STRAIGHTFORWARD BUT VERY PROTRACTED. TO YOUR RIGHT IS BUTTERTUBS PASS. IDEAL FOR A WEEKEND RUN OUT IN THE CAR
SHEEP FOLD
LARGE PILE OF STONES
PATH CLEAR ALONG RIDGE
LESSER TRACK. THIS IS THE HEARNE COAL ROAD. IT LEADS TO BLEA POT
PATH TO COTTERDALE
091
GATE IN TRACK
56
KEEP LEFT
WALLED LANE ENDS. OPEN FELL FROM HERE ON
MAP 57
0 1/4 mile
0 APPROX SCALE 500m
2 HRS–2 HRS 30 MINS TO SUMMIT OF GT SHUNNER FELL (MAP 59) FROM HARDRAW (MAP 56)
2 HRS–2 HRS 30 MINS FROM SUMMIT OF GT SHUNNER FELL (MAP 59) TO HARDOW (MAP 56)

some rooms can be combined for groups of up to five. They have a **bunkhouse** (1 x 6-bed en suite, 2 x 2-, 5 x 4-, 1 x 5-, 1 x 6-, 1 x 8-bed rooms share facilities; from £18pp) with a basic kitchen. The bunkhouse may be booked by groups so it is worth checking availability beforehand, but the range of options here means you're unlikely to end up sleeping rough. The evening menu (**food** served daily noon-3pm & 5.30-8.30pm but variable in the low season) includes fried lamb's liver & mash (£11.50), and steak & ale pie (£12.95). There is live music most Saturday nights in the summer; see p14 for details of the brass-band contest held here in September. You can visit the impressive **Hardraw Force** (waterfall; daily 8am to dusk in summer; winter 10am-5.30pm) behind the pub.

Cart House Tea Rooms (☎ 01969-667691; 🐕 in one part only; Easter-end Oct daily 10am-5pm) serve snacks, light lunches and afternoon teas. They also manage ***Old Hall Cottage Campsite*** (☎ same as Cart House, 💻 oldhallcottage campsite.co.uk; Easter to end Oct weather permitting) where walkers can camp for £7pp. Shower (50p) and toilet facilities are available and the tea rooms will make breakfast for campers if arranged in advance. Note that they accept cash only in the tea room and for camping; also dogs are not allowed on this site.

To the east of the village the very quiet ***Shaw Ghyll Campsite*** (☎ 01969-667359, 💻 shawghyll.co.uk; 🐕 on lead; Apr to end Oct) charges £10-20 for up to two walkers in a tent.

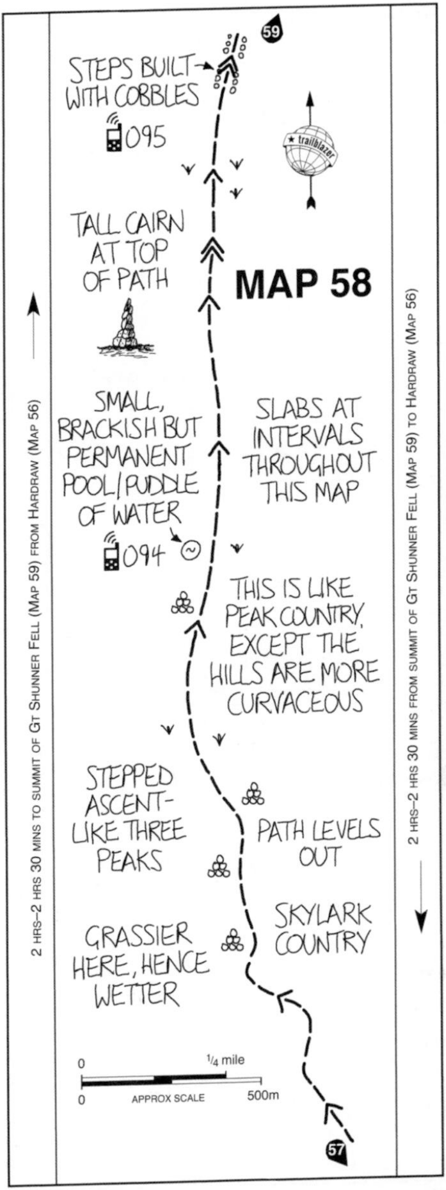
MAP 58
STEPS BUILT WITH COBBLES
095
TALL CAIRN AT TOP OF PATH
SMALL, BRACKISH BUT PERMANENT POOL/PUDDLE OF WATER
094
SLABS AT INTERVALS THROUGHOUT THIS MAP
THIS IS LIKE PEAK COUNTRY, EXCEPT THE HILLS ARE MORE CURVACEOUS
STEPPED ASCENT - LIKE THREE PEAKS
PATH LEVELS OUT
GRASSIER HERE, HENCE WETTER
SKYLARK COUNTRY
59
57
trailblazer
0 1/4 mile
0 APPROX SCALE 500m
2 HRS–2 HRS 30 MINS TO SUMMIT OF GT SHUNNER FELL (MAP 59) FROM HARDRAW (MAP 56)
2 HRS–2 HRS 30 MINS FROM SUMMIT OF GT SHUNNER FELL (MAP 59) TO HARDRAW (MAP 56)

[**Hardraw** *cont'd*] Booking is advised at all times. There are shower facilities (50p) and a toilet block.

If you're not too muddy or sweaty and feel like some luxury, treat yourself at ***Simonstone Hall Hotel*** (☎ 01969-667255, 🖳 simonstonehall.com; 5D or T/13D, all en suite; ☕; Ⓛ; 🐕). **B&B** costs £70-100pp (sgl occ £120-180); dinner bed & breakfast rates are also available – the ***restaurant*** (Mon-Sat 6-9pm, Sun 1-8pm) is open to non-residents. You won't want to leave.

Hardraw is a stop on Little White Bus's No 113 **bus** service (see pp54-9).

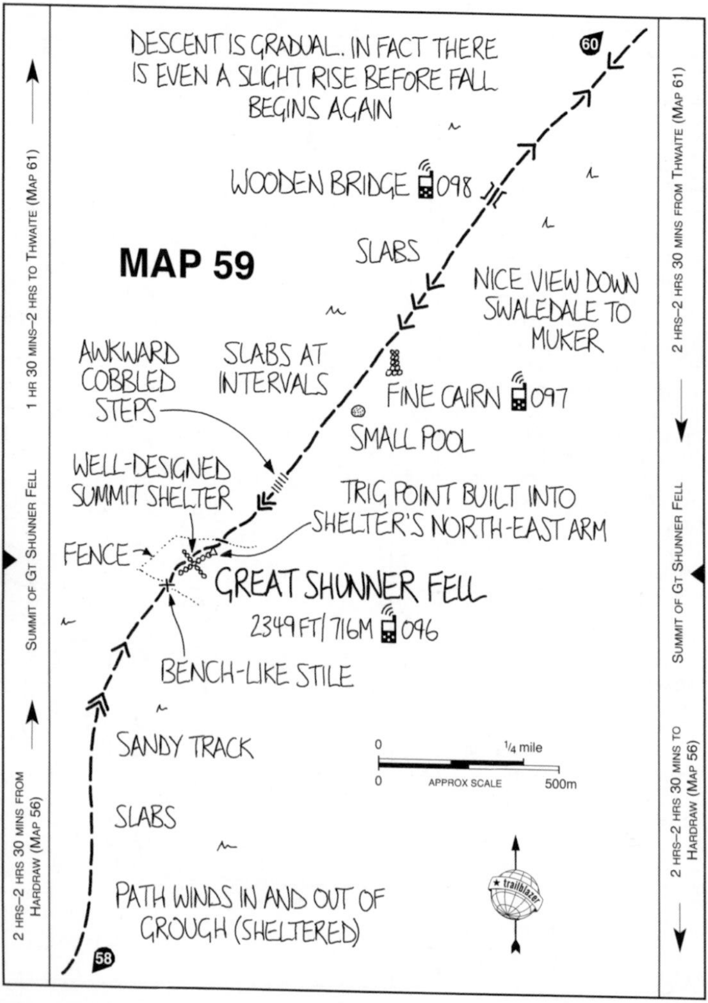

MAP 59
DESCENT IS GRADUAL. IN FACT THERE IS EVEN A SLIGHT RISE BEFORE FALL BEGINS AGAIN
60
WOODEN BRIDGE 098
SLABS
NICE VIEW DOWN SWALEDALE TO MUKER
AWKWARD COBBLED STEPS
SLABS AT INTERVALS
FINE CAIRN 097
SMALL POOL
WELL-DESIGNED SUMMIT SHELTER
TRIG POINT BUILT INTO SHELTER'S NORTH-EAST ARM
FENCE
GREAT SHUNNER FELL
2349FT/716M 096
BENCH-LIKE STILE
SANDY TRACK
SLABS
PATH WINDS IN AND OUT OF GROUGH (SHELTERED)
58
0 ¼ mile
0 APPROX SCALE 500m
trailblazer
1 HR 30 MINS–2 HRS TO THWAITE (MAP 61)
SUMMIT OF GT SHUNNER FELL
2 HRS–2 HRS 30 MINS FROM HARDRAW (MAP 56)
2 HRS–2 HRS 30 MINS FROM THWAITE (MAP 61)
SUMMIT OF GT SHUNNER FELL
2 HRS–2 HRS 30 MINS TO HARDRAW (MAP 56)

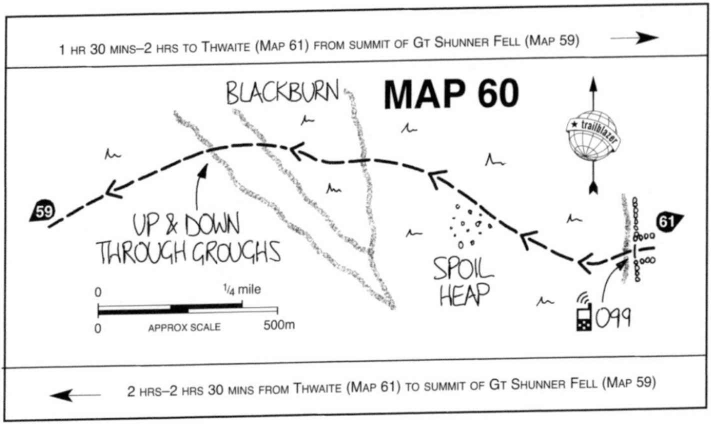

1 HR 30 MINS–2 HRS TO THWAITE (MAP 61) FROM SUMMIT OF GT SHUNNER FELL (MAP 59)
BLACKBURN
MAP 60
trailblazer
59
61
UP & DOWN THROUGH GROUGHS
SPOIL HEAP
0 1/4 mile
0 APPROX SCALE 500m
099
2 HRS–2 HRS 30 MINS FROM THWAITE (MAP 61) TO SUMMIT OF GT SHUNNER FELL (MAP 59)

THWAITE [Map 61, p177]

The village is notable for the welcome **café** at ***Kearton Country Hotel*** (☎ 01748-886277, 🖳 keartoncountryhotel.co.uk; 2S/6D/2T/2Tr, all en suite; ☕; Ⓛ) where you can have morning coffee, tea with a home-made biscuit or scones, a pint with bar meals or choose something from the proper lunch menu; the cappuccinos alone deserve an industry award. **B&B** costs from £59pp (sgl occ £64, £72.50pp for dinner, bed & breakfast). The café is open daily (Mon-Fri 11am-5pm, Sat & Sun 10am-5pm; lunch is served noon-3pm). An evening meal is served in the restaurant at 7pm, non residents are welcome but must book.

Just over half a mile east through the meadows towards Muker brings you to the **campsite** at ***Usha Gap*** (☎ 01748-886110, 🖳 ushagap.co.uk; 🐕), a lovely riverside field. The rate is from £8pp; showers and toilets are available along with a drying room, phone-charging points and a fridge freezer.

Little White Bus's No 30 (Keld–Richmond) is the only **bus** service calling here (see pp54-9 for details).

❑ Field barns

As you pass through the Yorkshire Dales the prevalence of field barns will have been obvious. Swaledale is particularly noted for these isolated stone barns which are also known as laithes. It has been estimated that within a 1000-metre radius of the village of Muker there are 60 barns of this type. They were part and parcel of the traditional farming methods of the area which saw grazing land enclosed between stone walls, the cattle kept in the barns between October and May, fed on hay stored in the upper roof space of the barn. Cows were milked where they stood and their manure was spread on the surrounding fields. Typically, a field barn would house four or five cows, hence a farmer with a large herd would need plenty of barns to keep them in.

Today, field barns are largely redundant due to farmers making hay on a semi-industrial basis with automated machinery, the hay being baled and stored in huge modern barns close to the farm buildings for convenience. In some cases farmers have converted them into tourist accommodation, thanks to the availability of grants encouraging them to do so.

MUKER [off Map 61]

Another half a mile through the fields beyond Usha Gap and you reach Muker.

This is a very pleasant little place and a favourite of James Herriot (the Yorkshire vet who wrote *All Creatures Great and Small*). It has a church, a small **shop** and a fine pub, the ***Farmers Arms*** (☎ 01748-886297, 🖳 farmersarmsmuker.co.uk; 🐕; food served daily noon-2.30pm & 6-8.30pm; note that the pub is closed 2.30-6pm on Mon in the winter months and the bar may close earlier than 11pm in the evening), which serves a range of dishes from Yorkshire puddings with a selection of fillings (£8.85) to steak (from £13.75).

Muker Village Store and Teashop (☎ 01748-886409; 🖳 mukerteashop@btinternet.com) comprises the **village shop** (end Mar to end Oct Mon 10am-4pm, Wed-Sun to 5pm, end Oct to end Mar Thur-Sun 10am-noon), a **tearoom** (no WI-FI; 🐕; end Mar to end Oct Wed-Mon 10.30am-5pm but they will stay open later if people are around) and they provide **B&B** (1D, en suite; Ⓛ; from £40pp, sgl occ full room rate).

If not, there are a couple of other options including ***Stone Leigh*** (☎ 01748-886375, 🖳 stoneleighcottage.co.uk; 2D en suite, 1T private facilities; Ⓛ), which charges from £40pp (sgl occ £50), and the last house in the village, ***Bridge House*** (☎ 01748-886461, 🖳 bridgehousemuker.co.uk; 2D, both en suite; Ⓛ) with rooms from £45pp (sgl occ full room rate). Note that all bookings are online now, not via the phone.

Feeling chilly? Then you'll be delighted to learn that for over 30 years Muker has also been the home of **Swaledale Woollens** (☎ 01748-886251, 🖳 www.swaledalewoollens.co.uk), its products made from the yarn of Swaledale sheep as well as Wensleydale and Welsh Hill wool. The **shop** (daily Mar-Oct 10am-5pm, Nov-Dec 10am-4pm, Jan & Feb Mon, Wed & Fri-Sun 10am-4pm) boasts that it actually saved the village following the depression caused by the collapse of the mining industry. Following a meeting in the pub, a decision was made to set up a local cottage industry producing knitwear, and today about 30 home-workers are employed in knitting the jumpers, hats and many other items available in the store, which is near the pub.

See p14 for details about Swaledale's Arts Festival held here in May.

Little White Bus's No 30 (Keld–Richmond) and Arriva's seasonal No 830 are the only **bus** services calling here (see pp54-9 for details).

KELD [Map 62, p178]

For a short while in Keld the Pennine Way and the popular Coast to Coast Path meet. Thus the town can be busy though the accommodation situation has improved.

Little White Bus's No 30 (to Richmond) and Arriva's seasonal No 830 are the only **bus** services calling here (see pp54-9 for details).

You can **camp** at ***Rukin's Park Lodge Campsite*** (☎ 01748-886274, 🖳 rukins-keld.co.uk; 🐕) from £7pp for walkers. There are toilet and (free) shower facilities; there's also a **café** (Easter to end Sep daily 9am-6pm) with some snacks and cakes and a sparsely provisioned **shop** (same hours) but no mobile phone reception.

Half a mile west of Keld is ***Keld Bunk Barn*** (Park House; ☎ 01748-886549, 🖳 keldbunkbarn.com; Ⓛ; 🐕). The **bunkhouse** (1D en suite, 1Tr/1Qd bunk rooms with shared facilities) is a great resource for hikers on a budget who used to find little on offer in Keld. A bunk bed costs from £22pp (sgl occ from £56) and the double room is from £31.50pp (sgl occ £63) a night. The bunkhouse has a communal area with a kitchen.

Swaledale Yurts (☎ 01748-886159, 🖳 swaledaleyurts.com) offers a pitch at the riverside **campsite** (£7-8pp; Ⓛ; 🐕; Mar to end Oct) where dogs are allowed to stay for free. They also have five **yurts** (Ⓛ; 🐕; Mar to end Oct) which sleep 2-5 people (£59-89 for two sharing plus £15 per additional person; these are so huge you are unlikely to miss them as you approach the site. The campers' barn has some cooking facilities.

(cont'd on p180)

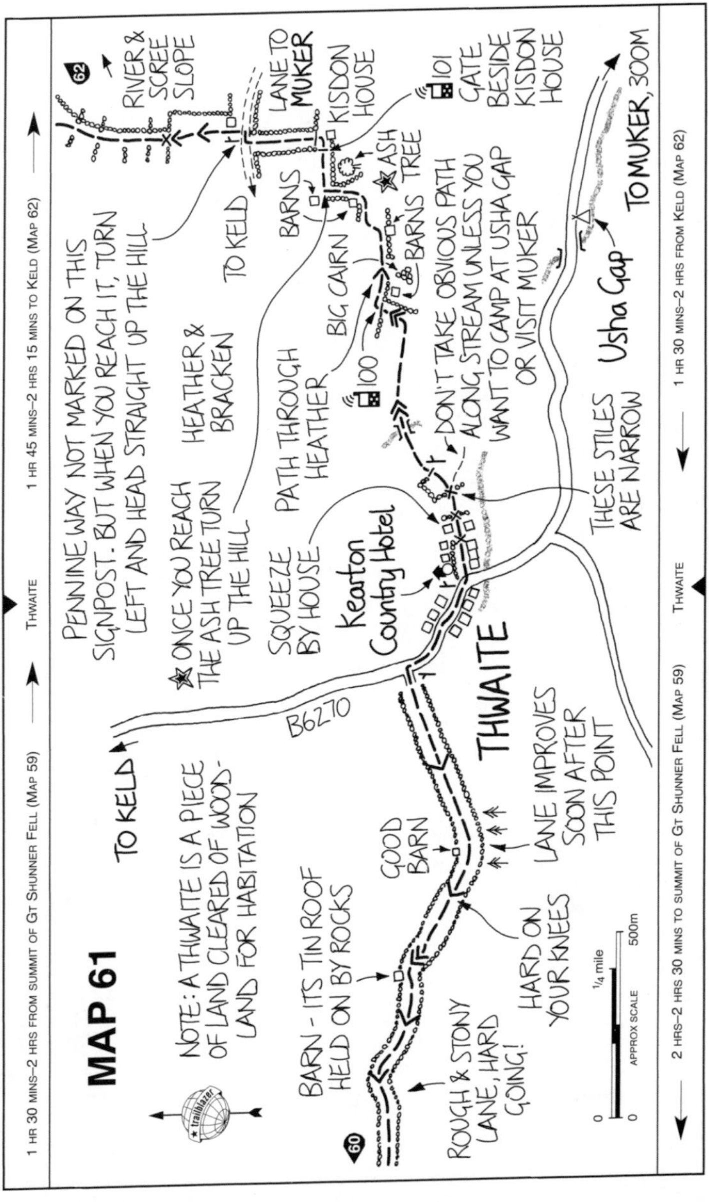
1 HR 30 MINS–2 HRS FROM SUMMIT OF GT SHUNNER FELL (MAP 59)
THWAITE
1 HR 45 MINS–2 HRS 15 MINS TO KELD (MAP 62)
MAP 61
NOTE: A THWAITE IS A PIECE OF LAND CLEARED OF WOOD-LAND FOR HABITATION
TO KELD
PENNINE WAY NOT MARKED ON THIS SIGNPOST. BUT WHEN YOU REACH IT, TURN LEFT AND HEAD STRAIGHT UP THE HILL
ONCE YOU REACH THE ASH TREE TURN UP THE HILL
SQUEEZE BY HOUSE
Kearton Country Hotel
PATH THROUGH HEATHER
HEATHER & BRACKEN
BIG CAIRN
BARNS
TO KELD
LANE TO MUKER
RIVER & SCREE SLOPE
62
KISDON HOUSE
ASH TREE
BARNS
100
101 GATE BESIDE KISDON HOUSE
DON'T TAKE OBVIOUS PATH ALONG STREAM UNLESS YOU WANT TO CAMP AT USHA GAP OR VISIT MUKER
THESE STILES ARE NARROW
Usha Gap
TO MUKER, 300M
THWAITE
B6270
LANE IMPROVES SOON AFTER THIS POINT
GOOD BARN
BARN - ITS TIN ROOF HELD ON BY ROCKS
HARD ON YOUR KNEES
ROUGH & STONY LANE, HARD GOING!
60
trailblazer
APPROX SCALE
0
1/4 mile
0
500m
2 HRS–2 HRS 30 MINS TO SUMMIT OF GT SHUNNER FELL (MAP 59)
THWAITE
1 HR 30 MINS–2 HRS FROM KELD (MAP 62)

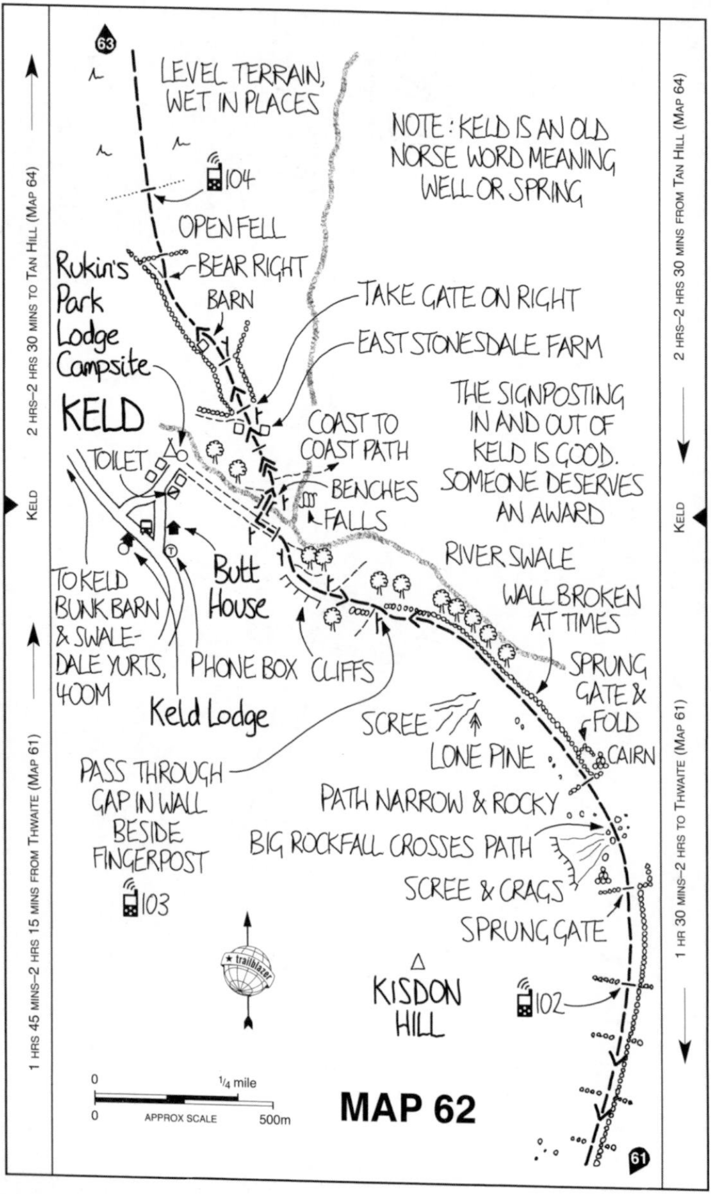

LEVEL TERRAIN, WET IN PLACES
NOTE: KELD IS AN OLD NORSE WORD MEANING WELL OR SPRING
104
OPEN FELL
Rukin's Park Lodge Campsite
BEAR RIGHT
BARN
TAKE GATE ON RIGHT
EAST STONESDALE FARM
KELD
THE SIGNPOSTING IN AND OUT OF KELD IS GOOD. SOMEONE DESERVES AN AWARD
COAST TO COAST PATH
TOILET
BENCHES
FALLS
RIVER SWALE
Butt House
TO KELD BUNK BARN & SWALE-DALE YURTS, 400M
PHONE BOX
CLIFFS
WALL BROKEN AT TIMES
SPRUNG GATE & FOLD
Keld Lodge
SCREE
LONE PINE
CAIRN
PASS THROUGH GAP IN WALL BESIDE FINGERPOST
PATH NARROW & ROCKY
BIG ROCKFALL CROSSES PATH
SCREE & CRAGS
103
SPRUNG GATE
KISDON HILL
102
0
¼ mile
0
APPROX SCALE
500m
MAP 62
63
61
2 HRS–2 HRS 30 MINS TO TAN HILL (MAP 64)
KELD
1 HRS 45 MINS–2 HRS 15 MINS FROM THWAITE (MAP 61)
2 HRS–2 HRS 30 MINS FROM TAN HILL (MAP 64)
1 HR 30 MINS–2 HRS TO THWAITE (MAP 61)

ROUTE GUIDE AND MAPS

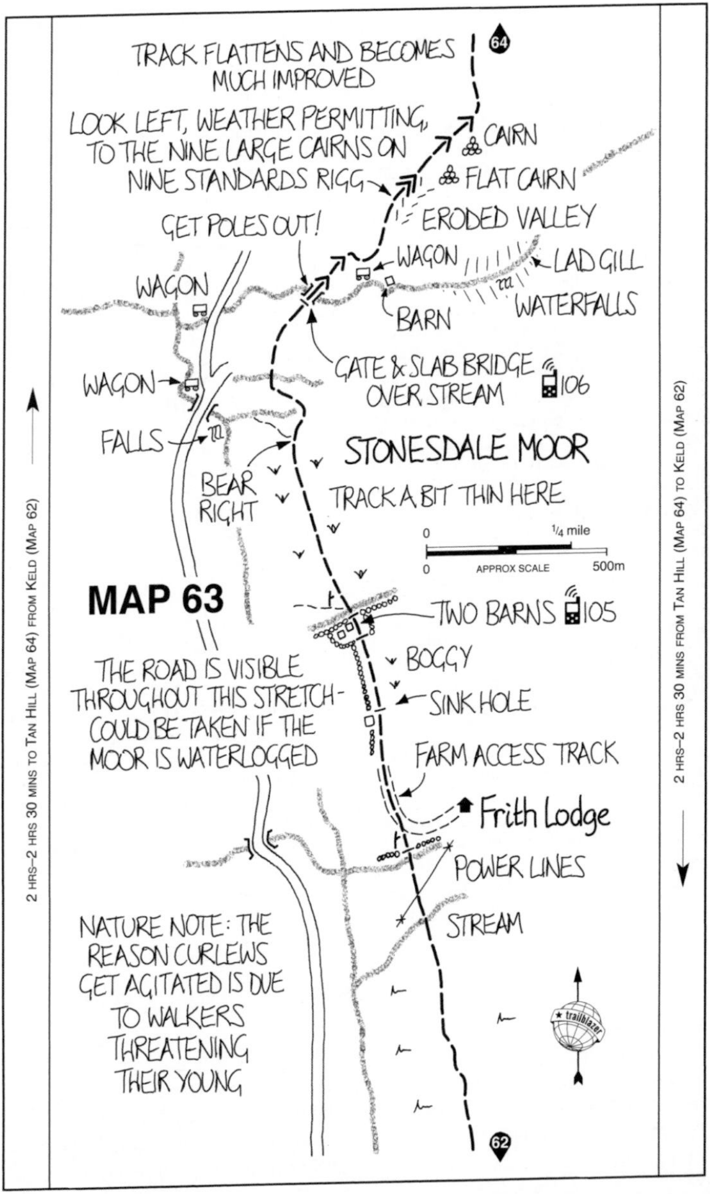
TRACK FLATTENS AND BECOMES MUCH IMPROVED
64
LOOK LEFT, WEATHER PERMITTING, TO THE NINE LARGE CAIRNS ON NINE STANDARDS RIGG
CAIRN
FLAT CAIRN
ERODED VALLEY
GET POLES OUT!
WAGON
LAD GILL
WAGON
WATERFALLS
BARN
GATE & SLAB BRIDGE OVER STREAM
106
WAGON
FALLS
STONESDALE MOOR
BEAR RIGHT
TRACK A BIT THIN HERE
0
1/4 mile
0
APPROX SCALE
500m
MAP 63
TWO BARNS
105
BOGGY
THE ROAD IS VISIBLE THROUGHOUT THIS STRETCH - COULD BE TAKEN IF THE MOOR IS WATERLOGGED
SINK HOLE
FARM ACCESS TRACK
Frith Lodge
POWER LINES
STREAM
NATURE NOTE: THE REASON CURLEWS GET AGITATED IS DUE TO WALKERS THREATENING THEIR YOUNG
trailblazer
62
2 HRS–2 HRS 30 MINS TO TAN HILL (MAP 64) FROM KELD (MAP 62)
2 HRS–2 HRS 30 MINS FROM TAN HILL (MAP 64) TO KELD (MAP 62)

(cont'd from p176) It also provides an indoor sitting area for campers, a place you may not want to vacate as Keld can be rather popular with midges too.

Whether camping or in a barn/yurt, if booked in advance you can get an evening **meal** (£8.95-9.95); breakfast baguettes (from £3.50) and packed lunches are available too.

Keld Lodge (☎ 01748-886259, 🖳 keldlodge.com; 3S/4D/3T/1Tr, all en suite, 2S share facilities; Ⓛ; 🐕; Feb-Oct) is a small licensed hotel with en suites from £52.50pp (sgl from £45, sgl occ £72.50). Along with a bar (daily noon-9.30pm) there's a **restaurant** (daily Apr-Oct 5.30-7.30pm, rest of year open only when they have guests; main courses cost £9.50-13.50) – **but booking is essential** in the high season as they get so busy; they also have a **drying room**.

Butt House (☎ 01748-886374, 🖳 butthousekeld.co.uk; 1S/2T/1D/1Tr, all en suite; ☕; Ⓛ; Mar-Oct) has been a mainstay of the accommodation scene in Keld for many years and knows exactly what walkers want, including alcohol. There is a boot room which can be used as a drying room, a laundry service (£8.50 per load) and if booked in advance they can provide an evening meal too. B&B costs from £46pp (sgl £52, sgl occ rates on request).

Just over a mile from Keld itself but right on the Pennine Way, ***Frith Lodge*** (see Map 63; ☎ 01748-886489, 🖳 frithlodgekeld.co.uk; 3D/2T, all en suite; Ⓛ; Apr-end Sep) is pretty much as lonely as B&Bs get on the trail. Being so far from anywhere it's pretty much essential that they serve an evening meal – which they do, thankfully, for £15.50/18.50 for two/three courses. B&B costs from £47.50pp (sgl occ rates on request).

East View (☎ 01748-886436, 🖳 eastviewkeld.co.uk; 1S/1D/1T, shared facilities; ☕; Ⓛ; mid Apr to mid Oct) is run by Doris, a Chinese-Filipino who is married to a Brit. B&B costs from £40pp (sgl/sgl occ £40/80). The evening meal (£16/20 for 2/3 courses) 'was Chinese influenced (spring rolls and mild curry & rice), which was a nice change after days of pub grub'.

TAN HILL [Map 64]

Tan Hill Inn (☎ 01833-628246, 🖳 tanhillinn.com; 3D/3T/1Tr, all en suite; ☕; Ⓛ; 🐕) prides itself on being the highest pub (1732ft/528m above sea level) in Britain. **B&B** costs £45-55pp (sgl occ from £60). There are also two **bunkrooms** (1 x 6-, 1 x 8-bunk-bed room; communal bathroom and mixed-sex dorms); a bed with breakfast costs £30pp. Besides the pub there are no facilities here apart from some rocks to shelter behind but at £5pp (which goes to charity), **camping** round the back is pretty much as cheap as it gets. There is a tap and outside loo and you can use the staff shower. A camper's breakfast is available (£8) if booked in advance. The pub itself is open all day year-round. **Food** (daily noon-3pm & 6.30-9pm) is standard but reasonable value pub fare (mains from £8.95) and light bites and sandwiches are available even when the kitchen is closed.

By day the inn is a peaceful place for a cup of tea but at night at weekends in the summer months it can get much more raucous with live music and other events held most weeks.

TAN HILL TO MIDDLETON-IN-TEESDALE MAPS 64-72

Route overview

16½ miles (26.5km) – 1700ft (518m) of ascent – 7¼-9¾ hours

You could be forgiven for thinking you're going in the wrong direction as you leave Tan Hill Inn the next morning – the route starts out downhill! This is hardly surprising, however, bearing in mind the pub's location and altitude. The route may be downhill, but the crossing of **Sleightholme Moor** (Map 65) could be the wettest section of the Pennine Way yet experienced. The peaty path becomes waterlogged after prolonged rain and you may find yourself jumping across peat groughs in what will probably be a vain attempt to keep your boots dry.

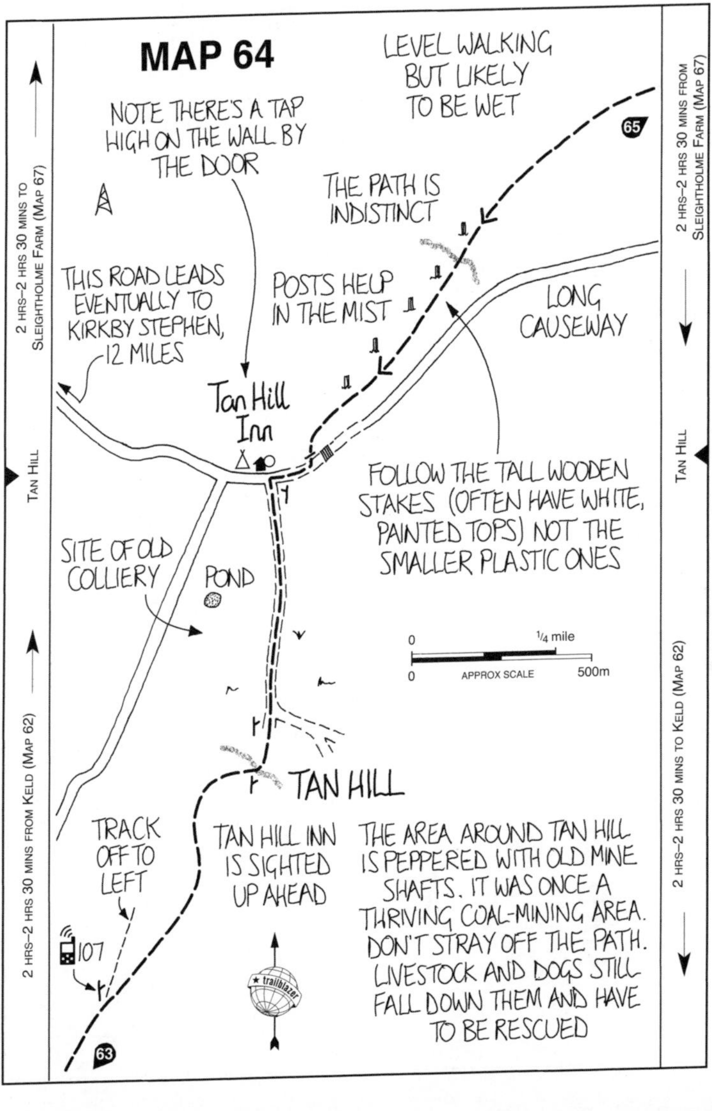
MAP 64
LEVEL WALKING BUT LIKELY TO BE WET
NOTE THERE'S A TAP HIGH ON THE WALL BY THE DOOR
THE PATH IS INDISTINCT
65
2 HRS–2 HRS 30 MINS TO SLEIGHTHOLME FARM (MAP 67)
2 HRS–2 HRS 30 MINS FROM SLEIGHTHOLME FARM (MAP 67)
THIS ROAD LEADS EVENTUALLY TO KIRKBY STEPHEN, 12 MILES
POSTS HELP IN THE MIST
LONG CAUSEWAY
Tan Hill Inn
TAN HILL
TAN HILL
FOLLOW THE TALL WOODEN STAKES (OFTEN HAVE WHITE, PAINTED TOPS) NOT THE SMALLER PLASTIC ONES
SITE OF OLD COLLIERY
POND
0
1/4 mile
0
APPROX SCALE
500m
2 HRS–2 HRS 30 MINS FROM KELD (MAP 62)
2 HRS–2 HRS 30 MINS TO KELD (MAP 62)
TAN HILL
TRACK OFF TO LEFT
TAN HILL INN IS SIGHTED UP AHEAD
THE AREA AROUND TAN HILL IS PEPPERED WITH OLD MINE SHAFTS. IT WAS ONCE A THRIVING COAL-MINING AREA. DON'T STRAY OFF THE PATH. LIVESTOCK AND DOGS STILL FALL DOWN THEM AND HAVE TO BE RESCUED
107
trailblazer
63

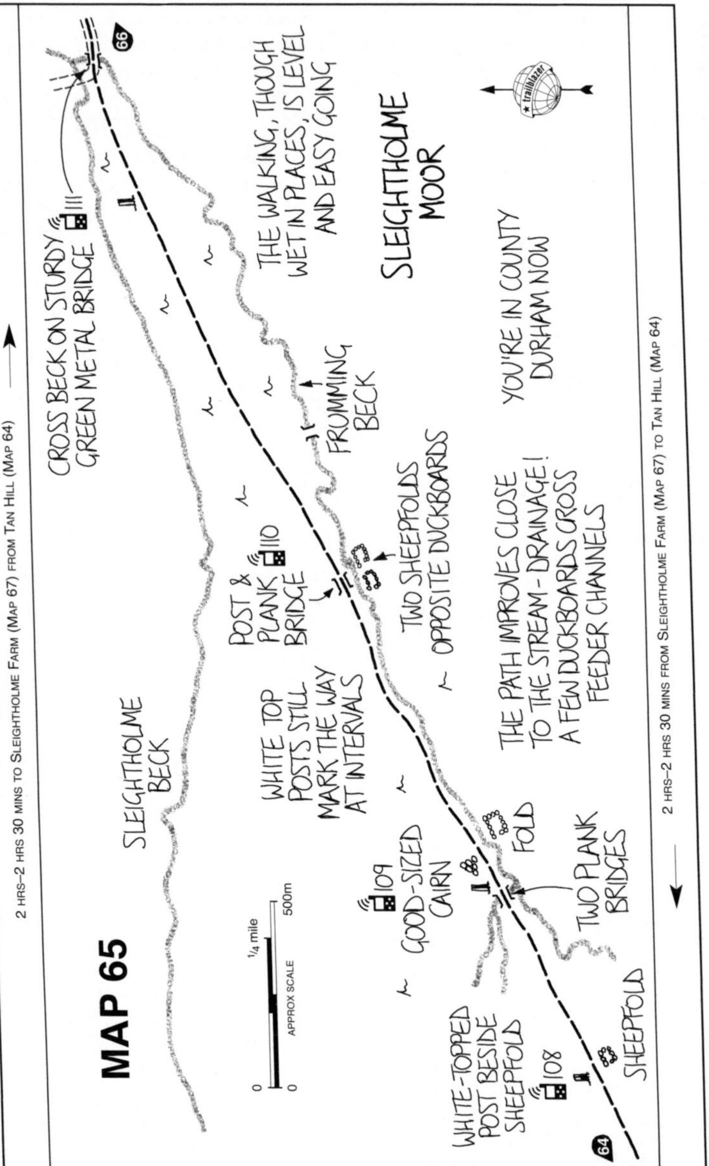
MAP 65
2 HRS–2 HRS 30 MINS TO SLEIGHTHOLME FARM (MAP 67) FROM TAN HILL (MAP 64)
2 HRS–2 HRS 30 MINS FROM SLEIGHTHOLME FARM (MAP 67) TO TAN HILL (MAP 64)
CROSS BECK ON STURDY GREEN METAL BRIDGE
THE WALKING, THOUGH WET IN PLACES, IS LEVEL AND EASY GOING
SLEIGHTHOLME MOOR
YOU'RE IN COUNTY DURHAM NOW
FRUMMING BECK
POST & PLANK BRIDGE
110
TWO SHEEPFOLDS OPPOSITE DUCKBOARDS
THE PATH IMPROVES CLOSE TO THE STREAM - DRAINAGE! A FEW DUCKBOARDS CROSS FEEDER CHANNELS
WHITE TOP POSTS STILL MARK THE WAY AT INTERVALS
SLEIGHTHOLME BECK
FOLD
TWO PLANK BRIDGES
109
GOOD-SIZED CAIRN
SHEEPFOLD
WHITE-TOPPED POST BESIDE SHEEPFOLD
108
1/4 mile
0
500m
APPROX SCALE
64
66
trailblazer

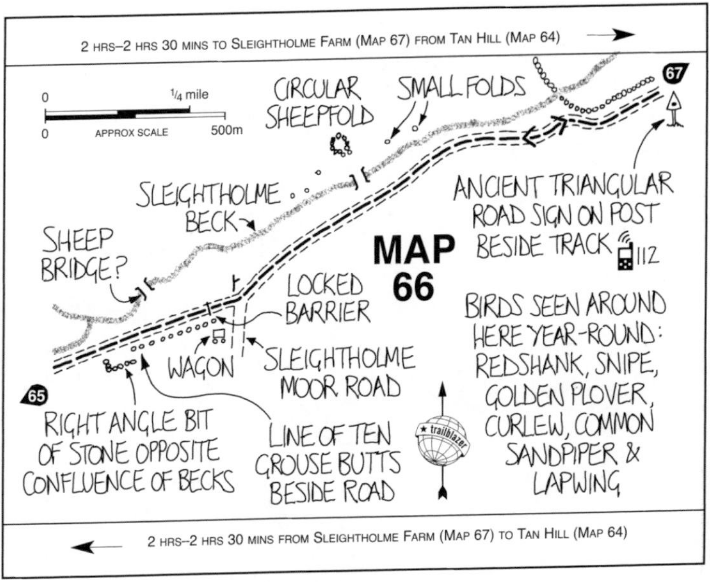
2 HRS–2 HRS 30 MINS TO SLEIGHTHOLME FARM (MAP 67) FROM TAN HILL (MAP 64)
0
¼ mile
0
APPROX SCALE
500m
CIRCULAR SHEEPFOLD
SMALL FOLDS
67
SLEIGHTHOLME BECK
ANCIENT TRIANGULAR ROAD SIGN ON POST BESIDE TRACK
112
SHEEP BRIDGE?
MAP 66
LOCKED BARRIER
BIRDS SEEN AROUND HERE YEAR-ROUND: REDSHANK, SNIPE, GOLDEN PLOVER, CURLEW, COMMON SANDPIPER & LAPWING
WAGON
SLEIGHTHOLME MOOR ROAD
65
RIGHT ANGLE BIT OF STONE OPPOSITE CONFLUENCE OF BECKS
LINE OF TEN GROUSE BUTTS BESIDE ROAD
trailblazer
2 HRS–2 HRS 30 MINS FROM SLEIGHTHOLME FARM (MAP 67) TO TAN HILL (MAP 64)

Once you've crossed **Frumming Beck**, however, things get easier, a stony track, much cursed on the descent into Horton, is now hailed in equal measure and it brings you to **Sleightholme Farm** (Map 67) and beyond it a decision; the **Bowes Loop** (see below), or the direct route to Baldersdale? The Bowes Loop adds about four miles (6.4km). To the delight of many a Pennine Way walker, The Ancient Unicorn pub (see below) has reopened therefore enabling you to break two long sections – between Hawes and Middleton-in-Teesdale – into three shorter ones. The Bowes Loop also takes a slightly drier path, avoiding Cotherstone Moor.

Bowes Loop (alternative route) [Maps 67a-c]

The Bowes Loop (8½ miles/13.7km) came about as an alternative route for those seeking a bed, or a meal, in Bowes (see below); it takes 1-1½hrs from the start of the route to Bowes and about 2hrs from Bowes to the point where the paths converge at Baldersdale (Map 69, p191).

At **Trough Heads Farm** (Map 67, p184) a branch of the Pennine Way heads off east to **Bowes** (Map 67a) where the ***Ancient Unicorn*** (☎ 01833-628576, 🖳 ancientunicorn.com; 8D/1T/1Tr en suite, 1D/1T shared facilities; ☛; Ⓛ; 🐕) provides both accommodation and food. **Room** rates vary according to the season though expect to pay £25-42.50pp (sgl occ £40-85). **Food** can be had either at their ***coffee shop*** (daily 8am-6pm), or in the pub itself (daily noon-8pm). They have also opened up ***The Bowes*** restaurant (daily noon-8pm) with mains starting at about £10 for their steak & ale pie. The only other reason to visit is to wander around the ruins of **Bowes Castle**. *(cont'd on p188)*

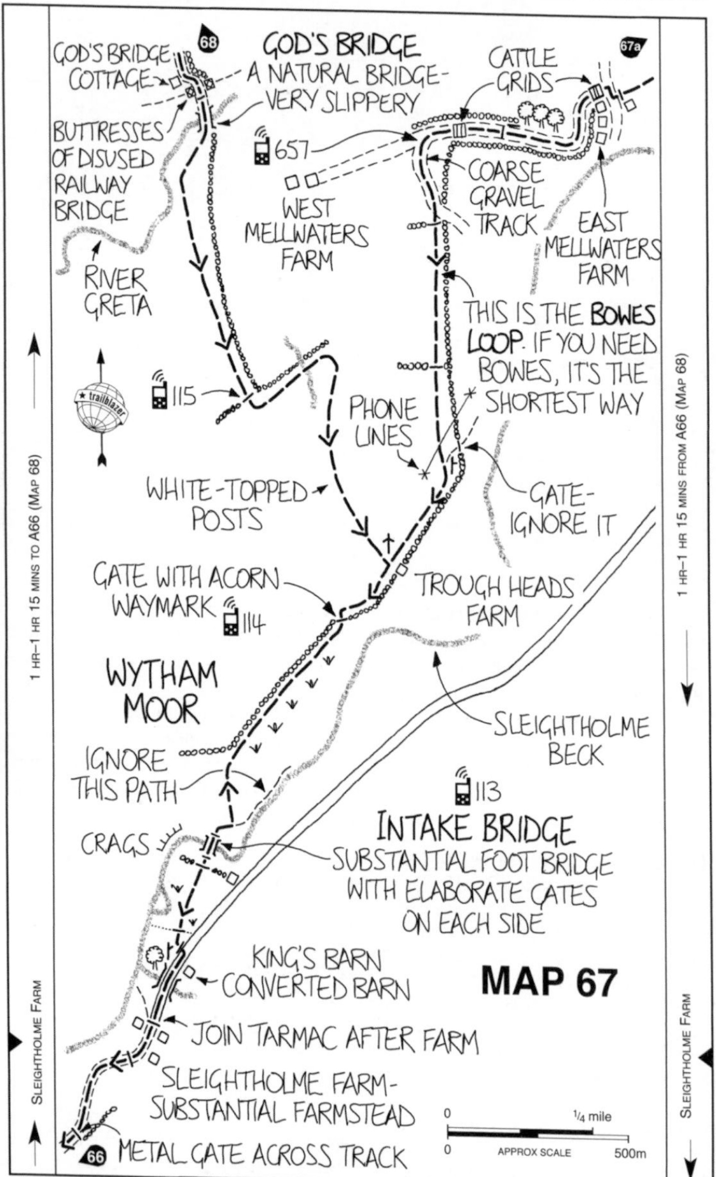
GOD'S BRIDGE COTTAGE
68
GOD'S BRIDGE
A NATURAL BRIDGE - VERY SLIPPERY
CATTLE GRIDS
67a
BUTTRESSES OF DISUSED RAILWAY BRIDGE
657
WEST MELLWATERS FARM
COARSE GRAVEL TRACK
EAST MELLWATERS FARM
RIVER GRETA
THIS IS THE BOWES LOOP. IF YOU NEED BOWES, IT'S THE SHORTEST WAY
115
PHONE LINES
GATE - IGNORE IT
WHITE-TOPPED POSTS
GATE WITH ACORN WAYMARK
114
TROUGH HEADS FARM
WYTHAM MOOR
SLEIGHTHOLME BECK
IGNORE THIS PATH
113
INTAKE BRIDGE
CRAGS
SUBSTANTIAL FOOT BRIDGE WITH ELABORATE GATES ON EACH SIDE
KING'S BARN CONVERTED BARN
MAP 67
JOIN TARMAC AFTER FARM
SLEIGHTHOLME FARM - SUBSTANTIAL FARMSTEAD
METAL GATE ACROSS TRACK
66
0
1/4 mile
0
APPROX SCALE
500m
1 HR–1 HR 15 MINS TO A66 (MAP 68)
1 HR–1 HR 15 MINS FROM A66 (MAP 68)
SLEIGHTHOLME FARM
SLEIGHTHOLME FARM

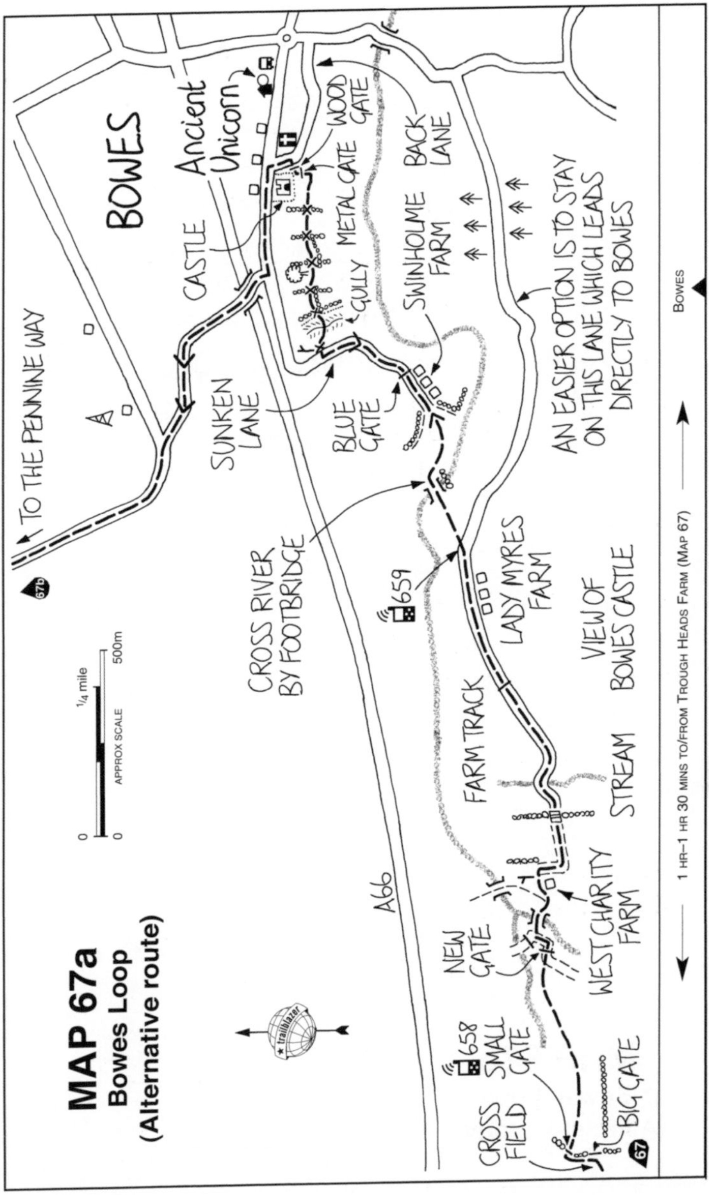
MAP 67a
Bowes Loop
(Alternative route)
APPROX SCALE
0
0
1/4 mile
500m
67b
TO THE PENNINE WAY
BOWES
Ancient Unicorn
CASTLE
WOOD GATE
METAL GATE
GULLY
BACK LANE
SWINHOLME FARM
SUNKEN LANE
BLUE GATE
CROSS RIVER BY FOOTBRIDGE
AN EASIER OPTION IS TO STAY ON THIS LANE WHICH LEADS DIRECTLY TO BOWES
659
LADY MYRES FARM
VIEW OF BOWES CASTLE
FARM TRACK
STREAM
A66
NEW GATE
WEST CHARITY FARM
658
SMALL GATE
CROSS FIELD
BIG GATE
67
1 HR–1 HR 30 MINS TO/FROM TROUGH HEADS FARM (MAP 67)
BOWES

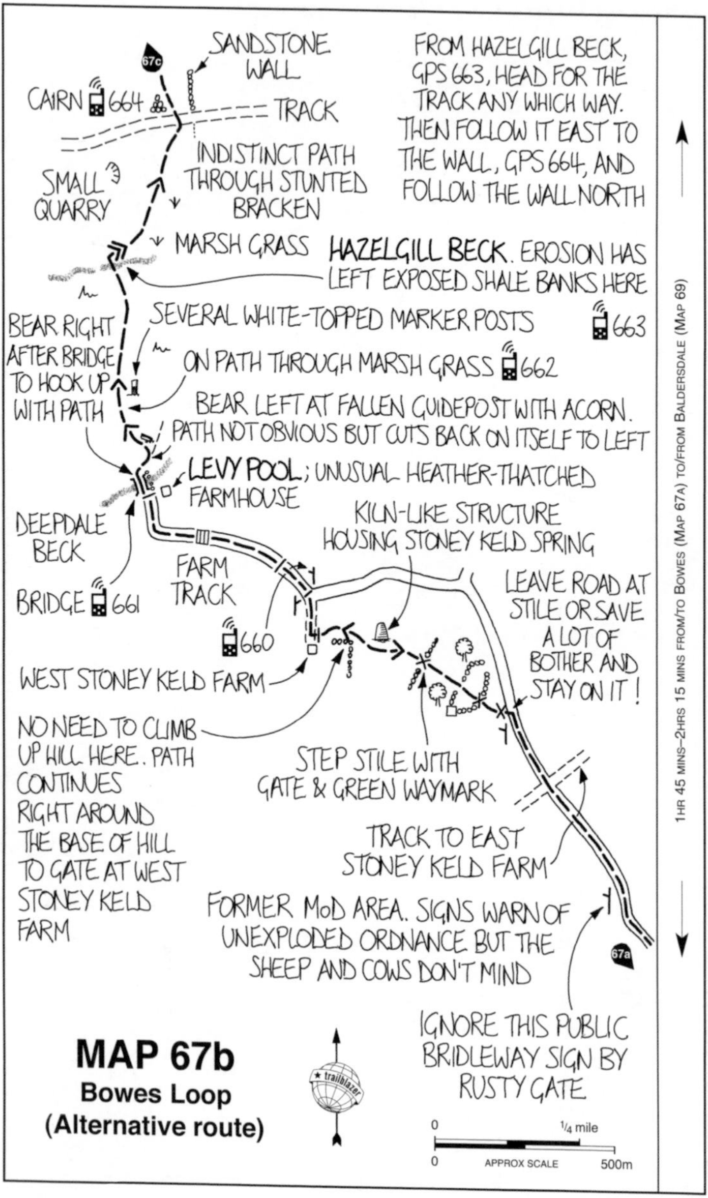
SANDSTONE WALL
CAIRN 664
TRACK
FROM HAZELGILL BECK, GPS 663, HEAD FOR THE TRACK ANY WHICH WAY. THEN FOLLOW IT EAST TO THE WALL, GPS 664, AND FOLLOW THE WALL NORTH
INDISTINCT PATH THROUGH STUNTED BRACKEN
SMALL QUARRY
MARSH GRASS
HAZELGILL BECK. EROSION HAS LEFT EXPOSED SHALE BANKS HERE
SEVERAL WHITE-TOPPED MARKER POSTS
663
BEAR RIGHT AFTER BRIDGE TO HOOK UP WITH PATH
ON PATH THROUGH MARSH GRASS 662
BEAR LEFT AT FALLEN GUIDEPOST WITH ACORN. PATH NOT OBVIOUS BUT CUTS BACK ON ITSELF TO LEFT
LEVY POOL; UNUSUAL HEATHER-THATCHED FARMHOUSE
DEEPDALE BECK
KILN-LIKE STRUCTURE HOUSING STONEY KELD SPRING
FARM TRACK
BRIDGE 661
LEAVE ROAD AT STILE OR SAVE A LOT OF BOTHER AND STAY ON IT!
660
WEST STONEY KELD FARM
NO NEED TO CLIMB UP HILL HERE. PATH CONTINUES RIGHT AROUND THE BASE OF HILL TO GATE AT WEST STONEY KELD FARM
STEP STILE WITH GATE & GREEN WAYMARK
TRACK TO EAST STONEY KELD FARM
FORMER MoD AREA. SIGNS WARN OF UNEXPLODED ORDNANCE BUT THE SHEEP AND COWS DON'T MIND
IGNORE THIS PUBLIC BRIDLEWAY SIGN BY RUSTY GATE
67c
67a
MAP 67b
Bowes Loop
(Alternative route)
trailblazer
0 1/4 mile
0 APPROX SCALE 500m
1HR 45 MINS–2HRS 15 MINS FROM/TO BOWES (MAP 67A) TO/FROM BALDERSDALE (MAP 69)

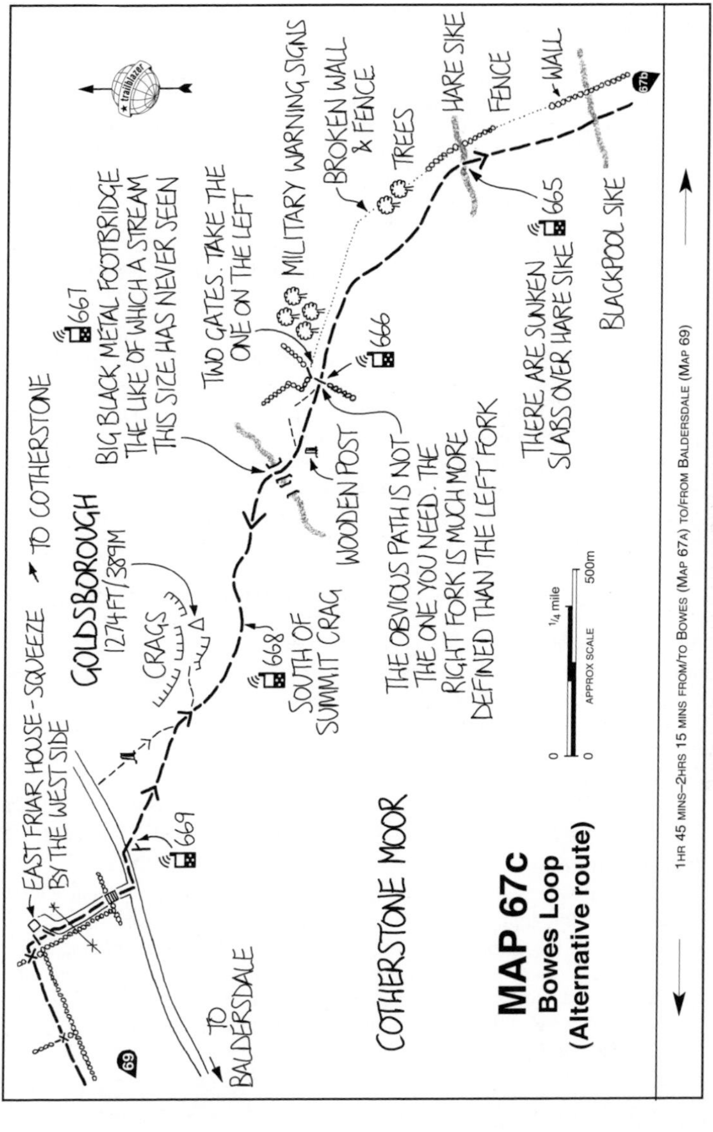
MAP 67c
Bowes Loop
(Alternative route)
EAST FRIAR HOUSE - SQUEEZE BY THE WEST SIDE
TO COTHERSTONE
GOLDSBOROUGH
1274FT/389M
CRAGS
BIG BLACK METAL FOOTBRIDGE THE LIKE OF WHICH A STREAM THIS SIZE HAS NEVER SEEN
667
TWO GATES. TAKE THE ONE ON THE LEFT
MILITARY WARNING SIGNS
BROKEN WALL & FENCE
TREES
HARE SIKE
FENCE
WALL
67b
665
THERE ARE SUNKEN SLABS OVER HARE SIKE
BLACKPOOL SIKE
666
WOODEN POST
THE OBVIOUS PATH IS NOT THE ONE YOU NEED. THE RIGHT FORK IS MUCH MORE DEFINED THAN THE LEFT FORK
668
SOUTH OF SUMMIT CRAG
669
69
TO BALDERSDALE
COTHERSTONE MOOR
0
1/4 mile
APPROX SCALE
0
500m
1HR 45 MINS–2HRS 15 MINS FROM/TO BOWES (MAP 67A) TO/FROM BALDERSDALE (MAP 69)

(cont'd from p183) The castle is a Norman keep dating from around 1087 and it is managed by English Heritage; you are free to visit at any time. Scarlet Band's **bus** No 72 goes to Barnard Castle (see pp54-9).

This longer route has noticeably **fewer ups and downs** and is a little more scenically appealing, although route finding can have **a few irritating moments**: care is needed after crossing the **bridge** at Levy Pool farmhouse (Map 67b). The Pennine Way guide post should point you on your way across the moor to Hazelgill Beck and the obvious path from the bridge leads you north-east towards the wall that can be seen ahead. Make sure to bear right for just a few yards after crossing the bridge, before turning left (north) to pick up the thin path through the tall grass. If you're using a GPS, aim for GPS Waypoint 662 after crossing the bridge. If all else fails head for the wall mentioned above and follow that north to a track where you will meet the Pennine Way again.

The Pennine Way climbs up and over **Wytham Moor** and drops down to the natural stone span of **God's Bridge** after which it meets the **A66** trunk road (Map 68). For once you don't have to scurry across between the rushing vehicles as a thoughtful subway, unthoughtfully laid a couple of hundred yards off the direct line, takes you beneath the tarmac instead.

A long steady ascent follows, out of **Stainmore Gap**, past a scattering of rocks that glory in the name of '**Ravock Castle**', and down to the possibly very welcome shelter of a shooting hut beside **Deepdale Beck**, before climbing again to the wall at **Race Yate** (Map 69) and the immense views ahead to Lunedale and the hills beyond Weardale.

Drop down the squelchy moorland to **Baldersdale** where the Way passes between two more reservoirs and, more significantly, reaches the halfway mark! Pat yourself on the back, many people don't make it this far, but you've obviously got the stuff that Pennine Wayfarers are made of; surely only injury can stop you from finishing now. The day's exertions haven't finished yet though, there are still 7 miles (11km) to Middleton-in-Teesdale and close to 1000ft (305m) of ascent over **Mickleton Moor** (Map 70) and **Harter Fell** (Map 71). Depending on the plans of the new owners, you *may* be able to find refuge at Clove Lodge (see p190) in Baldersdale, but **Middleton-in-Teesdale** (Map 72) offers many more options and will set you up nicely for the next (big) stage.

Navigation notes

Sleightholme Moor is vast and desolate, but for all that the track is fairly well defined and white-topped stakes help mark the way. In really bad conditions a combination of the tarmac road from Tan Hill Inn and the Sleightholme Moor Road (track) could help you avoid the worst of the moor. The field boundaries around the lower slopes of Harter Fell (Map 71) can be confusing and somehow the route on the ground seems to be much longer than that shown on the map, so be patient and the waypoints marked on the map will come eventually.

❑ Important note – walking times

All times in this book refer only to the time spent walking. You will need to add 20-30% to allow for rests, photography, checking the map, drinking water etc.

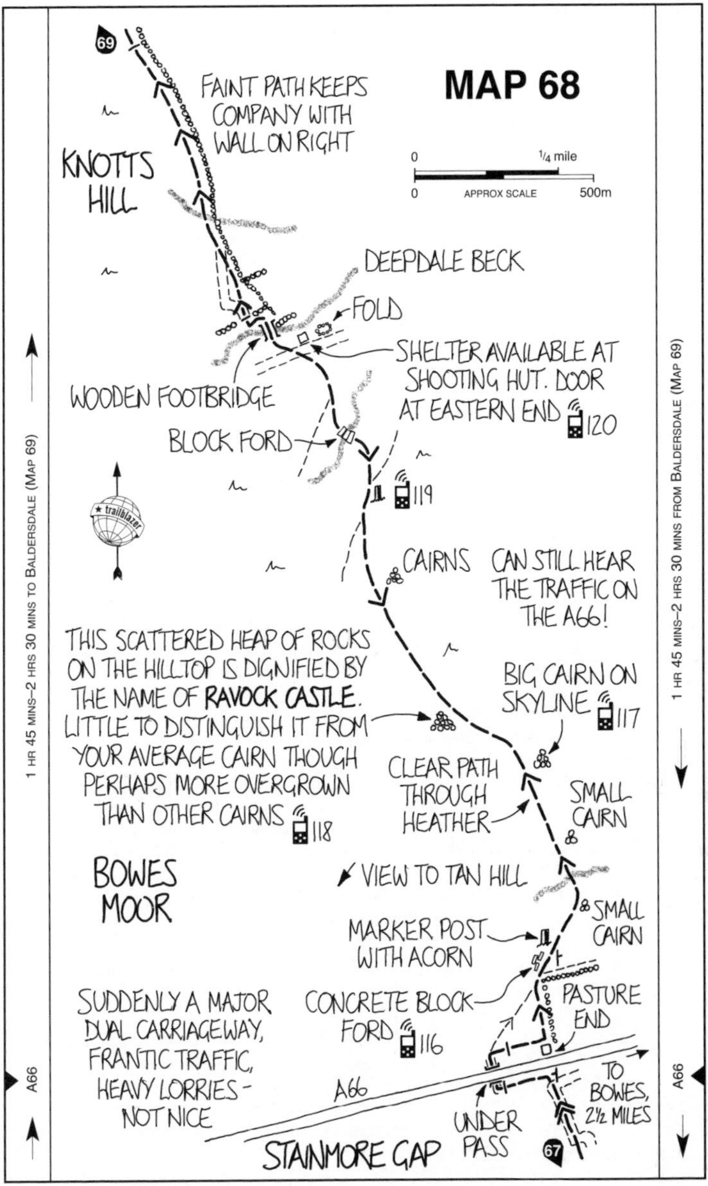
MAP 68
0 1/4 mile
0 APPROX SCALE 500m
69
FAINT PATH KEEPS COMPANY WITH WALL ON RIGHT
KNOTTS HILL
DEEPDALE BECK
FOLD
SHELTER AVAILABLE AT SHOOTING HUT. DOOR AT EASTERN END 120
WOODEN FOOTBRIDGE
BLOCK FORD
119
trailblazer
CAIRNS
CAN STILL HEAR THE TRAFFIC ON THE A66!
THIS SCATTERED HEAP OF ROCKS ON THE HILLTOP IS DIGNIFIED BY THE NAME OF RAVOCK CASTLE. LITTLE TO DISTINGUISH IT FROM YOUR AVERAGE CAIRN THOUGH PERHAPS MORE OVERGROWN THAN OTHER CAIRNS 118
BIG CAIRN ON SKYLINE 117
CLEAR PATH THROUGH HEATHER
SMALL CAIRN
BOWES MOOR
VIEW TO TAN HILL
SMALL CAIRN
MARKER POST WITH ACORN
SUDDENLY A MAJOR DUAL CARRIAGEWAY, FRANTIC TRAFFIC, HEAVY LORRIES - NOT NICE
CONCRETE BLOCK FORD 116
PASTURE END
A66
TO BOWES, 2½ MILES
UNDER PASS
STAINMORE GAP
67
1 HR 45 MINS–2 HRS 30 MINS TO BALDERSDALE (MAP 69)
1 HR 45 MINS–2 HRS 30 MINS FROM BALDERSDALE (MAP 69)
A66
A66

BALDERSDALE [Map 69]

Clove Lodge Bunk Barn (☎ 01833-650650, 💻 clovelodge.co.uk) changed hands in 2018 and the new owners are refurbishing the bunkhouse (sleeps 8) and planning to reopen in March 2019. With the path passing right through its garden, and being almost exactly halfway along the trail, this was always a popular stop. There's a shower room and kitchen facilities so self-catering will be possible. B&B, evening meals and packed lunches may also be provided but contact the new owners for more details.

COTHERSTONE [off Map 67c]

The Fox and Hounds (☎ 01833-650241, 💻 cotherstonefox.co.uk; 2D/1T, all en suite; ☕; Ⓛ; 🐕); has pleasant rooms and they can pick you up from the trail and drop you off the next morning, a service which is included in the room rates from £45pp (sgl occ £50). However, note that a time needs to be pre-arranged as the phone signal is not good. They also serve **food** (daily noon-2pm, Sun-Thur 6-8.30pm, Fri & Sat to 9pm). Scarlet Band No 95 & 96 **bus** services (see pp54-9) run through the village.

LUNEDALE [Map 71, p193]

There's not much for walkers in Lunedale aside from scattered homesteads and farms but two miles (3km) along the B6276 (ie a stone's throw from Middleton itself by road) is the **campsite** at ***Highside Farm*** (off Map 71; ☎ 01833-640135, 💻 www.highsidefarm.co.uk; 🐕), Bow Bank. Pitching at the small site costs £10pp. *(cont'd on p194)*

❑ Hannah Hauxwell

Right on the edge of Blackton Reservoir beside the Pennine Way stands the farm of Low Birk Hat (see Map 69), home for many years to a remarkable woman. Hannah Hauxwell came to public attention through a number of television programmes and books (both formats are still available) telling the story of the life of someone living at subsistence level in Baldersdale as recently as the 1970s. With a cow which had one calf a year, she allowed herself £250 a year for living expenses, without electricity or gas, surviving the harsh winters by the simple expedient of putting on another coat.

Later Hannah Hauxwell became famous for her courage and her natural understanding of the world and its follies when she travelled for the cameras recording her impressions of cities around the world. Her curiosity and common-sense enabled her to put her finger on the unusual and get pleasure from the commonplace.

Hannah died in 2018 at the age of 81 but will be long remembered by those who followed her adventures. Her farm where at one time her father alone supported a family of seven, both sets of parents, himself, his wife and their daughter, has since been much modernised and a glimpse over the wall reveals merely an echo of the hard livelihood it once accommodated. See also box p204.

Hannah's Meadow (see Map 70) Part of the legacy of Hannah Hauxwell has been the preservation of her farmland which has been given the status of a study area for meadow grasses and wild flowers.

Purchased by Durham Wildlife Trust in 1988, the site was later designated a Site of Special Scientific Interest (see p61) qualifying by having 23 of the 47 species of rare and characteristic plants listed by Natural England. The meadows were never ploughed, being cut for hay in August and thereafter grazed by cows resulting in herb-rich meadows. Numerous varieties of birds are visitors to the meadows and no fewer than 16 kinds of dung-beetle have been identified.

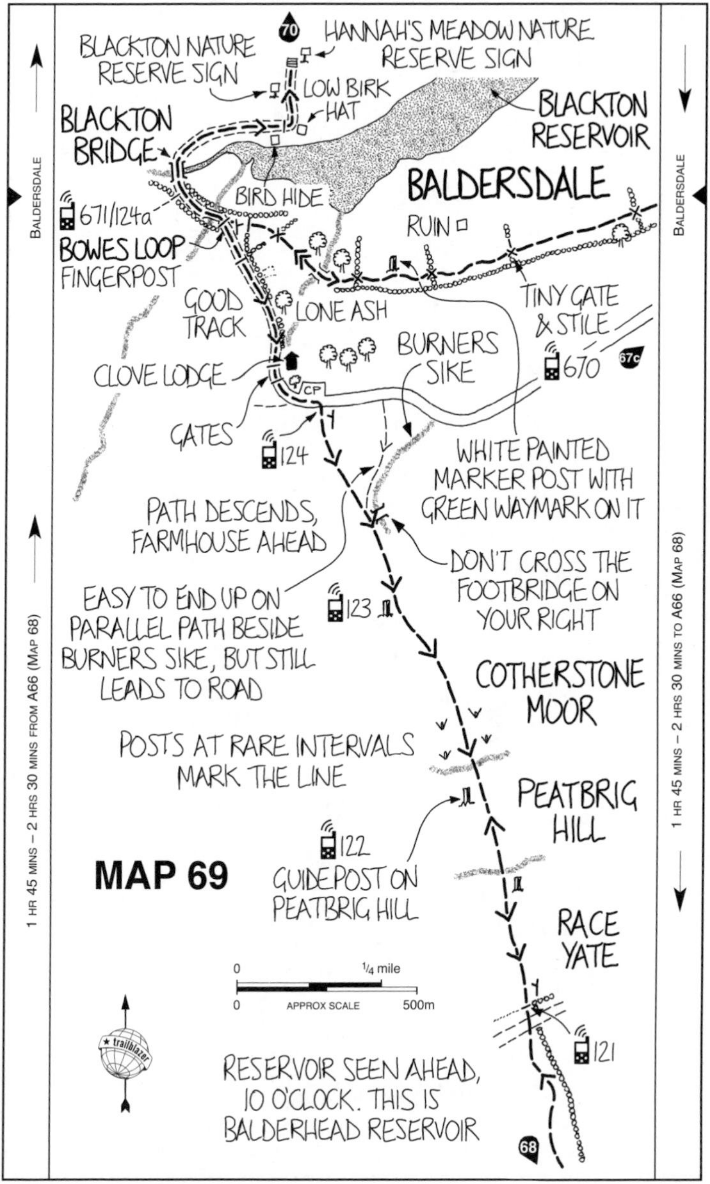
BALDERSDALE
BALDERSDALE
1 HR 45 MINS – 2 HRS 30 MINS FROM A66 (MAP 68)
1 HR 45 MINS – 2 HRS 30 MINS TO A66 (MAP 68)
70
HANNAH'S MEADOW NATURE RESERVE SIGN
BLACKTON NATURE RESERVE SIGN
LOW BIRK HAT
BLACKTON BRIDGE
BLACKTON RESERVOIR
BIRD HIDE
BALDERSDALE
671/124a
BOWES LOOP FINGERPOST
RUIN
GOOD TRACK
LONE ASH
TINY GATE & STILE
BURNERS SIKE
CLOVE LODGE
CP
670
67c
GATES
124
WHITE PAINTED MARKER POST WITH GREEN WAYMARK ON IT
PATH DESCENDS, FARMHOUSE AHEAD
DON'T CROSS THE FOOTBRIDGE ON YOUR RIGHT
EASY TO END UP ON PARALLEL PATH BESIDE BURNERS SIKE, BUT STILL LEADS TO ROAD
123
COTHERSTONE MOOR
POSTS AT RARE INTERVALS MARK THE LINE
PEATBRIG HILL
122
MAP 69
GUIDEPOST ON PEATBRIG HILL
RACE YATE
0
1/4 mile
0
APPROX SCALE
500m
trailblazer
121
RESERVOIR SEEN AHEAD, 10 O'CLOCK. THIS IS BALDERHEAD RESERVOIR
68

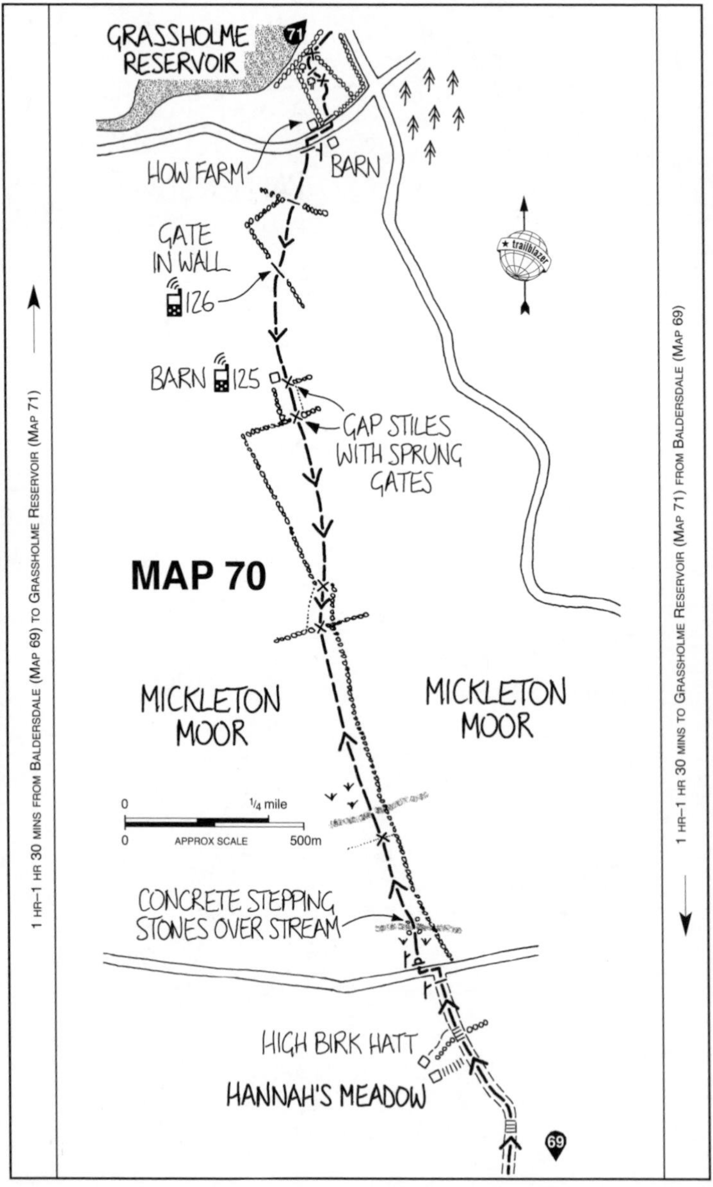
GRASSHOLME RESERVOIR
71
HOW FARM
BARN
GATE IN WALL
126
BARN
125
GAP STILES WITH SPRUNG GATES
MAP 70
MICKLETON MOOR
MICKLETON MOOR
0
1/4 mile
0
APPROX SCALE
500m
CONCRETE STEPPING STONES OVER STREAM
HIGH BIRK HATT
HANNAH'S MEADOW
69
1 HR–1 HR 30 MINS FROM BALDERSDALE (MAP 69) TO GRASSHOLME RESERVOIR (MAP 71)
1 HR–1 HR 30 MINS TO GRASSHOLME RESERVOIR (MAP 71) FROM BALDERSDALE (MAP 69)

1 HR 30 MINS–2 HRS TO MIDDLETON-IN-TEESDALE (MAP 72)

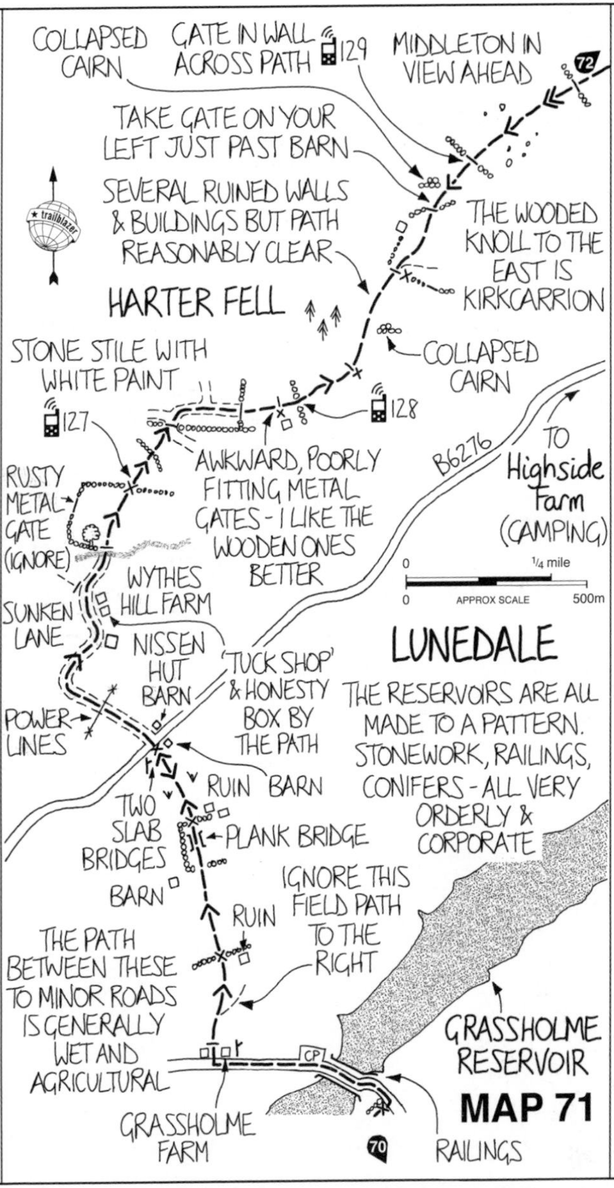
COLLAPSED CAIRN
GATE IN WALL ACROSS PATH
129
MIDDLETON IN VIEW AHEAD
72
TAKE GATE ON YOUR LEFT JUST PAST BARN
SEVERAL RUINED WALLS & BUILDINGS BUT PATH REASONABLY CLEAR
THE WOODED KNOLL TO THE EAST IS KIRKCARRION
trailblazer
HARTER FELL
STONE STILE WITH WHITE PAINT
COLLAPSED CAIRN
127
128
B6276
TO Highside Farm (CAMPING)
RUSTY METAL GATE (IGNORE)
AWKWARD, POORLY FITTING METAL GATES - I LIKE THE WOODEN ONES BETTER
0
1/4 mile
0
APPROX SCALE
500m
WYTHES HILL FARM
SUNKEN LANE
NISSEN HUT BARN
'TUCK SHOP' & HONESTY BOX BY THE PATH
LUNEDALE
THE RESERVOIRS ARE ALL MADE TO A PATTERN. STONEWORK, RAILINGS, CONIFERS - ALL VERY ORDERLY & CORPORATE
POWER LINES
BARN
RUIN
TWO SLAB BRIDGES
PLANK BRIDGE
BARN
IGNORE THIS FIELD PATH TO THE RIGHT
RUIN
THE PATH BETWEEN THESE TO MINOR ROADS IS GENERALLY WET AND AGRICULTURAL
GRASSHOLME RESERVOIR
CP
GRASSHOLME FARM
70
RAILINGS
MAP 71

GRASSHOLME RESERVOIR

1 HR 30 MINS–2 HRS FROM MIDDLETON-IN-TEESDALE (MAP 72)

GRASSHOLME RESERVOIR

ROUTE GUIDE AND MAPS

(cont'd from p190) There are showers, toilets and washing facilities. However, at the time of research the farm had just been taken over by new people and they expect to do work on the campsite so things may change.

MIDDLETON-IN-TEESDALE

[Map 72a]

On the banks of the River Tees, this small town thrived during the 19th century when the now defunct lead-mining industry was in its heyday. It's mostly laid out along one street, with handsome architecture interspersed with a few quirky buildings.

See p14 for details of Middleton Carnival held here in early August.

Services

The **tourist information centre** (TIC; ☎ 01833-641001; Tue 10am-1pm, other days 10am-1pm if volunteers are available), 10 Market Place, has limited opening hours but sells some interesting publications on the North Pennines and also has free information on the area.

For groceries there is a large, well-stocked Co-op **supermarket** (daily 7am-10pm). Next door in the Utass centre is a **post office** (Tue 9.45am-12.30pm, Fri 1-3.30pm), and very near to that is G&J **newsagents**. There is also a **pharmacy** (Mon, Tue, Thur & Fri 9am-5.30pm, Wed & Sat 9am-1pm). The Barclays Bank here has an **ATM**. Early closing day for most of the town is Wednesday.

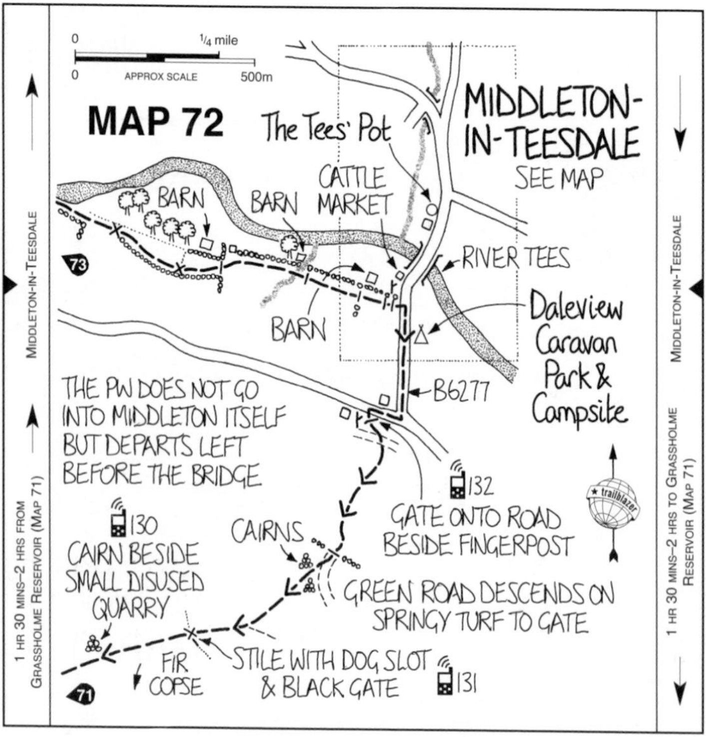
MAP 72
0 ¼ mile
0 APPROX SCALE 500m
MIDDLETON-IN-TEESDALE
SEE MAP
The Tees' Pot
BARN
BARN
CATTLE MARKET
RIVER TEES
BARN
Daleview Caravan Park & Campsite
B6277
THE PW DOES NOT GO INTO MIDDLETON ITSELF BUT DEPARTS LEFT BEFORE THE BRIDGE
132
GATE ONTO ROAD BESIDE FINGERPOST
130
CAIRN BESIDE SMALL DISUSED QUARRY
CAIRNS
GREEN ROAD DESCENDS ON SPRINGY TURF TO GATE
STILE WITH DOG SLOT & BLACK GATE
FIR COPSE
131
73
71
MIDDLETON-IN-TEESDALE
1 HR 30 MINS–2 HRS FROM GRASSHOLME RESERVOIR (MAP 71)
1 HR 30 MINS–2 HRS TO GRASSHOLME RESERVOIR (MAP 71)
trailblazer

Middleton-in-Teesdale MAP 72a

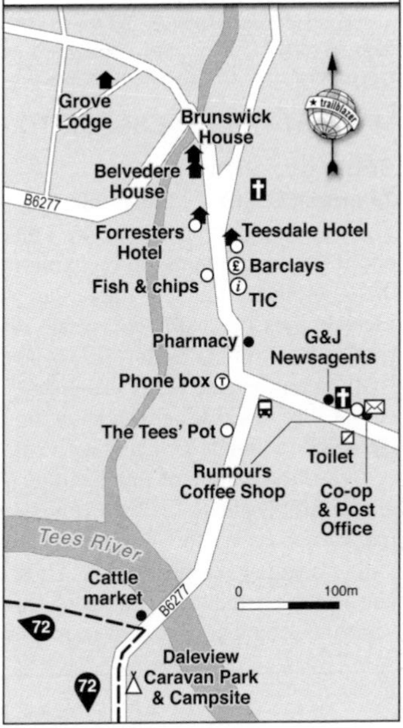
Grove Lodge
Brunswick House
Belvedere House
B6277
Forresters Hotel
Teesdale Hotel
Barclays
Fish & chips
TIC
Pharmacy
G&J Newsagents
Phone box
The Tees' Pot
Toilet
Rumours Coffee Shop
Co-op & Post Office
Tees River
Cattle market
B6277
0
100m
72
72
Daleview Caravan Park & Campsite
trailblazer

Transport

[See pp54-9] The nearest railway station is Darlington, 25 miles (40km) away and a stop on both LNER and TransPennine Express services. To get there take Scarlet Band's No 95 or 96 **bus** service to Barnard Castle and change there for the service to Darlington. Hodgsons No 73 and Cumbria Classic Coaches No 572 call here but only on a Wednesday.

Where to stay

Unless The Rolling Stones decide to play Middleton Village Hall, there is always going to be plenty of choice. The most convenient **campsite** is ***Daleview Caravan Park and Camp Site*** (☎ 01833-640233, 🖳 daleviewcaravanpark.com; 🐕; Mar-Oct) which you pass on your way into town. They accept hikers and charge from £5pp including a shower. Book in advance for bank holiday weekends.

Don't be put off by the grand appearance of ***Grove Lodge*** (☎ 01833-640798, 🖳 grovelodgemiddletoninteesdale.co.uk; 3T/3D, all en suite; ☕; Ⓛ; 🐕) just outside the far side of town and with great views back to Kirkcarrion and Harter Fell; they welcome walkers as long as you don't shake yourself off in the hallway like a wet dog. B&B costs from £42.50pp (sgl occ £65). The twin (with kitchen) and double in the garden rooms can be separate, or connected for a group of up to four people. They can provide an evening meal (from an à la carte menu) with dishes costing from £6.50.

Brunswick House (☎ 01833-640393, 🖳 brunswickhouse.net; 2T/3D, all en suite; ☕; Ⓛ) is more central and B&B costs from £42.50pp (sgl occ £60).

Forresters Hotel (☎ 01833-641435, 🖳 www.forrestersmiddleton.co.uk; 1S/3D/3D or T, all en suite; ☕; Ⓛ; clean 🐕) is a flashy place (all chrome fittings and shiny floors) with a modern bar. B&B costs £40-55pp (sgl/sgl occ from £55), though if you forego breakfast the rate is reduced by £15pp.

For a change of style head over the road to ***The Teesdale Hotel*** (☎ 01833-640264, 🖳 teesdalehotel.co.uk; 2S/2D or T/1T/7D/1Qd, all en suite; ☕; Ⓛ; 🐕), an old stone-built coaching inn, charging £37.50-49pp (sgl/sgl occ £40-50).

Belvedere House (☎ 01833-641277, 🖳 thebelvederehouse.co.uk; 1D/1T private bathroom, 1D/1T en suite; ☕) charges from £32.50pp (sgl occ £45).

Where to eat and drink

Closest to the Way is ***The Tees'pot*** (☎ 01833-640717, 🖳 the-teespot.business.site; no WI-FI; 🐕; daily summer 9am-5pm, winter 10am-4pm though often closed Jan-Feb). Food is available to take away or eat in and you can get bacon, sausage or egg baps for just £2/2.50 eat in/takeaway; they also serve paninis, meat pies and quiches.

There are a couple more cafés with outside terraces, including ***Rumours Coffee Shop*** (Fri-Wed 10am-5pm, winter

Sat-Wed 10am-4pm), with toasties for around £4.

Opposite the TIC is a **fish & chip** shop (Tue, Thur & Sat 11.30am-2pm & 4-8pm, Wed pm only, Fri 11.30am-8.30pm).

Food at ***Forresters*** (see Where to stay; food Wed-Fri 5-8pm, Sat noon-9pm) is served at the bar (the menu includes a reasonable variety of baguettes from £5.95) and at a restaurant which specialises in French food; that menu includes beef bourguignon (£15.95).

At ***Teesdale Hotel*** (see Where to stay; daily noon-2.30pm & 5.30-9pm, hours variable in winter) mains start at £11, with their fish pie for £13.

MIDDLETON-IN-TEESDALE TO DUFTON MAPS 72-83

Route overview

20 miles (32km) – 2300ft (701m) – 9¾-10¾ hours

There are only two days that are longer than this on the Pennine Way (and only one if you're planning on breaking up the last section into Kirk Yetholm), but this is probably the best single day walk of the lot. The highlights get increasingly impressive as the day wears on, culminating in one of the best sights in England. If you like waterfalls, you're in for an extra-special treat! For a linear, south to north walk, today is unusual in that it finishes further south than it started out, but this just goes to show how important the day is in terms of spectacle and how much the planners wanted to include this section of path.

The first couple of miles out of Middleton may leave you wondering what all the fuss is about, the path is hampered with a tedious series of stiles and too many trees impair the long views, but the river is ever present on the right providing adequate compensation. **Holwick** (Map 74) offers both accommodation and food and then you arrive at **Low Force** (Map 75), an impressive double waterfall, quickly surpassed in magnitude by High Force. After Low Force the

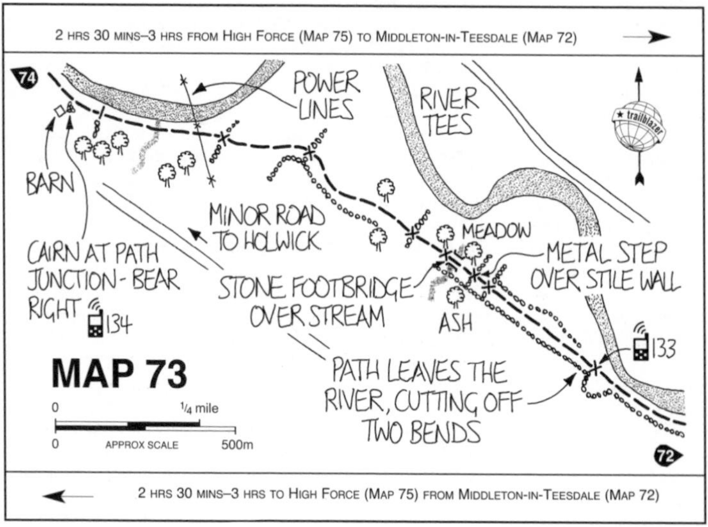

2 HRS 30 MINS–3 HRS FROM HIGH FORCE (MAP 75) TO MIDDLETON-IN-TEESDALE (MAP 72)
74
POWER LINES
RIVER TEES
BARN
MINOR ROAD TO HOLWICK
MEADOW
METAL STEP OVER STILE WALL
CAIRN AT PATH JUNCTION - BEAR RIGHT
134
STONE FOOTBRIDGE OVER STREAM
ASH
133
MAP 73
0
¼ mile
0
APPROX SCALE
500m
PATH LEAVES THE RIVER, CUTTING OFF TWO BENDS
72
2 HRS 30 MINS–3 HRS TO HIGH FORCE (MAP 75) FROM MIDDLETON-IN-TEESDALE (MAP 72)

2 HRS 30 MINS–3 HRS FROM HIGH FORCE (MAP 75) TO MIDDLETON-IN-TEESDALE (MAP 72)
75
SLABS
STEPPING STONES OVER STREAM
NEWBIGGIN
COBBLY PATH HERE
135
MOOR HOUSE/ UPPER TEESDALE NNR SIGN
POWER LINES
B6277
SEABERRY BRIDGE (WOODEN)
Low Way Farm
Camping Barn & Camping
RESCUE LIFEBELT
TO MIDDLETON
HOLWICK
BACK TO RIVER LEVEL
FARMLAND
HOLWICK SCAR
CONCRETE BRIDGE
FENCE ENCLOSES PATH HERE
Strathmore Arms
Farmhouse Kitchen
LOW WAY FARM
MAP 74
WILD GARLIC
0
1/4 mile
PATH HIGH AGAIN
73
0
APPROX SCALE
500m
TREES BETWEEN RIVER & PATH
2 HRS 30 MINS–3 HRS TO HIGH FORCE (MAP 75) FROM MIDDLETON-IN-TEESDALE (MAP 72)

Tees river gets wider and runs faster and at **High Force** (see p198 and box p200) it spills over 70ft (21m) in a magnificent display of power and white water. Beyond High Force the scenery improves significantly and short excursions above the river provide views along its length and into the surrounding hills.

Soon you cross the Tees at **Cronkley Bridge** (Map 77) where your day can end among the scattered, whitewashed communities of **Forest-in-Teesdale** and **Langdon Beck**. At **Widdy Bank Farm** the scene changes again and you are soon walking between rising cliffs, along the boulder-strewn, ankle-twisting margins of the river at **Falcon Clints** (Map 78).

The huge waterfall of **Cauldron Snout** is almost stumbled upon as you round a corner of cliff and without the knowledge that a path lay up the right side of the falls, you would wonder where to go next. A short scramble later and you'll stand beneath the concrete walls of **Cow Green Reservoir** which feeds the snout. The wilderness is temporarily muted as the Way scoots along the access road to the isolated farmstead of **Birkdale** (Map 79; see box p190). But once through the farmyard it leads out on the open moors again, crossing **Grain Beck** and facing the only mildly noteworthy climb of the day to a crest alongside **Rasp Hill** and its long-abandoned mine workings.

The walk along the wide, open valley of **Maize Beck** (Maps 80 & 81) is a delight, but quickly becomes forgotten when you reach the highlight of the day, and possibly the whole walk; **High Cup** (also known as **High Cup Nick**; Map 81). Suddenly the land drops away in front of you in a textbook U-shaped demonstration of the aftermath of glacial erosion. The sides are rimmed with strata of hard rock, basalt or dolerite, interspersed with jumbled scree and twinkling rivulets and from the head of the valley Maize Beck trickles down when it's not getting blown back in your face. A perfect example of glacial erosion, this impressive scooped-out bowl of a valley is a genuine feast for the eyes. If the wind isn't howling up 'the Nick', sit and gawp as long as you can – you're only an hour or two from Dufton, four miles (6.4km) along an old miners' track and it's all downhill.

Dufton (Map 83) has few services but is a lovely place to recharge your batteries and prepare for the ascent of the infamous Cross Fell.

Navigation notes

It's hard to see where one could go wrong on this stage. The path is nearly always obvious and even when it isn't it is following a river.

HOLWICK [Map 74, p197]

Low Way Farm (☎ 01833-640506, 🖳 lowwayfarm.co.uk), a family-run Upper Teesdale working farm, offers basic **camping** for £5pp and **camping barn** accommodation in two barns (1 x 8-, 1 x 20- beds) for £8.50pp or £10 if single occupancy; however, bedding is not provided and booking is recommended as the barns are sometimes taken by groups for sole use. There are basic cooking facilities in the barns but there are no electric sockets or pans, nor is there crockery or cutlery; also lighting and the fridge are on a meter (£1 coins). Note: dogs are not allowed in the barn *or* on the campsite. If prebooked breakfast (£8) and evening meals (two courses from £14) are available on Sat and Sun at the Farmhouse Kitchen by the main farm buildings. ***Farmhouse Kitchen*** (Easter till end Oct Sat & Sun 10am-5pm) serves country café fare such as soups, sandwiches, pies and baked potatoes; Sunday lunch (£13.50) is available all year if prebooked. There is a sign from the trail and the barns are only about 200 metres off the route.

Just over half a mile from the Way is ***Strathmore Arms*** (☎ 01833-640362, 🖳 strathmoregold.co.uk; 2D/1T, all en suite; Ⓛ; 🐕; closed Tue year-round), a pub with rooms where **B&B** costs £37.50-42.50pp (sgl occ full room rate). **Food** is served Mon & Wed-Sat noon-8pm, Sun noon-3pm.

The only **bus** service is Hodgsons No 73 (see pp54-9) on a Wednesday, but the bus stop is 20 minutes away in **Newbiggin**.

HIGH FORCE [Map 75]

High Force Hotel (☎ 01833-622336, 🖳 thehighforcehotel.co.uk; 1S/1T/2D/1T or D/1Tr, all en suite; ☕; Ⓛ; 🐕) charges £40-50pp for **B&B** (single same price, or £65 for sgl occ). **Food** is served (Sun-Thur 11am-8pm, Fri & Sat to 8.30pm) and they have a specials board and also serve real ales.

Hodgsons No 73 **bus** service calls here on a Wednesday; see pp54-9.

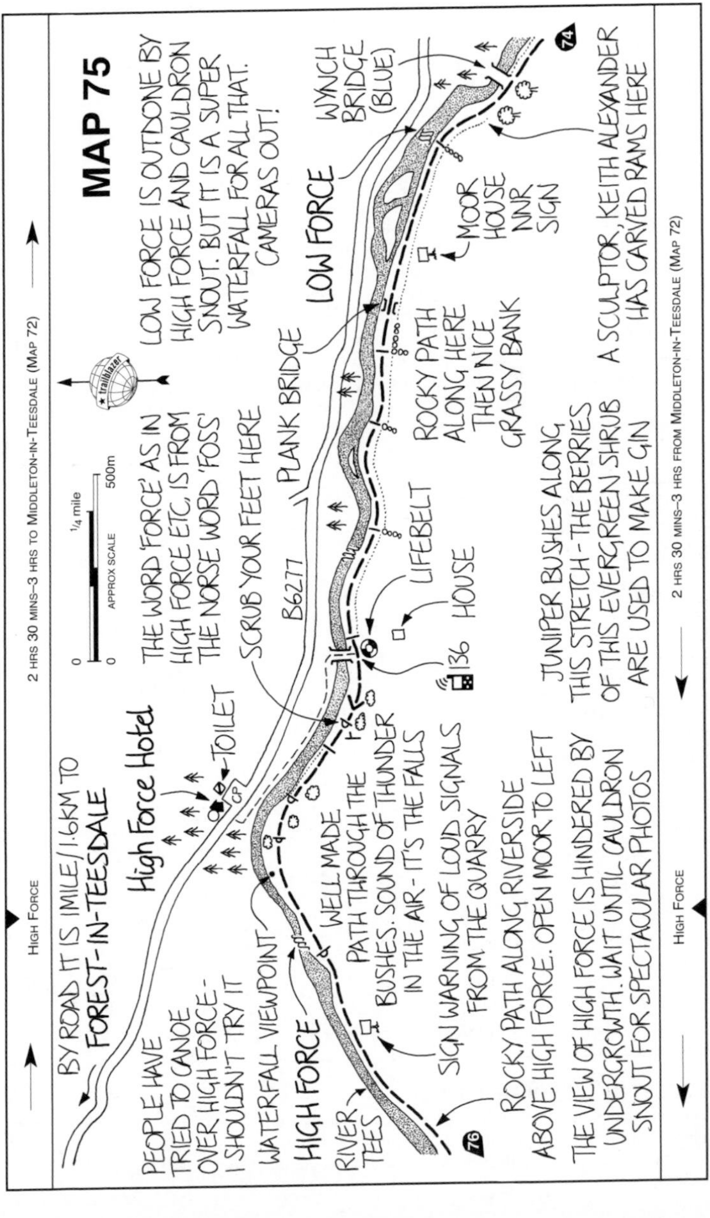
MAP 75
2 HRS 30 MINS–3 HRS TO MIDDLETON-IN-TEESDALE (MAP 72)
HIGH FORCE
2 HRS 30 MINS–3 HRS FROM MIDDLETON-IN-TEESDALE (MAP 72)
HIGH FORCE
APPROX SCALE
0
1/4 mile
0
500m
BY ROAD IT IS 1MILE/1.6KM TO
FOREST-IN-TEESDALE
High Force Hotel
TOILET
CP
PEOPLE HAVE TRIED TO CANOE OVER HIGH FORCE - I SHOULDN'T TRY IT
WATERFALL VIEWPOINT
HIGH FORCE
RIVER TEES
WELL MADE PATH THROUGH THE BUSHES. SOUND OF THUNDER IN THE AIR - IT'S THE FALLS
SIGN WARNING OF LOUD SIGNALS FROM THE QUARRY
ROCKY PATH ALONG RIVERSIDE ABOVE HIGH FORCE. OPEN MOOR TO LEFT
THE VIEW OF HIGH FORCE IS HINDERED BY UNDERGROWTH. WAIT UNTIL CAULDRON SNOUT FOR SPECTACULAR PHOTOS
76
THE WORD 'FORCE' AS IN HIGH FORCE ETC, IS FROM THE NORSE WORD 'FOSS'
SCRUB YOUR FEET HERE
B6277
PLANK BRIDGE
LIFEBELT
HOUSE
136
ROCKY PATH ALONG HERE THEN NICE GRASSY BANK
JUNIPER BUSHES ALONG THIS STRETCH - THE BERRIES OF THIS EVERGREEN SHRUB ARE USED TO MAKE GIN
LOW FORCE IS OUTDONE BY HIGH FORCE AND CAULDRON SNOUT. BUT IT IS A SUPER WATERFALL FOR ALL THAT. CAMERAS OUT!
LOW FORCE
MOOR HOUSE NNR SIGN
WYNCH BRIDGE (BLUE)
A SCULPTOR, KEITH ALEXANDER HAS CARVED RAMS HERE
74

❑ High Force
[Map 75, p199]

High Force is so big it has to claim some distinction over others. The highest? The biggest? These seem to belong elsewhere so what they say is it's the highest unbroken fall of water in England; the drop is 21 metres (70ft). It's certainly impressive, especially after rain when the water appears the colour of tea, tinged with the peat from the moors.

W A Poucher, the celebrated photographer and writer of a series of guides during the 1960s and '70s, said that it is a difficult subject to photograph well, facing north-east, hence having the wrong light conditions for effective photography. Its other problem, at least from the Pennine Way side of the river, is access for a good view. There are places where you can scramble through the undergrowth and cling on to the cliff edge but few where you can wield the camera effectively.

People have done some strange things here. Some have gone off the top, ending their lives in the torrent. Two boaters were stopped at the last minute from attempting to kayak off the top and a visitor from abroad slipped on the flat shelf at the lip and though saving himself, catapulted the infant on his back over the edge to its doom. There is an odd fascination about raging water which seems to compel some people to get just that little bit too close.

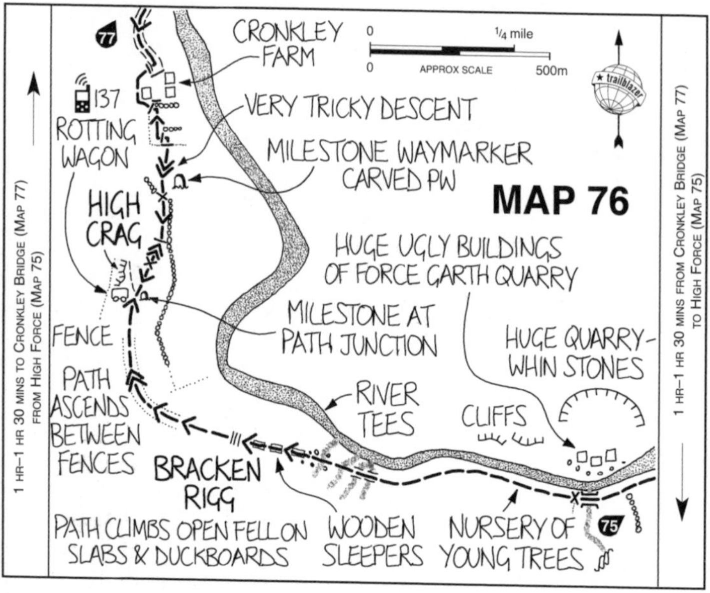
1 HR–1 HR 30 MINS TO CRONKLEY BRIDGE (MAP 77)
FROM HIGH FORCE (MAP 75)
77
137
ROTTING WAGON
HIGH CRAG
FENCE
PATH ASCENDS BETWEEN FENCES
BRACKEN RIGG
PATH CLIMBS OPEN FELL ON SLABS & DUCKBOARDS
CRONKLEY FARM
0
1/4 mile
0
APPROX SCALE
500m
trailblazer
VERY TRICKY DESCENT
MILESTONE WAYMARKER CARVED PW
MAP 76
HUGE UGLY BUILDINGS OF FORCE GARTH QUARRY
MILESTONE AT PATH JUNCTION
HUGE QUARRY-WHIN STONES
RIVER TEES
CLIFFS
WOODEN SLEEPERS
NURSERY OF YOUNG TREES
75
1 HR–1 HR 30 MINS FROM CRONKLEY BRIDGE (MAP 77)
TO HIGH FORCE (MAP 75)

FOREST-IN-TEESDALE [off Map 77]

On reaching Cronkley Bridge the nearest place with accommodation is Forest-in-Teesdale, a scattered collection of houses along the B6277. The only regular **bus** service is Hodgsons No 73 on a Wednesday; see pp54-9 for details.

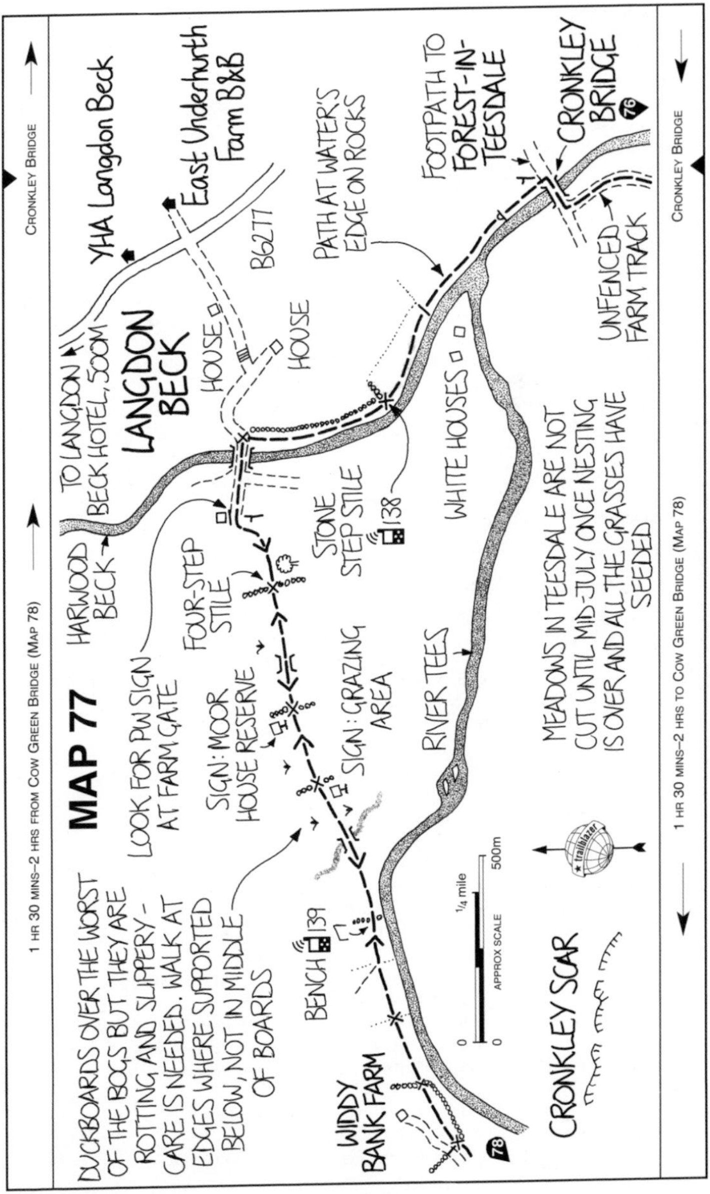

1 HR 30 MINS–2 HRS FROM COW GREEN BRIDGE (MAP 78)
CRONKLEY BRIDGE
MAP 77
DUCKBOARDS OVER THE WORST OF THE BOGS BUT THEY ARE ROTTING AND SLIPPERY – CARE IS NEEDED. WALK AT EDGES WHERE SUPPORTED BELOW, NOT IN MIDDLE OF BOARDS
LOOK FOR PW SIGN AT FARM GATE
SIGN: MOOR HOUSE RESERVE
FOUR-STEP STILE
HARWOOD BECK
TO LANGDON BECK HOTEL, 500M
LANGDON BECK
HOUSE
HOUSE
YHA Langdon Beck
East Underhurth Farm B&B
B6277
PATH AT WATER'S EDGE ON ROCKS
FOOTPATH TO FOREST-IN-TEESDALE
CRONKLEY BRIDGE
76
BENCH
139
SIGN: GRAZING AREA
STONE STEP STILE
138
WHITE HOUSES
RIVER TEES
UNFENCED FARM TRACK
WIDDY BANK FARM
78
APPROX SCALE
0
1/4 mile
0
500m
CRONKLEY SCAR
trailblazer
MEADOWS IN TEESDALE ARE NOT CUT UNTIL MID-JULY ONCE NESTING IS OVER AND ALL THE GRASSES HAVE SEEDED
1 HR 30 MINS–2 HRS TO COW GREEN BRIDGE (MAP 78)
CRONKLEY BRIDGE

[**Forest-in-Teesdale** *cont'd*] ***The Dale*** (☎ 01833-622303; 1D or T/1D, shared bathroom; ☕; no WI-FI; Ⓛ; 🐕; Mar-end Oct) is one of those stalwarts among Pennine Way B&Bs. Mrs Bonnett has catered for walkers for many years and knows how to please them, with comfortable beds and a coal fire to sit by on cold days. Mr Bonnett works at the High Force waterfall and has some tales to tell. **B&B** costs from £28pp (sgl occ £28) which represents outstanding value for money, particularly as it includes a lift to Langdon Beck Hotel and back in the evening for dinner. You can find them by first locating the school then turning right at the top of the lane.

LANGDON BECK [Map 77, p201]

YHA Langdon Beck (☎ 0345-371 9027, 🖳 yha.org.uk/hostel/langdon-beck; 1 x 5-bed room en suite, 2 x 2-, 4 x 4-, 1 x 8-bed room shared facilities; Ⓛ; Mar-end Oct) will be the chosen destination for many walkers, but note that the hostel gets booked up, particularly in the summer months. A dorm bed costs from £15pp and a private room from £29. The hostel is licensed and meals are available; there are also laundry facilities and a drying room.

The warden is helpful and knowledgeable about the PW and local wildlife.

If the hostel is full try the nearby ***East Underhurth Farm*** (☎ 01833-622062, 🖳 eastunderhurthfarm@hotmail.co.uk; 1D/1Tr, shared facilities; ☕; Ⓛ; 🐕), a working hill farm and a lovely place to stay; **B&B** costs from £35pp (sgl occ £35). Booking is recommended.

About a quarter of a mile north of the hostel is ***Langdon Beck Hotel*** (☎ 01833-622267, 🖳 langdonbeckhotel.com; 2T en suite, 2S/2D/1T share bathrooms; ☕; Ⓛ; 🐕). **B&B** costs £40-50pp (sgl/sgl occ from £50/60-70). They are happy for walkers to

❑ Lead mining in the Pennines

The history of digging in the earth for lead in the Pennine hills goes back to the Romans and probably earlier, evidence having been uncovered that Romans further exploited existing workings soon after they arrived.

The growth in the building of abbeys and castles increased the demand for lead for the roofs and stained-glass windows but it was not until the 19th century that mining assumed industrial proportions as the demand for lead increased.

The industry started to suffer when cheaper foreign sources threatened local production and by the early years of the 20th century mining was in decline. Today there is no lead mining in Britain although some of the old pits have been re-opened to exploit other minerals found there such as barytes and fluorspar. The ore, galena, also has a use in producing X-ray equipment.

The ruins evident around Alston, and around Keld in Swaledale, are a reminder of the extensive industry involved in lead mining at one time. Old spoil tips, ruined mine buildings and the occasional remains of a chimney are all that is left of this activity, now long discarded as uneconomic. Traces of bell pits are often to be seen as hollows in the ground. They used to sink a shaft to a certain level then widen the bottom of the hole until it was unsafe to go further. Everything dug out went to the surface in a bucket, firstly by hand and then by a winch, sometimes drawn up on a wheel by a horse walking in a circle. It was a primitive industry in the early days, reliant on the muscle power of the miners themselves. With the advent of engineering, ways were found to mechanise production and so multiply the output, increasing profits for the owners.

Around Middleton-in-Teesdale mining rights were held by the London Lead Mining Company, a Quaker concern, active from the latter part of the 1700s until early in the 1900s when they pulled out in the face of cheap imported ore from Europe.

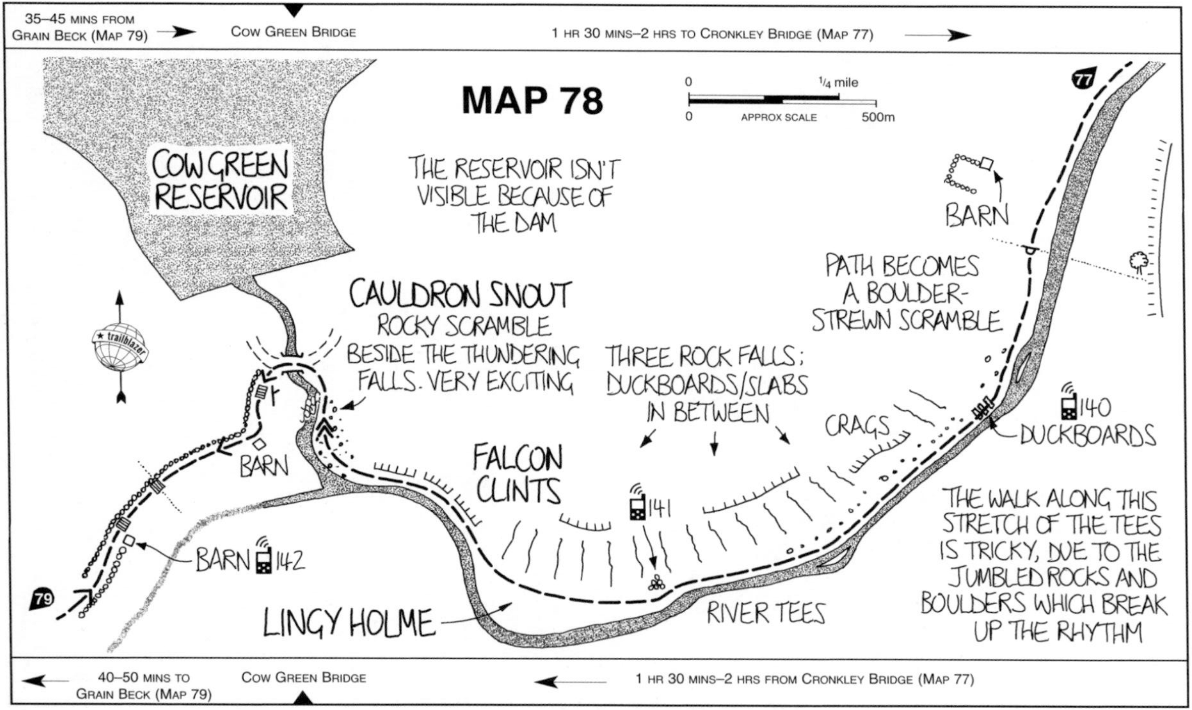
35–45 MINS FROM GRAIN BECK (MAP 79)
COW GREEN BRIDGE
1 HR 30 MINS–2 HRS TO CRONKLEY BRIDGE (MAP 77)
MAP 78
0 1/4 mile
0 APPROX SCALE 500m
77
COW GREEN RESERVOIR
THE RESERVOIR ISN'T VISIBLE BECAUSE OF THE DAM
BARN
PATH BECOMES A BOULDER-STREWN SCRAMBLE
trailblazer
CAULDRON SNOUT
ROCKY SCRAMBLE BESIDE THE THUNDERING FALLS. VERY EXCITING
THREE ROCK FALLS; DUCKBOARDS/SLABS IN BETWEEN
140
DUCKBOARDS
CRAGS
BARN
FALCON CLINTS
141
THE WALK ALONG THIS STRETCH OF THE TEES IS TRICKY, DUE TO THE JUMBLED ROCKS AND BOULDERS WHICH BREAK UP THE RHYTHM
BARN
142
79
LINGY HOLME
RIVER TEES
40–50 MINS TO GRAIN BECK (MAP 79)
COW GREEN BRIDGE
1 HR 30 MINS–2 HRS FROM CRONKLEY BRIDGE (MAP 77)

put their boots to dry in front of one of the fires. **Food** is served (Easter to early Oct Mon-Sat noon-2pm & 7-9pm, Sun noon-2.30pm & 7-8.30pm, rest of year Tue-Sat noon-2pm & 7-9pm, Sun noon-2.30pm & 7-8.30pm) but note that the hotel is closed completely on Mondays between the first Monday in October and the Monday before Easter.

The pub has a great menu including a 9oz Teesdale sirloin steak with a plateload of trimmings for £14.25 as well as a few veggie options from £7.95. They also have specials such as cottage pie and steak pie; most of the food is home made.

Hodgsons No 73 **bus** runs from here to Middleton-in-Teesdale but only on a Wednesday; see pp54-9.

❑ *Too Long a Winter*

Even though these days a sealed road leads to it, walking past the front of Birkdale Farm (Map 79) you can't help but be struck by the homestead's strikingly remote location. Said to be the highest occupied farmhouse in England, it makes Emily Bronte's Withins Height (see p119) look like a shed at the back of the garden.

In the 1970s the farmer whose family had long rented the property from Lord Barnard's extensive Raby Estate was the subject of a TV documentary. The show depicted three groups of local characters: Brian and Mary Bainbridge farming at Birkdale, a brief glimpse of a chauffeur-driven Mrs Field from Middleton, a preposterous caricature cut out of an Agatha Christie novel, and the soon-to-become famous Hannah Hauxwell (see box p190). Brian Bainbridge, who helped dig out the Cow Green Reservoir behind Cauldron Snout, was followed as he and his wife returned to the empty homestead after several years' absence to give the place another go. He was filmed from a circling helicopter rounding up sheep (or perhaps chasing them as they fled from the chopper) and staggering around the snowbound fells, staff in hand, hauling strays out of snow drifts. A decade earlier the disastrous winter of 1963 wiped out the then young farmer's entire flock and led him to eventually abandon Birkdale. He described that tragic year as just 'too long a winter' for the sheep and so gave the programme its title.

Among other characters, a smiling, ruddy-faced fellow herder George Haw, was asked about the attraction of life on the moors. 'Well I don't know, it's just a living that's all... I can't say there's any attraction to it, like'. Mary Bainbridge is mildly more upbeat to the same query 'I love the hills, the sheep, the loneliness'.

Too Long a Winter also set the 46-year-old Daleswoman Hannah Hauxwell on her path to fame. Her story and presence are no less moving. Like a character out of a children's fairy tale, she is seen dragging her prize bull to market on a sleety winter's day; the outcome set to meet her financial needs for the coming year. Resigned but not necessarily devoted to a solitary life, she observes the wrong husband would not be worth having and is filmed at Mrs Field's annual harvest do tapping her feet in her giant-lapelled overcoat while all around her dance gaily. Like the Bainbridges (but not at all like the batty Mrs Field) Hauxwell's ingenuous innocence and ready acceptance of life's hardships set her apart and led to a staggering response from the viewing public; letters and food parcels came in from all over the country. Over the next 20 years other TV shows and books followed. On her husband's death in 2006 Mary Bainbridge said, 'He always thought the TV programme was a bit of a farce. Neither he nor I ever met Miss Hauxwell. I thought she was rather exploited.'

The video of *Too Long a Winter* is easily found on Amazon or eBay for a few pounds, along with what might be called the Hannah Hauxwell boxed set. Tracing this prodigious output of 'Hannobilia' by director/producer Brian Cockcroft, ending in Hannah USA, you can't help feeling Mary Bainbridge may have had a point.

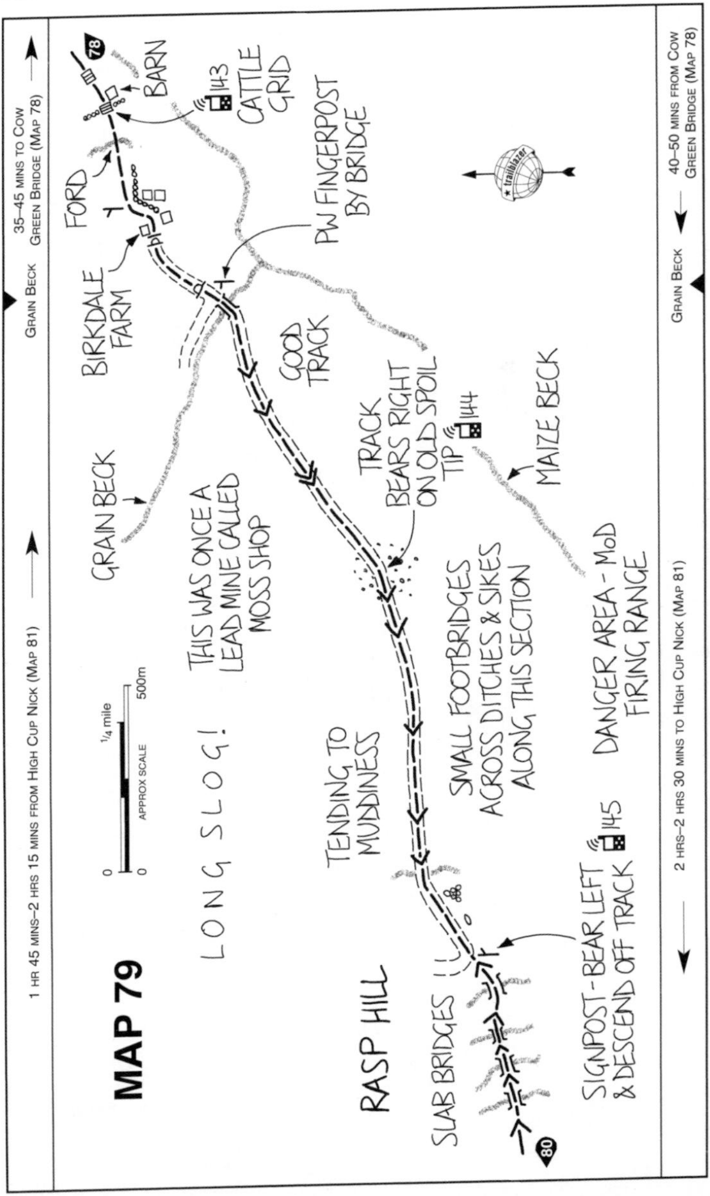
MAP 79
1 HR 45 MINS–2 HRS 15 MINS FROM HIGH CUP NICK (MAP 81)
GRAIN BECK
35–45 MINS TO COW GREEN BRIDGE (MAP 78)
78
BARN
143
CATTLE GRID
FORD
BIRKDALE FARM
PW FINGERPOST BY BRIDGE
GOOD TRACK
GRAIN BECK
THIS WAS ONCE A LEAD MINE CALLED MOSS SHOP
TRACK BEARS RIGHT ON OLD SPOIL TIP
144
MAIZE BECK
trailblazer
0 1/4 mile
APPROX SCALE
0 500m
LONG SLOG!
TENDING TO MUDDINESS
SMALL FOOTBRIDGES ACROSS DITCHES & SIKES ALONG THIS SECTION
DANGER AREA - MoD FIRING RANGE
RASP HILL
SLAB BRIDGES
145
SIGNPOST - BEAR LEFT & DESCEND OFF TRACK
80
40–50 MINS FROM COW GREEN BRIDGE (MAP 78)
GRAIN BECK
2 HRS–2 HRS 30 MINS TO HIGH CUP NICK (MAP 81)

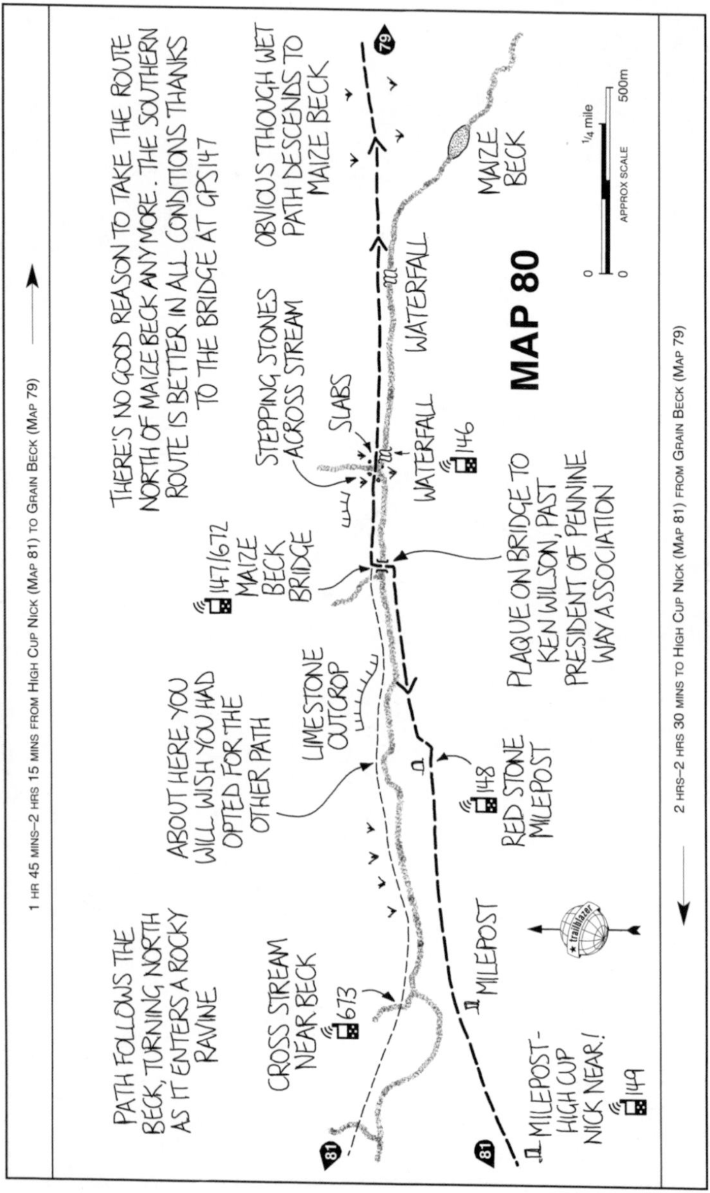
1 HR 45 MINS–2 HRS 15 MINS FROM HIGH CUP NICK (MAP 81) TO GRAIN BECK (MAP 79)
MAP 80
THERE'S NO GOOD REASON TO TAKE THE ROUTE NORTH OF MAIZE BECK ANYMORE. THE SOUTHERN ROUTE IS BETTER IN ALL CONDITIONS THANKS TO THE BRIDGE AT GPS147
OBVIOUS THOUGH WET PATH DESCENDS TO MAIZE BECK
79
STEPPING STONES ACROSS STREAM
SLABS
WATERFALL
146
WATERFALL
MAIZE BECK
147/672 MAIZE BECK BRIDGE
PLAQUE ON BRIDGE TO KEN WILSON, PAST PRESIDENT OF PENNINE WAY ASSOCIATION
LIMESTONE OUTCROP
ABOUT HERE YOU WILL WISH YOU HAD OPTED FOR THE OTHER PATH
148 RED STONE MILEPOST
MILEPOST
PATH FOLLOWS THE BECK, TURNING NORTH AS IT ENTERS A ROCKY RAVINE
673 CROSS STREAM NEAR BECK
149 MILEPOST- HIGH CUP NICK NEAR!
81
81
0 1/4 mile
0 500m
APPROX SCALE
2 HRS–2 HRS 30 MINS TO HIGH CUP NICK (MAP 81) FROM GRAIN BECK (MAP 79)

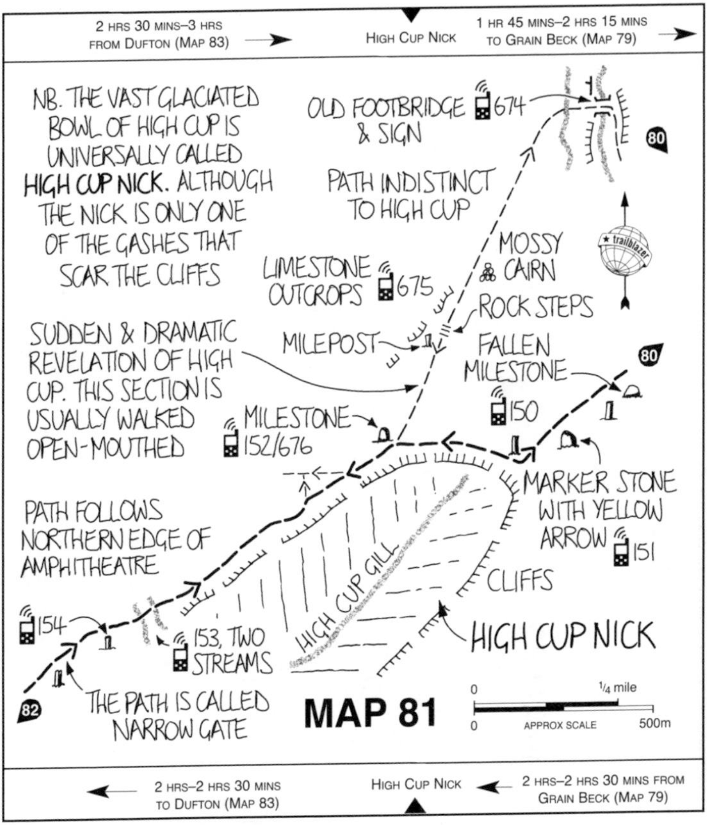
2 hrs 30 mins–3 hrs from Dufton (Map 83)
High Cup Nick
1 hr 45 mins–2 hrs 15 mins to Grain Beck (Map 79)
NB. THE VAST GLACIATED BOWL OF HIGH CUP IS UNIVERSALLY CALLED HIGH CUP NICK. ALTHOUGH THE NICK IS ONLY ONE OF THE GASHES THAT SCAR THE CLIFFS
OLD FOOTBRIDGE & SIGN
674
80
PATH INDISTINCT TO HIGH CUP
MOSSY CAIRN
LIMESTONE OUTCROPS
675
ROCK STEPS
SUDDEN & DRAMATIC REVELATION OF HIGH CUP. THIS SECTION IS USUALLY WALKED OPEN-MOUTHED
MILEPOST
FALLEN MILESTONE
80
150
MILESTONE
152/676
MARKER STONE WITH YELLOW ARROW
151
PATH FOLLOWS NORTHERN EDGE OF AMPHITHEATRE
HIGH CUP GILL
CLIFFS
154
153, TWO STREAMS
HIGH CUP NICK
82
THE PATH IS CALLED NARROW GATE
MAP 81
0
1/4 mile
0
APPROX SCALE
500m
2 hrs–2 hrs 30 mins to Dufton (Map 83)
High Cup Nick
2 hrs–2 hrs 30 mins from Grain Beck (Map 79)

The Maize Beck Gorge route **[Map 80; Map 81]**

In the days before the footbridge was built at GPS waypoint 147/672 there used to be stepping stones over Maize Beck at that point and these would regularly become submerged and treacherous as the river rose after rain. An alternative route, using another footbridge on the northern side of the beck was therefore suggested to walkers by signs at Cow Green Reservoir. This is all water under the bridge (or over the stepping stones) now and the need for the Maize Beck Alternative, as it became known, is redundant.

It's hard to imagine when the route along the northern bank of Maize Beck would be preferable to the official route along the southern side; it is rougher, less well defined, muddier after rain and longer. Some, no doubt, will wonder why even the 2015 editions of the OS Explorer and Landranger maps persist in showing it as an alternative and these notes are for those inquisitive souls, or for repeat Pennine Wayfarers who want a change of scenery. *(cont'd on p210)*

2 HRS 30 MINS–3 HRS FROM DUFTON (MAP 83) TO HIGH CUP NICK (MAP 81) →

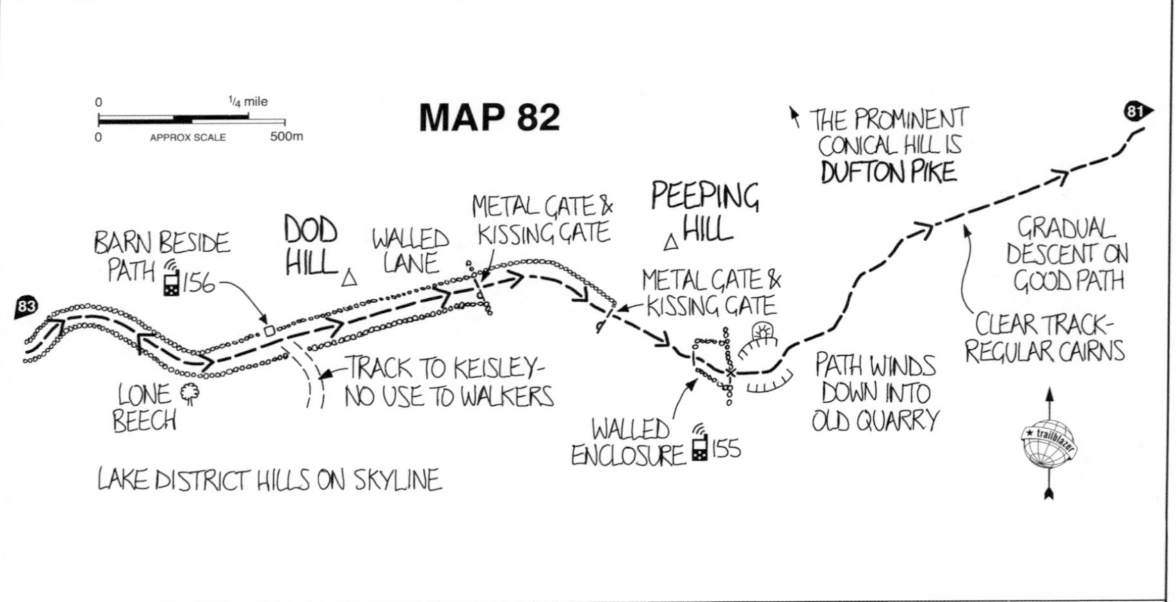
MAP 82
0 1/4 mile
0 APPROX SCALE 500m
83
BARN BESIDE PATH 156
DOD HILL
WALLED LANE
METAL GATE & KISSING GATE
PEEPING HILL
METAL GATE & KISSING GATE
THE PROMINENT CONICAL HILL IS DUFTON PIKE
81
GRADUAL DESCENT ON GOOD PATH
CLEAR TRACK-REGULAR CAIRNS
PATH WINDS DOWN INTO OLD QUARRY
WALLED ENCLOSURE 155
TRACK TO KEISLEY-NO USE TO WALKERS
LONE BEECH
LAKE DISTRICT HILLS ON SKYLINE
trailblazer

← 2 HRS–2 HRS 30 MINS TO DUFTON (MAP 83) FROM HIGH CUP NICK (MAP 81)

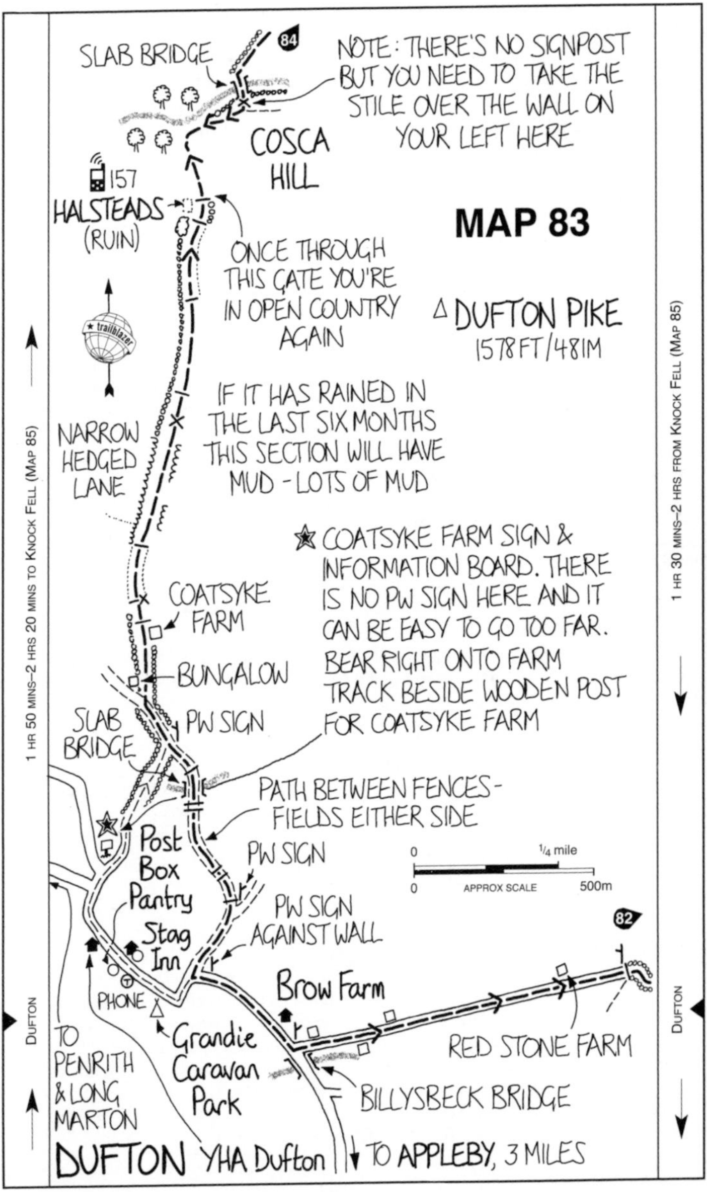

84
SLAB BRIDGE
NOTE: THERE'S NO SIGNPOST BUT YOU NEED TO TAKE THE STILE OVER THE WALL ON YOUR LEFT HERE
COSCA HILL
157
HALSTEADS (RUIN)
MAP 83
ONCE THROUGH THIS GATE YOU'RE IN OPEN COUNTRY AGAIN
DUFTON PIKE 1578 FT/481M
trailblazer
IF IT HAS RAINED IN THE LAST SIX MONTHS THIS SECTION WILL HAVE MUD - LOTS OF MUD
NARROW HEDGED LANE
COATSYKE FARM SIGN & INFORMATION BOARD. THERE IS NO PW SIGN HERE AND IT CAN BE EASY TO GO TOO FAR. BEAR RIGHT ONTO FARM TRACK BESIDE WOODEN POST FOR COATSYKE FARM
COATSYKE FARM
BUNGALOW
PW SIGN
SLAB BRIDGE
PATH BETWEEN FENCES - FIELDS EITHER SIDE
Post Box
Pantry
PW SIGN
0 1/4 mile
0 APPROX SCALE 500m
Stag Inn
PW SIGN AGAINST WALL
82
PHONE
Brow Farm
Grandie Caravan Park
RED STONE FARM
TO PENRITH & LONG MARTON
BILLYSBECK BRIDGE
DUFTON
YHA Dufton
TO APPLEBY, 3 MILES
1 HR 50 MINS–2 HRS 20 MINS TO KNOCK FELL (MAP 85)
1 HR 30 MINS–2 HRS FROM KNOCK FELL (MAP 85)
DUFTON
DUFTON

(cont'd from p207) There will be many faint paths, made by walkers and sheep alike, between the main path on the ground and High Cup Nick, but it's generally best to stick to the longer, more established route and use these waypoints as backup. The 'old footbridge' at GPS 674 (Map 81) spans a beautiful rocky gorge and the path beyond becomes very faint at times. A couple of low cairns will be reassuring and GPS 675 marks a distinctive area of limestone, before the revelation of High Cup.

DUFTON [Map 83, p209]

This quiet and attractive little village is a lovely place to stop after a great day's walking, whichever direction you're taking. There is an agricultural show here in August; see p14 for details.

YHA Dufton (bookings ☎ 0345-371 9734, 🖳 yha.org.uk/hostel/dufton; 1 x 2-bed room en suite, 1 x 2-, 4 x 4-, 2 x 6-bed rooms shared facilities; Ⓛ; Mar-end Oct), opposite the pub, is one of the best on the Way. A dorm bed costs from £15pp, private rooms from £29. The hostel is licensed and meals are available but there is also a self-catering kitchen. Note that the hostel is sometimes booked by groups so reservations are recommended.

Camping at ***Grandie Caravan Park*** (aka **Dufton Caravan Park**; ☎ 01768-353582, 🖳 duftoncaravanpark.co.uk; 🐕; Apr-Oct) costs £7-8pp. There are two toilet /shower blocks. They now have three Hobbit Huts (2 x 2 single beds from £25 per night, 1 x 4 with bunk beds from £40 electricity and heating inc but not bedding); booking is particularly recommended for weekends for these. They also have a wooden hut with seats and table where campers can escape the rain.

Brow Farm (☎ 01768-352865, 🖳 browfarm.com; 1T/2D, all en suite; ▼; Ⓛ) offers B&B in comfortable rooms from £38pp (sgl occ £45).

A recent and welcome addition to the village services is the ***Post Box Pantry*** (☎ 07903-358081, 🖳 postboxpantry.co.uk; 🐕; Easter-end Sep Mon-Wed & Fri 10am-4pm, Sat & Sun to 5pm), on the village green. They serve tea and coffee and a wide selection of snacks, sandwiches, cakes and ice-cream, as well as a small selection of useful items such as bread, milk, canned foods and toiletries. An absolute gold mine, particularly if you're self-catering at the YHA hostel.

The Stag Inn (☎ 01768-351608, 🖳 thestagdufton.co.uk; 🐕 in parts of the pub) is known for its substantial meals (**food** summer Tue 6-8.30pm, Wed-Sat noon-2pm & 6-8.30pm, Sun noon-2pm & 6-7.30pm) in the £10-16 range. Note that the pub only opens at 6pm on Mondays and Tuesdays and food is never served on a Monday. The menu is very limited, with often only a couple of mains to choose from, but the food is good and the prices are reasonable.

Robinson's No 573 **bus** service (Fri only; see pp54-9) operates on a circular route to Appleby, 3 miles along the road (despite what the road sign near the campsite says).

APPLEBY

Appleby (🖳 visitcumbria.com/evnp/appleby) is an attractive country town on the Carlisle–Leeds railway (Northern Rail; see box p59) with banks, several pubs and a bakery or two, all settled around a bend in the River Eden. If you're due for a day off, you could do a lot worse than scheduling it around Dufton and Appleby. Be warned, however, that in June there's the annual **horse fair**, the largest of its kind in the world and one that attracts a vast population of travellers, many arriving in their traditional gypsy caravans. It's quite a spectacle but can be very crowded and more than a little chaotic at this time.

DUFTON TO ALSTON MAPS 83-94

Route overview

19½ miles (31.5km) – 3500ft (1066m) of ascent – 6½-8 hours

Today the challenge is tackling the highest point on the Pennine Way; Cross Fell stands at 2930ft (893m) above sea level and with Dufton standing at only 600ft (183m), alas, there is quite a haul ahead. This is a serious mountain walk and it should not be undertaken lightly, not least because the Helm Wind, one of the strongest in England, can be dangerous to unexpecting and ill-equipped walkers. Come prepared, and be careful.

The Pennine Way may be a National Trail, but don't leave Dufton without proper waterproof clothing, compass (and GPS if you have one) as well as food and water to sustain you for the whole day – there is no re-supply option until Garrigill and possibly not there either depending on the day and time of arrival. Take heart though, you're a battle-scarred veteran of Kinder, Bleaklow and Pen-y-ghent; this is just another notch waiting to be cut into your walking pole.

The official route just skims the edge of Dufton, using a narrow path between fields on the village's south-eastern edge, but most will continue to use the 'unofficial' route through the village and along a quiet lane until both paths join before Coatsyke Farm. A muddy track leads to the old ruin of **Halsteads** and the final

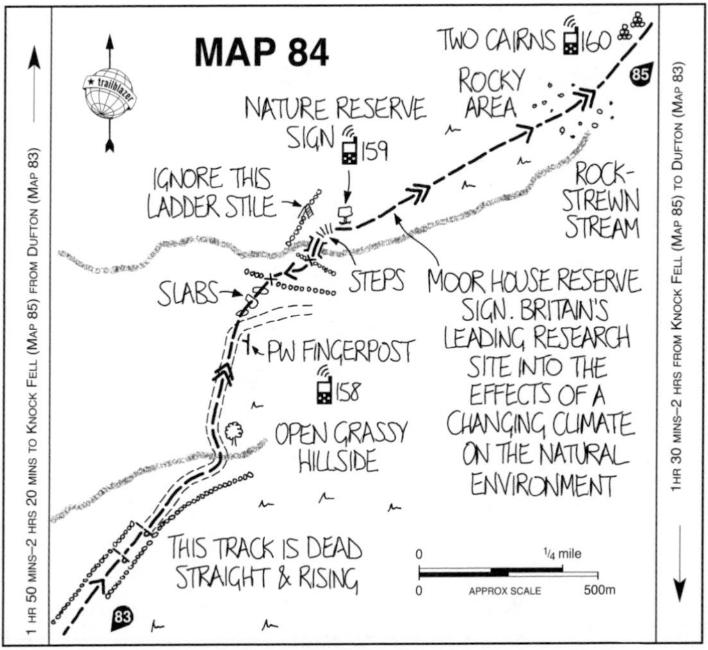
MAP 84
trailblazer
TWO CAIRNS 160
85
ROCKY AREA
NATURE RESERVE SIGN 159
ROCK-STREWN STREAM
IGNORE THIS LADDER STILE
SLABS
STEPS
MOOR HOUSE RESERVE SIGN. BRITAIN'S LEADING RESEARCH SITE INTO THE EFFECTS OF A CHANGING CLIMATE ON THE NATURAL ENVIRONMENT
PW FINGERPOST
158
OPEN GRASSY HILLSIDE
THIS TRACK IS DEAD STRAIGHT & RISING
0
¼ mile
0
APPROX SCALE
500m
83
1 HR 50 MINS–2 HRS 20 MINS TO KNOCK FELL (MAP 85) FROM DUFTON (MAP 83)
1HR 30 MINS–2 HRS FROM KNOCK FELL (MAP 85) TO DUFTON (MAP 83)

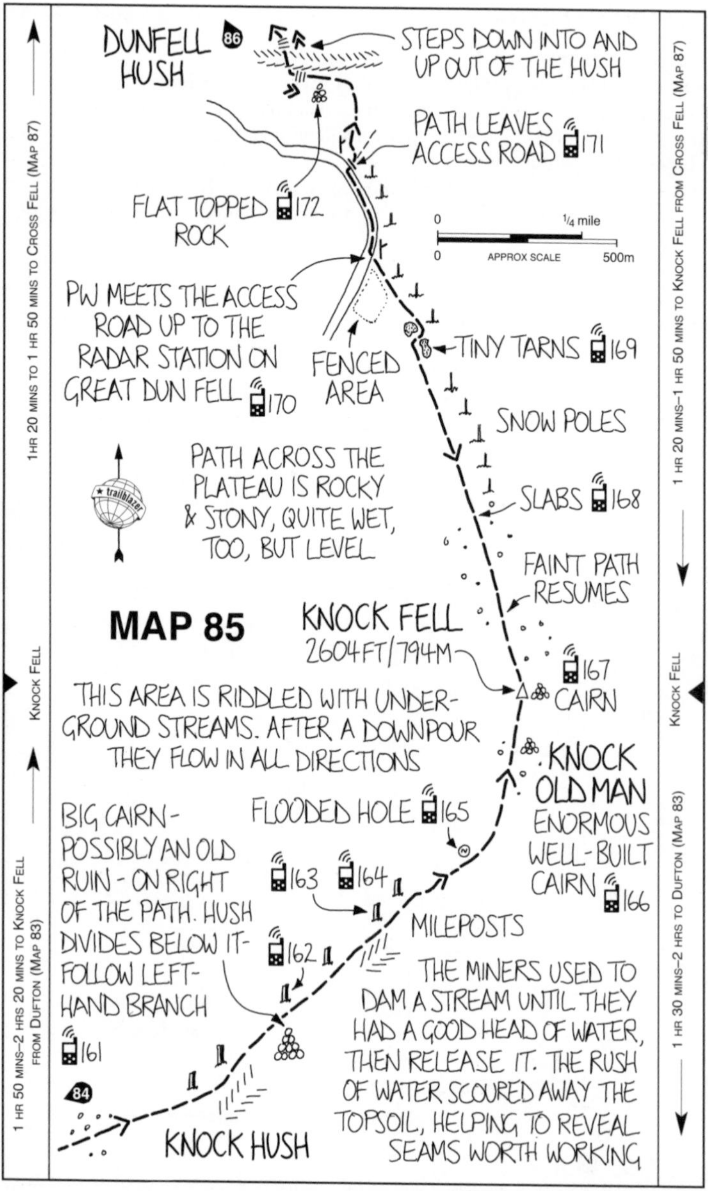
DUNFELL HUSH
86
STEPS DOWN INTO AND UP OUT OF THE HUSH
PATH LEAVES ACCESS ROAD 171
FLAT TOPPED ROCK 172
0 1/4 mile
0 APPROX SCALE 500m
PW MEETS THE ACCESS ROAD UP TO THE RADAR STATION ON GREAT DUN FELL 170
FENCED AREA
TINY TARNS 169
SNOW POLES
trailblazer
PATH ACROSS THE PLATEAU IS ROCKY & STONY, QUITE WET, TOO, BUT LEVEL
SLABS 168
FAINT PATH RESUMES
MAP 85
KNOCK FELL 2604FT/794M
167 CAIRN
THIS AREA IS RIDDLED WITH UNDERGROUND STREAMS. AFTER A DOWNPOUR THEY FLOW IN ALL DIRECTIONS
KNOCK OLD MAN
ENORMOUS WELL-BUILT CAIRN 166
FLOODED HOLE 165
BIG CAIRN - POSSIBLY AN OLD RUIN - ON RIGHT OF THE PATH. HUSH DIVIDES BELOW IT - FOLLOW LEFT-HAND BRANCH
163
164
MILEPOSTS
162
THE MINERS USED TO DAM A STREAM UNTIL THEY HAD A GOOD HEAD OF WATER, THEN RELEASE IT. THE RUSH OF WATER SCOURED AWAY THE TOPSOIL, HELPING TO REVEAL SEAMS WORTH WORKING
161
84
KNOCK HUSH
1 HR 20 MINS TO 1 HR 50 MINS TO CROSS FELL (MAP 87)
KNOCK FELL
1 HR 50 MINS–2 HRS 20 MINS TO KNOCK FELL FROM DUFTON (MAP 83)
1 HR 20 MINS–1 HR 50 MINS TO KNOCK FELL FROM CROSS FELL (MAP 87)
KNOCK FELL
1 HR 30 MINS–2 HRS TO DUFTON (MAP 83)

gate into open country. The ascent is gentle to begin with, but once beyond the ladder stile over the final access wall, the gradient increases significantly.

The next couple of miles up to **Knock Fell** (Map 85) account for almost 1500ft (457m) of today's total ascent, so be sure to turn and look across to the Lake District as you catch your breath. If the weather is in your favour the white dome of the radar station on **Great Dun Fell** (Map 86) becomes your next goal, but in mist you may need to resort to compass or GPS to find the route off Knock Fell, though soon slabs and snow poles will act as a guide.

Two more ascents and another couple of miles will see you over the top of **Little Dun Fell** and standing on the summit of **Cross Fell** (Map 87) the roof of the Pennines, hopefully with a grand vista stretched before you. The route off the summit is not obvious in mist and a compass bearing may be needed from the trig point or shelter. A short, possibly boggy, descent takes you to the track that leads down to Garrigill.

You may feel a rush of relief at reaching the firm footing of **Corpse Road** (so called because in the past it was the route coffins had to be taken to reach consecrated ground as there was nowhere in Garigill) and at being able to put

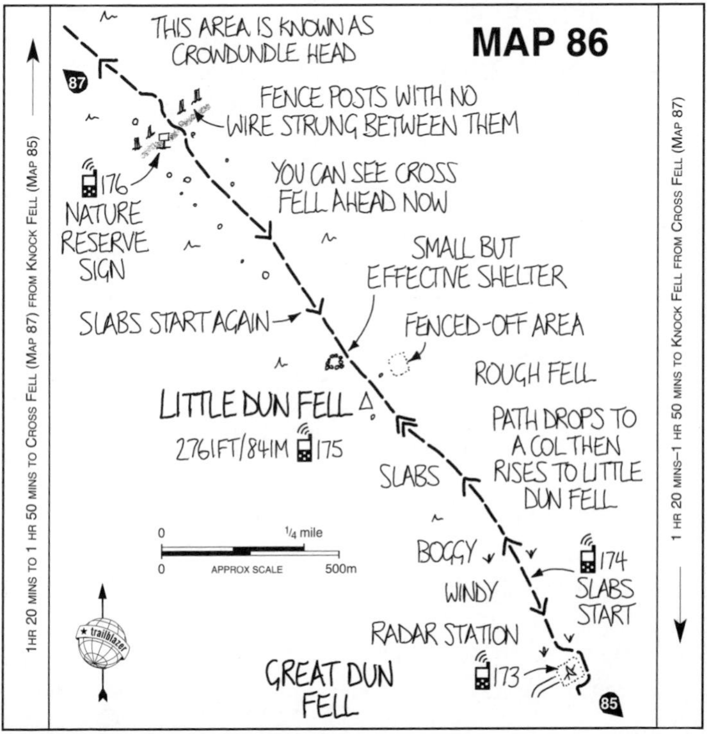
MAP 86
1HR 20 MINS TO 1 HR 50 MINS TO CROSS FELL (MAP 87) FROM KNOCK FELL (MAP 85)
1 HR 20 MINS–1 HR 50 MINS TO KNOCK FELL FROM CROSS FELL (MAP 87)
THIS AREA IS KNOWN AS CROWDUNDLE HEAD
87
FENCE POSTS WITH NO WIRE STRUNG BETWEEN THEM
176
NATURE RESERVE SIGN
YOU CAN SEE CROSS FELL AHEAD NOW
SMALL BUT EFFECTIVE SHELTER
SLABS START AGAIN
FENCED-OFF AREA
ROUGH FELL
LITTLE DUN FELL
2761FT/841M 175
PATH DROPS TO A COL THEN RISES TO LITTLE DUN FELL
SLABS
0 1/4 mile
0 APPROX SCALE 500m
BOGGY
WINDY
174 SLABS START
RADAR STATION
trailblazer
GREAT DUN FELL
173
85

away your map and compass, but this will be short lived as the miles into Garrigill begin to hammer at the soles of your feet and your knees begin to creak and groan under the constant descent. It's enough to make those who cross Cross cross. A brief respite can be found in **Greg's Hut** (see box opposite); before you leave add your experiences to the visitors' book.

The descent continues and the sight of the road stretching ahead can be soul (and sole) destroying, but eventually Garrigill comes into sight and the worst is soon over. If you've timed it right the pub and shop in **Garrigill** (Map 91) may be open, but you're just as likely to find them both shuttered and silent. If you're pushing on to Alston the final few miles along the river may well be easier than Corpse Road, but they are no picnic; an obstacle course of stiles and sprung gates has been laid for you, but **Alston** (Map 94) is an oasis of refreshments and services galore.

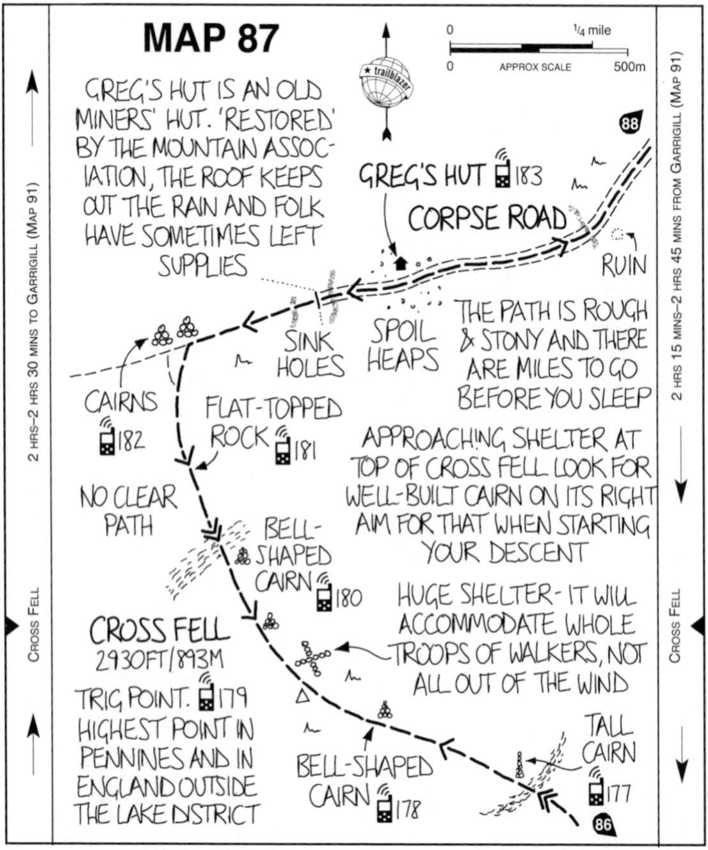
MAP 87
0 ¼ mile
0 APPROX SCALE 500m
trailblazer
88
2 HRS–2 HRS 30 MINS TO GARRIGILL (MAP 91)
2 HRS 15 MINS–2 HRS 45 MINS FROM GARRIGILL (MAP 91)
GREG'S HUT IS AN OLD MINERS' HUT. 'RESTORED' BY THE MOUNTAIN ASSOCIATION, THE ROOF KEEPS OUT THE RAIN AND FOLK HAVE SOMETIMES LEFT SUPPLIES
GREG'S HUT 183
CORPSE ROAD
RUIN
SINK HOLES
SPOIL HEAPS
THE PATH IS ROUGH & STONY AND THERE ARE MILES TO GO BEFORE YOU SLEEP
CAIRNS 182
FLAT-TOPPED ROCK 181
APPROACHING SHELTER AT TOP OF CROSS FELL LOOK FOR WELL-BUILT CAIRN ON ITS RIGHT AIM FOR THAT WHEN STARTING YOUR DESCENT
NO CLEAR PATH
BELL-SHAPED CAIRN 180
CROSS FELL
CROSS FELL 2930FT/893M
HUGE SHELTER - IT WILL ACCOMMODATE WHOLE TROOPS OF WALKERS, NOT ALL OUT OF THE WIND
TRIG POINT. 179 HIGHEST POINT IN PENNINES AND IN ENGLAND OUTSIDE THE LAKE DISTRICT
TALL CAIRN 177
BELL-SHAPED CAIRN 178
86

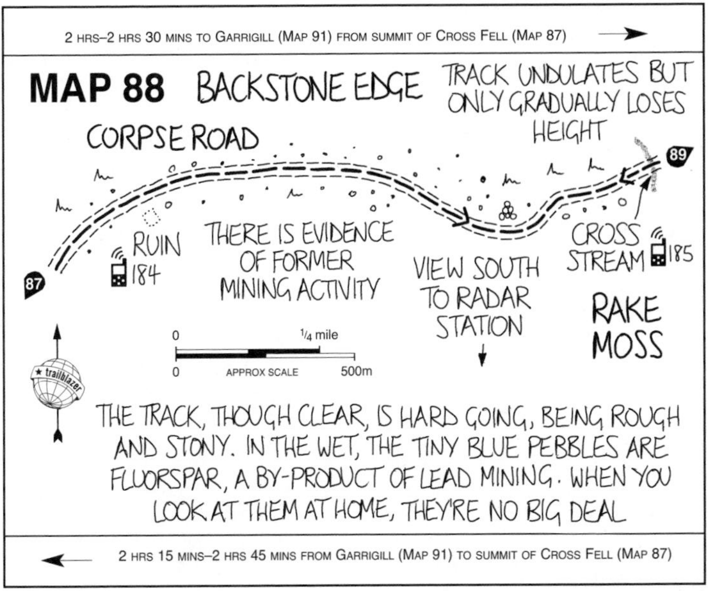
2 HRS–2 HRS 30 MINS TO GARRIGILL (MAP 91) FROM SUMMIT OF CROSS FELL (MAP 87)
MAP 88 BACKSTONE EDGE
TRACK UNDULATES BUT ONLY GRADUALLY LOSES HEIGHT
CORPSE ROAD
89
RUIN
184
87
THERE IS EVIDENCE OF FORMER MINING ACTIVITY
VIEW SOUTH TO RADAR STATION
CROSS STREAM
185
RAKE MOSS
0
1/4 mile
0
APPROX SCALE
500m
trailblazer
THE TRACK, THOUGH CLEAR, IS HARD GOING, BEING ROUGH AND STONY. IN THE WET, THE TINY BLUE PEBBLES ARE FLUORSPAR, A BY-PRODUCT OF LEAD MINING. WHEN YOU LOOK AT THEM AT HOME, THEY'RE NO BIG DEAL
2 HRS 15 MINS–2 HRS 45 MINS FROM GARRIGILL (MAP 91) TO SUMMIT OF CROSS FELL (MAP 87)

❑ Greg's Hut [Map 87]

Greg's Hut is a welcome and well-maintained bothy just over the summit of Cross Fell where walkers can take refuge or just pop in for a nose around. It holds a special place in the heart of many wayfarers. Originally it was used by lead miners whose tailing can be seen all around. They would stay here all week and walk home at the weekend. 'Greg' was actually John Gregory, a climber who died following an epic climbing accident in the Alps in 1968 in spite of the heroic efforts of his companion who held him on the rope and tended his injuries all night. Rescuers arrived too late.

Thanks to the efforts of the Mountain Bothies Association, the hut has been repaired and maintained. There are two rooms, the inner one has a raised sleeping platform with a stove, although fuel is scarce. Certainly you're unlikely to find any on the surrounding fell. This is a classic mountain bothy, unique along the Pennine Way, and it's hard to drag yourself out of it in horrible conditions. The visitors' book could be published as it stands, telling a multitude of stories, most of them epics of embellishment or endurance.

Navigation notes

With good visibility, today's route poses no real problems, other than the lack of an obvious path off the summits of Knock Fell and, in particular, Cross Fell, both of which require a change of direction in order to keep on the Way. In mist or low cloud, however, the story changes significantly and the dome of the radar station cannot be relied on as a guide. The rock-strewn summit of Knock Fell

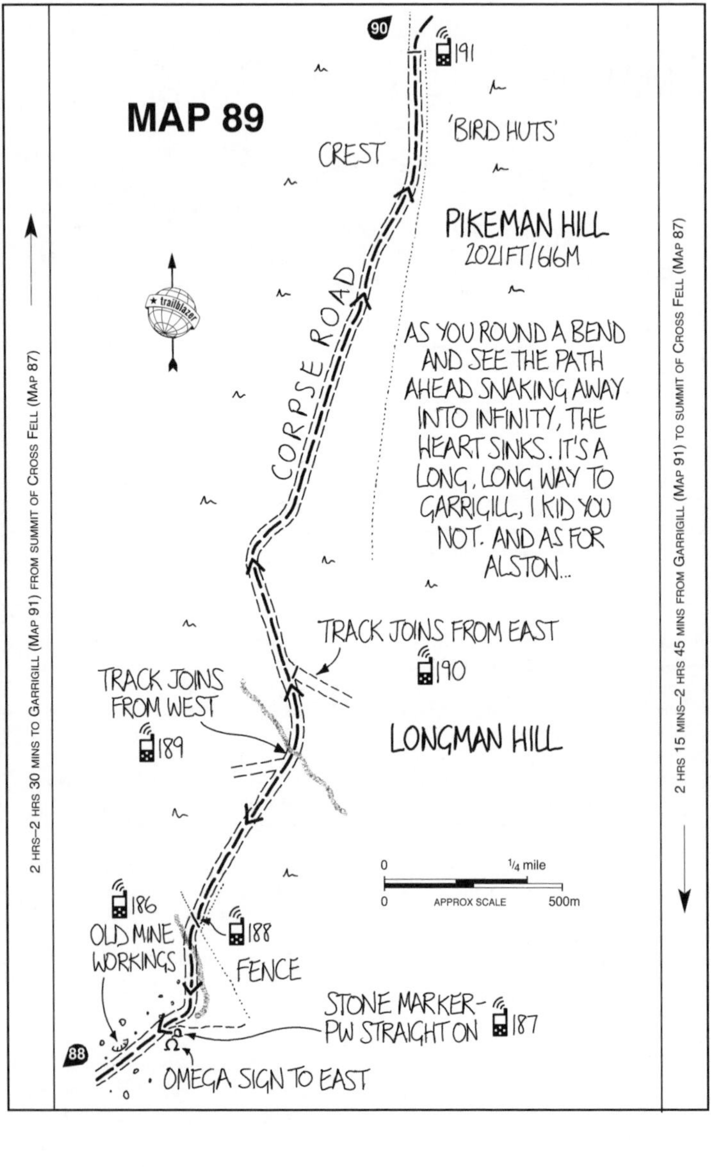
MAP 89
90
191
'BIRD HUTS'
CREST
PIKEMAN HILL
2021FT/616M
CORPSE ROAD
AS YOU ROUND A BEND AND SEE THE PATH AHEAD SNAKING AWAY INTO INFINITY, THE HEART SINKS. IT'S A LONG, LONG WAY TO GARRIGILL, I KID YOU NOT. AND AS FOR ALSTON...
TRACK JOINS FROM EAST
190
TRACK JOINS FROM WEST
189
LONGMAN HILL
0
1/4 mile
0
APPROX SCALE
500m
186
OLD MINE WORKINGS
188
FENCE
STONE MARKER-PW STRAIGHT ON
187
88
OMEGA SIGN TO EAST
2 HRS–2 HRS 30 MINS TO GARRIGILL (MAP 91) FROM SUMMIT OF CROSS FELL (MAP 87)
2 HRS 15 MINS–2 HRS 45 MINS FROM GARRIGILL (MAP 91) TO SUMMIT OF CROSS FELL (MAP 87)

does not hold a clear path, hence the proliferation of GPS waypoints along this section. Similarly on Cross Fell, the change in direction can be confusing, especially if you've rested in the shelter and lost your bearings. A line of small cairns leads north off Cross Fell, but more reliably, the GPS waypoints are there. Better still, a compass bearing can be taken from the trig point.

The path from Garrigill to Alston is never far from the river, except when it climbs to Bleagate (Map 93). Although it can be somewhat confusing at times, the signage is fairly good and there aren't too many alternative footpaths leading off the main path.

2 HRS–2 HRS 30 MINS TO GARRIGILL (MAP 91) FROM SUMMIT OF CROSS FELL (MAP 87)

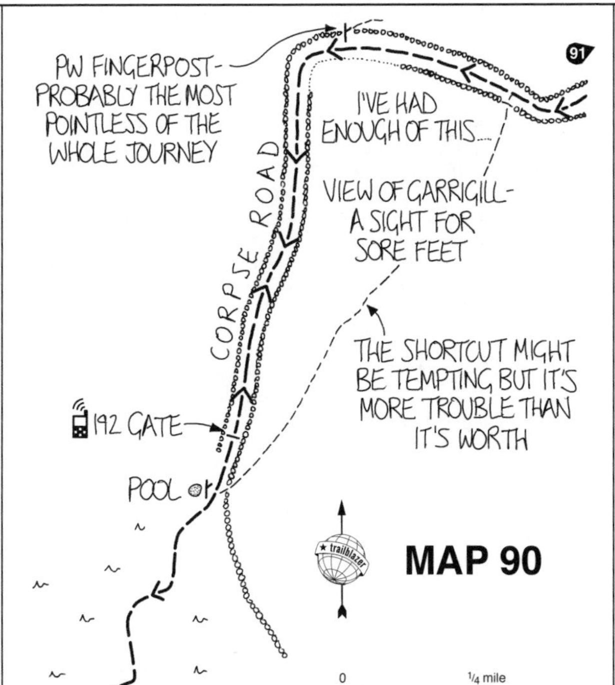

PW FINGERPOST-
PROBABLY THE MOST
POINTLESS OF THE
WHOLE JOURNEY
91
I'VE HAD
ENOUGH OF THIS....
CORPSE ROAD
VIEW OF GARRIGILL-
A SIGHT FOR
SORE FEET
THE SHORTCUT MIGHT
BE TEMPTING BUT IT'S
MORE TROUBLE THAN
IT'S WORTH
192 GATE
POOL
trailblazer
MAP 90
0
1/4 mile
0
APPROX SCALE
500m
89

2 HRS 15 MINS–2 HRS 45 MINS FROM GARRIGILL (MAP 91) TO SUMMIT OF CROSS FELL (MAP 87)

ROUTE GUIDE AND MAPS

❑ **Important note – walking times**
All times in this book refer only to the time spent walking. You will need to add 20-30% to allow for rests, photography, checking the map, drinking water etc.

❑ Where to stay: the details

☛ means at least one room has a bath; Ⓛ signifies that a packed lunch is available if requested in advance; 🐕 signifies that dogs are welcome in at least one room but always by prior arrangement. A charge may also be payable (see also p82).

WI-FI is now available at most hostels, pubs and cafés as well as places offering B&B-style accommodation (but not always at campsites) so it is no longer specified.

GARRIGILL [Map 91]

Don't be disturbed to find the shutters up on Garrigill's **post office**, these are to protect the antique windows when the shop is closed; when open (Mon & Wed-Fri 9am-5.30pm, Tue & Sat 9am-12.30pm) it transacts the usual business and includes a sparsely provisioned **shop** (same hours) as well as selling **hot drinks** (£1.50). It's also home to ***Garrigill Post Office Guesthouse*** (☎ 01434-381257, 🖳 garrigill-guesthouse.co.uk; 2T shared bathroom; ☛; Ⓛ; 🐕; Easter to Sep). It's clean and comfortable – and has been providing B&B for over half a century now! B&B costs from £35pp.

Nearby you'll also find ***East View*** (☎ 01434-381561, 🖳 garrigillbedandbreakfast.co.uk; 1D en suite, 1Tr private bathroom; ☛; Ⓛ; 🐕) with B&B for £37.50-40pp (sgl occ from £50).

If you want to **camp** at Garrigill, you can pitch up behind the village hall. The cost is £5, with use of the drying facilities and a shower is £2 extra; note that no dogs are allowed.

The village pub, ***George & Dragon*** (☎ 01434-382691, 🖳 garrigillpub.co.uk; 🐕; food served Mon-Fri 6-9pm, Sat & noon-9pm) is serving **food** once more, with excellent value mains usually around the £8-10 mark; everything is home made and it really is great to see this place up and running again.

They also have some basic **accommodation** (1S/1T shared facilities) and charge £15pp (sgl/sgl occ £20) for the room at the moment; a full English breakfast costs around £12pp extra. At the time of writing the bar is open daily (Mon-Fri 5-11.30pm, Sat & Sun noon-11pm), but they hope to open earlier and also to serve tea and coffee etc during the day.

ALSTON [Map 94a, p222]

Alston is England's highest market town (although it no longer holds a regular weekly market) and its steep cobbled streets and 18th-century buildings give it a bit of character. It has an excellent range of services for walkers and is a welcome site following two days of remote hiking.

Services

The **tourist information centre** (TIC; ☎ 01434-382244, 🖳 visiteden.co.uk; Mar to mid Oct Mon-Sat 10am-5pm, Sun 11am-3pm, mid Oct to Mar Mon & Fri 10am-5pm, Tue-Thur & Sat 10am-3pm) is in the Town Hall on Front St.

Hi-Pennine Outdoor (🖳 www.visitnorthpennines.co.uk; summer Mon-Sat 10am-5pm, Sun 11am-5pm; winter Mon-Sat 10am-4.30pm, Sun 11am-4.30pm), an **outdoor equipment shop**, is a good spot to replace worn-out socks, blister patches and the like.

Alston Wholefoods (🖳 alstonwholefoods.com; end Mar-end Oct Mon-Sat 9am-5pm, Sun 10.30am-4.30pm, rest of year same but Sun 11am-4pm) sells Fairtrade chocolate, over 40 varieties of local cheese and delicatessen items and environmentally friendly goods.

There are also two **supermarkets**; a Spar (daily 6am-10pm) at a petrol station, which has an **ATM**, and a Co-op (daily 7am-10pm), and a **chemist** (Mon & Wed-Fri 9am-5.30pm, Tue & Sat to 12.30pm). There is also a **post office** (Mon-Fri 9am-1pm & 2-5.30pm, Sat 9am-12.30pm).

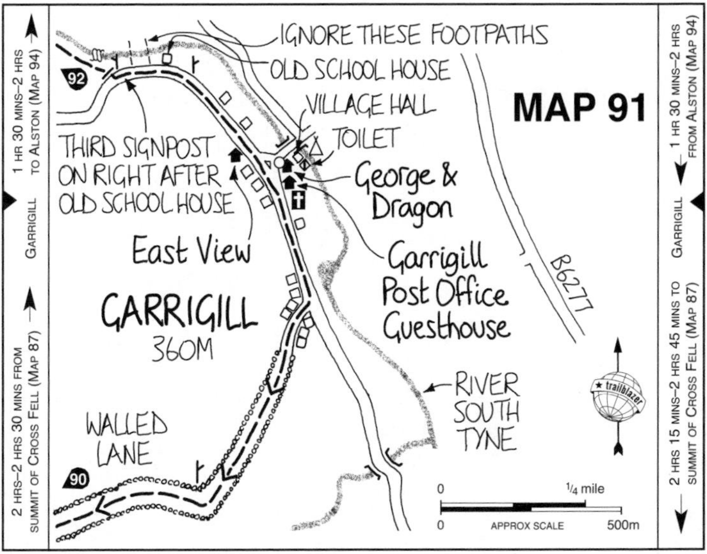
1 HR 30 MINS–2 HRS TO ALSTON (MAP 94)
GARRIGILL
2 HRS–2 HRS 30 MINS FROM SUMMIT OF CROSS FELL (MAP 87)
1 HR 30 MINS–2 HRS FROM ALSTON (MAP 94)
GARRIGILL
2 HRS 15 MINS–2 HRS 45 MINS TO SUMMIT OF CROSS FELL (MAP 87)
MAP 91
IGNORE THESE FOOTPATHS
OLD SCHOOL HOUSE
VILLAGE HALL
TOILET
THIRD SIGNPOST ON RIGHT AFTER OLD SCHOOL HOUSE
George & Dragon
East View
Garrigill Post Office Guesthouse
GARRIGILL
360M
B6277
RIVER SOUTH TYNE
WALLED LANE
92
90
0
1/4 mile
0
APPROX SCALE
500m

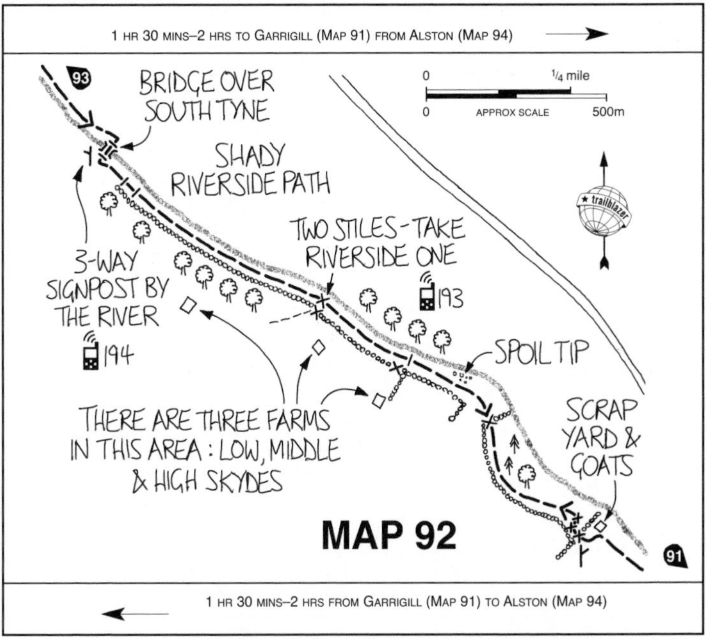
1 HR 30 MINS–2 HRS TO GARRIGILL (MAP 91) FROM ALSTON (MAP 94)
93
BRIDGE OVER SOUTH TYNE
SHADY RIVERSIDE PATH
3-WAY SIGNPOST BY THE RIVER
194
TWO STILES-TAKE RIVERSIDE ONE
193
SPOIL TIP
SCRAP YARD & GOATS
THERE ARE THREE FARMS IN THIS AREA : LOW, MIDDLE & HIGH SKYDES
MAP 92
91
0
1/4 mile
0
APPROX SCALE
500m
1 HR 30 MINS–2 HRS FROM GARRIGILL (MAP 91) TO ALSTON (MAP 94)

1 HR 30 MINS–2 HRS FROM GARRIGILL (MAP 91) TO ALSTON (MAP 94)

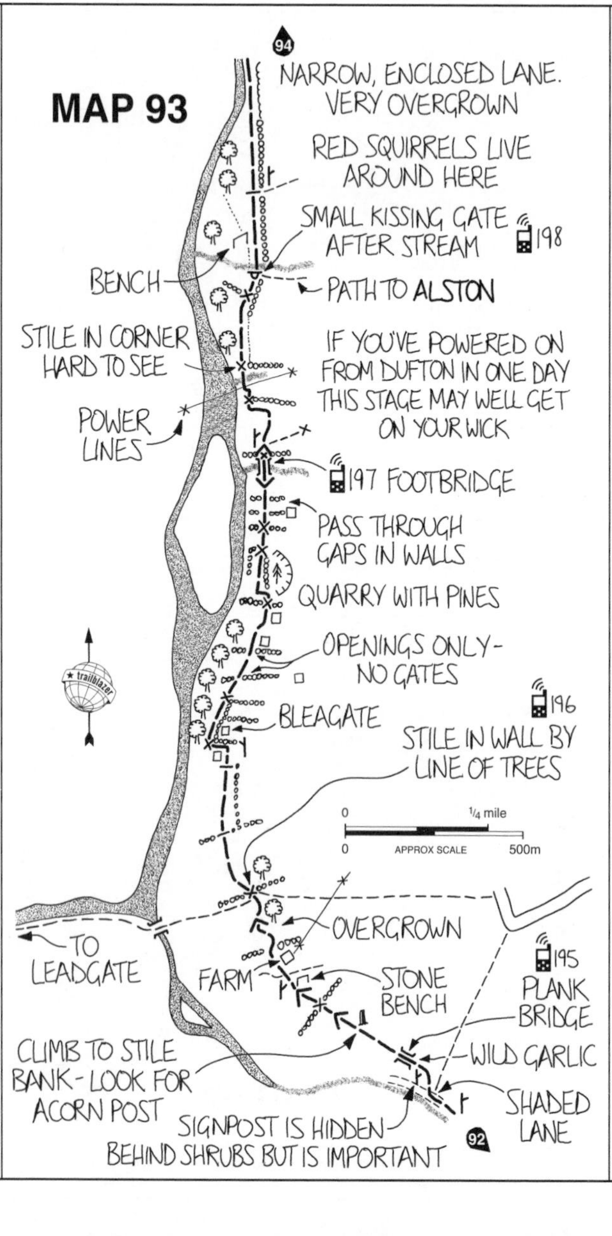
MAP 93
94
NARROW, ENCLOSED LANE. VERY OVERGROWN
RED SQUIRRELS LIVE AROUND HERE
SMALL KISSING GATE AFTER STREAM
198
BENCH
PATH TO ALSTON
STILE IN CORNER HARD TO SEE
IF YOU'VE POWERED ON FROM DUFTON IN ONE DAY THIS STAGE MAY WELL GET ON YOUR WICK
POWER LINES
197 FOOTBRIDGE
PASS THROUGH GAPS IN WALLS
QUARRY WITH PINES
OPENINGS ONLY - NO GATES
trailblazer
196
BLEAGATE
STILE IN WALL BY LINE OF TREES
0
1/4 mile
0
APPROX SCALE
500m
OVERGROWN
TO LEADGATE
195
PLANK BRIDGE
FARM
STONE BENCH
CLIMB TO STILE BANK - LOOK FOR ACORN POST
WILD GARLIC
SHADED LANE
SIGNPOST IS HIDDEN BEHIND SHRUBS BUT IS IMPORTANT
92

1 HR 30 MINS–2 HRS TO GARRIGILL (MAP 91) FROM ALSTON (MAP 94)

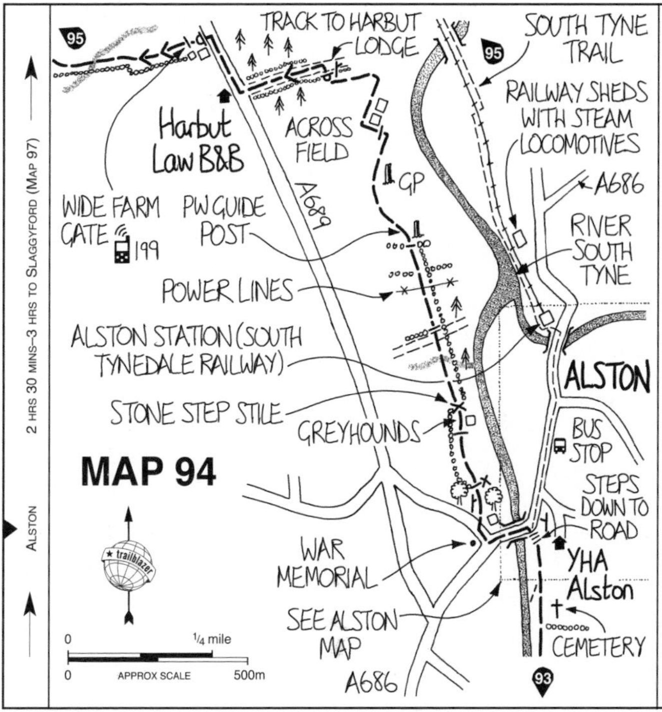
TRACK TO HARBUT LODGE
SOUTH TYNE TRAIL
RAILWAY SHEDS WITH STEAM LOCOMOTIVES
Harbut Law B&B
ACROSS FIELD
GP
A686
A689
WIDE FARM GATE
199
PW GUIDE POST
RIVER SOUTH TYNE
POWER LINES
ALSTON STATION (SOUTH TYNEDALE RAILWAY)
ALSTON
STONE STEP STILE
GREYHOUNDS
BUS STOP
MAP 94
STEPS DOWN TO ROAD
WAR MEMORIAL
YHA Alston
SEE ALSTON MAP
CEMETERY
A686
0 1/4 mile
0 APPROX SCALE 500m
2 HRS 30 MINS–3 HRS TO SLAGGYFORD (MAP 97)
2 HRS 30 MINS–3 HRS FROM SLAGGYFORD (MAP 97)
ALSTON
95
93

Transport
[See pp54-9] Go North East's 681 **bus** service heads to Haltwhistle and their X81 to Hexham. Telford Coaches' (limited) No 680 bus also calls here. For a **taxi** try Alston Taxis (☎ 07990-593855).

❑ South Tynedale Railway

South Tyndedale Railway (☎ 01434-382828, 💻 south-tynedale-railway.org.uk; daily late July to early Sep, Tue, Thur, Sat & Sun late Mar to late July & early Sep to end Oct) operates trains to Slaggyford (approx 5 miles) on 'England's highest narrow-gauge railway'. Steam locomotives are used on some services; see the website or phone them for details. The line originally went to Haltwhistle and volunteers are now hoping to restore the line all the way there.

Where to stay

Campers should make their way past lots of derelict cars behind the Texaco garage to ***Tyne Willows Caravan Park*** (☎ 01434-382515; 🐕; Mar to end Oct). It costs £5pp to **camp** on the bit of grass allocated for tents; there are basic toilet and shower facilities. Booking is recommended for bank holiday weekends.

YHA Alston (☎ 0345 260 2489, ☎ 01434-381509, 💻 yha.org.uk/hostel/alston; Ⓛ) overlooks the South Tyne river. It has 30 beds (2 x 2-, 2 x 4-, 3 x 6-bed rooms, shared facilities); a dorm bed costs from £20.50pp (private rooms from £36). The hostel offers meals and it also has laundry facilities and a drying room. Check-in at this hostel is from 5pm.

There are several pubs, some past their prime; you may find traditional B&Bs a better bet. Pubs with rooms include ***Victoria Inn*** (☎ 01434-381194; 4S/2D/2Tr, some en suite, others share facilities; Ⓛ; 🐕 bar only) which charges £27.50-32.50pp (sgl £33-38, sgl occ rates on request). ***The Angel Inn*** (☎ 01434-381363, 🖳 kennethlittle1@hotmail .com; 1T/2D, all en suite; Ⓛ; 🐕 bar only) down the hill does B&B for £29.50pp (sgl occ £35-45) and is used to walkers.

Cumberland Hotel (☎ 01434-381875, 🖳 cumberlandalston.co.uk; 2D/3Tr, all en suite; ▼; Ⓛ; 🐕) charges from £45pp (sgl occ £60) for B&B; room only rates also available. ***Alston House Hotel*** (☎ 01434-382200, 🖳 alstonhousehotel.co.uk; 1T/1D/4Tr/1Qd, all en suite; ▼; Ⓛ; 🐕) is the pick of the crop in town; B&B costs £45-60pp (sgl occ £70-75). It has great food (see Where to eat and drink).

About a mile north of Alston, where the Pennine Way crosses the A689, is ***Harbut Law*** (see Map 94; ☎ 01434-381950, 🖳 cumbria-cottages.co.uk; 1D/ 1Tr, both en suite; Ⓛ; Mar-Oct) a comfortable B&B charging from £35pp (sgl occ £45).

High Field B&B (☎ 01434-382182, 🖳 kalinkaleo@gmail.com; 1D en suite/1T shared bathroom; ▼; Ⓛ), Bruntley Meadows, charges from £30pp (no sgl occ supplement). Refreshments are offered on arrival. ***Gilderdale B&B*** (☎ 07460-177683, or ☎ 07410-598059, 🖳 jane.strickland@ hotmail.co.uk; 1D private facilities), 3 Townfoot, is self-contained and ingredients

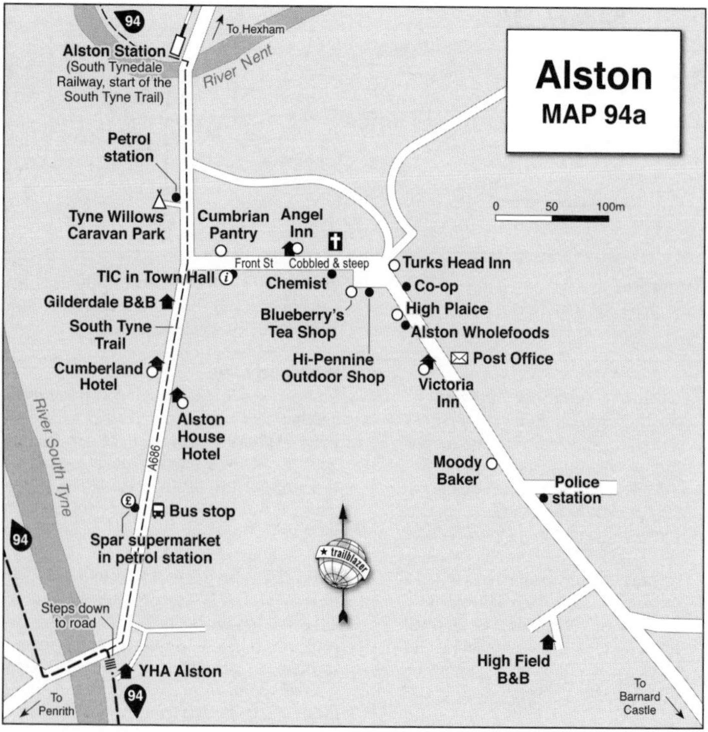
Alston
MAP 94a
94
To Hexham
River Nent
Alston Station
(South Tynedale Railway, start of the South Tyne Trail)
Petrol station
Tyne Willows Caravan Park
Cumbrian Pantry
Angel Inn
Front St
Cobbled & steep
Turks Head Inn
TIC in Town Hall
Chemist
Co-op
Gilderdale B&B
Blueberry's Tea Shop
High Plaice
Alston Wholefoods
South Tyne Trail
Hi-Pennine Outdoor Shop
Post Office
Cumberland Hotel
Victoria Inn
River South Tyne
Alston House Hotel
A686
Moody Baker
Police station
Bus stop
Spar supermarket in petrol station
trailblazer
Steps down to road
YHA Alston
High Field B&B
To Penrith
To Barnard Castle
0
50
100m

for a continental breakfast are left in the room. There is also a couch bed in the room so it can be used as a twin. They charge from £32.50pp (sgl occ £60).

Where to eat and drink

Not all the pubs do great food; try ***The Angel Inn*** (see Where to stay; food served Mon-Thur noon-2pm & 7-9pm, Fri-Sun noon-3pm & 6-9pm; food is not served on Tue night in the winter months).

Alston House Hotel (see Where to stay) serves food in its ***House Café*** (Mon-Sat 10am-4pm), with daytime snacks and salads, as well as in its bar and **restaurant** (summer Mon-Fri 6-9pm, Sat & Sun 10am-9pm, winter same but not on Mon); the extensive menu includes dishes such as lamb shoulder (£16.95). ***Cumberland Hotel*** (see Where to stay) also serves food (daily noon-3pm & 6-9pm).

Blueberry's Tea Shop (☎ 01434-381928; Mon-Sat 9am-5pm, Sun 10am-5pm, but they may close earlier in the winter) serves lunches and a fabulous all-day breakfast from £4.20. Dogs are not allowed inside but there is outside seating.

High Plaice (Mon 4-8pm, Tue-Thur noon-8pm, Fri noon-10pm, Sat noon-11.30pm, Sun noon-6pm) is, not surprisingly, a fish & chip shop. The nearby ***Moody Baker*** (☎ 01434-382003; Mon-Sat 9am-4pm) co-operative has an excellent range of home-made food to take away; the food is all baked on the premises and they focus on using local produce and organic ingredients where possible.

Cumbrian Pantry (☎ 01434-381406; summer daily 9am-3pm, open some evenings 5-8pm for takeaway only, winter hours variable) prepares meals to be eaten in as well as food, such as sandwiches and cakes, to be eaten in or taken away; they also serve fresh-ground coffee. The fish & chips costs £5.50 to takeaway. If you sit in you have free wi-fi access.

Victoria Inn (see Where to stay; Tue-Sun 6-10pm) does curries.

The best place for a drink is ***Turks Head Inn*** which does real ales.

ALSTON TO GREENHEAD — MAPS 94-102

Route overview

16½ miles (26.5km) – 2000ft (610m) of ascent – 7½-9½ hours

It's hard to justify the allure of the Pennine Way over that of the South Tyne Trail in the first part of today's walk. The Pennine Way selects a bizarre, pedantic route through fields, farms and over countless stiles and gates whereas the South Tyne Trail meanders like an unbroken, gradient-free ribbon of contentment beside it. Admittedly when the planners laid down the Way, the South Tyne Trail didn't exist, but you now have a choice: traditionalist or pragmatist. Today marks the end of the Pennine chain and the transition slowly to the Southern Upland range just beyond Hadrian's Wall; the hills are no less impressive though and there are many delights to come. This stage can be broken almost exactly in half by staying in Knarsdale but it's not particularly strenuous compared to the last couple of days, so push on to Greenhead and the Wall.

Whether you followed the Pennine Way or the South Tyne Trail, the first settlement is **Slaggyford** (Map 97), a forgotten platform on a small, quiet railway line in a tiny hamlet of houses; the only reason to stop is to take Go North East's 681 **bus** service (see pp54-9) between Alston and Haltwhistle.

A mile beyond Slaggyford both the Pennine Way and South Tyne Trail allow for a diversion to **Knarsdale** (see p226) where shelter, beer and food are available to anyone wanting to break this day into two. Any pragmatists following the South Tyne Trail need to drop down to the left, off the far end of the viaduct by

2 HRS 30 MINS–3 HRS FROM ALSTON (MAP 94) TO SLAGGYFORD (MAP 97) →

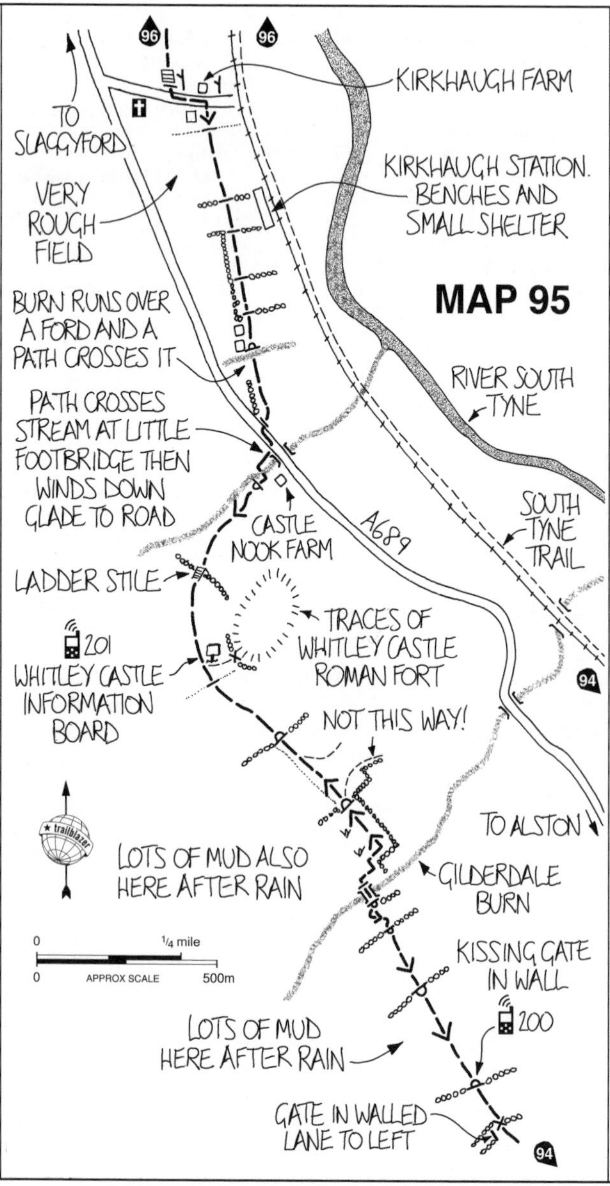
96
96
KIRKHAUGH FARM
TO SLAGGYFORD
KIRKHAUGH STATION. BENCHES AND SMALL SHELTER
VERY ROUGH FIELD
MAP 95
BURN RUNS OVER A FORD AND A PATH CROSSES IT
RIVER SOUTH TYNE
PATH CROSSES STREAM AT LITTLE FOOTBRIDGE THEN WINDS DOWN GLADE TO ROAD
SOUTH TYNE TRAIL
CASTLE NOOK FARM
A689
LADDER STILE
TRACES OF WHITLEY CASTLE ROMAN FORT
201
WHITLEY CASTLE INFORMATION BOARD
94
NOT THIS WAY!
TO ALSTON
trailblazer
LOTS OF MUD ALSO HERE AFTER RAIN
GILDERDALE BURN
0
1/4 mile
0
APPROX SCALE
500m
KISSING GATE IN WALL
200
LOTS OF MUD HERE AFTER RAIN
GATE IN WALLED LANE TO LEFT
94

← 2 HRS 30 MINS–3 HRS TO ALSTON (MAP 94) FROM SLAGGYFORD (MAP 97)

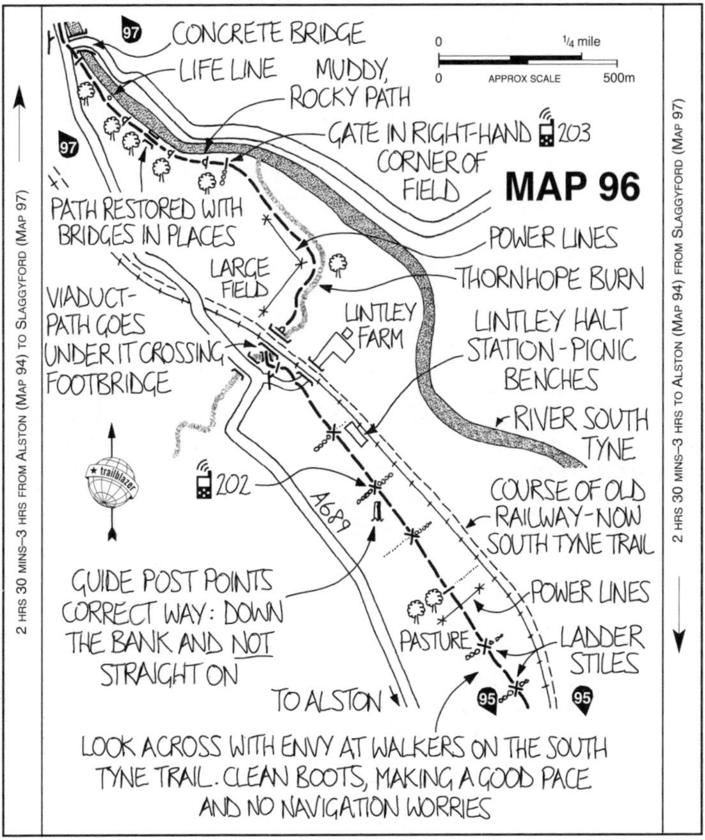
CONCRETE BRIDGE
LIFE LINE
MUDDY, ROCKY PATH
GATE IN RIGHT-HAND CORNER OF FIELD
203
MAP 96
0 ¼ mile
0 APPROX SCALE 500m
PATH RESTORED WITH BRIDGES IN PLACES
POWER LINES
LARGE FIELD
THORNHOPE BURN
VIADUCT- PATH GOES UNDER IT CROSSING FOOTBRIDGE
LINTLEY FARM
LINTLEY HALT STATION - PICNIC BENCHES
RIVER SOUTH TYNE
202
A689
COURSE OF OLD RAILWAY - NOW SOUTH TYNE TRAIL
GUIDE POST POINTS CORRECT WAY: DOWN THE BANK AND NOT STRAIGHT ON
POWER LINES
PASTURE
LADDER STILES
TO ALSTON
97
95
LOOK ACROSS WITH ENVY AT WALKERS ON THE SOUTH TYNE TRAIL. CLEAN BOOTS, MAKING A GOOD PACE AND NO NAVIGATION WORRIES
2 HRS 30 MINS–3 HRS FROM ALSTON (MAP 94) TO SLAGGYFORD (MAP 97)
2 HRS 30 MINS–3 HRS TO ALSTON (MAP 94) FROM SLAGGYFORD (MAP 97)

the farmhouse of Burnstones (Map 97), to meet the tarmac lane and take the Pennine Way up the hill and out of the valley.

The path has now joined the **Maiden Way** (Maps 97 to 98), an old Roman Road that brought troops and supplies to the Wall. A rare wild camp opportunity along this stretch presents itself by the idyllic **Glendue Burn** (Map 98), just beyond Knarsdale.

Make the most of the firm footing, because once you climb out of **Hartley Burn** (Map 99) and pass **Greenriggs Farm** (Map 100) you enter the quagmire that is **Blenkinsopp Common**. This is perhaps the wettest and boggiest section of the whole Way; even after a 12-week drought you're still going to get wet across here. ***Kellah Farm*** (see p231) provides a B&B option near Greenriggs. You may breathe a sigh of relief as you reach the wall with its nearby trig point at **Black Hill**. It would be premature however; the Black Hill crossed on day two may have been tamed by slabs, but this one isn't and a squelchy crossing is almost a certainty.

Only when the track at GPS 228 (Map 101) is reached should you look for a stream to wash the mud off your boots, calves, thighs.... This track leads to the A69 where you need to scurry across between the trucks and then up the other side to walk beside the **golf course** down into Greenhead village. Here various places will feed, water and house you, in preparation for another big day!

Navigation notes

If you follow the South Tyne Trail from Alston to Burnstones there are no navigational issues at all, the path is clear, well laid (until the last mile or so) and impossible to lose. Traditionalists on the Pennine Way should be aware that signage isn't great along this section. The loop from Harbut Law B&B to Castle Nook Farm (Map 95) is a prime example of this; one eye on the map and the other on the ground is needed at all times.

The knot of tracks and footpaths at Knar Burn (Map 97), just after leaving Slaggyford, needs care too as the Pennine Way and the South Tyne Trail cross and diverge. If you've committed to the Trail no problem, otherwise the navigation of the gardens at Merry Knowe can be confusing.

At the ruin at High House (Map 99), just before you drop down to Hartley Burn, be sure to keep left as you descend. If anything err on the side of caution and bear too far left rather than stray right. Just a little further ahead, as you leave Ulpham Farm (Map 100), watch for the change of direction, through the gate, instead of along the very obvious lane.

The path beyond Greenriggs is almost non existent, a vast grassy swathe stretches ahead across Round Hill; soggy at best, down-right swampy the rest of the time. You won't keep your feet dry here no matter what line you take, so if in doubt, head for the fence line to the west and follow this due north. The path beside and across Greenhead Golf Course (Map 102) is easy enough and better signed than the previous few miles.

KNARSDALE [Map 97]

Just a couple of hundred yards from the Pennine Way you can **camp** at ***Stonehall Farm*** (☎ 01434-381349; 🐕 on lead). At £5pp it's basic, there's an outside toilet and a cold water tap. The pub, Kirkstyle Inn, is just 200 metres down the road but note that it does not serve food every evening.

Pennine Wayfarers are always looking for an excuse to stop at ***Kirkstyle Inn*** (☎ 01434-381559, 💻 kirkstyleinn.co.uk; 🐕; bar Mon 7-11pm, Wed-Sat noon-2pm & 6-11pm, though if it is quiet they may close at 9pm, Sun noon-2pm only; **food** served Wed-Sun noon-2pm & Wed-Sat 6-9pm, Oct-Mar no food on Wed). From the choice of beers to the tasty bar menu and the atmosphere, this place has everything walkers like and is the sort of hostelry you'll be hallucinating about when you're halfway between Byrness and Kirk Yetholm.

❑ Important note – walking times

All times in this book refer only to the time spent walking. You will need to add 20-30% to allow for rests, photography, checking the map, drinking water etc.

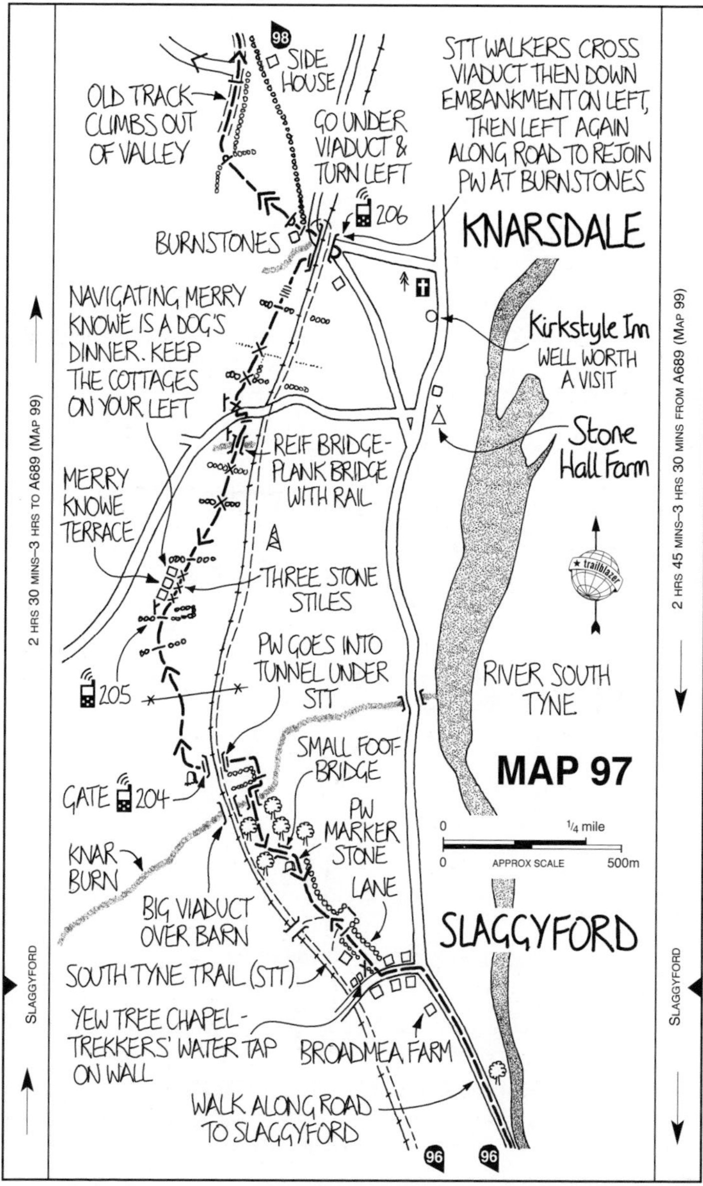
98
SIDE HOUSE
OLD TRACK CLIMBS OUT OF VALLEY
GO UNDER VIADUCT & TURN LEFT
STT WALKERS CROSS VIADUCT THEN DOWN EMBANKMENT ON LEFT, THEN LEFT AGAIN ALONG ROAD TO REJOIN PW AT BURNSTONES
206
BURNSTONES
KNARSDALE
NAVIGATING MERRY KNOWE IS A DOG'S DINNER. KEEP THE COTTAGES ON YOUR LEFT
Kirkstyle Inn
WELL WORTH A VISIT
Stone Hall Farm
REIF BRIDGE-PLANK BRIDGE WITH RAIL
MERRY KNOWE TERRACE
THREE STONE STILES
trailblazer
205
PW GOES INTO TUNNEL UNDER STT
RIVER SOUTH TYNE
SMALL FOOT-BRIDGE
MAP 97
GATE 204
PW MARKER STONE
0
1/4 mile
0
APPROX SCALE
500m
KNAR BURN
BIG VIADUCT OVER BARN
LANE
SLAGGYFORD
SOUTH TYNE TRAIL (STT)
YEW TREE CHAPEL-TREKKERS' WATER TAP ON WALL
BROADMEA FARM
WALK ALONG ROAD TO SLAGGYFORD
96
96
2 HRS 30 MINS–3 HRS TO A689 (MAP 99)
2 HRS 45 MINS–3 HRS 30 MINS FROM A689 (MAP 99)
SLAGGYFORD
SLAGGYFORD

ROUTE GUIDE AND MAPS

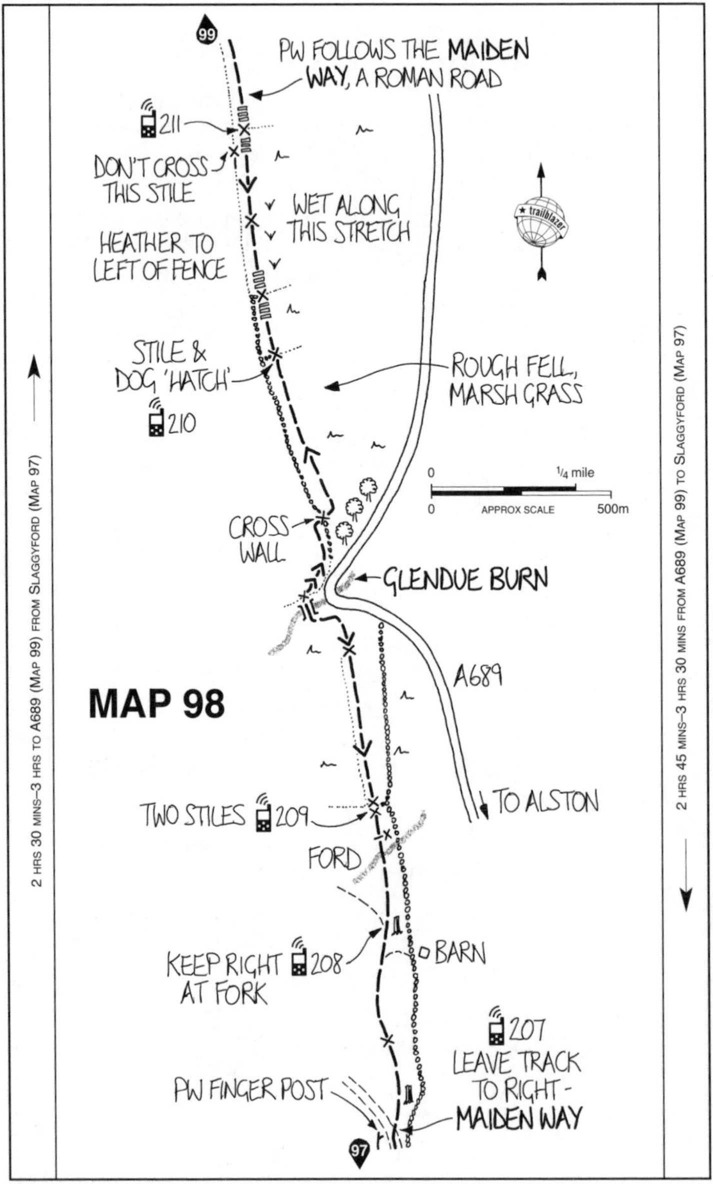

MAP 98
2 HRS 30 MINS–3 HRS TO A689 (MAP 99) FROM SLAGGYFORD (MAP 97)
2 HRS 45 MINS–3 HRS 30 MINS FROM A689 (MAP 99) TO SLAGGYFORD (MAP 97)
99
PW FOLLOWS THE MAIDEN WAY, A ROMAN ROAD
211
DON'T CROSS THIS STILE
WET ALONG THIS STRETCH
HEATHER TO LEFT OF FENCE
trailblazer
STILE & DOG 'HATCH'
210
ROUGH FELL, MARSH GRASS
0
1/4 mile
0
APPROX SCALE
500m
CROSS WALL
GLENDUE BURN
A689
TO ALSTON
TWO STILES
209
FORD
KEEP RIGHT AT FORK
208
BARN
207
LEAVE TRACK TO RIGHT - MAIDEN WAY
PW FINGER POST
97

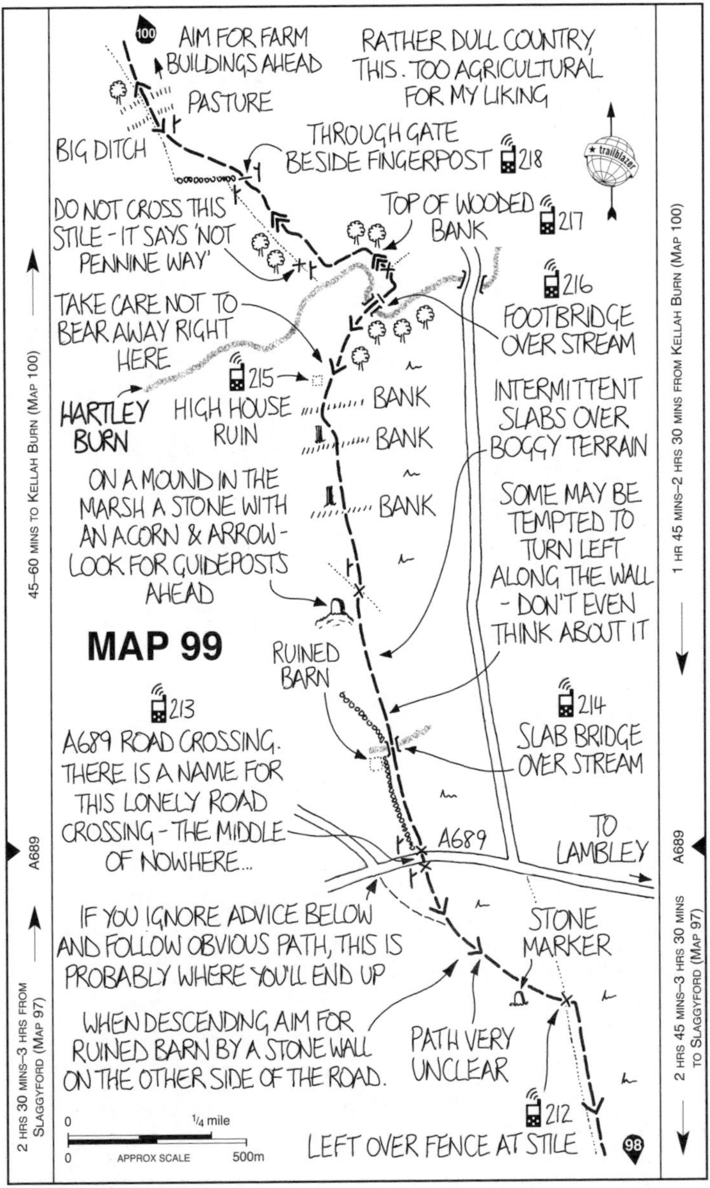
100
AIM FOR FARM BUILDINGS AHEAD
RATHER DULL COUNTRY, THIS. TOO AGRICULTURAL FOR MY LIKING
PASTURE
BIG DITCH
THROUGH GATE BESIDE FINGERPOST
218
trailblazer
DO NOT CROSS THIS STILE - IT SAYS 'NOT PENNINE WAY'
TOP OF WOODED BANK
217
216
FOOTBRIDGE OVER STREAM
TAKE CARE NOT TO BEAR AWAY RIGHT HERE
215
HARTLEY BURN
HIGH HOUSE RUIN
BANK
BANK
BANK
INTERMITTENT SLABS OVER BOGGY TERRAIN
ON A MOUND IN THE MARSH A STONE WITH AN ACORN & ARROW - LOOK FOR GUIDEPOSTS AHEAD
SOME MAY BE TEMPTED TO TURN LEFT ALONG THE WALL - DON'T EVEN THINK ABOUT IT
MAP 99
RUINED BARN
213
214
A689 ROAD CROSSING. THERE IS A NAME FOR THIS LONELY ROAD CROSSING - THE MIDDLE OF NOWHERE...
SLAB BRIDGE OVER STREAM
A689
TO LAMBLEY
IF YOU IGNORE ADVICE BELOW AND FOLLOW OBVIOUS PATH, THIS IS PROBABLY WHERE YOU'LL END UP
STONE MARKER
WHEN DESCENDING AIM FOR RUINED BARN BY A STONE WALL ON THE OTHER SIDE OF THE ROAD.
PATH VERY UNCLEAR
212
LEFT OVER FENCE AT STILE
98
0 1/4 mile
0 APPROX SCALE 500m
45–60 MINS TO KELLAH BURN (MAP 100)
A689
2 HRS 30 MINS–3 HRS FROM SLAGGYFORD (MAP 97)
1 HR 45 MINS–2 HRS 30 MINS FROM KELLAH BURN (MAP 100)
A689
2 HRS 45 MINS–3 HRS 30 MINS TO SLAGGYFORD (MAP 97)

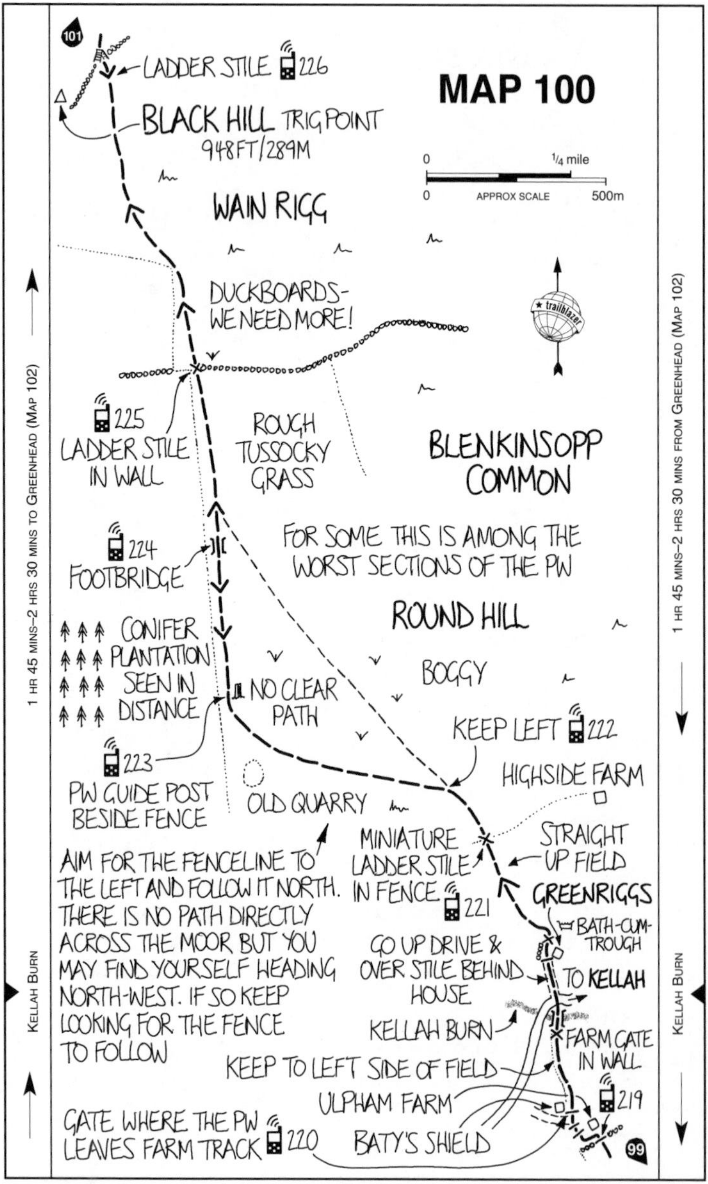
MAP 100
0 1/4 mile
0 APPROX SCALE 500m
trailblazer
101
LADDER STILE 226
BLACK HILL TRIG POINT
948FT/289M
WAIN RIGG
DUCKBOARDS-
WE NEED MORE!
225
LADDER STILE
IN WALL
ROUGH
TUSSOCKY
GRASS
BLENKINSOPP
COMMON
224
FOOTBRIDGE
FOR SOME THIS IS AMONG THE
WORST SECTIONS OF THE PW
ROUND HILL
CONIFER
PLANTATION
SEEN IN
DISTANCE
NO CLEAR
PATH
BOGGY
KEEP LEFT 222
223
PW GUIDE POST
BESIDE FENCE
OLD QUARRY
HIGHSIDE FARM
MINIATURE
LADDER STILE
IN FENCE 221
STRAIGHT
UP FIELD
AIM FOR THE FENCELINE TO
THE LEFT AND FOLLOW IT NORTH.
THERE IS NO PATH DIRECTLY
ACROSS THE MOOR BUT YOU
MAY FIND YOURSELF HEADING
NORTH-WEST. IF SO KEEP
LOOKING FOR THE FENCE
TO FOLLOW
GREENRIGGS
BATH-CUM-
TROUGH
GO UP DRIVE &
OVER STILE BEHIND
HOUSE
TO KELLAH
KELLAH BURN
FARM GATE
IN WALL
KEEP TO LEFT SIDE OF FIELD
ULPHAM FARM
219
GATE WHERE THE PW
LEAVES FARM TRACK 220
BATY'S SHIELD
99
1 HR 45 MINS–2 HRS 30 MINS TO GREENHEAD (MAP 102)
KELLAH BURN
1 HR 45 MINS–2 HRS 30 MINS FROM GREENHEAD (MAP 102)
KELLAH BURN

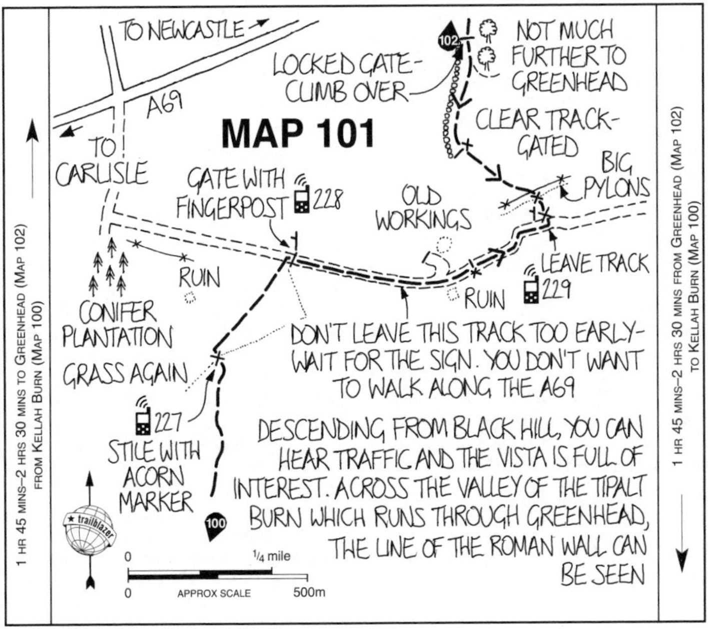
MAP 101
TO NEWCASTLE
A69
TO CARLISLE
LOCKED GATE - CLIMB OVER
NOT MUCH FURTHER TO GREENHEAD
CLEAR TRACK - GATED
BIG PYLONS
GATE WITH FINGERPOST 228
OLD WORKINGS
RUIN
LEAVE TRACK 229
CONIFER PLANTATION
GRASS AGAIN
DON'T LEAVE THIS TRACK TOO EARLY - WAIT FOR THE SIGN. YOU DON'T WANT TO WALK ALONG THE A69
227
STILE WITH ACORN MARKER
DESCENDING FROM BLACK HILL, YOU CAN HEAR TRAFFIC AND THE VISTA IS FULL OF INTEREST. ACROSS THE VALLEY OF THE TIPALT BURN WHICH RUNS THROUGH GREENHEAD, THE LINE OF THE ROMAN WALL CAN BE SEEN
102
100
trailblazer
0 1/4 mile
0 APPROX SCALE 500m
1 HR 45 MINS–2 HRS 30 MINS TO GREENHEAD (MAP 102) FROM KELLAH BURN (MAP 100)
1 HR 45 MINS–2 HRS 30 MINS FROM GREENHEAD (MAP 102) TO KELLAH BURN (MAP 100)

KELLAH **[off Map 100]**

Kellah Farm (☎ 01434-320816, 💻 kellah.co.uk; 3D/2Tr, all en suite; ☕; Ⓛ) is about a third of a mile off the path. The accommodation is smart and the owners are helpful. Rates for **B&B** are £36-38pp (sgl occ from £55). For dinner in the evening, you can either take a taxi to the closest pub (around £10 each way to the Blenkinsop Castle or, for more choice, to Haltwhistle), order from the local takeaway (pizzas, fish & chips etc) that delivers to the farm, or you can enjoy one of the simple frozen meals made by the farm (around £7 for a meal).

GREENHEAD **[Map 102, p233]**

Having arrived in the rather dispersed hamlet of Greenhead, you can take solace from the fact that you're very near Britain's geographical centre; a point equidistant from all shores. Not a lot of people know that.

Carvoran Roman Army Museum (☎ 016977-47485, 💻 vindolanda.com; daily Feb-Mar & Oct 10am-5pm, Apr-Sep 10am-6pm; Nov-Feb weekends only 10am-4pm; £6.60, combined ticket with Vindolanda £11.60) is well worth the short detour to see some fascinating Roman artefacts including coins, shoes and nails. The museum features include a 3D film of a visualisation of the top of the wall from here to Vindolanda and additional exhibits about life in the Roman army.

Transport

The Newcastle to Carlisle railway line runs through Greenhead but services do not stop here. However, they do stop at Haltwhistle, (see Northern Rail, box p59), which is three miles away.

However, Arriva's **bus** No 685 (operated in conjunction with Stagecoach) travels between Carlisle and Newcastle (and thus almost the entire length of the Wall too) via the A69 near Greenhead. Go North East also operates the No 185 to Haltwhistle and the seasonal AD122 bus (the designated route 'AD122' is in honour of the Wall's inauguration by the Emperor Hadrian); see pp54-9 for details.

Where to stay, eat & drink

A converted Methodist chapel houses ***Greenhead Hostel*** (☎ 01697-747411; 2 x 8-, 4 x 6-bed rooms; no WI-FI; Ⓛ; 🐕), owned by the hotel (see below) over the road. A bed costs from £15.50pp; breakfast (£9.95 for a full English, £1 less for the veggie option) and evening meals are available in the hotel. They also have a self-contained **flat** sleeping five (1S/2D) for £85 per night. As mentioned earlier in this guide, the hostel stands out as the only one on the route that allows dogs to stay, too.

Nearby ***Four Wynds*** (☎ 01697-747972, 🖳 hadriansholidays.com; Ⓛ; 🐕) have two lovely, well-appointed '**B&B lodges**' (1T/1D, both en suite) from £37.50pp (sgl occ £55) for B&B; breakfast is served in the lodge.

Greenhead Hotel (see Greenhead Hostel for contact details; 2D or T/2Tr, all en suite; ☕; Ⓛ; 🐕), in the middle of the village, offers B&B in spacious rooms from £42.50pp (sgl occ £55). The hotel is your best bet for a feed in the evening; meals (**food** served daily noon-8.30pm) are served in both the bar and the restaurant.

Back on the Way, half a mile north of the village, ***Holmhead Guest House*** (☎ 01697-747402, 🖳 bandb-hadrianswall.co.uk; 1D or T/3D, all en suite; Ⓛ; 🐕 on lead and for campers/barn only) is a multiple accommodation complex for Wall-bound wayfarers. The pleasant walk there crosses a river, follows a track along the bank, through sheep fields and thence to the homestead. **B&B** costs £36-41pp (sgl occ from £72). The **camping barn** (from £13.50pp plus £3.50 to hire a sleeping bag) sleeps six and has a kitchenette and shower/toilet facilities. There is also a **bunk barn** which sleeps up to six people and has access to shower and toilet facilities. Reservations are recommended as the barns are often booked by groups. They also have a small area where you can **camp** (£5-7pp; Mar-end Oct); basic toilet/shower facilities are available and an outside tap). Reservations also recommended for campers.

The ***Village Tearooms*** (summer only, daily 10am-4pm) serve snacks on home-made bread and an all-day breakfast.

Alternatively try the ***café*** (Easter to end Oct daily 10am-5pm) in Walltown car park where you can get soup & a roll for £2.

Ald White Craig Cottages (☎ 01434-321069, 🖳 aldwhitecraigcottages.co.uk; four cottages, two with 2D and two sleeping up to six people; ☕; 🐕 on lead) are self-catering cottages and they are about halfway between Haltwhistle and B6318. The proprietors charge £40-100 per cottage and will accept stays of only one night. If arranged in advance they can provide a continental breakfast. Also if they are available and have time they will pick guests up from the PW and take them back the next day and also if necessary take you to a supermarket for provisions.

❑ Thirlwall Castle [Map 102]

Thirlwall Castle was built in the 14th century by the powerful like-named family for protection and defence against border raiders. At that time the castle must have represented an impregnable stronghold to men armed only with spear and sword but by the 17th century these lawless times had passed and the Thirlwall family moved to more comfortable quarters in Hexham. As a reminder of a time when the Borders were the scene of raids and struggles, Thirlwall serves a purpose but there are more absorbing antiquities than this to investigate. Ahead lies The Wall (from which the castle procured much of its building materials!).

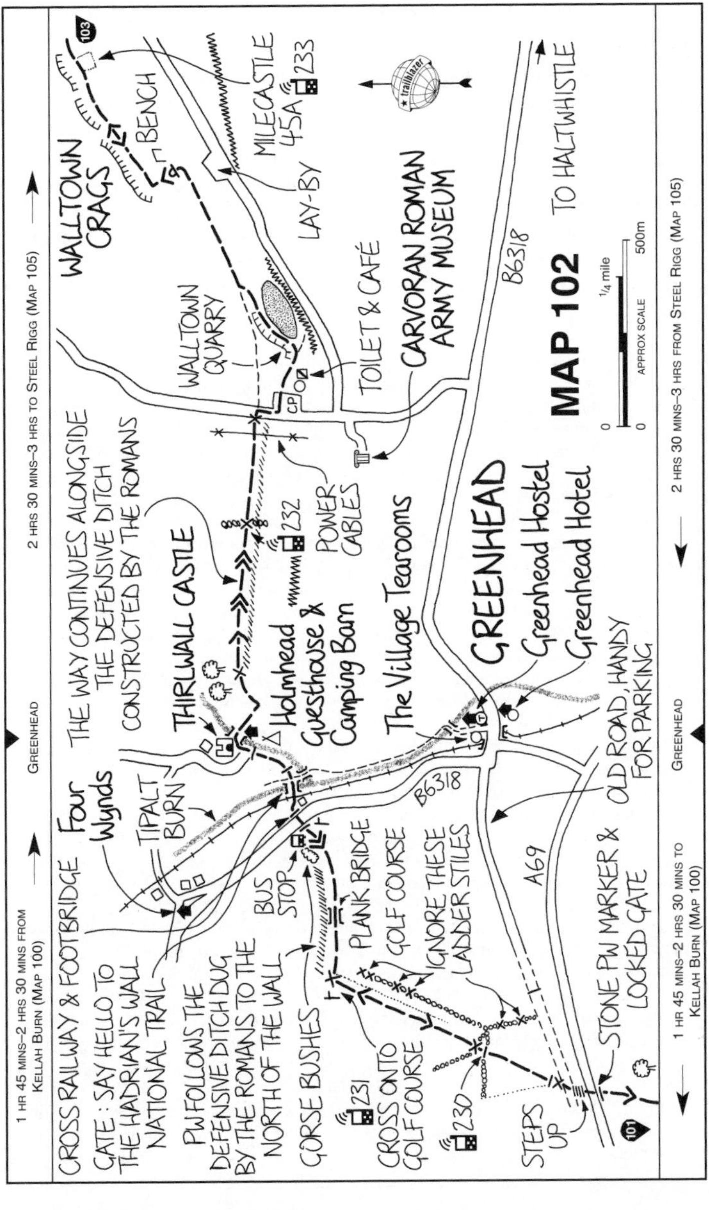
1 HR 45 MINS–2 HRS 30 MINS FROM KELLAH BURN (MAP 100)
GREENHEAD
2 HRS 30 MINS–3 HRS TO STEEL RIGG (MAP 105)
CROSS RAILWAY & FOOTBRIDGE
GATE : SAY HELLO TO THE HADRIAN'S WALL NATIONAL TRAIL
PW FOLLOWS THE DEFENSIVE DITCH DUG BY THE ROMANS TO THE NORTH OF THE WALL
GORSE BUSHES
231
CROSS ONTO GOLF COURSE
230
STEPS UP
101
Four Wynds
TIPALT BURN
BUS STOP
PLANK BRIDGE
GOLF COURSE
IGNORE THESE LADDER STILES
A69
STONE PW MARKER & LOCKED GATE
OLD ROAD, HANDY FOR PARKING
B6318
THE WAY CONTINUES ALONGSIDE THE DEFENSIVE DITCH CONSTRUCTED BY THE ROMANS
THIRLWALL CASTLE
Holmhead Guesthouse & Camping Barn
232
POWER CABLES
The Village Tearooms
GREENHEAD
Greenhead Hostel
Greenhead Hotel
WALLTOWN QUARRY
CP
TOILET & CAFÉ
CARVORAN ROMAN ARMY MUSEUM
B6318
MAP 102
0 ¼ mile
0 APPROX SCALE 500m
WALLTOWN CRAGS
BENCH
LAY-BY
MILECASTLE 45A
233
trailblazer
TO HALTWHISTLE
103
1 HR 45 MINS–2 HRS 30 MINS TO KELLAH BURN (MAP 100)
GREENHEAD
2 HRS 30 MINS–3 HRS FROM STEEL RIGG (MAP 105)

GREENHEAD TO BELLINGHAM MAPS 102-112

Route overview

21½ miles (34.5km) – 3100ft (945m) of ascent – 9-10½ hours

Fasten your *caligae* (Roman legionary sandals) firmly, shoulder your *sarcina* (legionary marching pack) and thank the gods that you're not carrying the 90-110lbs (40-50kg) of equipment regularly packed onto the back of a Roman soldier. Today is a tough one if you intend to walk the full length from Greenhead to Bellingham, having only slightly less ascent than the day over Cross Fell.

At weekends and in the high season you may want to leave early in order to avoid the inevitable crowds that will throng the Wall close to the various car parks along this section. This is the best-preserved length of Hadrian's Wall and

❑ Hadrian's Wall

The Roman Emperor Hadrian first conceived the project after visiting Britain in AD122 and finding out for himself the extent of the difficulty faced by the occupying army in northern Britain. It was impossible to hold any kind of control over the lawless tribes in the area that is now called Scotland so, as the Chinese had done nearly 400 years earlier, it was decided to build a defensive wall. The line of the wall, drawn from the Solway to the Tyne, followed the fault-line of the Whin Sill, an 'escarpment' of resistant dolerite which acted as a natural east–west barrier.

The Wall ran for approximately 80 Roman miles (73 modern miles, or 117km) and had turrets or milecastles every (Roman) mile and larger forts at intervals along its length. The forts would have had a garrison of 500 cavalry or 1000 foot soldiers, and milecastles were manned by 50 men. The Wall was made of stone and turf and would have been five metres high and with a defensive ditch, the *vallum*, set between two mounds of earth, running the length of the southern side. Behind that ran a road to supply and provision the troops manning the wall. In addition to the vallum, they also dug a defensive ditch along the northern side of the Wall.

The construction of the Wall was supervised by the Imperial Legate, Aulus Platorius Nepos, and it took 10 years. The Wall remained in use for 200 years but as the Romans withdrew it fell into disuse and gradually the stones were plundered to build farmsteads and roads. **Thirlwall Castle** (see box p232 & Map 102) is among the many local buildings with stones from the Roman Wall.

Today English Heritage, the National Trust and the National Park authorities preserve and protect what remains of the Wall, keeping it tidy and providing the information needed to help imagine what it was all for. It's well worth visiting **Housesteads Fort** (off Map 106; ☎ 01434-344363; daily Apr-Sep 10am-6pm, Oct to early Nov 10am-5pm, Nov-Mar 10am-4pm; adult/concessions £7.80/7; free to NT and English Heritage members), just before the Way heads north. You'll be pleased to know the communal latrines are particularly well preserved.

The information about the history of the Wall is fragmentary and circumstantial, historians having disputed for centuries over the finer details. What is certain is that the Wall is an extraordinary example of military might whilst demonstrating perhaps the futility of human endeavour. How can you hold back the tide of human expansion by anything so transient as a wall? Impressive, inspiring, unique, yes, but ultimately a failure. When you turn your back on it and head north into Wark Forest, the sight of the Whin Sill is like a breaking wave. The Wall blends into the landscape. The northern tribes had only to wait.

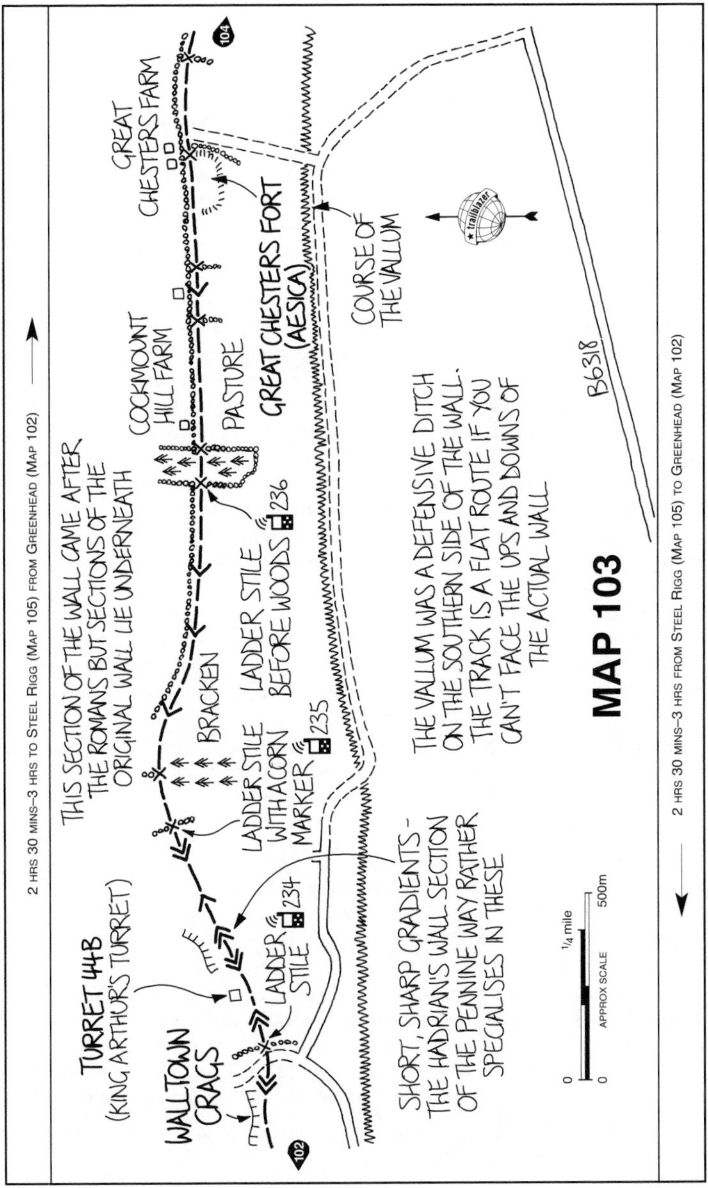
2 HRS 30 MINS–3 HRS TO STEEL RIGG (MAP 105) FROM GREENHEAD (MAP 102)
2 HRS 30 MINS–3 HRS FROM STEEL RIGG (MAP 105) TO GREENHEAD (MAP 102)
MAP 103
104
102
GREAT CHESTERS FARM
GREAT CHESTERS FORT (AESICA)
COURSE OF THE VALLUM
COCKMOUNT HILL FARM
PASTURE
THIS SECTION OF THE WALL CAME AFTER THE ROMANS BUT SECTIONS OF THE ORIGINAL WALL LIE UNDERNEATH
LADDER STILE BEFORE WOODS
236
BRACKEN
LADDER STILE WITH ACORN MARKER
235
THE VALLUM WAS A DEFENSIVE DITCH ON THE SOUTHERN SIDE OF THE WALL. THE TRACK IS A FLAT ROUTE IF YOU CAN'T FACE THE UPS AND DOWNS OF THE ACTUAL WALL
B6318
TURRET 44B (KING ARTHUR'S TURRET)
WALLTOWN CRAGS
LADDER STILE
234
SHORT, SHARP GRADIENTS - THE HADRIAN'S WALL SECTION OF THE PENNINE WAY RATHER SPECIALISES IN THESE
0
1/4 mile
APPROX SCALE
0
500m
trailblazer

draws tens of thousands of visitors every year. You won't have seen crowds like this since Hawes or Malham. Much of the day's ascent figures are comprised of steep little climbs, as the Wall sticks to the edge of the escarpment. The first good section of Wall is found at **Walltown Crags** (Map 102) and this is followed a couple of miles later by the faint outline of **Great Chesters Fort** (Map 103), or Aesica as the Romans would have called it. Those staying at ***Hadrian's Wall Campsite*** (see p238) may want to turn off at **Caw Gap** (Map 104) and head south.

A more detailed exploration of the Wall and its associated archaeological sites (see box p234) can be achieved by breaking this day at **Once Brewed** (Map 105); this has the added benefit of reducing the remaining stretch to Bellingham to a much more palatable 15 miles or so.

Keep an eye open for the iconic **lone Sycamore tree**, possibly the most photographed tree in England, before reaching **Rapishaw Gap** (Map 106) where you say farewell to the day-walking 'civilians' and other 'wallkers' and head north into the forest. If you're lucky the paths amongst the trees will be dry and springy, a joy to walk on, but forestry paths are notorious for cutting up easily and as the Way tries to avoid the harsh logging roads you could end up with muddy boots here. Shortly after entering **Wark Forest** (Map 107), campers can avail themselves of the sturdy walls of ***Haughtongreen Bothy*** (🖳 mountainbothies.org.uk), only a short diversion from the Way.

Leaving the trees to cross **Haughton Common** (Map 108) you may be rewarded with a view of the Cheviots, now not so distant. On the far side of the common, logging leaves a nasty scar before the final section of forest.

The next goal, visible from several miles away, is a radio transmitter station above **Shitlington Crag** (Map 111) which is reached through a mostly pleasant series of pasture, farmland and quiet country lanes. The mast can seem elusive but is eventually reached after a brief scramble up a rocky escarpment and a long steady climb across fields.

A final descent through more rough pasture brings you to a roadside walk into **Bellingham** (Map 112). Metaphorically (if not geographically) it's all downhill to the end from here; no-one gives up now!

Navigation notes

Despite the path through the forest and the many field boundaries later in the day, this section is mostly free of navigation difficulties. The Wall makes the perfect hand-rail for the first part of the day and once you head into the badlands of the former cattle-thieving barbarians the signage is mostly excellent thanks to the sterling work of Northumberland National Park Authority.

The first of a couple of areas to be careful in, is the crossing of Warks Burn (Map 109). As you climb away from the tiny footbridge, be on the lookout for a right turn about halfway up the bank, marked by a large stone. If you miss this you will reach a wide farm gate at the top of the bank; turn sharp right through the gate, along the fence, to pick up the path again. Just beyond are the buildings at The Ash (Map 110); the number and position of gates can be confusing here, so try to keep the buildings to your left and you should keep to the path.

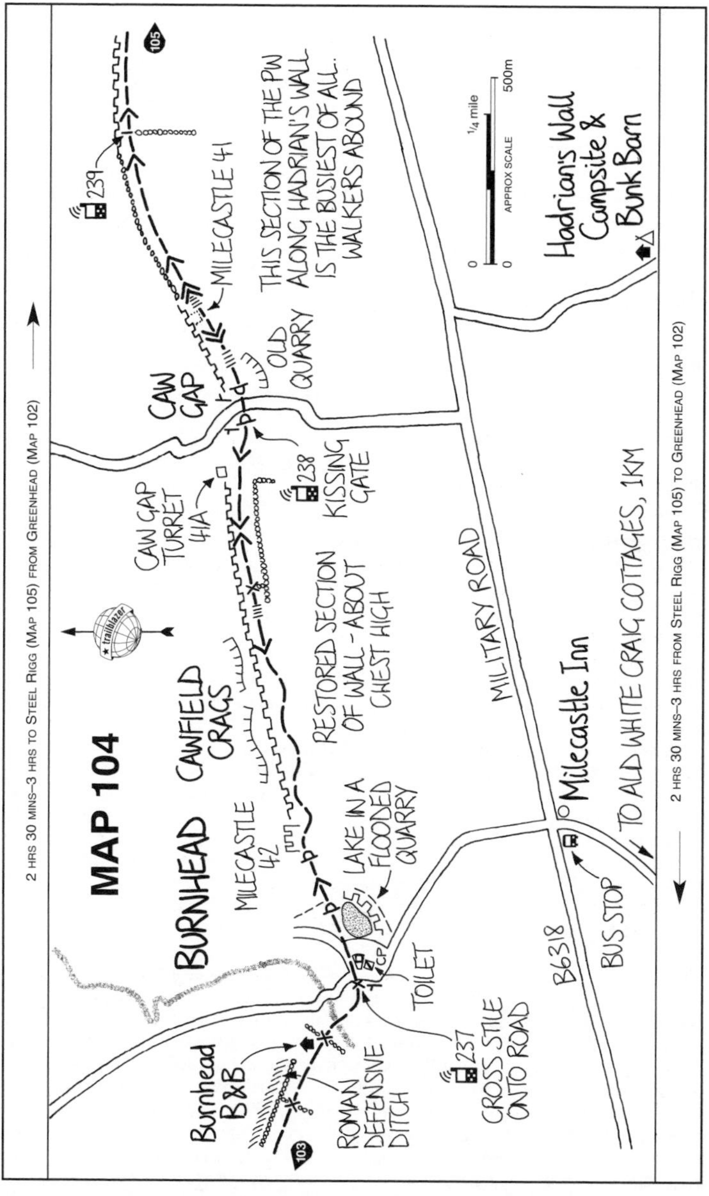
2 HRS 30 MINS–3 HRS TO STEEL RIGG (MAP 105) FROM GREENHEAD (MAP 102)
MAP 104
BURNHEAD
CAWFIELD CRAGS
MILECASTLE 42
LAKE IN A FLOODED QUARRY
RESTORED SECTION OF WALL - ABOUT CHEST HIGH
CAW GAP TURRET 41A
238
KISSING GATE
CAW GAP
OLD QUARRY
MILECASTLE 41
239
THIS SECTION OF THE PW ALONG HADRIAN'S WALL IS THE BUSIEST OF ALL. WALKERS ABOUND
105
103
1/4 mile
0
0
500m
APPROX SCALE
Hadrian's Wall Campsite & Bunk Barn
MILITARY ROAD
Milecastle Inn
TO ALD WHITE CRAIG COTTAGES, 1KM
BUS STOP
B6318
Burnhead B&B
ROMAN DEFENSIVE DITCH
237
CROSS STILE ONTO ROAD
TOILET
CP
2 HRS 30 MINS–3 HRS FROM STEEL RIGG (MAP 105) TO GREENHEAD (MAP 102)

Complacency may set in as you approach Bellingham, so keep an eye open for the change in direction as you descend from the relay station. The natural course is to stay on the track beside the wall, but you need to cut left, across the rough pasture where the fingerpost points, even though the path may initially seem non-existent.

A revision of the path into Bellingham, not reflected on the 2015 edition of the OS Explorer map, may also be confusing. In an attempt to avoid the busy B6320 the Pennine Way follows a path through Kings Wood, staying to the left of the road for around 500 yards before using a footpath beside the road. This is not currently well marked.

BURNHEAD [Map 104, p237]

Right on the Pennine Way so you may well walk into it, you'll get a warm welcome at ***Burnhead*** (☎ 01434-320841, 🖳 burnhead bedandbreakfast.co.uk; 2T, both en suite; Ⓛ); they charge from £42.50pp (sgl occ £45). They are happy to dry wet clothes.

Milecastle Inn (☎ 01434-321372, 🖳 milecastle-inn.co.uk; **food** served Easter to end Oct daily noon-8.30pm, Nov to Easter daily noon-2pm & 6-8.30pm) on Military Road is just 10 minutes' walk away for an evening meal. Note that the pub closes in the afternoon (3-5pm) in the winter.

Go North East's seasonal AD122 **bus** service stops at the pub (see pp54-9).

ONCE BREWED [Map 105]

Not really a village, Once Brewed is about half a mile south of the Way on the B6318, better known for nearly two millennia as the 'Military Road'.

Doubtless the origins of this place's name torment your curiosity. The Twice Brewed Inn, a staging post between Carlisle and Newcastle, gained its name around 1710 when General Wade found the local ale so weak he advised that it be brewed again. When the hostel was opened in the 1930s, the YHA's patron, Lady Trevelyan, remarked that she hoped her cup of tea would be brewed once, not twice like the General's ale, and so the name was born.

See p14 for details of the Roman Wall show held here in June.

Services

The former tourist office at Once Brewed has been knocked down and replaced with the enormously impressive **Sill National Landscape Discovery Centre** (🖳 thesill .org.uk; Mar-Oct daily 9.30am-6pm). As well as a ***café*** (daily summer 9.30am-5pm, winter 10am-3pm), shop and toilets, the centre also hosts exhibitions on the local area; and while it does not act as a tourist office per se, the staff are all local and pretty knowledgeable about the area.

The website 🖳 visithadrianswall.co.uk also has lots of valuable advice on the area, including regional accommodation.

Internet access is available at The Twice Brewed Inn (see Where to stay).

Transport

[See pp54-90] Go North East's seasonal AD122 **bus** service stops at the visitor centre. The service also stops at Haltwhistle railway station from where there are regular **train** services on the Carlisle–Newcastle line (Northern Rail).

For a **taxi**, call Sprouls Taxis (☎ 07712-321064).

Where to stay and eat

A popular place to **camp** is ***Hadrian's Wall Campsite*** (see Map 104; ☎ 01434-320495, 🖳 hadrianswallcampsite.co.uk; 🐕), though it's about a mile west of the pub and The Sill, at **Melkridge**, about 400m south of the B6318. Still, it's a friendly place with good facilities – showers (24hrs), laundry room with a small fridge freezer; and a cook house with free gas for hikers.

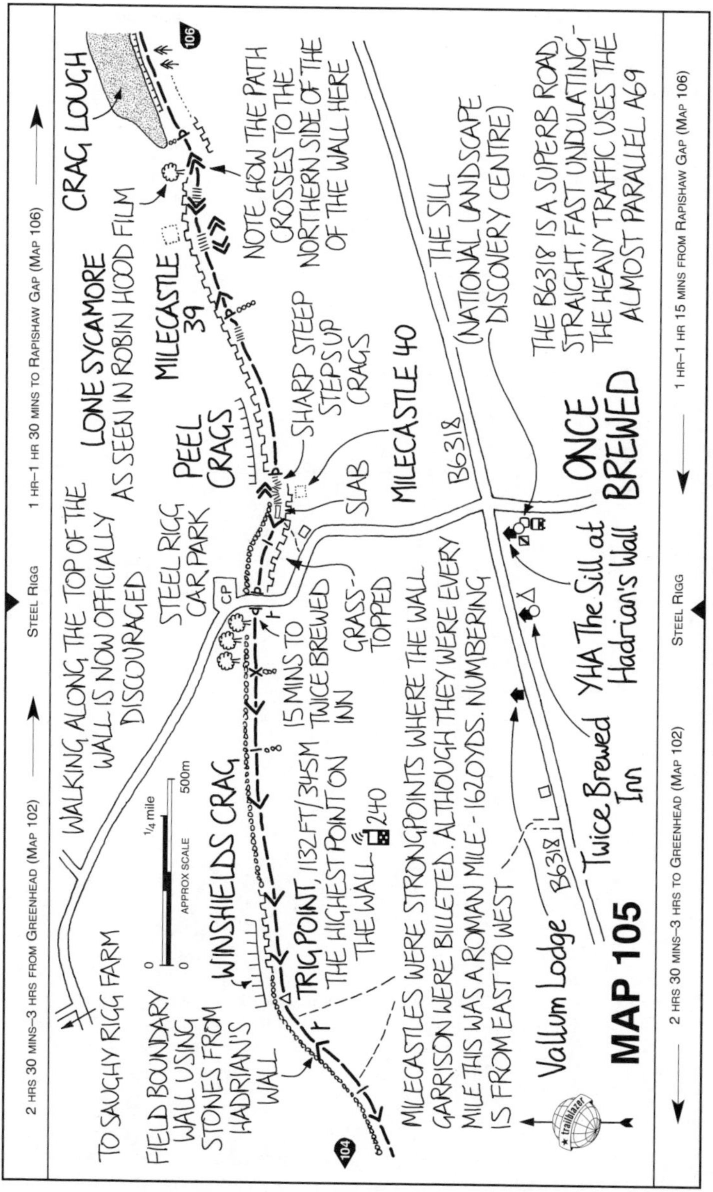
2 HRS 30 MINS–3 HRS FROM GREENHEAD (MAP 102)
STEEL RIGG
1 HR–1 HR 30 MINS TO RAPISHAW GAP (MAP 106)
TO SAUGHY RIGG FARM
WALKING ALONG THE TOP OF THE WALL IS NOW OFFICIALLY DISCOURAGED
CRAG LOUGH
106
LONE SYCAMORE AS SEEN IN ROBIN HOOD FILM
FIELD BOUNDARY WALL USING STONES FROM HADRIAN'S WALL
0 1/4 mile
0 500m
APPROX SCALE
WINSHIELDS CRAG
STEEL RIGG CAR PARK
CP
PEEL CRAGS
MILECASTLE 39
NOTE HOW THE PATH CROSSES TO THE NORTHERN SIDE OF THE WALL HERE
TRIG POINT, 1132FT/345M THE HIGHEST POINT ON THE WALL
240
15 MINS TO TWICE BREWED INN
GRASS-TOPPED
SLAB
SHARP STEEP STEPS UP CRAGS
MILECASTLE 40
THE SILL (NATIONAL LANDSCAPE DISCOVERY CENTRE)
B6318
MILECASTLES WERE STRONGPOINTS WHERE THE WALL GARRISON WERE BILLETED. ALTHOUGH THEY WERE EVERY MILE THIS WAS A ROMAN MILE - 1620YDS. NUMBERING IS FROM EAST TO WEST
104
Vallum Lodge
B6318
Twice Brewed Inn
YHA The Sill at Hadrian's Wall
ONCE BREWED
THE B6318 IS A SUPERB ROAD, STRAIGHT, FAST UNDULATING - THE HEAVY TRAFFIC USES THE ALMOST PARALLEL A69
MAP 105
2 HRS 30 MINS–3 HRS TO GREENHEAD (MAP 102)
STEEL RIGG
1 HR–1 HR 15 MINS FROM RAPISHAW GAP (MAP 106)

[**Once Brewed** *cont'd*] They also have a **bunk barn** that sleeps up to 10 people (1 x 6-, 1x 4-bed room; booking is recommended) and they charge £15 per bunk (plus £5 per stay if bedding is required). Camping costs £10/13 for one/two hikers in a tent.

Ensure you arrive before 8pm as the site is locked then.

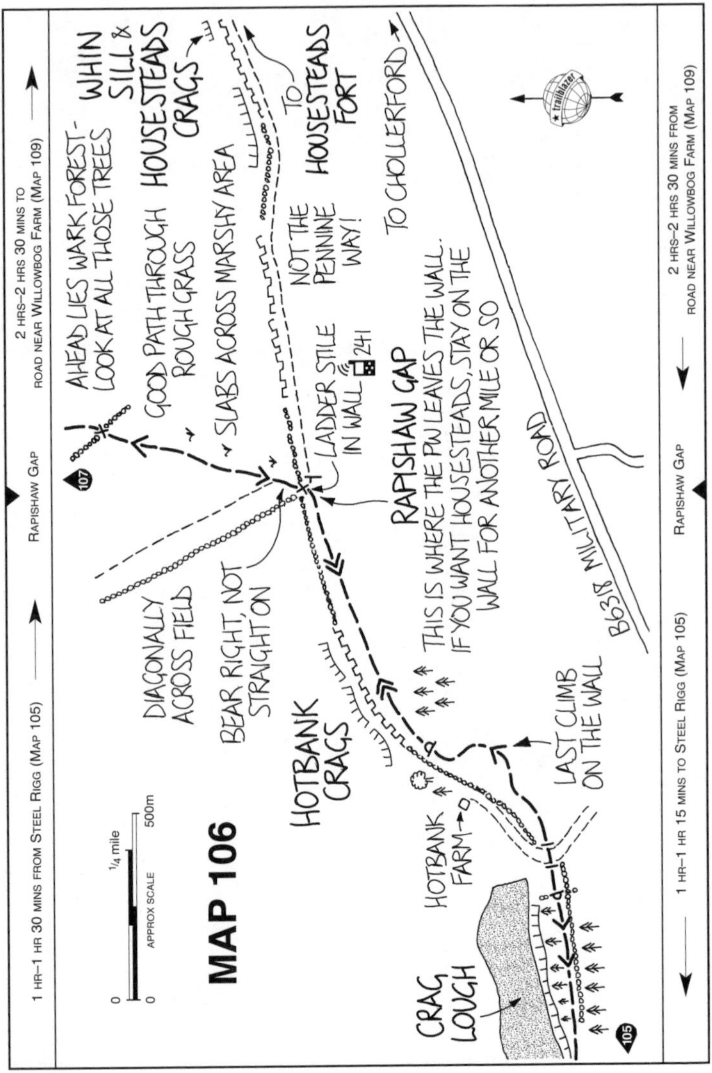

MAP 106
APPROX SCALE
0 1/4 mile
0 500m
1 HR–1 HR 30 MINS FROM STEEL RIGG (MAP 105)
RAPISHAW GAP
2 HRS–2 HRS 30 MINS TO ROAD NEAR WILLOWBOG FARM (MAP 109)
1 HR–1 HR 15 MINS TO STEEL RIGG (MAP 105)
2 HRS–2 HRS 30 MINS FROM ROAD NEAR WILLOWBOG FARM (MAP 109)
CRAG LOUGH
HOTBANK FARM
HOTBANK CRAGS
LAST CLIMB ON THE WALL
DIAGONALLY ACROSS FIELD
BEAR RIGHT, NOT STRAIGHT ON
THIS IS WHERE THE PW LEAVES THE WALL. IF YOU WANT HOUSESTEADS, STAY ON THE WALL FOR ANOTHER MILE OR SO
B6318 MILITARY ROAD
RAPISHAW GAP
LADDER STILE IN WALL
241
NOT THE PENNINE WAY!
TO CHOLLERFORD
SLABS ACROSS MARSHY AREA
GOOD PATH THROUGH ROUGH GRASS
AHEAD LIES WARK FOREST- LOOK AT ALL THOSE TREES
HOUSESTEADS CRAGS
WHIN SILL &
TO HOUSESTEADS FORT
trailblazer
105
107

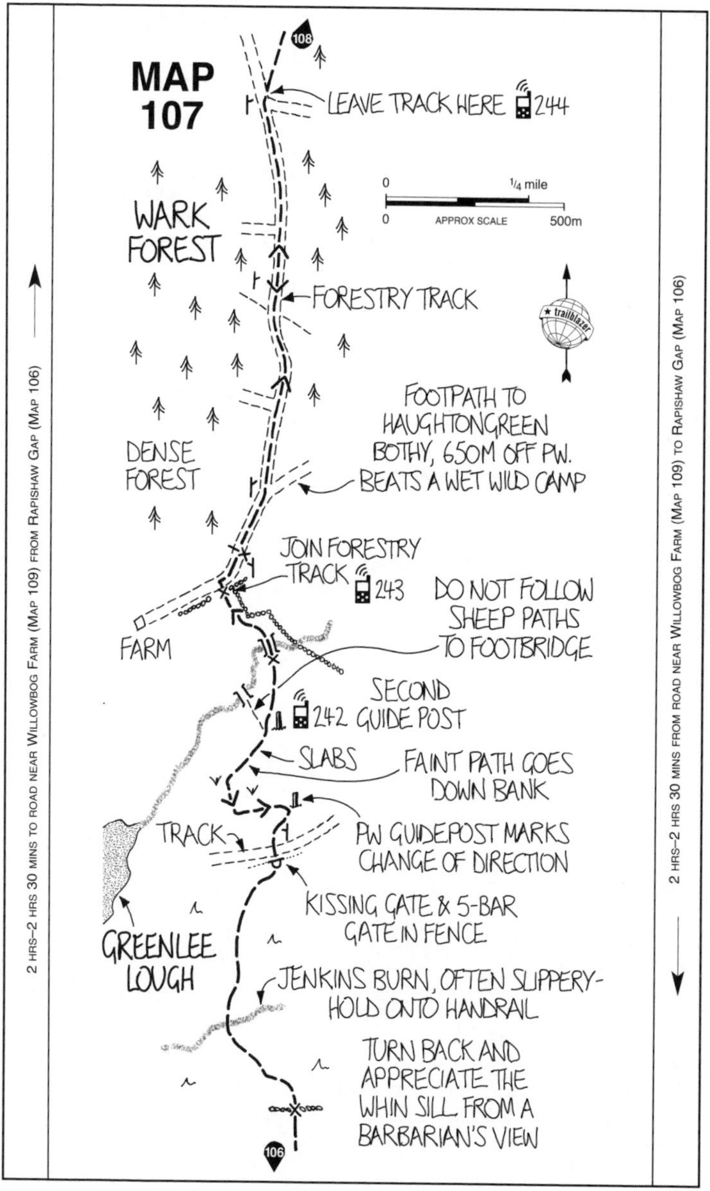
MAP 107
LEAVE TRACK HERE 244
WARK FOREST
0 ¼ mile
0 APPROX SCALE 500m
FORESTRY TRACK
trailblazer
FOOTPATH TO HAUGHTONGREEN BOTHY, 650M OFF PW. BEATS A WET WILD CAMP
DENSE FOREST
JOIN FORESTRY TRACK 243
DO NOT FOLLOW SHEEP PATHS TO FOOTBRIDGE
FARM
SECOND GUIDE POST
242
SLABS
FAINT PATH GOES DOWN BANK
TRACK
PW GUIDEPOST MARKS CHANGE OF DIRECTION
KISSING GATE & 5-BAR GATE IN FENCE
GREENLEE LOUGH
JENKINS BURN, OFTEN SLIPPERY- HOLD ONTO HANDRAIL
TURN BACK AND APPRECIATE THE WHIN SILL FROM A BARBARIAN'S VIEW
108
106
2 HRS–2 HRS 30 MINS TO ROAD NEAR WILLOWBOG FARM (MAP 109) FROM RAPISHAW GAP (MAP 106)
2 HRS–2 HRS 30 MINS FROM ROAD NEAR WILLOWBOG FARM (MAP 109) TO RAPISHAW GAP (MAP 106)

[**Once Brewed** *cont'd*] ***YHA The Sill at Hadrian's Wall*** (☎ 0345-260 2702, 💻 yha.org.uk/hostel/yha-the-sill-at-hadrians-wall; 8 x 2-, 2 x 3-, 8 x 4-bed all en suite, 8 x 4-bed shared facilities; Ⓛ) is a brand new purpose-built hostel built on the site of the old one. A dorm bed costs from £15pp and from £29 for a private room. The hostel is licensed and has its own ***café*** (daily breakfast 7.30-9am, food 3-8pm, drinks to 11pm) for residents. Check-in is from 3pm and there is 24hr access; there are also laundry facilities and a drying room.

Other accommodation in the area includes the superior ***Vallum Lodge*** (☎ 01434-344248, 💻 vallum-lodge.co.uk; 3T/4D, all en suite; ☕; Ⓛ; Apr-Oct) charging from £45pp (sgl occ £90) for B&B. They also have a 'snug' (1D en suite; kitchen and lounge area) which costs £110 per night including breakfast.

Between the YHA hostel and Vallum Lodge is ***The Twice Brewed Inn*** (☎ 01434-344534, 💻 twicebrewedinn.co.uk; 10D or T/8D all en suite; ☕; Ⓛ; 🐕) with **B&B** from £45pp (sgl occ £70). (*cont'd on p244*)

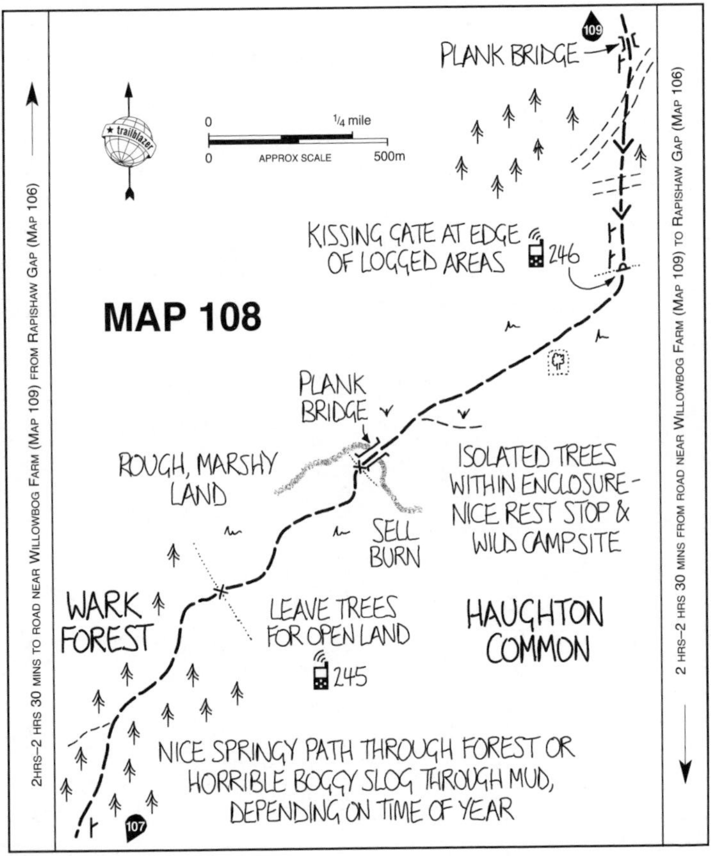
2HRS–2 HRS 30 MINS TO ROAD NEAR WILLOWBOG FARM (MAP 109) FROM RAPISHAW GAP (MAP 106)
2 HRS–2 HRS 30 MINS FROM ROAD NEAR WILLOWBOG FARM (MAP 109) TO RAPISHAW GAP (MAP 106)
trailblazer
0
1/4 mile
0
APPROX SCALE
500m
109
PLANK BRIDGE
KISSING GATE AT EDGE OF LOGGED AREAS
246
MAP 108
PLANK BRIDGE
ROUGH, MARSHY LAND
ISOLATED TREES WITHIN ENCLOSURE - NICE REST STOP & WILD CAMPSITE
SELL BURN
WARK FOREST
LEAVE TREES FOR OPEN LAND
245
HAUGHTON COMMON
NICE SPRINGY PATH THROUGH FOREST OR HORRIBLE BOGGY SLOG THROUGH MUD, DEPENDING ON TIME OF YEAR
107

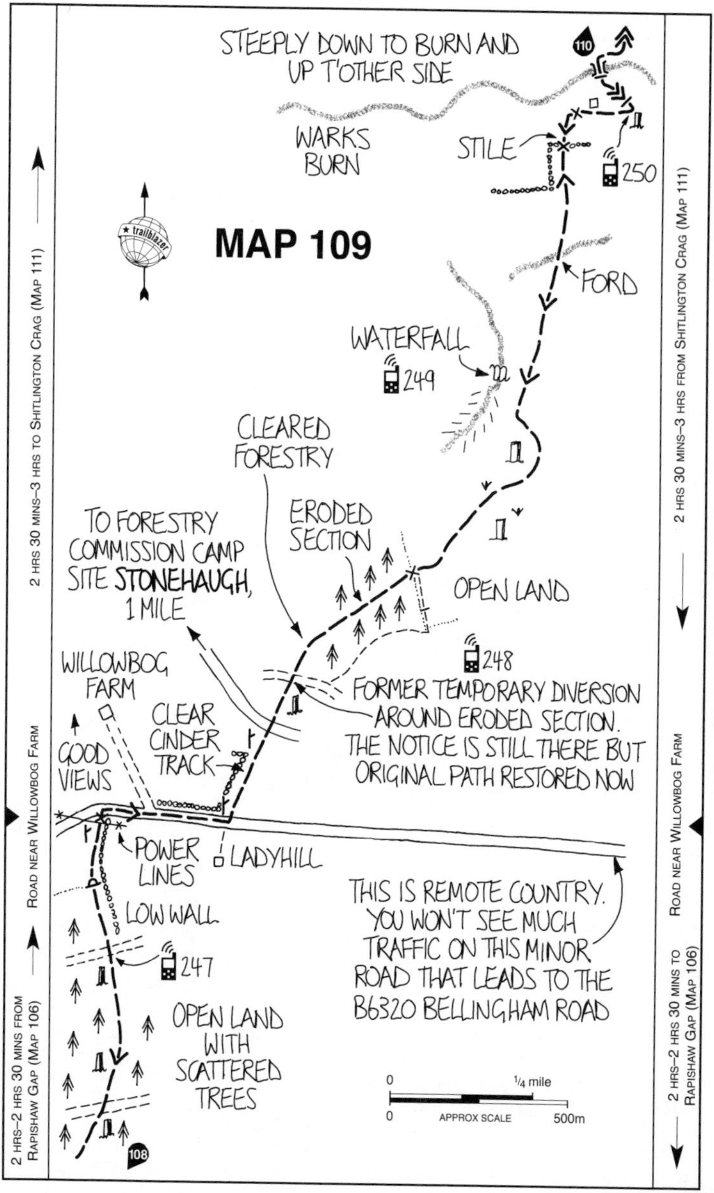
STEEPLY DOWN TO BURN AND UP T'OTHER SIDE
110
WARKS BURN
STILE
250
MAP 109
trailblazer
FORD
WATERFALL
249
CLEARED FORESTRY
ERODED SECTION
TO FORESTRY COMMISSION CAMP SITE STONEHAUGH, 1 MILE
OPEN LAND
248
WILLOWBOG FARM
GOOD VIEWS
CLEAR CINDER TRACK
FORMER TEMPORARY DIVERSION AROUND ERODED SECTION. THE NOTICE IS STILL THERE BUT ORIGINAL PATH RESTORED NOW
POWER LINES
LADYHILL
LOW WALL
THIS IS REMOTE COUNTRY. YOU WON'T SEE MUCH TRAFFIC ON THIS MINOR ROAD THAT LEADS TO THE B6320 BELLINGHAM ROAD
247
OPEN LAND WITH SCATTERED TREES
0
1/4 mile
0
APPROX SCALE
500m
108
2 HRS 30 MINS–3 HRS TO SHITLINGTON CRAG (MAP 111)
ROAD NEAR WILLOWBOG FARM
2 HRS–2 HRS 30 MINS FROM RAPISHAW GAP (MAP 106)
2 HRS 30 MINS–3 HRS FROM SHITLINGTON CRAG (MAP 111)
ROAD NEAR WILLOWBOG FARM
2 HRS–2 HRS 30 MINS TO RAPISHAW GAP (MAP 106)

[**Once Brewed** *cont'd*] The menu (**food** served Mon-Sat noon-5pm & 6-9pm, Sun noon-8pm) has some good meaty options. They now make own beer in the brewery here – The Twice Brewed Brewhouse – and offer tours (Mon-Fri). There's **camping** here (£10 for up to two people; shower and toilet facilities available) but booking is recommended.

Another great spot is ***Saughy Rigg Farm*** (off Map 105; ☎ 01434-344747, 💻 saughyriggfarm.com) but the only problem is that they are moving more towards the self-catering side of the industry, though they do say that they can probably offer B&B in some double/twin rooms (all en suite; ☕; Ⓛ; 🐕) during the week in the main walking season. If they do, B&B will cost £40-42.50pp (sgl occ £55-60). They have drying facilities and may provide evening meals if booked in advance. The pleasingly isolated farm is about half a mile north of Hadrian's Wall along the road from the Steel Rigg car park.

STONEHAUGH [off Map 109, p243]

Aside from licking dew off the grass, there are hardly any opportunities for refreshments on the route today except at the forestry outpost of Stonehaugh, eight miles from Bellingham, where, if you feel that you simply cannot walk any further, you could head for the Forestry Commission's ***Stonehaugh Camp Site*** (☎ 01434-230798, 💻 stonehaughcampsite.com; 🐕; Ⓛ; Easter to end Sep), which charges £10pp (plus £1pp over bank holiday weekends); cash payment only is accepted. The rate includes use of the shower/toilet facilities. It's a mile off the route and there are no shops for five miles although they can supply provisions and a packed lunch if you advise them about two weeks in advance.

BELLINGHAM [Map 112a, p248]

This old market town on the North Tyne is the last place on the Pennine Way offering most things you may need. Note Bellingham is pronounced Belling-jam.

The **Heritage Centre** (Map 112; ☎ 01434-220050, 💻 bellingham-heritage.org.uk; Easter to end Oct Mon-Sat 10am-4pm, Sun 11-4pm; £4), on Woodburn Rd out of town to the east, has displays on local history and tea rooms (see Where to eat).

See p14 for details of the show held here in August.

Services

The volunteers at the Heritage Centre (see above) are happy to help with **tourist information** queries if they can but this is no longer an official TIC; however, there are some leaflets.

There's a **chemist** (Mon-Fri 9am-12.30pm & 1.30-5.30pm, Sat am only), **bakery** (see Where to eat), Thompson's **butcher**, and a Co-op **supermarket** (daily 7am-10pm) with an **ATM**. This is the last ATM on the route; that said, there aren't many places left on the route where you can actually spend money either! If that's not working you can try withdrawing money from the **post office** (Mon-Fri 6.30am-6pm, Sat 8am-1pm). Bellingham Garage Services, on the way out of the village, sells **Coleman fuel and gas canisters** as well as general groceries.

Transport

[See also pp54-9] Bellingham is a stop on Go North East's No 680 **bus** service and also ADAPT's 694 (Tue & Fri only), with both heading to Hexham.

For a **taxi** call Bellingham Taxis ☎ 01434-220570.

Where to stay

Before the bridge on your way into town you'll pass ***Bellingham Camping and Caravan Club*** (see Map 112; ☎ 01434-220175, 💻 campingandcaravanningclub.co.uk; 🐕; Mar to early Jan) which charges £6.30-9.25pp (members £5.30-7.80pp) for backpackers and has four **wooden camping pods** (sleeping up to three) for £45 (members £35-45); the place has a wealth of facilities apart from the almost obligatory toilets and showers, including a kitchen with fridge-freezer, a drying room and even a social area with a log-burning stove. Booking is essential for the pods and there may be a minimum stay requirement for them over bank holiday weekends.

Closer to the town centre, ***Demesne Farm Campsite and Bunkhouse*** (☎ 01434-220258, 💻 demesnefarmcampsite.co.uk) has **camping** (May-Oct; 🐕) for £8pp. It also has a 15-bed (1 x3-, 1 x 4-, 1 x 8-bed room) self-catering **bunkhouse** (from £22pp; 🐕). Bedding is provided but not towels (£2 to hire). It has a drying room, a well-equipped kitchen and there is a sitting area for people staying in the bunkhouse. It is essential to book for the bunkhouse, particularly in the peak season.

(cont'd on p248)

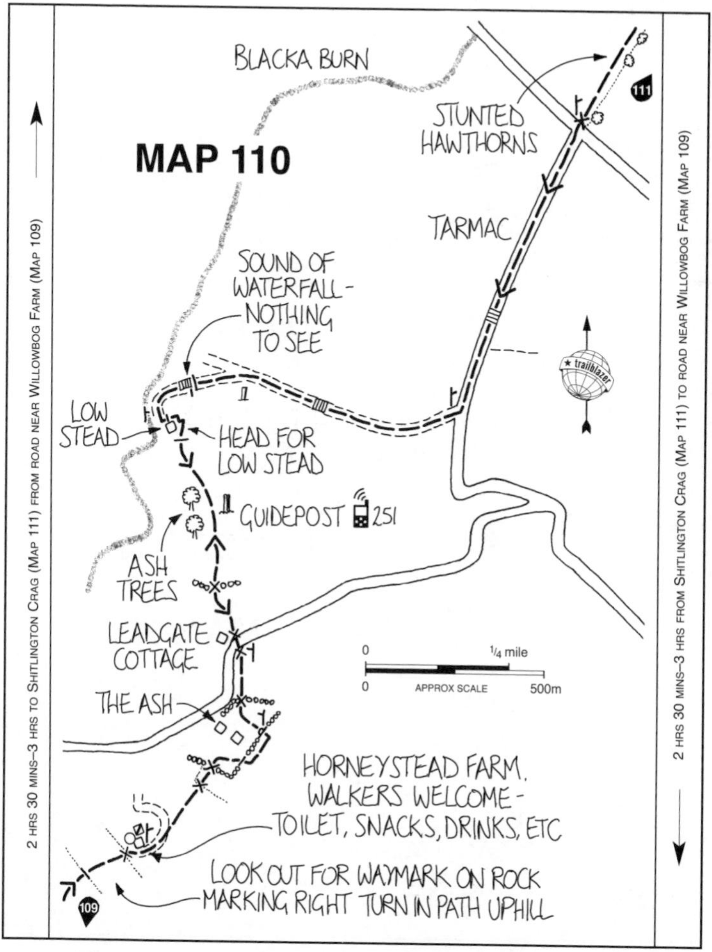
MAP 110
BLACKA BURN
STUNTED HAWTHORNS
111
TARMAC
SOUND OF WATERFALL - NOTHING TO SEE
LOW STEAD
HEAD FOR LOW STEAD
GUIDEPOST 251
ASH TREES
LEADGATE COTTAGE
THE ASH
0 1/4 mile
0 APPROX SCALE 500m
HORNEYSTEAD FARM. WALKERS WELCOME - TOILET, SNACKS, DRINKS, ETC
LOOK OUT FOR WAYMARK ON ROCK MARKING RIGHT TURN IN PATH UPHILL
109
trailblazer
2 HRS 30 MINS–3 HRS TO SHITLINGTON CRAG (MAP 111) FROM ROAD NEAR WILLOWBOG FARM (MAP 109)
2 HRS 30 MINS–3 HRS FROM SHITLINGTON CRAG (MAP 111) TO ROAD NEAR WILLOWBOG FARM (MAP 109)

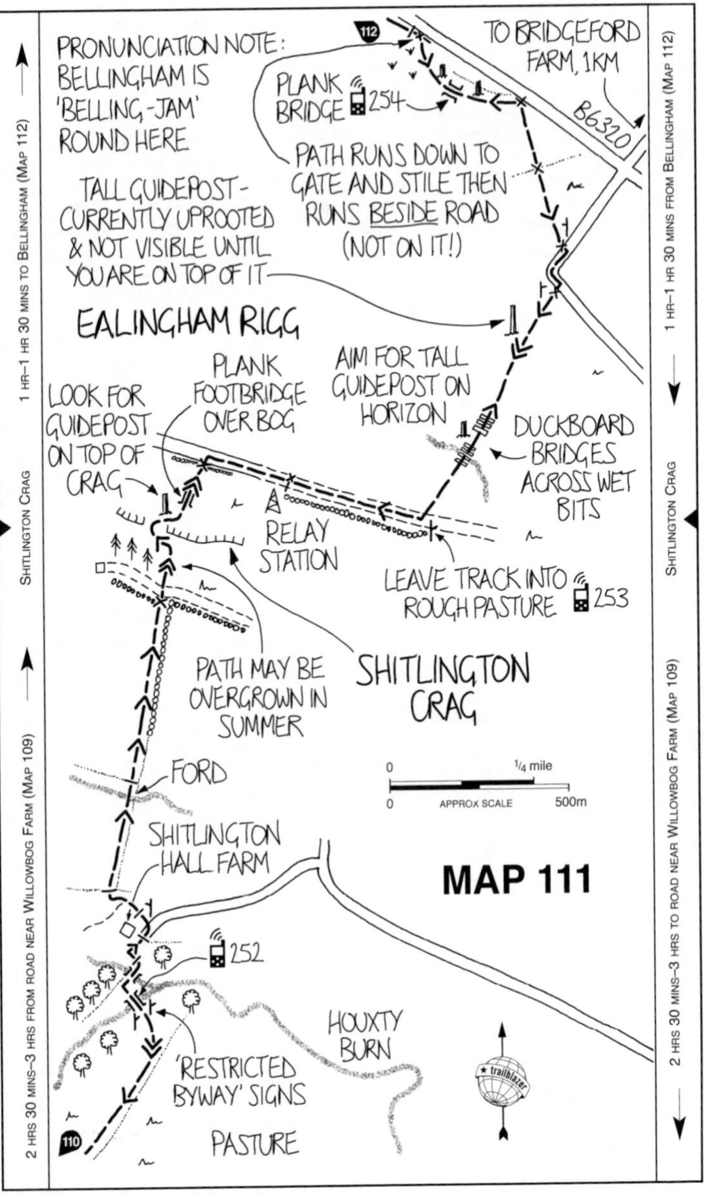
1 HR–1 HR 30 MINS TO BELLINGHAM (MAP 112)
SHITLINGTON CRAG
2 HRS 30 MINS–3 HRS FROM ROAD NEAR WILLOWBOG FARM (MAP 109)
1 HR–1 HR 30 MINS FROM BELLINGHAM (MAP 112)
SHITLINGTON CRAG
2 HRS 30 MINS–3 HRS TO ROAD NEAR WILLOWBOG FARM (MAP 109)
112
PRONUNCIATION NOTE: BELLINGHAM IS 'BELLING-JAM' ROUND HERE
TO BRIDGEFORD FARM, 1KM
PLANK BRIDGE 254
B6320
PATH RUNS DOWN TO GATE AND STILE THEN RUNS BESIDE ROAD (NOT ON IT!)
TALL GUIDEPOST - CURRENTLY UPROOTED & NOT VISIBLE UNTIL YOU ARE ON TOP OF IT
EALINGHAM RIGG
PLANK FOOTBRIDGE OVER BOG
AIM FOR TALL GUIDEPOST ON HORIZON
LOOK FOR GUIDEPOST ON TOP OF CRAG
DUCKBOARD BRIDGES ACROSS WET BITS
RELAY STATION
LEAVE TRACK INTO ROUGH PASTURE 253
PATH MAY BE OVERGROWN IN SUMMER
SHITLINGTON CRAG
FORD
0
1/4 mile
0
APPROX SCALE
500m
SHITLINGTON HALL FARM
MAP 111
252
HOUXTY BURN
'RESTRICTED BYWAY' SIGNS
PASTURE
110

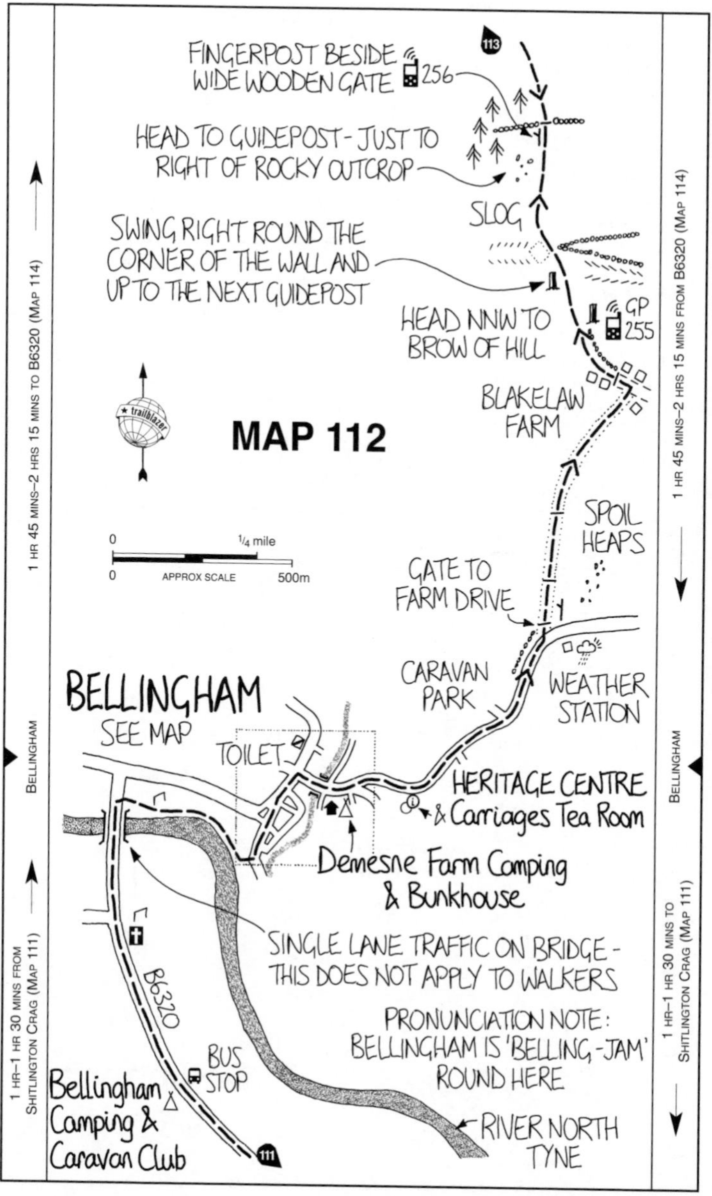
1 HR 45 MINS–2 HRS 15 MINS TO B6320 (MAP 114)
BELLINGHAM
1 HR–1 HR 30 MINS FROM SHITLINGTON CRAG (MAP 111)
1 HR 45 MINS–2 HRS 15 MINS FROM B6320 (MAP 114)
BELLINGHAM
1 HR–1 HR 30 MINS TO SHITLINGTON CRAG (MAP 111)
113
FINGERPOST BESIDE WIDE WOODEN GATE
256
HEAD TO GUIDEPOST - JUST TO RIGHT OF ROCKY OUTCROP
SLOG
SWING RIGHT ROUND THE CORNER OF THE WALL AND UP TO THE NEXT GUIDEPOST
HEAD NNW TO BROW OF HILL
GP 255
BLAKELAW FARM
MAP 112
trailblazer
0
1/4 mile
0
APPROX SCALE
500m
SPOIL HEAPS
GATE TO FARM DRIVE
CARAVAN PARK
WEATHER STATION
BELLINGHAM SEE MAP
TOILET
HERITAGE CENTRE & Carriages Tea Room
Demesne Farm Camping & Bunkhouse
SINGLE LANE TRAFFIC ON BRIDGE - THIS DOES NOT APPLY TO WALKERS
B6320
PRONUNCIATION NOTE: BELLINGHAM IS 'BELLING-JAM' ROUND HERE
BUS STOP
Bellingham Camping & Caravan Club
RIVER NORTH TYNE
111

ROUTE GUIDE AND MAPS

(cont'd from p245) The bunkhouse can also be booked through the YHA where it is called **YHA Bellingham,** though the rate is the same.

Lyndale Guest House (☎ 01434-220361, 💻 lyndaleguesthouse@hotmail.com; 1S/1T/2D, most en suite; ☕; Ⓛ) is a bright and friendly place. B&B costs from £45pp (sgl £50, sgl occ en suite £70). They are happy to do washing/drying (£7 per bag) and also have a drying room for boots.

If you'd like to stay in a pub ***The Cheviot Hotel*** (☎ 01434-220696; 7D or T/1Tr, all en suite; ☕; Ⓛ; 🐕) is the best choice with B&B from £45pp (sgl occ £55).

Bridgeford Farm (☎ 01434-220940, 💻 www.bridgefordfarmbandb.co.uk; 2D/1T, all en suite; ☕; Ⓛ) is about a mile before you get to Bellingham; however, if arranged in advance they provide a pick up and drop off service. For B&B they charge from £40pp (sgl occ £50).

Where to eat and drink

As you enter the village on the Way, the first place serving food you see will be the ***Rocky Road Café*** (daily 8.30am-4.30pm) which does meals and hot drinks as well as packed lunches. Note that dogs are not allowed in here, though they are in the ***Fountain Cottage Tea Room*** (daily 9am-4pm; 🐕), at the northern end of the village, which does light lunches and teas.

Tea is also served in a converted railway carriage at ***Carriages Tea Room*** (☎ 01434-221151, 💻 carriages-tearoom.co.uk;

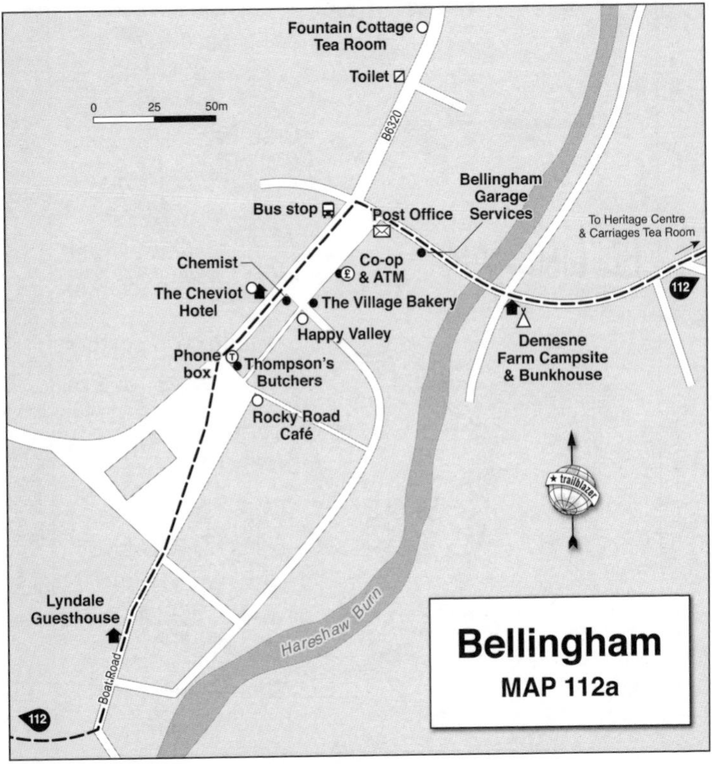
Fountain Cottage Tea Room
Toilet
0 25 50m
B6320
Bellingham Garage Services
Bus stop
Post Office
To Heritage Centre & Carriages Tea Room
Chemist
Co-op & ATM
The Cheviot Hotel
The Village Bakery
112
Happy Valley
Demesne Farm Campsite & Bunkhouse
Phone box
Thompson's Butchers
Rocky Road Café
trailblazer
Lyndale Guesthouse
Hareshaw Burn
Boat Road
112
Bellingham
MAP 112a

daily 10am-4.30pm but in the summer they may stay open till 6pm) at the Heritage Centre (see p244).

The Cheviot Hotel (see Where to stay; food served daily noon-2.30pm & 6-9pm; takeaways available 6-10pm) is the best of the pubs. If you only have one burger on the Pennine Way, make sure it's here; there is a wide selection and all are home-made, along with other favourites such as steak & ale pie, or fish & chips (also available as takeaway). Starters cost £5-10 and mains are £10-20.

The Village Bakery (Mon-Fri 7am-5pm, Sat 8am-2.30pm) is a great place to stop as you set out in the morning, they open early enough to supply a snack for the road. There's also a Chinese takeaway, ***Happy Valley*** (Mon & Wed-Sun 4.30-10.30pm), opposite.

BELLINGHAM TO BYRNESS — MAPS 112-120

Route overview

15 miles (24km) – 1800ft (549m) of ascent – 7¼ to 9 hours

At a modest 15 miles, today's walk is something of a warm-up for tomorrow's mountain marathon over the Cheviot range. Take it easy today, enjoy the relatively low-level route with its diverse scenery of green fields, heather moorland, forestry tracks and riverside paths, for tomorrow is high, rolling hills and open skies all day.

The day starts, as usual, with a climb out of the village and into the green fields around **Blakelaw Farm** (Map 112). This soon turns to rough pasture as you approach **Hareshaw House** (Map 113) and beyond this last outpost of civilisation you enter heather moorland; the track is little more than the width of two boots and marked by occasional guide posts.

The delightfully named **Deer Play** (Map 114) gives glorious views, soon surpassed by those from **Whitley Pike** (Map 115) and from the path around **Padon Hill** (Map 116).

The heather is left behind as you begin the steep ascent of **Brownrigg Head**, using an old broken wall to avoid the perpetually sodden edge of the forest. Celebration would be premature though, as you are now faced with a squelchy 1½ miles between the plantation's northern perimeter and a boundary fence which will almost certainly leave you with wet feet.

It is with some relief then, that you reach the forestry road in **Redesdale Forest** (Map 117); a firm surface at last. Unfortunately, where the Forestry Commission has cleared sections of the forest the landscape is particularly harsh and bleak. It also soon becomes apparent that you've swapped one extreme for another, as the harsh stone surface begins to take its toll on your feet. Three miles of forestry road wind away into the distance, broken only by two pedantic side excursions through tall grass and bracken that most walkers rightly avoid. If you're lucky you won't be covered in dust by a speeding timber lorry!

You can finally wriggle your abused toes in the grass at the picnic benches at **Blakehopeburnhaugh** (Map 119), before continuing through pleasant woodland beside the **River Rede** down to **Byrness village** (Map 120) and the A68. A varied and mostly undemanding day has hopefully set you up nicely for the immense undertaking of The Cheviot traverse that awaits.

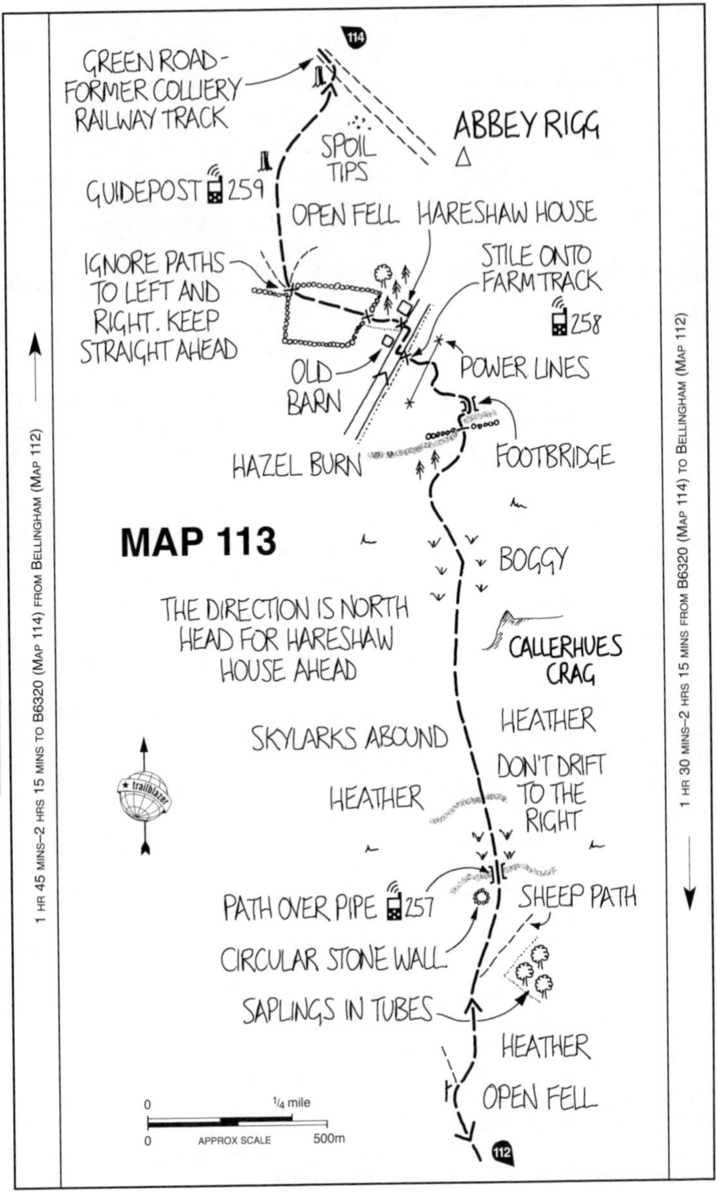
GREEN ROAD - FORMER COLLIERY RAILWAY TRACK
114
ABBEY RIGG
SPOIL TIPS
GUIDEPOST 259
OPEN FELL
HARESHAW HOUSE
IGNORE PATHS TO LEFT AND RIGHT. KEEP STRAIGHT AHEAD
STILE ONTO FARM TRACK
258
OLD BARN
POWER LINES
FOOTBRIDGE
HAZEL BURN
MAP 113
BOGGY
THE DIRECTION IS NORTH HEAD FOR HARESHAW HOUSE AHEAD
CALLERHUES CRAG
HEATHER
SKYLARKS ABOUND
HEATHER
DON'T DRIFT TO THE RIGHT
trailblazer
PATH OVER PIPE 257
SHEEP PATH
CIRCULAR STONE WALL
SAPLINGS IN TUBES
HEATHER
OPEN FELL
0
1/4 mile
0
APPROX SCALE
500m
112
1 HR 45 MINS–2 HRS 15 MINS TO B6320 (MAP 114) FROM BELLINGHAM (MAP 112)
1 HR 30 MINS–2 HRS 15 MINS FROM B6320 (MAP 114) TO BELLINGHAM (MAP 112)

Navigation notes

In very bad visibility the route may get a little thin as it branches around a bog below Callerhues Crag (Map 113) on the way to Hareshaw House, but a generally northern direction will bring you to the wall before Hazel Burn; head for the trees if they are visible.

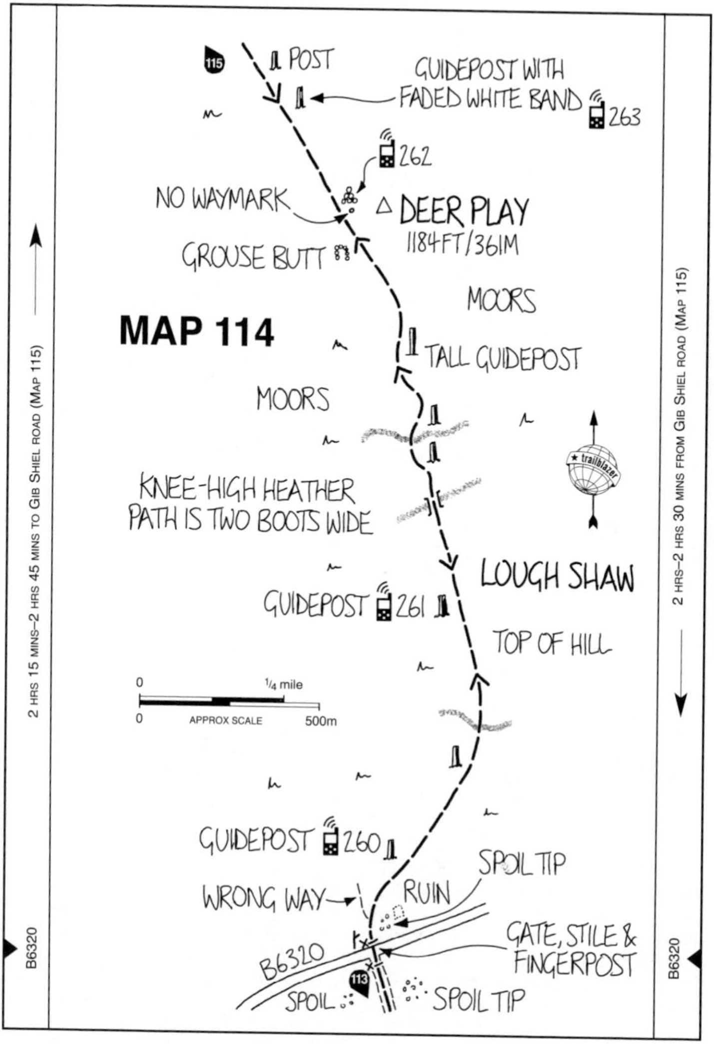
2 HRS 15 MINS–2 HRS 45 MINS TO GIB SHIEL ROAD (MAP 115)
2 HRS–2 HRS 30 MINS FROM GIB SHIEL ROAD (MAP 115)
B6320
B6320
115
POST
GUIDEPOST WITH
FADED WHITE BAND
263
262
NO WAYMARK
DEER PLAY
1184FT/361M
GROUSE BUTT
MOORS
MAP 114
TALL GUIDEPOST
MOORS
KNEE-HIGH HEATHER
PATH IS TWO BOOTS WIDE
trailblazer
LOUGH SHAW
GUIDEPOST
261
TOP OF HILL
0
1/4 mile
0
APPROX SCALE
500m
GUIDEPOST
260
SPOIL TIP
WRONG WAY
RUIN
GATE, STILE &
FINGERPOST
B6320
113
SPOIL
SPOIL TIP

Soon after, at the B6320 a PW fingerpost helps you set off at the right bearing, NNW, to lock on to the line of guideposts leading to Deer Play hill (Map 114) then down and up again to Whitley Pike (Map 115). The path through the heather is fairly easy to follow.

Leaving Whitley Pike, be sure to bear right as you cross the fence, as an obvious path wants to draw you too far left. If in doubt, head for GPS 266 which marks the start of the slabs across the moor.

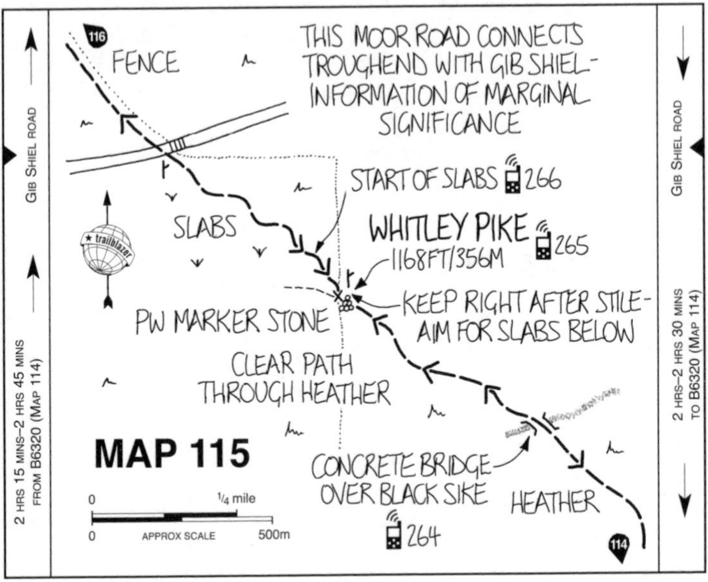
116
FENCE
THIS MOOR ROAD CONNECTS TROUGHEND WITH GIB SHIEL - INFORMATION OF MARGINAL SIGNIFICANCE
GIB SHIEL ROAD
GIB SHIEL ROAD
START OF SLABS 266
SLABS
WHITLEY PIKE 265
1168FT/356M
trailblazer
PW MARKER STONE
KEEP RIGHT AFTER STILE - AIM FOR SLABS BELOW
CLEAR PATH THROUGH HEATHER
2 HRS 15 MINS–2 HRS 45 MINS FROM B6320 (MAP 114)
2 HRS–2 HRS 30 MINS TO B6320 (MAP 114)
MAP 115
0
¼ mile
0
APPROX SCALE
500m
CONCRETE BRIDGE OVER BLACK SIKE
HEATHER
264
114

ROUTE GUIDE AND MAPS

❑ Important note – walking times

Unless otherwise specified, **all times in this book refer only to the time spent walking**. You will need to add 20-30% to allow for rests, photography, checking the map, drinking water etc, not to mention time simply to stop and stare. When planning the day's hike count on 5-7 hours' actual walking.

BYRNESS **[Map 120, p257]**

These days this collection of buildings strung out along the A68 offers **barely enough** to fortify you for the final hurdle, so arrive prepared.

Forest View Walkers Inn (☎ 07928-376677, or ☎ 01830-520425, 🖳 forestview byrness.co.uk; 2S private facilities, 2D/2T/1Tr all en suite; Ⓛ; 🐕; Apr-Oct) provides dinner, bed & breakfast from £60pp; for any walker booking two nights DB&B (from £114pp) they provide a free pick up service from and to the halfway point on the final section of the Way. Booking is recommended. **Camping** is available if

2 HRS 30 MINS–3 HRS TO BLAKEHOPEBURNHAUGH (MAP 119) FROM GIB SHIEL ROAD (MAP 115)

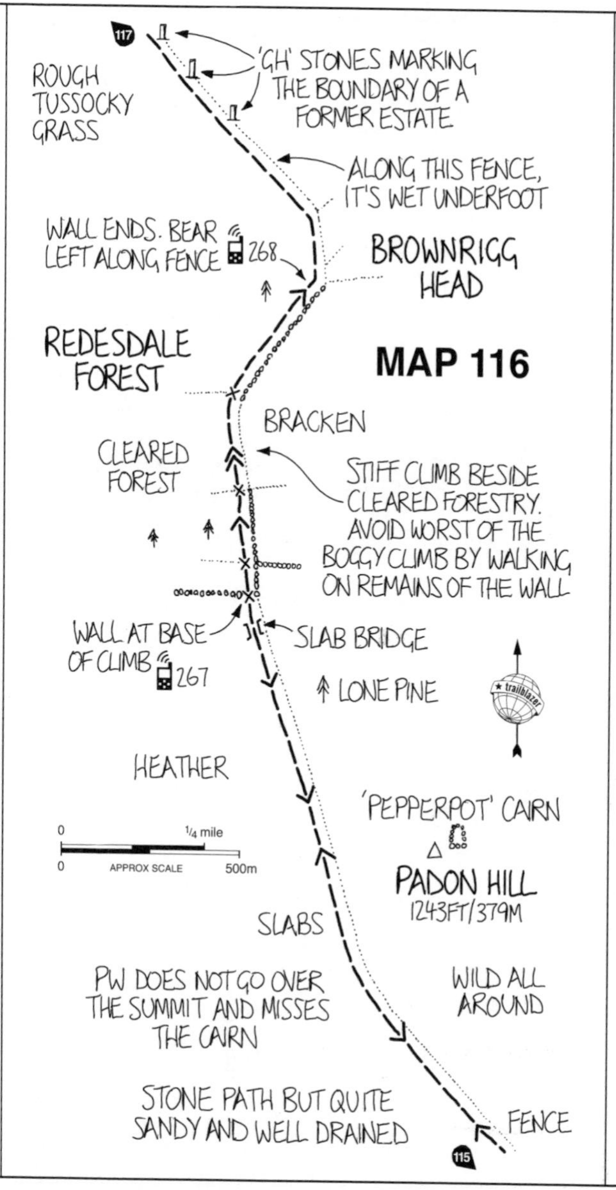
117
'GH' STONES MARKING THE BOUNDARY OF A FORMER ESTATE
ROUGH TUSSOCKY GRASS
ALONG THIS FENCE, IT'S WET UNDERFOOT
WALL ENDS. BEAR LEFT ALONG FENCE 268
BROWNRIGG HEAD
REDESDALE FOREST
MAP 116
BRACKEN
CLEARED FOREST
STIFF CLIMB BESIDE CLEARED FORESTRY. AVOID WORST OF THE BOGGY CLIMB BY WALKING ON REMAINS OF THE WALL
WALL AT BASE OF CLIMB 267
SLAB BRIDGE
LONE PINE
trailblazer
HEATHER
'PEPPERPOT' CAIRN
0
1/4 mile
0
APPROX SCALE
500m
PADON HILL
1243FT/379M
SLABS
PW DOES NOT GO OVER THE SUMMIT AND MISSES THE CAIRN
WILD ALL AROUND
STONE PATH BUT QUITE SANDY AND WELL DRAINED
FENCE
115

2 HRS 30 MINS–3 HRS FROM BLAKEHOPEBURNHAUGH (MAP 119) TO GIB SHIEL ROAD (MAP 115)

arranged in advance; campers have access to shower/toilet facilities and a drying room. There is also ***Foresters Restaurant & Bar*** (food served daily 6-7.45pm) and a **shop** (daily 4-10pm) selling basic supplies. Forest View also provide a transfer service (£17 for up to two bags Bellingham to Byrness, £28 for Byrness to Kirk Yetholm; all bags must be under 20kg) for anyone preferring to do the last stage without their baggage.

You'll pass round the back of ***Border Forest Holiday Park*** (see Map 119; ☎ 01830-520259, 💻 borderforest.com; 🐕) with **camping** for Pennine Way walkers only from £8pp including use of

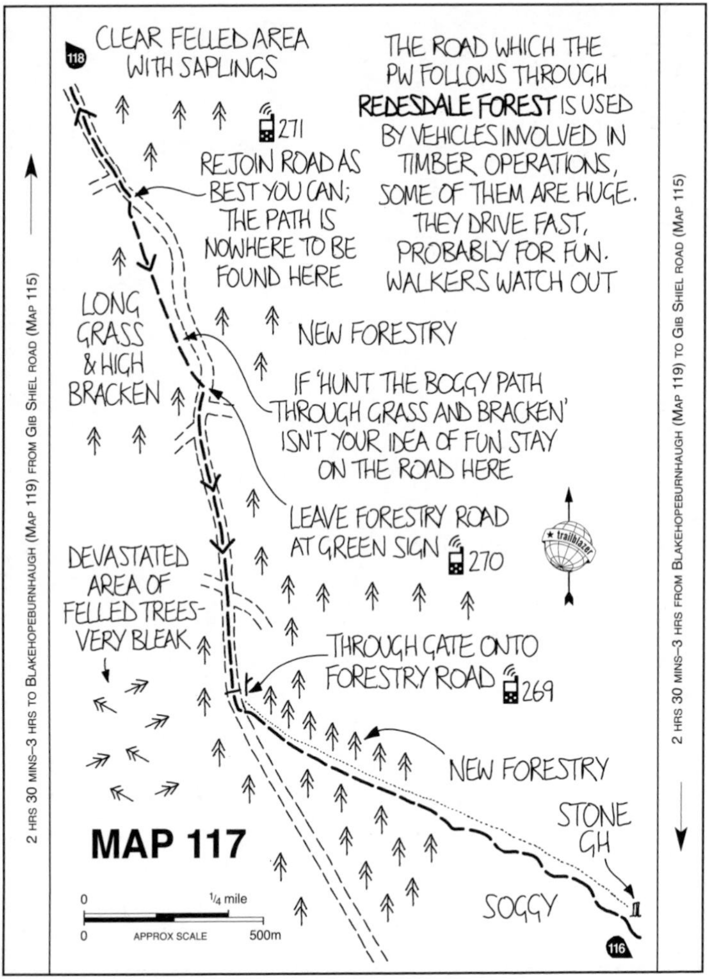

118
CLEAR FELLED AREA WITH SAPLINGS
271
THE ROAD WHICH THE PW FOLLOWS THROUGH REDESDALE FOREST IS USED BY VEHICLES INVOLVED IN TIMBER OPERATIONS, SOME OF THEM ARE HUGE. THEY DRIVE FAST, PROBABLY FOR FUN. WALKERS WATCH OUT
REJOIN ROAD AS BEST YOU CAN; THE PATH IS NOWHERE TO BE FOUND HERE
LONG GRASS & HIGH BRACKEN
NEW FORESTRY
IF 'HUNT THE BOGGY PATH THROUGH GRASS AND BRACKEN' ISN'T YOUR IDEA OF FUN STAY ON THE ROAD HERE
LEAVE FORESTRY ROAD AT GREEN SIGN
270
trailblazer
DEVASTATED AREA OF FELLED TREES- VERY BLEAK
THROUGH GATE ONTO FORESTRY ROAD
269
NEW FORESTRY
STONE GH
SOGGY
116
MAP 117
0
1/4 mile
0
APPROX SCALE
500m
2 HRS 30 MINS–3 HRS TO BLAKEHOPEBURNHAUGH (MAP 119) FROM GIB SHIEL ROAD (MAP 115)
2 HRS 30 MINS–3 HRS FROM BLAKEHOPEBURNHAUGH (MAP 119) TO GIB SHIEL ROAD (MAP 115)

2 hrs 30 mins–3 hrs to Blakehopeburnhaugh (Map 119) from Gib Shiel road (Map 115)

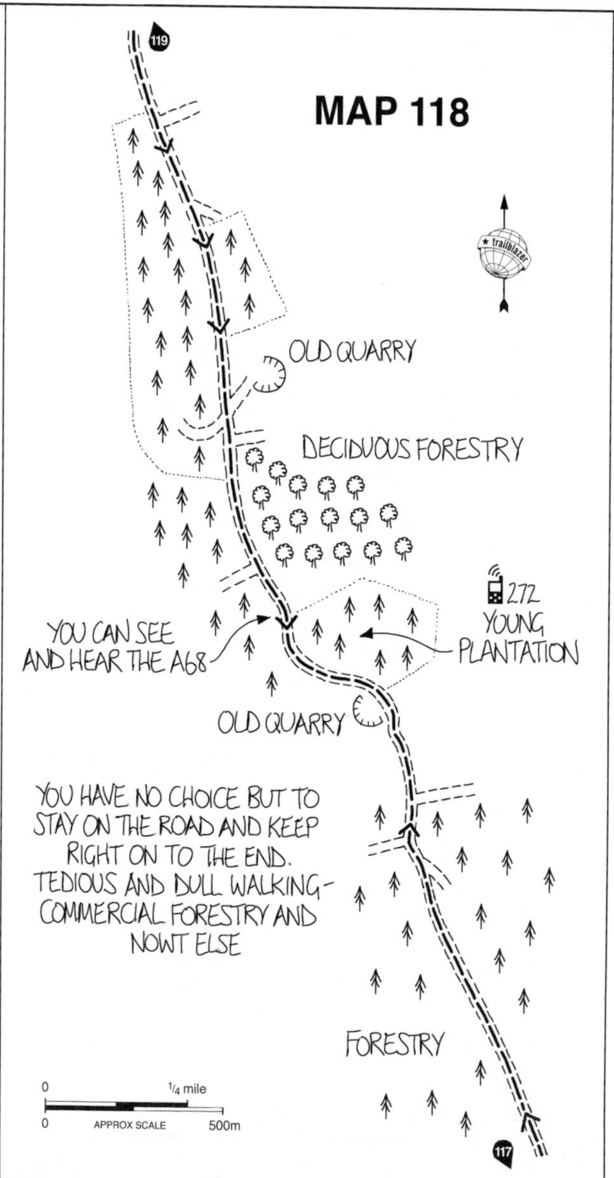
MAP 118
119
OLD QUARRY
DECIDUOUS FORESTRY
272
YOUNG PLANTATION
YOU CAN SEE AND HEAR THE A68
OLD QUARRY
YOU HAVE NO CHOICE BUT TO STAY ON THE ROAD AND KEEP RIGHT ON TO THE END. TEDIOUS AND DULL WALKING-COMMERCIAL FORESTRY AND NOWT ELSE
FORESTRY
0
1/4 mile
0
APPROX SCALE
500m
117

2 hrs 30 mins–3 hrs from Blakehopeburnhaugh (Map 119) to Gib Shiel road (Map 115)

shower/toilet facilities. They also three offer **pods** (£35-45 per pod); each pod has lighting and heating and can sleep up to three adults but there are no beds so you need to bring your own bedding. Booking is essential for the pods. There is no shop, bar or restaurant on site but they do have a kitchen area with a microwave oven and a fridge/freezer.

Peter Hogg of Jedburgh operate a **bus** service (No 131; Jedbergh–Newcastle) via here (see pp54-9).

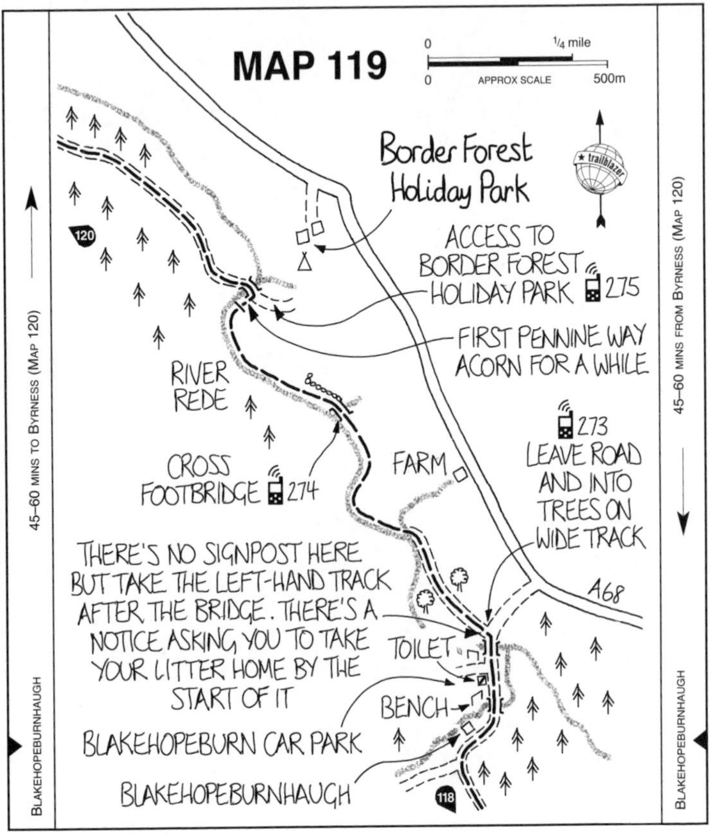
MAP 119
0
¼ mile
0
APPROX SCALE
500m
trailblazer
Border Forest Holiday Park
ACCESS TO BORDER FOREST HOLIDAY PARK 275
FIRST PENNINE WAY ACORN FOR A WHILE
RIVER REDE
CROSS FOOTBRIDGE 274
FARM
273 LEAVE ROAD AND INTO TREES ON WIDE TRACK
A68
THERE'S NO SIGNPOST HERE BUT TAKE THE LEFT-HAND TRACK AFTER THE BRIDGE. THERE'S A NOTICE ASKING YOU TO TAKE YOUR LITTER HOME BY THE START OF IT
TOILET
BENCH
BLAKEHOPEBURN CAR PARK
BLAKEHOPEBURNHAUGH
120
118
45–60 MINS TO BYRNESS (MAP 120)
45–60 MINS FROM BYRNESS (MAP 120)
BLAKEHOPEBURNHAUGH
BLAKEHOPEBURNHAUGH

BYRNESS TO KIRK YETHOLM — MAPS 120-135

Route overview

25½ miles (41km) – 4800ft (1463m) of ascent – 10½-13 hours

This is possibly one of the longest single day walks you'll ever do, but you're ready; let's face it, you've been training for this for the last two weeks! It may

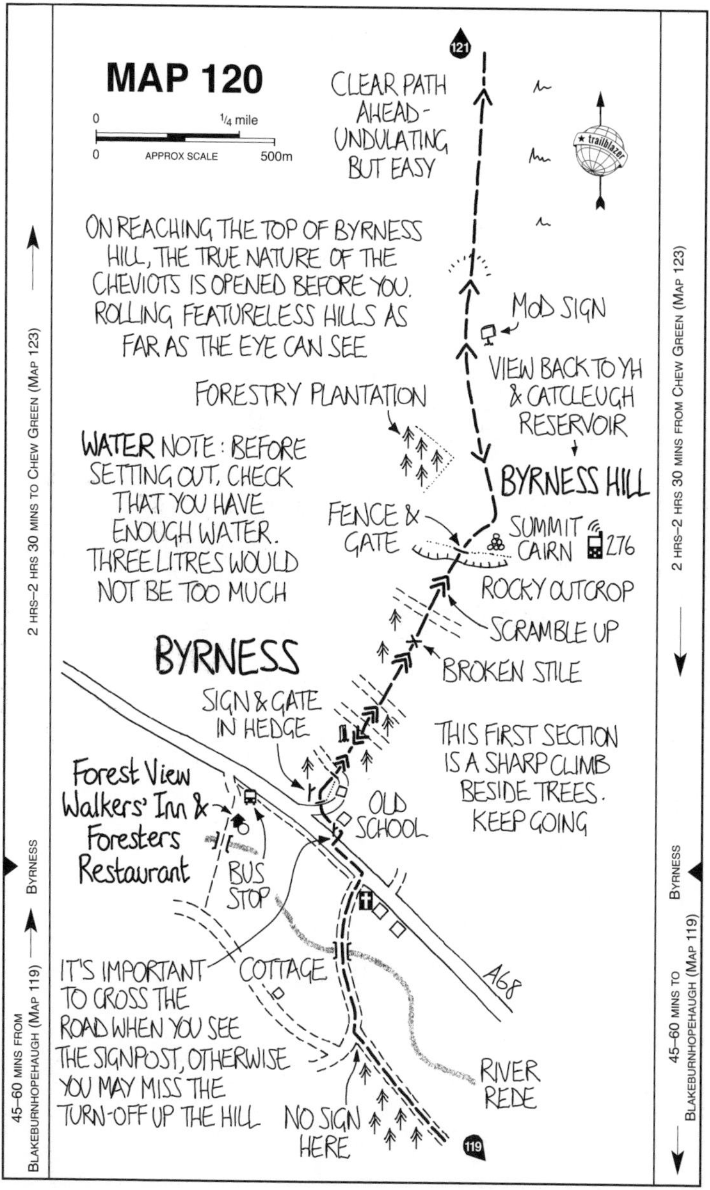
MAP 120
0 1/4 mile
0 APPROX SCALE 500m
121
CLEAR PATH AHEAD - UNDULATING BUT EASY
trailblazer
ON REACHING THE TOP OF BYRNESS HILL, THE TRUE NATURE OF THE CHEVIOTS IS OPENED BEFORE YOU. ROLLING FEATURELESS HILLS AS FAR AS THE EYE CAN SEE
MOD SIGN
VIEW BACK TO YH & CATCLEUGH RESERVOIR
FORESTRY PLANTATION
WATER NOTE: BEFORE SETTING OUT, CHECK THAT YOU HAVE ENOUGH WATER. THREE LITRES WOULD NOT BE TOO MUCH
BYRNESS HILL
FENCE & GATE
SUMMIT CAIRN
276
ROCKY OUTCROP
SCRAMBLE UP
BYRNESS
BROKEN STILE
SIGN & GATE IN HEDGE
THIS FIRST SECTION IS A SHARP CLIMB BESIDE TREES. KEEP GOING
Forest View Walkers' Inn & Foresters Restaurant
OLD SCHOOL
BUS STOP
A68
IT'S IMPORTANT TO CROSS THE ROAD WHEN YOU SEE THE SIGNPOST, OTHERWISE YOU MAY MISS THE TURN-OFF UP THE HILL
COTTAGE
RIVER REDE
NO SIGN HERE
119
2 HRS–2 HRS 30 MINS TO CHEW GREEN (MAP 123)
BYRNESS
45–60 MINS FROM BLAKEBURNHOPEHAUGH (MAP 119)
2 HRS–2 HRS 30 MINS FROM CHEW GREEN (MAP 123)
BYRNESS
45–60 MINS TO BLAKEBURNHOPEHAUGH (MAP 119)

2 HRS–2 HRS 30 MINS TO CHEW GREEN (MAP 123) FROM BYRNESS (MAP 120)

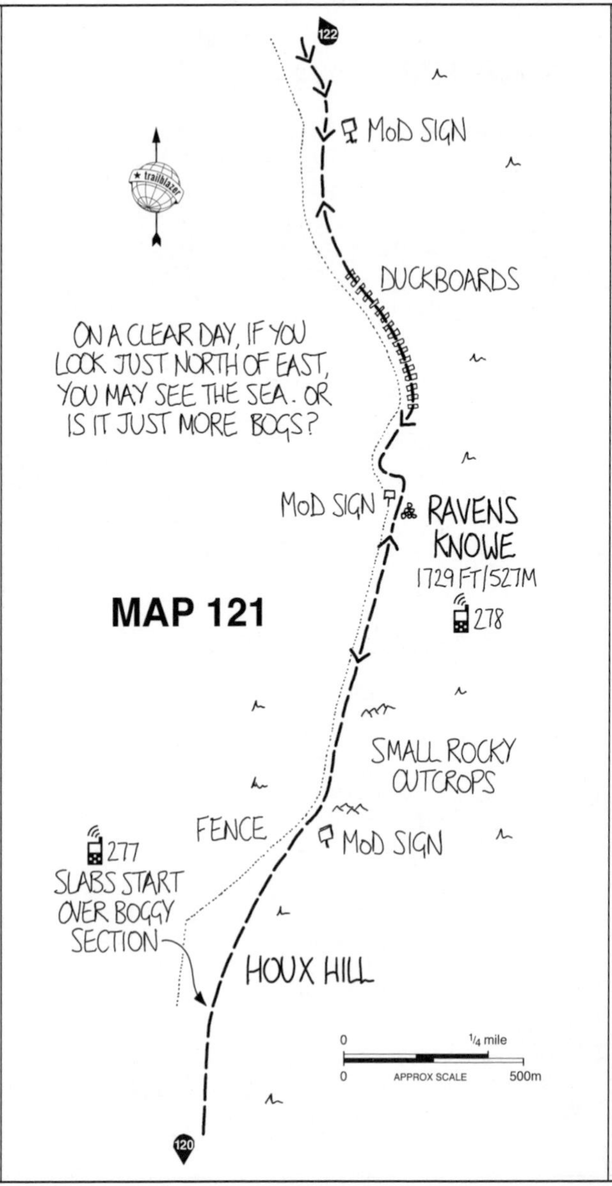
MOD SIGN
DUCKBOARDS
ON A CLEAR DAY, IF YOU LOOK JUST NORTH OF EAST, YOU MAY SEE THE SEA. OR IS IT JUST MORE BOGS?
MOD SIGN
RAVENS KNOWE
1729FT/527M
278
MAP 121
SMALL ROCKY OUTCROPS
FENCE
MOD SIGN
277
SLABS START OVER BOGGY SECTION
HOUX HILL
0
1/4 mile
0
APPROX SCALE
500m
122
120
trailblazer

2 HRS–2 HRS 30 MINS FROM CHEW GREEN (MAP 123) TO BYRNESS (MAP 120)

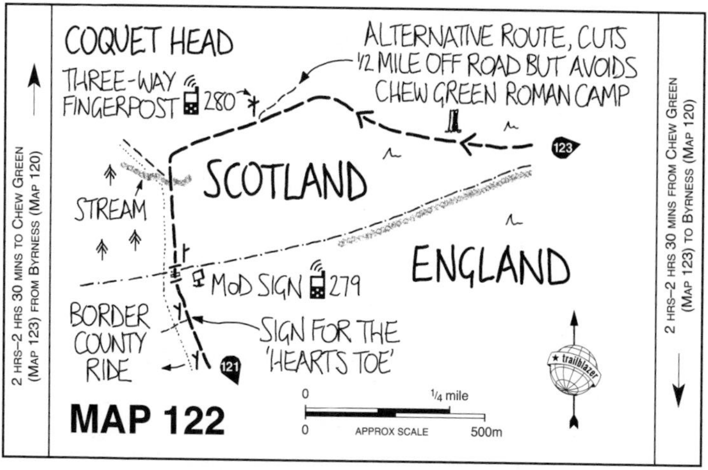
COQUET HEAD
THREE-WAY FINGERPOST 280
ALTERNATIVE ROUTE, CUTS ½ MILE OFF ROAD BUT AVOIDS CHEW GREEN ROMAN CAMP
123
SCOTLAND
STREAM
ENGLAND
MoD SIGN 279
BORDER COUNTY RIDE
SIGN FOR THE 'HEARTS TOE'
121
MAP 122
0
¼ mile
0
APPROX SCALE
500m
trailblazer
2 HRS–2 HRS 30 MINS TO CHEW GREEN (MAP 120) FROM BYRNESS (MAP 123)
2 HRS–2 HRS 30 MINS FROM CHEW GREEN (MAP 123) TO BYRNESS (MAP 120)

be almost as long as a marathon and have nearly a whole mile of vertical ascent, but thousands of Pennine Wayfarers have done it and so can you.

You would be advised to start early and give yourself plenty of time to complete this section; the accommodation options in Byrness are used to early departures. You may not get a cooked breakfast, or even a cheery wave at 5am, but you will be able to set out early.

Make sure you are carrying plenty of water when you set out, especially if warm weather is forecast, as there are almost no places to find running water, unless you're prepared to drop off the ridge and find a spring. The only exception is at Chew Green (see Map 123) and is marked on that map in this book, though even here you will need to treat the water – there are a lot of sheep grazing nearby. Ideally you should also be looking to have enough food/snacks for at least two meal breaks – it's a long day.

For those who decide to make two days of it, you'll enjoy it even more. Wild camping offers the freedom of the hills but it might be necessary to drop down off the exposed plateau. Alternatively you could spend the night in one of two identical **refuge huts** (Map 125 and Map 131) with room for up to six on the floor. There's no water at either although notes tell you where to look. Just after the second refuge hut, about six or seven miles before Kirk Yetholm, a path leads down to Mounthooly Bunkhouse (see p262).

Aside from wild camping, the refuge huts and the bunkhouse, the only accommodation options between Byrness and Kirk Yetholm are those provided at Barrowburn Farm (see p271) in Upper Coquetdale, usually reached from the summit of Windy Gyle (Map 127). This is a 3½-mile detour, losing over 300 metres of height along a good path from Windy Gyle.

Remember, this is one more option for those looking to stretch the walk over two days: if you have booked two nights at Forest View Walkers' Inn, or

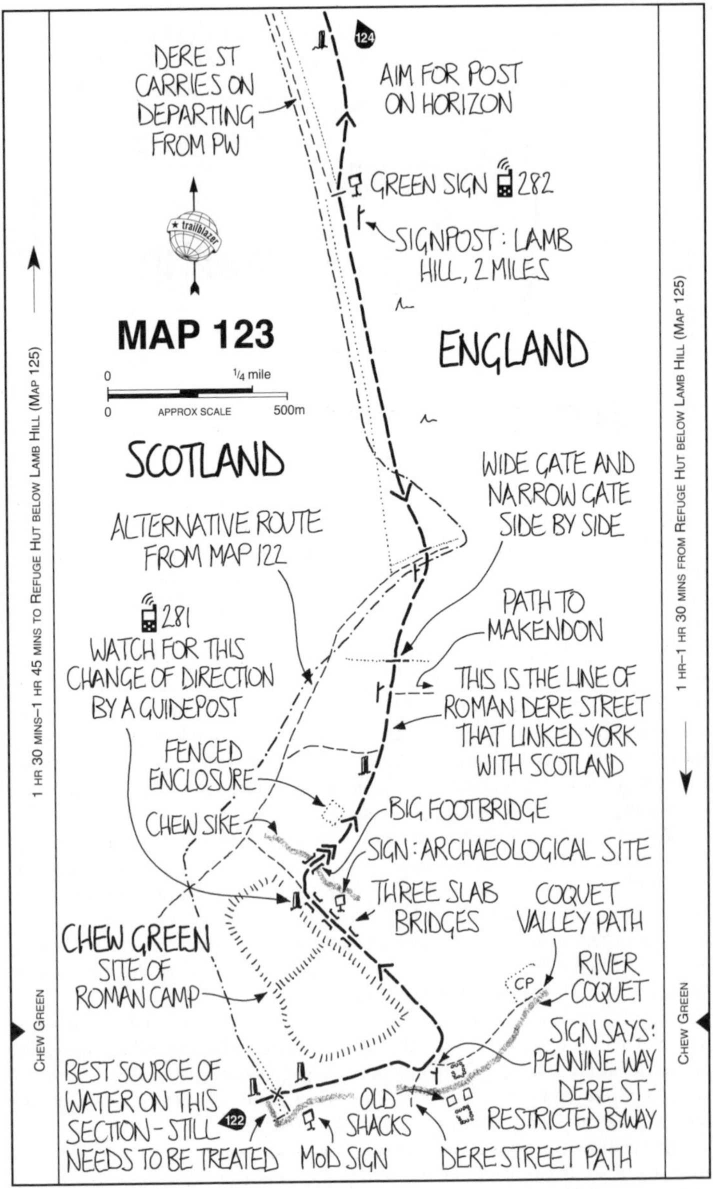
MAP 123
0 1/4 mile
0 APPROX SCALE 500m
1 HR 30 MINS–1 HR 45 MINS TO REFUGE HUT BELOW LAMB HILL (MAP 125)
1 HR–1 HR 30 MINS FROM REFUGE HUT BELOW LAMB HILL (MAP 125)
124
DERE ST CARRIES ON DEPARTING FROM PW
AIM FOR POST ON HORIZON
GREEN SIGN 282
SIGNPOST: LAMB HILL, 2 MILES
ENGLAND
SCOTLAND
WIDE GATE AND NARROW GATE SIDE BY SIDE
ALTERNATIVE ROUTE FROM MAP 122
PATH TO MAKENDON
281
WATCH FOR THIS CHANGE OF DIRECTION BY A GUIDEPOST
THIS IS THE LINE OF ROMAN DERE STREET THAT LINKED YORK WITH SCOTLAND
FENCED ENCLOSURE
BIG FOOTBRIDGE
CHEW SIKE
SIGN: ARCHAEOLOGICAL SITE
THREE SLAB BRIDGES
COQUET VALLEY PATH
CHEW GREEN
SITE OF ROMAN CAMP
RIVER COQUET
CP
SIGN SAYS: PENNINE WAY DERE ST- RESTRICTED BYWAY
BEST SOURCE OF WATER ON THIS SECTION - STILL NEEDS TO BE TREATED
122
OLD SHACKS
MoD SIGN
DERE STREET PATH
CHEW GREEN
CHEW GREEN

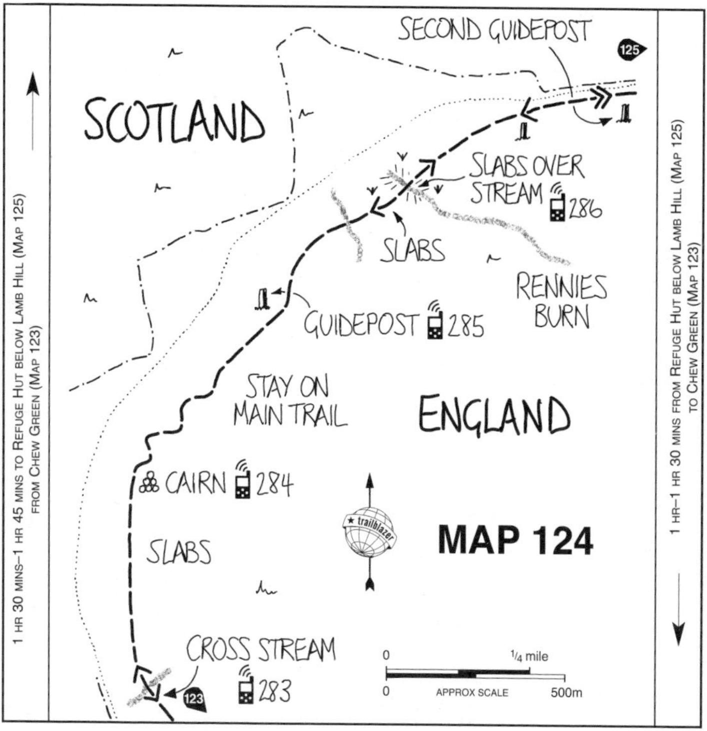
1 HR 30 MINS–1 HR 45 MINS TO REFUGE HUT BELOW LAMB HILL (MAP 125)
FROM CHEW GREEN (MAP 123)
SECOND GUIDEPOST
125
SCOTLAND
SLABS OVER STREAM 286
SLABS
RENNIES BURN
GUIDEPOST 285
STAY ON MAIN TRAIL
ENGLAND
CAIRN 284
SLABS
MAP 124
CROSS STREAM
283
123
0 ¼ mile
0 APPROX SCALE 500m
1 HR–1 HR 30 MINS FROM REFUGE HUT BELOW LAMB HILL (MAP 125)
TO CHEW GREEN (MAP 123)

Mill House B&B at Kirk Yetholm (see p271), they will pick you up and drop you off from the track at Cocklawfoot, about two miles south of Windy Gyle.

Leaving Byrness you're faced with the inevitable steep climb up between trees to the airy summit of **Byrness Hill** (Map 120). Take a breather and enjoy the incredible views behind and ahead, but don't linger too long, there is a long way to go. Some slabs help you cross the previously appalling bog on **Houx Hill** (Map 121) and over **Ravens Knowe** to some anonymous grassy lumps; all that remains of the Roman Camp at **Chew Green** (Map 123).

The slabs are intermittent along the whole of the ridge; they help navigation, reduce the chances of being swallowed by the bogs and act as rhythm-maintaining tram rails.

The roller-coaster ridge can take its toll on your legs and you'll be pleased to arrive at the first **Refuge Hut** at the foot of **Lamb Hill** (Map 125), about eight miles (12.9km) and four hours into the walk. A wonderful respite from wind and rain and a pleasant wooden bench to sit on in the sun.

The next eight miles are undoubtedly the hardest, with long ascent followed by long descent, seemingly ad infinitum. The trig point on **Windy Gyle** (Map

127) marks the approximate halfway point and the climb up **King's Seat** (Map 129) and up to the foot of **The Cheviot** (Map 130) will seem never-ending. The optional diversion to The Cheviot's summit is skipped by most full-length walkers, for obvious reasons and you'll be wishing you could skip the knee-crunching descent from **Auchope Cairn** too. A short break in the **second Refuge Hut** (Map 131) may recharge your batteries for the steepest ascent of the day, up to The Schil.

Just after the refuge hut a path leads down to ***Mounthooly Bunkhouse*** (off Map 131; ☎ 01668-216210, 💻 college-valley.co.uk/Mounthooly.htm; 1 x 4-bed en suite, 1T & 2 x 9-bed rooms shared facilities; no WI-FI; 🐕). Showers, cooking facilities, bedding and a drying room are provided. A bed costs from £17pp (£14 for students; private room from £65); book in advance particularly in the summer months. The bunkhouse is about 1½ miles from the Pennine Way and involves a steep descent of over 200 metres into College Valley and a steep climb back up the next day.

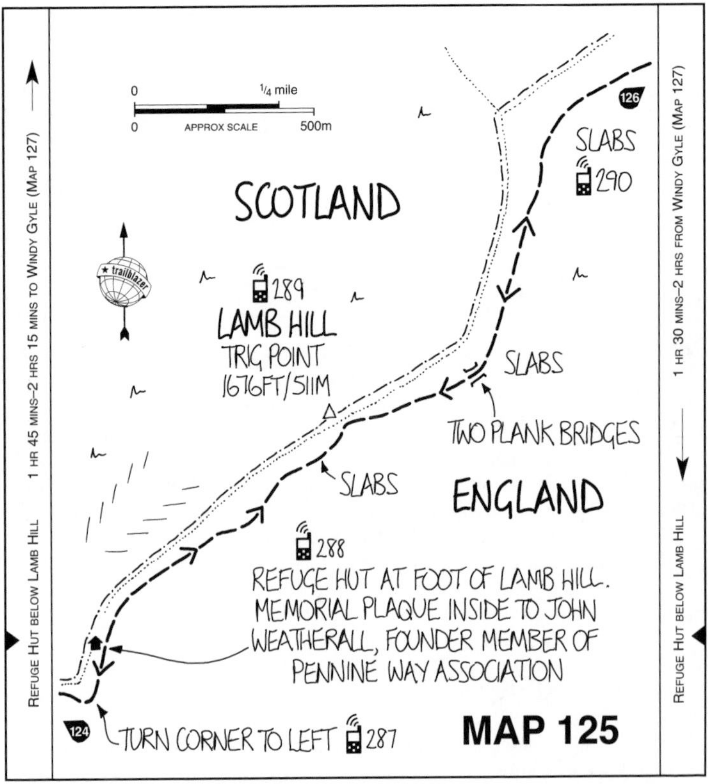
1 HR 45 MINS–2 HRS 15 MINS TO WINDY GYLE (MAP 127)
REFUGE HUT BELOW LAMB HILL
1 HR 30 MINS–2 HRS FROM WINDY GYLE (MAP 127)
REFUGE HUT BELOW LAMB HILL
0
1/4 mile
0
APPROX SCALE
500m
126
SLABS
290
SCOTLAND
289
LAMB HILL
TRIG POINT
1676FT/511M
SLABS
TWO PLANK BRIDGES
SLABS
ENGLAND
288
REFUGE HUT AT FOOT OF LAMB HILL.
MEMORIAL PLAQUE INSIDE TO JOHN
WEATHERALL, FOUNDER MEMBER OF
PENNINE WAY ASSOCIATION
124
TURN CORNER TO LEFT
287
MAP 125

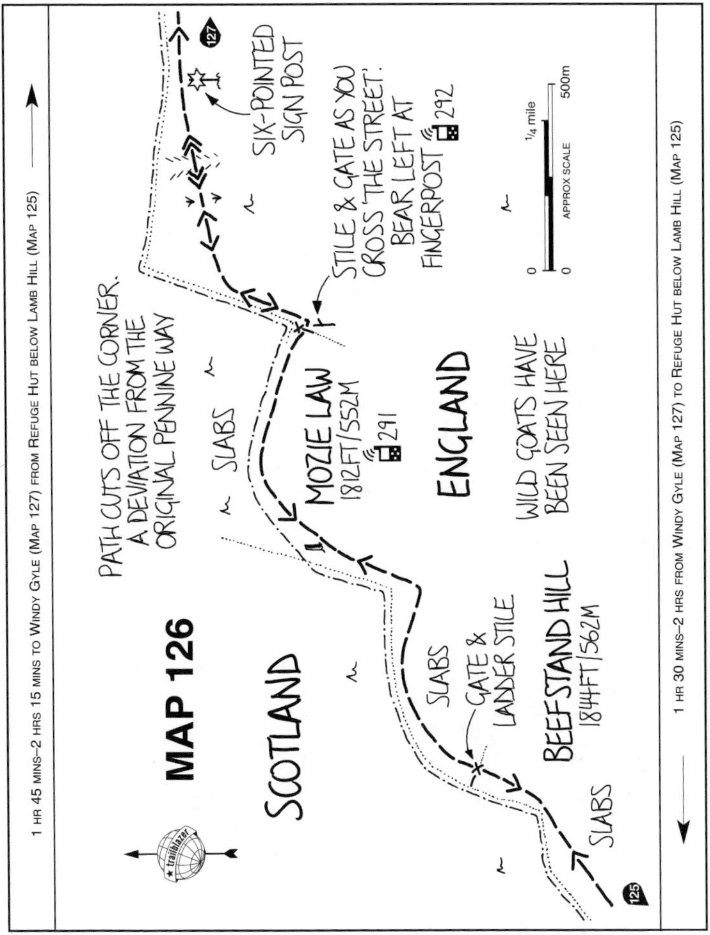
1 HR 45 MINS–2 HRS 15 MINS TO WINDY GYLE (MAP 127) FROM REFUGE HUT BELOW LAMB HILL (MAP 125)
MAP 126
SCOTLAND
PATH CUTS OFF THE CORNER. A DEVIATION FROM THE ORIGINAL PENNINE WAY
SLABS
MOZIE LAW 1812FT/552M
291
ENGLAND
WILD GOATS HAVE BEEN SEEN HERE
STILE & GATE AS YOU CROSS 'THE STREET'. BEAR LEFT AT FINGERPOST
292
SIX-POINTED SIGN POST
127
GATE & LADDER STILE
BEEFSTAND HILL 1844FT/562M
125
0 1/4 mile
0 500m
APPROX SCALE
1 HR 30 MINS–2 HRS FROM WINDY GYLE (MAP 127) TO REFUGE HUT BELOW LAMB HILL (MAP 125)

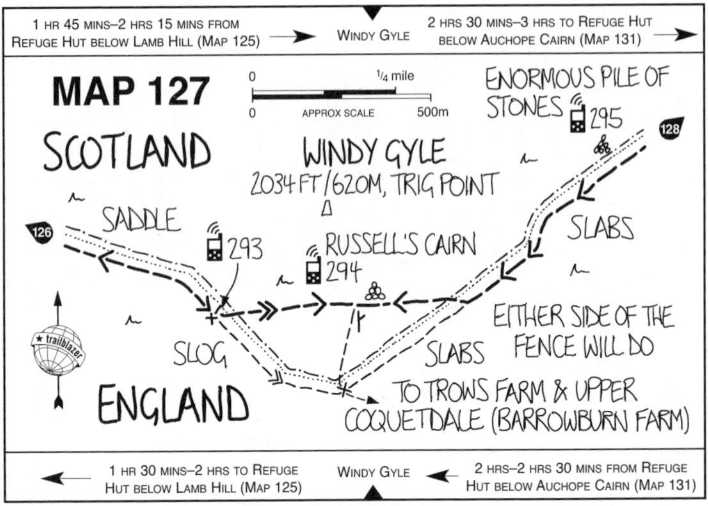
1 HR 45 MINS–2 HRS 15 MINS FROM REFUGE HUT BELOW LAMB HILL (MAP 125)
WINDY GYLE
2 HRS 30 MINS–3 HRS TO REFUGE HUT BELOW AUCHOPE CAIRN (MAP 131)
MAP 127
0 1/4 mile
0 APPROX SCALE 500m
ENORMOUS PILE OF STONES
295
128
SCOTLAND
WINDY GYLE
2034 FT/620M, TRIG POINT
126
SADDLE
293
RUSSELL'S CAIRN
294
SLABS
EITHER SIDE OF THE FENCE WILL DO
SLOG
SLABS
ENGLAND
TO TROWS FARM & UPPER COQUETDALE (BARROWBURN FARM)
1 HR 30 MINS–2 HRS TO REFUGE HUT BELOW LAMB HILL (MAP 125)
WINDY GYLE
2 HRS–2 HRS 30 MINS FROM REFUGE HUT BELOW AUCHOPE CAIRN (MAP 131)

Just beyond **The Schil**, you have to choose between more roller-coaster hills along the high route, or the more mundane, but easier, lower route. The high route is the official path and is well worth the effort it will require.

(cont'd on p269)

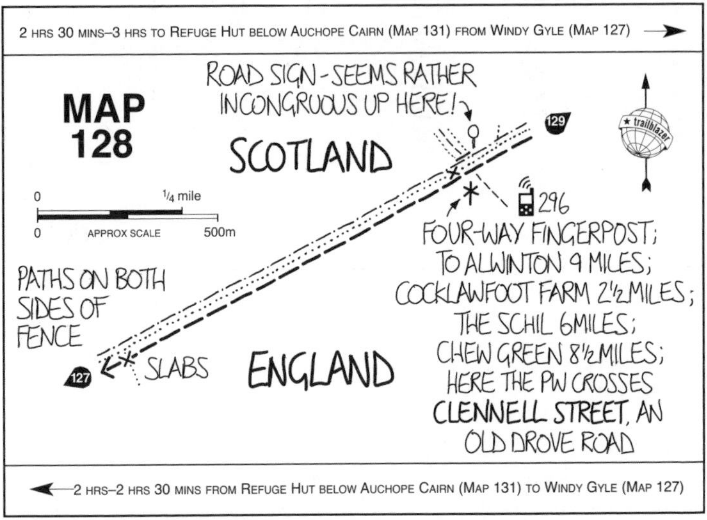
2 HRS 30 MINS–3 HRS TO REFUGE HUT BELOW AUCHOPE CAIRN (MAP 131) FROM WINDY GYLE (MAP 127)
MAP 128
ROAD SIGN - SEEMS RATHER INCONGRUOUS UP HERE!
129
SCOTLAND
0 1/4 mile
0 APPROX SCALE 500m
296
FOUR-WAY FINGERPOST; TO ALWINTON 9 MILES; COCKLAWFOOT FARM 2½ MILES; THE SCHIL 6MILES; CHEW GREEN 8½ MILES; HERE THE PW CROSSES CLENNELL STREET, AN OLD DROVE ROAD
PATHS ON BOTH SIDES OF FENCE
127
SLABS
ENGLAND
2 HRS–2 HRS 30 MINS FROM REFUGE HUT BELOW AUCHOPE CAIRN (MAP 131) TO WINDY GYLE (MAP 127)

2 HRS 30 MINS–3 HRS TO REFUGE HUT BELOW AUCHOPE CAIRN (MAP 131) FROM WINDY GYLE (MAP 127)

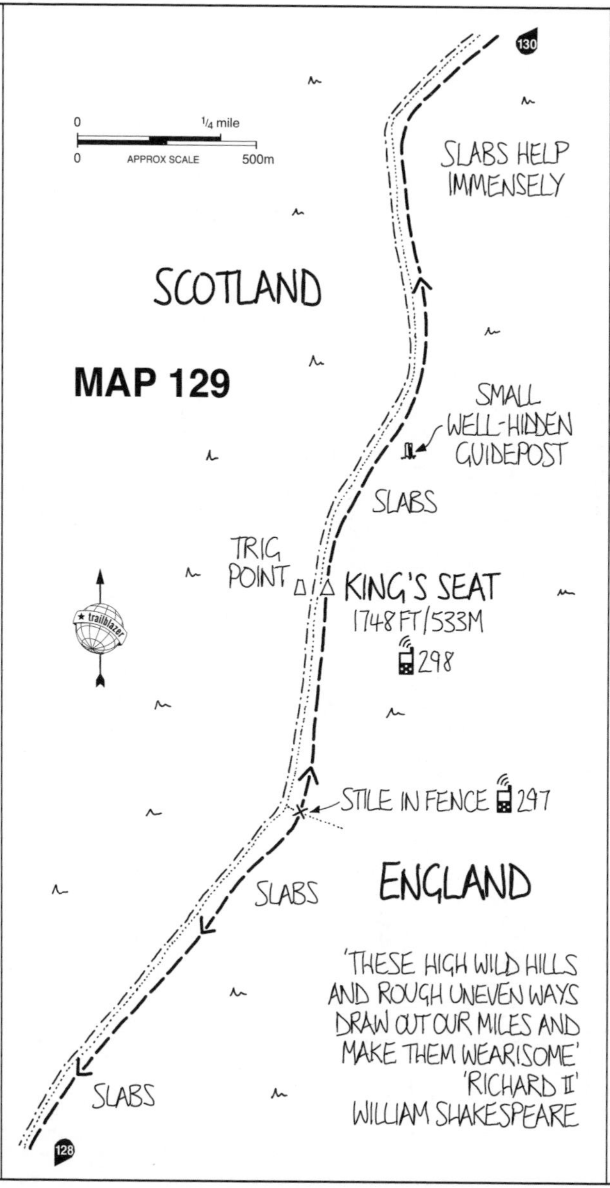
130
0
1/4 mile
0
APPROX SCALE
500m
SLABS HELP IMMENSELY
SCOTLAND
MAP 129
SMALL WELL-HIDDEN GUIDEPOST
SLABS
TRIG POINT
KING'S SEAT
1748 FT/533M
298
★ trailblazer
STILE IN FENCE
297
ENGLAND
SLABS
'THESE HIGH WILD HILLS AND ROUGH UNEVEN WAYS DRAW OUT OUR MILES AND MAKE THEM WEARISOME'
'RICHARD II'
WILLIAM SHAKESPEARE
SLABS
128

2 HRS–2 HRS 30 MINS FROM REFUGE HUT BELOW AUCHOPE CAIRN (MAP 131) TO WINDY GYLE (MAP 127)

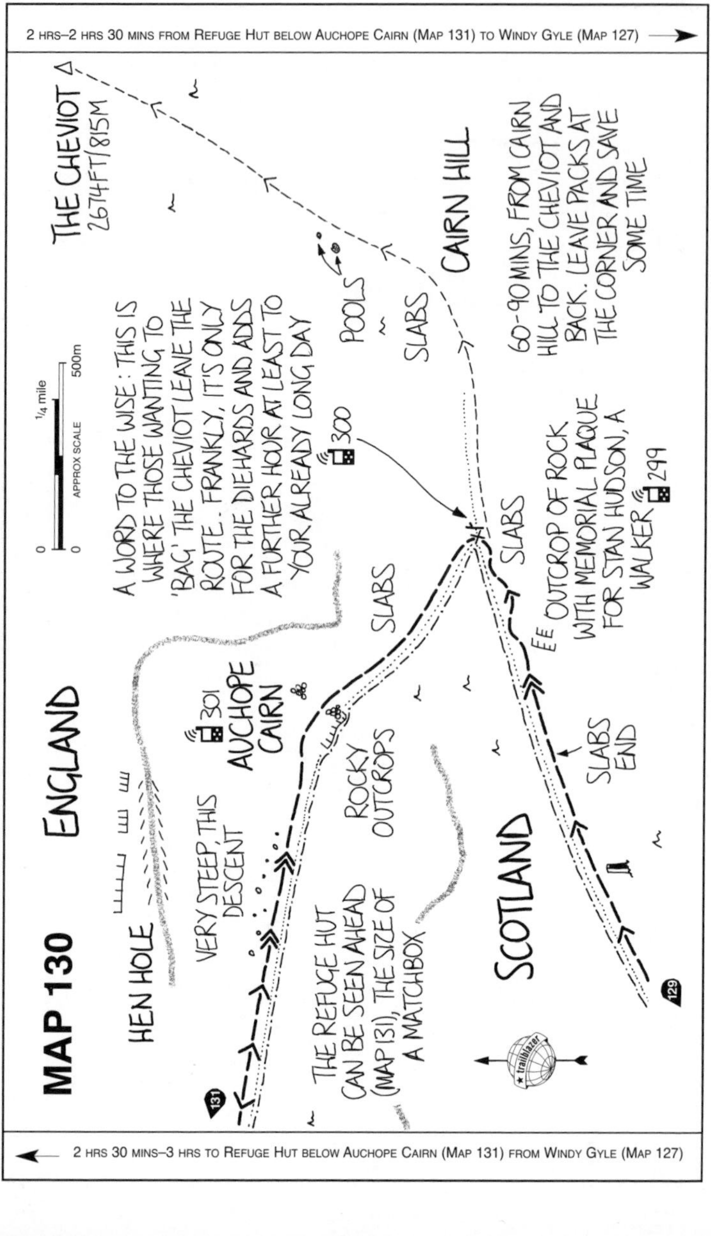
2 HRS–2 HRS 30 MINS FROM REFUGE HUT BELOW AUCHOPE CAIRN (MAP 131) TO WINDY GYLE (MAP 127)
MAP 130
ENGLAND
SCOTLAND
HEN HOLE
VERY STEEP, THIS DESCENT
THE REFUGE HUT CAN BE SEEN AHEAD (MAP 131), THE SIZE OF A MATCHBOX
ROCKY OUTCROPS
301
AUCHOPE CAIRN
SLABS
A WORD TO THE WISE : THIS IS WHERE THOSE WANTING TO 'BAG' THE CHEVIOT LEAVE THE ROUTE. FRANKLY, IT'S ONLY FOR THE DIEHARDS AND ADDS A FURTHER HOUR AT LEAST TO YOUR ALREADY LONG DAY
300
0 APPROX SCALE 1/4 mile 0 500m
POOLS
SLABS
THE CHEVIOT
2674FT/815M
CAIRN HILL
60-90 MINS, FROM CAIRN HILL TO THE CHEVIOT AND BACK. LEAVE PACKS AT THE CORNER AND SAVE SOME TIME
SLABS
OUTCROP OF ROCK WITH MEMORIAL PLAQUE FOR STAN HUDSON, A WALKER
299
SLABS END
131
129
trailblazer
2 HRS 30 MINS–3 HRS TO REFUGE HUT BELOW AUCHOPE CAIRN (MAP 131) FROM WINDY GYLE (MAP 127)

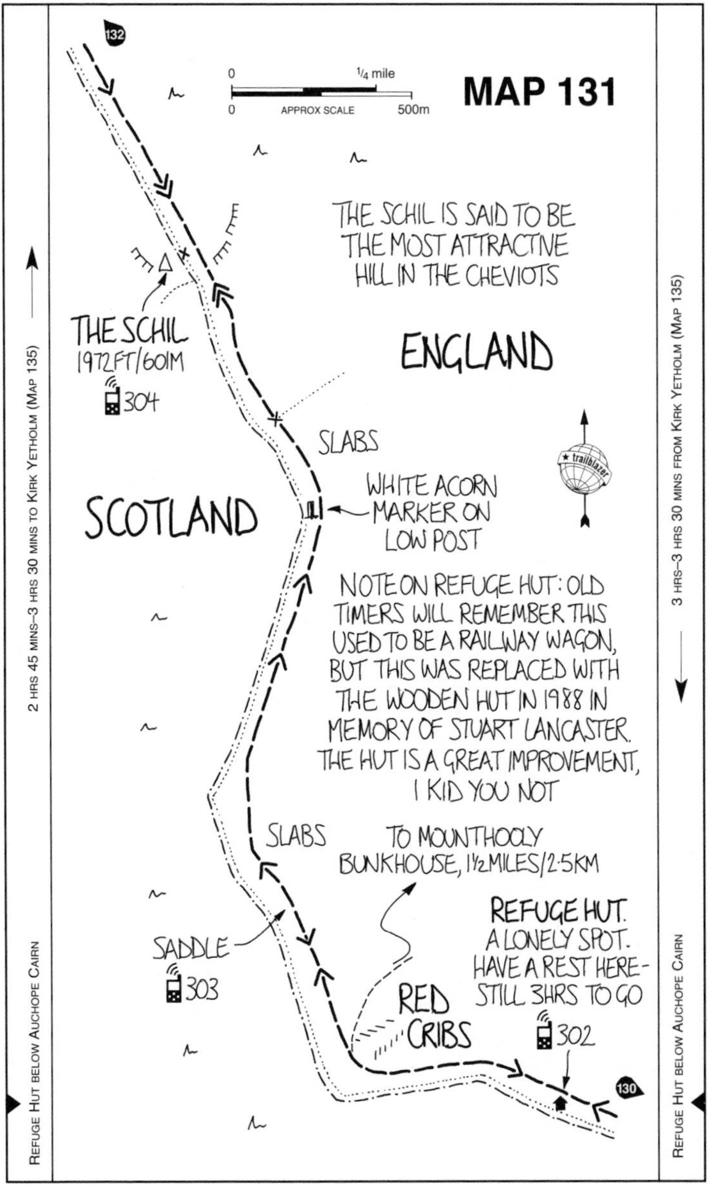
MAP 131
0 1/4 mile
0 APPROX SCALE 500m
THE SCHIL IS SAID TO BE THE MOST ATTRACTIVE HILL IN THE CHEVIOTS
THE SCHIL 1972FT/601M
304
ENGLAND
SCOTLAND
SLABS
WHITE ACORN MARKER ON LOW POST
NOTE ON REFUGE HUT: OLD TIMERS WILL REMEMBER THIS USED TO BE A RAILWAY WAGON, BUT THIS WAS REPLACED WITH THE WOODEN HUT IN 1988 IN MEMORY OF STUART LANCASTER. THE HUT IS A GREAT IMPROVEMENT, I KID YOU NOT
SLABS
TO MOUNTHOOLY BUNKHOUSE, 1½MILES/2.5KM
REFUGE HUT. A LONELY SPOT. HAVE A REST HERE - STILL 3HRS TO GO
SADDLE
303
RED CRIBS
302
132
130
2 HRS 45 MINS–3 HRS 30 MINS TO KIRK YETHOLM (MAP 135)
3 HRS–3 HRS 30 MINS FROM KIRK YETHOLM (MAP 135)
REFUGE HUT BELOW AUCHOPE CAIRN
REFUGE HUT BELOW AUCHOPE CAIRN

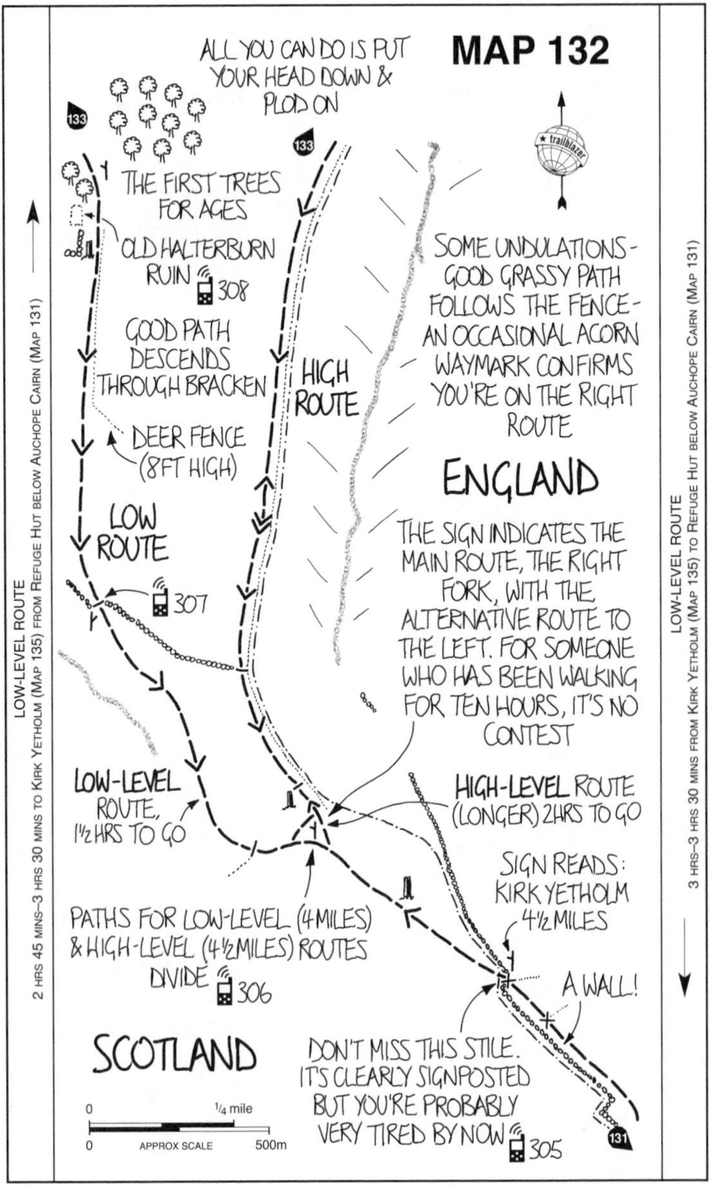
MAP 132
ALL YOU CAN DO IS PUT YOUR HEAD DOWN & PLOD ON
133
133
THE FIRST TREES FOR AGES
OLD HALTERBURN RUIN 308
GOOD PATH DESCENDS THROUGH BRACKEN
DEER FENCE (8FT HIGH)
LOW ROUTE
HIGH ROUTE
SOME UNDULATIONS - GOOD GRASSY PATH FOLLOWS THE FENCE - AN OCCASIONAL ACORN WAYMARK CONFIRMS YOU'RE ON THE RIGHT ROUTE
ENGLAND
THE SIGN INDICATES THE MAIN ROUTE, THE RIGHT FORK, WITH THE ALTERNATIVE ROUTE TO THE LEFT. FOR SOMEONE WHO HAS BEEN WALKING FOR TEN HOURS, IT'S NO CONTEST
307
LOW-LEVEL ROUTE, 1½ HRS TO GO
HIGH-LEVEL ROUTE (LONGER) 2HRS TO GO
SIGN READS: KIRK YETHOLM 4½ MILES
PATHS FOR LOW-LEVEL (4 MILES) & HIGH-LEVEL (4½ MILES) ROUTES DIVIDE 306
A WALL!
SCOTLAND
DON'T MISS THIS STILE. IT'S CLEARLY SIGNPOSTED BUT YOU'RE PROBABLY VERY TIRED BY NOW 305
131
0 ¼ mile
0 APPROX SCALE 500m
LOW-LEVEL ROUTE
2 HRS 45 MINS–3 HRS 30 MINS TO KIRK YETHOLM (MAP 135) FROM REFUGE HUT BELOW AUCHOPE CAIRN (MAP 131)
LOW-LEVEL ROUTE
3 HRS–3 HRS 30 MINS FROM KIRK YETHOLM (MAP 135) TO REFUGE HUT BELOW AUCHOPE CAIRN (MAP 131)

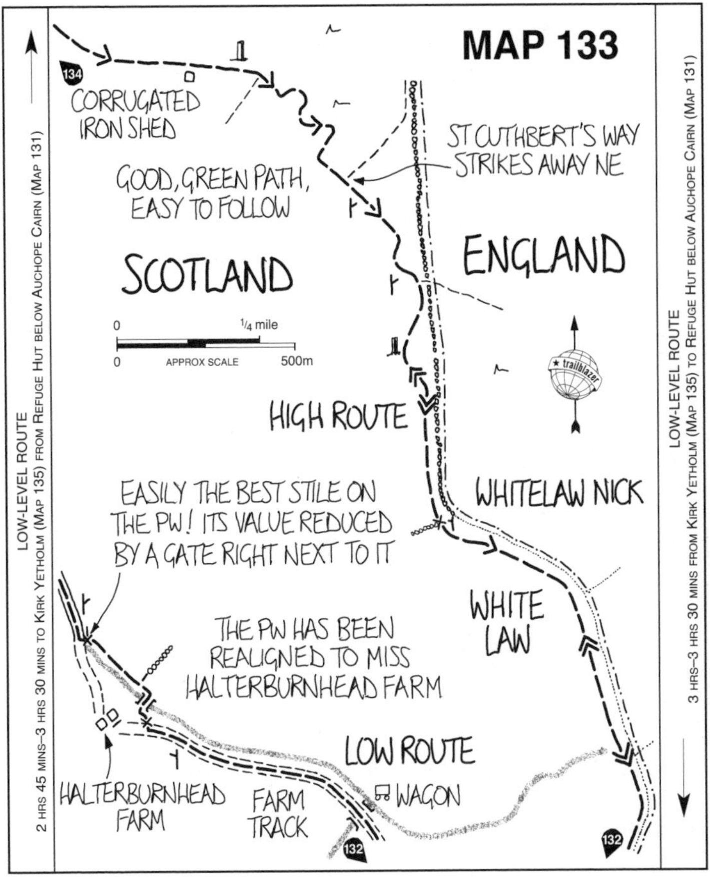
MAP 133
LOW-LEVEL ROUTE
2 HRS 45 MINS–3 HRS 30 MINS TO KIRK YETHOLM (MAP 135) FROM REFUGE HUT BELOW AUCHOPE CAIRN (MAP 131)
LOW-LEVEL ROUTE
3 HRS–3 HRS 30 MINS FROM KIRK YETHOLM (MAP 135) TO REFUGE HUT BELOW AUCHOPE CAIRN (MAP 131)
134
CORRUGATED IRON SHED
GOOD, GREEN PATH, EASY TO FOLLOW
ST CUTHBERT'S WAY STRIKES AWAY NE
SCOTLAND
ENGLAND
0
1/4 mile
0
APPROX SCALE
500m
trailblazer
HIGH ROUTE
WHITELAW NICK
EASILY THE BEST STILE ON THE PW! ITS VALUE REDUCED BY A GATE RIGHT NEXT TO IT
WHITE LAW
THE PW HAS BEEN REALIGNED TO MISS HALTERBURNHEAD FARM
LOW ROUTE
HALTERBURNHEAD FARM
FARM TRACK
WAGON
132
132

(cont'd from p264) It also offers the last wild camp options of the walk and the opportunity to watch your final Pennine Way sunset, perhaps from the summit of White Law (Map 133). However, no-one will blame you if you head downhill.

At last you pull back your shoulders and pick up your dragging feet. There's no point in looking beaten. The villagers in **Kirk Yetholm** (Map 135) don't care one way or the other, but you have your pride. That said, given the number of Pennine Way walkers they must see the Border Hotel extends a welcome to those that have completed the entire trail that is satisfyingly celebratory, with certificates and your free half-pint offered without quibble. You should also sign their book, and you can read in there the comments of fellow lengthsmen and women, mostly nonchalant or triumphant, some philosophical. Add yours if you

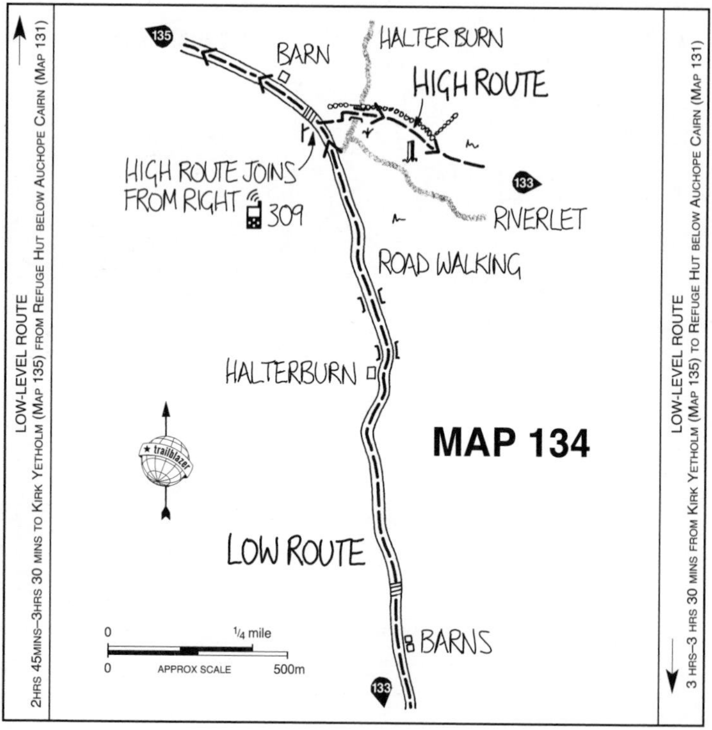
LOW-LEVEL ROUTE
2HRS 45MINS–3HRS 30 MINS TO KIRK YETHOLM (MAP 135) FROM REFUGE HUT BELOW AUCHOPE CAIRN (MAP 131)
135
BARN
HALTER BURN
HIGH ROUTE
HIGH ROUTE JOINS FROM RIGHT
309
133
RIVERLET
ROAD WALKING
HALTERBURN
MAP 134
trailblazer
LOW ROUTE
0
1/4 mile
0
APPROX SCALE
500m
BARNS
133
LOW-LEVEL ROUTE
3 HRS–3 HRS 30 MINS FROM KIRK YETHOLM (MAP 135) TO REFUGE HUT BELOW AUCHOPE CAIRN (MAP 131)

like: you have, after all, just completed what is arguably Britain's most challenging long-distance trail.

Navigation notes

Leaving Byrness is the most likely cause for confusion today; the path runs straight as an arrow up the hill but the scramble up the final section isn't marked and you are left to follow the track on the ground until the cairn on Byrness Hill appears over the top. Even after here there is little indication that you are on the correct path until you reach the border with Scotland for the first time. Once the slabs appear, however, there's very little to distract you from the path. From Auchope Cairn (Map 30) the knee-popping descent to the second refuge hut is well trodden, as is the trail round and up to The Schil (Map 131) and down to the ladder stile leading to the high or low route divide, both of which roll unambiguously down to Kirk Yetholm.

All in all, even in poor visibility this very long day is made much easier by reasonable waymarking and orientation aids (aka 'slabs and fence lines'). All you have to do is last the distance.

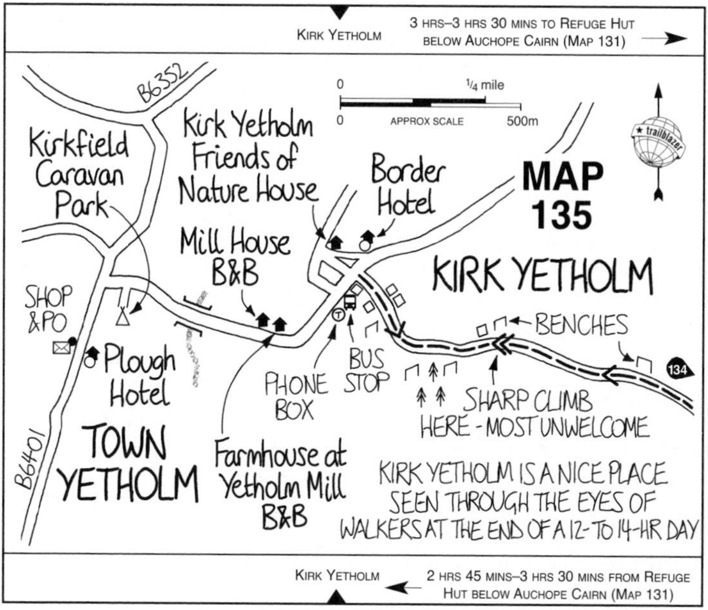
Kirk Yetholm
3 hrs–3 hrs 30 mins to Refuge Hut below Auchope Cairn (Map 131)
B6352
0 ¼ mile
0 APPROX SCALE 500m
trailblazer
MAP 135
Kirkfield Caravan Park
Kirk Yetholm Friends of Nature House
Border Hotel
Mill House B&B
KIRK YETHOLM
SHOP &PO
BENCHES
Plough Hotel
BUS STOP
PHONE BOX
134
SHARP CLIMB HERE - MOST UNWELCOME
B6401
TOWN YETHOLM
Farmhouse at Yetholm Mill B&B
KIRK YETHOLM IS A NICE PLACE SEEN THROUGH THE EYES OF WALKERS AT THE END OF A 12- TO 14-HR DAY
Kirk Yetholm
2 hrs 45 mins–3 hrs 30 mins from Refuge Hut below Auchope Cairn (Map 131)

UPPER COQUETDALE

[off Map 127, p264]

Upper Coquetdale is about 1½ miles from Windy Gyle. ***Barrowburn Farm*** (☎ 01669-650059, 💻 barrowburnfarm.com) has a **camping barn** which sleeps up to 15 people and is primarily for groups, though individuals can book and stay there for just £15pp. There is a sleeping platform (but no bedding), a kitchen and some chairs/tables; there are toilets and sinks in a separate outbuilding but no showers at the time of research. Their **Deer Hut** sleeps up to six people (2T plus a sofa bed in the living room; basic kitchen; ☕; 🐕) and is available for £65-70 per night on a self-catering basis; they prefer a minimum booking of two nights at weekends. Bedding is provided for the twin beds but not the sofa bed. They also offer **camping** at £5pp; there are toilets but no showers at the time of research. This is an excellent place and the only downside is that it is a long walk off the route. However, it is the only option if you don't want to get a lift to or from your accommodation.

KIRK YETHOLM [Map 135]

It's probably fair to say that only a fraction of the people who have heard of this pleasant little village would have done so if the Pennine Way did not end here. As it is, it offers a perfect and well-appointed spin down to your big walk.

See p14 for details of Yetholm Festival week held in June; for general information visit 💻 yetholmonline.org.

Transport

[See pp54-9] Peter Hogg of Jedburgh and Borders Buses operate the No 81/81A/ 81B **bus** services to Kelso (20-35 mins) from where you can either catch Borders Buses' No 52 to Edinburgh, for rail and coach connections, or their No 67 to Galashiels and Berwick-upon-Tweed. Peter Hogg's No 20 service goes to Hawick via Jedburgh.

Peter Hogg also operate a **taxi** service (☎ 01835-863755; Mon-Fri 9am-3pm) and they provide luggage transfer but only limited days/hours. Other options, both of which are recommended, are **Hownam Taxis** (☎ 07768 070818), pronounced 'whonam', and **Border Villager Taxi** (☎ 01668-482888, or ☎ 07765-791348, 🖳 bordervillagertaxi.co.uk).

Places to stay, eat and drink

Campers should head to Town Yetholm (see below) where there's a decent campsite.

As for **B&Bs**, ***Mill House*** (bookings ☎ 01573-420604, after booking ☎ 07721 463547, 🖳 millhouseyetholm.co.uk; 2D or T/1D/1Qd, all en suite; ☕; Ⓛ) is a comfortable place to stay and it offers a laundry service (£5 for wash and £5 for dry) and drying room for walking gear. B&B costs £40-47.50pp (sgl occ £60-75). They offer a pick-up and drop-off service (£25 each way) for Pennine Way walkers from/to Cocklawfoot Farm, thereby dividing the last day into two halves.

Border Hotel (☎ 01573-420237, 🖳 borderhotel.co.uk; 2D/2D or T/1Tr, all en suite; ☕; Ⓛ; 🐕) has a characterful bar where you can ask for the Pennine Way visitors book and get a certificate. Anyone who has finished the Pennine Way is stood a free half pint courtesy of Hadrian Border Brewery. **B&B** costs £40-50pp (sgl occ £55-65). The menu (**food** served Mon-Sat noon-2pm & 6-8.30pm, Sun noon-8pm) here offers a knee-weakening range of dishes to help pile back the calories burned up during the haul over from Byrness. You may need to book if you want to eat in the restaurant. Non-residents can have breakfast here (daily 8-9am; £10).

Round the corner ***Kirk Yetholm Friends of Nature House*** (bookings ☎ 01573-420639, 🖳 thefriendsofnature.org.uk/houses/kirk-yetholm; 1 x 7-, 1 x 5-, 1 x 4-, 1 x 2-bed bunk rooms, 2 x 2-bed; all shared facilities; Easter-end Oct) costs from £18pp. The hostel is self-catering only but bedding is provided and there are drying facilities.

The excellent ***Farmhouse at Yetholm Mill*** (☎ 01573-420505, 🖳 thefarmhouseatkirkyetholm.com; 1D en suite/1D or T private facilities; ☕ Jacuzzi; Ⓛ; 🐕) charges £37.50-40pp (sgl occ £50-55) for B&B. They also have a cottage (1D/1D or T, both en suite) which can be booked for B&B if it is available. If requested in advance they will arrange for a taxi to pick you up at Cocklawfoot and take you back there the next day to break up The Cheviot traverse.

TOWN YETHOLM [Map 135, p271]

It could be one half mile too many but in Town Yetholm you'll find a **shop** (Mon-Fri 7am-7pm, Sat 7am-5pm, Sun 9am-5pm) and a **post office** (closed afternoons, Wed and Sat). There's also ***Kirkfield Caravan Park*** (☎ 07791-291956 or ☎ 01573-420346, 🖳 kirkfieldcaravanpark.co.uk; no WI-FI; 🐕; Apr-end Oct) a fairly smart and peaceful place where you can pitch your tent (£8pp) in the corner of the site; shower and toilet facilities are available.

There's also ***Plough Hotel*** (☎ 01573-420215, 🖳 theploughhotelyetholm.co.uk; 1D/1T/1D or T/1Tr, all en suite; ☕; Ⓛ; 🐕) where **B&B** costs £42.50-47.50pp (sgl occ from £68). The menu (**food** served daily noon-2pm, Sun-Thur 5.30-7.45pm, Fri & Sat to 8.30pm) changes but almost always includes a pie of the day (£12.50). They also have a takeaway menu which is available daily 5-7pm.

Peter Hogg of Jedburgh and Borders Buses operate the No 81/81A/81B **bus** services to Kelso (20-35 mins). See pp54-9.

APPENDIX A: MAP KEY

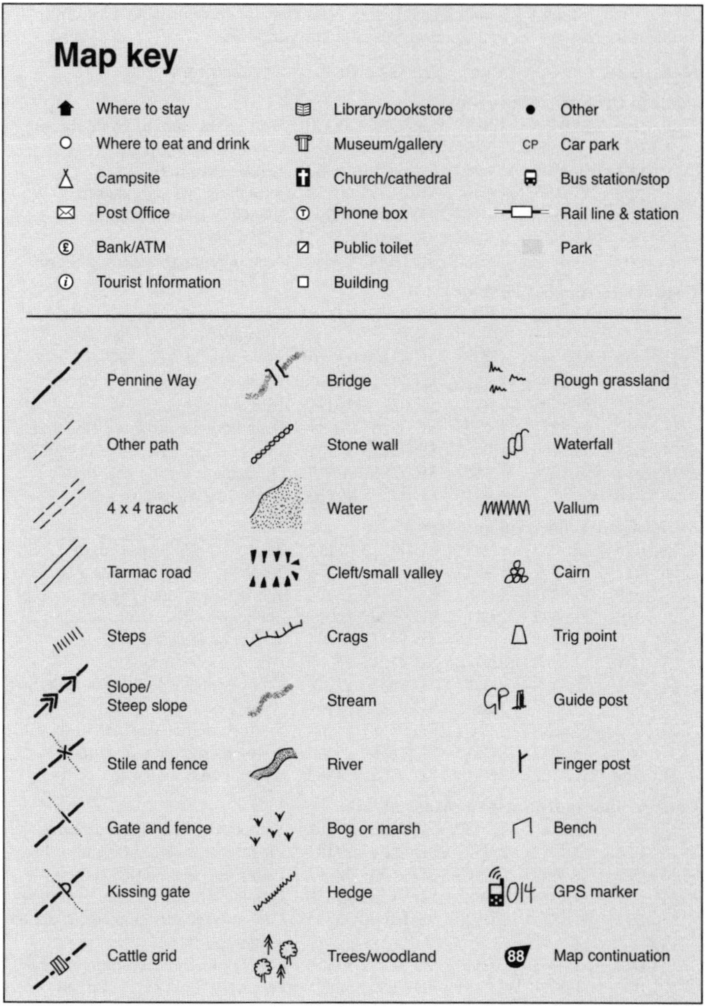

Map key
Where to stay
Where to eat and drink
Campsite
Post Office
Bank/ATM
Tourist Information
Library/bookstore
Museum/gallery
Church/cathedral
Phone box
Public toilet
Building
Other
CP Car park
Bus station/stop
Rail line & station
Park
Pennine Way
Other path
4 x 4 track
Tarmac road
Steps
Slope/
Steep slope
Stile and fence
Gate and fence
Kissing gate
Cattle grid
Bridge
Stone wall
Water
Cleft/small valley
Crags
Stream
River
Bog or marsh
Hedge
Trees/woodland
Rough grassland
Waterfall
Vallum
Cairn
Trig point
GP Guide post
Finger post
Bench
014 GPS marker
88 Map continuation

APPENDIX B: GPS WAYPOINTS

Each GPS waypoint was taken on the route at the reference number marked on the map as below. This list of GPS waypoints is also available in downloadable form from the Trailblazer website – trailblazer-guides.com/gps-waypoints.

Map	GPS	Lat	Long	OS Grid Ref	Description
Edale to Crowden (Maps 1-9)					
3	001	53.3753	-1.8818	SK 07860 86530	Bear left at cairn to Edale Rocks
3	002	53.3803	-1.8835	SK 07751 87079	Kinder Low trig point
4	003	53.3972	-1.8765	SK 08209 88962	Kinder Downfall
4	004	53.4088	-1.9061	SK 06241 90254	Straight ahead at guidepost
7	005	53.4613	-1.8597	SK 09311 96096	Bleaklow Head summit
7	006	53.4656	-1.8628	SK 09108 96582	Milestone
8	007	53.4753	-1.9060	SK 06237 97649	Gate in fence above Reaps Farm
Crowden to Standedge (Maps 9-15)					
10	008	53.5220	-1.9100	SE 05967 02849	Cross stream joining Crowden Great Brook
11	009	53.5299	-1.9035	SE 06396 03730	Cross stile in fence line
12	010	53.5387	-1.8836	SE 07711 04710	Black Hill summit
12	011	53.5505	-1.8772	SE 08138 06022	Path begins to bear left
13	012	53.5781	-1.9204	SE 05267 09084	Drop into valley, beside fingerpost
14	013	53.5756	-1.9485	SE 03412 08802	Cross bridge between reservoirs
15	014	53.5774	-1.9567	SE 02867 09000	Go through kissing gate in fence
15	015	53.5816	-1.9610	SE 02578 09470	Green PNFS signpost #357
Standedge to Calder Valley (Maps 15-22)					
15	016	53.5903	-1.9829	SE 01132 10434	Trig point (Millstone Edge)
16	017	53.5977	-1.9947	SE 00351 11264	Stone marker by Oldham Way
17	018	53.6151	-2.0157	SD 98960 13194	White Hill summit trig point
18	019	53.6408	-2.0417	SD 97242 16059	Shelter of sorts
18	020	53.6438	-2.0436	SD 97117 16394	Trig point (Blackstone Edge)
18	021	53.6500	-2.0418	SD 97240 17086	Aiggin Stone, turn left
18	022	53.6494	-2.0477	SD 96850 17018	Cross drainage ditch, then turn right
19	023	53.6684	-2.0555	SD 96335 19131	'Packhorse'-style bridge
20	024	53.6917	-2.0654	SD 95681 21727	Slabs start after Warland Reservoir
20	025	53.7047	-2.0515	SD 96597 23165	4-way marker on tall signpost
21	026	53.7192	-2.0314	SD 97927 24783	Straight on beside wall
Calder Valley to Ickornshaw (Maps 22-31)					
22	027	53.7389	-2.0480	SD 96833 26974	Signpost to Badger Fields Farm
23	028	53.7584	-2.0527	SD 96527 29141	Fingerpost by Mount Pleasant Farm
24	029	53.7639	-2.0579	SD 96183 29752	Path meets wall beside fingerpost
24	030	53.7736	-2.0822	SD 94582 30839	Pennine Bridleway sign; turn right
25	031	53.7871	-2.0820	SD 94600 32335	Layby; leave road and cut corner at fingerpost
26	032	53.7963	-2.0540	SD 96442 33356	Cross drain on metal bridge
26	033	53.8011	-2.0481	SD 96832 33895	Fingerpost points right up hill
27	034	53.8159	-2.0281	SD 98150 35536	Japanese fingerpost
28	035	53.8236	-2.0045	SD 99704 36395	Turn left at signpost down lane
28	036	53.8267	-2.0040	SD 99735 36736	Switchback left at fingerpost
28	037	53.8312	-2.0188	SD 98762 37244	Leave tarmac onto green path before gate

Map	GPS	Lat	Long	OS Grid Ref	Description
Calder Valley to Ickornshaw (Maps 22-31) ***(cont'd)***					
29	038	53.8362	-2.0187	SD 98769 37794	Leave track (turn left) at fingerpost
29	039	53.8465	-2.0324	SD 97867 38938	Guidepost beside path where wall ends abruptly, open moor ahead
29	040	53.8500	-2.0404	SD 97345 39331	Rank green pool beside path
29	041	53.8577	-2.0424	SD 97213 40191	Stone building
30	042	53.8579	-2.0440	SD 97109 40207	Stone shelter
30	043	53.8651	-2.0484	SD 96815 41013	Stone (shooting) hut
31	044	53.8707	-2.0457	SD 96995 41629	Door to garden and hut
31	045	53.8722	-2.0441	SD 97101 41798	Metal gate, change of direction
31	046	53.8859	-2.0546	SD 96412 43323	Spring; turn right through gate
Ickornshaw to Malham (Maps 31-41)					
32	047	53.8967	-2.0607	SD 96012 44527	Turn right onto road
32	048	53.9184	-2.0661	SD 95658 46938	Bench beside path
32	049	53.9202	-2.0739	SD 95149 47142	Two planks across ditch
33	050	53.9209	-2.0863	SD 94333 47225	Pinhaw Beacon trig point
33	051	53.9240	-2.1015	SD 93338 47565	Leave road bear left beside wall
33	052	53.9315	-2.1257	SD 91744 48402	PW fingerpost in farmyard
35	053	53.9415	-2.1406	SD 90774 49519	Leave lane, go through gate into field
35	054	53.9615	-2.1316	SD 91366 51737	Leave lane, go right into field through gate
36	055	53.9706	-2.1234	SD 91903 52753	Stone water tank
36	056	53.9739	-2.1188	SD 92211 53123	4-way fingerpost on Scaleber Hill
37	057	53.9791	-2.1137	SD 92546 53697	Right turn through gate into field by fingerpost
37	058	53.9911	-2.1166	SD 92358 55030	Stile in wall on right
38	059	54.0027	-2.1281	SD 91603 56330	Fingerpost by gate
38	060	54.0073	-2.1301	SD 91473 56832	Path between walls
38	061	54.0094	-2.1317	SD 91368 57072	Lone Pennine Way sign
38	062	54.0189	-2.1424	SD 90668 58132	Left off road after crossing bridge
39	063	54.0324	-2.1492	SD 90228 59627	Slab bridge over beck
39	064	54.0463	-2.1544	SD 89888 61174	Stone steps up to road
40	065	54.0510	-2.1529	SD 89991 61707	Fingerpost by wall corner
Malham to Horton-in-Ribblesdale (Maps 41-48)					
41	066	54.0732	-2.1584	SD 89633 64172	Bear left along wall
42	067	54.0816	-2.1670	SD 89076 65104	Bear right at fork, keep to wall
42	068	54.0869	-2.1644	SD 89245 65693	Fingerpost and gate at road
43	069	54.1018	-2.1721	SD 88745 67353	Leave track at gate in wall
43	070	54.1178	-2.1782	SD 88353 69140	Across cattle grid onto farm lane
44	071	54.1256	-2.1903	SD 87563 70005	Bear right at fingerpost
44	072	54.1438	-2.2036	SD 86698 72030	Wall stile
45	073	54.1433	-2.2183	SD 85738 71977	Path meets wall on descent
46	074	54.1506	-2.2523	SD 83526 72800	Fingerpost shows way to Horton avoiding Pen-y-ghent
46	075	54.1560	-2.2486	SD 83766 73397	Summit of Pen-y-ghent
46	076	54.1634	-2.2505	SD 83648 74227	Bear left at fingerpost
47	077	54.1640	-2.2726	SD 82206 74300	Gate in walled lane
48	078	54.1484	-2.2907	SD 81011 72562	Bench beside track
Horton-in-Ribblesdale to Hawes (Maps 48-55)					
49	079	54.1694	-2.2923	SD 80919 74900	PW & 3 Peaks fingerpost by gate in wall

Map	GPS	Lat	Long	OS Grid Ref	Description
Horton-in-Ribblesdale to Hawes (Maps 48-55) *(cont'd from p275)*					
49	080	54.1900	-2.2879	SD 81214 77189	Acorn on gate; don't follow obvious path ahead
50	081	54.1962	-2.3048	SD 80114 77889	Barn beside path
50	082	54.2193	-2.3057	SD 80069 80457	Cam End forestry road
52	083	54.2402	-2.2752	SD 82066 82779	Join tarmac here
53	084	54.2459	-2.2628	SD 82876 83409	Leave tarmac before Kidhow Gate
54	085	54.2772	-2.2426	SD 84205 86889	Leave West Cam Road for grassy path
54	086	54.2785	-2.2415	SD 84276 87032	Cairn on rocky outcrop in middle of path
54	087	54.2857	-2.2326	SD 84861 87823	Half-size wooden gate
54	088	54.2915	-2.2231	SD 85478 88473	Gate after prominent cairn
55	089	54.2999	-2.2018	SD 86868 89403	Gate onto road opposite houses
Hawes to Tan Hill (Maps 55-64)					
56	090	54.3122	-2.1929	SD 87450 90766	Stone bench with view
57	091	54.3242	-2.2203	SD 85676 92113	Gate in track
57	092	54.3341	-2.2359	SD 84662 93213	Gate next to stile
57	093	54.3344	-2.2355	SD 84691 93243	Fingerpost to Cotterdale
58	094	54.3496	-2.2409	SD 84344 94940	Permanent puddle to left of path
58	095	54.3653	-2.2394	SD 84445 96682	Steps built with cobbles
59	096	54.3708	-2.2346	SD 84763 97291	Great Shunner Fell summit
59	097	54.3769	-2.2271	SD 85252 97969	Fine cairn
59	098	54.3818	-2.2198	SD 85723 98520	Wooden bridge
60	099	54.3812	-2.1926	SD 87492 98444	Gate after stream
61	100	54.3811	-2.1612	SD 89533 98424	Gate beside barns
61	101	54.3824	-2.1515	SD 90160 98569	Gate beside Kisdon House
62	102	54.3908	-2.1483	SD 90373 99503	Wide gate in wall
62	103	54.4020	-2.1567	NY 89828 00752	Go through gap in wall by fingerpost
62	104	54.4138	-2.1678	NY 89111 02069	Gate in fence line
63	105	54.4279	-2.1731	NY 88768 03638	Two barns
63	106	54.4358	-2.1752	NY 88638 04520	Gate and slab bridge over stream
64	107	54.4430	-2.1674	NY 89147 05320	PW fingerpost
Tan Hill to Middleton-in-Teesdale (Maps 64-72)					
65	108	54.4662	-2.1378	NY 91070 07889	White-topped post beside sheepfold
65	109	54.4680	-2.1320	NY 91446 08094	Good-sized cairn
65	110	54.4718	-2.1216	NY 92120 08511	Post and plank bridge opp sheepfolds
65	111	54.4763	-2.1005	NY 93490 09015	Cross beck on sturdy metal bridge
66	112	54.4844	-2.0730	NY 95272 09913	Ancient triangular road sign on metal post beside track
67	113	54.4913	-2.0680	NY 95596 10674	Intake Bridge
67	114	54.4956	-2.0628	NY 95930 11152	Gate with acorn waymark
67	115	54.5031	-2.0668	NY 95674 11986	Gate in wall
68	116	54.5129	-2.0707	NY 95426 13078	Concrete block ford
68	117	54.5197	-2.0733	NY 95258 13837	Big cairn on skyline
68	118	54.5222	-2.0771	NY 95010 14116	'Ravock Castle' (Rock cairn)
68	119	54.5264	-2.0782	NY 94939 14588	Marker post
68	120	54.5281	-2.0813	NY 94739 14775	Shelter in shooting hut
69	121	54.5402	-2.0910	NY 94116 16123	Gate in fence on Race Yate
69	122	54.5453	-2.0931	NY 93975 16686	Post on Peatbrig Hill
69	123	54.5486	-2.0961	NY 93785 17056	Guide post on left side of path

Map	GPS	Lat	Long	OS Grid Ref	Description
Tan Hill to Middleton-in-Teesdale (Maps 64-72) *(cont'd)*					
69	124	54.5538	-2.1006	NY 93494 17635	Path meets tarmac at fingerpost
69	124a	54.5582	-2.1040	NY 93275 18129	Bowes Loop fingerpost
70	125	54.5812	-2.1101	NY 92884 20687	Barn by gap stile
70	126	54.5835	-2.1114	NY 92799 20945	Gate in wall
71	127	54.6025	-2.1207	NY 92204 23059	Stone stile with white paint
71	128	54.6048	-2.1156	NY 92535 23315	Gap in wall
71	129	54.6084	-2.1086	NY 92984 23712	Gate in wall across path
72	130	54.6117	-2.1028	NY 93358 24082	Cairn beside small disused quarry
72	131	54.6137	-2.0924	NY 94034 24304	Stile with dog slot and black gate
72	132	54.6187	-2.0854	NY 94486 24852	Gate onto road beside fingerpost
Bowes Loop Route (Map 67-69)					
67	657	54.5079	-2.0586	NY 96202 12530	Bear right over cattle grid
67a	658	54.5101	-2.0491	NY 96820 12765	Small gate beside big gate
67a	659	54.5125	-2.0291	NY 98117 13032	Leave track and enter field
67b	660	54.5316	-2.0442	NY 97138 15160	Fingerposts beside gate
67b	661	54.5343	-2.0512	NY 96690 15460	Bridge over Deepdale Beck
67b	662	54.5354	-2.0514	NY 96675 15587	On path through marsh grass
67b	663	54.5392	-2.0528	NY 96582 16012	Splash through Hazelgill Beck
67b	664	54.5427	-2.0503	NY 96747 16397	Cairn marks path
67c	665	54.5477	-2.0533	NY 96554 16957	Sunken slabs over Hare Sike
67c	666	54.5497	-2.0552	NY 96427 17181	Through gate in wall
67c	667	54.5518	-2.0631	NY 95921 17413	Big black metal footbridge
67c	668	54.5532	-2.0720	NY 95342 17571	South of summit crag
67c	669	54.5561	-2.0816	NY 94725 17892	Meet road beside fingerpost
69	670	54.5575	-2.0920	NY 94054 18047	Tiny gate and stone stile
69	671	54.5582	-2.1040	NY 93275 18129	Bowes Loop fingerpost
Middleton-in-Teesdale to Dufton (Maps 72-83)					
73	133	54.6249	-2.1030	NY 93350 25550	Step stile in wall
73	134	54.6309	-2.1236	NY 92022 26217	Cairn at path junction bear right
74	135	54.6415	-2.1426	NY 90800 27399	Stepping stones over stream
75	136	54.6496	-2.1734	NY 88813 28300	Bridge, keep left
76	137	54.6488	-2.2135	NY 86223 28221	Rotting wagon
77	138	54.6635	-2.2243	NY 85535 29864	Stone step stile in wall
77	139	54.6632	-2.2480	NY 84005 29830	Bench beside stile in wall
78	140	54.6519	-2.2623	NY 83078 28576	Duckboards
78	141	54.6478	-2.2742	NY 82307 28127	Large cairn
78	142	54.6494	-2.2985	NY 80743 28304	Barn beside path
79	143	54.6404	-2.3175	NY 79513 27317	Cattle grid
79	144	54.6405	-2.3175	NY 79507 27324	Old spoil tip on Moss Shop
79	145	54.6375	-2.3444	NY 77774 26998	Signpost. Bear left; descend off track
80	146	54.6358	-2.3571	NY 76950 26807	Waterfall
80	147	54.6357	-2.3636	NY 76532 26806	Maize Beck Bridge
80	148	54.6347	-2.3724	NY 75963 26701	Red stone milepost
80	149	54.6333	-2.3865	NY 75055 26543	Milepost (near High Cup Nick)
81	150	54.6308	-2.3906	NY 74790 26265	Fallen milestone
81	151	54.6299	-2.3931	NY 74625 26170	Marker stone with yellow arrow
81	152	54.6298	-2.4012	NY 74102 26155	Milestone at junction of paths
81	153	54.6270	-2.4101	NY 73525 25858	Two streams
81	154	54.6259	-2.4122	NY 73388 25733	Way marker

MAP	GPS	LAT	LONG	OS GRID REF	DESCRIPTION
Middleton-in-Teesdale to Dufton (Maps 72-83) *(cont'd from p277)*					
82	155	54.6193	-2.4316	NY 72130 25008	Walled enclosure
82	156	54.6195	-2.4505	NY 70913 25038	Barn beside path
Maize Beck alternative route (Maps 80-81)					
80	672	54.6357	-2.3636	NY 76532 26806	Maize Beck Bridge
80	673	54.6351	-2.3832	NY 75265 26745	Cross stream near beck
81	674	54.6376	-2.3904	NY 74805 27022	Old footbridge
81	675	54.6327	-2.3970	NY 74375 26483	Limestone outcrops
81	676	54.6298	-2.4012	NY 74102 26155	Milestone at junction of paths
Dufton to Alston (Maps 83-94)					
83	157	54.6375	-2.4800	NY 69020 27051	Halsteads (ruin)
84	158	54.6485	-2.4693	NY 69722 28266	Pennine Way fingerpost
84	159	54.6516	-2.4654	NY 69977 28606	Nature reserve sign
84	160	54.6539	-2.4574	NY 70495 28861	Two cairns
85	161	54.6571	-2.4476	NY 71129 29213	Big cairn (possibly an old ruin)
85	162	54.6607	-2.4436	NY 71388 29611	Milepost
85	163	54.6621	-2.4402	NY 71610 29772	Milepost
85	164	54.6637	-2.4390	NY 71686 29943	Milepost
85	165	54.6640	-2.4389	NY 71691 29980	Flooded hole
85	166	54.6651	-2.4353	NY 71924 30096	Knock Old Man cairn
85	167	54.6665	-2.4334	NY 72046 30254	Knock Fell cairn
85	168	54.6695	-2.4349	NY 71956 30594	Slabs
85	169	54.6726	-2.4355	NY 71917 30934	Tiny tarns
85	170	54.6770	-2.4397	NY 71652 31423	PW meets access road
85	171	54.6787	-2.4414	NY 71542 31615	Path leaves access road
85	172	54.6803	-2.4453	NY 71289 31794	Flat-topped rock
86	173	54.6833	-2.4493	NY 71038 32129	Radar station on Great Dun Fell
86	174	54.6855	-2.4522	NY 70851 32379	Slabs start
86	175	54.6914	-2.4603	NY 70330 33042	Little Dun Fell summit
86	176	54.6974	-2.4695	NY 69745 33707	Nature reserve sign
87	177	54.7011	-2.4767	NY 69284 34123	Tall cairn
87	178	54.7022	-2.4816	NY 68968 34247	Bell-shaped cairn
87	179	54.7029	-2.4868	NY 68633 34329	Cross Fell summit
87	180	54.7048	-2.4873	NY 68604 34539	Bell-shaped cairn
87	181	54.7082	-2.4901	NY 68425 34923	Flat-topped rock
87	182	54.7108	-2.4921	NY 68300 35213	Cairn at track
87	183	54.7128	-2.4814	NY 68985 35429	Greg's Hut
88	184	54.7174	-2.4690	NY 69793 35929	Ruin
88	185	54.7168	-2.4498	NY 71025 35864	Cross stream
89	186	54.7181	-2.4457	NY 71290 35997	Old mine workings
89	187	54.7185	-2.4441	NY 71398 36048	Stone marker; PW straight on
89	188	54.7214	-2.4406	NY 71624 36366	Gate in fence
89	189	54.7255	-2.4369	NY 71864 36817	Track joins from west
89	190	54.7272	-2.4360	NY 71924 37009	Track joins from east
89	191	54.7420	-2.4310	NY 72254 38659	Gate
90	192	54.7513	-2.4210	NY 72903 39681	Gate
92	193	54.7780	-2.4249	NY 72670 42663	Two stiles – take riverside one
92	194	54.7800	-2.4301	NY 72338 42883	3-way signpost by the river
93	195	54.7827	-2.4340	NY 72088 43190	Plank bridge
93	196	54.7848	-2.4388	NY 71783 43418	Stile in wall by line of trees

Map	GPS	Lat	Long	OS Grid Ref	Description
Dufton to Alston (Maps 83-94) ***(cont'd)***					
93	197	54.7976	-2.4411	NY 71642 44848	Footbridge
93	198	54.8033	-2.4418	NY 71600 45478	Small kissing gate over stream
Alston to Greenhead (Maps 94-102)					
94	199	54.8205	-2.4566	NY 70662 47397	Wide farm gate
95	200	54.8211	-2.4651	NY 70116 47470	Kissing gate in the wall
95	201	54.8306	-2.4794	NY 69208 48531	Whitley Castle information board
96	202	54.8511	-2.4862	NY 68789 50813	Short ladder stile in wall
96	203	54.8574	-2.4899	NY 68551 51522	Gate in right-hand corner of field
97	204	54.8703	-2.5122	NY 67132 52968	Gate after tunnel under old railway
97	205	54.8735	-2.5146	NY 66981 53319	Wide gate beside fingerpost
97	206	54.8831	-2.5076	NY 67436 54384	Go under viaduct and turn left
98	207	54.8875	-2.5123	NY 67142 54876	Leave track to right (Maiden Way)
98	208	54.8914	-2.5120	NY 67160 55311	Keep right at fork
98	209	54.8937	-2.5116	NY 67192 55574	Two stiles
98	210	54.9086	-2.5173	NY 66837 57224	Stile and dog hatch
98	211	54.9159	-2.5195	NY 66704 58045	Duckboards either side of stile in fence
99	212	54.9187	-2.5208	NY 66621 58353	Left over fence at stile
99	213	54.9211	-2.5267	NY 66244 58620	A689 road crossing
99	214	54.9243	-2.5282	NY 66154 58981	Slab bridge over stream
99	215	54.9323	-2.5303	NY 66021 59871	High House ruin
99	216	54.9345	-2.5286	NY 66134 60122	Footbridge over stream
99	217	54.9357	-2.5292	NY 66098 60249	Top of wooded bank
99	218	54.9373	-2.5336	NY 65814 60435	Through gate beside fingerpost
100	219	54.9404	-2.5397	NY 65425 60775	Farm gate in wall
100	220	54.9409	-2.5411	NY 65342 60840	Gate where PW leaves farm track
100	221	54.9483	-2.5434	NY 65198 61655	Miniature ladder stile in fence
100	222	54.9495	-2.5461	NY 65029 61798	Keep left at faint fork in path
100	223	54.9513	-2.5558	NY 64409 61997	PW guide post beside fence
100	224	54.9539	-2.5559	NY 64400 62290	Footbridge
100	225	54.9580	-2.5563	NY 64378 62744	Ladder stile in wall
100	226	54.9656	-2.5600	NY 64148 63592	Ladder stile
101	227	54.9696	-2.5624	NY 64001 64044	Stile with acorn marker
101	228	54.9731	-2.5616	NY 64054 64428	Gate with fingerpost beside it
101	229	54.9731	-2.5451	NY 65110 64424	Leave track at fingerpost
102	230	54.9824	-2.5459	NY 65066 65455	Gate in fence
102	231	54.9860	-2.5432	NY 65246 65850	Cross onto golf course
Greenhead to Bellingham (Maps 102-112)					
102	232	54.9878	-2.5256	NY 66371 66048	Stile through wall
102	233	54.9906	-2.5094	NY 67412 66350	Milecastle 45a
103	234	54.9949	-2.4939	NY 68406 66824	Ladder stile
103	235	54.9933	-2.5010	NY 67951 66643	Ladder stile with acorn marker
103	236	54.9954	-2.4787	NY 69377 66872	Ladder stile before woods
104	237	54.9927	-2.4520	NY 71085 66556	Cross stile onto road
104	238	54.9957	-2.4281	NY 72615 66882	Kissing gate at road
104	239	54.9999	-2.4120	NY 73649 67339	Gate in wall
105	240	55.0020	-2.4046	NY 74120 67571	Winshield Crags trig point
106	241	55.0117	-2.3441	NY 77997 68633	Ladder stile in wall
107	242	55.0258	-2.3452	NY 77933 70207	Second guide post
107	243	55.0305	-2.3460	NY 77884 70731	Join forestry track

Map	GPS	Lat	Long	OS Grid Ref	Description
Greenhead to Bellingham (Maps 102-112) *(cont'd from p279)*					
107	244	55.0411	-2.3443	NY 77999 71902	Leave track
108	245	55.0489	-2.3378	NY 78422 72773	Leave trees for open land
108	246	55.0566	-2.3197	NY 79581 73622	Kissing gate at edge of logged area
109	247	55.0648	-2.3166	NY 79781 74538	Cross forestry track
109	248	55.0746	-2.3089	NY 80281 75618	Start of old diversion
109	249	55.0813	-2.2983	NY 80959 76367	Waterfall
109	250	55.0873	-2.2949	NY 81176 77025	Left at guide post through gate
110	251	55.0978	-2.2888	NY 81573 78202	Guide post beside trees
111	252	55.1124	-2.2692	NY 82831 79815	Footbridge
111	253	55.1241	-2.2570	NY 83614 81114	Leave track into rough pasture
111	254	55.1344	-2.2555	NY 83713 82257	Plank bridge
Bellingham to Byrness (Maps 112-120)					
112	255	55.1542	-2.2415	NY 84611 84466	Guide post
112	256	55.1598	-2.2437	NY 84477 85088	Fingerpost by wide wooden gate
113	257	55.1677	-2.2431	NY 84518 85968	Path over pipe
113	258	55.1801	-2.2469	NY 84279 87343	Stile onto farm track
113	259	55.1852	-2.2516	NY 83981 87910	Guidepost
114	260	55.1914	-2.2495	NY 84120 88600	Guide post beside path
114	261	55.1985	-2.2470	NY 84282 89387	Guide post
114	262	55.2063	-2.2506	NY 84051 90257	Deer Play summit
114	263	55.2086	-2.2544	NY 83809 90514	Guide post with white band
115	264	55.2129	-2.2609	NY 83402 91003	Concrete bridge over Black Sike
115	265	55.2151	-2.2698	NY 82833 91248	Whitley Pike summit
115	266	55.2164	-2.2724	NY 82672 91387	Slabs start
116	267	55.2351	-2.2935	NY 81338 93474	Wall at base of climb
116	268	55.2429	-2.2901	NY 81554 94340	Wall ends bear left along fence
117	269	55.2542	-2.3182	NY 79773 95603	Through gate onto forestry road
117	270	55.2612	-2.3197	NY 79686 96389	Leave forestry road at green sign
117	271	55.2668	-2.3229	NY 79481 97009	Rejoin forestry road
118	272	55.2789	-2.3332	NY 78835 98366	Young plantation
119	273	55.2965	-2.3403	NT 78394 00326	Leave road and into trees
119	274	55.3019	-2.3466	NT 78000 00924	Cross footbridge
119	275	55.3051	-2.3506	NT 77745 01281	Access to Border Forest Holiday Park
Byrness to Kirk Yetholm (Maps 120-135)					
120	276	55.3231	-2.3570	NT 77347 03289	Byrness Hill summit cairn
121	277	55.3382	-2.3585	NT 77264 04968	Slabs start over boggy section
121	278	55.3495	-2.3483	NT 77916 06220	Ravens Knowe summit
122	279	55.3583	-2.3529	NT 77630 07199	MoD sign
122	280	55.3671	-2.3506	NT 77782 08184	3-way (alternative route) fingerpost
123	281	55.3725	-2.3372	NT 78635 08782	Guide post, watch for change of direction
123	282	55.3887	-2.3351	NT 78771 10575	Green sign
124	283	55.3944	-2.3359	NT 78724 11209	Cross stream
124	284	55.3992	-2.3347	NT 78807 11746	Cairn
124	285	55.4021	-2.3308	NT 79056 12072	Guide post
124	286	55.4054	-2.3254	NT 79398 12437	Slabs over stream
125	287	55.4067	-2.3133	NT 80163 12579	Turn corner to left
125	288	55.4095	-2.3109	NT 80314 12892	Refuge hut at foot of Lamb Hill
125	289	55.4135	-2.3007	NT 80961 13334	Lamb Hill trig point

Byrness to Kirk Yetholm (Maps 120-135) ***(cont'd)***

Map	GPS	Lat	Long	OS Grid Ref	Description
125	290	55.4198	-2.2939	NT 81399 14031	Slabs again
126	291	55.4286	-2.2721	NT 82780 15003	Mozzie Law summit
126	292	55.4285	-2.2624	NT 83394 14985	Stile & gate bear left at fingerpost
127	293	55.4307	-2.2359	NT 85076 15232	Gate and stile in fence
127	294	55.4306	-2.2300	NT 85446 15212	Russell's Cairn
127	295	55.4335	-2.2207	NT 86036 15534	Enormous pile of stones
128	296	55.4380	-2.2049	NT 87035 16030	4-way fingerpost at Clennell Street
129	297	55.4454	-2.1941	NT 87722 16850	Stile in fence
129	298	55.4498	-2.1930	NT 87793 17344	King's Seat trig point
130	299	55.4666	-2.1709	NT 89192 19216	Outcrop of rock with memorial plaque
130	300	55.4680	-2.1662	NT 89495 19364	Corner of path to summit
130	301	55.4724	-2.1741	NT 88998 19859	Auchope Cairn
131	302	55.4752	-2.1961	NT 87608 20169	Auchope Hill refuge hut
131	303	55.4839	-2.2052	NT 87036 21139	Saddle
131	304	55.4949	-2.2082	NT 86848 22371	Access to The Schil summit
132	305	55.5033	-2.2174	NT 86271 23301	Stile over wall
132	306	55.5053	-2.2243	NT 85835 23524	Low- & high-level routes divide
132	307	55.5122	-2.2365	NT 85063 24301	Gate in wall
132	308	55.5206	-2.2360	NT 85103 25228	Old Halterburn ruin
134	309	55.5424	-2.2559	NT 83854 27665	High route rejoins from right

❑ St Cuthbert's Way and other continuations

For those who want to extend their walk, St Cuthbert's Way is a 66-mile (106km) trail that runs from Melrose, via Kirk Yetholm, to Lindisfarne Castle on Holy Island, reached via a causeway off the Northumberland coast. That would round off your adventure in tremendous style. If the Pennine Way is being used as part of a Land's End to John O'Groats (or better still to Cape Wrath) journey, the Scottish National Trail (SNT) may suit your purposes perfectly. Although not yet a National Trail, this 540-mile (864km) route links Kirk Yetholm with Cape Wrath, using scenic routes even through the urban choke-point of Scotland between Glasgow and Edinburgh. It runs through Fort William, thereby linking you to the West Highland Way and the Great Glen Way, for a route to John O'Groats, or stay on the SNT for Cape Wrath.

The pastime of walking the long-distance trails grows on you. Getting back to normal life is hard. You're likely to find that everyday cares are less important now that you've communed with curlews and breathed the wind on Windy Gyle. One of the attractions of walking is the tangible sense of being out of the everyday world yet bonded to a community with different values from the common herd:

© Jim Manthorpe

We are Pilgrims, Master; we shall go
Always a little further: it may be
Beyond that last blue mountain barred with snow,
Across that angry or that glimmering sea.

So it is that the Trailblazer marketing department feels compelled to alert you to the full range of its British Walking Guides series listed on pp292-4. For you my friend, the walking is not over.

APPENDIX C: TAKING A DOG

TAKING DOGS ALONG THE WAY

Many are the rewards that await those prepared to make the extra effort required to bring their best friend along the trail. But you shouldn't underestimate the amount of work involved. Indeed, just about every decision you make will be influenced by the fact that you've got a dog: how you plan to travel to the start of the trail, where you're going to stay, how far you're going to walk each day, where you're going to rest and where you're going to eat in the evening etc. But if you're sure your dog can cope with (and will enjoy) walking 10 miles or more a day for several days in a row, and you can cope with the responsibility of looking after him or her, then you need to start preparing accordingly.

Looking after your dog

To begin with, you need to make sure that your dog is fully **inoculated** against the usual doggy illnesses, and also up to date with regard to **worm pills** (eg Drontal) and **flea preventatives** such as Frontline – they are, after all, following in the paw-prints of many a dog before them, some of whom may well have left fleas or other parasites on the trail that now lie in wait for their next meal to arrive.

Pet insurance is also a very good idea; if you've already got insurance, do check that it will cover a trip such as this.

On the subject of looking after your dog's health, perhaps the most important implement you can take with you is the **plastic tick remover**, available from vets for a couple of quid. These removers, while fiddly, help you to remove the tick safely (ie without leaving its head behind buried under the dog's skin).

All dogs now have to be **microchipped** but make sure your dog also has a **tag with your contact details on it** (a mobile phone number would be best if you take one with you). Being in unfamiliar territory also makes it more likely that you and your dog could become separated.

When to keep your dog on a lead

- **When crossing farmland**, particularly in the lambing season (March to May) when your dog can scare the sheep, causing them to lose their young. Farmers are allowed by law to shoot at and kill any dogs that they consider are worrying their sheep. During lambing, most farmers would prefer it if you didn't take your dog at all. The exception is if your dog is being attacked by cows (see box opposite).
- **On National Trust land**, where it is compulsory to keep your dog on a lead.
- **Around ground-nesting birds** It's important to keep your dog under control when crossing an area where certain species of birds nest on the ground. Most dogs love foraging around in the woods but make sure you have permission to do so; some woods are used as 'nurseries' for game birds and dogs are only allowed through them if they are on a lead.
- **On hill and cliff tops** It's a sad fact that, every year, a few dogs lose their lives falling over the edge of the cliffs. It usually occurs when they are chasing rabbits (which know where the cliff-edge is and are able, unlike your poor pooch, to stop in time).

What to pack

You've probably already got a good idea of what to bring to keep your dog alive and happy, but the following is a checklist:

- **Food/water bowl** Foldable cloth bowls are popular with walkers, being light and taking up little room in the rucksack. You can get also get a water-bottle-and-bowl combination, where the bottle folds into a 'trough' from which the dog can drink.
- **Lead and collar** An extendable one is probably preferable for this sort of trip. Make sure both lead and collar are in good condition – you don't want either to snap on the trail, or

❑ Walking through fields of cattle

The Pennine Wayfarer will meet cattle almost every day of the walk; there will be dozens of encounters with these large, mostly docile creatures and the vast majority of people will complete the walk without any adverse incident at all. However, there are very rare cases of walkers being attacked by cattle, resulting in serious injury and sometimes even death. Cows are most nervous when they see a dog in their field and this can be heightened significantly if they have calves with them.

In most cases cows won't even raise their heads from the grass and if you remain calm they will too. If you really wish to avoid them you are permitted to walk around the field boundary and rejoin the path beyond them. In some cases cows will approach you, or follow you, through curiosity or in the expectation of food, but they usually keep a respectable distance from you. Ramblers (see box p50) offer the following guidelines for safely crossing fields of cattle:

- Try not to get between cows and their calves
- Be prepared for cattle to react to your presence, especially if a dog is with you
- Move quickly and quietly, and if possible walk around the herd
- Keep your dog close and under effective control, ideally on a lead
- Don't hang onto your dog, if you are threatened by cattle, let it go as the cattle will chase the dog
- Don't put yourself at risk, find another way round the cattle and rejoin the footpath as soon as possible
- Don't panic or run, most cattle will stop before they reach you, if they follow just walk on quietly.

you may end up carrying your dog through sheep fields until a replacement can be found.

- **Bedding** A simple blanket may suffice, or you can opt for something more elaborate if you aren't carrying your own luggage.
- **Food/water** Remember to bring treats as well as regular food to keep up the mutt's morale. That said, if your dog is anything like mine the chances are they'll spend most of the walk dining on rabbit droppings and sheep poo anyway.
- **Medication** You'll know if you need to bring any lotions or potions.
- **Tick remover** See opposite.
- **Poo bags** Essential.
- **Raingear** It can rain!
- **Old towels** For drying your dog.
- **Hygiene wipes** For cleaning your dog after it's rolled in stuff.
- **A favourite toy** Helps prevent your dog from pining for the entire walk.
- **Corkscrew stake** Available from camping or pet shops, this will help you to keep your dog secure in one place while you set up camp/doze.

When it comes to packing, I always leave an exterior pocket of my rucksack empty so I can put used poo bags in there (for deposit at the first bin reached). I always like to keep all the dog's kit together and separate from the other luggage (usually inside a plastic bag inside my rucksack). I have also seen several dogs sporting their own 'doggy rucksack', so they can carry their own food, water, poo etc – which certainly reduces the burden on their owner!

Cleaning up after your dog

It is extremely important that dog owners behave in a responsible way when walking the path. Dog excrement should be cleaned up. In towns, villages and fields where animals graze or which will be cut for silage, hay etc, you need to pick up and bag the excrement.

Staying (and eating) with your dog

In this guide we have used the symbol 🐕 to denote where a place welcomes dogs. However, this always needs to be arranged in advance; some places don't make an additional charge but others do, though this may be per night or per stay).

Many B&B-style places have only one or two rooms suitable for people with dogs; hostels do not permit them unless they are an assistance (guide) dog; smaller campsites tend to accept them, but some of the larger holiday parks do not – however, in either case it is likely the dog will have to be on a lead. Before you turn up always double check whether the place you would like to stay accepts dogs and whether there is space for them.

When it comes to **eating**, some cafés accept dogs and most landlords allow dogs in at least a section of their pubs, though few restaurants do. Make sure you always ask first and ensure your dog is on a lead and secured to your table or a radiator so it doesn't run around.

❑ Walking the Pennine Way – a personal experience

I never intended to walk the Pennine Way. I spent a day and a half walking from Gargrave to Horton-in-Ribblesdale, just for something to do over a long weekend away. Yet at the end I found myself staring at Ingleborough and Whernside, thinking that I could do with a bit more of this. Six months later I was back staring at those same hills, ready to set off to do some more. Having never done any long-distance walking before, I was suddenly hooked.

Walking in stages, fitted in when my annual leave allowed, it took three years to complete the whole thing, mostly completed in spring and autumn, when the weather was often at its worst. More than once I arrived at a B&B or hostel soaking wet, wondering why I was doing this, but the magic of those wild moorlands and hills kept me going. Well, that and the thought of a reviving pint in one of the many pubs along the way. It was an amazing experience – and a great pub crawl – and I have every intention of doing it again one day, preferably all in one go, and maybe even going north to south for a change. One thing is for sure, I'll do it in the summer when it might (hopefully) be just a bit drier!

Andrew Bowden (Twitter: @RamblingManUK)

INDEX

Page references in **bold** type refer to maps

accents 48
access 76, 86
accidents 78-9
accommodation 19-24, 82
booking 22, 28-9
see also place name
Aiggin Stone 106, **109**
Airbnb 24
Aire, River 136, **141**, **142**, **143**, **144**, **145**
Airton 136, 142, **144**, 145
Alston 214, 218, 221, **221**, 222-3, **222**
altitude profiles 295-312
Appleby 210
apps, birds 67
Areas of Outstanding Natural Beauty (AONBs) 60-1
ATMs 27, 28, 34, 36
Auchope Cairn 262, **266**

Backpackers Club 50
baggage-transfer services 27-8, 44, 79
Bainbridge, Brian & Mary 204
Baldersdale 160, 188, 190, **191**
bank holidays 28
banks 28
Barber Booth 86, 159
bed & breakfasts (B&Bs) 21-2
B&B-style accommodation 23, 32, 35, 37
beers 26
Bellingham 236, 244-5, **247**, 248-9, **248**
birds 66-71
field guide 51, app 67
birdwatching 147
Birkdale Farm 198, 204, **205**
black grouse 68-9, 160
Black Hill (nr Crowden) 87, 98, **101**
Black Hill (Greenhead) 226, **230**
Black Moss Reservoir 103, **103**, **105**
Blackshaw Head 120
Blackstone Edge 106, 108, **109**, 110
Reservoir **111**
Blackton Reservoir 190, **191**
Blakehopeburnhaugh 249, **256**
Bleaklow Head 90, **95**
Blenkinsopp Common 225, **230**
blisters 79
booking accommodation 22, 28
books 51
boots 45
Bowes 183, **185**, 188
Bowes Loop 183, **184**, **185**, **186**, **187**, **191**
breweries 26
British Summer Time (BST) 29
Brontës of Haworth 126
Brontë Bridge/Way 119, 125, **125**, **127**
Brownrigg Head 249, **253**
Brun Clough Reservoir/car park 103, **105**
budgeting 32-3
bunkhouses 21, 22, 32, 35, 37
Burnhead **237**, 238
bus services **54**, **55**, 56-9
see also coach services
business hours 28
butterflies 73
Butterfly Conservation 62
Byrness 249, 252, 254, 256, **257**
Byrness Hill **257**, 261

Calder Valley 108, **115**
Calderdale Way **112**
Callerhues Crag **250**, 251
Callis Bridge **115**
Callis Wood 108, **115**
Cam End 160, **162**
Cam High Road 156, 160, **163**
camping/campsites 19-20, 32, 35, 37, 39
camping barns 20-1, 32, 35, 37
camping gear 48
camping pods 21
camping supplies 26
cash machines *see* ATMs
cattle 283
Cauldron Snout 197, **203**
Caw Gap 236, **237**
cell phones *see* mobile phones
Cheviot, The 262, **266**
Chew Green **260**, 261
climate 13-16
clothing 45-6, 78
Clough Edge 90, **96**
coach services
to Britain 52
within Britain 53
coal mining 149
Colden 119, 120, **121**
Coldwell Hill 106-7, **112**
compasses 47
conservation, of the Pennines 60-2
conservation organisations 62
Corpse Road 213, **214**, **215**, **216**, **217**
Cotherstone 190
Cotherstone Moor **187**, **191**
Countryside Code 77
Cow Green Reservoir 197-8, **203**, 204
Cowling 132, **133**, 134
cowlings **132**
Crag Lough **239**, **240**
Cronkley Bridge 197, 200, **201**
Cross Fell 213, **214**, 215, 217
Crowden **97**, 98
Crowden Great Brook 98, **99**, **100**, 103
curlews 69
currency 28

Dales Way **162**, **163**
day walks 39-42
daylight hours 16

Deepdale Beck 188, **189**
Deer Play 249, **251**
Devil's Dike 88, **94**, **95**
dialects 48, **101**
difficulty, of route 11
Diggle 104, **105**, 106
digital mapping 18-19, 49
direction of walk 38-9
distance chart 290-1
Dodd Fell 160, **164**
dogs, walking with 31, 77, 282-3
Douk Ghyll Scar **157**
driving
  to Britain 52
  within Britain 53
Dufton 198, **209**, 210
duration of walk 12
Durham Wildlife Trust 190

Earby 136, **138**
East Marton 134, 136, **139**, 140
Edale 83-6, **85**, 159
Edale Rocks 87, **91**
emergency services 29
emergency signals 88-9
Emley Moor Mast 103
English Heritage 62, 234
environmental impact 74-6
equipment 44-51
erosion 75, 87
Eshton Moor 136, **143**
European Health Insurance Cards (EHICs) 28-9
events, annual 14
exchange rates 28
exposure *see* hypothermia

Falcon Clints 197, **203**
fell running 156
Fellsman Hike 14, **164**
festivals 14
field barns 175
field guides 51
first-aid kit 47
flashlights *see* torches
flights to Britain 52
flora & fauna 63-73, 75
flowers 63-5
food 24-6, 47, 78
food shops/stores 35, 37
footwear 45
forecasts, weather 79
forests 65-6
Forest-in-Teesdale 197, 200, 202
Forestry Commission 61, 65
Fountains Fell 149, **152**, 156

Gargrave 134, 140-1, **141**, 142, **142**
Garrigill 214, 218, **219**
glamping 21, 35, 37
Glendue Burn 225, **228**
God's Bridge **184**, 188
Gordale Scar **146**
GPS 17-19, 49
GPS waypoints 274-81
gradients 11, 295-312
Graining Water 119, **123**
grasses 63-5
Grassholme Reservoir **192**, **193**
Great Chesters Fort **235**, 236
Great Dun Fell 213, **213**
Great Shunner Fell 170, 172, **174**
Greenhead 231-2, **233**
Greenwich Mean Time 29
Greg's Hut 214, **214**, 215
grouse 68-9, 160
grouse shooting 76
guesthouses 23
guided walking holidays 31

Hadfield 98
Hadrian's Wall 76, **233**, 234, **235**, 236, **237**, **239**, **240**
Halsteads **209**, 211
Hannah's Meadow 190, **192**
Hardraw 170, **171**, 172-4
Hardraw Force waterfall 170, **171**, 173
Harter Fell 188, **193**
Hartley Burn 225, **229**
hats 46
Haughton Common 236, **242**
Hauxwell, Hannah 190, 204
Hawes 160, 165-6, **167**, 168, **169**, 170
Haworth 119, 125-6, 128, **129**, 130
Hazelgill Beck **186**, 188
heat exhaustion 80
heatstroke 80
Hebden Bridge 108, 114, 116, **117**, 118
Hebden Bridge Loop 110, **113**, **121**
Heptonstall 110
Heptonstall Moor 119, **122**
Hern Clough 88, **95**
High Cup/High Cup Nick 198, **207**
High Force 197, 198, **199**, 200
history 9-10
  Kinder Scout 86
Historic England 61
Holme Moss Mast **101**, 103
Holwick 196, **197**, 198
Horton-in-Ribblesdale 149, 156, **157**, 158
hostels 21, 22, 32, 35, 37
hotels 23
Housesteads Fort 234
Houx Hill **258**, 261
hydration packs 26, 47
hyperthermia 80
hypothermia 80

Ickornshaw 119, 131-2, **133**
Ickornshaw Moor 119, 120, **132**
inns 23
insurance 28-9
Intake Bridge **184**
itineraries 38-43
  suggested 39, 40, 41

Jack Bridge 120, **121**
Jackdaw Hill 160, **161**
Jacob's Ladder 87, **91**, 159

karst 160
Keighley & Worth Valley Railway 126
Keld 171, 176, **178**, 180
Kellah 231
Kidhow Gate 160, **164**
Kinder Downfall 87, **92**
Kinder Low 90, **91**
Kinder Scout 86, 87, **89**, **91**
Kinder Scout route 87-8
King's Seat 262, **265**
Kirk Yetholm 269, 271-2, **271**

Kirkby Malham **144**, 145
Kirklees Way **101**, **102**
Kisdon Hill 170, **178**
Knar Burn 226, **227**
Knarsdale 223, 226, **227**
Knock Fell **212**, 213, 215

Laddow Rocks 98, **99**
Lamb Hill 261, **262**
lambing 76
Langdon Beck 197, **201**, 202, 204
lead mining 202
Leeds-Liverpool Canal 134, **139**, **141**, **142**
Light Hazzles Reservoir **111**
Ling Gill Bridge 159, 160, **162**
Ling Gill NNR 160
litter 74-5, 77
Little Dun Fell 213, **213**
Local Nature Reserves (LNRs) 61
Long Distance Walkers' Association, The 50
Longdendale Trail/Valley 90, **97**, 98
Lothersdale 134, **135**, 136
Low Force 196, **199**
luggage transfer
  see baggage transfer
Lumbutts 110, **112**
Lunedale 190, **193**, 194

Maiden Way 225, **228**
Maize Beck 198, **205**, **206**
Maize Beck Gorge route **206**, 207, **207**, 210
Malham 136, **146**, **147**, 147-8
Malham Cove **146**, 147, 149
Malham Tarn 149, **150**, **151**
mammals 71-3
Mankinholes 107, 110, **112**
map key 273
map scale 81
maps 48-50, 81-2
Marsden 104
Mickleton Moor 188, **192**
Middleton-in-Teesdale 188, 194-6, **194**, **195**
Mill Hill 88, **92**
Millstone Edge **105**, 106

minimum impact walking 74-7
mining *see* coal mining, lead mining
mobile phones 29, 47, 78, 79
money 27
Montane Spine Race 14
Moorland Centre, Edale 83, **85**, 87
Moors for the Future 87
Mozie Law **263**
mountain rescue 79
Mountain Weather Info Service (MWIS) 79
Muir, John 6
Muker 170, 176
Mytholm **115**, 119

National Nature Reserves (NNRs) 61
national holidays 28
National Parks (NP) 60
  centres 34, 36, 50, 83, 147, 166
national trails 50, 61
National Trust 62, 86, 234
Natural England 60-1, 190
Nether Booth 85, **85**
Newbiggin **197**, 198
North Pennines AONB 60
Northumberland NP 60

Old Bess Hill **131**
Oldham Way **107**
Once Brewed 236, 238, **239**, 240, 242, 244
opening hours 28
orchids 64

packhorse bridges **91**, **111**, 159, 160
packhorse roads/routes **105**, **109**, 159
Padfield 98
Padon Hill 249, **253**
Peak & Northern Footpath Society (PNFS) 84
  signs **96**, **102**, **107**
Peak District NP 60
  centres 83
peat/peat bogs 87, 88
Pennine Way Association (PWA) 50

Pen-y-ghent 149, **154**
peregrine falcons 70, 71, 147
Pinhaw Beacon 134, **137**
poles, walking 47
Ponden 119, 124, **127**, 128
post offices 27, 28, 34, 36
public holidays 28
public transport 51-9, 74
  services 51-3, **54-5**, 56-9
pubs 23, 25, 28
  see also place name

Race Yate 188, **191**
rail services
  to Britain 52
  within Britain 51-3, 59
rainfall 16
Ramblers 50
Rapishaw Gap 236, **240**
Rasp Hill 198, **205**
Ravens Knowe **258**, 261
Ravock Castle 188, **189**
real ales 26
red grouse 69, 160
Redbrook Reservoir 103, **105**
Redesdale Forest 249, **253**, **254**
Redmires 106, **109**
refuge huts 259, 261, 262, **262**, **267**
reptiles 73
restaurants *see place name*
Right to Roam 76, 86
Rochdale Canal 108, 114, **115**, 117
Rottenstone Hill 160, **165**
Round Hill 226, **230**
route finding 17
  troublespots 81
Royal Society for the Protection of Birds (RSPB) 62, 147
rucksacks 44

safety 78-80
Scaleber Hill 134, **140**
Schil, The 264, **267**
school holidays 28
Scottish National Trail 281
self-guided holidays 30-1
Sell Gill Holes **155**, 159
Shitlington Crag 236, **246**
shops, food 28, 35, 37

signposts 17, 84
Sill National Landscape Discovery Centre 238, **239**
Sites of Special Scientific Interest (SSSIs) 61, 190
Slaggyford 223, **227**
sleeping bags 47-8
Sleightholme Moor 180-1, **182**, 188
smoking 29
Snaizeholme Valley 160, **164**
Snake Pass 88, 93, **94**
South Tynedale Railway 221
South Tyne Trail **221**, 223, **224**, **225**, 226, **227**
Special Areas of Conservation (SACs) 61
St Cuthbert's Way **269**, 281
Stainmore Gap 188, **189**
Stanbury 124-5, **127**
Standedge 104, **105**, 159
Standedge Cutting 104, **105**
Stephenson, Tom 9
Stonehaugh 244
Stonesdale Moor 171, **179**
Stoodley Pike 107, **113**, 114
sunburn 80
supermarkets 28
Swaledale 170, 175
Swelland Reservoir 103, **103**
sycamore tree, lone 236, **239**

Tan Hill/Tan Hill Inn 171, 180, **181**
Tees, River 196, **196**, **197**, **198**, **199**, **200**, **203**
telephones 29, 47
temperatures 16
Thirlwall Castle 232, **233**, 234
Thornton-in-Craven 134, **138**
three-day walks 43
Three Peaks Challenge 14, 156, **161**
Three Peaks Cyclocross 14
Thwaite 170, 175, **179**
Time, British Summer (BST) 29
Todmorden 110
Todmorden Way **112**
toilets 75-6
Top Withins 119, **125**
torches 47, 78
Torside 93-4, **97**
Torside Clough 90, **96**
tourist information centres 34, 36, 50
Town Yetholm **271**, 272
town/village facilities 24-7
trail information 50
trail maps 81-2
train services *see* rail services
Trans-Pennine Trail **97**
transport *see* public transport
travel insurance 28-9
trees 65-6, 236, **239**
Twice Brewed Roman Wall Show 14
two-day walks 43

Upper Booth 87, 89, **90**
Upper Coquetdale 271

village/town facilities 34-7
visitor centres 50

Wainwright, Alfred 10
walkers' experiences 12, 30, 31, 33, 36, 37, 38, 42, 43, 284
walkers' organisations 50
walking holiday companies 27-31
walking poles 47
walking seasons 13-15
walking times 81
Walltown Crags **233**, **235**, 236
Walshaw Dean reservoirs 119, **123**, **124**
Wark Forest 236, **241**, **242**
Warks Burn 236, **243**
Warland Reservoir **111**, **112**
water, drinking 26-7, 78
water filters 26
water pouches 26
Watlowes Valley 149, **150**
waypoints 18, 274-81
weather forecasts 79
weekend walks 43
weights and measures 29
Wensleydale Creamery 165-6, **167**, **169**
Wessenden Head **101**, 103
Wessenden/Wessenden Head reservoirs **102**, 103
West Cam Road 160, **164**, **165**
West Marton 140
whistles 47, 78
White Hill 106, **108**
White Holme Reservoir **111**
Whitley Castle Roman fort remains **224**
Whitley Pike 249, **252**, 252
Widdop 120, **123**
wi-fi 27, 82
Wildboar Grain 90, **96**
wild camping 19-20, 39
wild flowers 63-5
wildlife 75
see also flora and fauna
Wildlife Trusts, The 62
Windy Gyle 261-2, **264**
Winshields Crag **239**
Withen's Gate 107, **112**
Withins Height 119, **125**
woods 65-6
Woodland Trust 62
Wytham Moor **184**, 188

Yetholm 14
see also Kirk Yetholm *and* Town Yetholm
YHA/YHA hostels 21, 35, 37
Yorkshire Dales NP 60
centres: Hawes 166
Malham 147

Opposite, top: Pausing to take in the view from Auchope Cairn. **Centre, left**: The final refuge of the walk (see p267) and a good place to prepare for your last steep ascent of the entire trail, up to the Schil. **Right**: Walking between Auchope Cairn and the final refuge hut on the Pennine Way – a tough walk whatever direction you're trekking. **Bottom**: Daisy finds a comfortable place for a short nap after descending from Windy Gyle.

HIGH
FIRE RISK
NO OPEN FIRES

	Edale	Upper Booth	Torside	Crowden	Standedge	Blackstone Edge	Mankinholes	Calder Valley	Blackshaw Head	Colden	Widdop	Ponden/Stanbury	Ickornshaw	Lothersdale	East Marton	Gargrave	Airton	Kirkby Malham
Edale	0																	
Upper Booth	1.5																	
Torside	15	13.5																
Crowden	16	14.5	1															
Standedge	27	25.5	12	11														
Blackstone Edge	32.5	31	17.5	16.5	5.5													
Mankinholes	38.5	37	23.5	22.5	11.5	6												
Calder Valley	41.5	40	26.5	25.5	14.5	9	3											
Blackshaw Head	43	41.5	28	27	16	10.5	4.5	1.5										
Colden	43.5	42	28.5	27.5	16.5	11	5	2	0.5									
Widdop	46	44.5	31	30	19	13.5	7.5	4.5	3	2.5								
Ponden/Stanbury	52	50.5	37	36	25	19.5	13.5	10.5	9	8.5	6							
Ickornshaw	57	55.5	42	41	30	24.5	18.5	15.5	14	13.5	11	5						
Lothersdale	59.5	58	44.5	43.5	32.5	27	21	18	16.5	16	13.5	7.5	2.5					
East Marton	65.5	64	50.5	49.5	38.5	33	27	24	22.5	22	19.5	13.5	8.5	6				
Gargrave	68	66.5	53	52	41	35.5	29.5	26.5	25	24.5	22	16	11	8.5	2.5			
Airton	72	70.5	57	56	45	39.5	33.5	30.5	29	28.5	26	20	15	12.5	6.5	4		
Kirkby Malham	73.5	72	58.5	57.5	46.5	41	35	32	30.5	30	27.5	21.5	16.5	14	8	5.5	1.5	
Malham	74.5	73	59.5	58.5	47.5	42	36	33	31.5	31	28.5	22.5	17.5	15	9	6.5	2.5	1
Horton-in-R'dle	89	87.5	74	73	62	56.5	50.5	47.5	46	45.5	43	37	32	29.5	23.5	21	17	15.5
Hawes	102.5	101	87.5	86.5	75.5	70	64	61	59.5	59	56.5	50.5	45.5	43	37	34.5	30.5	29
Hardraw	104	102.5	89	88	77	71.5	65.5	62.5	61	60.5	58	52	47	44.5	38.5	36	32	30.5
Thwaite	112	110.5	97	96	85	79.5	73.5	70.5	69	68.5	66	60	55	52.5	46.5	44	40	38.5
Keld	115	113.5	100	99	88	82.5	76.5	73.5	72	71.5	69	63	58	55.5	49.5	47	43	41.5
Tan Hill	119	117.5	104	103	92	86.5	80.5	77.5	76	75.5	73	67	62	59.5	53.5	51	47	45.5
Baldersdale	129	127.5	114	113	102	96.5	90.5	87.5	86	85.5	83	77	72	69.5	63.5	61	57	55.5
Lunedale	132	130.5	117	116	105	99.5	93.5	90.5	89	88.5	86	80	75	72.5	66.5	64	60	58.5
Middleton-in-T	135.5	134	120.5	119.5	108.5	103	97	94	92.5	92	89.5	83.5	78.5	76	70	67.5	63.5	62
Holwick	138	136.5	123	122	111	105.5	99.5	96.5	95	94.5	92	86	81	78.5	72.5	70	66	64.5
High Force	140.5	139	125.5	124.5	113.5	108	102	99	97.5	97	94.5	88.5	83.5	81	75	72.5	68.5	67
Dufton	155	153.5	140	139	128	122.5	116.5	113.5	112	111.5	109	103	98	95.5	89.5	87	83	81.5
Garrigill	170.5	169	155.5	154.5	143.5	138	132	129	127.5	127	124.5	118.5	113.5	111	105	102.5	98.5	97
Alston	174.5	173	159.5	158.5	147.5	142	136	133	131.5	131	128.5	122.5	117.5	115	109	106.5	102.5	101
Knarsdale	181.5	180	166.5	165.5	154.5	149	143	140	138.5	138	135.5	129.5	124.5	122	116	113.5	109.5	108
Greenhead	191	189.5	176	175	164	158.5	152.5	149.5	148	147.5	145	139	134	131.5	125.5	123	119	117.5
Burnhead	195	193.5	180	179	168	162.5	156.5	153.5	152	151.5	149	143	138	135.5	129.5	127	123	121.5
Once Brewed	197.5	196	182.5	181.5	170.5	165	159	156	154.5	154	151.5	145.5	140.5	138	132	129.5	125.5	124
Hetherington	208	206.5	193	192	181	175.5	169.5	166.5	165	164.5	162	156	151	148.5	142.5	140	136	134.5
Bellingham	212.5	211	197.5	196.5	185.5	180	174	171	169.5	169	166.5	160.5	155.5	153	147	144.5	140.5	139
Byrness	227.5	226	212.5	211.5	200.5	195	189	186	184.5	184	181.5	175.5	170.5	168	162	159.5	155.5	154
Kirk Yetholm	253	251.5	238	237	226	220.5	214.5	211.5	210	209.5	207	201	196	193.5	187.5	185	181	179.5

Pennine Way
DISTANCE CHART

miles (approx)

	Malham	Horton-in-Ribblesdale	Hawes	Hardraw	Thwaite	Keld	Tan Hill	Baldersdale	Lunedale	Middleton-in-Teesdale	Holwick	High Force	Dufton	Garrigill	Alston	Knarsdale	Greenhead	Burnhead	Once Brewed	Hetherington	Bellingham	Byrness
Horton-in-Ribblesdale	4.5																					
Hawes	3	13.5																				
Hardraw	.5	15	1.5																			
Thwaite	7.5	23	9.5	8																		
Keld	.5	26	12.5	11	3																	
Tan Hill	4.5	30	16.5	15	7	4																
Baldersdale	4.5	40	26.5	25	17	14	10															
Lunedale	7.5	43	29.5	28	20	17	13	3														
Middleton-in-Teesdale	1	46.5	33	31.5	23.5	20.5	16.5	6.5	3.5													
Holwick	3.5	49	35.5	34	26	23	19	9	6	2.5												
High Force	6	51.5	38	36.5	28.5	25.5	21.5	11.5	8.5	5	2.5											
Dufton	0.5	66	52.5	51	43	40	36	26	23	19.5	17	14.5										
Garrigill	6	81.5	68	66.5	58.5	55.5	51.5	41.5	38.5	35	32.5	30	15.5									
Alston	00	85.5	72	70.5	62.5	59.5	55.5	45.5	42.5	39	36.5	34	19.5	4								
Knarsdale	07	92.5	79	77.5	69.5	66.5	62.5	52.5	49.5	46	43.5	41	26.5	11	7							
Greenhead	16.5	102	88.5	87	79	76	72	62	59	55.5	53	50.5	36	20.5	16.5	9.5						
Burnhead	20.5	106	92.5	91	83	80	76	66	63	59.5	57	54.5	40	24.5	20.5	13.5	4					
Once Brewed	23	108.5	95	93.5	85.5	82.5	78.5	68.5	65.5	62	59.5	57	42.5	27	23	16	6.5	2.5				
Hetherington	33.5	119	105.5	104	96	93	89	79	76	72.5	70	67.5	53	37.5	33.5	26.5	17	13	10.5			
Bellingham	38	123.5	110	108.5	100.5	97.5	93.5	83.5	80.5	77	74.5	72	57.5	42	38	31	21.5	17.5	15	4.5		
Byrness	53	138.5	125	123.5	115.5	112.5	108.5	98.5	95.5	92	89.5	87	72.5	57	53	46	36.5	32.5	30	19.5	15	
Kirk Yetholm	78.5	164	150.5	149	141	138	134	124	121	117.5	115	112.5	98	82.5	78.5	71.5	62	58	55.5	45	40.5	25.5

TRAILBLAZER'S LONG-DISTANCE PATH (LDP) WALKING GUIDES

We've applied to destinations which are closer to home Trailblazer's proven formula for publishing definitive practical route guides for adventurous travellers. Britain's network of long-distance trails enables the walker to explore some of the finest landscapes in the country's best walking areas. These are guides that are user-friendly, practical, informative and environmentally sensitive.

'The same attention to detail that distinguishes its other guides has been brought to bear here'.
THE SUNDAY TIMES

● **Unique mapping features** In many walking guidebooks the reader has to read a route description then try to relate it to the map. Our guides are much easier to use because walking directions, tricky junctions, places to stay and eat, points of interest and walking times are all written onto the maps themselves in the places to which they apply. With their uncluttered clarity, these are not general-purpose maps but fully edited maps drawn by walkers for walkers.

● **Largest-scale walking maps** At a scale of just under 1:20,000 (8cm or 3¹/₈ inches to one mile) the maps in these guides are bigger than even the most detailed British walking maps currently available in the shops.

● **Not just a trail guide – includes where to stay, where to eat and public transport** Our guidebooks cover the complete walking experience, not just the route. Accommodation options for all budgets are provided (pubs, hotels, B&Bs, campsites, bunkhouses, hostels) as well as places to eat. Detailed public transport information for all access points to each trail means that there are itineraries for all walkers, for hiking the entire route as well as for day or weekend walks.

● **Includes dowloadable GPS waypoints** – Marked on our maps and downloadable from the Trailblazer website.

Cleveland Way *Henry Stedman*, 1st edn, ISBN 978-1-905864-91-1, 208pp, 58 maps
Coast to Coast *Henry Stedman*, 8th edn, ISBN 978-1-905864-96-6, 268pp, 110 maps
Cornwall Coast Path (SW Coast Path Pt 2) *Stedman & Newton*, 6th edn, ISBN 978-1-912716-05-0, 352pp, 142 maps
Cotswold Way *Tricia & Bob Hayne*, 4th edn, ISBN 978-1-912716-04-3, 204pp, 53 maps,
Dales Way *Henry Stedman*, 1st edn, ISBN 978-1-905864-78-2, 192pp, 50 maps
Dorset & South Devon (SW Coast Path Pt 3) *Stedman & Newton*, 2nd edn, ISBN 978-1-905864-94-2, 336pp, 88 maps
Exmoor & North Devon (SW Coast Path Pt I) *Stedman & Newton*, 2nd edn, ISBN 978-1-905864-86-7, 224pp, 68 maps
Great Glen Way *Jim Manthorpe*, 1st edn, ISBN 978-1-905864-80-5, 192pp, 55 maps
Hadrian's Wall Path *Henry Stedman*, 5th edn, ISBN 978-1-905864-85-0, 224pp, 60 maps
Norfolk Coast Path & Peddars Way *Alexander Stewart*, 1st edn, ISBN 978-1-905864-98-0, 224pp, 75 maps,
North Downs Way *Henry Stedman*, 2nd edn, ISBN 978-1-905864-90-4, 240pp, 98 maps
Offa's Dyke Path *Keith Carter*, 4th edn, ISBN 978-1-912716-03-6, 240pp, 98 maps
Pembrokeshire Coast Path *Jim Manthorpe*, 5th edn, ISBN 978-1-905864-84-3, 236pp, 96 maps,
Pennine Way *Stuart Greig*, 5th edn, ISBN 978-1-912716-02-9, 272pp, 138 maps
The Ridgeway *Nick Hill*, 4th edn, ISBN 978-1-905864-79-9, 208pp, 53 maps
South Downs Way *Jim Manthorpe*, 6th edn, ISBN 978-1-905864-93-5, 204pp, 60 maps
Thames Path *Joel Newton*, 2nd edn, ISBN 978-1-905864-97-3, 256pp, 99 maps
West Highland Way *Charlie Loram*, 7th edn, ISBN 978-1-912716-01-2, 218pp, 60 maps

'The Trailblazer series stands head, shoulders, waist and ankles above the rest. They are particularly strong on mapping ...'
THE SUNDAY TIMES

TRAILBLAZER
British Walking Guides
SEE OVERLEAF FOR FULL TITLE LIST
West Highland WAY
Coast to Coast PATH
Cleveland WAY
Norfolk Coast Path AND PEDDARS WAY
Dales Way
North Downs WAY
trailblazer
Orkney
Thurso
Stornoway
Scottish Highlands Hillwalking Guide
Inverness
Skye
Great Glen Way
Aberdeen
Fort William
SCOTLAND
Mull
West Highland Way
Edinburgh
Milngavie
Glasgow
Berwick upon Tweed
Arran
Kirk Yetholm
Pennine Way
Hadrian's Wall Path
Bowness-on-Solway
Wallsend
Newcastle upon Tyne
. IRELAND
Carlisle
Belfast
Coast to Coast
St Bees
Robin Hood's Bay
Bowness-on-Windermere
Filey
Dales Way
Helmsley
Cleveland Way
Isle of Man
Ilkley
York
EP. OF
ELAND
Pennine Way
Leeds
Hull
IRISH SEA
Liverpool
Manchester
Edale
Norfolk Coast Path & Peddars Way
Dublin
Prestatyn
Anglesey
Bangor
Crewe
Lincoln
Nottingham
Cromer
Norwich
ENGLAND
Great Yarmouth
Offa's Dyke Path
Birmingham
Cotswold Way
Cambridge
Knettishall Heath
Cardigan
The Ridgeway
Chipping Campden
WALES
Pembrokeshire Coast Path
Amroth
Ivinghoe Beacon
Kemble
Chepstow
London
Thames Path
Cardiff
Bristol
Bath
Overton Hill
Canterbury
Exmoor & N Devon Coast Path
Winchester
Farnham
Dover
Minehead
Salisbury
North Downs Way
Bude
Eastbourne
Portsmouth
Brighton
Exeter
Poole
Cornwall Coast Path
Isle of Wight
South Downs Way
Plymouth
Dorset & S Devon Coast Path
0 50 100km
0 25 50 miles
es of
cilly
ENGLISH CHANNEL

Kilimanjaro
THE TREKKING GUIDE TO
AFRICA'S HIGHEST MOUNTAIN
HENRY STEDMAN
trailblazer

Tour du
Mont Blanc
trailblazer

TRAILBLAZER TITLE LIST

Adventure Cycle-Touring Handbook
Adventure Motorcycling Handbook
Australia by Rail
Cleveland Way (British Walking Guide)
Coast to Coast (British Walking Guide)
Cornwall Coast Path (British Walking Guide)
Cotswold Way (British Walking Guide)
The Cyclist's Anthology
Dales Way (British Walking Guide)
Dorset & Sth Devon Coast Path (British Walking Gde)
Exmoor & Nth Devon Coast Path (British Walking Gde)
Great Glen Way (British Walking Guide)
Hadrian's Wall Path (British Walking Guide)
Himalaya by Bike – a route and planning guide
Inca Trail, Cusco & Machu Picchu
Japan by Rail
Kilimanjaro – the trekking guide (includes Mt Meru)
Madeira Walks – 37 selected day walks
Moroccan Atlas – The Trekking Guide
Morocco Overland (4WD/motorcycle/mountainbike)
Nepal Trekking & The Great Himalaya Trail
New Zealand – The Great Walks
North Downs Way (British Walking Guide)
Offa's Dyke Path (British Walking Guide)
Overlanders' Handbook – worldwide driving guide
Peddars Way & Norfolk Coast Path (British Walking Gde)
Pembrokeshire Coast Path (British Walking Guide)
Pennine Way (British Walking Guide)
Peru's Cordilleras Blanca & Huayhuash – Hiking/Biking
The Railway Anthology
The Ridgeway (British Walking Guide)
Sahara Overland – a route and planning guide
Scottish Highlands – Hillwalking Guide
Siberian BAM Guide – rail, rivers & road
The Silk Roads – a route and planning guide
Sinai – the trekking guide
South Downs Way (British Walking Guide)
Thames Path (British Walking Guide)
Tour du Mont Blanc
Trans-Canada Rail Guide
Trans-Siberian Handbook
Trekking in the Everest Region
The Walker's Anthology
The Walker's Anthology – further tales
The Walker's Haute Route – Mont Blanc to Matterhorn
West Highland Way (British Walking Guide)

TREKKING IN THE
Everest
REGION
trailblazer

Scottish Highlands
THE HILLWALKING GUIDE
trailblazer

THE
Inca Trail
CUSCO &
MACHU PICCHU
trailblazer

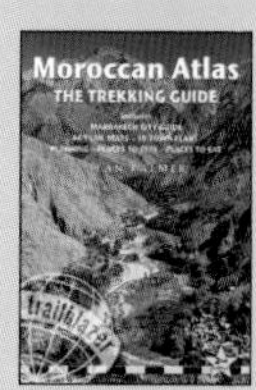
Moroccan Atlas
THE TREKKING GUIDE
trailblazer

PERU'S
Cordilleras Blanca &
Huayhuash
trailblazer

Morocco
OVERLAND
CHRIS SCOTT
trailblazer

Adventure
Cycle-Touring
HANDBOOK
trailblazer

Japan
BY RAIL
trailblazer

The Walker's
Anthology
FURTHER TALES

Trans-Siberian
HANDBOOK
trailblazer

For more information about Trailblazer and our expanding range of guides, for guidebook updates or for credit card mail order sales visit our website:

www.trailblazer-guides.com

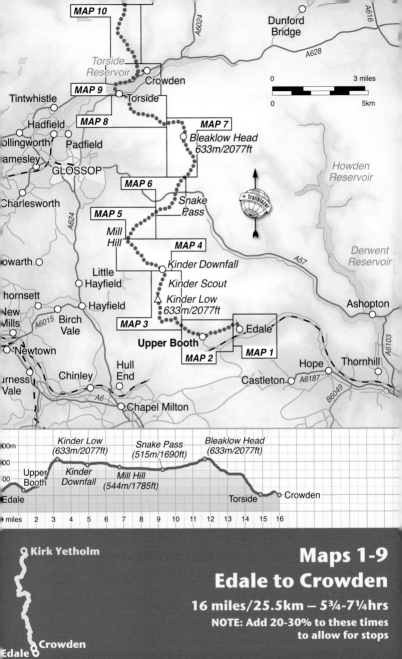

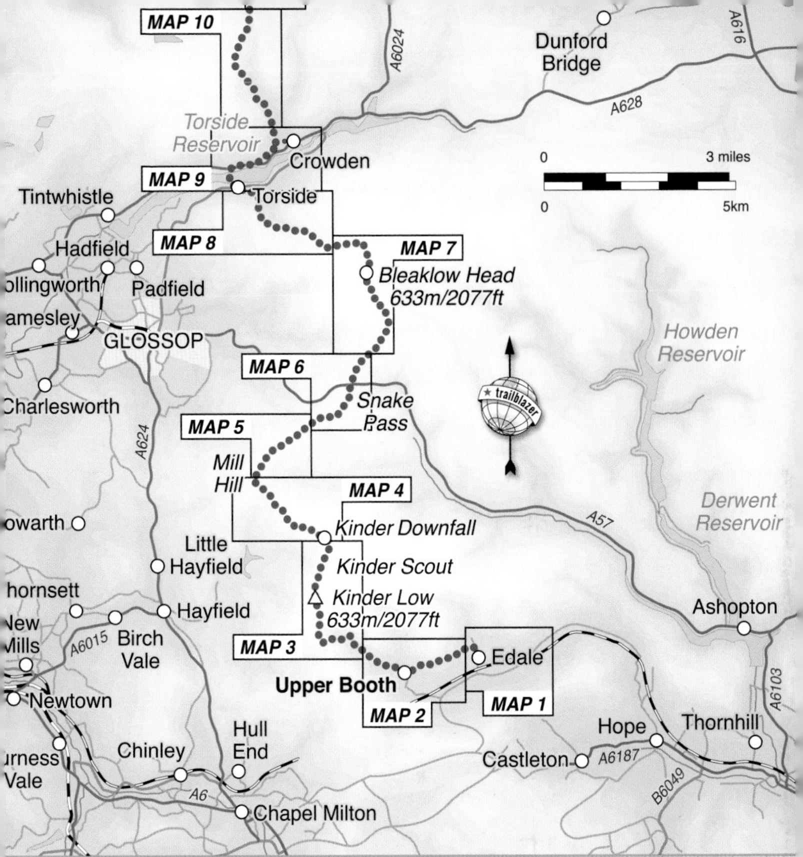
MAP 10
Dunford Bridge
A616
A6024
A628
Torside Reservoir
Crowden
0
3 miles
0
5km
MAP 9
Tintwhistle
Torside
MAP 8
Hadfield
MAP 7
Bleaklow Head 633m/2077ft
ollingworth
Padfield
amesley
GLOSSOP
Howden Reservoir
MAP 6
trailblazer
Snake Pass
Charlesworth
MAP 5
A624
Mill Hill
MAP 4
Derwent Reservoir
owarth
A57
Kinder Downfall
Little Hayfield
Kinder Scout
hornsett
Kinder Low 633m/2077ft
Hayfield
Ashopton
New Mills
A6015
Birch Vale
MAP 3
Edale
Upper Booth
Newtown
MAP 1
MAP 2
A6103
Hull End
Hope
Thornhill
Chinley
rness Vale
Castleton
A6187
A6
B6049
Chapel Milton

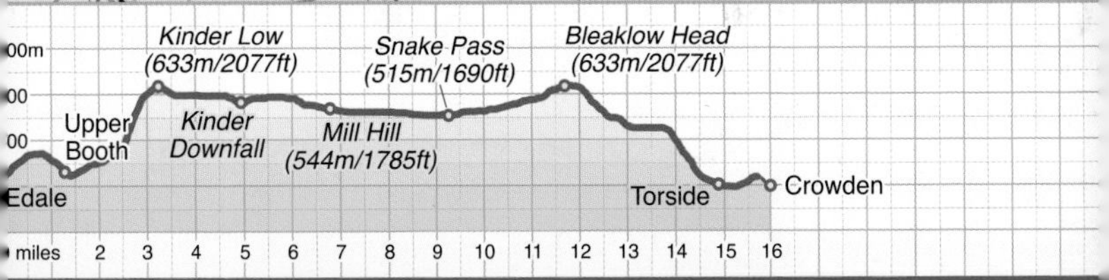
Kinder Low (633m/2077ft)
Snake Pass (515m/1690ft)
Bleaklow Head (633m/2077ft)
00m
00
00
Upper Booth
Kinder Downfall
Mill Hill (544m/1785ft)
Edale
Torside
Crowden
miles
2
3
4
5
6
7
8
9
10
11
12
13
14
15
16

Kirk Yetholm
Crowden
Edale

Maps 1-9
Edale to Crowden

16 miles/25.5km – 5¾-7¼hrs

NOTE: Add 20-30% to these times to allow for stops

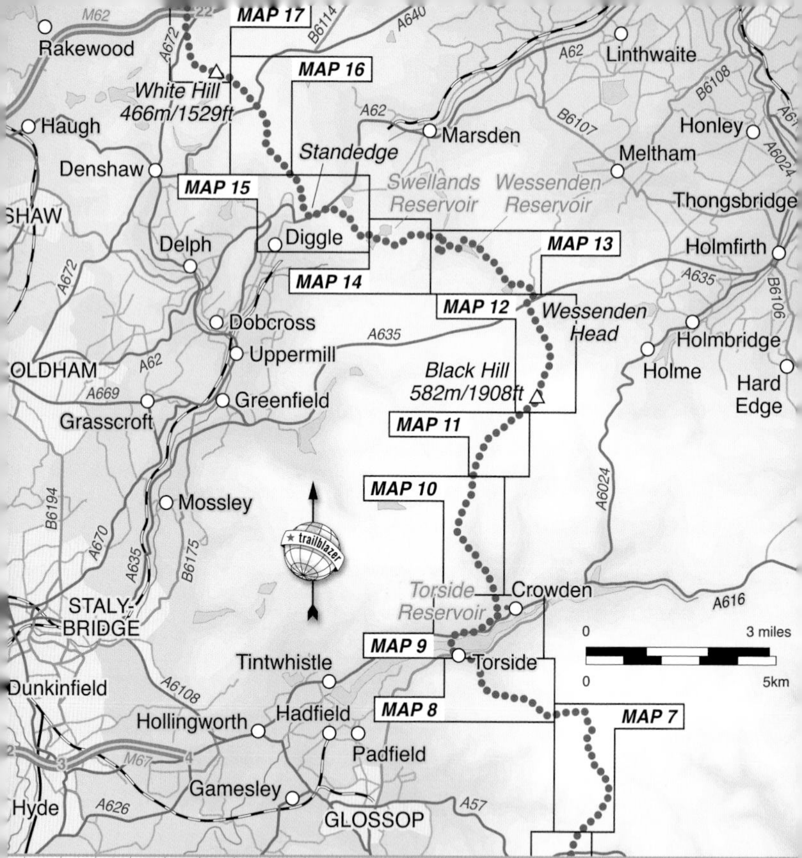

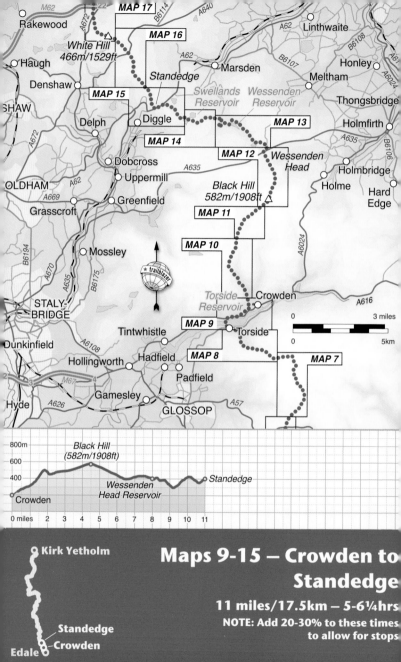

M62
22
MAP 17
B6114
A640
Rakewood
A672
White Hill
466m/1529ft
MAP 16
A62
Linthwaite
B6108
Haugh
A62
Marsden
B6107
Honley
A6024
Denshaw
Standedge
Meltham
MAP 15
Swellands Reservoir
Wessenden Reservoir
Thongsbridge
SHAW
Diggle
Delph
MAP 13
Holmfirth
A672
MAP 14
A635
MAP 12
Wessenden Head
B6106
Dobcross
A635
Holmbridge
Uppermill
OLDHAM
A62
Black Hill
582m/1908ft
Holme
A669
Greenfield
Hard Edge
Grasscroft
MAP 11
MAP 10
A6024
Mossley
B6194
A670
trailblazer
A635
B6175
Torside Reservoir
Crowden
A616
STALYBRIDGE
0
3 miles
MAP 9
Tintwhistle
Torside
0
5km
Dunkinfield
A6108
MAP 8
Hadfield
MAP 7
Hollingworth
Padfield
M67
Gamesley
Hyde
A626
A57
GLOSSOP

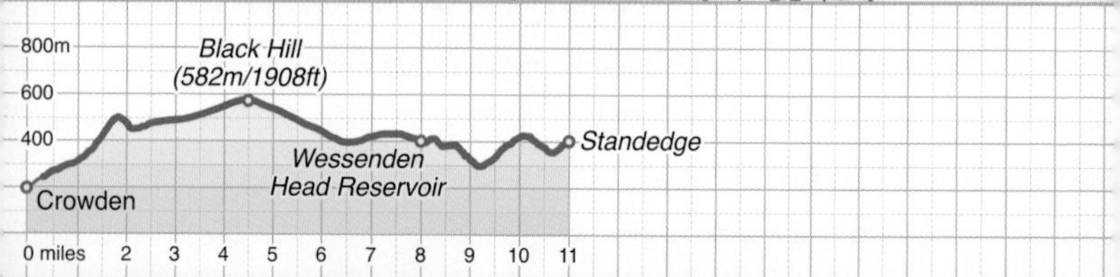

800m
600
400
Black Hill
(582m/1908ft)
Wessenden Head Reservoir
Standedge
Crowden
0 miles
2
3
4
5
6
7
8
9
10
11

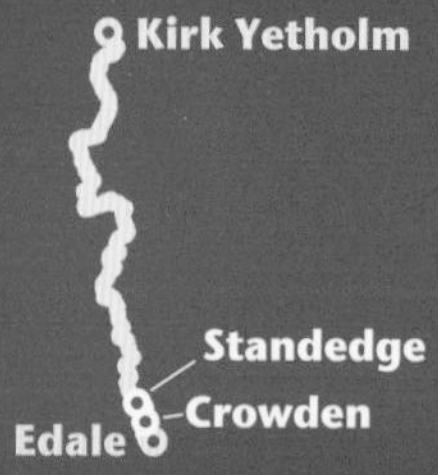

Kirk Yetholm
Standedge
Crowden
Edale

Maps 9-15 – Crowden to Standedge

11 miles/17.5km – 5-6¼hrs

NOTE: Add 20-30% to these times to allow for stops

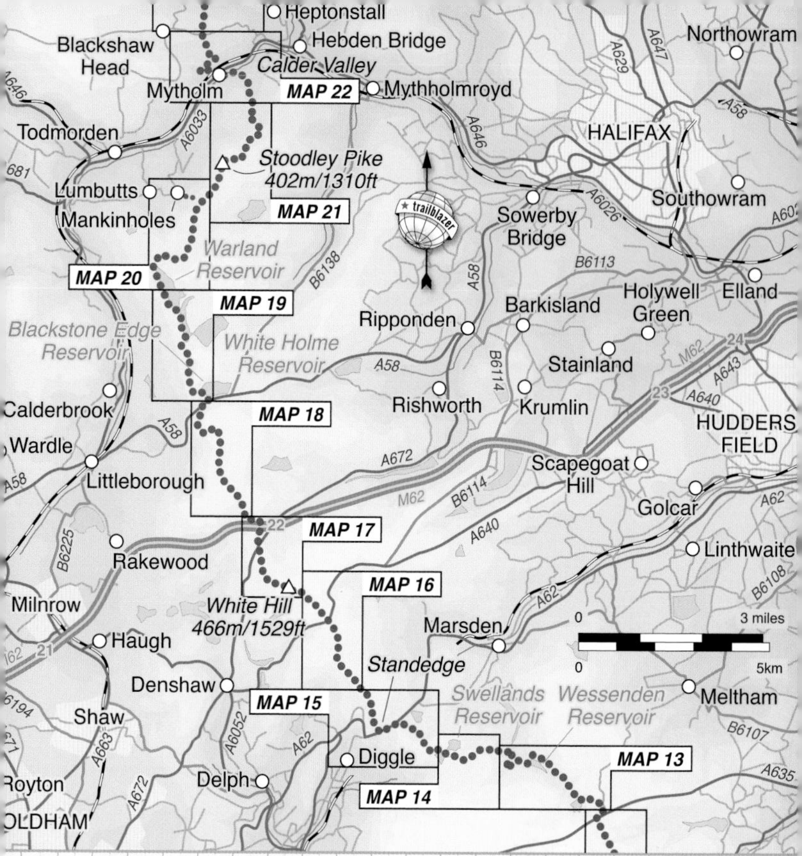

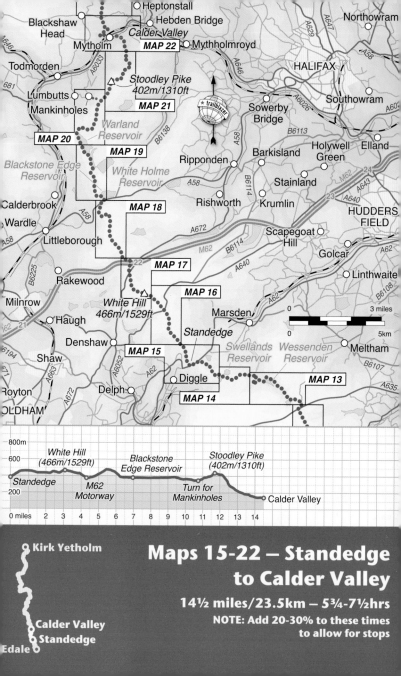

Heptonstall
Blackshaw Head
Hebden Bridge
Calder Valley
Northowram
Mytholm
MAP 22
Mythholmroyd
A629
A647
A646
A58
HALIFAX
Todmorden
A6033
Stoodley Pike 402m/1310ft
Lumbutts
Mankinholes
MAP 21
trailblazer
A6026
Southowram
Sowerby Bridge
Warland Reservoir
B6138
B6113
MAP 20
MAP 19
A58
Holywell Green
Elland
Barkisland
Ripponden
Blackstone Edge Reservoir
White Holme Reservoir
A58
B6114
Stainland
M62
A643
24
A640
23
Calderbrook
MAP 18
Rishworth
Krumlin
HUDDERSFIELD
Wardle
A58
A672
Scapegoat Hill
Littleborough
M62
B6114
Golcar
A62
A640
22
MAP 17
B6225
Rakewood
Linthwaite
MAP 16
B6108
White Hill 466m/1529ft
Milnrow
A62
Marsden
0
3 miles
Haugh
0
5km
21
Standedge
Denshaw
Swellands Reservoir
Wessenden Reservoir
Meltham
MAP 15
Shaw
A6052
A62
B6107
A663
Diggle
MAP 13
A635
Delph
MAP 14
Royton
A672
OLDHAM

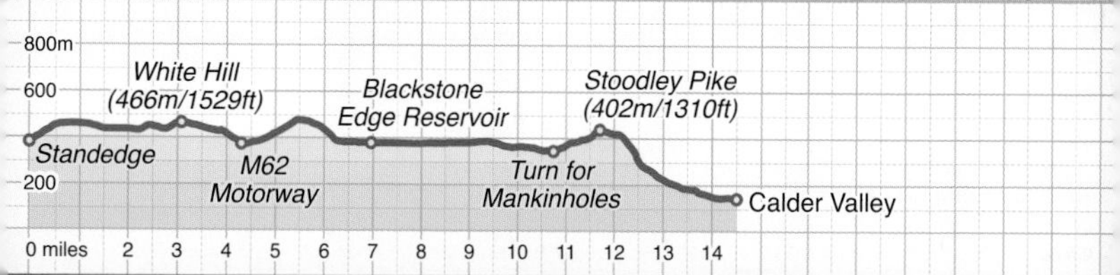

800m
600
200
White Hill (466m/1529ft)
Blackstone Edge Reservoir
Stoodley Pike (402m/1310ft)
Standedge
M62 Motorway
Turn for Mankinholes
Calder Valley
0 miles
2
3
4
5
6
7
8
9
10
11
12
13
14

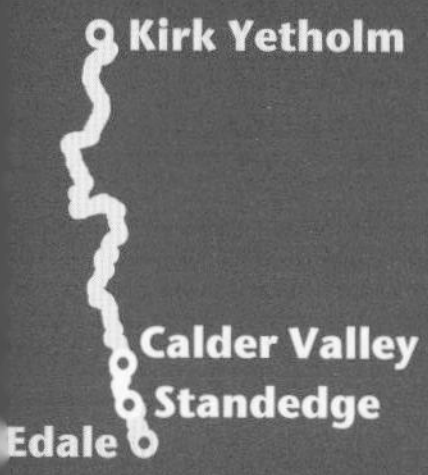

Kirk Yetholm
Calder Valley
Standedge
Edale

Maps 15-22 – Standedge to Calder Valley

14½ miles/23.5km – 5¾-7½hrs

NOTE: Add 20-30% to these times to allow for stops

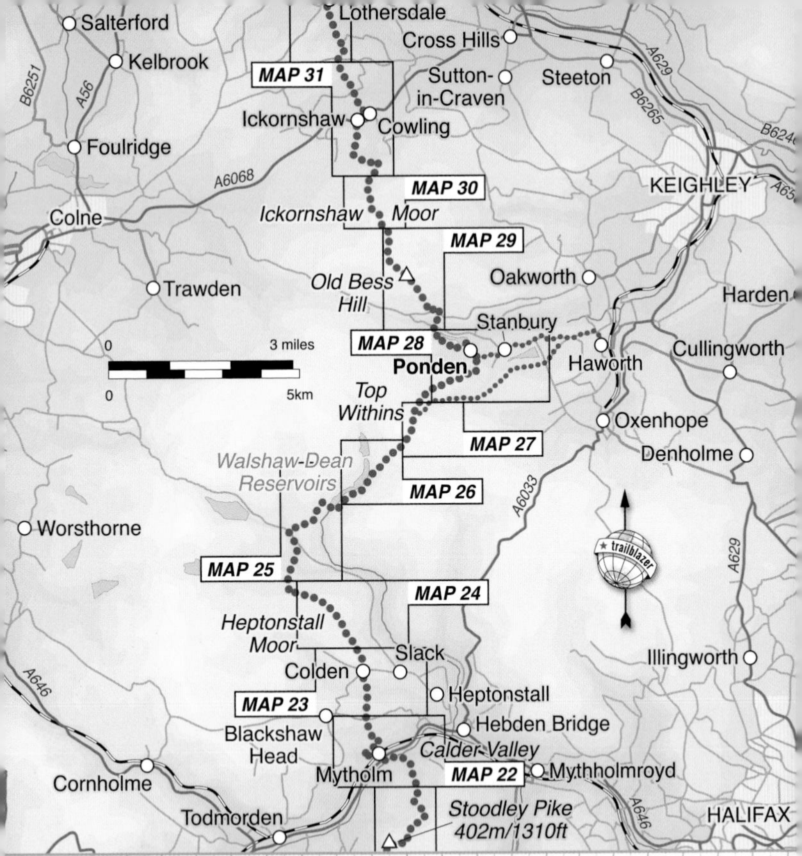

Lothersdale
Salterford
Cross Hills
Kelbrook
MAP 31
Sutton-in-Craven
Steeton
A629
B6251
A56
B6265
Ickornshaw
Cowling
B624
Foulridge
A6068
MAP 30
KEIGHLEY
A65
Colne
Ickornshaw Moor
MAP 29
Old Bess Hill
Oakworth
Trawden
Harden
Stanbury
0
3 miles
MAP 28
Haworth
Cullingworth
Ponden
0
5km
Top Withins
Oxenhope
MAP 27
Denholme
Walshaw-Dean Reservoirs
MAP 26
A6033
Worsthorne
trailblazer
A629
MAP 25
MAP 24
Heptonstall Moor
Slack
Illingworth
Colden
A646
Heptonstall
MAP 23
Hebden Bridge
Blackshaw Head
Calder Valley
Cornholme
Mytholm
MAP 22
Mythholmroyd
A646
Todmorden
Stoodley Pike 402m/1310ft
HALIFAX

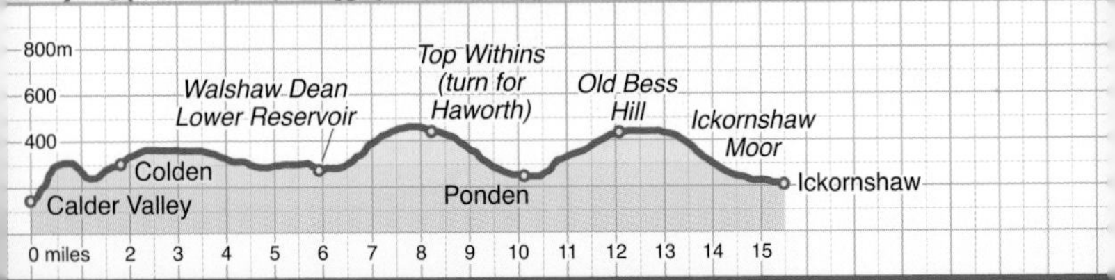

800m
600
400
Walshaw Dean Lower Reservoir
Top Withins (turn for Haworth)
Old Bess Hill
Ickornshaw Moor
Colden
Calder Valley
Ponden
Ickornshaw
0 miles
2
3
4
5
6
7
8
9
10
11
12
13
14
15

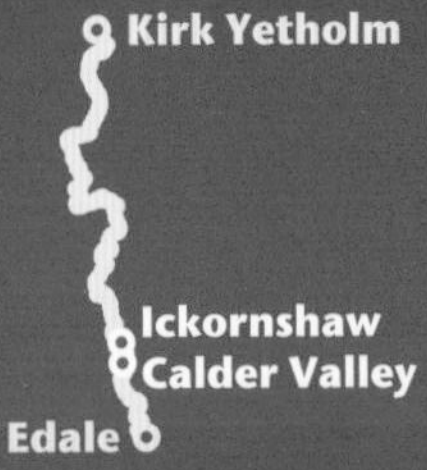

Kirk Yetholm
Ickornshaw
Calder Valley
Edale

Maps 22-31
Calder Valley to Ickornshaw

15½ miles/25km – 5½-7½hrs

NOTE: Add 20-30% to these times to allow for stops

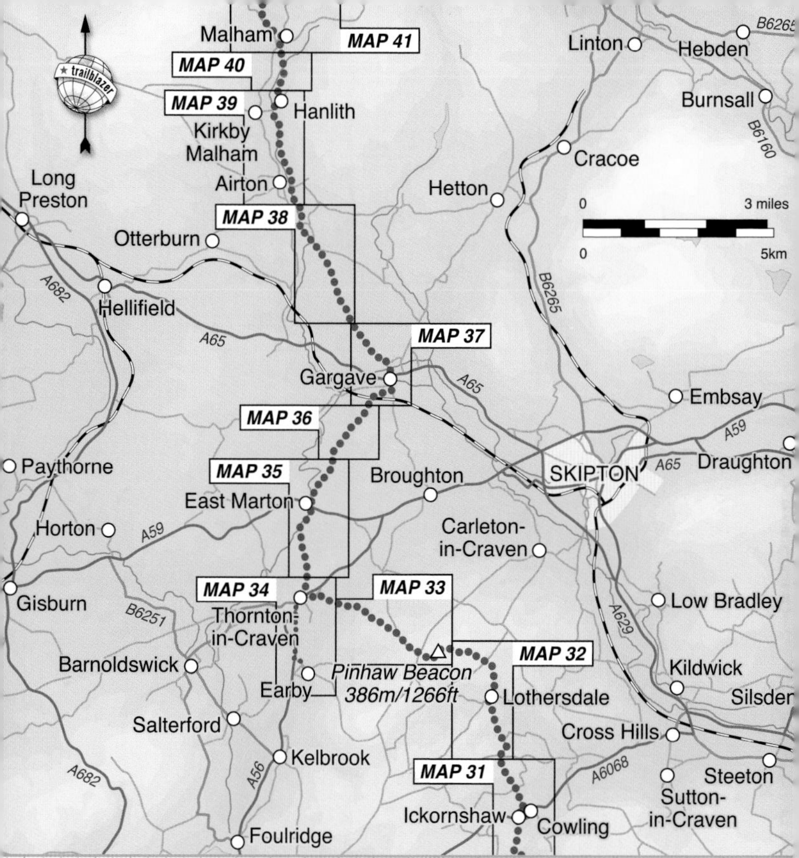
Malham
MAP 41
MAP 40
MAP 39
Hanlith
Kirkby
Malham
Airton
Long
Preston
Otterburn
MAP 38
Hellifield
A682
A65
Gargrave
MAP 37
A65
MAP 36
MAP 35
Paythorne
East Marton
Broughton
Horton
A59
Gisburn
MAP 34
Thornton-
in-Craven
B6251
Barnoldswick
Earby
MAP 33
Pinhaw Beacon
386m/1266ft
MAP 32
Lothersdale
Salterford
Kelbrook
A56
A682
MAP 31
Ickornshaw
Cowling
Foulridge
Linton
Hebden
B6265
Burnsall
B6160
Cracoe
Hetton
0
3 miles
0
5km
B6265
Embsay
A59
SKIPTON
A65
Draughton
Carleton-
in-Craven
Low Bradley
A629
Kildwick
Silsden
Cross Hills
A6068
Steeton
Sutton-
in-Craven
trailblazer

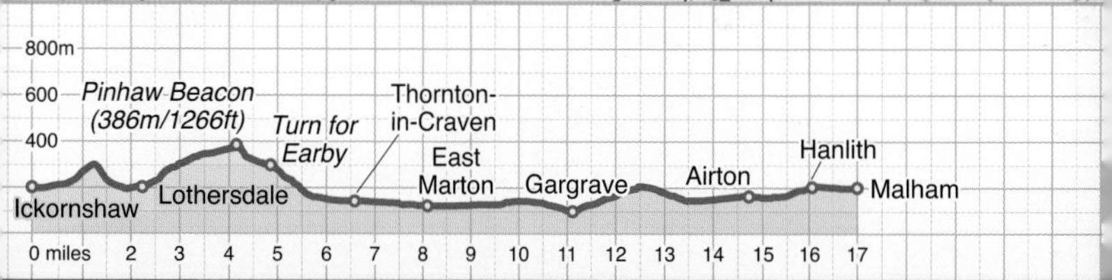
800m
600
400
Pinhaw Beacon
(386m/1266ft)
Turn for
Earby
Thornton-
in-Craven
East
Marton
Gargrave
Airton
Hanlith
Malham
Ickornshaw
Lothersdale
0 miles
2
3
4
5
6
7
8
9
10
11
12
13
14
15
16
17

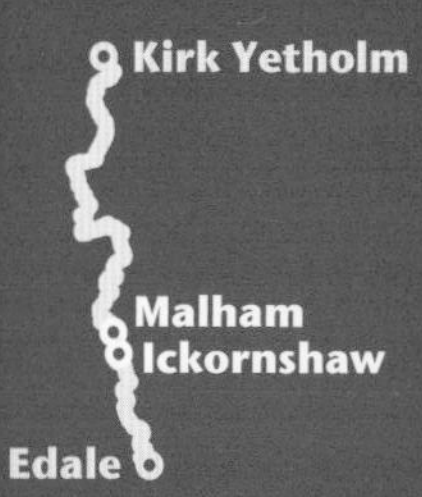
Kirk Yetholm
Malham
Ickornshaw
Edale

Maps 31-41
Ickornshaw to Malham

17 miles/27.5km – 6¾-9¾hrs

NOTE: Add 20-30% to these times to allow for stops

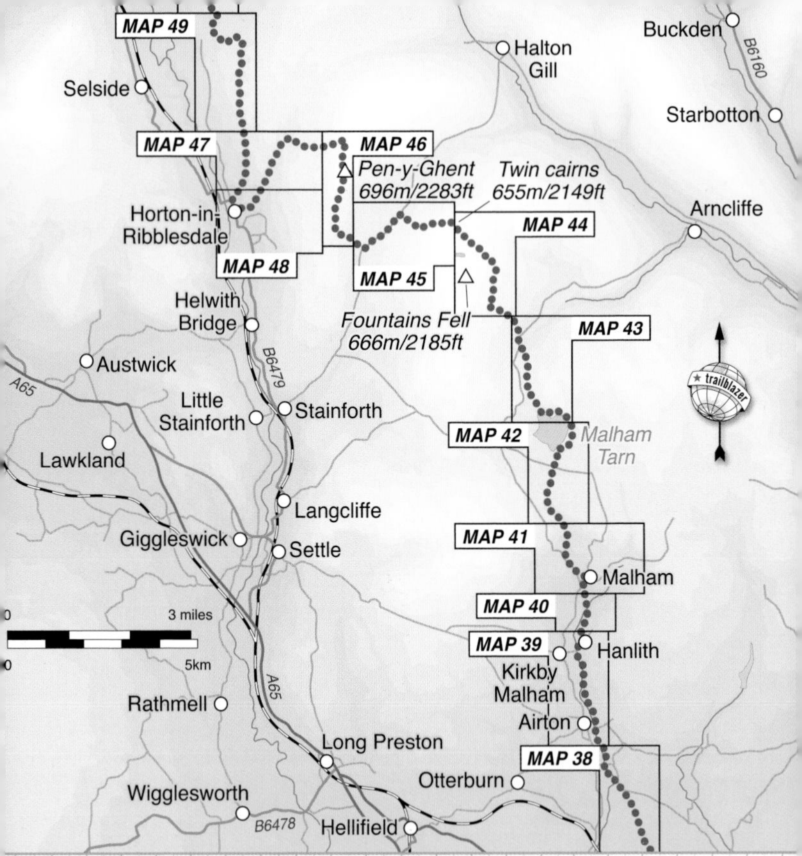
MAP 49
MAP 47
MAP 46
MAP 44
MAP 48
MAP 45
MAP 43
MAP 42
MAP 41
MAP 40
MAP 39
MAP 38
Selside
Halton Gill
Buckden
B6160
Starbotton
Pen-y-Ghent 696m/2283ft
Twin cairns 655m/2149ft
Arncliffe
Horton-in-Ribblesdale
Fountains Fell 666m/2185ft
Helwith Bridge
B6479
Austwick
A65
Little Stainforth
Stainforth
Lawkland
Malham Tarn
Langcliffe
Giggleswick
Settle
Malham
0
3 miles
0
5km
Hanlith
Kirkby Malham
Rathmell
Airton
Long Preston
Otterburn
Wigglesworth
B6478
Hellifield
trailblazer

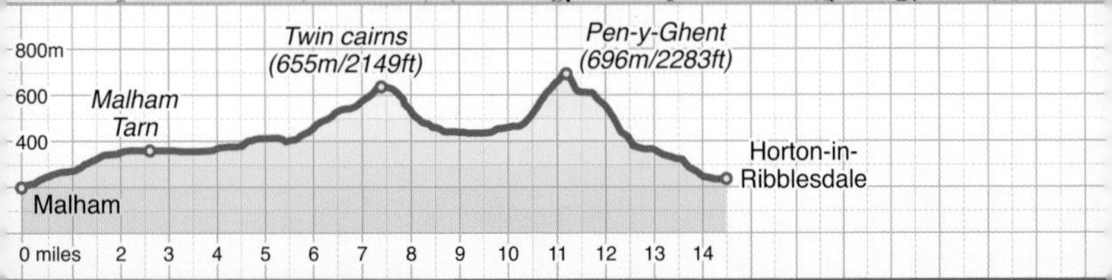
800m
600
400
Malham Tarn
Twin cairns (655m/2149ft)
Pen-y-Ghent (696m/2283ft)
Horton-in-Ribblesdale
Malham
0 miles
2
3
4
5
6
7
8
9
10
11
12
13
14

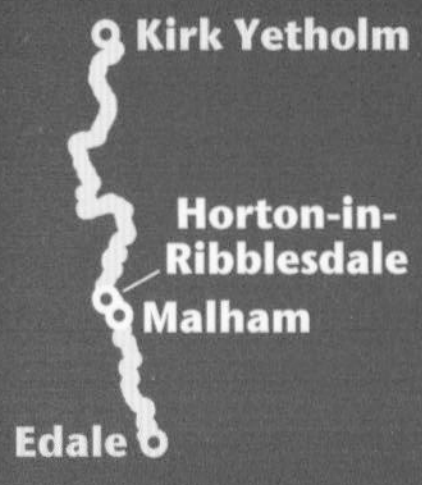
Kirk Yetholm
Horton-in-Ribblesdale
Malham
Edale

Maps 41-48 – Malham to Horton-in-Ribblesdale

14½ miles/23.5km – 6-8hrs

NOTE: Add 20-30% to these times to allow for stops

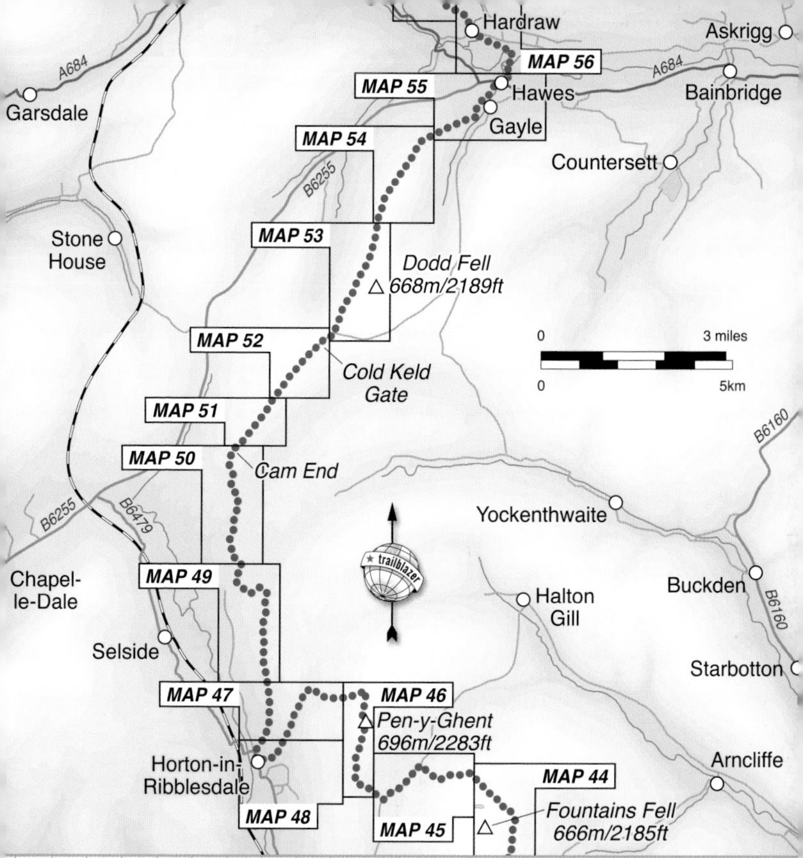
Hardraw
Askrigg
MAP 56
A684
MAP 55
Hawes
A684
Bainbridge
Garsdale
Gayle
MAP 54
Countersett
B6255
MAP 53
Stone
House
Dodd Fell
668m/2189ft
MAP 52
0
3 miles
Cold Keld
Gate
0
5km
MAP 51
B6160
MAP 50
Cam End
B6255
B6479
Yockenthwaite
trailblazer
Chapel-
le-Dale
MAP 49
Buckden
Halton
Gill
B6160
Selside
Starbotton
MAP 47
MAP 46
Pen-y-Ghent
696m/2283ft
Horton-in-
Ribblesdale
Arncliffe
MAP 44
MAP 48
MAP 45
Fountains Fell
666m/2185ft

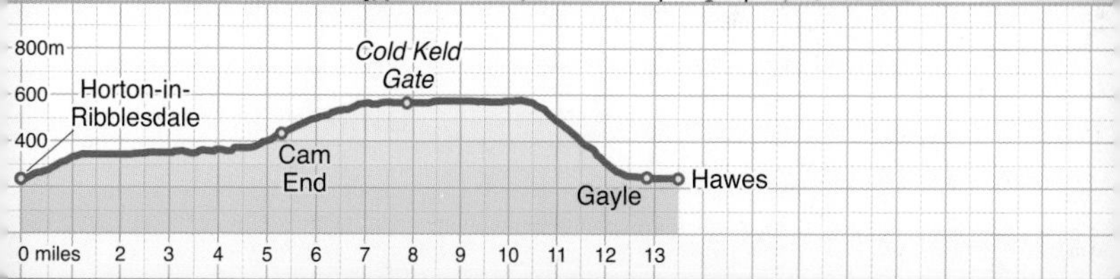
800m
600
400
Horton-in-
Ribblesdale
Cold Keld
Gate
Cam
End
Gayle
Hawes
0 miles
2
3
4
5
6
7
8
9
10
11
12
13

Kirk Yetholm
Hawes
Horton-in-
Ribblesdale
dale

Maps 48-55 Horton-in-Ribblesdale to Hawes

13½ miles/21.5km – 6¼-6¾hrs

NOTE: Add 20-30% to these times to allow for stops

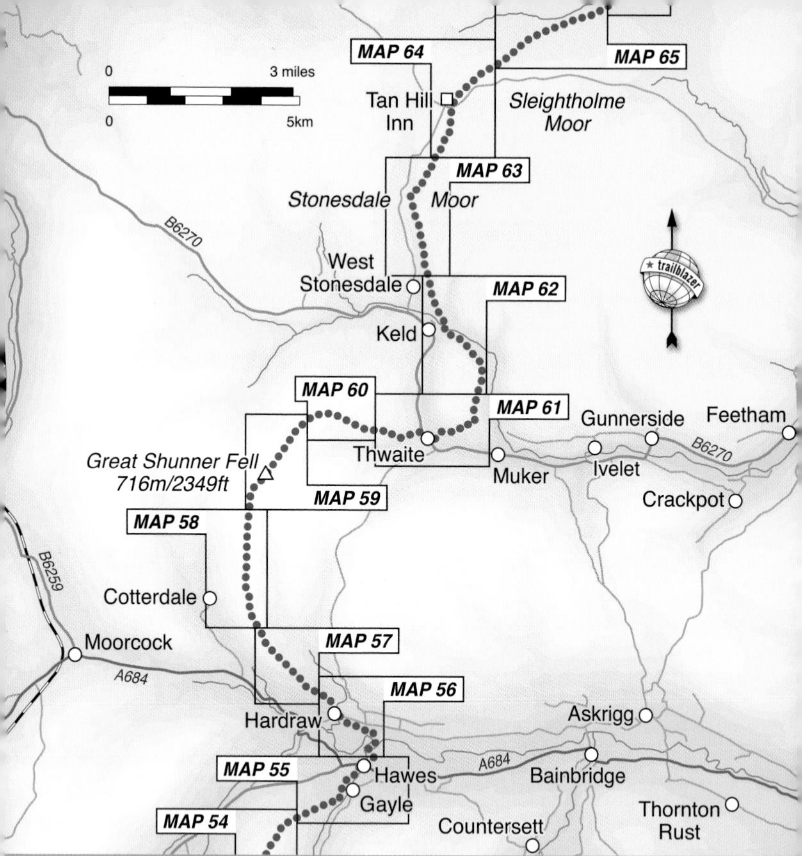
0
3 miles
0
5km
MAP 64
MAP 65
Tan Hill
Inn
Sleightholme
Moor
MAP 63
Stonesdale
Moor
B6270
West
Stonesdale
MAP 62
Keld
trailblazer
MAP 60
MAP 61
Gunnerside
Feetham
Thwaite
Muker
Ivelet
B6270
Great Shunner Fell
716m/2349ft
MAP 59
Crackpot
MAP 58
B6259
Cotterdale
Moorcock
MAP 57
A684
MAP 56
Hardraw
Askrigg
MAP 55
Hawes
A684
Bainbridge
Gayle
Thornton
Rust
MAP 54
Countersett

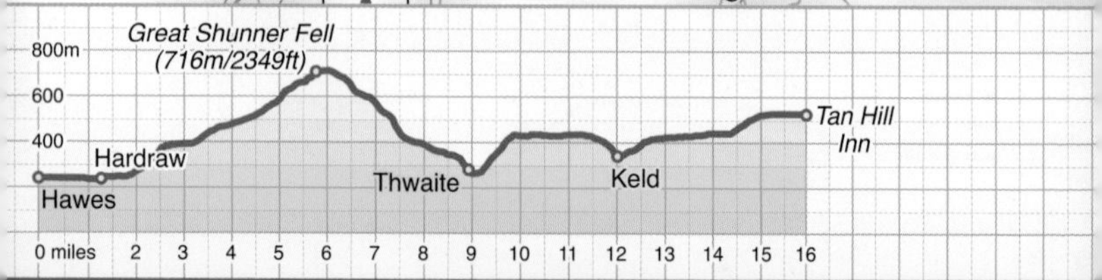
Great Shunner Fell
(716m/2349ft)
800m
600
400
Hardraw
Hawes
Thwaite
Keld
Tan Hill
Inn
0 miles
2
3
4
5
6
7
8
9
10
11
12
13
14
15
16

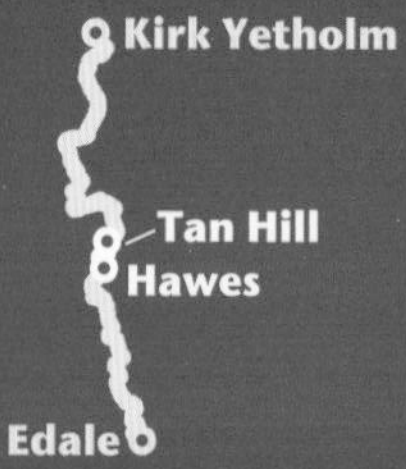
Kirk Yetholm
Tan Hill
Hawes
Edale

Maps 55-64
Hawes to Tan Hill

16 miles/25.5km – 8-10hrs

NOTE: Add 20-30% to these times to allow for stops

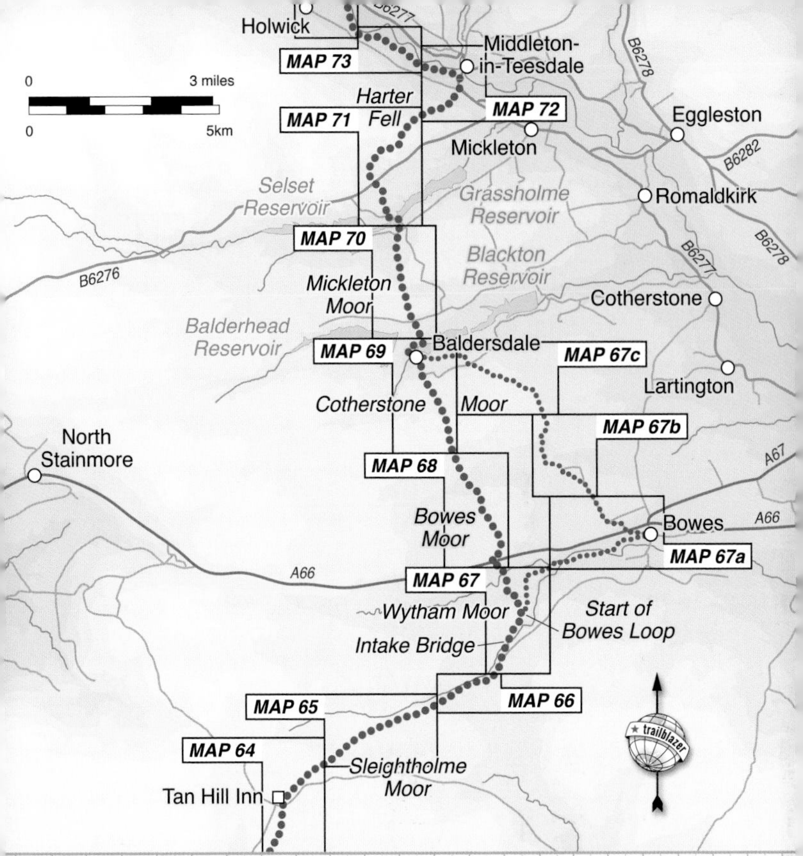
Holwick
B6277
Middleton-in-Teesdale
MAP 73
0
3 miles
0
5km
Harter Fell
MAP 71
MAP 72
Eggleston
Mickleton
B6278
B6282
Selset Reservoir
Grassholme Reservoir
Romaldkirk
MAP 70
B6278
B6277
B6276
Blackton Reservoir
Mickleton Moor
Cotherstone
Balderhead Reservoir
MAP 69
Baldersdale
MAP 67c
Lartington
Cotherstone
Moor
MAP 67b
North Stainmore
MAP 68
A67
Bowes Moor
Bowes
A66
MAP 67a
A66
MAP 67
Wytham Moor
Start of Bowes Loop
Intake Bridge
MAP 66
MAP 65
trailblazer
MAP 64
Sleightholme Moor
Tan Hill Inn

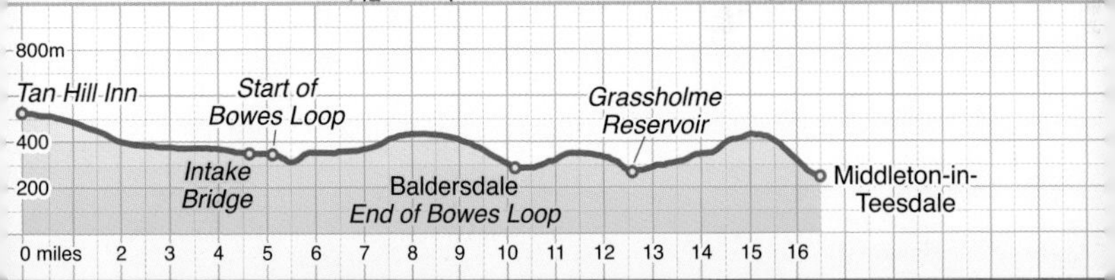
800m
Tan Hill Inn
Start of Bowes Loop
Grassholme Reservoir
400
Intake Bridge
200
Baldersdale
End of Bowes Loop
Middleton-in-Teesdale
0 miles
2
3
4
5
6
7
8
9
10
11
12
13
14
15
16

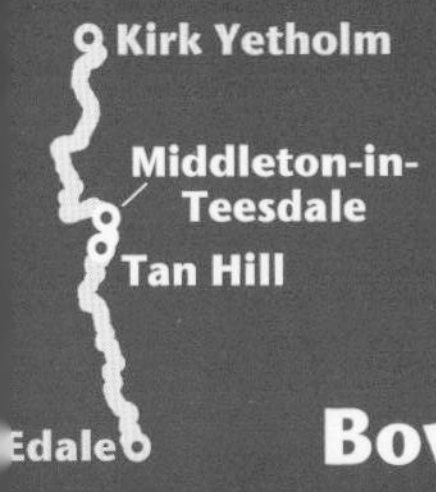
Kirk Yetholm
Middleton-in-Teesdale
Tan Hill
Edale

Maps 64-72 – Tan Hill to Middleton-in-Teesdale

16½ miles/26.5km – 7¼-9¾hrs

Maps 67, 67a-67c & 69 Bowes Loop

8½ miles/13.7km – 3-3½hrs

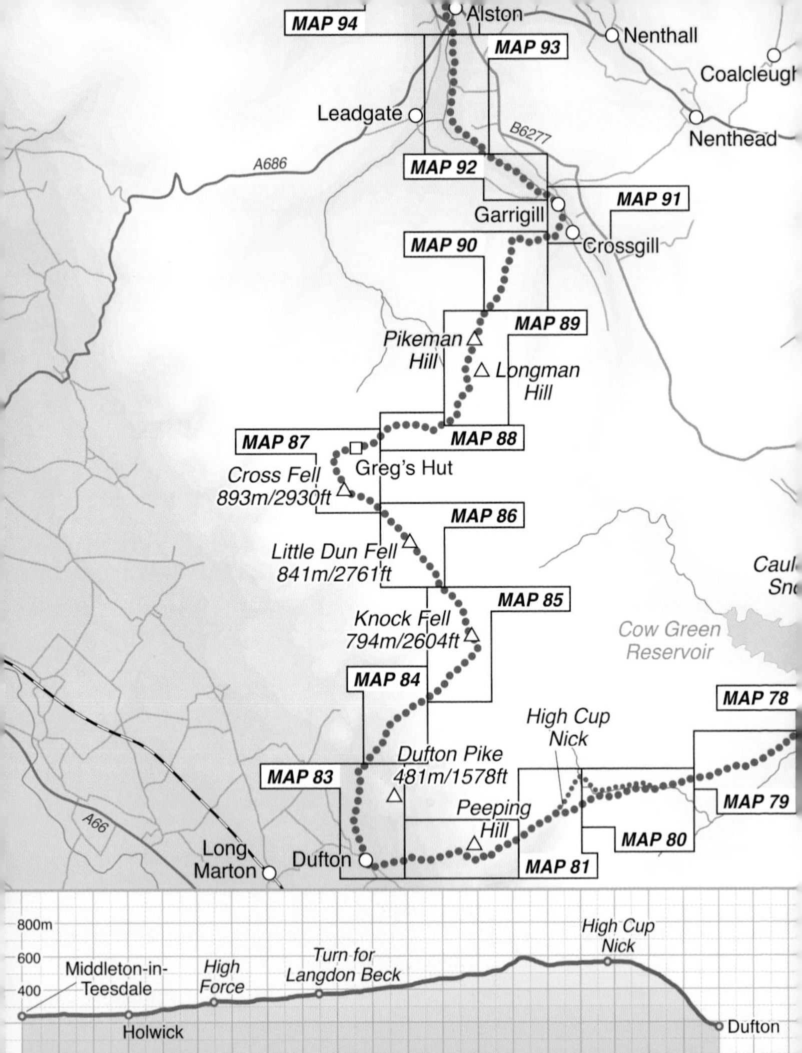

MAP 94
Alston
Nenthall
MAP 93
Coalcleugh
Leadgate
B6277
Nenthead
A686
MAP 92
MAP 91
Garrigill
Crossgill
MAP 90
MAP 89
Pikeman Hill
Longman Hill
MAP 87
MAP 88
Greg's Hut
Cross Fell 893m/2930ft
MAP 86
Little Dun Fell 841m/2761ft
MAP 85
Knock Fell 794m/2604ft
Cow Green Reservoir
MAP 84
MAP 78
High Cup Nick
Dufton Pike 481m/1578ft
MAP 83
MAP 79
Peeping Hill
MAP 80
A66
Long Marton
Dufton
MAP 81

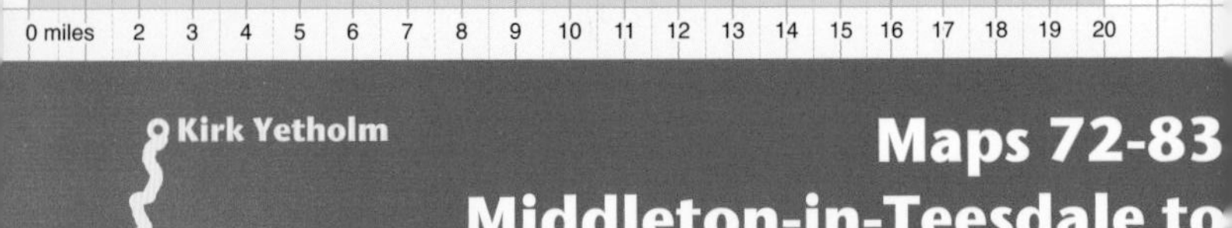

800m
600
400
Middleton-in-Teesdale
Holwick
High Force
Turn for Langdon Beck
High Cup Nick
Dufton
0 miles
2
3
4
5
6
7
8
9
10
11
12
13
14
15
16
17
18
19
20

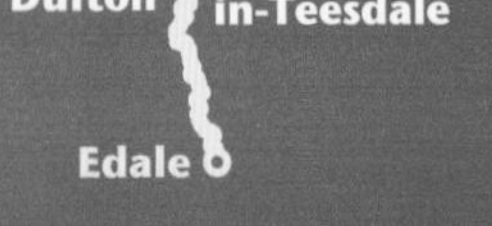

Kirk Yetholm
Middleton-in-Teesdale
Dufton
Edale

Maps 72-83 Middleton-in-Teesdale to Dufton

20 miles/32km – 9¾-10¾hrs

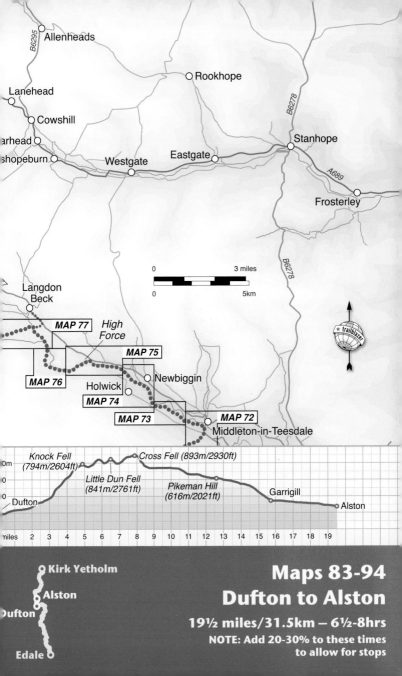

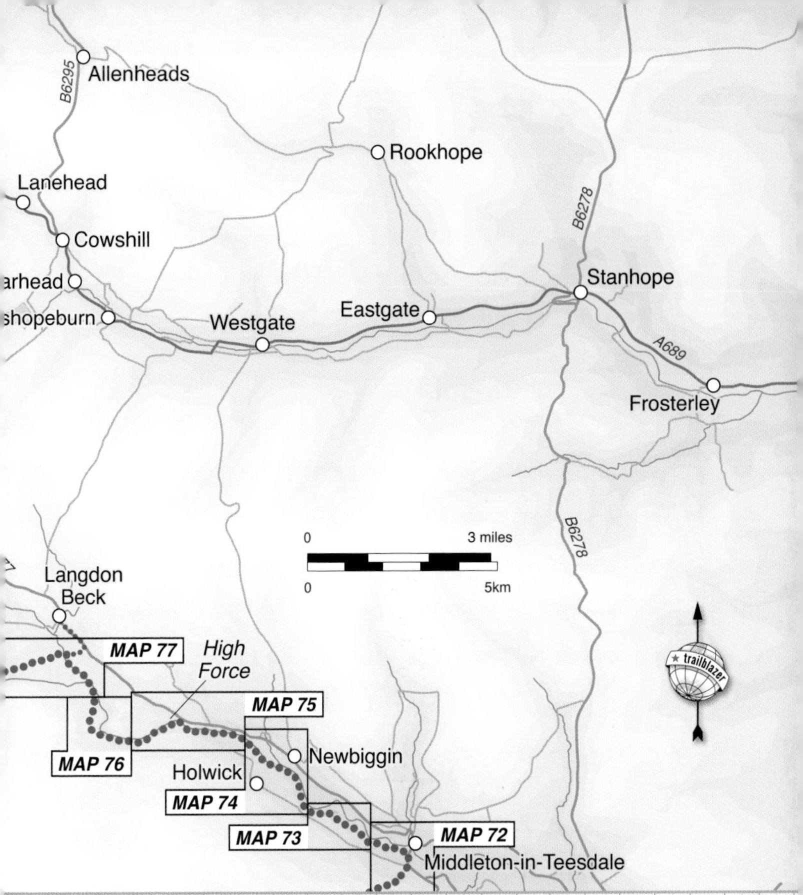
Allenheads
B6295
Rookhope
Lanehead
Cowshill
arhead
shopeburn
Westgate
Eastgate
Stanhope
B6278
A689
Frosterley
0
3 miles
0
5km
Langdon
Beck
MAP 77
High
Force
MAP 75
MAP 76
Newbiggin
Holwick
MAP 74
MAP 73
MAP 72
Middleton-in-Teesdale
trailblazer

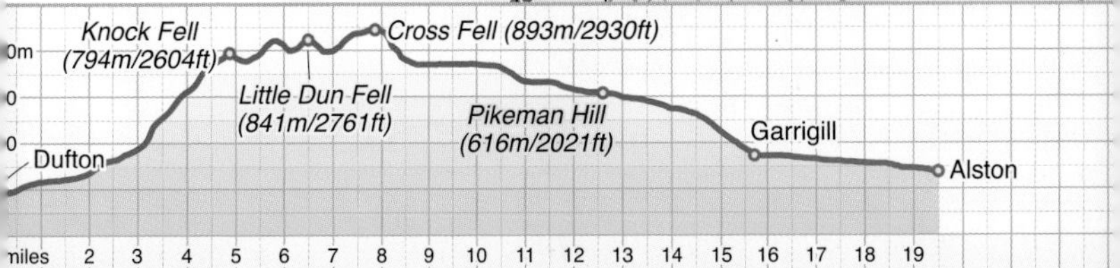
Knock Fell
(794m/2604ft)
Cross Fell (893m/2930ft)
Little Dun Fell
(841m/2761ft)
Pikeman Hill
(616m/2021ft)
Garrigill
Dufton
Alston
miles 2 3 4 5 6 7 8 9 10 11 12 13 14 15 16 17 18 19

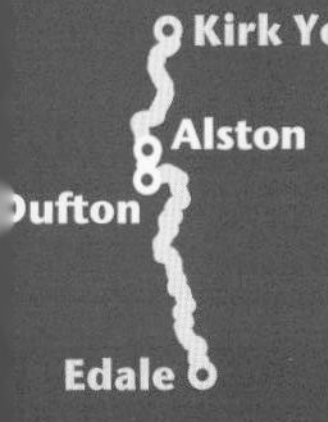
Kirk Yetholm
Alston
Dufton
Edale

Maps 83-94
Dufton to Alston

19½ miles/31.5km – 6½-8hrs

NOTE: Add 20-30% to these times to allow for stops

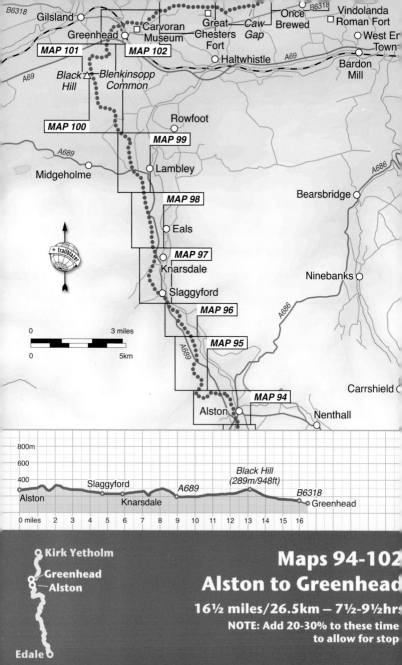

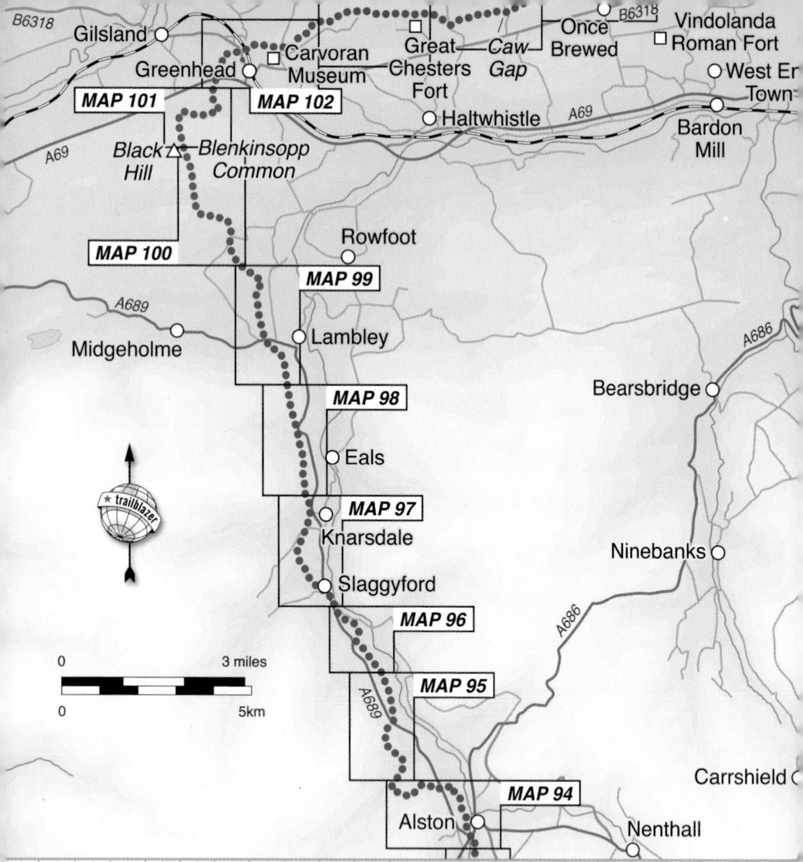
B6318
Gilsland
Greenhead
Carvoran
Museum
Great
Chesters
Fort
Caw
Gap
Once
Brewed
B6318
Vindolanda
Roman Fort
West End
Town
MAP 101
MAP 102
Haltwhistle
A69
Bardon
Mill
A69
Black
Hill
Blenkinsopp
Common
Rowfoot
MAP 100
MAP 99
A689
Midgeholme
Lambley
A686
Bearsbridge
MAP 98
Eals
trailblazer
MAP 97
Knarsdale
Ninebanks
Slaggyford
MAP 96
A686
0
3 miles
0
5km
MAP 95
A689
Carrshield
MAP 94
Alston
Nenthall

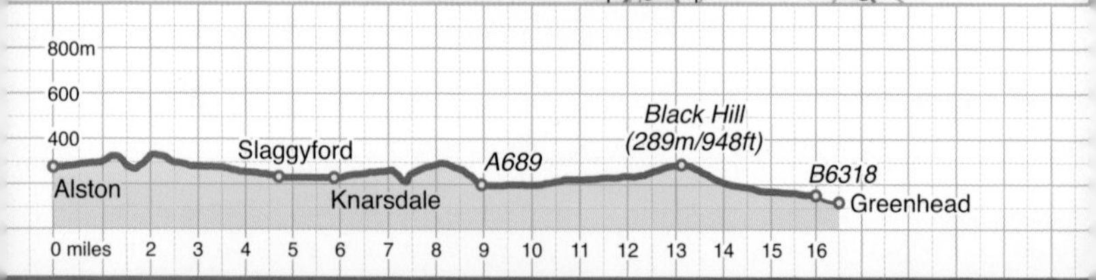
800m
600
400
Alston
Slaggyford
Knarsdale
A689
Black Hill
(289m/948ft)
B6318
Greenhead
0 miles
2
3
4
5
6
7
8
9
10
11
12
13
14
15
16

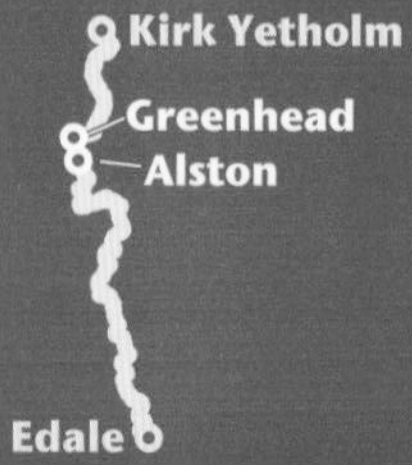
Kirk Yetholm
Greenhead
Alston
Edale

Maps 94-102
Alston to Greenhead

16½ miles/26.5km – 7½-9½hrs

NOTE: Add 20-30% to these times to allow for stops

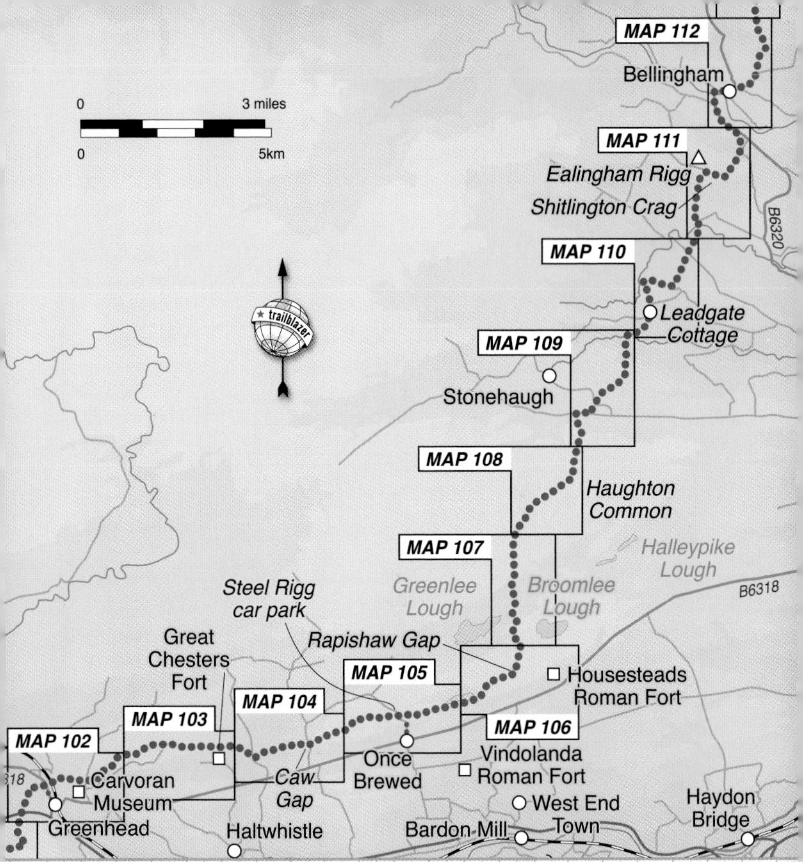

MAP 112
Bellingham
0
3 miles
0
5km
MAP 111
Ealingham Rigg
Shitlington Crag
B6320
MAP 110
trailblazer
Leadgate
Cottage
MAP 109
Stonehaugh
MAP 108
Haughton
Common
MAP 107
Halleypike
Lough
Greenlee
Lough
Broomlee
Lough
B6318
Steel Rigg
car park
Rapishaw Gap
Great
Chesters
Fort
MAP 105
Housesteads
Roman Fort
MAP 104
MAP 103
MAP 106
MAP 102
Once
Brewed
Vindolanda
Roman Fort
Carvoran
Museum
Caw
Gap
West End
Town
Haydon
Bridge
Greenhead
Haltwhistle
Bardon Mill

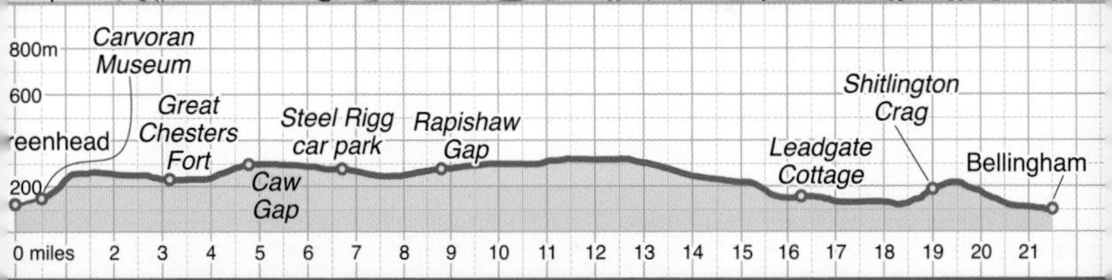

800m
600
200
Carvoran
Museum
Greenhead
Great
Chesters
Fort
Caw
Gap
Steel Rigg
car park
Rapishaw
Gap
Leadgate
Cottage
Shitlington
Crag
Bellingham
0 miles
2
3
4
5
6
7
8
9
10
11
12
13
14
15
16
17
18
19
20
21

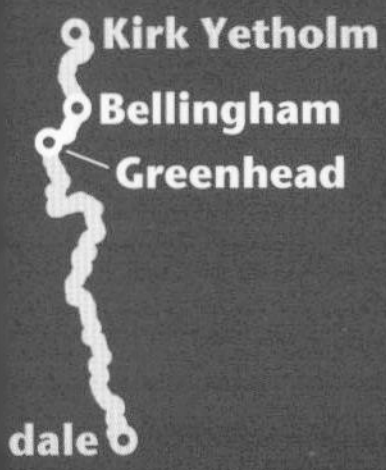

Kirk Yetholm
Bellingham
Greenhead
dale

Maps 102-112
Greenhead to Bellingham

21½ miles/34.5km – 9-10½hrs

NOTE: Add 20-30% to these times to allow for stops

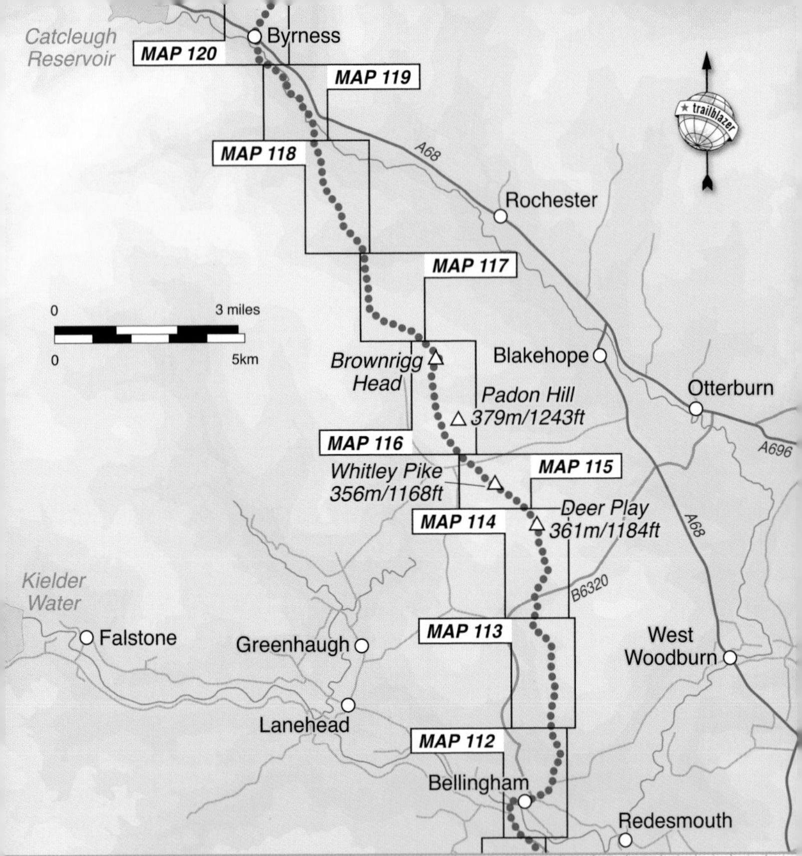
Catcleugh Reservoir
MAP 120
Byrness
MAP 119
trailblazer
A68
MAP 118
Rochester
MAP 117
0
3 miles
0
5km
Brownrigg Head
Blakehope
Padon Hill 379m/1243ft
Otterburn
A696
MAP 116
Whitley Pike 356m/1168ft
MAP 115
Deer Play 361m/1184ft
MAP 114
A68
B6320
Kielder Water
Falstone
Greenhaugh
MAP 113
West Woodburn
Lanehead
MAP 112
Bellingham
Redesmouth

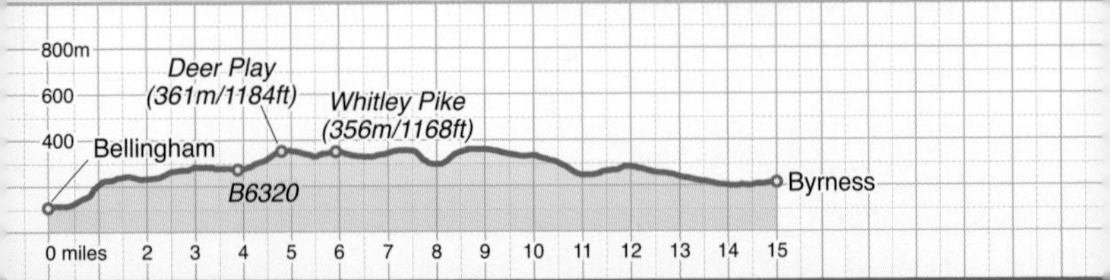
800m
600
400
Bellingham
Deer Play (361m/1184ft)
Whitley Pike (356m/1168ft)
B6320
Byrness
0 miles
2
3
4
5
6
7
8
9
10
11
12
13
14
15

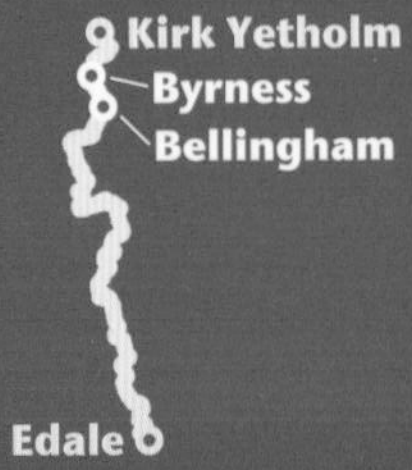
Kirk Yetholm
Byrness
Bellingham
Edale

Maps 112-120
Bellingham to Byrness

15 miles/24km – 7¼-9hrs

NOTE: Add 20-30% to these times to allow for stops

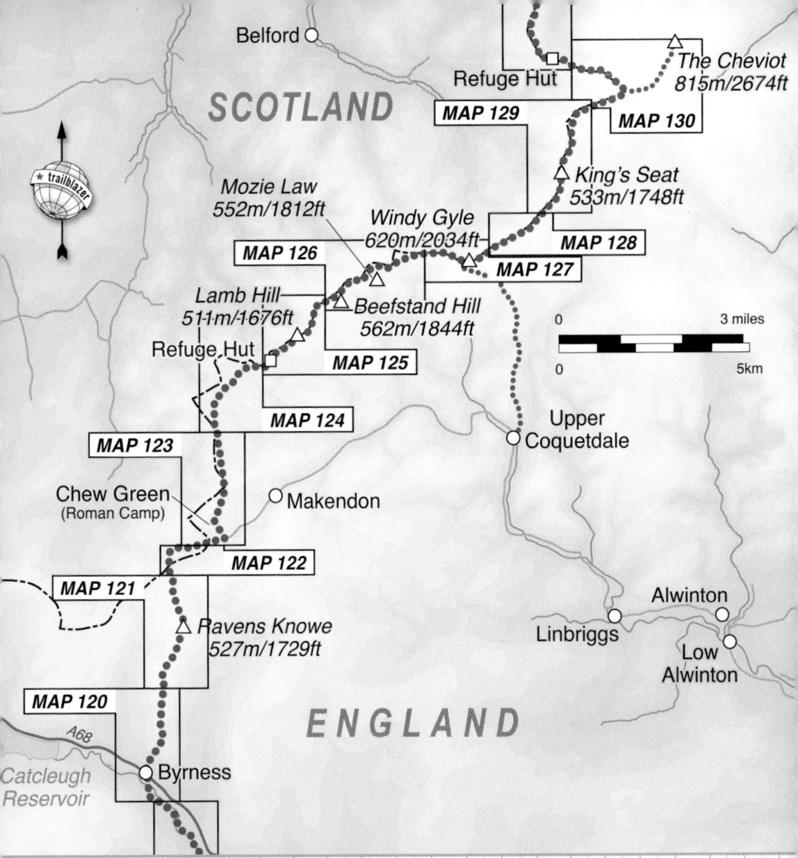
Belford
SCOTLAND
Refuge Hut
The Cheviot
815m/2674ft
MAP 129
MAP 130
trailblazer
King's Seat
533m/1748ft
Mozie Law
552m/1812ft
Windy Gyle
620m/2034ft
MAP 128
MAP 126
MAP 127
Lamb Hill
511m/1676ft
Beefstand Hill
562m/1844ft
0
3 miles
Refuge Hut
MAP 125
0
5km
MAP 124
Upper
Coquetdale
MAP 123
Chew Green
(Roman Camp)
Makendon
MAP 122
MAP 121
Alwinton
Ravens Knowe
527m/1729ft
Linbriggs
Low
Alwinton
MAP 120
ENGLAND
A68
Catcleugh
Reservoir
Byrness

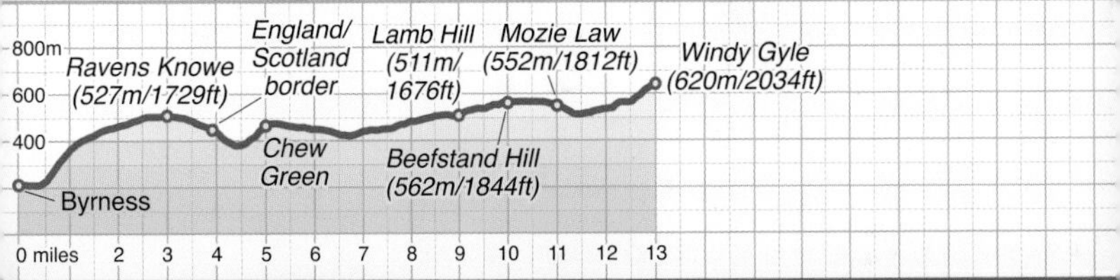
800m
600
400
England/
Scotland
border
Lamb Hill
(511m/
1676ft)
Mozie Law
(552m/1812ft)
Windy Gyle
(620m/2034ft)
Ravens Knowe
(527m/1729ft)
Chew
Green
Beefstand Hill
(562m/1844ft)
Byrness
0 miles
2
3
4
5
6
7
8
9
10
11
12
13

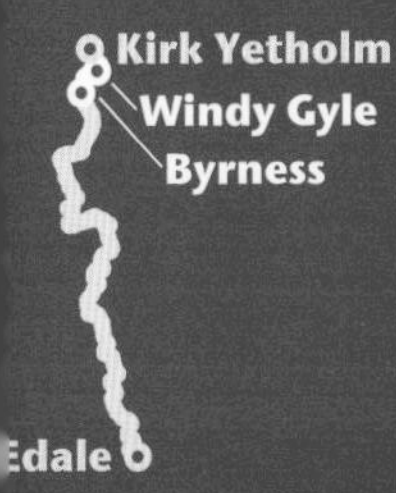
Kirk Yetholm
Windy Gyle
Byrness
Edale

Byrness to Kirk Yetholm

Maps 120-127 – Byrness to Windy Gyle

13 miles/21km – 5¼-6½hrs

NOTE: Add 20-30% to these times to allow for stops

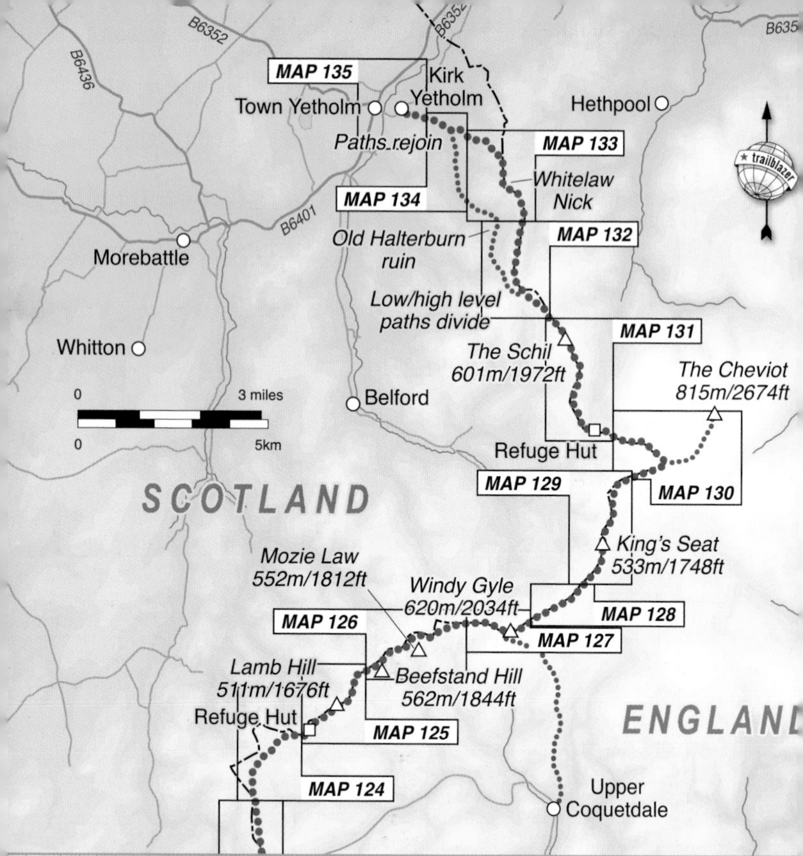
B6352
B6352
B635
B6436
MAP 135
Kirk
Yetholm
Town Yetholm
Hethpool
Paths rejoin
MAP 133
Whitelaw
Nick
MAP 134
B6401
Old Halterburn
ruin
MAP 132
Morebattle
Low/high level
paths divide
MAP 131
The Schil
601m/1972ft
Whitton
The Cheviot
815m/2674ft
0
3 miles
0
5km
Belford
Refuge Hut
MAP 129
MAP 130
SCOTLAND
King's Seat
533m/1748ft
Mozie Law
552m/1812ft
Windy Gyle
620m/2034ft
MAP 126
MAP 128
MAP 127
Lamb Hill
511m/1676ft
Beefstand Hill
562m/1844ft
Refuge Hut
MAP 125
ENGLAND
MAP 124
Upper
Coquetdale

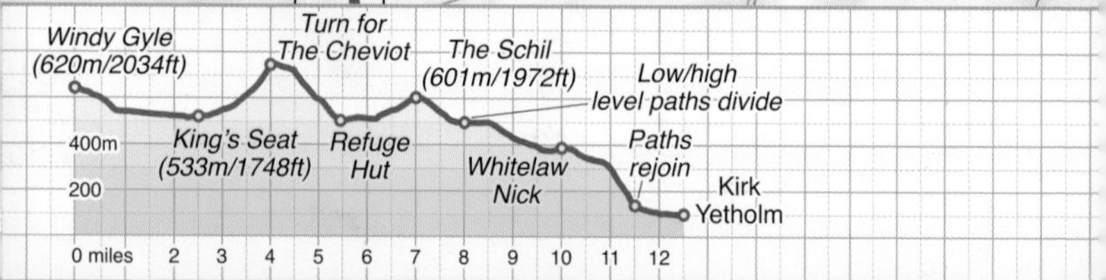
Windy Gyle
(620m/2034ft)
Turn for
The Cheviot
The Schil
(601m/1972ft)
Low/high
level paths divide
400m
King's Seat
(533m/1748ft)
Refuge
Hut
Paths
rejoin
200
Whitelaw
Nick
Kirk
Yetholm
0 miles
2
3
4
5
6
7
8
9
10
11
12

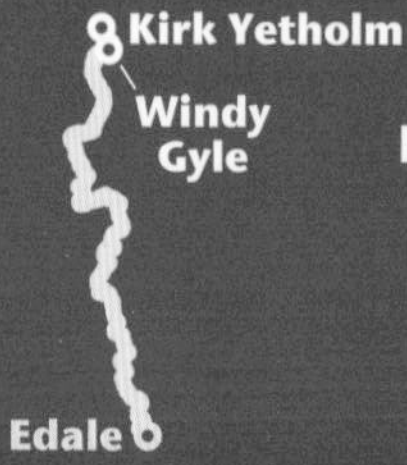
Kirk Yetholm
Windy
Gyle
Edale

Byrness to Kirk Yetholm

Maps 127-135 – Windy Gyle to Kirk Yetholm

12½ miles/20km – 5¼-6½hr

NOTE: Add 20-30% to these times to allow for stops

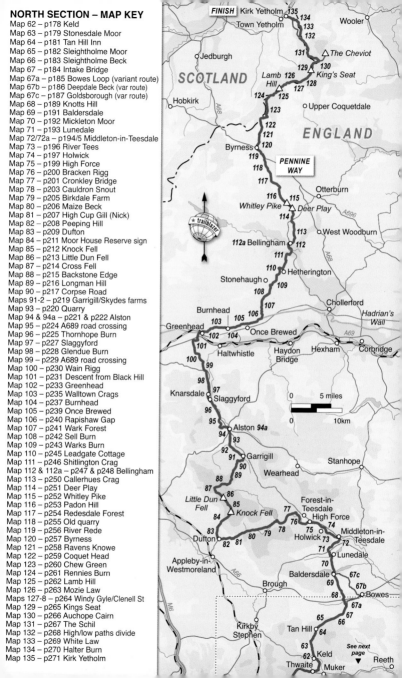

NORTH SECTION – MAP KEY

Map 62 – p178 Keld
Map 63 – p179 Stonesdale Moor
Map 64 – p181 Tan Hill Inn
Map 65 – p182 Sleightholme Moor
Map 66 – p183 Sleightholme Beck
Map 67 – p184 Intake Bridge
Map 67a – p185 Bowes Loop (variant route)
Map 67b – p186 Deepdale Beck (var route)
Map 67c – p187 Goldsborough (var route)
Map 68 – p189 Knotts Hill
Map 69 – p191 Baldersdale
Map 70 – p192 Mickleton Moor
Map 71 – p193 Lunedale
Map 72/72a – p194/5 Middleton-in-Teesdale
Map 73 – p196 River Tees
Map 74 – p197 Holwick
Map 75 – p199 High Force
Map 76 – p200 Bracken Rigg
Map 77 – p201 Cronkley Bridge
Map 78 – p203 Cauldron Snout
Map 79 – p205 Birkdale Farm
Map 80 – p206 Maize Beck
Map 81 – p207 High Cup Gill (Nick)
Map 82 – p208 Peeping Hill
Map 83 – p209 Dufton
Map 84 – p211 Moor House Reserve sign
Map 85 – p212 Knock Fell
Map 86 – p213 Little Dun Fell
Map 87 – p214 Cross Fell
Map 88 – p215 Backstone Edge
Map 89 – p216 Longman Hill
Map 90 – p217 Corpse Road
Maps 91-2 – p219 Garrigill/Skydes farms
Map 93 – p220 Quarry
Map 94 & 94a – p221 & p222 Alston
Map 95 – p224 A689 road crossing
Map 96 – p225 Thornhope Burn
Map 97 – p227 Slaggyford
Map 98 – p228 Glendue Burn
Map 99 – p229 A689 road crossing
Map 100 – p230 Wain Rigg
Map 101 – p231 Descent from Black Hill
Map 102 – p233 Greenhead
Map 103 – p235 Walltown Crags
Map 104 – p237 Burnhead
Map 105 – p239 Once Brewed
Map 106 – p240 Rapishaw Gap
Map 107 – p241 Wark Forest
Map 108 – p242 Sell Burn
Map 109 – p243 Warks Burn
Map 110 – p245 Leadgate Cottage
Map 111 – p246 Shitlington Crag
Map 112 & 112a – p247 & p248 Bellingham
Map 113 – p250 Callerhues Crag
Map 114 – p251 Deer Play
Map 115 – p252 Whitley Pike
Map 116 – p253 Padon Hill
Map 117 – p254 Redesdale Forest
Map 118 – p255 Old quarry
Map 119 – p256 River Rede
Map 120 – p257 Byrness
Map 121 – p258 Ravens Knowe
Map 122 – p259 Coquet Head
Map 123 – p260 Chew Green
Map 124 – p261 Rennies Burn
Map 125 – p262 Lamb Hill
Map 126 – p263 Mozie Law
Maps 127-8 – p264 Windy Gyle/Clenell St
Map 129 – p265 Kings Seat
Map 130 – p266 Auchope Cairn
Map 131 – p267 The Schil
Map 132 – p268 High/low paths divide
Map 133 – p269 White Law
Map 134 – p270 Halter Burn
Map 135 – p271 Kirk Yetholm

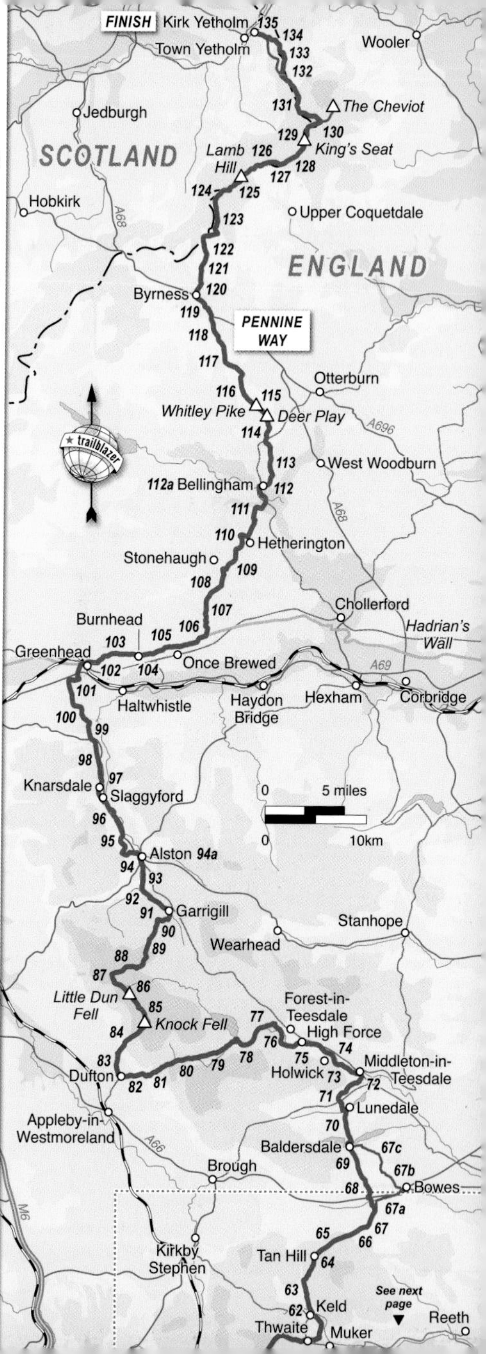

FINISH
Kirk Yetholm
Town Yetholm
Wooler
The Cheviot
King's Seat
Jedburgh
SCOTLAND
Lamb Hill
Hobkirk
A68
Upper Coquetdale
ENGLAND
Byrness
PENNINE WAY
Otterburn
Whitley Pike
Deer Play
A696
trailblazer
West Woodburn
112a Bellingham
A68
Hetherington
Stonehaugh
Chollerford
Hadrian's Wall
Burnhead
Greenhead
Once Brewed
A69
Haltwhistle
Haydon Bridge
Hexham
Corbridge
Knarsdale
Slaggyford
0 5 miles
0 10km
Alston 94a
Garrigill
Stanhope
Wearhead
Little Dun Fell
Knock Fell
Forest-in-Teesdale
High Force
Holwick
Middleton-in-Teesdale
Dufton
Lunedale
Appleby-in-Westmoreland
A66
Baldersdale
Brough
Bowes
M6
Kirkby Stephen
Tan Hill
Keld
Thwaite
Muker
Reeth
See next page
135 134 133 132 131 130 129 128 127 126 125 124 123 122 121 120 119 118 117 116 115 114 113 112 111 110 109 108 107 106 105 104 103 102 101 100 99 98 97 96 95 94 93 92 91 90 89 88 87 86 85 84 83 82 81 80 79 78 77 76 75 74 73 72 71 70 69 68 67c 67b 67a 67 66 65 64 63 62

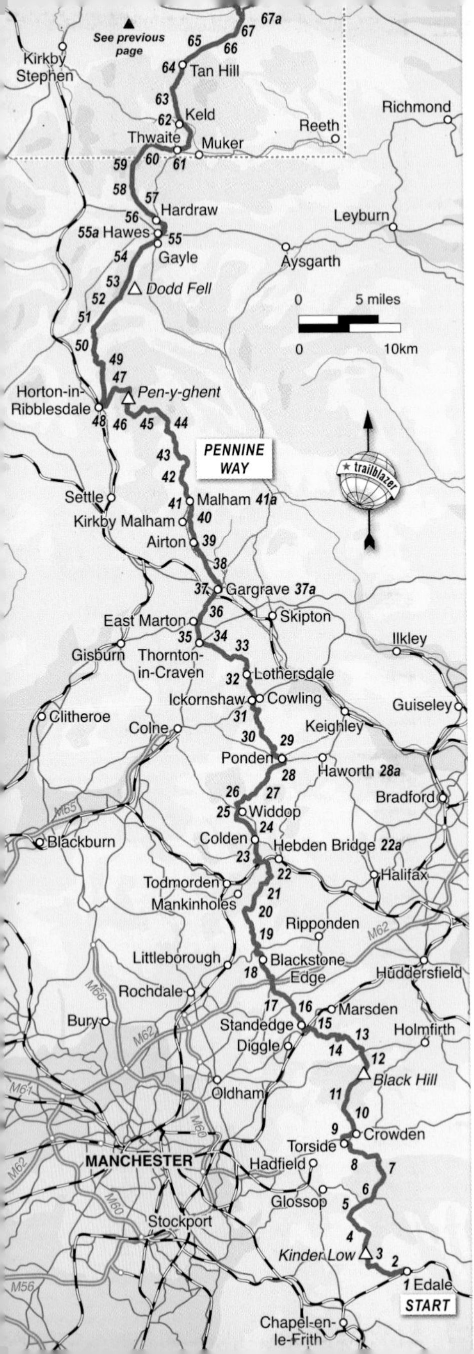
See previous page
Kirkby Stephen
Tan Hill
Keld
Thwaite
Muker
Reeth
Richmond
Hardraw
Hawes
Gayle
Leyburn
Aysgarth
Dodd Fell
0
5 miles
0
10km
Horton-in-Ribblesdale
Pen-y-ghent
PENNINE WAY
trailblazer
Settle
Malham 41a
Kirkby Malham
Airton
Gargrave 37a
East Marton
Skipton
Gisburn
Thornton-in-Craven
Ilkley
Lothersdale
Ickornshaw
Cowling
Guiseley
Clitheroe
Colne
Keighley
Ponden
Haworth 28a
Bradford
Widdop
M65
Blackburn
Colden
Hebden Bridge 22a
Todmorden
Halifax
Mankinholes
Ripponden
M62
Littleborough
Blackstone Edge
Huddersfield
M66
Rochdale
Marsden
Bury
Standedge
Holmfirth
M62
Diggle
Black Hill
M61
Oldham
M60
Crowden
Torside
MANCHESTER
Hadfield
M62
M60
Glossop
Stockport
Kinder Low
M56
1 Edale
START
Chapel-en-le-Frith

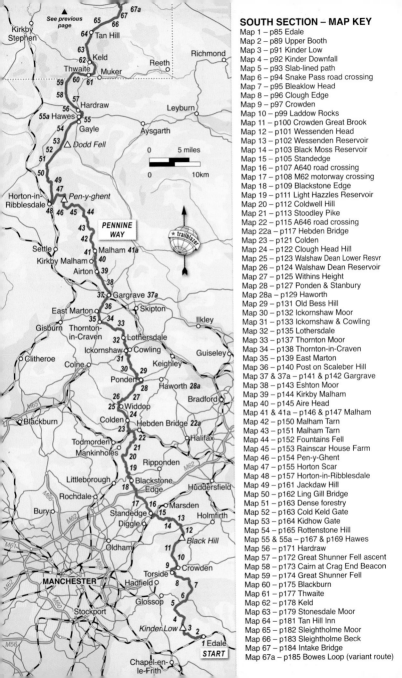

SOUTH SECTION – MAP KEY

Map 1 – p85 Edale
Map 2 – p89 Upper Booth
Map 3 – p91 Kinder Low
Map 4 – p92 Kinder Downfall
Map 5 – p93 Slab-lined path
Map 6 – p94 Snake Pass road crossing
Map 7 – p95 Bleaklow Head
Map 8 – p96 Clough Edge
Map 9 – p97 Crowden
Map 10 – p99 Laddow Rocks
Map 11 – p100 Crowden Great Brook
Map 12 – p101 Wessenden Head
Map 13 – p102 Wessenden Reservoir
Map 14 – p103 Black Moss Reservoir
Map 15 – p105 Standedge
Map 16 – p107 A640 road crossing
Map 17 – p108 M62 motorway crossing
Map 18 – p109 Blackstone Edge
Map 19 – p111 Light Hazzles Reservoir
Map 20 – p112 Coldwell Hill
Map 21 – p113 Stoodley Pike
Map 22 – p115 A646 road crossing
Map 22a – p117 Hebden Bridge
Map 23 – p121 Colden
Map 24 – p122 Clough Head Hill
Map 25 – p123 Walshaw Dean Lower Resvr
Map 26 – p124 Walshaw Dean Reservoir
Map 27 – p125 Withins Height
Map 28 – p127 Ponden & Stanbury
Map 28a – p129 Haworth
Map 29 – p131 Old Bess Hill
Map 30 – p132 Ickornshaw Moor
Map 31 – p133 Ickornshaw & Cowling
Map 32 – p135 Lothersdale
Map 33 – p137 Thornton Moor
Map 34 – p138 Thornton-in-Craven
Map 35 – p139 East Marton
Map 36 – p140 Post on Scaleber Hill
Map 37 & 37a – p141 & p142 Gargrave
Map 38 – p143 Eshton Moor
Map 39 – p144 Kirkby Malham
Map 40 – p145 Aire Head
Map 41 & 41a – p146 & p147 Malham
Map 42 – p150 Malham Tarn
Map 43 – p151 Malham Tarn
Map 44 – p152 Fountains Fell
Map 45 – p153 Rainscar House Farm
Map 46 – p154 Pen-y-Ghent
Map 47 – p155 Horton Scar
Map 48 – p157 Horton-in-Ribblesdale
Map 49 – p161 Jackdaw Hill
Map 50 – p162 Ling Gill Bridge
Map 51 – p163 Dense forestry
Map 52 – p163 Cold Keld Gate
Map 53 – p164 Kidhow Gate
Map 54 – p165 Rottenstone Hill
Map 55 & 55a – p167 & p169 Hawes
Map 56 – p171 Hardraw
Map 57 – p172 Great Shunner Fell ascent
Map 58 – p173 Cairn at Crag End Beacon
Map 59 – p174 Great Shunner Fell
Map 60 – p175 Blackburn
Map 61 – p177 Thwaite
Map 62 – p178 Keld
Map 63 – p179 Stonesdale Moor
Map 64 – p181 Tan Hill Inn
Map 65 – p182 Sleightholme Moor
Map 66 – p183 Sleightholme Beck
Map 67 – p184 Intake Bridge
Map 67a – p185 Bowes Loop (variant route)